Enjoy!!

Bonnie

FRED LODGE'S
Diaries

A Quiet Man's Journey Through Hell

L/Cpl FREDERICK THOMAS LODGE

EDITED BY JAMES HYATT AND BONNIE (LODGE) FRASER

 FriesenPress

Suite 300 - 990 Fort St
Victoria, BC, V8V 3K2
Canada

www.friesenpress.com

Edited by James Hyatt and Bonnie (Lodge) Fraser.
bleelodge@gmail.com and dieppepow@bell.net

ISBN
978-1-5255-4039-4 (Hardcover)
978-1-5255-4040-0 (Paperback)
978-1-5255-4041-7 (eBook)

1. Biography & Autobiography, Military

Distributed to the trade by The Ingram Book Company

DEDICATION

"WE SHARE THESE DETAILED WW II DIARIES AND
MEMORIES OF OUR HERO—OUR DAD."

Bonnie, Carol, Fred Jr.

TABLE OF CONTENTS

INTRODUCTION

On August 19, 1942 the Canadian 2nd Division attempted a raid on the French coastal city of Dieppe; it was a disaster, poorly planned, badly led and costly. Of the 4,963 Canadians who embarked from England for the operation, only 2,210 returned, and many of them were wounded. Casualties totaled 3,367, including 916 dead and 1,946 prisoners of war. One of these prisoners was Lance-Corporal Fred Lodge, a member of the Queen's Own Cameron Highlanders of Canada.

Frederick Thomas Lodge was born in Kenora, Ontario, Canada in January, 1913. He was the ninth and final child of William and Emily Lodge. The Lodge family had emigrated to Canada in 1908, taking advantage of a Canadian Government sponsorship program designed to attract laborers and farmers to Canada. The Lodges were poor, hard working and patriotic. The father, William and oldest son, William known as Bill, served in the Canadian Army overseas during World War One with the son killed by a gas shell near Passchendaele, Belgium on November 11th,1917.

Fred Lodge grew up a "Kenora" boy, a skilled outdoorsman, often listening to stories about life in the Army and the courage of his brother, Bill, who had been a signaler in a machine gun company on the Western Front. Fred was an athlete, rowing for the Kenora Rowing Club, and an excellent marksman. His athleticism, dark complexion and good looks made him very popular with the local girls.

When war was declared against Germany in September, 1939, Fred Lodge was keen to join the Army and emulate his older brother. It took months for the Canadian government to organize the recruitment and training of large numbers of volunteers and Fred Lodge enlisted in 1940 in the Queen's Own Cameron Highlanders of Canada.

Fred traveled by train from Kenora to Winnipeg, Manitoba early in September, 1939 to join the Cameron Highlanders, a storied infantry regiment. He was 26 years old and chose the infantry because he was fit, athletic, and wanted to be trained as a sniper or signaler like his older brother.

The Camerons were officially notified of the impending war on September 1st, 1939 when the unit was ordered to mobilize and recruit up to 807 all ranks. Within seventeen days the battalion was at full strength. With a general mobilization, barrack space was at a premium. For the first two months most of the Camerons returned to their homes at the end of each day. Temporary quarters were eventually found at the Robinson Store on Main Street in Winnipeg.

In April 1940 the Camerons turned in their kilts, and were issued new battle-dress trousers and jackets. They would not fight in the traditional highland uniforms as had their fathers twenty-five years earlier. On May 24th, 1940, the battalion moved to Camp Shilo, Manitoba. At Shilo, unit training from section to battalion level took place as well as more complex brigade exercises. Fred enjoyed his initial training in Winnipeg and quickly made some good friends.

The battalion embarked for overseas on December 16th, 1940, arriving in the UK on Christmas Eve. Billeted at Cove, Hampshire, the battalion was assigned a defensive task adjacent to Aldershot in the Surrey area.

Numerous training exercises and inspections highlighted 1941. By July the Camerons were training in the Newhaven area of the channel coast near Sussex, England in a coastal defense role.

On August 19th, 1942 the Camerons landed at Pourville Beach, near Dieppe, France. Their objectives were the Dieppe-Saint Aubins airfield; battery 265 at Rouxmosnel-Calment and a suspected German divisional headquarters at nearby Arques-la-Battaile. Although the Camerons made the deepest penetration of the day, the main landing at Dieppe had been unsuccessful, and as

German resistance stiffened, the battalion was unable to reach its objectives. Of 503 Camerons on the raid, 346 were casualties: 60 killed in action; 8 dead of wounds after evacuation; 167 prisoners of war (8 of whom died of wounds). Of the 268 returning to England, 103 were wounded. The concept and value of the raid is a matter of controversy. However, the lessons learned were later thought by some to be useful in planning the Normandy invasion-still two years away.

The Cameron Highlanders battalion had come all the way across the English Channel in their little R-boats and landed about 06:00 in the morning led by a piper standing in the bow of the lead boat playing his pipes while in full view of the Germans. The Commanding Officer, Lieutenant-Colonel Gosling, was killed when the first boats reached the beach and he stood up. Fred Lodge was a signaller in the Headquarters Company so he would have run ashore with that image fresh in his mind. It would be the first of many dreadful events he would experience that day.

Fred spent his last few hours of freedom in France trailing his Company Commander, carrying a heavy Mark 18 radio transceiver on his back, maps and code books in his small pack, ammunition and a Lee-Enfield rifle in his hand. They moved under German fire the whole time and crawled, walked or ran more than 5 kilometers that day. When their withdrawal was finally ordered they returned to the Pourville beach under heavy German mortar and machine gun fire. There were not enough boats to take them all off the beach and the enemy fire was heavy and effective. When Fred's turn came the last boat was full so he clung to the side, hoping to be towed to a ship. The heavy radio was still strapped to his back and as the boat left the beach the weight and water resistance on the radio dragged him down and away from the boat. Luckily, Fred was a good swimmer and he managed to get rid of the radio and swim to shore despite his heavy, waterlogged clothing. He crawled ashore and up the beach to the seawall seeking shelter from the rain of German bullets and mortar bombs. He was soaking wet, exhausted and apprehensive but he was unhurt. Fred felt his bigger problem was the commando dagger strapped to his belt. Rumor had it that the Germans would shoot a prisoner out of hand if they found a dagger in his possession; Fred found a loose stone in the sea wall and managed to create a cavity large enough to hold the dagger and wedged the stone back in place, pledging to return someday and retrieve it. After a few minutes not even the constant machine gun ricochets and mortar bomb explosions could keep him awake. The next thing he knew he was being kicked and ordered to get up, "hande hoch." He was a prisoner.

Later a Canadian POW told Fred that a good number of people in England and at home think we gave in without trying at Dieppe. Fred said, "If that is true, I wish those people had of been there. To feel the clinging sand dragging on their feet while trying to run with an eighteen set strapped to their backs and weighed down by ammunition while Ack-Ack tracers, machine gun and rifle fire snapped past their ears and kicked up sand around their feet. I'd like to have seen them trying to climb over a barbed wire capped sea wall in the face of a deadly crossfire. Men hanging helpless on the cruel barbs riddled with bullets, their blood dripping on the shoulders and upturned faces of their comrades. I wish they had been in the streets of Pourville, crawling over rough cobble stones while the deadly accurate four-inch German mortars in inaccessible hill positions, showered them with accurately placed bombs. I would have liked to have seen them crossing the ridge under a crackling barrage of machine gun fire from strong indiscernible pill boxes across the valley and dodging across a grain field with only one or two stooks of grain for shelter from the penetrating, searching hail of lead; to see their buddies pitch, scream and thrash around on the ground with a fatal burst of machine gun slugs in their vitals. I wish they had been there when we met a solid front of entrenched troops supported by tanks against which our puny rifles and bayonets had no effect; then the retreat to the beach, in blistering noon day heat, through mortar, machine gun, rifle and grenade fire only to find the tide out and the boats unable to land. I wish they had been there."

Fred had collapsed exhausted beside the seawall on the beach in front of the tiny village of Pourville, he was barely conscious of the bullets passing close overhead, fired by the many German MG-42 machine guns covering the beach. Nor did he pay any attention to the mortar rounds constantly exploding close by as the German gunners searched for surviving Canadian soldiers. Fred no longer even saw the many Camerons and South Saskatchewan Regiment soldiers lying dead and wounded around him; he was cold, wet, mentally and physically exhausted. Later in the afternoon the German fire relented as the last Allied ships passed out of sight and it was apparent that any remaining Canadians were either dead, wounded or about to surrender. German soldiers began moving along the beach taking prisoners into custody, collecting and treating the Canadian wounded and marking the dead for later retrieval. Fred lay on the sea side of the Pourville seawall so he was among the last prisoners to be found.

The Germans used unwounded Canadians as stretcher bearers to collect the wounded and dead for treatment or burial. When the task was complete they were marched to the rear under guard to an assembly area where they were counted and their military details recorded. Those POWs capable of walking were then marched about 20 kilometres to Verneuil where they spent the night in an old factory. The following day they were loaded into crowded box cars en route by train to Stalag VIII (B) Prisoner of War camp in Lambsdorf, Germany.

Though travelling by cattle car was standard practice for European armies, POWs moved in this way were usually overcrowded and undersupplied with food, water and other necessities. Sometimes conditions in the boxcars were truly barbarous. One British officer who saw the Canadians arrive in Germany had quite unpleasant recollections of their state about eight to ten days after the Dieppe Raid: "These people just fell out — absolutely whacked. Covered in excreta and in a terrible state. They'd been in there for days. Things we'd read about, and impossible to describe — the stench, the horror, the tragedy of it all."[1]

Fred Lodge was a committed diarist, and he diligently recorded his wartime experience in the series of diaries that follow. He experienced the best and the worst of wartime service, surviving the 1942 Dieppe Raid and three years as a prisoner of war with honour and optimism despite the horrors he saw firsthand.

---

1   Dr. William S. Holden interview by Charles G. Roland OHA, HCM 32-85, 25 March 1985, p .23. as quoted by Charles G. Roland in On the Beach and in the Bag, The Fate of Dieppe Casualties Left Behind.

After the war ended, Fred returned to Canada, trained as a radio technician, married his wife, Bernice (Bunny), and raised three children while living out his life in Kenora. He seldom worked as a radio technician but instead became a foreman on a large paper machine, working at the Ontario & Minnesota paper mill in Kenora.

Fred Lodge died in June, 1976, a man proud of his family and his military service. This is his story.

LCol (Ret'd) James O. Hyatt CD

FRED LODGE DIARY
January 1, 1940 to October 21, 1940

Daily Diary:
H19859, F. T. Lodge,
Camerons of Canada (C.A.S.F.) Canada
Book No. 1

Started at the request of my sister, Nelle, and in case of fatal "accident" please mail to
Miss Nelle Lodge
Box 165
Kenora, Ontario,
Canada

Time of enlistment:
Dec. 4, 1939
with the Queen's Own Cameron Highlanders of Canada
Robertson Building
City of Winnipeg, Canada

JAN. 1ST, 1940

Set out to find Bobby and finally succeeded at the Clarendon Hotel after making a trip up to Groves. Missed her yesterday so didn't have much time today. Was greatly disappointed at the little time we had together and peeved at myself for not going to the Clarendon last night.

JAN. 2

Detailed for Barrack guard today. Started a letter to Rose. Got a letter from Nelle. Almost lost $2.00.

JAN. 3

Paraded to the Y.M.C.A. for a swim this A.M. Nice. Blancoed and polished my equipment this P.M. for inspection tomorrow. Was issued with two suits of underwear. About time I think as the one suit I had was nearly falling off and I was scared to wash it because it might of dissolved before my eyes.

JAN. 4

Had my bunk changed from No. 5 to No. 13. Didn't go out on parade on account of no uniform.

JAN. 5

Stayed in again today. Had lectures on musketry in the Mess Hall. Wrote some letters.

JAN. 6

Complimented on my blanket roll. Applied for transfer to signals. Got a letter from Jack.

JAN. 7

Darned my socks and mended my pants. Hear we are getting uniforms tomorrow (old ones). Wrote a letter to Gibsons.

JAN. 8

Almost got a uniform today; maybe tomorrow. Went to Minto (Armouries) with full kit for rifle drill. Saw the Jam Session tonight. Good.

JAN. 9
No uniform yet. Going to keep worrying him for it. Went to Minto again today. Nothing doing in Barracks tonight.

JAN. 10
Went to Minto again today. Wrote a letter to B & B today.

JAN. 11
Bath parade today. Had a travel talk in the Grace United Church this P.M. Slipped on street car track while marching and have a sore elbow now.

JAN. 12
Minto barracks again today. Wrote a letter to Bobbie. Blancoed my kit for inspection tomorrow.

JAN. 13
Nothing of any importance. Have a hunch I will be on fatigue next week. Went to see Donna. She wasn't home. Got a uniform and it doesn't fit.

JAN. 14
Sewed my trouser. Tunic is in the tailor being altered. Washed a shirt, pair of socks and five hankies. Went on church parade this A.M.

JAN. 15
Detailed for Sergeant's Mess. Not bad. I took advantage of the good grub and had three darn good meals. I think it is an all week job, I hope. Working with Pat Maloney, a former teamster on the highway. I think Jack would remember him.

JAN. 16
Went out for an observation march. We came back and had to answer questions on direction and unusual things that we passed and saw.

JAN. 17
Detailed for kitchen fatigue, pretty rough. Went to the Beacon and saw "Fast and Loose" and "Mutiny in the Big House."

JAN. 18
Had rifle instruction in the Mess Hall in the A.M. Went out for a route march in the P.M. followed by a lecture by the Coy. C.O. Finally salvaged my tunic from the tailor; it still doesn't fit, yet, but will fix it myself. Started a letter to B & B. I'm getting behind in my letter writing. I'll have to do better.

JAN. 19, FRI.
Detailed to sweep and scrub the main floor. Started a 24 hour stretch of fire picquet at 6:00 P.M. What a job, 24 hour session.

JAN. 20, SAT.
Finished fire picquet at 6:00P.M. Went to a show with George Wilson.

JAN. 21, SUN.
Wrote a letter to Nelle and one to Jack. Took a shower tonight. Spoke to Corporal Rankine about my getting into the signals. May have some luck.

JAN. 22, MON.
The Battalion went to Minto for Battalion drill. The N.C.O.'s and officers are getting tough. They seem to be rushing the training which may indicate something happening in the near future. Mailed a letter to Jack tonight. I wish some of the guys I loaned money to would pay it back. No word from Cpl. Rankine yet.

JAN. 23, TUES.
My birthday. Received hankies from Bobbie, cigs from Roy, socks from Em. Letters from Rose, Nelle, Bezzie, June, Em and Bobbie. What a birthday. Had a hard day at Minto getting ready for the big inspection. Dead tired and broke tonight.

JAN. 24, WED.

We were all changed around today and had our sleeping allocations changed. I am in No. 23 platoon which is anti-tank. There are only supposed to be 22 men in the anti-tank and we have 44 so I guess 22 of us will be transferred to something else. Still trying to get into the signals.

JAN. 25, THURS.

Went for a route march this A.M. and then went for a swim afterwards.

JAN. 26, FRI.

Went out to Minto this A.M. and didn't get back until after 1:00 P.M. Had a rifle lecture in the Mess Hall and then went for a short route march before supper. Learned how to fold our greatcoats. Blancoed and polished my webbing and rifle. Saw Corporal Rankine again and told him of my radio experience. He is going to see the Lieut. this week.

JAN. 27, SAT.

Supposed to have inspection today but if we did I didn't notice it. I will have to postpone all letter writing until pay-day: no stamps. May go up and see Donna tonight. I had my issue mitts stolen today. The Q.M.S. won't do anything about so will have to take someone else's. Went up to see Donna but she wasn't home; came back to bed.

JAN. 28, SUN.

Only two meals today. Started a letter to Nelle. Washed a towel, pair of socks and six hankies. Did a little studying.

JAN. 29, MON.

Supposed to have had a full marching pack inspection. Stood from ten A.M. till noon with full pack but no inspection. Handed in our rifles for a check-up today.

JAN. 30, TUES.

Hard day at Minto Armouries. Went up to Donna's again but she wasn't in. Raining and freezing here tonight. Streets are pretty slick. The roof is leaking in a dozen places.

JAN. 31, WED.

Payday. Detailed for Barrack Room Guard until 9:30P.M. Drew out two pair of fatigue pants, size 46 W. & 33 L. and 36 W. & 33 L. Why do they make them so doggone big? Took my uniform trouser to the tailors for alterations. Had my rifle checked by the armourer and as I suspected it was duly condemned. No rifle now for a few days. Am going to blow myself to a 40¢ meal tomorrow.

FEB. 1, THURS.

Had a good meal and did considerable shopping then went to a show.

FEB. 3, SAT.

Mess hall fatigue in the A.M.; went to a show this afternoon; had supper at the Denver Café again; did some more shopping and took in another show.

FEB. 4, SUN.

Attended church parade this A.M. Wrote a letter to Bobbie this afternoon. Went out for supper and came back for the free show in the Mess Hall. Good show. Hope we get out new hats tomorrow.

FEB. 5, MON.

Had a tiring day at Minto. We didn't get our new hats. It's like everything else, delays and false alarms. Getting tired of this "E" company business. We are never included in any battalion plans or events, we are always the last to be issued with anything and on top of all that there is a chance that I may be among the 150 of "E" Coy. That remain behind when the Battalion goes away. Wrote a letter to Nelle.

FEB. 6, TUES.

Went to a lecture on Arms and ammunition given by Lieut. Rutherford in the Army Hut on Main Street. Received letters from Nelle, Connie and Mommie Sharpe. My mail is sure piling up on me. Every day finds me closer to the time when I will lose control of myself and get into trouble. Things don't seem to be so smooth in this outfit. Took in a show until 2400 hrs.

FEB. 7, WED.

Bath parade today in the A.M. Supposed to have a kit inspection this P.M. Hung around for 3 hours and no inspection. They seem to have lots of fun seeing us standing around. Issued with a housewife (sewing kit) today. Wrote a letter to Mr. Gibson.

FEB. 8, THURS.

Went to the Army Hut for another lecture in the A.M. Had a blanco parade this afternoon. Went down to the station to see a bunch of replacements for the Seaforth Highlanders go through and had a good time doing it. Wouldn't be surprised if we left around the twentieth of next month which is not at all too soon to suit me. I'll have to go up and see Donna tomorrow night and inspect her pressing facilities as I have to press my trouser for the D.C.O.'s inspection next week. Bad time to apply for a leave of absence.

FEB. 9, FRI.

Paraded to the Y.M. for a swim. I prefer the Y to the Sherbrooke Baths; we have more fun at the Y. Saw some fellows from the Battery at Kenora, in the Y this afternoon; George Kerr, Sonny Oulette, Bill Mitchel and a few others. They are leaving for Kingston on Tues. the 13th. Went out to St. Boniface this afternoon for company drill; had a hard time in the deep snow. We learned when we got back that we are duty company from today until next Friday. So they get rid of us until after the inspection. I am detailed for basement fatigue tomorrow.

Went up to see Donna again tonight but she wasn't home. Had a midnight pass but booked in at 9 o'clock.

Completely and positively fed up and disgusted. We don't know where we stand in this "E" Company.

FEB. 10, SAT.

Detailed for basement fatigue. Wrote two letters, one to Con and one to Nelle. May have another nephew soon. Didn't go out tonight.

FEB. 11, SUN.

Went to church parade today. Wrote letters to Rosie and Mrs. Sharpe.

FEB. 12, MON.

Kitchen fatigue. Got a midnight pass and once more tried to find Donna. Wonders of wonders, she was in and had quite an evening. Promised to go back tomorrow night. She is pretty lonely for home town folk.

FEB. 13, TUES.

Worked all day in the Mess Hall, scrubbing tables and floor. Went up to Donna's again tonight and she pressed my uniform, including my greatcoat. I went up for supper and had a very good evening. Got in at 2400 hrs. Completely out of tobacco and hate to borrow more.

FEB. 15, THURS.

On guard duty all last night and today until 6:00P.M. Had a midnight pass and went up to see Donna. Had a real good time. She wants me to go to so many places with her I can't remember them. She really has not changed as much as I first thought the night I saw her first. Almost broke again.

FEB. 16, FRI.

Went up to Minto until after twelve noon and I seemed to be dumber than usual today. Had a short route march and sort of enjoyed it.

Took in a show at the Lyceum tonight. Three of the fellows, Albert Perry, J. L. Hill (60) and Dunbar are fooling around pulling each others' bunks apart. They are sure raising a big noise around here.

FEB. 17, SAT.

Had kit inspection this A.M. and nothing much came of it. They, at least, walked around and glanced at the kits this time. Went to a show this afternoon and had supper at the Denver Café and then took in another show.

I offered to change seats with a young lady who was sitting beside me right behind a pillar but she refused. She wouldn't even move when there were better seats available.

FEB. 18, SUN.

Went on church parade this A.M. Went up to Donna's for supper and then went to church with her. She really hasn't changed much. I have a good time up there and have lots of fun. I help her with her studies and we have some good talks, comparing people and places. Due to the number of late passes I am getting, the fellows are beginning to think I am going to the dogs. What a laugh.

FEB. 19, MON.

Had a three hour route march this A.M. and had trouble with my shoes. There are two holes in the soles and the snow packs in between the soles making marching a painful ordeal. The shoes are in the shoemaker's and Lord only knows when I'll be getting them back. In the meantime, I will have to keep out of sight so that they won't tack a fatigue on me as I can't go on parade without shoes. I think I should blanco my web equipment.

FEB. 20, TUES.

Put my first day in at the musketry school. It's going alright so far. Wrote a little note to Bobs tonight. I can't figure out when would be the best time to get my home leave. I think I'll wait until pay day; I may have more money then. Some of the C.B. boys are doing pack drill tonight. I hope they enjoy it. I was the only Private who took notes at school today and now the other fellows are asking for them.

FEB. 21, WED.

Had a good day at the school. Got myself a pass and called on Donna again; helped her with her first aid lesson. If Donna doesn't happen to be home when I call, I just walk in and wait for her. Getting to know her friends and neighbours fairly well.

FEB. 22, THURS.

Attended school in the day time. Was given the job of making out passes for our section. Am supposed to be second in command of our section and still wish I wasn't.

FEB. 24, SAT.

Had a preliminary test at the school today and had trouble with my rifle jamming in rapid fire; didn't do so good. Weekend passes given away wholesale this weekend but didn't take one as I have no where to go and no money. Mailed letters to Bobbie, Nelle and Jack. There is another call for potential signalers but I am not sure if I should apply or not. If I did get in I may not get my two weeks leave.

Lazed around all night until Tattoo.

FEB. 25, SUN.

Had to shave in cold water this morning because the heaters had failed during the night. Scrubbed my equipment this morning and blancoed it this afternoon. Will have to polish the brass tonight. Barrack Room inspection by Brig. Gen. Browne of G.H.Q. tomorrow and everything has to be perfect.

FEB. 26, MON.

School today. Went up to see Donna. She had her first aid exam and she thinks she passed alright.

FEB. 27, TUES.

School. Went up to help Donna study; had a good time and learned a lot about ancient history.

FEB. 28, WED.

School. Went to the Ice Carnival on a free pass and met Herb there. Herb is a next door neighbour of Donna's and he is a real decent chap. He is too young to be anything else. She also has a Cameron by the name of Harvey, for a neighbour. He is in "A" company.

FEB. 29, THURS.

Had our examination today and made third highest score. Pay parade today.

MARCH 2, SAT.

Roy dropped in to see me along with Maurice Crawford and George Pearce. They wanted me to go with them but I had a date with Donna which I felt I couldn't break.

MARCH 3, SUN.

Dad came in and greatly surprised me. He must think I am a big heel and a bum. Being short of time I couldn't talk to him as long as I wanted to. I only had half an hour to get ready for church parade. I also bummed a dollar off him for tobacco. Went up to the Institute for supper with Dave and Hugh, two of Donna's fellow students and then went to the Norski Baptist Church with them. I wouldn't blame Roy for thinking the same thing as I think Dad thinks.

MARCH 4, MON.

I have been here three months today. We had a route march today led by Sergeant Major Dunsheath and he had all the boys, including the officers, saying Uncle. We were all mighty tired and glad to get back.

MARCH 5, TUES.

Put in for a midnight pass this morning. Went up to Minto and had P.T., small arms training and arms drill, then marched back for dinner. We had to scrub all our bunks and the floor around them for some reason or other. Maybe it was because someone thought they were dirty.

Issued with a new pair of boots this morning and got them a little nearer my size (8½E). We all have two pair now. We also got another brush, button stick, a can of dubbin and a can of polish (shoe). The big problem now is, where shall I put it all.

Went up to Donna's and helped her study. Just how I help her is a mystery to me. Maybe it's moral support.

MARCH 6, WED.
Went for P.T. and swim parade at the Y.M.C.A. then marched up to Minto for rifle drill and ceremonial march. A hard day. Stayed in tonight and washed my head. Got a pair of gloves from Nelle today; a real pair of gloves.

MARCH 7, THURS.
Minto again this morning. Was stiff and slow during drill this morning because of the P.T. yesterday. Had a lecture by our C.O., Lieut. Ross, on various things that the boys have been doing and shouldn't and things they should be doing and haven't. I didn't mind it a bit as we just sat and listened for two hours. I am feeling intensely disgusted with everything tonight; particularly myself. I guess I'll have to get a few days leave to get myself in a better frame of mind.

MARCH 8, FRI.
Went to Minto for the day. Had P.T. and bayonet fighting in the morning and ceremonial march in the afternoon.

Went up to Donna's tonight and had the usual good time there.

MARCH 9, SAT.
Had C.O.'s inspection this morning and then had a short route march. Blancoed my outfit right after dinner and Mr. Gibson dropped in with Walter Bradley. He invited me to the Kenora-Brandon hockey match tonight. Saw Eric and Janet and they gave me a ticket to the game. Sat beside Bert Nilson. Kenora won 3-2 after a very fast and rough game. Brandon is eliminated now. Eric also made arrangements with Orald Holmes, Jr., son of the manager of the amp. For me to secure tickets for the next two play-off games. Also have

me two dollars to pay for the tickets. I think that was darned decent of him. Saw loads of Kenora people at the game. My voice is ruined for a while after the hollering I did at the game. Had lots of fun.

MARCH 10, SUN.
Went to church parade this A.M. and took a little walk this P.M. before supper. Didn't see any Kenora people during my walk so I guess they have all gone home. Attended the free show but it didn't turn out as good due to a defect in the projector.

MARCH 11, MON.
Had equipment parade this morning and to me it was just a waste of time as I have all of my equipment. Received a letter from Bobbie. Detailed for first aid class tonight under Sergeant Bement. I'll have to phone Donna and tell her I'll be late getting there. My voice is gradually coming back again.

MARCH 12, TUES.
Was told today that anyone on First Aid Class can't get furlough until the course is completed six weeks from now. I think I'll try again Friday morning. Went out to Minto this A.M. and a short route march this P.M. Had our shooting tests today on the indoor range and made eight bull's eyes and two inners out of ten shots. The officer in charge said I did very good. That completes my T.O.E.T. and I have no doubts that I have passed okay.

MARCH 13, WED.
Went for a P.T. and swim parade at the Y.M.C.A. and they sure gave us a workout. Marched up to Minto for lunch and then took part in the ceremonial practice. We were complimented on our showing and the officers seemed highly pleased and happy about the whole thing. Took in a show tonight called, "Shipyard Sally" starring Gracie Fields. I am going up on "orders" tomorrow to try for 3½ days' leave. Tomorrow is pay day.

MARCH 14, THURS.
Went up on orders this A.M. about my pass, advised to wait until next weekend as it will be a long one, from Thursday night to Monday night.

Went to Minto until noon and then came back for pay parade. Took an hour's instruction in Anti-Tank Rifle. Went up to see Donna but she didn't come home until ten.

MARCH 15, FRI.

Had a hard day at Minto, pretty tired tonight. Some of the boys have their battle dress. We expect ours tomorrow. Went up to Donna's for supper then went to a church away up on Burnett and Alverstone where there was a special service with a minister from the States. I think his name was Rev. Jarden, but I am not sure. Met a few more of Donna's student friends. They were singing duets and solos for the service. The minister was a very forceful talker with an accent I couldn't place.

MARCH 16, SAT.

Had line inspection this A.M. and were told the company fund was to be liquidated. Also, there is a possibility that the reinforcements will be split up among the other companies and the Reinforcements done away with. Anyone who is not lucky enough to be transferred will be placed in depot which means he will not go with the battalion when it moves. Here's hoping I get a transfer of some kind. We are supposed to get our Battle Dress on Monday but I'll believe it when I see it. Albert Perry from Saskatchewan is being transferred to "B" company tomorrow. Took in two shows tonight.

MARCH 17, SUN.

Had a battalion church parade today. The Chaplain told the men and officers to take their wives and kiddies to their own churches next Sunday as it might be their last chance to do so. I wonder if that means something, or everything or anything. Wrote a letter to Bobs, Em and Nelle. I am becoming quite a letter fiend. If I don't get one a day something seems to be lacking. No free show tonight, no reason given.

Went down town for my supper. An extravagant luxury. The splitting up of old "E" company seems to be almost certain now. I wonder when it will take place. Surely not during the Easter holidays. Will be washing dishes tomorrow I think. Headquarters had orders today to have all passes completed as soon as possible. May move out within a month. It's time I did some study-ing for first aid, second class tomorrow night.

MARCH 18, MON.
Washed dishes in the Mess Hall for an hour after every meal. Kit inspection today. The beginning of the end of the First Reinforcements started today. I asked for a transfer to signals. Other fellows who also applied are: big Bill Richardson, MacKay, Bill Robertson and few others I am not so familiar with. Every man in the 1ˢᵗ Rein. will be transferred to one of the other companies.

This shake has to come just when I am trying to get leave. We will know for sure tomorrow where we go. Went to First Aid class tonight and Palmer and I were doing bandages that the class hasn't even taken yet. The bandaging is fairly easy if one studies the book carefully.

MARCH 19, TUES.
Went to Minto on the last parade for the Reinforcements. Had a pretty stiff workout. Was transferred to the Signallers today. The only one out of eight that applied. The rest of the eight are in transport with the remainder of other companies. Things for me are very unsettled at present. They couldn't find a bunk for me in the signal section so I am placed far removed from the proper sleeping place, but they tell me it is only temporary. I'll have to see Sgt. Rankine about a number of things; I'll have to see the H.Q. Sergeant Major about a leave of absence tomorrow morning and will most likely get my new battle dress.

The Lodge Jinx is working again. Before the Signals were exempt from all fatigues but now that I am in it they are doing just as much work as any one.

Went up to Donna's tonight and Mary was there. Donna is going home for Easter Holidays with Mrs. & Mr. Blanket. I sure hope I can get my elusive leave of absence about the same time.

MARCH 20, WED.
Saw the H.Q. C.S.M. this morning and as luck would have it, Capt. Shankland is away on leave and won't be back until Tuesday, at which time I

am supposed to go down and see him again. He left orders that no one who had joined after Nov. 15 could receive leave unless it was absolutely necessary, so I guess that is that.

Went for a bath and P.T. parade this morning. Got our new battle dress today. Nothing for looks but made for comfort. Tried to get my Easter holidays this weekend but it was no go. Wrote a hasty letter to Nelle. Blancoed my outfit.

MARCH 21, THURS.
Had a Lewis Gun lecture in the Mess Hall just to pass the time but it was all old stuff to me. I wish they would find a bunk for me in the signals lines. Received another letter from Bobbie today. Fooled around all afternoon doing practically nothing. Went up to see Donna before she went home for Easter; wrote a note to Mommie for her to take with her. Listened to the last of the first Elmwood-Kenora game. Kenora won 4-5. I tried my darnedest to get home for Easter but I am glad now they refused as I may be able to get six days instead of four and we get paid on Thursday.

MARCH 22, FRI.
Good Friday. Had a little fatigue this A.M. which we finished in about half an hour. Went to a show this afternoon; had supper at the Denver Café; ran into Freddie Brinkman there. He said he is up for a week's holiday.

Received a letter from Nelle and one from Connie today. I am away behind in my letter writing now. Started a letter to Bobbie tonight. Would like to get home for awhile. I guess I have a bad case of homesickness. I haven't been detailed for fatigues yet although I have been in H.Q. three days now. Maybe they can't remember my name. I only hope it lasts until after the Holidays when some other company takes over the duties. I think I'll try and borrow Cpl. Rankine's signalling manual and do a little studying.

MARCH 23, SAT.
Hardly did a thing all morning. Borrowed a signalling book from Corporal Richardson through Corporal Rankine. I almost think I am in this signalling platoon. As far as the electrical part goes it is just a review to me. I'll have to study the semaphore for a little more. Went up to Donna's room tonight to

do some studying but who should drop in but Jack and Mary. We talked for awhile then studied a little more, then we had a lunch. I came back to barracks soon after and left them holding the fort. Heard a lot about Altoona or Altona from them and I told them a lot about the Lake and Kenora. All in all, it wasn't a bad evening. Maybe I should of left a little sooner and given them a chance to get caught up but I didn't know how to make an exit gracefully.

MARCH 24, SUN.
Did nothing all morning. Went up to Donna's room at 2 o'clock this afternoon and studied or read until 11 o'clock this evening. Also wrote a letter to Connie. Met Godfrey Campbell on Portage Avenue when I was coming back. He is going home with Nick Krantz tonight.

MARCH 25, MON.
Detailed for kitchen fatigue today, but got the job of peeling onions and got off at 11 o'clock. Went up to Donna's room for an afternoon of study; had supper at the Denver. Went to see "Four Feathers." Met Godfrey Campbell again tonight and he told me Kenora had won the game 7-2 thus winning the Manitoba Championship. Godfrey is trying to join the army but his chances are poor just now.

MARCH 26, TUES.
Went on my first parade with the signals to Minto. Had some practice at sending Morse code by flag. Went over to the Code school this afternoon and made a mess of my first buzzer test. It was in Polish which did not help matters much. I need a little practice after the long lay-off. My keying was alright. Spent a quiet evening with Donna.

MARCH 27, WED.
Went up to Minto for the day and had two hours semaphore. There is persistent rumours that we are going to Shilo this spring which is meeting with unanimous disapproval.

Applied for C.P.R. fare voucher today as I may go home tomorrow. Studied the Signal Manual tonight.

MARCH 28, THURS.

Went to Minto for the morning and had Morse flag practice. Pay parade today and had a little trouble getting paid due to recent transfer. We had to scrub our bunks before we could get our passes, I got mine around 4:30 and caught the 7:00 o'clock train for home. Mrs. Blair and Peggy Yorkton were on the train and we talked nearly all the way down. Went straight to Em's from the train and didn't get home until after midnight. Finally turned in about 3:00A.M.

MARCH 29, FRI.

Pressed my uniform and went for a walk down town with Jack. Met Bobbie at 9:30 in front of Williams. She had to work overtime. Tomorrow being Saturday she will have to work late again. Stayed at Em's until after midnight again.

MARCH 30, SAT.

Jack and I partly worked out and partly guessed Bobbie code message. Went down to Bezzie's this afternoon and stayed for supper. Midnight before I got home again.

MARCH 31, SUN.

Didn't do much all day except a little signal practice. Had my picture taken a few times. Paid a visit to Gibson's and found only Olga home. Spent the evening over at Connie's. After midnight again tonight.

APRIL 1, MON.

April Fool's Day. The outfit took in 100 new men today. There isn't much use of Jack coming up as the men are flocking around the door. Talked to Oscar Martin coming back on the train today. Kind of glad to get back but would have liked to stay away longer. Kenora won the Thunder Bay championship tonight. I hope they go right through. The Camerons took in about 80 more men today and there are still a crowd around the door.

APRIL 2, TUES.

Went to Minto this morning. Had two periods of Morse flag drill and one of bayonet fighting. Spent an hour and a half on the buzzer this P.M. I'll have to study procedure some more. Had a nice evening at Donna's. Caught another cold.

APRIL 3, WED.

Feel exceedingly miserable tonight due to a cold, sore throat and headache. Had a hard day having been thoroughly soaked by a very wet snow storm. Some sort of special parade tomorrow but didn't have the ambition to find out what. I am getting to bed at 10:00 o'clock for the first time in a week. It may do me good.

APRIL 4, THURS.

Went up to Minto for the morning and had my first experience at station work. I was supposed to be in charge of the station as it is the easiest job of the lot. All I had to do was sit and watch the other fellows work.

Semaphore practice in the C.N. yards this afternoon. Went up to Donna's this evening and met Elsie Redman and Hilda Fieten or something like that. They left early and Donna and I got some studying in. I felt pretty miserable and was running a slight temperature.

APRIL 5, FRI.

Spent the entire A.M. practicing semaphore with Carl Sund, at Minto. I learned quite a lot and am improving daily. Had ceremonial march practice in the afternoon. Stayed in tonight to doctor my cold.

APRIL 6, SAT.

Had a foot inspection this morning and a route march. Wrote a letter to Jack and one to Nelle this afternoon. Saw Godfrey Campbell again tonight. He is up here trying to get in again.

APRIL 7, SUN.

Church parade today. Went up to Donna's this afternoon and pressed my uniform. We went for a walk around the parliament buildings, then Donna cooked a good supper. Went to service at the Alliance with Donna and Herb, then attended the student's service at the school. Had a lunch with Mary and Donna at Donna's place. I don't mind going to church so much now.

APRIL 8, MON.

Two new men in the signals; one was an instructor sergeant in the Royal Signals and the other has had experience at radio operating. They are both plenty good and may be the cause of me being dropped. Had a good day at the code school today and I know lots more about procedure. Was taking about eight words a minute on the buzzer. I wasn't included in the first aid class tonight so stayed in and started a letter to Rose.

APRIL 9, TUES.

Had semaphore practice all morning at Minto. Me, a three week signaller teaching a man that has been in it for three or four months. Screwy. Had my first experience signalling during field formations. It's interesting. Got a letter from Bobbie saying she was coming up and to buy tickets for the game with three dollars she enclosed. Tickets are all sold up here. Made arrangements for a Reveille pass for Wednesday and sent Bobbie an answer. Went up to Donna's this evening; she had to go to a social so I slept until she got back.

APRIL 10, WED.

Swim parade at the Y.M.C.A. until 10:00 o'clock, then code school until noon. Back to school again this afternoon for some more practice. I think I am improving every day. Met the special at 5:10P.M. and Bobs and I had supper at the Denver Café. We walked up to the Amph on the off chance of buying tickets for the game. We were exceptionally lucky in being able to buy seats No.'s 38 and 39 that some one had just canceled.

Enjoyed the game immensely. After seeing Bobs off home I finally turned in around 1:30A.M.

APRIL 11, THURS.

A very easy day all around. Had one hour on target finding, 2 hours at map reading. Had a little instruction in hand grenades this A.M. Went up to Donna's for the evening and slept for an hour. Studied for a while and then listened to Donna read Anne of Green Gables.

APRIL 12, FRI.

Went to buzzer practice this morning and had a good session. Had map reading this afternoon. Wrote a little to Nelle; also finished one to Jack. Listened to the hockey match for awhile; score up to now 2-1 for Edmonton with 11 penalties at the end of the first period. It will get rough later on.

APRIL 13, SAT.

Foot inspection and pay parade today. Was in the Guard of Honour for Brig. Brown during the Trooping of the Colours today. Went to a show, then came back and blancoed my outfit. Heard part of the Kenora-Edmonton game, the score at the end of the second period was 2-2. I wonder if Kenora can pull through with another win? I couldn't get a pass tonight as I have had my full allotment for this week. Blancoed my outfit tonight.

APRIL 14, SUN.

Polished the brass on my web and then had a fatigue which lasted for one hour. Spent all afternoon and the evening with Donna.

APRIL 15, MON.

Spent the morning at some badly needed buzzer practice. Improved a little. An hour of buzzer again this afternoon. Attended a lecture on gas for the last hour.

Had supper out and then took in a show. Started a letter to Bobbie tonight.

APRIL 16, TUES.

Went on an eighteen mile route march today and sort of enjoyed it. Went up to Donna's tonight and she and I did some good studying. We also listened to the Oshawa-Kenora game. Kenora lost 1-0.

APRIL 17, WED.

P.T. and swim parade at the Y.M. They had a broadcast of our sing song and the band playing then they marched us around to the booth on Portage for free coffee. The booth is fixed up like a sand bag shelter. We then proceeded to Minto and had a half an hour's rifle drill before dinner.

In the afternoon we had station work in conjunction with the platoons of the company. Wrote a letter to Rose tonight and copied more notes. I am writing this with my feet in a basin of water. They have needed soaking for quite some time.

APRIL 18, THURS.

Went to code school for the A.M. Had semaphore station work this P.M. Listened to a hockey broadcast. Kenora lost again 4-1.

APRIL 19, FRI.

Went to the code school for two hours then proceeded to Minto where we had a mess tin inspection. One hour of semaphore station work this afternoon with me sending on flags. Not so good. One hour of ceremonial marching. Had a good shower tonight and wrote a letter to Nelle. Hope her answer to my watch proposition is favourable.

APRIL 20, SAT.

Had kit inspection this A.M. followed by a short route march. They gave me a weekend pass and as is usually the case, I was broke so just walked around town as I thought maybe Bobbie had come up but there was no special so gave up. Listened to the hockey broadcast in front of a store on Portage. Kenora 4-3. Saw Rod Gibson who promised to send Ted's address. Exceedingly pleased that Ted has finally got a start in aviation even if it is the Air Force. He is a second class aircraftman and I hope he doesn't get like the rest of that self satisfied branch of the service. I don't think he will.

APRIL 21, SUN.

Didn't go on church parade because I had a weekend pass. Went up to Donna's this afternoon and evening. Attended the Third Year Class Service at the school this evening.

APRIL 22, MON.

Code school this morning. I am getting fast enough to move to a faster table. Semaphore this afternoon at Minto.

APRIL 23, TUES.

Starvation parade at Minto today. That is, we didn't have dinner until 1:30P.M. Station work all morning. Did a little sending today. Code school this afternoon and moved to a faster table. Learned how not to send by listening to others.

Went up to Donna's this evening to tell her that I wouldn't be able to attend the Class Day Exercises. Some military plans will interfere.

APRIL 24, WED.

Swim and P.T. parade at the Y. until 11:00A.M. Then to Minto for station work with Morse flag. Ceremonial for rest of the afternoon. Night march tonight from 7:30P.M. until 2:00A.M. Scared a few farmers half to death.

APRIL 25, THURS.

Practically lazed around all morning; had kit inspection and a short route march as a muscle loosener. Went to Code school this afternoon.

APRIL 26, FRI.

Went to Code school for a while this A.M. then to Minto. Had ceremonial this afternoon. Attended the Graduation Service for the school this evening, nicely arranged and carried out.

APRIL 27, SAT.

Had kit inspection and then scrubbed our bunks. Blancoed this afternoon.

Went down town with Al Perry and sold my watch for $2.00. Al and I went to a show and had a bite to eat afterward. We walked around until 12:30A.M.

APRIL 28, SUN.
Started a letter to Bobbie at 1100 hrs and finished it at 1500 hours. Paid a call to Mrs. Groves. I'll have to go up more often.

APRIL 29, MON.
Went to buzzer school this morning and afternoon. Received a letter from Bobbie with a dollar from Em in it.

Went up to see Donna for the last time before she goes to Herriots. She will only be there a week then she is going home.

APRIL 30, TUES.
Code school all day. Payday so I bought a 15 jewel wrist watch for $19.95, Serial No. 9180 with a luminous dial. Went to a couple of shows tonight.

APRIL 31, WED.
Code school until 1000hrs. then a swim at the Y.M.C.A. then Code school until 1145hrs. School again from 1400hrs until 1545hrs. I have a hunch I'll be running short of smokes this week.

MAY 1, THURS.
Went to Code school this morning. Was granted a 48 hour embarkation leave and travelling time. But it is not going to do me much good as I haven't the fare to go home. This ought to be the last chance to see the folks at home.

MAY 2, THURS.
Applied for 48 hour leave again. I am optimistic and hope to be able to borrow enough. Was at the Code school all day today. A wire from Jack placed $8.00 at my disposal which solved the problem of train fare. I have to pack up and get out of here.

Arrived in town at 15 minutes to 10 or 0945hrs. Stayed at Em's until 2100hrs. Got to bed 0200hrs. Friday morning.

MAY 3, FRI.

Lazed around all morning. Went to a show with Jack. Went up to Bobbie's this evening and had a good time.

MAY 4, SAT.

Did some visiting in the morning. Went down to Bezzie's for supper and had a good time. Visited the Gibson's about eight o'clock. Accompanied Olga down town and had quite a lot of fun. Finally got home at 0200hrs in the morning.

MAY 5, SUN.

Went bicycling with Bobbie this morning and enjoyed the ride very much. Caught No. 1 this afternoon and arrived in Winnipeg at eight P.M. Phoned Donna but she wasn't at home. Went to the Denver Café for something to eat then came back and handed my pass in, thus ending my 48 hour embarkation leave.

MAY 6, MON.

Code school all day today. Delivered Connie's letter and fare money to Donna tonight and arranged for her to go on the 6:45 train tomorrow night. Met Vera on Portage and she asked me to phone her mother after Friday. Vera has changed quite a lot; she looks a lot thinner and has blonde hair. I didn't recognize her until she stopped me.

MAY 7, TUES.

Code school all day where we were honoured(?) by a visit of the District Signalling Officer.

Went down to see Donna off but must have missed her in the crowd. Now I don't know if she has gone home or not. May have to wear kilts on Decoration Day parade.

MAY 8, WED.

Wrote a letter to Bobbie tonight.

MAY 9, THURS.

Code school this morning. Was ordered to get another hair cut as this one is not short enough. We were told today that the advance party will leave for Shilo on the 21st and we will leave Shilo within a month for the east. Went to Minto for ceremonial this afternoon. Stayed in again tonight and slept and read. There isn't much else to do these days.

MAY 10, FRI.

Code school all day. Things are getting more interesting now. We had our first lecture in the use, care and operation of the heliograph today and I found it very interesting. Things are coming so fast now I find it hard to record it all. Due for a short haircut tomorrow. Received a note from Vera inviting me up to Elliott's on Sunday evening. Was told today by Lieut. Kent that I would be operating a D III or D Mark 3, a combination phone and code set for the inspection when and if it were necessary to put on demonstration for Inspector General Ashton. We soon will be having qualification tests and we are not so sure we are ready for it.

MAY 11, SAT.

We had to scrub our bunks this morning for O.C. inspection. Had a reveille pass tonight but no way of using it.

MAY 12, SUN.

The big church parade went through with hardly a hitch as far as I could see. Finally got around to see Vera and found that she is a welcome diversion from army routine. Learning things I never knew about her before. Anyway, I had a good time.

MAY 14, TUES.

At last the big day dawned and we were duly inspected by his nibs who turned out to be a fairly decent sort. He was very pleased with the signal demonstration when he sent a message and it passed through eleven stations without a hitch. I finally ended up "flashing the glam." Went up to see Vera again tonight and had quite a talk with Mrs. Elliott. I am going up to Strathcona St. If I can find my way up there.

MAY 15, WED.

Eight of us so called signallers were detailed to establish and maintain communication between the butts and the firing pits at the St. Charles Rifle Range today. It lasted all day and was the easiest day I have spent in the army to date. "A" and "D" were doing the shooting, our job was to report any required checks on the targets.

MAY 16, THURS.

School all morning. Went to Minto this morning with the Decoration Day detail for kilts. We were issued with a full kilt outfit and Balmoral. Saw Vera tonight.

MAY 17, FRI.

On the phone all day at the St. Charles rifle range. Stayed in tonight to fix my kilt and Balmoral. These Balmorals look like a flattened wash basin.

MAY 18, SAT.

Spent most of the day fixing my kilt for tomorrow. Wore the kilt for first time when I took Vera to a show. Had my picture taken on Portage Avenue during the rush hour by three pretty young ladies from the States. I still don't know if they took it because of my good looks or the uniform or both. Balmoral and kilts, what a combination. Am glad that no one from Kenora is here.

MAY 19, SUN.

Decoration Day parade and a hot tiring time we had of it too. Went up to Elliott's for supper and had a real good meal.

MAY 20, MON.

Spent the day taking my shooting tests at St. Charles range and did fairly well despite the crosswind.

MAY 21, TUES.

Left for Camp Shilo this morning at 9:00A.M. Arrived here at 12:30 and worked from 3:30P.M. to 8:00P.M.

MAY 22, WED.

Worked all day putting up tents and getting the camp ready for the Battalion on Friday. I am in the same tent with "Doc" Draper, Jim Whittaker and "Mac" McGuire.

MAY 23, THURS.

Spent the day working around camp, changing some of the tents and filling palliases with straw. Wrote to Nelle tonight.

MAY 24, FRI.

The Battalion arrived today and completely shattered the peace and tranquility of our camp. Sgt. Rankine made "Doc" move out and put in L/cp. Suttlehan. Sorry to see "Doc" moved as he is lots of fun.

Doc and I have something in common, we both like lakes, pine trees and rocky hills and we both have a distinct dislike for this flat land all around here.

MAY 25, SAT.

It's kind of tough shaving in the morning as it is pretty cold at that time of day and cold water isn't the best of liquid to use for that purpose; besides, my razor blades are all exceedingly dull. I didn't do much all day and I slept this afternoon. "Doc" wants me to go for a walk tomorrow to the River which is four miles away and forms one of the Camp boundaries. Had a chat with Doc before "lights out" and we compared experiences in canoeing, boating, driving, etc. I like to listen to his flying experiences. Fort Garry House pulled in today. Calgary Highlanders are due tomorrow.

MAY 26, SUN.

Almost had a fight this morning with the fireman over hot water. I got my hot water okay. Word just came around for the advance guard to stand by at a moment's notice. There will be no signallers on it so I guess I am stuck in this god forsaken place.

Spent most of the day at lectures on map reading, code practice, heliograph, lamp and D III's. G.H.Q. suddenly decided to give us a classification test tomorrow and no one is ready for it. Received a letter from Bobbie with stamps and a dollar enclosed in it which came in mighty handy, as I was entirely out of tobacco. I have missed Bobbie's letters a lot lately. I answered it tonight. Studying is what is required right now but I can't settle down to it.

MAY 27, MON.
Hard at it today getting ready for our classifications which was postponed until tomorrow. Roy Miller, Leich, Smith, McGuire and myself nearly walked to the river tonight. We had loads of fun watching the people walking around in Brandon, 18 miles away from here, with signalling telescopes (15 power).

MAY 28, TUES.
Had our tests today; everybody failed, but we will have another chance at it ten day's from now. Wrote a letter to Vera tonight. Received one from Nelle.

MAY 29, WED.
Lamp and semaphore practice all day. Practiced semaphore with Reg Langston after supper. Lieut. Kent took us out to show us how a lamp looked at night. Wrote a letter to Jack.

SUMMARY OF THE TIME BETWEEN LAST ENTRY AND THIS DATE, JUNE 7, 1940.
We have done little else but read the lamp daytime and night, compulsory and voluntarily.

Had another qualification test and was one of the seven that passed. Taking quite a riding from the boys that failed. Their kidding is getting Whittaker down.

JUNE 8, SAT.
It started to rain about noon but we wouldn't let it interfere with our prearranged plans. Doc, Sgt. Rankine and I went for a walk to the river despite the downpour and had lots of fun. "Doc" and the Sgt. are firmly convinced that I am an Indian. They have called me all kinds of names all starting with big chief. They even told Lieut. Kent of my supposed ability to read trail signs.

JUNE 9, SUN.
Sunday, which turned out to be a wet miserable cold day which nobody enjoyed.

JUNE 10, MON.
Station work with D III's this morning. Map reading this afternoon.

JUNE 11, TUES.
Station work with D III's again this morning. We were signalling six miles this afternoon with heliograph: very interesting. Had some fun tonight blanket tossing. Yep, I got tossed and went back for more.

JUNE 12, WED.
We had a signalling system with heliograph going this morning. Doc was in charge of the first station near the camp. I had charge of the next station six miles distant and Lieut. Kent had the third station 16 miles from Doc's station. Had buzzer practice this afternoon in one of the Marquees. Started a letter to Bobbie tonight.

JUNE 17, MON.
I was placed in charge of No. 2 group today. They are the fellows who had a little tough luck in the last test. Why he picked me still remains somewhat of a mystery as anyone of them can tell me things about signalling. Had to attend an N.C.O.'s meeting as a potential L/cpl. Not so fussy about that job especially in this platoon. Both Doc and I go.

JUNE 18, TUES.
Attended another demonstration today, and Lt. Col. McBrayne spoke to us.

No. 1 platoon has to erect a telephone system between 6th Brigade, H.Q. and the three units. Sid Sutton informs me that Jack has joined up. I sincerely wish him luck. He may be a lot better off than I am. We finished the phone line about 8:00P.M.

JUNE 19, WED.

In charge of No. 2 group again and they didn't give me as much trouble as I thought they would. Code practice this afternoon. Had a Lewis gun practice session tonight which lasted for 1 hour. Fooled around for the rest of the evening.

JUNE 20, THURS.

Had a swell lamp scheme going this morning. I had a station to myself and had to do my own reading, writing and sending. Detailed for phone duty at the rifle range this evening. We got our new equipment today and it's a cinch compared to the old stuff.

I just happen to think I have been in over six months and I am entitled to furlough.

JUNE 22, SAT.

Got up at 3:30P.M. today for the purpose of shooting my Lewis gun qualifications. Had the guns all set up and targets up, then it started to rain so it was postponed. Spent all morning cleaning and drying the guns off. Back on the range again this afternoon (soldier's half holiday). Made a score of 137 out of a possible 150. I learned later that it was expert shooting.

JUNE 23, SUN.

On duty all day as an exchange operator in the Battalion Orderly Room; learned a lot of procedure. Lot of visitors came in today. The new Y.M.C.A. Hut opened officially this morning.

JUNE 24, MON.

Issued with respirators at noon so spent all afternoon learning how to use them. I was just starting a letter to Nelle, tonight when Sid Sutton came in and said his father and mother left him holding a bag. A bag full of eats and he wanted some help at disposing of it. I didn't refuse. Butterscotch pie, chocolate cakes, tarts, etc. Some feed. Reminded me of when George and I used to raid the pantry.

JUNE 25, TUES.

Went up on orders today to try for a week or so furlough and the C.S.M. said he would check the records and would advise me this afternoon. I won't say anything to the family until I am sure of getting it. If I don't get it no one will be disappointed. Had gas drill all day today and it gets awfully tiresome.

The C.S.M. failed to do anything about my furlough but says he will tomorrow. I was on phone duty at the range for three hours tonight. We got our new light canvas shoes today to wear after parade hours. Started a letter to Nelle last night but that is as far as I've gone. Gee, I hope they see fit to give me my furlough, three to six days at home, boy, what a thought. There is no further word about my rumoured promotion, as yet, I doubt very much if I will ever get it. It's starting to rain.

JUNE 26, WED.

Had lamp reading practice until 10:00A.M. then we were shoved through the gas chamber in a hurry. We will be getting the special signal respirator soon which means a couple of more trips to the gas chamber.

I saw the C.S.M. about my furlough and he informs me that he thinks he has it all lined up and will know for sure tomorrow. Went in and had a gander at Lister's code machine: pretty good. Got a letter from Jack and wrote one to Nelle.

JUNE 27, THURS.

Showers today so we spent the morning in one of the Marquees on code practice and theory. Got our new water bottles today and had to sign our pay books. Got another letter from Bobbie.

JUNE 28, FRI.

Payday today. Was promised today by the C.S.M. that if I stayed in camp for duty this weekend I would get ten days furlough next weekend. I was on phone duty again tonight with Beck.

JUNE 29, SAT.
Missed fatigues today by saying I was on phone duty tomorrow. Went to Brandon with Tully, where we were supposed to meet Doc at the Carlton Café at 8:00P.M. Doc turned up at 10:00 which didn't matter a great deal as I had a chance of getting better acquainted with "Shorty" a young lady that I have talked to on former visits. Had a new mainspring put in my watch, also bought a dictionary to aid in my correspondence.

JUNE 30, SUN.
Got up at 9:30 this morning: it's the first morning that I am able to remember since I joined up when I haven't heard Reveille blown. Went on phone duty at 12:00 noon with Tully and came off 10:00P.M. Wrote letters to Nelle, Bobbie, Jack and Vera.

JULY 1, MON.
Got out of fatigues by saying I was on phone duty all day Sunday and it worked again. Went to Brandon to take in the fair and this time Tully and I had to hitch as the train had been cancelled. Got a ride for four miles from camp, walked two and were finally picked up by the Manager of the Greyhound Bus Lines in his private car and rode right into Brandon. Talked to "Shorty" while waiting for "Doc." I know her name and address now. Doc finally arrived in a state of high anger because the Brandon Flying Club's one plane was unfit for flying today. Took in the Brandon Fair. Had a hard time finding room in a Shilo bound bus; finally made it at 4:30A.M.

JULY 2, TUES.
Another qualification test for the boys who failed to pass the last time. I was put to work teaching four new fellows the Morse Code. Didn't do too badly.

JULY 3, WED.
Tackled the C.S.M. again about my leave and was told that it would start at 4:30P.M. Had quite a time before I got away, what with all the necessary things that had to be attended to before I could leave: finally caught the 7:30 bus to Brandon. Train doesn't leave until 5:00A.M. so will have a long wait.

JULY 4, THURS.
Home at last. I have a hunch that these ten days are going to go awfully fast.

JULY 5, FRI.
Paid Harry and Bezzie a visit tonight and spent a very enjoyable and somewhat lazy evening with B & B, Bobbie, Bern and Len Page. It's good to be home again even if there isn't much doing.

JULY 6, SAT.
Paid visits to Mommie's and Biddie's and had a look at the daughter. Made a date with Donna for Tuesday night.

Connie's kiddies are measuring up to and greatly surpassing everything that I have been told about them in my various letters. They are four great little youngsters. Of course, little Holly isn't much of a conversationalist yet but give her time.

Went down town tonight for the second time since I have been home. The people seem to derive great amusement from the Balmoral or maybe it's all my imagination.

JULY 7, SUN.
Went for a walk with Bobbie this afternoon. Ended the day at Em's. Bobbie and I read Bill's diaries for a couple of hours. I should write a letter to Jack, and one to "Shorty." I suppose I should send some sort of explanation to BB too but I don't know how to go about it, so I want to discourage certain aspects of that angle. I am developing a certain degree of independence which is causing me to gamble with other people's estimation of myself.

Looking ahead, I wonder if they will all greet me so enthusiastically, when I get my "civvies" on again, as they do now? I am afraid I am getting myself into some very deep water in a number of ways. Narrow minded people put a great strain on my otherwise stable patience.

JULY 8, MON.

Went over to Sharpe's for a while and spent a couple of hours talking to Donna and Bid, then we had a cup of tea. Went over to Gibson's in the evening and phoned Buddo from there. They want me to go on a wiener roast tomorrow night which I wouldn't miss for anything. Found Donna and took her out for a walk tonight instead of tomorrow.

JULY 9, TUES.

Went down town this A.M. and met Mr. Gibson; we called in at Janet's for a while then went home to Gibson's. Olga made me a lunch with a little wholesome kidding on the part of both parties, which was very favourable to the lunch. It's a pleasure to meet Olga when I go over there not to mention the rest of the family. I may as well say now what I have been thinking for a good number of years. It's a pleasure and a lucky break to have the privilege of knowing the whole "famn damily" of them, including their wives and husbands. Janet, herself, has treated me as well as any brother has been treated in any good family and Mrs. Gibson treated me better than a son, more like a guest of honour all the time I had known her until she passed away a short time ago. "Old Tom" treats me like a friend and one of the family and the rest of the family have also made me glad to associate with them. Ted, Rod, Janet, Harry, Helen, Eric, Olga, Nan, Bob and Mr. & Mrs. Gibson, I thank you for everything; the door was never locked, the ice box easily accessible whenever I went there. Maybe I didn't do a very good job of showing my appreciation during all these years, but I do owe them all a debt of gratitude.

Went out to Bavery's camp on the Lake of Two Mountains on a wiener roast with Harry and Bezzie and enjoyed myself immensely. Met a crowd of new people; Ed Leblue, the towerman, a regular guy who knows something about radio. Chic Johnston, Charlotte's boyfriend and can she pick them. Uncle Henry, Jean, Bezzie's sister who is everything that people have told me she was. Felicie treated me swell and made sure I had a wiener on my stick all the time, when the dog was done she was standing there with a bun and mustard.

Marcelle interesting me especially; I think she would make interesting company. Was given an invitation to go out to the camp Thursday night and stay until Friday night. Very much inclined to accept.

JULY 10, WED.

Attended Dawn's birthday party this afternoon and had a very good time. Bobbie gave Dawn a two wheeled bicycle for her birthday. Bobbie and I called in to Harry's and settled arrangements for tomorrow night.

JULY 11, THURS.

Went down to Bezzie's for supper and Uncle Henry was there. Boy is that man a talker. Accepted Marcelle's and Felicie's invite to their camp. Arrived there about eight o'clock. Bobbie came out for the ride with Bezzie, Harry, Junie, Teddy, Uncle Henry and myself. Climbed the tower again with Bobbie, Felicie and Bezzie. Bobbie, Harry, Bezzie, Junie and Teddy left for home about eleven o'clock, leaving me with Jean, Felicie, Marcelle and Ed Leblue. We talked until nearly 1:00A.M., then decided to retire. Marcelle had promised Harry that she would take care of me and even tuck me into bed, which she did very motherly and which I thought was pretty pleasant to say the least. Soon after we had all settled down there was a disturbance, caused by a wild animal that seemed to be trying to woo Mimi, the family's pet cat. Got to sleep at 3:00A.M.

JULY 12, FRI.

Got up at 7:15, lit the fire, put the kettle on and woke up Marcelle by tickling her nose with a piece of paper. She woke up with a smile. I liked that. Had a very good breakfast cooked by Marcelle. Then she, Georgie, Audrey (Jean's little girl) and I went out fishing until 11:30. Came back to an equally good dinner prepared by Jean and Felicie. Lemon pie, raisin pie and all the trimmings.

Went up to the tower for a couple of hours with Ed and spoke to Les Hines stationed at Pine, over the 5 meter radio transmitter. Had a real old confab and enjoyed it very much. I have finally mastered my "mike fright."

Took Felicie, Jean, Audrey and Marcelle picking water lilies; got back at 4:15P.M. Rested on the veranda with Mars until supper was ready. She asked me to write to her when I got back to Shilo; I was hoping she would, as I think she writes a very good letter. Had another very good meal. Harry, Bezzie, Mr. Bavery, Teddy and Junie arrived soon after and Marcelle, Jackie (quite a little gentleman), Audrey and Junie and myself went fishing again. Very nice on the lake, a perfect night for a canoe ride. Marcelle got the first pickerel (walled eyed pike) ever caught in the Lake of the Two Mountains. Quite an occasion; Marcelle gave me an appropriate reward for helping her. Went up to the tower with Felicie, Bezzie and Marcelle. Marc and I got better acquainted on the way up; she is a swell kid and no kidding. We all talked to Lyle Kerr at Dogtooth and had lots of fun. Before I left for town, Marcelle and I were acquainted as well as anyone could be in such a short time and she promised to send a picture of herself. I would really like to know her better; maybe I will if we correspond long enough.

I owe Harry a lot for supplying transportation and grub; I think it was Bezzie's and Marcelle's idea and Marcelle, Felicie and Jean with Ed's share thrown in gave me one of the best times I had in my life. They bid me goodbye as if I was their brother except Marcelle and that needs no explanation.

Arrived home about 1300 hours and found Bobbie there. Things are getting complicated but there is only one solution. Started home with Bobbie and noticed that Gibson's were still up and remembered my promise to drop in tonight. I told Bobbie about the promise and she made me go back while she went home alone. Got back and found Gibson's in bed so I didn't go in.

JULY 13, SAT.
Spent the morning packing up for return trip. Said goodbye to the folks who wouldn't be down at the train. Went up to Emmy's at 1:30, Bobbie's dinner hour. Bobbie translated the shorthand message and it greatly increased my worries about her. Bought a pickerel bait for Marcelle. Left Kenora at 4:30P.M. in a downpour of rain and arrived in Brandon at 1:05A.M. and was in camp at 4:40A.M.

JULY 14, SUN.
Church parade. Wrote a letter to Marcelle. I wish I had stayed an extra day, I could have gotten away with it. Pretty dead in camp after ten days with the home folk.

JULY 15, MON.
Drew out my rifle and respirator. Awfully tired. The signals formed two teams for softball today. Dots and Dashes. I am on the Dashes. Played a game tonight and lost.

JULY 16, TUES.
Nothing of any importance today.

JULY 17, WED.
Detailed for phone duty in the Battalion Orderly Room. Due for dental parade tomorrow.

JULY 18, THURS.
Dental parade at 1:30P.M. Complained about my upper plate being too loose so they are making me a new one. They wouldn't tighten the old ones. So I have no teeth again and I am taking a riding from the boys. McGuire and I put up an aerial in the officer's lines.

JULY 19, FRI.
I am not eating much due to the lack of molars. Mac and I went up to see a show at the "Y" but we had seen it before.

JULY 20, SAT.
Fatigues this morning. Received a letter from Mars which I have been anxiously waiting for all week. She writes a better letter than I even expected.

Washed my summer uniform and had a shower this afternoon. Phone duty again with Cossar at five o'clock. Started a long letter to Marcelle and posted one each to Jack and Bobbie. Came off duty at ten after a busy session.

JULY 21, SUN.
Attended church parade this morning and lost a lot of poundage from the heat. Finished a pretty lengthy letter to Marcelle that I started last night and wrote another to Harry and Bezzie. Altered the position of the flags on my tunic which were too high and forward. Sewed up my mattress which has

been emitting straw for the past week. Read a couple of stories and finished re-copying my diary from the small book to this one here. It looks like we are going to get a storm soon.

Now that my teeth are in hock, they have changed the diet from stews and soups to salads and steaks and I can't eat them. I have to make a bowl of porridge last me all day. I have spent nearly all of my tobacco money on chocolate bars which I have lived on since Thursday. I am afraid there is a financial crisis looming between now and next pay day, ten days away.

What a day! Up until 5:30P.M. it was sweltering hot and couldn't keep cool no matter how much we tried. Then a real dust storm came up which blew over quite a few tents and it's rumoured that one of the new bunk houses toppled over; we had to wear our respirators so that we could peg the tents down. Everything is covered with dust inside the tents and I suppose we will be eating it for a week. Then the thunder storms started to appear on all sides. It's very interesting to watch the lightening which is flashing continuously. The kind of a storm that I like. The storm is just about ready to beak and I want to go and watch it until the rain comes.

JULY 22, MON.

A hot blistering day. Lamp reading this morning; the heat was stifling. I must have strained a ligament in my knee during P.T.; it's getting stiff and sore. A miracle happened today, in fact two of them. We had to attend a gas decontamination center demonstration this afternoon which took about an hour. Then they told us to take off our equipment and puttees, grab a towel and fall in again. They loaded us onto trucks and took us down to the river, 3 miles away for a swim. Miracle No. 1. The ride down there was dusty as was the ride back but the time we spent in the river was worth all of the discomfiture of the dusty rides. Arrived back in camp six-thirty and they gave us "ICE-CREAM" for supper. Miracle No. 2. the ice cream was in the form of Revels and sure tasted good.

I am getting very proficient at guessing at the weather. The fellows have gotten into the habit of coming to me when they want to know when it will rain. Lieut. Kent asked me, down at the river, if it was going to rain tonight and I took the bit in my teeth and went whole hog and told him there would be a very bad storm after supper. As luck would have it, about 7:30 a real humdinger came out of the south-west. It blew like a gale and rained like a fire hose. The thunder was continuous and the lightening was flashing all the time. Some more tents went down so we had to get out and secure the other ones that were left. A good storm is about the only diversion I get around here. It looks like "Chief Wahoo" is going to stick to me. Some times it's cut to just "Wahoo."

JULY 23, TUES.
P.T. and bayonet fighting this A.M. I don't mind it so much. Had a little lamp reading and first aid for the remainder of the morning. Had some buzzer practice this afternoon. Received a letter from Nelle and started to answer it. I had to go on phone in the B.O.R. (Battalion Orderly Room) for an hour and a half because the two fellows who were supposed to be on didn't show up until 8:30P.M.

Another rip-snorting storm came up around 10:00P.M. which blew down four marquees and eight sleeping tents as far as I could count from my tent. Greatest lightening display that I have seen for some time. One Marquee was ripped from stem to stern but it was still standing after it was all over. I think I would be safe in predicting a storm every night if this hot spell hangs on.

JULY 24, WED.
Started the day by going to the Dental Clinic to get my new upper plate which turned out to be looser than the old ones. I have to go back Friday afternoon to have them fixed. Finally recollected where I had seen the dentist before. He had an orchestra for a couple of summers at the rowing club; his name is Joe Rumberg, now Lieut. Rumberg.

We were engaged with code reading practice for the rest of the morning. This afternoon was sports day so we were taken for a ride down to the river where we swam, played ball and otherwise had a good time. Got back in camp about 7:45P.M. I think we will get another storm late tonight. I'll have to try and finish Nelle's letter tonight. I am bumming tobacco from the boys now.

JULY 25, THURS.

Had to move in with Doc today which suits me okay for obvious reasons, beside the fact that I needed a change. Doc, Reg, Tully and I went out with helio this evening but it was too cloudy for practical use of same. Went up to the "Sally Ann" and Doc treated me to a lunch and I have access to his tobacco whenever I run short which I am now. Doc figures that he will be leaving in three weeks. Mailed a letter to Nelle tonight and received one from Bobbie and one from Harry & Bezzie. Marc hasn't answered my last letter yet.

JULY 26, FRI.

Buzzer practice for an hour this morning, one hour lamp reading and two hours Bren Gun instruction. Kept an appointment with Lieut. Rumberg (dentist) at 1330 hours. He checked my new plate and pronounced it satisfactory. He took an impression for a partial lower plate and told me to report back on Monday at the same time. I think we spent as much time talking about Kenora and the people we both know as it took to do the dental work. When he was making the impression he made me laugh when I had a mouth full of "plasto mud" and water and darned near choked me. They put a handful of mud in a holder and press it down over the teeth and vacant spots. The doc holds the thing down while his assistant squirts cold water over it with a small hose. The results of cracking a joke at that particular time can well be imagined.

More than half of the signal platoon is detailed for kitchen fatigue tomorrow and we are all in a belligerent mood tonight and most of us are ready to apply for a transfer. One man is responsible for that and he hates us signallers and seems to be laying for us particularly after the Brigadier said that we were the best on ceremonial parade. This one man doesn't hold such a high rank but he seems to have the last word in the running of the company. I started a letter to Bobbie tonight but don't like the results so will make a fresh start on Sunday, if I am not on fatigues again.

JULY 27, SAT.

On kitchen fatigue all day today and didn't mind it as much as I thought I would It is a lot easier than I thought it would be. The cook baked a few pies for us this afternoon.

There was a big change in the camp today. Nearly all of the 6th Infantry Brigade moved into the new huts today. There are no bunks yet so there are only about half of the intended number of men; consequently the other half has to sleep elsewhere until the bunks arrive. The elsewhere is in marquees close to the huts except for a few who are in bell tents close to the marquees. Doc, Reg, Tully and I are sleeping in a bell tent right beside the road. We just moved today and we are referred to as a tent full of lunatics already. Of course, it is only temporary until the huts are ready for their full compliment of manpower which will be in a couple of days. We are using the new mess halls now and they are quite an improvement on the old system. I let Reg read some of my diary and I am not so sure of just what he thought of it.

JULY 28, SUN.
Raining today so there was no church parade for which I was extremely thankful. We had a very good dinner today; maybe it wasn't so good compared to home cooked meals but as far as army eats go it was fair to middling. Finished a letter to Bobbie and sent another one to Easton's inquiring about a book on army wireless. Wandered around camp with Langston tonight.

JULY 29, MON.
Lamp reading in the A.M. with a little P.T. and bayonet fighting thrown I. Dental parade at 1330 hours and had an impression tested for shape. He said he would let me know when the set was ready.

JULY 30, TUES.
A lamp and line telegraphy scheme today which lasted from 8:00A.M. to 4:00P.M. Was in charge of signal center and I am afraid I made a lot of mistakes. I'll have to study the duties of the personnel of the signal center.

"Shorty" and her girlfriend came out this evening and we had quite a time. The girls were supposed to be on the bus by 9:30P.M. but they didn't bother trying to catch it, so we retired to a copse just east of the camp. We spent the rest of the time dodging guards until 11:30 when we headed for the station to try and get the girls on the 11:45 train to Brandon, the same which we missed. We were lucky to catch another train about half an hour later. Shorty said I was like a big brother, the same which made me kind of peeved as there is no fun being a big brother when there are girls like Shorty around. Doc and I finally got back to camp without being caught by any guards. We dropped in at the latrine and took off our puttees, undid our shoes, and tunics, put our hats under our tunics, which didn't improve their shape any, just in case the camp guard stopped us. There is no law or regulation stopping a man from going to the latrine at 1:00 o'clock in the morning. We finally got to bed without even seeing a guard.

JULY 31, WED.
Pay parade this A.M. and a lecture in the signal tent. Swim parade this afternoon which is more work than pleasure. Every one seems to be tight tonight but a few. Sent $8.00 to Dad and mailed a letter to Marcelle.

AUGUST 1, THURS.
Lamp station work this morning. Had an early lunch and went to the ranges for our Bren Gun qualifications. I made 50% of the possible score. Washed my shorts and shirt for tomorrow's ceremonial drill. Went up to the Sally Anne for the show there this evening. Ross and Mills were picked for the advance guard today. General opinion is that they will go on Sunday with the rest of the Battalion going soon after, I hope. Almost got caught in a storm tonight. We have no windows in this hut as yet and the rain is blowing in. Reg says they ought to give this country back to me and my Indian friends. Shucks, these guys don't seem to like a good storm. They are the best feature this desert can boast of.

AUGUST 2, FRI.
Rained all day, so we spent the morning in the Marquee. Applied for a Reveille pass for Saturday. Went to a Scotch concert at the Y.M.C.A. this evening with "Mac." The concert wasn't bad.

AUGUST 3, SAT.
Detailed for ration party but was taken off so as I could go on the ceremonial parade, during which we were told that we would be definitely in England by the end of the month. The boys refuse to believe it until it actually happens so the announcement was met with almost silence, compared to the usual welcome such a statement rates.

Went to Brandon this afternoon with Reg, MacKenzie, Comack and Corhonan. Made a date with Shorty for 1:00A.M. Had my watch fixed which didn't cost a cent while I was in town. Had quite a time with Reg up until 1:00A.M. at which time I kept my date with Shorty. Took Shorty home at 1:00A.M and stayed there until 3:00A.M. I could have stayed another half hour but her father was due home at three.

AUGUST 4, SUN.
Church parade this A.M. Phone duty in the Battalion Orderly Room from 1300 hours to 2200 hours.

AUGUST 5, MON.
Nothing of any importance.

AUGUST 6, TUES.
Lamp reading this morning and buzzer line scheme. Helped Doc make Lamp Batteries tonight.

AUGUST 7, WED.
Big Battalion Scheme which was a *[censored]* to the Cameron organization. Terribly disgusted tonight, as are Doc and Reg. Started a letter to Jack tonight but couldn't finish it due to the day's activity.

AUGUST 8, THURS.
Feel terrible today. Caught cold somehow and it's getting me down. Rumours are plentiful around here now regarding our going away and I am not inclined to believe them. I haven't finished that letter to Jack yet. Mail is scarce this week for some reason. Completely fed up and very disgusted.

A SUMMARY OF EVENTS BETWEEN THE DATE OF THE LAST ENTRY UP TO THE PRESENT DATE. *(AUGUST 13)*
Had a night scheme on Friday which helped to compensate for the poor showing of Wednesday. It lasted until twelve o'clock. Line orderly on Sunday. A big scheme at Carberry yesterday. I was with the defending force ("A"

Company) and the town was captured as per plan. Had some fun last night, doc played the piano and the sticks.

AUGUST 14, WED.
Doc is almost certain to be going to the Air Force, possibly next week. I wish I was going with him. Thinking seriously of writing to the Air Force in the 'Peg, not that it will do much good. Reg is going in to see the Navy about a transfer. I guess I will have to do something. If both Reg and Doc leave, I'll be on my own again.

AUGUST 15, THURS.
Payday. This camp is getting me down. The fellows are getting on my nerves.

AUGUST 16, FRI.
Heard today that the advance parties have been cancelled or postponed again. The O.C. was heard to remark that he doesn't know how this leaving business is effecting the men but it is driving him nuts. Personally, I am disgusted with the whole outfit.

AUGUST 17, SAT.
Interior Economy this morning which when put in plain language means scrubbing the floor. Wrote letters to Bobbie and Marcelle. Took in a show at the Y this evening.

AUGUST 18, SUN.
Church parade this morning with only about 100 men out of the entire battalion on parade. We had a brass band in front and the Calgary band (pipe) behind, consequently, our marching was such that it would be rated as bad even for a brand new bunch of recruits.

Gracie Fields' parade at 1145 hours and I think I'll go.

AUGUST 19, MON.
The advance party is supposed to go Wednesday. I wish to blazes they would make up their minds and get things going here.

AUGUST 20, TUES.

The advance guard has been postponed until Friday. We didn't do anything all afternoon. It was supposed to be sports day and we were playing ball if anyone should have asked us although we were all laying in our bunks all afternoon.

AUGUST 21, WED.

Well, well, who would of thought it, the advance parties for us Camerons and the S.S.R.'s and the whole of the Calgary Highlanders got under way today. I wish I could have warned the folks because it will give them an awful scare when they see those Balmorals sticking out of the windows. Lord only knows when we will follow them.

Doc was ordered to pack up and go to Winnipeg pending his discharge. It's funny how one comes to like another and he doesn't realize it until one has to leave. Doc and I have had lots of fun together and I wish I could have gone with him. When we were shaking hands he said he had a good mind to chuck everything and stay. We may see each other sometimes, either by design or accident. I am going to miss Doc.

AUGUST 22, THURS.

Nothing of any importance today except a lot of rumours about the time when we leave. Nothing yet.

AUGUST 23, FRI.

Reg and I made arrangements for a trip to Brandon tomorrow. We had a night march tonight which was no cinch. It lasted from 8:30 to 12:30 and going at a near gallop most of the way.

AUGUST 24, SAT.

Interior Economy this morning (scrubbing the floor). On dental parade also this morning and got my lower bridge which has one portion loose and which hurts on the right side. I will have to get ready for Brandon.

5:00A.M. SUNDAY MORNING

Just got back from Brandon and am feeling awfully tired which is no wonder. Saw a bunch of Kenora fellows from the 16th Battery in town tonight. Took "Shorty" home at one o'clock and she tells me she is going to get married in a few weeks. Why is it that nearly all the girls I go with up and get married to someone else? Maybe I have personality in reverse. She wants me to go in and see her again before we leave.

AUGUST 25, SUN.

Church parade this A.M. Reg and I were out brushing up on our semaphore this afternoon and a Sgt. Major was trying to tell us how we should do it. He wasn't so good at it himself.

AUGUST 26, MON.

The usual parade today. Went on a night scheme tonight and I was in charge of a station. We had to follow a compass course while travelling by truck. It was lots of fun. We got back about midnight.

AUGUST 27, TUES.

A battalion scheme this afternoon which I got out of by claiming I had to go to the dentist. I got my lower bridge which completes my dental work.

AUGUST 28, WED.

Line station work this morning. Sports day today so we laid on our beds all day. Another night scheme tonight which was cut short because of a heavy mist.

AUGUST 29, THURS.

Went up on orders this morning to apply for a four day pass. Was told that it was out of the question as we may get orders to move this weekend. The weekend passes may be cancelled too.

AUGUST 30, FRI.

I was called from the field today to go up on orders about my pass again. I think I will get it okay. Another night march tonight which are getting on my nerves. The Orderly Sergeant hinted that I would be getting my pass alright.

AUGUST 31, SAT.

Gas drill today which lasted forty minutes, practically the entire time it took to scrub the barrack room floor. Packed up and on my way to Brandon where I caught the eastbound train. Ran into the holiday crowd at Winnipeg and had quite a time manipulating my packs through the dense crowds.

Gave the folks a surprise as they weren't expecting me. Roy and Doug came home on the same train. It's good to get home for awhile again for a few days.

SEPT. 1, SUN.

Jack surprised us all this morning by walking in unexpectedly, quite a reunion. Spent all morning trying to fix the front wheel on Harry's bike. Had my picture taken with the rest of the soldier members of the family and relations. Took Bobbie home and stayed for supper. Maurice and Elsie Crawford were there too. Stayed till nearly twelve.

SEPT. 2, MON.

Went down town with Jack where we hunted up Major "Bill" McLeod and Jack got an extra day tacked on his pass.

Went over to Gibson's and had my picture taken with Olga. Called in to Bezzie's and picked plums for awhile. We had supper then Bezzie and I went to a show. Finally got home about 12 midnight.

SEPT. 2, TUES.

Went down town this morning with Jack after saying goodbye to Mommie Sharpe. Obtained a supply of Vogue papers at a nickel a package, quite a lucky break.

Went over to say goodbye to Olga and promised to write to her when I got back. Caught the 4:30 train for Winnipeg after a lot of fond farewells.

Arrived in Brandon at 1:05A.M. where I met Reg. Got back to camp at 4:30A.M. Travelled from home to camp with Jackson and Gab Byington, Gab being 15 days A.W.O.L.

SEPT. 4, WED.
Awfully sleepy on parade today and I slept for 45 minutes during the morning. No sign or word from Marc yet. Very hot and dusty here today and I feel many times more disgusted than I did before I went home. Slept this afternoon for awhile, also this evening. Sgt. Rankine gave me the directions for some wood carving.

SEPT. 5, THURS.
All day scheme with the S.S.R. and R.W.R. which lasted until after five this afternoon. Met Roy this evening and we were together until nearly 9:30P.M.

SEPT. 6, FRI.
It rained this morning so we had buzzer practice in one of the mess halls until noon. Ceremonial again this afternoon with a signalling scheme tonight from 8:00P.M. until 10:30P.M. They gave us a lunch before we hit the hay.

SEPT. 7, SAT.
Interior economy which means floor scrubbing, this morning. Started a letter to Bobbie and studied a while this afternoon.

Took in a show at the Y tonight and came away ashamed to be in uniform. The performance was put on by a troupe from Winnipeg and the show itself was excellent. What I can't understand is why as soon as a majority of the fellows don a uniform they turn into loud mouthed, primitive-like foul tongued individuals who, if a girl doesn't do as they want them to, they have to insult and embarrass her. The fellows in the show tonight were bellowing crude remarks to the girls on the stage and otherwise insulting them, every time they made their appearance. I came away absolutely ashamed to be wearing a uniform.

SEPT. 8, SUN.

Went to church parade today. Wrote letters to Rose, Bobbie and Olga. I should write one to Vera and find out what the score is. We still have no idea as to when we are going east and the latest rumour off the press is that we are in the Fourth Division and will be in the Fifth in the near future. Pretty soon we will be demobilized if it keeps on. Precipitation is very abundant today, much to the discomfort of the usual Sunday visitors. This coming week is going to be pretty busy if all I heard is true. Tomorrow was originally set aside for our old complaint, ceremonials: on Tuesday and Thursday we go on a two day scheme (by foot) to Souris, a distance of 35 miles and the S.S.R. signallers and us have to establish communication along the route and from Souris to camp. We don't know whether the system will be lamp or line or a combination of both. Anyhoo, I think it will be interesting at least, even though it will probably mean a lot of extra work for us.

SEPT. 9, MON.

We had a visit from Colonel Ralston, Minister of National Defense today. He inspected the huts and lines this morning and he held a general inspection of the entire camp, after which he gave a speech in which he uttered some mighty broad hints but nothing definite. Spent the evening checking over equipment for the two day bivouac scheme which starts tomorrow.

SEPT. 10, TUES.

A big rush to get away this morning. We had a very cold ride on trucks to Souris, 35 miles away. The Signals rode the whole distance and nearly froze but the rest of the Battalion walked from camp to Douglas 10 miles, then rode from there to Souris. A few stations were put out with the idea of contacting the S.S.R. signallers who were working from Shilo to the Brandon Hills. Our job was to set up a communication scheme from Souris to the Hills, thus forming a chain of stations from Camp to Souris. There was mistakes, blunders and misunderstandings so as a result communication wasn't completed until 8 or 9 o'clock in the evening. I went on duty on our last station which was in contact with the S.S.R.'s last station at 9:30P.M. Was talking to a guy by the name of Ford or Foryd, by lamp for the rest of our schedule, 11:30P.M. Closed down at 11:45 and then slept out on the "bald headed" prairie.

SEPT. 11, WED.

Got up at 0500 hours and it was exceedingly cold for awhile. Had breakfast about 8:30A.M. being unable to contact the station north of us. Finally got in contact but they were very hard to read. Set up a heliograph and established communication from our station to Camp. We were unable to get through to Souris until an hour later, and then by heliograph as well. There are very few men in the platoon who have any idea about aligning these Helios's and consequently I had a few heated arguments but I think I came out on top. Anyway we had the system working just in time to pass a message from Souris to Shilo which went through our station with little trouble. Left for camp at 11:30A.M. and arrived back here at 4:00P.M.

We finally got something definite regarding our departure which is just a matter of days. I'll have to send a note to the family to let them know.

SEPT. 12, THURS.

The signals were on fatigues this morning as only half of the battalion is here. We had a pay parade this afternoon. Left camp for Winnipeg at six o'clock. Arrived in Winnipeg about nine o'clock and met Doc in the station; he introduced me to Kay Tully, Jack's sister. Had my supper then proceeded to the Oxford Hotel where I took a room. By that time it was too late to call on Mrs. Groves so I got a magazine and read until 2:00A.M. These clean sheets are going to feel good.

SEPT. 13, FRI.

Got up at 9:00A.M. after a very good night's sleep. Had breakfast of waffles and sausages in the Malted Waffle Shop hard by the hotel, then had a new bracelet put on my watch, a job which I am sure I could have done a lot better and faster. Phoned Doc but he was out flying so I went back to my room and read for an hour. Reg and Doc walked in on me about eleven A.M. but Reg had to see some friends and didn't stay long. I volunteered to help Doc pack as he was leaving on No. 4 this evening for the Manning Pool in Toronto. Afterwards we visited Jack Tully's family and stayed there until 4:30P.M. at which time we proceeded down to the Air Force offices where Doc had to report at 4:45P.M. Finally got down to the train and saw Doc off on his Air Force Career; thus I lose another friend who I probably won't see again . I took Mrs. and Kay Tully home and stayed there until 9:30P.M. then went back and checked out at the hotel and sauntered leisurely toward the C.N. station. Met Kay and Eileen, Kay's girlfriend and walked down to the station with them. Caught the eleven o'clock train back to camp; thus ending a very expensive day in Winnipeg.

SEPT. 14, SAT.
Confined to camp until further notice but still don't believe we are moving. Ceremonials this afternoon. Went to a concert at the Y tonight.

SEPT. 15, SUN.
Church parade this morning and read all afternoon. Received a telegram from Harry saying that Bob had died last night. Tried to find some one of authority so as I could apply for leave to go home and ran into Rankine at 9:30 which was too late to do anything. Sent a telegram to Em.

SEPT. 16, MON.
Tried to go up on orders again this morning but was unsuccessful because we have to leave on a scheme to Carberry at 7:00A.M. Got caught in the rain coming back and was drenched through. It was the worst storm we have had at Shilo this summer.

SEPT. 17, TUES.
Went up on orders this morning and after wading through miles of red tape, finally obtained a two and a half day pass and an eight dollar advance. Arrived home about 10:30P.M. hot, dirty and tired and too late for the funeral.

SEPT. 18, WED.
Visited Emmy, Bobbie and Roy this afternoon and found them quite cheerful despite the tough time they were having. Went down to Bezzie's for supper after which Harry went to pick up Emmy and Mrs. Groves and called for Marcelle. Bobbie and Shirley came in, followed by Roy a little later and we had quite an enjoyable time. Marc is a swell person. I wish I had gotten to

know her sooner, before I joined this army. Another couple of days leave would be just the thing now.

SEPT. 19, THURS.

Spent the morning packing my kit for the return trip to camp and calling on a few of our neighbours and Connie. Phoned Marcelle this morning to ask her about the truck which was a good excuse to call her up about. She called for me at one o'clock and drove me down to Harry's and up to Emmy's. I took Bobbie to work, met Rod Gibson, ran into Felicie and brought her back to Emmy's with me. Emmy gave me a lunch and five dollars. It seems to me that Emmy is always giving me something that I am never able to pay back. Had three pictures taken with Mar, Felicie and Bezzie and enjoyed taking them. I found it very hard to say goodbye today especially to Marcelle. Why didn't I get to know her sooner? There is a certain time in every man's life when he wonders what a certain young lady thinks of him and how he rates in her estimation. I think I have reached that stage now, I would give anything to know what Marc thinks of me. Two more days leave and I might have found out. Aw hell, what's the use; she will most likely marry someone else before this war is all over.

SEPT. 20, FRI.

Arrived in camp at 4:30A.M. and went to bed until 8:00. Had my breakfast over at the Chink's and had quite a battle with the swarm of flies; finding a long Chinaman's hair in my food was the last straw and I didn't finish the meal.

Spent the whole day writing a four page letter to Marcelle. I didn't say what I wanted to because it's kind of hard when I haven't the least idea of how she feels toward me. I think she will tell me in her next letter whether she does or she doesn't.

Went up to the sing song at the Y this evening. It was led by a lady from Dryden and when the show was beginning to peter out she asked us all to write our names and numbers down on a sheet of paper as she wants to write to us when we leave.

Bert Pope and I visited the 37th hut and saw quite a few of the Kenora Boys. I was talking to Maurice for awhile and he is going home tomorrow for the weekend. Also was speaking to Ed Noseworthy, Tommy Markham, Bill Rimstead and a few more.

Feeling downright disgusted again tonight because I could have had two more days at home as the battalion will not be back until Sunday. That old saying, "Why doesn't someone tell me those things," is very appropriate right here.

SEPT. 21, SAT.
Helped mop out the Barrack room this morning which took exactly half an hour. Read and started a letter to Bobbie this afternoon and went to hear Jeff Waddington and his orchestra at the Y.M.C.A. this evening and enjoyed the show very much. We had electric lights in the hut for the first time tonight.

SEPT. 22, SUN.
I read all morning until I heard the Battalion coming in, then I hiked up to the Sally Anne and finished Bobbie's letter and wrote one to Nelle. Went out on the ranges this afternoon to fire The Bren Gun, came away mad because I should have fired fifteen shots and only got five away. The five I did manage to get away were all on the target with three bull's eyes. When I changed to automatic action the gun wouldn't fire and as they were pressed for time they gave me a score of ten hits and let it go at that. The way I was shooting I am sure I could have gotten almost, if not all, most of the shots on target.

SEPT. 23, MON.
P.T. and bayonet fighting for 1 ½ hours this morning, then lamp reading for the rest of the morning. Buzzer practice this afternoon. The Y.M.C.A., Sally Anne and the Knights of Columbus as well as other units, were placed out of bounds because the M.O. is afraid that we will catch the measles and they can't take any chances at this particular time. Rumours reached a new high this evening and some of them sound pretty good: too good to be true, in fact.

SEPT. 24, TUES.

Heliograph work all day today; I had to instruct four or five men on the theory, setting up and operation of the instrument. I have come to the conclusion that the fellows don't want to learn it or it's too deep for them.

The rest of the camp is out of bounds for the Camerons due to measles. The Camerons are the only unit in camp who hasn't cases of measles in the ranks and they are taking steps to guard us against it. I have a splitting headache from reading the Helio this afternoon.

SEPT. 25, WED.

P.T. and bayonet fighting this morning until 10:00A.M. then buzzer reading until noon. Got the afternoon off today as it was sports day.

Received a letter from Marc and answered it tonight. I have a bad head cold which is making life miserable, just now, for me.

SEPT. 26, THURS.

Lamp practice this morning, long distance reading by telescope. Long distance helio scheme this afternoon, during which I had an argument (friendly) with Sgt. Rankine about the difference between hell divers and loons. We had a long distance lamp scheme tonight lasting from 8:00P.M. until 11:00P.M. Got to bed by midnight.

SEPT. 27, FRI.

Was awakened at 5:00A.M. by Sgt. Rankine and was told off for phone duty at the rifle range with Reg. The job lasted until 11:00A.M. We were paid as soon as we got back and were informed that the battalion was receiving a 48 hour leave, starting from 4:00P.M.

We bought fare to Winnipeg where Bert Pope, Sid Sutton and Stew Randall had supper at Paul's Cafe. Left for the C.P.R. freight yards about 10:30 in search of the stock train. It pulled out at 12:30 with the four of us hidden on a timber car.

SEPT. 28, SAT.

Arrived home about 7:00A.M. and found everybody in bed. Made a hurried call to the Department of Highways for Doug's check and walked home with Rod to say hello to Olga. She gave me a dinner of spaghetti on toast and preserved blueberries. Shaved in a hurry and scurried up to Em's to catch Bobbie at her dinner hour. Walked down to work with Bobs and ran into Sid Sutton but he hadn't seen anything of Bert Pope who promised to pay back a dollar he owes me, a dollar very much in need now. Saw "Hot Dog" Smith for the first time in four years and had quite a time with him until five thirty, at which time I went to Bezzie's for supper. I had a very good time until it was time to meet Bobbie as per arranged. All five of us went down in Harry's car, picked Bobbie up and we all went up to Em's where we had lunch and a good time. Finally got home between 11:00 and 12:00P.M. very disappointed to find that Marcelle has gone down to Fort William for the weekend.

SEPT. 29, SUN.

The military influence was felt by myself this morning when I woke up at 5:30A.M. when I had intended on sleeping until nine or ten. I got up at 7:30A.M. I phoned Bert to see when he was leaving, washed some hankies and went over to see Connie, Doug and family. Nelle gave me the necessary cash for bus fare, my riding freights doesn't appeal to her.

Emmy and Bobbie came up right after lunch and when they left, I said goodbye to all the folks and went with them. Sid Sutton phoned and asked me if I wanted to ride to Winnipeg in their car. I didn't hesitate to answer yes. Had supper at Em's and then walked down to the Post Office with Bobbie where I was to meet the car. Said goodbye to Bobs and finally got under way at 20 minutes to seven.

We got into Winnipeg at 10P.M. just enough time to have a bite to eat before train time. The car trip cost me a dollar for gas; Mr. Sutton paid for our lunch. Mrs. Sutton kissed the four of us goodbye at the C.N. station; a few minutes later we were on our way to camp. I can't help thinking about how there is people bidding me very fond farewells now who never hardly spoke to me before I joined. I still think the uniform has something to do with it: it certainly can't be my personality. How many more times am I going to have to say goodbye to relatives and friends? How many more times will I witness the confusion in the Winnipeg station when friends, wives, sisters and mothers come down to see the boys off to Shilo, thinking it is the last time they will see them only to have to repeat the whole performance two weeks later? Why don't we get a chance at something besides ceremonials, even if it is only dodging bombs and standing guard over a portion of the coast line?

SEPT. 30, MON.
P.T. and bayonet fighting this morning. Buzzer practice from 10:00A.M. until noon. Map reading test this afternoon and more buzzer practice.

Roy came down after supper and we talked for awhile before going up to the Y.M.C.A. where Roy stayed to write a few letters and I came back to the hut after buying two much-needed pencils.

OCT. 1, TUES.
Buzzer practice this morning from 10:00A.M. to noon. Lamp station work this afternoon. I let the new fellows get some much-needed practice while I read a Readers' Digest. Roy came in again tonight with the news that they are going east on Thursday. I gave him all my English addresses of relatives there. He had a tooth pulled today and I think his mouth was sore. I wished him luck as it will probably be the last time I will see him for some time as we are going on a bivouac tomorrow and we are supposed to end up in Winnipeg Monday or Tuesday. I wrote a letter to Doc this evening in answer to the one sent a few days ago. He is doing left and right turn by numbers and rifle drill. After his being in the army a year, I think it is just a waste of time for him. Last post is just sounding: I hope it is the last one that I will hear in this God-forsaken place.

OCT. 2, WED.
We left for the Old Camp Hughes site at 5:00P.M. in trucks and it started to rain lightly soon after we started. Arrived our camp ground about 7:30 and after a bowl of bean soup, sadly diluted by the rain, we started to get ready for bed.

We had to sleep in our great coat with a ground sheet underneath or on top, according to the individual's opinion of its maximum efficiency. I put mine on top. I was supposed to go on a patrol tour at 0100 hours but they called it off which met with my approval. They didn't decide until after they had awakened me so I hied myself to the improvised kitchen and got a mug of hot tea and then back to my watery bed. Reveille at 3:30A.M., three hours before dawn. We had another mug of hot tea then set out for Camp Hughes, on foot, to attack the defenders, the S.S.R.'s Once again old Camp Hughes echoed to the sound of marching feet and the flat explosions of dummies used in sham battles. "Very lights" *(flares)* soared up into the wet black morning sky and we did a nose dive into the wet grass and sand. My cold seemed a lot worse and I had to cough at the most critical times; I counteracted the result a little by putting my Balmoral over my face every time I felt a cough coming. We tripped and fell into trenches and barbed wire that was dug and strung there during the last war. Finally the battle was over and we went back for breakfast.

It started to rain as we fell in for breakfast; consequently, I had to chase my "spot of jam" all around my mess tin because the rain set it afloat. Soon after breakfast word came around that the rest of the scheme was called off so we arrived in camp at 11:30A.M.

OCT. 4, FRI.

Spent the morning getting ready for the Winnipeg bivouac and ceremonials. Went up to say so long to Roy who leaves for the east at 6:30. Left on trucks on the first leg of our journey at 1:00P.M. We went north to Douglas then turned west on No. 10 Highway to Brandon. We turned south at Brandon on No. 2 Highway for quite awhile, then turned east through Nesbit and Wawanesa. At Wawanesa there is a large sunken basin with towering clay cliffs on their sides. By the looks of things this clay cliff is always crumbling as we saw large sections of it ready to fall.

We turned south on No. 12 to Ninette, situated on Pelican Lake among some fairly high hills. Finally we arrived at Killarney, the location of our first overnight stay. We bivouaced beside Lake Killarney in a small summer resort. We had supper and then walked to the town proper to see what we could see; we didn't have much trouble seeing all that there was to see but Reg met the owner of the Golden Flake Lunch whom he knew in Winnipeg, so we talked to him for quite awhile. Reg and I got back to the camp site and had an exceedingly difficult time finding our bed rolls in the pitch black of the stormy night. A strong wind was blowing off the lake and it wasn't long before it started to rain so Reg, Hughie Comack and I commandeered a tarpaulin covered truck and moved in. It wasn't too bad sleeping in there and the main advantage was that we got up dry next morning.

OCT. 5, SAT.

Left Killarney early this morning and marched for an hour, then back into the trucks again. We travelled east on No. 3 through Cartwright, Clearwater, Crystal City to Pilot Mound where we had ceremonials and lunch. Pilot Mound donated six cases of apples for our dinner. On the road again by 1:30P.M. and passed through La Riviere Manitou to Mordon where we bivouaced in the old grand stand in the old race track grounds. We had supper and after a quick wash and shave we were paraded into Morden where we held a march past and were welcomed by the Mayor. The town was pretty busy as it was Saturday night (farmers' night.) Reg, L/Cpl Hatch and I went to see Shirley Temple in a picture called, "Bluebird" after which we came back to camp and hit the hay, I mean planks. A grandstand seat isn't the best material to use for a bed but we are getting used to sleeping in these difficult places.

OCT. 6, SUN.

Held church service in the city park and the minister of Morden gave us a roaring sermon; marched through town again back to camp. We had lunch and then got underway again. We travelled north through Rosebank to Carmen where we marched through the town, led by the local band (phewee) which boasted of a baton swinging majorette; we embussed again on the other side of town. We headed east on No. 3 highway through Brunkile, Sanford, Oak Bluff, Fort White and on to Winnipeg. Proceeded to Polo Park which is to be our home for the next four or five days. Just about supper time I was informed that my sister was waiting for me at the gate. I got over there as soon as possible and found Emily and Mrs. Groves waiting there; I sure was glad to see them. They had been waiting pretty long and were almost frozen and as I couldn't get away for some time we made arrangements to meet at Mrs. Groves' place later on. Arrived at Groves about 7:00P.M. having been given a lift by an understanding motorist. Mrs. Groves made me a lunch of tomato and lettuce sandwiches, cookies, cake and tea while I washed and shaved. The lunch, shave and wash sure were appreciated by myself. My cold kept bothering me so Mr. Groves made up a concoction from honey, vinegar and codeine to stop the coughing. Met George and Edith Steward and at eleven o'clock we had another lunch which met with immediate gastronomical approval. Emmy gave me car fare (50¢) and I finally got to bed about 2400 hours.

OCT. 7, MON.

Ceremonial practice at Minto this morning with lunch at Polo Park. Took things easy in the afternoon. Went up to Groves' again this evening and found Vera there. Mrs. Groves has the flu probably brought on by getting chilled yesterday afternoon while waiting for us to come in.

Emmy, Vera and I went to the Lyceum and Emmy nearly climbed up on an Air Force Captain's lap during the Charlie Chan mystery thriller. Had lunch at Groves and then took Vera home. It was quite a walk as she works away down at Westgate. Grabbed myself a handful of street car at the corner of Portage and Maryland and got back to camp at 0005 hours (12:05).

OCT. 8, TUES.

Had General Inspection this morning and we got the afternoon off so as we could take our sisters, sweethearts, mothers, etc. to the trooping of the colours. I called for Emmy at 1:00P.M. but we were unable to get into the armouries because of the crowd. We stood outside on the off chance of them holding it outside which they didn't do. Saw Mrs. Sutton there and a few other Kenora people; as there was no chance of seeing anything we came back to Groves. I met Eva Groves for the first time and Ida and her little girl Francis came in. We had afternoon tea soon after. Eva made supper and for once in a long time I had a good meal. I helped Eva with the dishes. Em had to catch the 6:45 train and we had to take a taxi. Made it with five minutes to spare. Em gave me another dollar before she left for what she called street car fare. On second thought she gave me the dollar on Tuesday night. After I had seen Em off I phoned Vera and made a date for tomorrow night. I took in a 15¢ show at the Oak, then walked back to Polo Park. A nice little distance.

OCT. 9, WED.
Detailed for phone duty at the St. Charles Rifle range. Ernie Kitchen told me that Ted was hunting for me at Minto yesterday. I saw an Air Force man there but it was too far to recognize Ted. Got back from the range at 4:30P.M., had supper and hung around thinking maybe Ted would drop in. started down town about 6:30P.M on the off chance of meeting Ted with no luck at all. Called for Vera at eight. I had the misfortune to lose 50¢ at the ranges today so Vera paid for the tickets to the show. We had lunch at the Stop-Inn then took Vera home. We had lots of fun and I didn't get home to the Park until 3:00A.M.

OCT. 10, THURS.
On the phone at the range again this morning and didn't get a chance to fire a shot. Got back to camp at Polo Park about 1:00A.M.

The training center bought 30 kegs of beer and about 3,000 men got very inebriated on the beverage. Made a call on the Groves to bid the goodbye and found Mrs. Groves much better. Phoned Mrs. A. Edwards for Ted but Helen said that Ted had gone home this morning. Phoned Vera and she had to stay in to work so said goodbye to her over the phone.

I was flat broke and there was no use going down town so I came back to camp. Found no one on the phone so I took over. Went to bed in the Battalion Orderly Room at 3:00A.M., the warmest night we have had since this bivouac started and I slept beside the stove.

OCT. 11, FRI.
Reveille at 0600 hours and we had breakfast then started back to Shilo. We marched from Polo up to Portage to the other side of the Deer Lodge Hospital where we got the trucks again. We arrived at Portage La Prairie at 1100 hours. After lunch we had platoon drill until 1600 hours. Moreau,

Tommy Suttlehan and I walked into and around town until 9:00P.M. but we had no money so we came back to camp. It was starting to rain so the three of us commandeered a truck and slept in the back under a tarpaulin.

OCT. 12, SAT.
We marched through and out of Portage La Prairie where we got into the trucks again for the run to the camp. Stopped for a march through at Carberry and then on our way again. Arrived in camp at 1:00P.M. and had lunch at 1:30.

Did a big washing this afternoon and I hope it is dry for tomorrow's full marching order muster parade. It will be a busy day tomorrow and how.

OCT. 13, SUN.
Reveille at 0600 hours and had all the beds apart and outside by 0700 hours. Church parade at 0900 hours and muster parade with full marching order, including all blankets.

Visitors are starting to arrive and there are a few in the hut. They are getting snatches of good old army cussing as some of the fellows fail to see them or forget they are there. After listening to the women talk I have come to the conclusion that they could teach the boys some very choice cuss words. The long awaited pay parade is scheduled for 2:30P.M. I guess we sleep on the floor tonight.

OCT. 14, MON.
Reveille at 0600 hours and emptied our palliases of straw. Reg, Tom Bell and I had to dismantle the antenna on the officer's mess, the same one that I helped to put up. That particular little duty was accomplished just in time to allow us to aid in massaging the bunk house floor with scrub brushes. In the afternoon we were obliged to pick up scrap paper, etc. around the lines.

I hightailed it across to the hot dog stand for a hot dog and a cup of coffee, around four o'clock but they had a Thanksgiving turkey dinner special on so "squandered" half a buck and enjoyed a darned good turkey dinner with all the trimmings including apple pie á la mode. There were customers waiting four deep for the seats; so soon as one was finished, another took his place.

I made it a point to see Mr. H.L. Brace of the Y.M.C.A. tonight regarding the free educational course sponsored by the Canadian Legion. He is a swell guy to talk to and he being an old school teacher advised me to take the secondary course which includes arithmetic, three courses in mathematics, science, physics and geometry after I had explained to him that mathematical problems were beating me in my radio studies. I hope I will be able to go through it okay as I can get a radio course when I finish this one.

Saw a show at the Sally Anne then we fell in for the march to the station. Finally got in our coaches and I was detailed for picquet *(watch)* at my end of the car for an hour. Charlie Longley had a seat or berth all picked out for him and I and we considered ourselves lucky for only half two, where the other fellows are sleeping three in a section. Charlie just got to bed when the senior batman came along and told Charlie he would have to move to another car so as to be closer to the officers. I have the section to myself now and thinking seriously of inviting Reg in for the night. My picquet shift is nearly up and I am ready for bed.

OCT. 15, TUES.
Woke up this morning with a feeling of motion and the sound of the wheels. We were finally on our way. I had the good fortune to be one of the first up and had a good chance to shave and wash before the rush started. Had a good breakfast prepared by the C.P.R. which consisted of porridge, bacon, pork sausages, potatoes, milk or coffee, bread and jam. It's the biggest breakfast I have eaten for years.

We hit the 'Peg on time, 0820 hours and found a good sized crowd despite the low temperature and freezing wind. It was well over an hour before we got under way again. A couple of hours and we will be in God's country. It's hard to write on a train. It zigs when I zag, consequently the writing is, to say the least, horrible.

Arrived in Kenora just before noon and managed to be excused from parade. All the family were there and a few special friends and some just friends. I appreciated the fact that there was no crying, in fact, I think they were just as pleased as I am that we are finally going east.

It seems that every time I shook hands there was money left in my hand; parcels and cigarettes were far from scarce too. Ten even dollars by shaking hands, $1.00 from Bob Gibson, one from Mr. Bodger, one from Mrs. McKelvie, one from Gertie Clark and a five dollar bill from some uncertain source. I am not sure, but I am going to find out. Reg sure appreciated Bobbie's little parcel and says he is going to write to her. I have a lot of letter writing to do when I get to Quebec.

Sgt. Rankine and I watched for deer and moose until dark this evening but 60 miles an hour isn't exactly the appropriate speed for sighting game in this dense bush. Got a cinder in my eye and had to go to the M.O. to get it out.

OCT. 16, WED.

Awoke this morning covered with coal dust which had seeped in the window during the night. Marched for 10 minutes through Chapleau. It froze last night and there is a little snow on the ground. We sure are getting swell meals on this train; last night for supper we had good ham, cabbage, spuds, carrots, pudding and coffee. For dinner yesterday, roast pork with dressing, spuds and apricots. This morning there was scrambled eggs and bacon, fried spuds, bread and jam. They say we will be at our destination tomorrow morning so the fellows seem to think we are not going to Quebec after all. They seem to think it will be Montreal.

I certainly have seen some wonderful game country between here and Kenora. Sudbury interested me a lot but we only went through that place slow. The amount of rock in that locality even surprised me and I am kind of used to it to a certain extent. We are just slowing down for Mattawa and the boys weren't slow in getting the windows up. I'll have to take a look. Some nice girls there on the station. We are moving again.

We marched through North Bay just before supper this afternoon and no matter what people say, there is hardly any difference that I could notice between the disposition or attitude of the people here and the people of the west. We are due in Quebec at noon tomorrow.

OCT. 17, THURS.

Woke up just as we were passing through the suburbs of Montreal, consequently we did not see much of that city. The farms appear as if they have been brought to reality from the pictures of old French farms that I have seen.

We passed through Three Rivers and arrived in Quebec City just before noon. The station's in Lower Town so we had to climb up a steep winding hill to Upper town. Some of the boys found it pretty tough, especially the boys from the prairies. In fact, one of the boys of the Anti-Tank died of heart failure while climbing the hill. His name is Rennie, a fellow who was consistently belligerent, and who joined up the same time or soon after I did.

The first thing we did was go out on the cliff to have a look at the River and the town of Levis across the stream. It sure is a wonderful sight and after seeing the height of the cliff I appreciate the feelings of General Wolfe when he sailed up the St. Lawrence to attack Quebec; it looks almost impossible to scale the face of the cliff, from the top and I can almost imagine how it looks from the bottom. Our camp is an old Internee Camp surrounded by a thick barbed wire fence and all the windows had barbed wire strung crisscross on the outside and it was exceedingly dirty. Altogether it was a very depressing sight which wasn't helped by the barbed wire entanglement.

It seems as if the advance guard and the first few men who ventured into town first created hard feelings and gave the natives a bad impression of the Camerons. The French M.P. has cracked a few Cameron heads already, without warning. From what we hear, the girls here are untouchable due to venereal diseases. We have been advised by a number of different sources, both military and civilian, not to go near them. Which means nothing to me as I won't go near them anyway.

OCT. 18, FRI.

Worked all day cleaning and scrubbing the hut and it still isn't clean. The C.B. was lifted tonight so Reg, Moreau, Comack and myself took a look around the town. There isn't a place in this Upper town that can be reached without climbing or descending a hill. In places the sidewalks and streets are so narrow two men can't walk abreast. The old houses and narrow twisting streets, which date back a couple of centuries, I found interesting. Ignorance of the French language isn't such a drawback as we first supposed, as it isn't hard to find someone who can speak English after a fashion. It must sound funny to hear us trying to speak French. We have been warned not to go down to Lower town unless we go in groups of four or five. We were quite a distance from camp at 9:15P.M. and 9:30 was the deadline so we came home by the Chateau Frontenac and cliff path (board walk along the edge of the cliff). We had to climb about 150 steps with a drop of a good few hundred feet on one side and the towering grey walls of the Citadel fortress on the other. The old cannon and cannon balls, the old bulwarks and ramparts, the old gates and archways, the crooked winding narrow streets, the statues and monuments, the armed freighters and the comparatively small ferries, the town of Levis across the river, the Quebec bridge, the path that Wolfe used to gain access to the plains of Abraham, the tide coming in, the occasional glimpse of a ship of the Royal Canadian Navy, the Isle of Orleans and a hundred and one other historic and modern places and things to see and investigate tends to make me think that this will be a very interesting stay here in Quebec.

OCT. 19, SAT.

We had to scrub the hut again this morning and now it is starting to look a little clean. Acquired a midnight pass and set forth for a tour of inspection of Lower town with Reg, and Harold Moreau. We located the Naval Headquarters and Reg got in touch with his uncle, Lieutenant-Commander Langston and he is to dine with gold braid tomorrow night. I have a strong premonition that we are going to lose Reggie now, through transfer to the Navy. Moreau and I made inquiries about transferring but although they need signal men, we may be blocked by the Camerons.

We explored the Lower Town very thoroughly during the course of the afternoon, having dined at a dirty little restaurant in Lower Town. I obtained a book called, "French, Self-Taught" and hope to learn enough French to get me by.

We increased our party to five during the evening and explored some very dark and very narrow alleys; we had no mishaps or trouble. Finally had a midnight lunch and strolled along the promenade back to camp. Wrote a letter to Nelle.

OCT. 20, SUN.
Church parade on the Heights beside the Citadel this morning, after which we had our pictures taken en mass by a professional photographer.

Comack, Carl Sund and I went to the Capitol Theatre to see Mickey Rooney and Judy Garland in "Strike Up the Band." The shows and most of the stores are open including beer parlors and liquor bars. We had supper downtown.

Came back to camp early and wrote a letter to Bobbie and read a magazine. It's snowing tonight. I don't think we will be here for the entire winter.

OCT. 21, MON.
We had to establish communication by lamp from the Plains of Abraham to the Battalion Orderly Room. I was stationed at the station on top of the Citadel hill all day and it was not so warm. About two inches of snow fell last night which was soft enough to cause wet feet this morning and there was a strong cold north wind blowing over the hill. The idea of the scheme is kind of obscure and has to be maintained during parade hours indefinitely. We are going to use the Plains of Abraham as a training area. There is a rumour going around that we are standing to again on short notice and there is talk of Valcartier. Moreau and I looked up the Royal Canadian Naval Reserve and inquired about transfers. The answer we got was very encouraging and surely warrants another visit and an interview with a higher rank. We looked all over town for a Winnipeg Free Press and got into some very interesting places, including the Chateau Frontenac. I should write some letters tonight but I can't seem to settle down to it.

The bigger part of Quebec has been put out of bounds and it includes the most interesting parts of the city. I'll have to work hard on these transfer potentialities. This is as good a time as any to bring this book to a close and to start a new volume tomorrow. Interesting or not, truthfully recorded or not, this is the end of book No. 1

Dec. 8, 1940
Quebec City, P.Q.

Dear Nelle:

Having read this account of my army life from January 1, 1940 to October 21, over again, I have come to the conclusion that diaries are funny things. There are portions written in anger, some during spells of melancholia, some very gloomy, some when I was feeling good, consequently, I have learned things about myself I never knew before and I'm not pleased.

There are parts in here which I could have left out and which are mostly sentimental but it's written now and I am leaving it as is.

There are some parts that might not meet with some people's approval and that couldn't be helped either.

As we are expecting to leave Canada in the very near future, I am sending this book home to you and hope it meets with your idea of a diary. I have done a better composing job in some of my letters than I have here and I suppose it could stand being revised in a lot of places.

I find that when writing a diary I seem to be under the impression that I am taking notes and the result isn't very satisfactory. Anyhow, here it is, I hope you find it to your liking. It will take you approximately 4 hours to read this providing you can understand the writing.

In some places the composition is childish and boastful, something which peeves me, no end. When I come home for good we will read it over together and maybe I can elucidate more fully on a few of the events recorded. As we expect to leave before the Yuletide, I'll wish you many Merry Christmases and many Happy New Years.

I am
Your Loving Brother
Fred.

FRED LODGE DIARY
October 23, 1940 to April 25, 1941

Book No. 2

Daily Diary:
H19859, F. T. Lodge,
Q.O.C.H. of C (C.A.S.F.)

Please mail to:
Miss N. Lodge
Box 165
Kenora, Ontario,
Canada

OCT. 23, WED.

I was one of the few detailed to help get the new signal stores and class rooms in shape.

During the course of the morning inquired about the pass that I applied for yesterday.

It was three o'clock in the afternoon before I arrived at the conclusion that my pass had been turned down. Today being sports day with no parades, Moreau, Reg and I decided to try getting out, which we accomplished very successfully.

We were granted an interview with the Naval Recruiting Officer, who turned out to be a Captain with a very friendly and obliging disposition. After hearing his explanation of the recruiting and transfer system we decided that a transfer to the Navy was impossible. When we were leaving the Captain said he was sorry he couldn't do something about it because they needed good men badly.

We had supper downtown and then did some more exploring in the vicinity of Rue St. Jean, Rue St. Roy and Cartier Avenue.

OCT. 24, THURS.

Still on the renovating of the new signal quarters, although we didn't do an awful lot of work, we did get the new class rooms ready for business, (after a fashion.) We had a battalion retreat parade this evening on the Earl Gray Point. I think it impressed, very much, the few citizens that were there to see it. Met Reg in front of the Capitol Theater and went in to see the "Return of Frank James." We had a late lunch down town before coming back to camp. I told him of my radio endeavours and failures to date and we both decided that we both had the ambition but no driving power. Reg is going to Montreal tomorrow to see his Aunt. He said he would try and introduce me to his Uncle on Sunday evening. His Uncle is a Lieut. Commander in the Royal Canadian Navy.

OCT. 25, FRI.

On parade today with a swim parade at the Y at 10:00 hrs. I decided that I had a too bad of a cold so didn't go swimming. Ceremonials on the Plains of Abraham this afternoon where we were inspected by the President of the Bank of Montreal.

Moreau and I went for a walk down to Wolfe's Cove and we fully agree with the historians in their assertions that Wolfe and his men had a very perilous climb to the plains above. There are stone pillars everywhere with Bronze tablets commemorating some great battle, person or event. We saw the monument supposedly erected on the spot where Wolfe died and which has been remodeled four times.

We finally ended up away down on St. Jean for a cup of java. We passed through the elite residential section and saw some houses that would knock Doug's eye out. Really beautiful places.

On the way home we spoke to a Sergeant of the Air Force about the possibilities of getting a transfer to that branch which resulted in our deciding to visit the recruiting offices tomorrow. I don't expect to get the answer I hope for but we are going to try anyway.

Rumours are circulating again which have us going to Halifax, Victoria, B.C., Valcartier and Winnipeg. I saw the Duchess of Athol, an ocean liner on her way back from Montreal after delivering a draft of airmen who are going to Brandon and Winnipeg. There is a guy eating toast here and I can't stand it much longer; he chews with his mouth open, smacks his lips and has a case of asthma; all of which doesn't help soothe my nerves.

OCT. 26, SAT.

Spent the morning erecting an antenna at the Officer's Mess. According to the height and length of the aerial itself and the loose rock where the ground pin is located I think I would be safe in saying that the whole set up is very inefficient.

Wrote a letter to Olga this afternoon copied more signal notes. Went to a show at the Cambrai. Received permanent midnight passes today.

The hankering to speak to a girl that talks English is getting chronic and I am afraid I'll have to make an effort to find one someplace. Planning on going skating this coming pay-day if I can get my skates down here in time.

OCT. 27, SUN.
Church parade this morning to the St. Andrew's Presbyterian. Stayed in this afternoon to write Nellie a letter and write notes on signalling and wireless. Sgt. Rankine asked me again if I wanted to transfer to the Navy yet. I explained the situation and told him I was going to try again at the next place we hit. I am thinking seriously of applying to the Air Force here. When I am applying here I am handicapped by the fact that I am not a Catholic and I can't speak French. Two strikes against me, as it were, and the third practically called because I can't read code fast enough.

Walked the streets of Quebec again tonight and it's beginning to get monotonous.

A fifteen mile route march to Quebec Bridge and back scheduled for tomorrow.

OCT. 28, MON.
Went on a route march along No. 1 highway past the Quebec Bridge, then we came back on No. 2. Some of the boys have very sore feet this evening. Reg went to a dance so I took in a show at the Empire Theater alone.

OCT. 29, TUES.
Detailed for station duty on the Earl Grey Terrace. Tommy asked a French girl for a date and got it. She had a friend so for the first time in my life I had a blind date.

We met the girls in front of the Y at 9:30PM and my partner turned out to be English, not bad looking. As we had no money except for 60¢ we decided to go to a dance. It didn't matter if I couldn't dance as I have made up my mind to learn. If Teresa Aikins doesn't like teaching me then I'll go out with the little nurse from Gaspè.

We couldn't find a dance so sat in a cafe for an hour getting acquainted. Teresa doesn't smoke, drink or neck which is okay with me. Finally took them home with understanding that we would phone them on Friday to make a date for Saturday. Tommy and I came in the back gate about 12:30AM.

OCT. 30, WED.

Detailed again this morning for station work on phone, being stationed in the Company Orderly Room. Everyone seems to delight in sending me messages and kept me busy from 8:30AM to 11:45AM. Mr. Kent seemed anxious to see how fast I could read the code and sent four or five messages at a speed ranging from 15 wpm to 20 wpm and I had very little trouble. I even surprised myself. I don't think it would take long for me to hit the twenty words a minute mark.

Copied notes and studied wireless all afternoon. Went to see a hockey game between Montreal Canadiennes and Quebec Aces and was very disappointed. I saw better games in the Junior and Juvenile leagues back home. I'd like to go skating.

OCT. 31, THURS.

I was unfortunate enough to have to go on parade today as we are taking turns on the station duties. Got paid today and I was selected to collect money for a radio for the platoon. They seem to think I am the man most fitted to select a good second hand radio that will cost no more than $13.00. I may be able to raise another five dollars tomorrow.

We are confined to camp tonight because the Colonel thinks the boys will indulge too much and get into trouble. They have arranged a concert in the reaction room with the recognized talent of the regiment performing. Pressed my trousers and Balmoral. Both Reg and I received letters from Bobbie today and Reg complained because the letter wasn't long enough.

I didn't attend the concert mainly because the place was crowded. They tell me it was a good show. I lent my questionable aid to the process of balancing the Platoon Fund accounts. The Radio Fund and making up of the duty list for tomorrow. When I go to bed, I'll have my head resting on exactly $120.00 which will be locked in my kit bag which I use for a pillow.

Jimmy Ellison received a telegram from home saying that his sister was very low. He had his pass and the extra financial requirements and was on his way to the station by 11:00PM.

NOV. 1, FRI.

I was taken off station work today to erect an aerial for the radio in the men's canteen. Roy Miller was told off to help me and we had trouble finding the necessary material in the way of guy wires and suitable masts. Finally completed the job at 3:00PM. In civilian life that little job would have netted me five dollars at least but in the army I was satisfied to be excused from ceremonial parades.

I finished collecting the radio fund and slept for a little while this evening. Sgt. Rankine said he would lend us the extra five dollars and we could pay him pack next pay day.

NOV. 2, SAT.

I have another aerial to put up in the Corporals' Mess but it's raining today so will have to wait until Monday. Reg, Roger Lacomte, Harold Ross, Hughie Comack and I set out in the rain to find a second hand radio. After walking the city for three hours, climbing hills and steps we finally found one for $23.00 but our highest price that we could pay was $18.00. We located the set in a little barber shop down in Lower town, a barber shop that sold beer, soft drinks, cent candies, radios and parts. The owner and his family lived in the rear of the store. Roger was our interpreter and he and the barber talked back and forth in French for over half an hour. During which time the rest of us were on pins and needles and the barber was scraping off whiskers all the time he was talking; once in awhile his wife put in a word in the dickering. Finally Roger heaved a heavy sigh and said, "she's yours for $18.00, boys." Quick witted Comack pipes up, "what the wife or the radio?" So we climbed the hundred and fifty steps back to camp bearing our precious radio. It's a 1938 Rogers with automatic tuning and I think it well worth the price; at least the boys are satisfied.

I paid 40¢ for a haircut in a barber shop situated in one of these narrow streets off the beaten path but the operation and result was worth the high price.

Reg, Tommy Suttlehan and I set out at 8:00 o'clock this evening, (still raining) to meet Theres, Louise and Pauline for an evening's fun. When the girls arrived at the meeting place it was too late for a show so we retired to a cafe where we sat and talked for a couple of hours.

A soldier from Valcartier came in and evidently he knew Theres (Teresa) and he started bothering her. She told him off and he left, just in time to prevent trouble because I had decided it was time for me to make it my business. I took her home in a taxi and left her at the house where she works with an understanding that I would phone her on Monday night for a date for Tuesday.

Teresa is English, although she was born at Valcartier. She has worked in Quebec City for two years. She doesn't smoke, drink or mush and she likes the winter season; she likes to skate, ski, etc. She is about as tall as I am, well proportioned, carries herself well and is quite good looking. I seem to have a knack of finding decent girls. Her full name is Teresa Aikins. I'll have to watch the other fellows as they think she is worth knowing.

NOV. 3, SUN.

Church parade was called off today for some unknown reason. Comack and I went to the Capitol theater to see a show then took supper in a very crowded and not so classy cafe. Was kind of glad to get out of it. Wrote letters this evening. Everyone seems satisfied with the radio.

NOV. 4, MON.

I accompanied the battalion on the 18 mile route march to Montmorency Falls and despite the tiring process of picking them up and putting them down, I sort of enjoyed it. The march seemed to be greatly enjoyed by the French girls who could be seen in windows, doors, on balconies, etc. Their shape sizes and colors were very varied but they all were French. Personally, I think getting a look at the Falls was compensation enough for the long walk.

Went down to the Y.M. to phone Teresa about tomorrow night. She tells me she may have to go out with her sister. Arranged to phone her again tomorrow night.

Went to the Cambrai Theatre to pass the time away. Held the door open for a pleasingly plump middle aged woman who had fire in her eye. She said, "Thanks very much, I am a little surprised to meet one of your Regiment who knows how to be polite." Having had my curiosity prodded by her attitude I asked her why she thought we were all so rude. She had been insulted by a very inebriated Cameron and was rip snorting mad for which I don't blame her. I tried to explain to her that there were a few who were like that and who made it hard for the rest of us. I don't know if she believed me or not but she walked away with a smiling good night.

NOV. 4, TUES.
With the help of Jack Tully I erected an aerial for the Corporal's mess. The Sergeants want one as do the Quartermasters Stores.

Received a parcel from Nellie today with my skates, key and ear phones inside. Went down to the Soucy Pharmacie on Cartier Ave. to phone Theresa but I guess I had left it too late and she had gone with her sister. Talked with an English speaking high school pupil for over 45 minutes and got a lot of information. Bought poppy from a girl in the Pharmacie. Finally got back to camp at nine P.M. It's a very miserable night in fact it has been that way since Friday night.

NOV. 6, WED.
Another wet, miserable day. We had map reading all morning. This afternoon we were inspected by a beer salesman from Winnipeg who is a friend of the O.C.'s. The inspection was held in the drill hall of the armories. Reg asked me if I would go on a blind date. I had to phone up Theresa to see if she was expecting me this evening and found out that she waited for me at the corner of Brown and Cyrille until 8:45 last night, consequently she thought I had stood her up and she had every indication of going on the warpath and the only satisfaction I got when I asked for a date tomorrow night was, "Call me at 7:20." So I guess all I can do is call her at the designated time. Having nothing in particular to do this evening I decided to help Reg out and go on the blind date. Reg phoned Pauline and told her he had a fellow for her girlfriend and when he left the phone he had a funny look on his

face. He told me the other girl was Louise, the girl that Tommy Suttlehan has been going out with and a friend of Theresa's. Things were beginning to get complicated and I didn't want to rile Theresa any more than I could help, so when Reg said he wasn't fussy about the date and asked me to go and phone Pauline that he had to go on guard duty. I snapped at the chance of getting out of a very potential embarrassing position. I felt sorry for Pauline when I phoned and told her that Reg had been unexpectedly called for guard duty.

Later, Reg and I walked down town and had a sandwich and a cup of coffee. Got back to camp at 10:30P.M.

NOV. 7, THURS.
Jack Tully and I were supposed to erect an aerial on the Sergeants' mess this morning but we found out that they didn't have a kit so as we had to find a ground pipe we spent a couple of hours before we found a suitable lengthy of pipe. We had map reading in the afternoon.

I called Theresa at 7:20 P.M. as per schedule and she was still a little sore about the misunderstanding the night before last. In fact, she insisted that she was going out with her sister again. As the sister is becoming all together too convenient as an excuse I hung up. In as much that I enjoy a show regardless if I am alone or not, I didn't let Theresa's refusal deter me from going to the Empire Theatre. I had a midnight lunch at the Empire Cafe, a few doors away from the theater.

NOV. 8, FRI.
Jack and I finally got started on the Sergeants' aerial and finished it around 2:15P.M. just in time to miss Ceremonial parade. Any notion that you may have that we made the job last until after Ceremonial Parade is hereby discredited by myself. It usually takes 6 hours for an aerial erecting operation but we did it in 5. Sent a letter and $7.00 home to Nelle this evening. It was drizzling and miserable out so stayed in barracks this evening until nine o'clock then went to bed.

NOV. 9, SAT.

Helped scrub the bunk house this morning. Reg, Sergeant Rankine and I went through the Museum this afternoon. Saw some darn good wood carvings on display as well as birds and animals of the wild outdoors, they were stuffed of course.

It was after five when we came out so we dropped into a little French café (one of those kind that is below the street level), and had a very good supper. From then until midnight we wandered around, in and out of stores, back alleys and streets and enjoyed ourselves after a fashion. Got to bed about 12:30A.M.

NOV. 10, SUN.

Attended church parade to St. Andrews Church. Stayed in during the afternoon and kept myself busy doing exactly nothing. Jack Tully and I went skating at the arena and had a fairly good time. The huge crowd of skating enthusiasts reminded me of the old crowd that used to go to the Thistle Rink on Tuesday and Friday nights on band nights. The crowd was so heavy that the ice started to melt after the first half an hour and to fall was a sure way of getting soaked.

Practically all the girls dress in short flaring skirts and most of them are actually very nice to look at, some could almost be classed as beautiful. I didn't feel up to maneuvering a partner through that crowd besides trying to talk to them so that they would understand so this first trip really developed into a reconnaissance patrol and the next time I go I'll have more fun.

NOV. 11, MON.

Remembrance Day. The Camerons were included in the ceremony at the Cenotaph which turned out to be very impressive. It started at 10:00 in the morning and lasted until one o'clock in the afternoon. We were applauded by three women as we march along the street so we came to the conclusion that they must have been Scotch; who else but Scotchman would cheer us down here?

I went up to Harry Guedesse's place to look at his radio and met his wife. Had quite a good evening finished off by a lunch. They are a very devoted couple and deserve a lot more from this world than they are getting. I wish them luck and plenty of it. It's pouring outside tonight but I suppose as usual it will stop just in time for the weekly route march tomorrow. Received and answered a letter from Marcelle this afternoon. According to the news tonight, this day appears to have been a very good from the Allies point of view, what with the earthquake in Romania's oil fields, the Greeks success against the Italians and the R.C.A.F.'s bombing raids on Germany.

NOV. 12, TUES.
It started to rain again just about parade time so we went to signal school for buzzer practice. We were broken off around 10:00 A.M. to polish our equipment in preparedness for inspection by General Brown (Brig. Brown of M.D.10) in the afternoon. The inspection didn't amount to much.

Moreau and I went up to a private residence for the evening. It's a nice way to spend a quiet evening listening to Captain Byron Hall tell of his experiences in the last war. The lady of the house is English and an interesting talker. They gave us plenty of refreshments and cigarettes and we enjoyed listening to a phonograph and an excellent selection of records. There is nothing exciting about the idea but it's very nice to have a place to go where the people are glad to have us.

They told us that anytime we wanted to go up again to just give them a ring and it would be alright.

NOV. 13, WED.
On station work all morning and found it very cold on the feet. Sport parade to the drill hall this afternoon and didn't do much but hang around until 4:00 o'clock. I wrote a letter to Doc this evening, then Reg and I went to the Capitol to see "The Northwest Mounted Police." Got back to bed between 10:30 and 11:00 P.M.

The O.C. told us that we would be getting eight day leaves at Christmas or New years but the train fare is $36.50, just a trifling sum but about $16.00 over my head. I may go to Montreal for Christmas, for no other reason but to look the place over.

NOV. 14, THURS.

Swim parade at the Y.M. this A.M. with a short route march afterward. During one of the breaks Major Otton told us that they were going to try and reduce the fare to $19.00 or $20.00 which gives us more than a chance.

We had ceremonial this afternoon during which we were inspected by Brig. Sergeant, the commander of the 6th Infantry Brigade. I was on phone duty from six to ten in the Batt. Ord. Room and I wrote a long letter to Olga, but I haven't mailed it yet because I can't remember if I have already written to her since we hit Quebec. I guess I'll have to take that chance and send it along. Now I remember, I did write to her because I told her about the hunting country north of Sudbury. All that time wasted last night; I'll have to tack somebody else's name on it, someone I haven't written to yet.

NOV. 15, FRI.

Heavy snowfall this morning with a strong wind from the Northeast. So far it is about three inches deep. Buzzer practice this morning and a little map reading.

Pay parade this afternoon and I collected nearly enough to pay for the radio; there is one or two yet to come across.

Reg, Red and myself had supper at the St. Jean Cafè then played pool for awhile. Pool is an interesting game where skill at figuring angles and tangents would come in mighty handy.

NOV. 16, SAT.

Detailed to help guard the roads around the firing range at Valcartier while the Anti-Aircraft and carrier platoons shot down gas filled balloons. The job lasted from 8:00 in the morning until after four in the afternoon. Went to see Deanna Durbin in "The Spring Parade" at the Capitol.

NOV. 17, SUN.

No parade today so spent the day writing letters. Someday I will hit a simple filing system to keep my correspondence straight.

Went to see Mickey Rooney in "Andy meets a Debutante" at the Cartier. Had a lunch in the Soucy Pharmacie. Sent five dollars home.

NOV. 18, MON.
Went for a route march this morning out past Sillery and it was exceedingly hard march with the slippery footing.

We started on a new studying idea this afternoon which will be alright if they continue along the same lines.

I received a letter from Marcelle this afternoon which I was very pleased to get. She sent a silk handkerchief and a gold ring for souvenirs. Especially pleased with the way she said good night. In fact it was a very nice letter all around.

Moreau and I visited Miss Banks and ex-Captain Hall again tonight and we had some fun playing Chinese checkers. Captain Hall started teaching us chess and I am getting interested in the game. If there were more people like Miss Banks and Captain Hall the life of the soldier would be much happier.

NOV. 19, TUES.
We had the Army Act read to us again this morning; the second time since I enlisted. Detailed to change the location of the radio in the Sergeant's mess. I had to find the necessary material myself and if they haven't found a double socket their radio isn't going yet.

We had lectures this afternoon in the signal school. The lectures are really reviews of work we have already taken.

Jim Ellison and I went skating this evening and met a few English speaking girls who live close to our barracks. The one I skated with twice, a very pretty blond, fairly tall, a little on the plump side. They are going skating again next Thursday. I received a letter from Olga today and it appears like she knows Marcelle. I started answering Marcelle's last letter before I went skating but didn't have time to finish it.

NOV. 20, WED.

Five of us were given the morning off because we were on picket duty at Valcartier last Saturday. That means we had the whole day off as this afternoon was sports day. Moreau and I went for a walk this afternoon and dropped in to the R.C.A.F.'s new recruiting offices for information on transfers. The clerk didn't seem very anxious to part with any information until we told him we wanted to get in as wireless operators then he explained the details and gave us an information pamphlet and an application form. As before when I tried the Navy, the first thing required is a letter from my Commanding Officer giving me permission to be discharged; something that is possible but virtually improbable. According to the pamphlet, the only position I could attain would be wireless operator on the ground (a wog.) I may try it later on when I get an accurate check up on my receiving speed. Sgt. Rankine, Cpl. Hatch and myself walked around town for awhile tonight. I mailed a letter to Marcelle.

NOV. 21, THURS.

Paraded to the Y.M.C.A. this morning for P.T. and swim parade and so had lots of time to read, write and play games or what have you. Buzzer practice this afternoon and we had our first look at up-to-date field telephone equipment; it's a vast improvement over the old stuff.

Jim Ellison and I went skating this evening and got so interested showing Audrey how to improve her skating the band was playing God Save The King before we realized it. I am in a quandary as to what to do about Christmas. If they bring the fare down I want to go home for New Year's because Marcelle will be in Fort William for Xmas, Doc has invited me down to his place in Toronto for Christmas and if the fare isn't reduced I may go down there; but I have to decide very soon which I am going to take, New Years or Xmas. If they could receive definite word about train fare the matter of settling the question would be easy.

NOV. 22, FRI.

We had a little experience at manipulating the new phone equipment and came to the conclusion that it is about a 200% improvement over the old gear for sensitivity, operating ease and efficiency. It's too bad that we will only have it until Monday morning when we have to take it back to the Royal Rifles of Canada from whom we borrowed it.

I paraded for new clothes this afternoon and got a whole new uniform; it is a much better fit than my old one. Treated myself to the Cameron's Concert, held at the Palaise Montcalm, tonight and enjoyed myself immensely. The place was packed, mostly by civilians and there were quite a number standing up. Another step toward making friends with this fair city of Quebec. I didn't see Audrey there; I guess there was too much of a crowd. I received a letter from Jack today.

NOV. 23, SAT.
Helped scrub the hut floor this morning which was completed at 10:00A.M. Jim Ellison and I went to a show at the Empire Theater then had supper in a café on St. Jean Ave.

Went for a walk with Reg this evening and got back 9:30P.M. Wrote a letter to Jack today.

NOV. 24, SUN.
Detailed for fatigues in the Sergeants quarters along with Stewie. Moreau and I went to a show at the Cartier then had supper down town after which we walked down to the Union Station in lower town. Found it very hard walking on these hills due to the ice.

NOV. 25, MON.
Buzzer reading practice until 2:15P.M, then two test messages, getting a mark of 99. Also test in elementary electricity with a mark of 100% and a test on map reading which is my pet headache, score 70%

Started a letter to Doc at noon but haven't finished it yet. Wrote my first exam paper of my mathematics course. I hope I did alright.

NOV. 26, TUES.

Found I had a question in map reading yesterday, right that was marked wrong so I got 70% instead of 25. List of marks for the tests: buzzer reading, plain English 99, Cypher 99, Elementary Electricity 100, Map Reading 70.

Went skating again last night and skated twice with Audrey and once with Kay. Found it exceedingly chilly this evening walking to and from the rink. I managed to make the two way trip with only one fall.

Reg walked back with me and we stopped at Gordon's Cafe for a cup of coffee. We sat beside an old Quebecer who gave us the low down on the girls that most of the Camerons are picking up, in no uncertain terms. Finally got to bed about midnight.

NOV. 27, WED.

Signal school all day with map reading and buzzer practice the main topic and activity. A blizzard started this morning and the snow has piled up quite a lot. It being sports day and me having no inclination for sports at this particular time I stayed in the hut and wrote letters and studied radio and mathematics. I managed to write and mail three letters, one to Connie which was long overdue, one to Vera and one to Doc. Feeling tired tonight. All this studying that I am doing on my own time seems so futile tonight.

NOV. 28, THURS.

Making good marks in code reading tests that we are having daily.

Went skating at the arena again this evening and had the usual two skates with Audrey. Also skated with a girl called Mable. After skating Jim and I walked home with Mable and she invited us in for coffee. They are a real nice family, seemingly athletic, judging from the cups they have for swimming, running, paddling and rowing. We had quite a confab with Mable's sister about rifles and pistols and archery. Another friend of Audrey's was there and she is a humdinger of a skater; I enjoyed my skate with her very much. I am beginning to classify the girls I know according to their skating ability.

NOV. 29, FRI.

Bath parade this morning and after having a good shower managed to start a letter to Marcelle.

Pay parade this afternoon and put $6.00 in the platoon fund toward my fare home, also bought a ticket for a raffle for $35.00 cash prize. Wrote and mailed letters to Marcelle and Rose.

NOV. 30, SAT.

We had indoor firing practice this morning and found I still have the tendency to pull to the right.

Went to the Cambrai Theater this afternoon after which I bought myself a very good 15¢ lunch at the Y.M.C.A. Came back to camp around 8:00 P.M. and wrote a fair sized note to Nelle.

DEC. 1, SUN.

Traded our old blankets for new ones today and it's about time. Finished a letter to Nelle this morning. Re-copied notes on radio and motors today and studied mathematics for awhile. I had a good shower tonight and would like to have one of the same every night.

I tried three times to get hold of Audrey to see if she and her friends were going skating, finally found out that she had gone to Levis with her Father.

DEC. 2, MON.

The usual routine today. Received two letters from Bobbie, one bawling me out for not answering her last letter and a note apologizing for the first letter.

Moreau and I made another visit to Miss Banks' apartment and as per usual had a good time. Mr. Hall related some more of his experiences from the last war and Harold and I played three games of chess. I won two of them, mostly by luck. I am beginning to like the game and may try carving a set of chessmen just for fun. We are to go up again next Friday.

DEC. 3, TUES.

Spent an hour in the drill hall this morning at my pet dislike, platoon drill; also an hour of lamp reading after which we had our daily buzzer practice. We had a written test on miscellaneous subjects this afternoon and have a premonition that I didn't do so well.

I wrote a letter to Olga this evening and mailed it.

Reg was talking to the radio operator of DA, a government station situated in the armories, and from Reg's account he sure has a mess of equipment over there. He invited Reg and any interested friend to go over sometime and he would show them around. So we may go over on Thursday and I have a feeling that I am going to enjoy the visit.

Rumours are going around again regarding future moves and it's not safe to go into detail except that it may interfere with our holiday leaves if the rumour turns out to be true.

DEC. 4, WED.

Spent the morning in the signal hut as per usual. The rumour I mentioned yesterday has been confirmed to a certain degree and until further notice, Xmas and New Year leaves have been cancelled. That means I'll have to inform certain people back home of the fact. The entire platoon wrapped their hands around thirty shovel handles this afternoon and banked the snow around the hut.

I went on phone duty at six o'clock and with the aid of L/Cpl Lister's code machine obtained an accurate check on my code receiving ability. If I remember rightly, I haven't reached the speed that brother Bill did; twenty words a minute. I can take eighteen with little trouble.

Started a long letter to Bobbie and I think she fully deserves it. Came off duty at 10:00P.M.

DEC. 5, THURS.

We had a very interesting lecture by Major "Tiger" Otton which took three hours, almost, but it was very interesting. He started out to explain how the signals would work in a battle and before he had finished he had, with the aid of maps, explained how they took various towns and places in the last war.

I finished an eight page letter to Bobbie which I mailed on my way to the rink. Had a fairly good skate this evening but the ice was awfully rough and hilly. Audrey and her friends weren't there. We were informed this evening by an obliging young Frenchman, that St Patrick Rink had much better ice and more English speaking people go there and so are we next time.

Came back to camp around ten o'clock and treated myself to a good hot shower in preparation for a physical examination tomorrow.

Seeing as the leaves are going to be cancelled, I may be able to send a few inexpensive gifts home at Christmas.

DEC. 6, FRI.

We had a physical examination this morning during which we were running around the hut in the altogether with snow, (hastily grabbed snow procured through rapidly opened and closed doors) very much in evidence. Later in the morning we had a clothing parade to the quartermaster's to rectify any deficiencies in our kits and to replace any worn out clothing.

We were given the afternoon off to scrub our webbing in preparation for something or other. Were told that there would be definitely no Christmas or New Year leaves which solves my two big problems efficiently, if not satisfactorily. After a couple of rumourless months, they have come back stronger and more fantastic than ever. We have no definite information regarding the leave cancellation but speculation is rife and the cussing eloquent.

Received a letter from Vera and Rose today and I answered Harry's and Bezzie and Rose's letters today. I am expecting at least two letters tomorrow, one from Marcelle and one from Nelle. If I remember rightly, the first Division left for overseas just before Christmas and I wouldn't be surprised to see history repeat itself in our case.

DEC. 7, SAT.

I guess I'll have to invest a couple of dollars in a new pen. Nursing this one along is getting my goat.

Interior economy this morning with the usual Saturday morning activities. Wrote a letter to Nelle this evening and one to Vera this morning. Also mailed my second mathematics paper this evening. I guess I can be safe in saying that we will be on the move again before Xmas unless the big shots change their minds again like they often do. Went to a mediocre picture at the Capitol this evening.

DEC. 8, SUN

I have been nailed for the line orderly's job today, although it doesn't entail very much work, the fact remains that I can't go out this afternoon and it sure is one swell day. I will be all through at 4:30 this afternoon so may go for a walk this evening. I may even go skating at the St. Patrick's rink. I am going to read over the first book of this diary, then send it home.

DEC. 9, MON.

Code practice and map reading all day. Stayed in this evening and studied.

DEC. 10, TUES.

Code and map reading practice all day. Got paid tonight at 9:30P.M. Things are being rushed now.

DEC. 11, WED.

We were all busy packing and loading trucks this morning. I had to tear down four aerials this afternoon. Moreau and I left camp at 5:30P.M. as we wanted to do a little shopping before going to Miss Banks' for supper.

They were ready for us with a big spread which they said would have to take the place of the real Christmas dinner which they had planned on giving. They presented each of us with a flashlight that must have cost them plenty. This sticker is a souvenir that Miss Banks gave me and I can't think of a more appropriate place for it. They gave us addresses of people in England who will be glad to see us when and if we call on them. We were also given a few coins for lucky charms and 75 cigarettes apiece. We were very sorry to have to leave them but whenever Quebec is mentioned I will remember our good friends Miss Banks and Captain Hall.

They had no particular reason to invite us up there twice a week, as far as we know but they seemed very pleased to have us and we were exceptionally pleased to go. They started us playing chess and I, at least, expect to play more of it.

DEC. 12, THURS.
So we left Quebec on this cold and frosty morning and said goodbye to quite a few friends that we had gotten to know in our short stay. We crossed the massive Quebec Bridge and then turned east through the little towns along the south shore of the St. Lawrence. Riviere de Loupe was reached around supper time and then came Porte Jolis where we went for a short march. This is the point where we turn southeast and head for New Brunswick. So the wheels turn and we are on the move again. I wonder what lies ahead? We will be in Halifax tomorrow morning, early.

Finally crossed the boundary between Quebec and New Brunswick at Matapedia and now we can't find a person on the station platforms who talks French. I got two addresses of girls in Tide Head.

Arrived in Campbelltown around 8:30P.M. and the fellows had quite a time with the girls. We caught our first glimpse of big water which happened to be the Gulf of St. Lawrence.

Our next big stop will be Moncton or Gloucester but I think we will all be in bed by that time.

Moreau and I just completed the mastication of a very swell lunch given to us by Miss Banks last night, which consisted of fruit cake, grapes and one chocolate duck apiece. I am having a grape pip shooting war with Reg who is perched very precariously on a top bunk trying to pen a letter when he isn't laying a careful aim on me, directly below. The direct hits are very few as we have to shoot around the edge of the berth without being seen. It should be a great battle if the grapes hold out.

DEC. 13, FRI.

Woke up this morning in time to shave and wash before arriving at Truro on the Bay of Fundy. We were informed by an early morning waker that the Black Devils are stationed a little west of here.

We are standing in the station now just getting ready for breakfast. It is raining pretty hard which makes the little snow that is on the ground very slushy. I wrote a short note to Bobbi last night which I mailed at Bathhurst, New Brunswick. I'd imagine that we are traveling the same route taken by Dad and Bill in the last war.

An hour or so later: we have passed through Brookfield, Shubenacadie, Milford and Grand Lake. I guess our next stop will be Windsor Junction then Halifax.

Arrived Halifax approximately 9:30P.M. and loaded right onto our boat the "Pasteur," a French luxury liner built recently and which has never had her passenger carrying maiden voyage. She is a swell ship and I am looking forward to sailing on her. A sailor informed us that she will carry (*crossed out*) men and (*crossed out*) crew members. We must have been the first unit to arrive as after we loaded a few more units or so we will pull out and anchor in the Bay to wait for the rest of the convoy to assemble. It promises to be a big convoy.

S.S. (Louis Pasteur at sea)

The Bay or Harbour life is very interesting to watch and I saw a Swedish freighter named Bauerspien pull in from the open sea. Another Freighter flying the Union Jack called the Swinbourne which sounds all Aussie to me. It soon will be time for our first meal aboard ship.

We had it and had our first experience with rationing; no tea or butter, which didn't meet with our approval in the least.

We may move out to anchor during the night as we are almost loaded now. We have reinforcements for the 1st Division on board, as well as the artillery. The exact number is unknown to such fellows as us and even if I did know I couldn't put it down here. This boat "Pasteur" has made four trips across the pond and has had three encounters with the enemy and has the privilege to claim credit for sinking one sub.

We were very fortunate in getting comparatively good sleeping accommodations as some of the fellows are sleeping in hammocks. Mine is Berth 2, Section L and Deck C. There are 88 bunks in this section with part being occupied by members of a French Canadian unit. Directly across the corridor is the mess hall and in the opposite direction is the canteen so we have everything handy.

DEC. 14, SAT.
Woke up this morning and found we were still moored to the pier. They say there is another few hundred men to come aboard so we may be here for a couple of days yet. I think I have walked every deck on this boat from stem to stern and now I am anxious to get going. I would like to be in London for Christmas, if we are going there.

I didn't do nothing much else but sleep this afternoon so can't say what went on outside or around the ship. They tried a new system of feeding us this evening which was a slight improvement over the system we were using.

Our partner unit in the brigade is in the Capetown Castle, another high class passenger ship moored directly behind us. We may get under way sooner than we expected.

I hear there is going to be a church parade tomorrow but I haven't heard any confirmation as yet. I have located the showers and I am looking forward to a good wash tomorrow. The boys are amusing themselves at bingo, crown & anchor and cards while we are waiting.

DEC. 15, SUN.

Still tied to the pier and it looks as if we will be carrying the overseas Xmas mail. The castle pulled away from her berth this morning but where she went we don't know. We had life boat station drill this morning, wearing life belts. By the looks of things I think we are going to have lots of fatigues on this trip. Some more troops came aboard this Afternoon and they finished loading the mail on board. Some girls were on the pier this P.M. and they sure got an assortment of souvenirs, sweaters, cigarettes, ha'pennies, etc. that the boys were throwing down to them. They, in turn, tied souvenirs to weighty objects and returned a trade souvenir by getting aid of a few husky sailors with good right arms.

We were issued with our tin hats today and the darn things are very heavy or at least, they feel heavy. They haven't finished loading the scow yet so I guess we will stay put for another day. Some more bushmen came aboard tonight with the possibility of more coming.

Took a couple of turns around the deck this evening before retiring for the night.

DEC. 16, MON.

We cleared the gang plank at 9:10A.M. and were gliding past the three mile limit by 10:10A.M. We are getting a good demonstration of how a convoy is run, with the large naval craft and the smaller destroyers, helped by the airplanes keeping up a constant watch for possible danger even though we haven't gone far as yet. The sea is not rough at all and there is very little roll noticeable when I am down here. The guns we carry look very businesslike and are all ready for action.

We had boat drill again this afternoon, at least, they did. I was a little late in getting on and they had changed our position from "B" deck to "A" deck.

I ran into Roy Miller who also was lost so we set out to find our company. In the course of our search we met Sgt.'s Rankine and Wilson who were wandering around in the same condition of confusion so we combined our forces and finally found the company on "A" deck just in time to see them break off. I have my ideas that Sgt. Major Dumma must be a superman or something because I'd leave or pass him at different spots and he always arrived at the next spot before me and by a different route.

We had the usual difficulty at supper tonight and for the fourth consecutive meal I filled up on bread and tea. The food is there and it's good eating but it takes so long to dish the vittles out that I don't want any of it when my turn comes. I understand we are making fairly good time over a choppy sea with the largest of our escort riding between our ship and the castle. There isn't much use going out on deck except for fresh air because everything is pitch black and very little can be seen. I have caught myself a head cold and it's making me feel a little miserable.

The old scow is starting to roll now so maybe there will be a few less in for breakfast in the morning. I found it extremely difficult to navigate the dark corridors and passageways this evening. Moreau and I were returning from the canteen a while ago and Moreau nearly stepped into a dark stairway.

Mr. Coate's idea of breathing with the ship (breath in when the ship comes up and out when it comes down) might be alright for small craft but this boat has a long roll and if I start breathing in on the up roll I have reached my capacity about half way up so I have to breath out on the last half of the roll and vice versa. She is starting to roll now so I think I will hit the hay.

DEC. 17, TUES.
Woke up this morning with the ship plowing through a heavy sea with poor visibility. Some of the boys are pretty sick. I had a good breakfast then went up on deck. They say it's only an average heavy sea but the waves are a good thirty feet high.

A starboard port hole blew in this morning injuring a couple of the boys slightly and we had to change our course so that the thing could be fixed. About the same time, the Castle broke her steering gear so we haven't seen the rest of the convoy since but we are supposed to rejoin them sometime this afternoon.

It's dusk and there is no sign of the convoy yet. A seaman said we will not rejoin the convoy until morning because of the danger of collision in the dark.

DEC. 18, WED.
As usual, I went out on deck this morning after breakfast and the first thing I saw was the convoy riding in its usual position. There is a freezing north wind blowing and the sea is far from smooth. We had a rifle inspection parade at eleven o'clock on the port promenade deck. We had a respirator inspection parade at 2:00P.M. on the starboard promenade deck. Major Otton gave us a few instructions about getting off the boat onto the train when we land.

So far I have managed to keep my stomach in its proper place and I have come to the conclusion that Mr. Coates knew what he was talking about.

The freighter rejoined the convoy this noon, settling the argument as to whether she had gone back with the destroyers or not.

We spotted a light off to the starboard this evening but I suppose we will never know who it belonged to. It may have been a neutral ship just passing. We are scheduled to arrive at a recognized "danger zone" tomorrow night and they say that stricter discipline will be enforced. It's very doubtful if we will land before Christmas.

DEC. 19, THURS.
Seventy-two hours out and by the height of the sun and the low temperature leads me to believe that we are sailing away north of the usual route. It's cold outside with the occasional snow flurry and a little too miserable to stay on deck long. We are still maintaining a speed of about 18 knots.

Nine other fellows and I searched for two hours this morning for the boatswain as he had a fatigue for us to do but we couldn't find him. Finally gave up and returned to our quarters only to be chased out again for General Inspection. We may have another boat drill this afternoon.

The boat drill failed to materialize but we did have another rifle inspection. Received our pay books today. I did a little studying tonight but the noise was too intense to make it very effective.

We met a west bound ship this evening which was running without lights also. She was right up on us before anyone was aware of her proximity but we managed to get through okay.

I partook of an ex-lax tablet this evening and hope it works well. The boys are all feeling lots better this evening and are actually indulging in a little horseplay.

DEC. 20, FRI.

The laxative is doing the job exceptionally well. The decks are covered with snow this morning and I couldn't see two of the ships of the convoy whether they are behind or obscured by snow, I don't know. They are kicking us out on deck at 8:30 this morning instead of nine thirty which means that we will have to stay on deck nearly three hours. I think the corporal has misunderstood orders. This scow can rock and roll now and I don't even notice it.

We had a sudden boat drill alarm this morning and the proceedings went along pretty smoothly and rapidly. We had our usual parade on the port deck this afternoon. We saw a ship going west but it was too far away to identify. Even at that, the castle moved back to give the battleship a clear line of fire and as soon as they ascertained that there was no danger she moved up into position again.

It seems funny that only a week ago we were safe in Canada and now we are keeping our eyes peeled for hostile sea craft and aircraft. What a difference a thousand miles make.

We are supposed to meet our additional armed escort from England sometime tomorrow. We expect to land pretty close to Xmas. All the boys are nearly back to normal and are feeling pretty chipper this evening.

Played a little "crown and anchor" tonight and came out 25¢ ahead. It's lots of fun and it helps to pass the time which seems to be dragging more than usual since we boarded ship. By the looks of things we may land in Scotland.

DEC. 21, SAT.

Got up this morning with a wind on our port bow and a light drizzle falling. Amused myself reading messages sent by lamp from the battleship. Some of the boys caught several varieties of hell for discussing the contents of the messages before other members of the different companies and units.

We were supposed to go on parade this morning at 11:00A.M. but I just got there in time to break off, which fails to cause me a particle of worry.

I think we must have reached the Gulf Stream because it has warmed up considerably, almost enough to go out on deck without a greatcoat, if it wasn't raining.

The convoy changed around this evening with the Revenge and our boat changing places. A little while after dusk the Revenge pulled out of sight. It's the general belief throughout the boat that we will be met with a strong escort to take us the rest of the way.

Lost sixty five cents in Bingo this evening but came close to winning a number of times. There is nothing much else to do and the silver is burning a hole in my pocket.

It's pitch black out tonight and all ships have closed in. Lights after dark has become a constant source of danger and it's to our own good to report any light within the convoy that might be noticed from outside. Our blackout lasts from 4:30P.M. to 9:45A.M. and God help the man who smokes on an open deck during those hours. Our life preservers are our constant companions now as we wear them wherever we go; meals, parades, etc. Reg is hollering for me to go and shave with him so I guess I had better go.

DEC. 22, SUN.

A fairly heavy sea rolling today although it isn't very cold. Watched the two smaller ships plowing through the water for awhile. We are still steaming along without an escort as the Revenge nor the expected destroyers have shown up as yet. The old tub is really rolling and pitching and a lot worse than last Tuesday but everyone seems to be enjoying it this time.

The meals aboard ship are of good quality consisting mainly of fish, roast beef, mutton stew and chops, sausages, soup, potatoes, cabbage, turnips, bread, butter and tea. For breakfast we usually have bacon and fried potatoes, bread, butter, jam and tea. For lunch either mutton stew or roast beef, etc. but no butter or tea; the tea is usually replaced with very good soup. We have gotten into the habit of saving a little of our breakfast butter for the noon day meal. For supper we might have any of the above mentioned but never the same as what we get for lunch. About two mornings a week we get "kippers" for breakfast. So there is plenty of variety and the food is good. We may be issued with iron rations sometime today.

We were issued with our iron rations or at least, part of them, viz: a can of bully beef. The sea is still kind of rough and darkness has come again with no sign of the convoy. It is rumored around that we should sight land sometime tomorrow. We seem to be keeping clear of the coast of Ireland for obvious reasons. Played Bingo again this evening with no luck, so I guess I am not meant to be a gambler.

DEC. 23, MON.
A high wind and a fairly rough sea today. I was detailed along with eight other fellows to sweep the sports deck which in itself is quite easily done if the wind stays in one direction like it didn't today.

They were steering a very zigzag course today with the four ships passing and re-passing beside and behind us all afternoon. There still isn't any sign of the convoy that we have been looking for two days and we haven't sighted land yet. I am enjoying this rough weather immensely and I seem kind of sorry that it will soon be over. I may endeavour to transfer to the navy again, maybe I'll have more luck in the Royal Navy.

There is a rumour going around that we will be split up with a company assigned to different villages and towns. The rumour also states that we will only be in England a few weeks but that is too unreliable to depend on. It has quietened considerably this evening which may mean that we are getting close to land and yet it may not. The fact remains that the boat is riding along with only a very slight roll. In all my life I have never had the misfortune to be in company with a group of men whose opinions and beliefs vary so widely. It would not be so annoying if they wouldn't take turns trying to change each other's opinions on the different subjects, but as it is there is hardly a subject mentioned that doesn't develop into a rip-snorting argument.

DEC. 24, TUES.

I spent most of the morning on the forward deck as the sea was like glass with only a very slight swell. Had quite a time watching the fish dashing away from the ship. They were anywhere from three to six feet long and they would swim just below the surface with an occasional surface-breaking leap. I decided that they might have been porpoises. We had another boat drill this morning at eleven o'clock during which we saw the first airplane of our air escort. It flew around a couple of times then it was joined by another; now the two of them have increased to four and they are flying around us in a wide circle. We also have a destroyer leading us so I guess we weren't forgotten after all. There is only two of us now as the other two ships forged ahead sometime during the night.

We saw a large convoy heading out to sea this afternoon which included well over twenty five ships of all sizes. Managed to get a haircut this afternoon. LAND HO! At 3:15 this afternoon. There is a little disagreement on whether it's the Orkney Islands, Shetland Islands or the west coast of Scotland. Most of the boys are overjoyed at sighting the long looked for "terra firma" but I think if I was working aboard a naval craft I wouldn't give a darn when I saw it. We have an abundant protection now with about ten destroyers all around and a flight of fighters above. We should be unloading by six tomorrow morning if all goes well.

We dropped anchor about 9:00P.M. which only requires a short river trip which will take about an hour, before we disembark. It's been the worse Christmas Eve that I have spent in many years and Christmas looks like it will be just as bad.

DEC. 25, CHRISTMAS DAY, WED.

The ship has been still for the first time since leaving our Canadian port. I understand that we will move up river at noon, possibly sooner. I have almost finished my packing except for a few minor articles so I might spend a great part of the morning on deck.

We moved from the Forth and headed up stream about nine thirty. As we were passing through the narrows we could see people in all the windows in the town waving what I took to be table clothes and aprons. We came to anchor among a flock of ships and water craft of every description, including mud scows. The harbour activity here is much greater than that of our embarkation port and from where we are it is quite difficult to see the town through the smoke. It is very interesting looking country with the ships in the harbour and the famous and much sung of hills behind as a background. I had my first glimpse of the now famous balloon barrage but on a lot smaller scale than I think London boasts. The houses along the shores are all built in the same manner; rectangular with the long side on the street. The material is gray appearing stone and by the number of chimney pots (that is what they call them I think) they must have two or more families living in them.

The gentleman that wrote that song roaming in the gloaming must have lived around here someplace. We were told late this morning that we will have to stay aboard ship until tomorrow at least as they haven't the train accommodation for all the troops to be unloaded in one day. We had a chicken dinner today which wasn't like home at all. The chicken was boiled and the peas were like bird shot and by the time my turn came there was no spuds; the pudding wasn't bad but like everything else that is cooked on a larger scale it could have been better. I wonder what they are doing at home.

Hugh Comack and I had a little fun this evening with four artillery sig's who were trying to read a lamp sending from the shore. After they had finished reading a message we asked them if they could read those flashes to which we received a firm reply to the positive. Then Hugh asked them what the message contained. We had also read the message so we knew they were stringing us a line when they tried to tell us. After they had the parts they had read correctly Hugh said "oh" and we walked away before we started laughing. We finally went back and asked them if they would like to know the true text of the message and without waiting for a yes or no, Hugh repeated the whole thing by memory.

They told us they had twelve weeks in a signal school and were qualified sigs. We left them soon after still calling out pips(p) for x-rays(x) and freddies(d) for London(L).

We came below and ran into a good feed of turkey that some of the boys had scrounged up someplace. Incidentally it didn't take long for the whole turkey to disappear and we sure had a good time while it lasted.

The ship's electrician informed us that we would experience our first air raid alarm tomorrow night so I guess we will continue our journey by land early in the morning. I may drop a line to cousin Wal one of these days, when there is more chance of mailing it easily.

DEC. 26, THURS.

I was detailed to sweep "A" deck this morning along with about ten others of the platoon but the job didn't take very long. We had lunch at 10:30 and boarded the tender at 1:15P.M. which took us to shore where we boarded the train. Nearly all of the boys were overjoyed to leave the old Pasteur. We pulled out of the sea port at 3:15P.M. There were six men to a compartment so there was no room to lie down for a sleep. In our compartment there were Steeds, Stewart, Dean, Ellison, Guedesse and myself. Steward isn't feeling so well and I think he didn't enjoy the train ride so very well. I was greatly impressed by the size and speed of these Old Country trains and although there seems to be trains dashing in every direction the transportation system is very efficient, at least it seems to be.

We stopped at Newcastle for awhile where some of the boys were given tea and cakes by some women's organization, we didn't stop long enough to allow everyone to be served. We saw a number of searchlights along the way which moved across the sky unceasingly, some of them were pretty close by the road.

We finally hit York at one o'clock in the morning where the ladies were waiting for us with tea and cakes, which they had loaded on four wheeled carts and parked beside each coach. Each man was given a large quantity of tea and two cakes which certainly hit the spot. There was plenty of refreshments left after the first round so we were given a second helping and as long as we stood on the platform our cups were never empty. Lots of the fellows have changed their opinion of the English people, for the better.

We arrived in Redding at 8:30 or 9:00A.M. Friday morning and learned that the ferries had laid off over Christmas but I don't think it was because of Adolf's holiday spirits. In Redding we saw two men push a locomotive around on a turntable simply by pushing it around by handles at each end of the table.

We arrived at our camp at 10:30A.M. where we had a very good breakfast. I met Clare Archer who has two stripes up now and who is leaving on Sunday for some course or other. We were issued with two blankets today now all I need to be comfortable is a mattress. There is no doubt that these are the best quarters we have had yet and the grub is much better than we had at Shilo. I went down town this evening and had quite a time navigating during the blackout. The air raid alarm sounded and a little later we could hear the bombs exploding miles away. We heard an enemy flight pass over a little later but they didn't drop any eggs. Finally started back to camp and after a little difficulty finding our way we arrived okay and hit the hay where I spent a miserable night due to the lack of a mattress.

DEC. 28, SAT.
A change of cooks and a change of grub for the worse this morning. We were issued with our gas capes, another blanket and two boxes of anti-gas paste. We were warned to have our respirators, capes and rifles in first class shape as we may be attacked any time now. It's hard to realize that we may be bombed any minute.

A Princess Pat man told me last night that Holly Sharpe is a Platoon Sergeant Major now. Also heard last night that a German radio station announced that they had sunk our entire convoy. I guess the folks at home must have had some very anxious days back home.

Reg and I went into town this afternoon and I discovered that the town looks vastly different in daylight than it does during a blackout. We visited the Toc. H Club for soldiers and I think it would be alright if it were a little bigger. I am finding the English monetary system a little confusing but it's getting clearer and clearer every day.

We met Forsythe a little later watching a football match and the three of us got quite a lot of fun out of it. Not because we liked football or rugby but because of their style of playing. Forsythe then invited us to take supper with him which cost 1'6 for two eggs, two big pieces of bacon, potato chips, coffee and two cakes per person. Then he took us to the Rex theatre where we saw a very good show. Coming back, Forsythe dropped into the dance at the Labour Hall and Reg and I groped our way back to camp.

There are no air raids tonight yet although the sky is clear as a bell, but there is a little fog starting to rise.

The Camerons have taken over the kitchens and so the system of feeding and the food have taken a decided turn for the worse.

I won't be able to get any letters away until Monday or Tuesday as I haven't any stamps or the money to buy any.

DEC. 29, SUN.

We had a muster parade this morning and I slept most of the afternoon instead of washing clothes like I intended. I understand Major "Tiger" Otton has been mess officer and Major Shankland is back with us as Company Commander. Also Major Dudley has been promoted and is taking charge of the Battalion. This is only hearsay as yet as there is no confirmation made of the changes.

The air raid alarm sounded again this evening and a short time after we heard the planes coming over. I believe they were after London again and we were treated to a fireworks display that paled any Fourth of July celebration I have ever seen. The bright fingers of the searchlight stabbing up into the partly clouded, star studded sky. The dull explosions and red glow of exploding bombs, the flash and explosions of the anti-aircraft guns with the flash of their death dealing missiles bursting against the scattered clouds.

There must have been a big fire started because there was a flash that lit up our vicinity quite plainly then it settled down to a steady glow which reflected from the clouds for long after. The all clear sounded about ten o'clock.

It seems crazy to me but here we have signed up to fight or be exterminated as the case may be and we stand at a comparatively safe distance and watch the innocent population being killed, maimed and made homeless and we can't do anything about it. Time for lights out.

DEC. 30, MON.

We were shown how to roll our gas capes this morning then we had a couple of hours of buzzer practice on the new DV's a sweet little instrument which is a pleasure to operate. We found out that we only have a portion of our anti-gas equipment; pretty soon we will have our respirator haversacks full up.

Reg and I may go to Aldershot soon for the purpose of buying a bona fide Balmoral and a hackle. The hackle is a plume of blue feathers worn behind our badges and it stands for Valour at Dunkirk. The Imperial Queen's Own Cameron Highlanders distinguished themselves at that battle and we are allowed to wear the hackle in their honour.

We had buzzer practice again this afternoon again for two and a half hours. Went to a free show this evening at the Garrison Theater here in camp and enjoyed it very much. A three piece orchestra called the "Three Crackers" that were really good, the drummer especially. The rest of the acts weren't far behind.

There hasn't been any air raid alarms as yet but the night is still young although there is a low ceiling and it feels like rain (I mean real rain).

I had canned salmon for the third dinner in a row tonight. The meals are getting decidedly worse and the system of feeding does not and cannot work with rationing. Half get a double ration and the other half get nearly nothing. Every day sees the men's tempers closer to the snapping point. There is a certain official that is headed for a lot of grief if he doesn't change his mind soon as the kitchen staff and the men are decidedly against the present system. I understand that we are supposed to have two uniforms and my kit bag is overflowing now.

I have come to the conclusion that men are still savages after all and still cling to most of their primitive instincts. If their girl friends and wives could listen in on some of their conversations and see them at meal times I am afraid they would not be able to recognize their different heart throbs.

Sometimes I have an overwhelming desire to get off by myself somewhere and regain my sense of social balance but as yet, that has been practically impossible. The solitude of a quiet lake surrounded by whispering pine trees seems very appealing tonight. The sighing of a fresh breeze, the lap of the waves and the whir of the reel would do me a world of good. Someone who would discuss things quietly and sensibly instead of shouting and babbling like this bunch, would be a treat worth fighting for. I have found that the best way to avoid arguments is to mind my own business and keep my opinions to myself.

DEC. 31, TUES.

Payday today and I received an even four pound and I can't send any home due to regulations and such. Spent the afternoon in the school doing buzzer work. Reg, Moreau and I went down town for supper which consisted of steak pudding and chips with bread and butter and tea. We went to a show afterwards then came back to camp. It's a heck of a way to spend New Year's Eve but like Christmas, it can't be helped. I can think of nothing better than to be home with a certain person and listen to the New Year being rung in. There is not a single indication that this is New Year's in this little town of Cove; the only time we hear New Year's mentioned is when one of the fellows suddenly expresses the desire to be home at this time, and tell of their experiences on other New Years' Eves. I would like to be able to wish someone a Happy and Prosperous New Year but it seems like so much mockery this year.

NEW YEAR'S DAY, 1941

Another year finished and the beginning of a new one. A whole year of recorded events, nothing very exciting or important but I have seen more of the world in the last 12 months than I ever did in all the years preceding 1940.

I have met loads of new people some of whom I am glad to rate as friends; I have come to know a person that I have known as far back as I can remember. I have lost track of my best friend entirely; I have seen the desolate wastes of Camp Shilo; I have learnt a lot about Winnipeg and things about the old home town I never knew before; I have been in Quebec and had the good fortune to meet two very good friends who I will be in debt to for some time. I have made an ocean trip under dangerous circumstances and travelled through Bonnie Scotland and part of England. I have watched air raids on London from the side lines and I have stumbled around in the blackouts. Every day, for the last month, has brought me closer to the actual battle field of this second world war. It is hard to realize that all the members of platoon who have annoyed me in their turn at one time or another will soon be facing the fury of a modern war and those who come back in one piece will be exceedingly fortunate.

I, like everyone else, have wondered how we as individuals will stand up under fire and each one, including myself, fervently hope that he won't show yellow when the time comes.

Today being a holiday I didn't do very much else than sleep and write letters. A few bombs were dropped on London this evening according to Carl Sund who visited there for a few hours although there was no alarms sounded in this vicinity. Played cards all evening until bed-time.

JAN. 2, THURS

Sergeant Richardson gave me the job of changing a phone from one room to another at the hospital this morning which necessitated a lot of wire changing. I am detailed for exchange duty next week so spent an hour in the exchange room learning the ropes.

Played cards again this evening until bed-time. The raid alarm sounded about 7:30 and I guess London got it again; the "all clear" went about 8:00P.M.

It's getting pretty cold here now having froze two nights in a row.

JAN. 3, FRI.

Buzzer reading all morning which gets exceedingly monotonous at its best. Lamp reading for the first hour this afternoon and then I was on the lamp key for the next hour. Played cards again this evening but had to stop to take a much needed shower which felt very good despite the chilliness of the room. The air raid alarm sounded again tonight and I saw the raid was west of us although some planes flew directly over head a couple of times. I may go to London tomorrow for half a day as the boys are hounding me to adapt our radio to this power line. I wrote a letter to Cousin Wally and hope to post it tomorrow. I didn't mail the first one I wrote because I had no idea when I could get leave.

JAN. 4, SAT.

"Interior economy" this A.M. We were informed that we will be going on our debarkation leave on the eighth so I had to write a third letter to Cousin Wal. I went down town this afternoon to find out about adapting our radio to this power line and I have to go back on Tuesday for an estimate on the job. I bought a genuine leather belt for five shillings while I was there.

We had a short air raid alarm this evening with the all clear sounding about eight o'clock. I finished a letter to Vera this evening which will go tomorrow.

The first batch of mail came in today but I was disappointed in not receiving a single letter. I feel like I am writing letters for nothing since I got over here.

JAN. 5, SUN.

I spent a few hours on the exchange this morning and this afternoon for purpose of gaining a little practice for tomorrow when I start on a week's exchange duty. I happened to draw the busiest period of the day.

I also went down again this evening for the air raid warnings but there happened to be none, due, no doubt, to the low ceiling. I caught another cold today and I have a feeling it will make me feel miserable tomorrow. My leave date has been changed three times up to now but it has finally settled down to the fifteenth. Due to the uncertainty of my leave I have come to the conclusion that I couldn't let Wal know when I would hit London so will have to look him up when I get there.

JAN. 6, MON.

On my first eight hours of exchange duty from 8A.M. to 4A.M. and had a very busy time of it for awhile this morning. I'll swear that there were eight or nine indicators showing at once and I didn't seem to have enough hands. I was relieved by Jim Ellison at 4A.M.

The exact time our leave is to start hasn't been decided as yet but at present it is back to the eighth or ninth. I played cards all evening to try and forget another head cold that I caught yesterday. I started a letter to Buddo and Bezzie but didn't get a chance to finish it.

JAN. 7, TUES.

Woke up this morning feeling downright miserable with this head cold and I am sore all over from coughing all night. I didn't have to go on parade today because I am on the exchange from 4P.M. to 12 midnight. We had to fall in for dental and trench mouth inspection which only took a few minutes.

We had to give an address of the place we are going to on our leave. Mackenzie and Ellison were stuck for an address so they put down the same one as I used which happened to be Cousin Wal's. They had to give one to receive their ration card but we were also told that we had to report to the address supplied once a day in case they had reasons to call us back before the leave was over. Some of the boys gave addresses which they had invented themselves, and I guess they are going to have a difficult time reporting every day.

I went down town this afternoon to get me some cough medicine and I managed to buy some that should be very effective because it certainly has a vile taste.

Went on duty again at four P.M. for an eight hour drag. I had an exceedingly difficult time getting outside calls through the Farnborough exchange.

There were no air raid alarms or warnings and the exchange quietened down around ten which gave me a chance to write a letter to Harry and Bezzie. Came off duty at midnight.

JAN. 8, WED.

I am off duty until midnight so I slept most of the morning. Up until now I have been trying to formulate a definite plan and budget for my trip to London but haven't reached any satisfactory conclusion as yet. It looks as if I will have to start my leave tomorrow morning sometime.

JAN. 9, THURS.

Ten A.M. found us on our way to London for six days. We landed at Waterloo station then took the Underground to Trafalgar Square; with the Beaver Club our first objective we started asking for directions. The Beaver Club is practically on Trafalgar Square beside The Mall.

We bought ourselves a lunch, a real good lunch and were sitting eating it trying to decide where to look for sleeping quarters, when two fairly good looking girls sat down opposite and pretty soon we were talking like old friends. One of the girls, Miss Rosemary Charrington, told us where to go for a good clean bed for nothing and she drew a map for us to help in the search.

After talking to the girls for awhile, playing ping pong for awhile we set out to find this place called the "Canteen." We walked down the Mall to Queen Victoria's Memorial, just in front of the Buckingham Palace, then decided we had better ask someone for some more directions. An elderly gentleman with a black top coat on and an umbrella in his hand happened to be nearest so he was the victim.

After a lengthy spiel regarding his knowledge fo the city he finally settled down to explaining how we might find our intended lodgings. During the course of his explanations he told us the age and history of every building and statue in sight. After a great deal of talking and map consulting he finally reached a point in his narrative where we decided we could find our destination okay. He decided to do us one last favour and show us the most beautiful scene in the whole of London. So he escorted us down to a little bridge spanning an unknown body of water just a hundred yards or so south of the Queen Victoria Memorial and showed us the wonderful scene. We stood on the bridge and looked eastward down the stream or creek, through leafless branches of some trees toward the War Offices. I still can't say if the War Offices were there or not as the haze and smoke was so thick the nearby trees even looked hazy. No doubt the scene would be nice on a clear summer day but as it was we had to strain our imagination too much to be fun.

We finally shook the old reprobate after he suggested we hire him as a guide and proceeded on our way past Buckingham Palace, up Constitution Hill to Piccadilly, across Piccadilly, then up Park Lane to the second street past the Dorchester House, then down this Street a block and there we saw a little sign wired to an iron fence signifying that there was the "Canteen."

After a hasty last minute conference we opened the portals giving access to the unknown and entered the house in a pessimistic frame of mind. The first thing we see is a bunch of policemen's top coats piled on chairs, so decided if the place was good enough for the law to hang out it should be perfect for three Camerons.

An interview with one of the ladies resulted in our attaining a bed a piece but as we were a little skeptical still, we only took it for one night.

The three of us, Ken Mackenzie, Jim Ellison and I set forth to find Cousin Wal's place this afternoon but it appears as if there is a Gloucester Rd. in every district, consequently, we found ourselves away down in south west London, around four o'clock in the afternoon so we grabbed a handful of tube train for Trafalgar Square then walked from there back to our diggings via Regent Street, Piccadilly to Park Lane.

We had a very good supper of stewed rabbit and vegetables during which we talked to a couple of "Bobbies" sitting on the opposite side of the table. While we were paying for our meal we heard the alarm go and the Ac Ac start firing so we hurried out to see the excitement. We walked for quite a ways trying to find the bombed areas but gave it up as hopeless. On the way home we stopped to watch the anti aircraft guns firing in Hyde Park. We finally came back to the Canteen, had a little lunch then went to bed.

JAN. 10, FRI.

We slept in until ten A.M. this morning, had a very good breakfast then went down to the Beaver Club before setting out on our search for Wal's place. We had a good dinner at the Club then inquired as to the best way to reach Tottenham in North London. We walked up to Leicester Square where we caught a tube to Wood Green. We boarded a bus, on the advice of a conductor, for some road on the other side of the reservoir where we got off to transfer to another bus. Another inquiry resulted in two conductors and two civilians holding a conference in which all four of them failed to agree on the locality of Gloucester Rd. Finally we had to back track quite a distance and we were lucky enough to find someone who knew where Gloucester Rd. was. We had to get off the bus about half way between Turnpike Lane and Wood Green, walked down some road to St. Philip Lane then to Gloucester Road. We located 88 very easily after that but it was empty with all the windows broken, presumably by a bomb which had demolished the house two doors away.

We knocked on three or four neighbor's doors before getting any answer and inquired over the whereabouts of the Turner family. The lady told me that a direct hit had been made on a bomb shelter, killing Wal's wife and causing concussion to Wal and the daughter. Wal and the girl had moved to the country and she didn't know their address but I gave her my address and she said she would get the information from a neighbour and send it to me. It will be quite a blow to Nell when she hears that.

JAN. 11, SAT.

We got up at nine this morning, had breakfast then proceeded to the Beaver club where we amused ourselves nearly all day playing billiards and table tennis. Met Moreau who had gone down to some other part of the country hunting for relatives, evidently he was unsuccessful in his search.

He and I tried to locate Mr. H. Stewart of the B.B.C. as Miss Banks asked us to but we were unable to find a single person who knew him. We all had supper at the Beaver Club after which Moreau left to keep an appointment. Mac, Jim, Ken Peters and I strolled down to Westminster Bridge hoping we would be able to participate in the incendiary bomb campaign.

We crossed Westminster walked along an embankment to the next bridge and were standing by the railing watching the fire bombs falling too far away to help put them out. Suddenly we were aware of a noise very much like a freight train approaching and as it was our first experience with a H.E. bomb we immediately prostrated ourselves on the bridge. The bomb landed about a quarter of a mile away so we picked ourselves up feeling a little foolish at our actions.

We stood there for awhile when we were startled to see fire bombs landing all around the place we just vacated. Jim and Peters high-balled for the opposite side of the bridge while Mac and I stood there like damn fools trying to decide to turn tail and follow the other two or go over and put out the incendiaries. Finally we decided on the latter course but we got there too late as the bombs were dealt with very quickly and efficiently by some warden. However, we did pick up one that had not exploded and carried it around for quite awhile before throwing it into the river.

There seemed to be a lot of activity south of the river so we proceeded in that direction until we came to a bunch of firemen trying to gain access to a bomb, burning on the top story of a booking agent's establishment but they had it under control so we kept going.

We finally came across a group of fire fighters running a hose into a church where a fire had gotten a good hold. After the hose was put into action we moved on a few hundred feet where we saw an old man trying to fight a blazing paper concern with an ordinary garden hose. He finally gave up and waited for the larger hose and pumps to come along. He said a number of incendiary bombs had landed on the roof and before he could get them all out they had burned through and dropped inside. After we had helped to lay the hose there we moved on until we came to a subway underneath which was a shelter so we stopped for a smoke. Then the H.E. came down like a freight train, people scurried for the shelter but the four of us who haven't witnessed the devastation of an exploding bomb waited until it struck. Luckily for us it was on the other side of the next row of houses which protected us from the concussion. The noise was deafening and we were running toward it before the debris had stopped falling, consequently we were among the first to reach the scene.

A four story house was completely leveled and a large water main had been broken which filled the gutters and alley with ankle deep rushing water. Following the example of the few wardens we went to all the houses adjacent to the one that was wrecked to see if any of the inmates were in need of help. By that time the First Aid workers were on the job so we aided in digging the unfortunates from the wreckage. I helped to uncover one old lady of about 75 years right from the bottom of the crater. I couldn't find out the extent of her injuries as she was soon on her way to a dressing station and there were more people to find under the piles of broken boards and masonry.

The next victim to be uncovered was an elderly lady around fifty or so whom must have been hurt pretty bad. She told the rescuers that there were two more in the place where she was but one of them was able to walk away under her own power. Finally everyone was accounted for and we were standing beside the broken main wondering how anyone could survive such an explosion when an old man came staggering over the pile of rubbish calling for his wife and failing to notice the hole, made by the gushing water, he stepped into it. Mac managed to get soaking wet up to his knees pulling the poor man out. During the excitement we lost track of Peters and as everything possible had been done at the spot, we waded through water a foot deep back to the subway. We couldn't find Peters there so we made our way around to the F.A.P. station but he wasn't there either, but we did have a short chat with a girl First Aid worker who came from Montreal; she had to rush off on another call before we learned her name.

All the fires and rescuing seemed to be under control in the immediate district so we started walking toward a big fire we could see a few blocks away partly hoping to be of more help and partly hoping to find Peters. We were suddenly aware that the bombs had stopped falling so we started back toward Waterloo Bridge, thinking that Peters may do the same thing. From the bridge we could see large fires burning about a mile down the river but the "all clear" sounded just as we reached the Strand.

We were wet, dirty and tired so we headed back to our diggings. We passed a place where a two ton bomb had landed which broke windows and wrecked store fronts for blocks. A policeman told us that there were two or three civilians killed in a subway where they had taken shelter when they heard the bomb coming. A soldier and his girl friend were killed by concussion from the same bomb as they were walking across a park and they didn't have time to find suitable shelter. We finally arrived at our billets and after a light lunch we were very glad to go to bed.

It made me mad to see children and old women being carried away from wrecked homes, and I am sure now that I will give no mercy to any Huns if and when I meet up with them. If they were bombing military objectives it wouldn't be so bad as every soldier has signed his life away for the purpose of fighting the enemy but when the bombs very seldom cause the death of men in khaki but cripple maim and kill innocent women and children then one becomes impatient to come to grips with the Germans. I was surprised at the courage and the determined attitude of the ordinary people also their cheerfulness in the face of danger. I saw it first hand and I know.

JAN. 12, SUN.
We slept in pretty late this morning so we skipped breakfast and waited for dinner. We went down to the Beaver Club this afternoon and heard that Peters had a narrow squeeze last night. A bomb landed pretty close to him and he says all he remembers is flying bricks and he woke up this morning in a private house. He says he wasn't hit at all but he still is unable to feel his leg. It must be a slight case of concussion. We had supper at the Beaver Club after going to see a show called "The Dictator," a Charlie Chaplin triumph.

Jim, Mac and I went out bomb hunting again this evening but the raid was too far south and too far for us to walk. We made our way back to our diggings where we had a light lunch then hit the hay.

JAN. 13, MON.
We had to get up early this morning because it is general cleaning day at the Canteen, it's a weekly procedure. We had breakfast at the Beaver Club which composed of four flapjacks with syrup and a milk shake. We hung around until one o'clock then had lunch. We had an appointment at the M.M. Club (Mainly Musicians) with a policeman we met at the "canteen" by the name of Liston.

Mac, Jim and I went to see "Spellbound" in one of the theaters then had supper at the Beaver Club around 7:00P.M. There are no air raids this evening as yet and I am afraid we will have to leave tomorrow sometime. I wrote letters and read until ten then we came home to the diggings and had a light lunch.

JAN. 14, TUES.

We sort of slept in for a while this morning and when we finally did manage to rouse ourselves and get down for breakfast who should be waiting on us but Miss Charrington. We had quite a lot of fun there, during breakfast with her, although we were a little late for the bacon and eggs.

We met Jarvis and Grant at the Beaver Club so the five of us went up to Madame Tussaud's Wax Museum. We had quite a lot of fun for about four hours. Some of the images, especially the ones of the old lady sitting on the chesterfield, asleep, and the doorman and the pretty blond behind the desk fooled us completely for quite awhile. We met Carl Sund there and he was trying to decide if the old lady on the chesterfield was alive. He found out soon after when he tried to pick up a book that she had supposedly dropped, it was a block of wood, painted like a book and glued to the floor. Mackenzie was raving about the beautiful blond at the desk all the time he was in the place and he nearly cried when he found out she was made of wax. I had a funny experience there once. There was a doorman standing with his hand on a door knob and I stood there for fully two minutes watching him. After I had fully convinced myself that he was another image, the son-of-a-gun blinked his eyes and opened the door nearly jolting me out of a year's growth. I must have had my mouth open because he turned around and smiled.

The "Sleeping Beauty" exhibit gives you a start when you first see it because her chest is rising and falling as if she was breathing. It is really surprising how they attain the life likeness in the statues, in some cases we thought some of them were going to speak to us.

We had supper at the Beaver Club then we played games and talked with Miss Charrington until after 9:30P.M. The whole three of us accompanied her home to Sloane Street and on our way passed many demolished houses and streets. In one case we had to make a detour because of a delayed action bomb that had not gone off yet. We left Miss Charrington at her door and made our way back to our diggings where we had our nightly snack. We left word with the little Dutch lady who calls us the "Three Musketeers" to call us at 5:30A.M. and then hit the hay.

JAN. 15, WED.
We were awakened by the Russian Princess at the desired time and in an hour we were on our way to the station. Imagine being gently shaken by a Russian Princess, it is the acme of something or other, or is it?

We caught the tube from Piccadilly to Waterloo station and managed to catch our train despite the general turmoil, by seconds to spare. We were back in camp in time for a gas demonstration parade at 9:30A.M.

The gas parade is the most unpleasant portion of our training we have hit yet. We had to walk through clouds of Nose and Throat Irritant Gas without our respirators on and believe me, what with this bad cold I have I sure had a sweet time. I coughed and sneezed until my chest ached and my nose and throat were sore. Some of the fellows were violently sick and had to drop out of the demonstration. The effects wore off by noon and we were able and willing to eat dinner.

We had buzzer and semaphore practice this afternoon with buzzer again for two hour this evening. Started a letter to Nelle.

JAN. 16, THURS.
I was on the exchange today from 8A.M. to 4P.M. and had a pretty good day as Sgt. Rankine spelled me off a number of times. Played cards for awhile this evening as well as reading.

JAN. 17, FRI.
I was on Signal Clerking all day and it was a new experience and which taught quite a lot in the practical line. I at least learned how to handle Dispatch Riders dockets and the signal register and the message procedure used by the R.C.C.S. I would like to get on again next Friday but I think we have to take

turns at that. I sure enjoyed the time I was on as the work was very interesting. Wrote letters and read this evening.

JAN. 18, SAT.

Interior economy this morning with the usual splashing good time. I washed my laundry and scrubbed my equipment this afternoon which is a good job done.

Played cards tonight. I am on the exchange again tomorrow.

JAN. 19, SUN.

Came on duty at 7:30A.M. and relieved Comack. Tuffy Chambers is signal clerk and as he is on for the first time I have to show him how the system peculates when it gets going. I had a big surprise this morning when Holly Sharpe walked in on me; it was a big surprise for two reasons. I wasn't expecting to see Holly come in and he is much fatter than he was the last time I saw him.

He stayed and we talked until 2:30 A.M. so we had lunch together in the NAAFI ("Naffi"). He had to catch a train at three and he left around 2:30.

Surprise No. 2 was a letter from cousin Ivy telling me where I could find them all. She said nearly all the family and families are staying in one place after they evacuated from London, following the death of Mrs. Walter Turner and she wants me to go down sometime and see them all. Most of the men folk are away with their units but two of them are coming home for leave in two weeks and she especially expressed the wish for my presence while they were home.

Cousin Wally is still in London, staying at his fire station, something which I should have known before. I think I'll write Ivy a letter tonight. It seems funny, but Bill's diaries had Ivy in them quite a lot and now it's creeping into mine. I think my path is running pretty well along the same lines as Bill's did a quarter of a century ago. The only difference is the people have changed and a younger generation has taken their place.

JAN. 20, MON.

We had to go out and learn, by experience, how to assemble and launch a pontoon foot bridge also how to assemble and handle assault boats. The boats procedure came easy and the bridge is fairly simple but it was raining out; there was slush and mud under foot and it was pretty cold in the bargain.

I received parcels from Marcelle and Harry and Bezzie as well as a letter from Vera and a card from Capt. Hall. There was no mail from home but I guess it will come soon. Received letters from Doc, Nelle, Marcelle, Bezzie and cards from Rose, Charlotte and a few others, this evening.

JAN. 21, TUES.

Buzzer reading this A.M. until noon, then semaphore reading this afternoon. I received another letter and a parcel containing two type 30 tubes from Nelle, cards from "Doc", Miss Banks, Felicie and a few more. Mail from the Murphy family hasn't arrived yet but it should be here any day now.

It is keeping me busy trying to answer all the mail I have received in the last three days. No air raids for the last couple of nights now.

JAN. 22, WED.

Made a very poor showing in lamp and buzzer tests this morning. We had more buzzer reading this afternoon, in which I read 18 words a minute, solid. We had semaphore practice outside this afternoon for awhile then a procedure lecture in the classroom.

I went down to the exchange for a while this evening to take a look at a wireless gadget called the "Beetle." No mail this evening so I am not holding much hope for receiving Emmy's and Bobbie's mail before the next convoy.

As I am going on exchange duty at midnight I went down for lunch at nine thirty. Started a letter to "Doc."

JAN. 23, THURS.

My birthday again. One year of my life in the army. I am not in the position to say it is wasted or not. Came on duty at 0001 hours (12:01A.M.) and wrote a letter to Doc. I have to copy everything that comes over the beetle

117

at every hour so there is no chance of cat napping. It took me two hours to get the fire going which caused me to miss the 2 o'clock broadcast. Quite probably I will catch seven varieties of hell for missing it but I suppose there isn't any use of making excuses.

I started a letter to Marcelle and managed to stay awake all night. Nothing doing in the line of duty from midnight on except the hourly reports from the "Beetle."

I was relieved at 8:00A.M. by Harold Steeds, then I had a breakfast of bread and jam after which I turned in and slept for four hours. I woke up in time for dinner then finished Marcelle's letter. I haven't heard anything of the broadcast I missed this morning.

JAN. 24, FRI.
Didn't do much else but read buzzer and semaphore and write letters.

JAN. 25, SAT.
I was on the exchange again today from 8 to 4 and was pretty busy for the first four hours. It slackened off this afternoon so I wrote a couple of short letters to people who had sent me cards. I was relieved by Mackenzie at four o'clock.

After supper I borrowed a book on wireless from Wally Mills and studied for awhile. Wrote a letter to Cousin Len and borrowed a shilling for stamps.

There hasn't been any air raid alarms for nearly a week. I wonder if Jerry is preparing for something or maybe the weather is unfavourable for flying.

JAN. 26, SUN.
Bribed out of bed this morning by a flapjack breakfast which was a little bit of alright. I finally kept a promise and wrote a letter to "Shorty" back in Brandon. Also wrote a letter to a Miss Iris Lawrence who sent me a Christmas card.

I didn't do much else than read for the rest of the day and evening.

JAN. 27, MON.

We had semaphore and buzzer reading this morning and afternoon. We went to a free show at the Garrison theater and it turned out to be a darn good bit of entertainment. The place was packed and they were standing in the aisles, maybe because it was a free show. I started a letter to Jack this evening which I didn't have time to finish.

JAN. 29, TUES.

Buzzer reading for awhile this morning. First, we started the day's activities by parading to a court martial sentencing session; the poor guy got 100 days in the glass house with forfeiture of pay. The whole thing only took about half an hour. I think they were trying to throw a scare into anyone else who was contemplating going A.W.O.L.

We had verbal message passing this morning for the first time and discovered it is very interesting. One man gives the message, which is usually full of figures and unusual phrases, verbally to another man, then that man has to repeat it to the next man and so on. The final message is compared with the original to see how far wrong or how many changes were made in the process. It is part of our training and very interesting.

We had our first daylight air raid alarm this afternoon but it must have been a stray plane because it only lasted twenty five or thirty minutes.

I came on exchange duty at four o'clock and will be on until midnight. I had a little fun pulling a fullerphone buzzer unit apart. I found the spring contacts on the armature loose so did the necessary tightening and the thing worked.

Mackenzie and I were considering the advisability of uncovering some of the mysteries of the exchange but luckily for us we were prevented from doing so by the arrival of Sgt. Rankine and Richardson. Some of these times my curiosity regarding the operation of different instruments and machines is bound to lead me into something very unpleasant.

Not long afterwards I finished my duty trick and left Mack holding the place against any incoming messages.

JAN. 29, WED.

My day off so I spent most of the morning in bed reading when I wasn't sleeping I finally tired of being there and not wanting to become bedridden, I roused myself and commenced the manufacture of a chess board. I finished that around two in the afternoon and although it's no masterpiece of workmanship, it's very effective. At least the squares are all square and the right colours.

By supper time the paint was still wet in spots but I wiped the surplus off and had a game with Wally Mills who had little trouble in trouncing me soundly. Finished the day off by reading until bedtime.

JAN. 30, THURS.

My presence was required on the ranges today for Bren Gun qualification firing which necessitated my early awakening and energetic activity to enable me to get ready for an early start. We were under way by 8:20A.M. and it was not long before we were well into the process of perforating inanimate targets with perfectly good metal. Things proceeded very well for me until we got back to the 300 yard range where I lost too many points on the rapid fire. By the time we were through shooting on this range a fog drifted in practically ruining the visibility so the rest of the procedure was called off. Despite my rapid fire showing I managed to make the highest score of the works with 103 points out of a possible 150.

Maybe I was lucky in having a very good gun and maybe I was just plain lucky but I am refusing to worry about it, the score still stands at 103. It was damp and cold out there and I heartily agreed when they decided to return to camp where we arrived at 2:00P.M. After we had dinner and had taken our hour and half off we decided it wasn't worth while getting ready for parade so spent the extra time in catching up on some lost sleep.

I borrowed half a Crown this evening so Mackenzie and I went to the Garrison Theater to see a very good show called "Captain Fury," after which we had an evening snack in the canteen. We finally retired having dispersed with the half crown but feeling that we had a very pleasant evening.

JAN. 31, FRI.

This being one of the days that getting off parade was definitely impossible I reconciled myself to attending the daily parades at least for one day and managed to get on parade without being late.

We had buzzer reading for a couple of hours then proceeded to place a small scale signaling scheme into operation. The scheme worked very well except for the pestilent presence of L/Cpl. Ross who persisted in amusing himself by cutting our wires. Consequently he is very much in disfavour with us all, in fact, he never occupied a place in our concerted estimation but I think he is decidedly in the dog house with all members of the platoon of private ratings.

Parade for pay this afternoon on which I received two pound ten. By supper time paying off various debts had rapidly dispersed of ten shillings of that.

I played two games of chess with Sgt. Rankine but he eliminated me two straight despite my best efforts. I came on exchange duty at midnight and will remain so occupied until eight A.M.

FEB. 1, SAT.

Sgt. Rankine stayed until two this morning when he finally finished his letter writing. I practiced on the fullerphone for awhile then fixed the buzzer unit, temporarily, it needs a new spring contact screw, two new spring contacts, in fact, it might save time and expense if they changed the whole buzzer unit, at least the armature.

I typed a letter to Janet (Mrs. Lindstrom) finished one to Cousin Louie and started one to Marc. Another 45 minutes and I will be off duty, then I can get four or five hours sleep in. Finally came off duty and hit the hay without bothering about breakfast. Slept until eleven o'clock then got up for dinner which I didn't bother to eat. Played Mackenzie a couple of games of chess and beat him both times. Went down town and bought a new fountain pen which cost 13 and 6. Moreau and I had supper in the Canteen and I was plenty hungry as it was my first meal today. Pressed my greatcoat this evening.

The weather finally cleared up and it's a very clear cold night but so far there has been no raid alarms this evening as yet. I received another letter from

Ivy this afternoon. I am afraid it is going to revive my old stamp problem again. Stamps cost 1½ pennies each and if the whole family writes letters and demands separate answers then I had better ask for a raise in salary or something.

I played Moreau three games of chess and won two. We are expecting something to happen soon and wouldn't be surprised if we swing into action in the near future. Everyone thinks it will break wide open pretty soon. It was a very clear night, last night and there was no raids as far as we know.

FEB. 2, SUN.

It was very cold getting up this morning so we stayed in bed as long as we could which happened to be when the breakfast call went. We had flapjacks for the second time since coming here.

Church parade at the Garrison Theater; our old friend Major Maclean delivered a short sermon. I played cards for awhile but couldn't seem to get interested in it so pulled out.

Reg, Moreau and I went down town to the Highway Cafe for supper then we went to the Rex Theater and saw "Love Affair" and "The Girl from Mexico." We got back to camp around 8:30 P.M. and had a snack in the Canteen. I played Mackenzie a game of chess and beat him after an hour and a half of play. Added a little more to a letter to Marcelle.

We are expecting Canadian mail in today or tomorrow and I am hoping there will be a letter from Bobbie for me. I mailed a letter to Cousin Louie this evening and I still have to answer Ivy's latest. I wonder if there will be as much mail from Canada this time as there was last.

FEB. 3, MON.

We woke up this morning to find it cold and snowing out so I guess we will have to wait a little longer for things to get moving. Everyone is sort of impatient to get this next chapter of the war over with as there is a chance that we may be sent home after it is finished. I think the length of the war will depend largely on the outcome of the next phase.

I am on exchange duty again today and find this little room lacking in heat. The thing is pretty busy this morning. The Sgt. insinuated that it might mean a stripe for me if I cancelled my application for a transfer to the Reconnaissance Squadron. I really haven't made up my mind as yet.

Mackenzie took my place on the exchange this afternoon while I completed a DV line to the officer's mess from the signal office. I tackled Mr. Kent about entering my qualification specifications in my pay book and received the same old answer. There isn't much use trying to transfer until that is fixed up. I played cards again this evening until ten o'clock.

FEB. 4, TUES.

I had some much needed semaphore practice this morning then the rest of the morning I spent in "group working," a very interesting signal arrangement.

Most of the platoon had to go out to the ranges again this afternoon to fire Bren Gun so there isn't many of us left for this afternoon activities.

We had some more much needed semaphore this afternoon which was finished off by some buzzer reading. Sgt. Richardson made a very good try to talk me out of transferring and he succeeded in that he sowed the seed of doubt in my mind. I can't see any advantage in my going to another unit if they are not going to use wireless. I wrote a letter to Marcelle, I mean I finished it after writing off and on for a few days. I also wrote one to Ivy this evening. We had our first night air raid alarm that we have had for two weeks, tonight.

FEB. 5, WED.

I spent all morning fixing a D5 telephone. I was supposed to be practicing group working but the phone failed to work so I proceeded to hunt for the trouble, consequently, my station was silent for three hours while I overhauled the instrument.

Paired up with Wally Mills for lamp reading this afternoon and had a good time despite the cold.

I studied map reading this evening as we are supposed to have a test tomorrow.

At last I got a break; we are taking over Brigade signal work in the morning. There are six of us going, three exchange operators, one Morse Code operator, one dispatch rider and Sgt. Rankine. I am the Morse operator which will be quite a job as I have to work back to divisional headquarters to the R.C.C.S. It's going to be well worth the time in experience gained. I'll have to start packing.

FEB. 6, THURS.
We were all ready to go early this morning but it was after nine thirty before we got started.

We had to wait until the Brigade signals had moved out so we didn't get started until after two in the afternoon.

There was not much to start with but by 10:00P.M. Sgt. Rankine and I, through our combined efforts, originality and resourcefulness, had rigged up an improvised but effective four line switch. It consisted of a piece of spring brass (purloined from an unused fuse block), four thumb tacks (obtained from the Orderly Room), a few small washers (from the same fuse block), a nail and a few pieces of cable.

We managed to make the operating table very neat looking. Before we quit for the night we tested the switch and the lines from the phone to the terminal board and found everything working perfectly. I will have to try and find two more lines that come into the building someplace.

We had our first meal with the F.M.R.s this evening and find they have a much better system of feeding than the C. of C. Every man providing he is there on time, gets his meal and there isn't near the amount of waiting in line as we had back at Delville. Also there is a better "NAAFI" here than at Delville in as much as there is more variety of cakes and the service is much faster.

We (six of us) have a whole room to ourselves, a room which would hold 28 men very easily. It is in the same building as where the rest of Brigade staff is housed. We have a wide choice of beds and we can use any three clothes closets if we wish.

FEB. 7, FRI.

Managed to rouse myself before breakfast time and was back at work by 07:45A.M. I tried to get through to 2nd Div. By Fullerphone but it was no go. The trouble is at their end. I discovered that I can use my own earphones on this fullerphone which is quite an improvement, also, I replaced the round knob on the key with my own Navy know so I am all ready to go. If I can figure out a satisfactory method I may replace the entire key, although this key isn't bad for sending but I want to get used to my own key.

I caught someone practicing on the S.S.R. line this morning and must have scared him out of a year's growth when I gave him an "R" for what he sent which happened to be "now is the time for all good men to come to the aid of the party." When I tried to send him a friendly message the poor guy had shut down.

I copied some notes on the Superimposing unit today and then Sgt. Rankine and I rigged one up and got it working satisfactorily. It was and still is more or less an experiment with the possibility that it will become of high value in the near future. Between the two of us we are not doing too badly. I had to receive a 52 group phonogram today and it's quite a job. The Sergeant took one of 157 groups today.

We fooled around with equipment right up until 11:00P.M. I received 300 cigarettes from the family today for a birthday present and boy were they welcome. Also received a letter from Louie.

FEB. 8, SAT.

Overslept this morning and as I had to be at work at 7:45A.M., I missed breakfast but I rectified the situation by taking a light lunch at the NAAFI canteen. I received a letter from Bobby, one from Rose and a card from "Hot Dog" Smith. We are going to erect a system of buzzers between this signal office and the exchange and bunk house, so as the night exchange operator will be able to wake us up on time in the morning.

We got the line up but complications set in which we eliminated by altering the original plan a little.

I finally received the parcel from Emmy and Bobby and was I ever pleased to get it. I was on duty in the signal office at the time so we had cookies and coffee for a lunch. Just why she sent a compass is beyond me, maybe she has no confidence in my ability to find my way around.

I stayed on duty until 11:00P.M. then had a shower and shave and went to bed.

FEB. 9, SUN.

The calling device worked like a charm and we were all up in plenty of time for breakfast. There was a purple air raid warning this morning at 7:30A.M. but the all clear came through before it developed into red. There isn't much doing this morning so think I'll start answering my mail. Started a letter to Louie this morning but the Sergeant and I started some more inventing, this time it is a receiver hook for our office phone. It consists of three staples which act as a hinge, a forked stick about ten inches long with tape wrapped around the two prongs and a contact about two inches from the fork. The other contact is on the bottom of our set of shelves, over the desk. The stick is fastened to the underneath surface of the shelf by means of the staple hinge and in such a position that the two contacts touch when the receiver is taken off the fork. Tension is obtained by means of three or four elastics wrapped around the fork and pinned to the top side of the shelf by means of a single thumb tack.

When the hand set is in the fork it's weight pulls the stick down and breaks the contact and when we want to make a call we only have to lift the hand set and we are connected to the exchange.

I finished the letter to Louie this evening but forgot to mail it. It was after twelve when I got to bed.

FEB. 10, MON.

Everyone seems to be going out on schemes today including nearly the entire Brigade staff so there hasn't been as much OR business as we were expecting. I got the afternoon off and Moreau and I took a walk down to the Delville

Barracks to see what was doing. While we were there we were issued with another uniform (Limey style) two gym outfits and a pair of running shoes.

We hear via the grapevine that the boys of the platoon have all been chosen for the different jobs but I can't find out what one is allotted to me. I am sure I could very easily get into the R.C.C.S. as an operator right now but can't make up my mind. I think I will talk to Captain Gilroy of "L" section the next time I see him.

I read some of Sergeant Rankine's sending for awhile this evening, then fixed a fullerphone. The usual evening activity saw another day finished.

FEB. 11, TUES.
I worked until noon then got the rest of the day off so I finished doing my laundry, a necessary operation which usually needs attending once and sometimes twice a week.

Went over to Delville to call for Reg as prearranged, and we went to a show at the Rex at Reg's expense. He insisted on paying for everything for some reason or other. I got back to my quarters at 11:15P.M. From that time on until midnight we were greeted to the amusing spectacle of Sgt. Rankine doing bicycle trick riding up and down the bunk house on one of our newly issued two-wheelers. A bunk house isn't exactly the best of places for such demonstrations and the results were hilarious, if not successful. His climaxing endeavour was trying to ride the conveyance backwards between two bunks but the said bunks persisted in getting in the way. That particular stunt got the better of him so he put the bicycle away and we all went to bed.

FEB. 12, WED.
A usual day at the signal office with the usual activity. Captain Adams came in again looking for data on a letter that had been lost but was unable to find the recordings of the document in question. It could not have gone through this office as we would have had the registration of it here. We worked until eleven again tonight.

FEB. 13, THURS.

Sergeant Rankine went off to trace a line we have here, to solve the mystery of its termination, without much success as he was stopped by impassable roads. We learned later that it ends up at 2nd Div. Another long day, having worked from 7:30A.M. until 11:00P.M.

FEB. 14, FRI.

I had to go down to Delville to run a line from the Sig office which was to be tee-ed into the Div. Line the Sgt. traced yesterday. I had the line almost completed when word came through that the R.C.C.S. were pulling the Div. Line down so I had to take my line down too.

Spent the rest of the afternoon installing a U.C. exchange at C of C sig office. I had supper at Delville.

Comack and I had quite a time navigating these roads on bicycles during the black out when we were coming home tonight. More than once we found ourselves running through deep mud puddles and almost smacking into people and objects along the road.

We all had a good lunch this evening around 11:30 but to mention the source of our supply would be very foolish as we can't afford to let the secret out.

We may start a telegraph sked with S.S.R., F.M.R. and C of C. on Monday then I will have a sweet time every day.

FEB. 15, SAT.

We received orders today to move our sleeping quarters to another wing so as to make room for the Reconnaissance Sqdn. Our new quarters are very nice but the L.A.D. boys seem dissatisfied at our intrusion which fails to bother us very much.

I went down to Delville again this afternoon to pay off some of my debts so I am all square again now. I took a nasty spill off of the bike yesterday but came through with little physical injury although my dignity was sadly disrupted at the time. Of course a girl cyclist had to be passing at the time and derived much amusement from my embarrassing predicament after she learned that my accident wasn't fatal. My wrist watch was badly damaged and will cost me a pound of hard earned English money to be repaired. If the jeweller runs true to the English standard of service, he might have it fixed by the end of the month. I took over this evening to allow Sergeant Rankine to have the night off.

The air raid siren is just outside the building and the noise of it fairly makes the building shake.

Had a little excitement this evening and thought for sure the moment had come. Sergeant Rankine phoned from Delville at 11:30 and told me to get the office ready for moving and I did. In half an hour I had everything disconnected and ready for loading on the truck. He came in around 01:30A.M. and was quite surprised when he saw the office. He had worded his message wrong and I took it the way it sounded, and was all ready for action. However, while him and Moreau were preparing lunch, I connected the dozens of wires and apparatus and had everything perking again before we turned in at three A.M.

FEB. 16, SUN.
Nothing else this morning but the daily busy period of getting the early dispatches away and receiving the incoming dispatches. Stayed on duty until 1:00P.M. then took the rest of the afternoon off. I made the trip to Delville again this afternoon for the primary purpose of getting something definite on this fullerphone communication scheme between the three units and brigade. I am particularly interested and anxious to get the scheme underway as I will be operating at Brigade which should prove valuable in the way of operating experience. I was unable to locate Mr. Kent so came away without the desired information and I still am ignorant of tomorrow's plans for this scheme. Came back again in time for supper then finished a letter to Bobbie.

FEB. 17, MON.
Slept in for an hour today and consequently missed my breakfast. Started an hourly schedule with the S.S.R.s on the fullerphone; still no word from the Camerons. I went down to the NAAFI right after my 10:00 o'clock sked and had a bite to eat.

A wet and drizzling day outside which makes it somewhat miserable. To increase the miserableness of the situation two fellows are cleaning the stove pipes, so it's chilly in here as well. That is one necessity I hate to witness, even when Dad used to clean the ones at home it used to spoil my entire day. I'll be glad when they complete this little job here and get a fire going again.

I had quite a time operating the fullerphone today working to the three units on hourly schedules. We had a little trouble with the C. of C. but they finally got their instrument perking alright and I am expecting a very good day tomorrow. It's too bad we haven't got a line to 2nd Div. H.Q. too then I would have some fun.

I was informed yesterday by a not so reliable source that I was going to be offered a stripe again and if they do that, I may surprise them and accept it. Sgt. Rankine has nearly convinced me that I would be very foolish to turn it down as if and when we do go into action I will most likely be placed in charge of a station which will entail all the duties and responsibilities of an N.C.O. and I may as well get paid for it. However, it is only hearsay as yet and I will believe it when they tell me in person.

FEB. 18, TUES.
Managed to keep the sked with the Camerons today but the S.S.R.'s were out on a scheme and I didn't hear a thing of them all day. The F.M.R.'s still do not understand what it's all about; I didn't bother explaining.

Same old stuff here in the signal office with DR's and the beetle. I had planned on going down to Delville this evening to speak to Wally about a transfer to the R.C.C.S. but I received a letter from Ivy so stayed here to answer it.

Played Sgt. Rankine a game of chess this evening and was beaten soundly.

About eleven o'clock Sgt. Rankine put the kettle on for tea and after that little operation was completed. I cooked the last of the bacon that we had managed to scrounge. Owing to the possibilities of punishment being inflicted on the person responsible for our obtaining the bacon and other nourishment, I am unable to mention any names.

The coal stove wasn't burning very well so I used the little coal oil heater, identical to the one we used to have at the house on Gold Street. I used a lid of a candy tin for a frying pan which was held by a pair of pliers. The result of burning paint from the lid, coal oil smoke from the stove and frying bacon was an odour very difficult to define and which permeated the entire building. It is very fortunate for us that the Brigadier wasn't around, the lateness of the hour was our ally. Despite the odour the bacon tasted swell. We washed it down with tea from Pepsi cola bottles as we had no cups. Incidentally, we had no plates either but we surmounted that little difficulty by using newspaper.

FEB. 19, WED.
I have been keeping some very good skeds with the C of C and S.S.R.'s today and it is sounding more and more like Hams talking back and forth. The F.M.R.'s do not seem inclined to join in the fun and every time I have a message for them I have to phone them up and tell them to put their fullerphone into operation. So I have given up hope of getting them working on a schedule.

I started a letter to Louie this evening but didn't have time to finish it. We are getting ready to go back to Delville tomorrow when the S.S.R. signals will take over.

I had a very hard time sending two messages over the fullerphone which had some very difficult groups in them. They were very difficult to send and I suppose they were equally hard to receive, but perseverance prevailed and the messages were delivered in reasonable time.

We spent the evening getting ready to go back to Delville in the morning.

FEB. 20, THURS.
The boys who are taking over the job arrived from the S.S.R.'s and we had to explain all the details to them. I finally met and shook hands with Ford, the man I worked to on the Souris scheme. He is taking over my job as telegraph operator.

We pulled out around two o'clock, Beck and I riding the bikes and the rest coming in the equipment truck. It seems funny to have nothing to do in the evening after working 17 hours a day for two weeks.

FEB. 21, FRI.

I had to go out on the rifle range this morning and shoot qualifications with great coat and full battle order on. It is very difficult to make a passing score with everything on and some of the boys were back there for their third and fourth time. I think I passed alright but I made the bigger part of my score at five hundred yards when I got six bulls eyes out of seven shots.

We got back at two in the afternoon and spent the remainder of the day cleaning our rifles.

FEB. 22, SAT.

Interior economy this morning and I got a good dose of nose and throat irritant gas, accidentally. I had to take an old mattress over to the incinerator and someone must have thrown a few gas capsules into the fire by mistake. I coughed and sneezed for the rest of the morning and part of the afternoon until my chest was so sore I could hardly breath. The wind was blowing from the incinerator toward camp and some of the other fellows had a slight touch of it. It's not fatal but it's damned uncomfortable.

I bummed a bar of washing soap from the Sanitary Corporal and washed my dirty laundry this evening.

I received three very welcome letters from Marcelle, Bobbie and Nelle.

FEB. 23, SUN.

Church parade this morning which was all over around 10:45A.M. Wrote a letter to Nelle but haven't mailed it yet. No mail for me this evening.

There were quite a few parcels came to the platoon so there was plenty to eat for a few hours. I was sort of hoping and expecting some cigarettes but I guess I will have to bum a few packages to last me until next payday. I had a darn good hot shower this evening as I may get two inoculations tomorrow.

FEB. 24, MON.

Had buzzer and semaphore reading practice this morning then had the two inoculations this afternoon. Sgt. Rankine and I finally found a way to put calls through the U.C. exchange over through the G.P.O. exchange and had it set up and working by three o'clock.

Wrote a letter to Marcelle today, at least I started it. No mail again tonight so borrowed three shillings off of Tommy Bell for cigarettes. The arm is plenty sore tonight.

FEB. 25, TUES.

Spent the morning writing letters and dodging from bed to bed getting away from the boys on interior economy. Spent the afternoon packing my kit properly in readiness for the scheme tomorrow. I am detailed as local operator stationed with Battalion H.Q.

FEB. 26, WED.

I was already to go at 9:00A.M. but there was a change of plans which postponed the start until later in the day. Dinner time came and passed as did supper time then we got an order to be ready to move at 7:30P.M. We were under way at 8:00P.M., Steward, Moreau and I sitting in a P.U. (small platoon truck) Steward with a small desk and signal registers in front of him; Moreau with an exchange in front of him and I with a D5 in front of me.

We progressed with numerous stops and starts, until two or three in the morning. It had started to rain around 10P.M. and by the time we arrived at our sleeping place it was pouring. Mr. Kent told me to take the first three hours on duty but if I had a chance to sleep to take it. Steward decided to take a try at sleeping outside while Moreau wrapped himself up in a blanket and propped his feet up on the exchange and got a couple of hours of sleep. Interruptions were too frequent to allow me to obtain much sleep. Steward poked his head in about 5:00A.M. and he was soaking wet. He said he was laying in two inches of water. From what I hear the rest of the fellows were sleeping in similar conditions.

FEB. 27, THURS.

We ate breakfast inside of the truck where it was dry then came the business of moving the trucks onto the road again. The camping grounds was a messy mass of mud, some of the boys were plastered from feet to waist. The carrier platoons did a good job with their tractor like carriers of pulling the big trucks out of the mire.

We had lunch in the rain and were under way again soon after. We rolled along main highways, dirt roads, country lanes until we hit a town called Petworth where we had one of those unexplainable stops.

Petworth is a cosy looking little town with winding streets and numerous high, moss covered walls. We were parked right in front of some private residences and we weren't there long before the lady of one of the houses started handing out tea to the boys. Soon her neighbours had followed suit. The tea was a very welcomed stimulant and it tasted like I always imagine tea made in the English style tasted. It was nearly six o'clock P.M. before we received word that the scheme was called off at 3:00P.M. and we could go home, a very welcome bit of news. It was nine P.M. before we pulled into camp.

So ended the scheme which was supposed to have lasted three days but due to adverse weather conditions only lasted 24 hours.

FEB. 28, FRI.

Slept in until nearly nine and so missed breakfast. Spent the morning restoring my equipment to its normal condition after the rough treatment it had yesterday.

Pay parade this afternoon and drew 1 pound 10 shillings, not near enough to take care of the expenses for the next two weeks. We start on another scheme tomorrow which will be completed late Sunday. This is a platoon scheme and will move a little faster than the larger schemes. I received a note from Len today.

Went to see the "Man in the Iron Mask" playing at the Garrison Theater; it wasn't a bad show. It's a clear night and I understand the "alert" is in effect. We go on another scheme tomorrow.

MAR. 1, SAT.

We were up early and ready for an early start on our little two day scheme. There happened to be a muster parade at 8:30A.M. so it was after nine before we pulled out. I was riding in the same P.U. truck with the same equipment and the same company.

There is no doubt about it, the country outside this immediate vicinity is much better looking and far more interesting.

We arrived at our destination soon after noon. Our camp for the two days was hop-pickers cabins, situated on a large farm just outside of a typical English town called Petersfield. After having lunch, prepared by Charlie Longley, those not unfortunate to be detailed for guard duty went to Petersfield for the evening. The town, as I said before, is typically English with its vine covered stone walls, narrow streets and well trimmed hedges. It also boasted a market square in the enter of which is a statue of a man on a horse.

Some of the houses were well aged, and in a number of places, the old fashioned architecture dated back scores of years. Some of the houses were built of an oak frame which was filled in between the beams with some sort of plaster. The beams are weather beaten and worm eaten with some very ancient iron spikes sticking in them here and there. The roofs are mostly tiled with a few here and there with a straw thatched roof.

Early in the evening the "alert" sounded and two bombs landed about three miles out in the country causing not the least bit of damage. Soon after, three flares came down lighting the countryside up like daylight but nothing else came down. The "all clear" sounded soon after.

We discovered a fish and chip shop open at eleven at night and the food was so good and reasonably priced that we each had two orders. We arrived back in camp around midnight and climbed into our pine board and blanket beds as soon as possible. We found an oil heater that some "hop-picking" family had left behind and that served us, very well, in heat.

MAR. 2, SUN.

I was awakened at 4:45A.M. for guard duty and it was blowing and raining out, miserably and forcibly. It took lots of fortitude to crawl out of my warm blankets and go out into the cold, wet morning to stand guard. Incidentally, a large truck was parked near my position of duty so I made use of the cab for protection against the elements. I was relieved at seven so I went back to bed until breakfast which was called at nine o'clock.

After breakfast we packed the trucks with everything except the material and utensils needed for lunch, which we had at 12:30P.M. By two o'clock we were on our way back to Delville, taking a slightly different but nonetheless interesting route. We arrived in camp around two o'clock and spent the rest of the day cleaning the mud off of my boots and uniforms and the rust off of my rifle.

MAR. 3, MON.

Started the day off with gas lectures but I was put on an exchange installation job which I made sure would last until noon. I went back to change a few worn plugs on the G.P.O. exchange but couldn't touch it as the G.P.O. service man was hovering in the vicinity but I managed to put the afternoon in puttering around with some faulty equipment and so missed the afternoon's boresome lecture on gas first aid.

For some unknown reason I was switched from battalion H.Q. operator to D company operator but I managed to talk the Company commander into letting me ride in the P.U. truck with him tomorrow. We were supposed to start on a scheme tonight but it was put off until the morning. I hope they don't start too early.

MAR. 4, TUES.

Roused out of bed at 1:30A.M. and after a hastily grabbed cup of cocoa, we were on our way. I managed to obtain a short nap while riding but the P.U. truck was a little too cramped for comfort.

At a certain point along the route we were ordered to disembark and before I could get my signalling equipment out, the truck pulled away down the road.

We marched about a mile up the road to a vacant lot along side of the road and breakfast, consisting of very good flapjacks, porridge, syrup, milk and tea, was prepared in short order.

Soon after breakfast the P.U. came back so I was able to procure my message forms, etc. and this time I hung them around my neck. A commanding officer's meeting was called for 09:00 hrs so I and Tully accompanied Mr. Honey when he set out to attend. We walked about four hundred yards down the road to a three hundred foot hill, the conference was being held on the very top because of the view of the surrounding country which was obtained from there. There were signallers, runners, wireless trucks from every conceivable branch of the service there. We stayed about half way up the hill and the officers went on up to the top. It was very misty out and it blanketed the view quite effectively. The mist cleared for a few moments disclosing a view which I thought was usually found on post cards produced by some artist's imagination. The mist closed in again shutting out the wonderful picture but if I could paint I think I could reproduce the scene in detail.

Finally the officers returned from their conference and things started to move. Trucks, heavy and light, motorcycles, bicycles, carriers and men marching could be seen everywhere, drawing into position for the big attack. Finally everything was ready, wire all laid, troops in position so we had lunch. Immediately after the attack started and progressed so rapidly it was almost impossible to keep the communication lines up with the troops.

It started to rain and we discovered a minor disadvantage with our phone sets. The rain shorted the key contacts causing the instruments to buzz which nearly drove the exchange operator crazy.

After the exchange truck had moved off leaving all the wires disconnected I could still talk to "A," "B" and "C" company over the lines without any visible connection whatsoever. It was a freak occurrence caused by the wet earth.

I was finally able to rejoin my company who had moved about a half a mile up the road, where we waited for word that the day's activity was finished. We had received information before that "A" company had "taken" the objective and we were anxious to be on our way home. After waiting two hours we received word to march a mile farther to a meeting place where supper would be waiting for us. The saturating rain was still making life miserable and we ploughed through four inches of gooey mud before we arrived at our destination. Upon arriving there, I asked Mr. Honey if he needed me anymore so he dismissed my services whereby I rejoined the signal platoon with whom I had supper. The whole platoon was dead tired from laying and reeling up the miles of cable we had used and as the original plan called for a march back to camp which would take seven hours the sergeants and Mr. Kent obtained permission for the signals to ride on the trucks. I rode on an open A.A. truck and as my clothes were soaked, found it a very cold ride.

I wasn't so cold that I didn't take notice of the country we passed through with the sunken roads, the huge vine covered trees, and towns. I have often described the villages and towns "typically English" but I will change that as it is English and I like it. I saw a pine forest today which I thought could only exist in the timber belt of Canada.

We arrived in camp around nine o'clock and soon after the alert sounded, which didn't delete the pleasure I felt at crawling into my warm blankets.

MAR. 5, WED.
We were allowed to sleep in until nine o'clock this morning and we had breakfast at 10:00. At breakfast we heard that the rest of the Battalion marched into camp around 01:00 this morning. Spent the day cleaning my rifle which was in good shape despite the rough treatment it received yesterday.

I went down to the signal office this evening to write letters and stayed there until one o'clock in the morning and managed to get letters off to Ivy, Louie, Jack and Vera. Also started to answer Bezzie's letter which had arrived today along with one from Jack and one from Vera.

MAR. 6, THURS.
We spent the first period this morning practicing cable splicing. After that it was all gas lectures which is necessary but awfully bore-some.

Right after dinner I was summoned to Mr. Kent's office along with Jim Ellison and Jim Beck and we had a good idea what it was all about before we got there. Each of us were offered a stripe each, temporarily without pay. Jim Beck refused point blank to take it but the new job connected with mine, interests me greatly.

I am to have a work bench in the signal stores and my official capacity will be equipment maintenance man. My job will be to repair all defective equipment and to keep the wireless sets in running order. The radio junk will be here pretty soon now. On schemes I will be in charge of a company signals station. I was given to understand that I would be receiving pay for the stripe in the near future. Jim Ellison accepted his as did Harold Steeds who took Beck's place after he had refused. There is going to be some big changes in the platoon very soon, I received some more letters this evening from Buddo, Rose, Nelle and Miss Banks of Quebec. Also received a valentine from Junie and Teddy and a lucky rabbits foot from the whole family. I received another surprise this evening when I was informed that I had to go out on Wednesday and fire the anti tank rifle. I understand that I was selected because I am classed as the only expert rifle shot in the platoon. This is the first I have heard of the results of my firing the other day.

Mackenzie loaned me the three pence for the show this evening so we saw the very excellent picture called, "Stanley and Livingston."

MAR. 7, FRI.
Buzzer reading practice to start with this morning then had gas training tests which was concluded at 2 this afternoon, the same which I think I have passed.

More mail came in this evening and I received a Valentine letter from Marcelle. There were no much needed smoking material so I had to borrow a package off of Roy Miller who had just received a carton of Sweet Caps. Started a letter to Bobbie which will have to be continued tomorrow.

MAR. 8, SAT.
I was conscientiously engaged in signal clerking from 8:00A.M. until 5:00P.M. and finished a letter to Bobbie. In the evening I went down and typed the letter out to save paper and eliminate the possibility of having to

pay postage on it. I asked Cormack to order rations for four and I stayed for lunch. I received a carton of British Consol cigarettes which Marcelle sent and found it very hard to express the appreciation I felt. I got to bed at 11:30P.M. after what I figured was a good day's work.

MAR. 9, SUN.
We went on a church parade this morning then washed my dirty laundry. I spent the afternoon writing a letter to Marcelle in which I made a poor attempt to thank her for the cigarettes. Also wrote a letter to Rose. I received a letter from Nellie and a parcel containing a scarf, sweater and a pair of socks from the Ladies Auxiliary to the 16th Medium Battery. I sent a letter of thanks to them.

MAR. 15, FRI.
Since the entry of Mar. 9 and this date quite a lot has happened which changes, to considerable extent, my status as a member of this battalion. They made me a lance corporal with pay effective on the 10th of this month with back pay from the 6th. On the tenth I also went before the paymaster and between us, we managed to make arrangements to have money sent home to Dad. I had made arrangements previously but they evidently had miscarried.

To do justice to my new rank and duties it was necessary to move into the signal stores with Ken Peters as a room mate. Ken and I had vastly different ideas of what a bedroom should look like which conflicted extensively with those of the former occupants of these quarters so we proceeded to carry out some alterations until it was to the satisfaction of ourselves. For the remaining time I have been terribly busy repairing the equipment and Ken has been equally busy straightening the stores and the inventories, which is the principle reason for the neglect to enter the daily events of the past week.

The air raids have, up until tonight, been fairly heavy although there has not been any bombs dropped in the immediate vicinity. For four or five hours on consecutive nights, last night included, the roar of planes was continuous although it must be realized that fifty percent or thereabouts, were our own night fighters. Other than that excepting a parcel of cookies from Marcelle and a very nice letter inside, and a carton of tobacco from Harry and about fourteen letters, two bundles of Miners. The last letters to arrive were from Doc Draper and Nelle.

MAR. 16, SAT.
I was in charge of a fatigue party cleaning out the signal stores building this morning and decided that habits die hard as I think I did as much work as anyone.

Reg and I made our first visit to Aldershot this afternoon where I bought two more text books on radio, "Foundations of Wireless" by a chap named Sowerby and "Handbook of Wireless Telegraphy" Vol II by the Admiralty, the mate of which, (Vol I), I already have. They are both good volumes and I think will prove very useful.

Aldershot, on a Saturday is no place to go for pleasure as the streets are crowded with soldiers and women from every branch of the service. I went in to see about my watch which has been in for repairs for over five weeks now and they are still waiting for material. As queer as it may seem it would have been just as quick or quicker to have sent the darn thing to Canada to be fixed. They told me to come back Tuesday.

Reg and I finally got tired of pushing our way through the crowd so caught the 5:50 bus back to Farnborough where we went to a show at the Rex. After the show we had a lunch at the Toc H club, then came back to camp.

One thing about these English people that was annoyingly emphasized today and that was their slowness at waiting on customers in the stores. Transactions that could have been completed in a few minutes took fifteen or twenty. Perhaps it is one of those qualities of wisdom which comes with age. The old English race is like an old man compared with young Canada and our similarity to the fast moving Americans and our fondness for fast moving action is brought out in increasing clarity.

MAR. 16, SUN.
Church parade this morning and I wrote letters all afternoon and all evening. I derived great pleasure in writing to Marcelle this evening and I surprised myself with some of the things I said. God knows what she will think of it.

MAR. 17, MON.

I had a little anti-tank rifle training this morning and we were supposed to have another T.O.E.T. exam today but I had to run a line into the stores for a phone and missed it. Cpl. Hatch informed me later that I passed it alright.

I couldn't do any work today because of the people getting underfoot. For some poor reason, the Dispatch riders have to wait here for their calls, consequently they are sitting at the writing table, at the work bench and laying on the beds. I'll have to complain about it and see if other arrangements can't be made.

I finally got around to doing my laundry, a job that has been hanging fire for a few days. I have an awful lot of studying to do before the qualifications but can't seem to get at it.

MAR. 18, TUES.

Worked all day renovating old antiquated D3's and repairing the new D5's in readiness for the qualification and inspection on Friday. Studied a little this evening but couldn't settle down to it. Somehow, I am not worrying a great deal about passing the examinations.

MAR. 19, WED.

The rest of the platoon had tests messages on lamp and semaphore and buzzer but I had to service one of the exchanges which had gone haywire. Slept all afternoon when I really meant to study. Reg and I had a little semaphore practice by ourselves this evening then came in and practiced doing a few map reading problems. Continued writing the long letter to Nelle which I had started the day before.

MAR. 20, THURS.

The qualifications are only a few hours away now and the studying I have done is negligible compared to what I need to do. I finished Nelle's letter at noon but managed to add four or five P.S.'s onto it before I mailed it this evening.

I got my boots back which I had taken in for repair about three weeks ago, also my watch was finally fixed after 1 month and 11 days. I had two after supper calls to locate and rectify phone trouble and so I still haven't accomplished much in the way of studying. I refuse to worry about the exams tomorrow; if I pass, alright, and if I don't, that's alright too.

MAR. 21, FRI.

The qualifications started off with a bang this morning when Mr. Kent was congratulated on the systematic arrangement and records of the stores by a high ranking official. Most of the credit goes to Peters who performed a wonderful job during such a short time. Every piece of equipment was in its place or accounted for and everything was operative.

I walked through the qualifications quite surprisingly and easily and am so sure I have passed I am sewing flags on my new uniform tomorrow. I feel happy about the whole thing.

I finished a letter to Ivy this evening which leaves me only Mommies letter to answer. Another bunch of Canadian mail came in tonight but was not surprised when there was none for me. I received such a pile of it last time. Rumours again but more of a personal nature, I may get a new and better job in the near future.

MAR. 22, SAT.

Interior economy this morning but I found myself unoccupied when a party came down in charge of Ellison (L/Cpl) which left me free to do as I pleased for the morning.

I washed my equipment this afternoon then wrote a letter to Mrs. Sharpe. I forgot to mail it. Some more veiled hints regarding big changes in the platoon. We haven't heard yet if we passed the tests yet. I had a little code reading on the Instructograph this evening.

MAR. 23, SUN.

I missed church parade this morning due to urgent repairs needed on one of the telephone lines, it has been causing me a lot of trouble recently but I think I have fixed it this time. I wrote letters all afternoon and evening and managed to answer all remaining mail that I had received some two weeks ago. Also answered a very nice letter from Felicie which I had received today along with one from Nelle. I wrote letters to Connie, Em and Dad which I have been promising to do for so long. Total number of letters written in 17 days comes to 25. It's a good thing I enjoy writing letters because I am afraid a lot of people would have to wait a lot longer than two months for an answer.

MAR. 24, MON.
Obtained a bad headache this morning from working on a couple of old D3's and it wasn't helped much when I had to wear a steel helmet for three hours this afternoon.

I wrote another letter to Nelle this evening and studied for awhile before turning in.

MAR. 25, TUES.
We had a Brigadier's inspection this morning which lasted until nearly 11:30A.M. I am not in the position to know whether he was satisfied with the turnout or not.

I whiled away a few hours this afternoon giving a U.C. 6 line telephone exchange a general check-up. I took it down and replaced the old one which is needing a thorough overhauling. At my usual evening pastime, writing letters and again to Nelle. Also studied radio again before concluding activities for the day. Headlines in the papers tonight say that Yugoslavia has signed the pact with Germany. I certainly wish them luck, which would probably be confiscated by Germany before she had it long.

MAR. 26, WED.
I overhauled another exchange this morning and had it finished by 10:00A.M. despite the questionable aid of one, Lieut. McManus. I will have to give the fellow credit he wants to help and he catches on quickly. It was necessary to explain the workings of the different parts to appease his insatiable curiosity which impeded my progress immensely.

Spent the afternoon and evening sewing on Canada badges and two sets of flags to my new Limey uniform. I was using a very effective but slow method of stitching but I am well satisfied that the time thus spent will be worth it.

We had three daylight air raid alarms this afternoon but my hopes of seeing a dog fight did not materialize. It rained all afternoon and the ceiling was pretty low which is probably the reason for my failure to see the raiders.

I heard today, that five men are going up to Brigade H.Q. to take over signalling duties again. There is a possible chance that I may go as N.C.O. in charge. I am not at all fussy about the job. Reg wants me to go and pose for a picture with him on pay day. I am giving it serious thought.

MAR. 27, THURS.

Right after breakfast we received short notice to get ready for an inspection and to load sufficient supplies for a small scale signalling scheme. We left camp around 10:15 and arrived at our destination around eleven. Rumours were very persistent that it was an inspection by the King and Queen.

We pulled up in a clearing in a thickly wooded area and commenced to camouflage truck and men. The clearing was fairly large with two roads running parallel through it. The S.S.R.'s were drawn up among the trees, directly across from us on a knoll and the F.M.R.'s were occupying a wood between us and the S.S.R.'s but to the right of our position. We were parked in between the two roads and in the form of a crude "L."

The signals received orders to establish a communication system using cable and phones on a miniature scale. We carried out the order in no time at all and soon had the system going with each station about 20 feet apart and camouflaged with tree limbs. Then we settled down to wait.

At 12:30 we had dinner which I found very difficult to eat mainly because I had forgotten to bring my knife, fork and spoon along and a clasp-knife isn't the most effective instrument with which to eat stew.

After dinner we were shown what we were supposed to do at one blast on the whistle. It consisted of breaking from cover and galloping across the clearing to within 10 yards of the road or so, then on two blasts on the whistle we would move forward to the edge of the road. At the same time the other two units would dash forward and take up similar positions on the other side of the road. Four times we rehearsed the procedure and four times we had to return to our original positions. Then came the 60 minute wait which seemed like an eternity. We all knew that the next whistle would be the real thing and were on edge waiting for it.

Finally it came, there was a mad dash across the clearing, everyone was doing his best to reach there first and be in the front row for the inspection. I was very fortunate in being able to obtain one of these valuable positions. My view was blocked to my left, the direction from which they were coming, consequently my first sight of the King was sudden and very close up. He looked much younger than he does in the various pictures I have seen of him and he looks every inch a soldier. He was dressed in his field marshal's uniform accompanied by army officers of high rank. He has light brown eyes which are penetrating and steady. I had a very good look at him but he soon passed on down the line.

Then came the leading lady of the Empire, the Queen herself. She appeared before me as suddenly as the King had. One moment she wasn't there and the next there she was, dressed in a blue coat with fur on the collar and cuffs. Her type of beauty is very seldom found in other women; her famous pleasant contagious smile gives one the feeling that she is about to speak. If she had of spoke I am afraid I would have been unable to answer, so great would be my surprise. The descriptions of other people were not exaggerated as I had thought, in fact, they were understatements. She has a radiant beauty, one that hits you like a ton of bricks. She passed on down the line followed by her maid-in-waiting and company. After they had finished inspecting us they crossed over to the F.M.R.'s where they took quite a few men then they proceeded to the S.S.R.'s. After they had finished there, they walked back to their car which was parked near the point on our right between the F.M.R.'s and our unit.

Then the whistle blew twice and we dashed for the road. Actually there was no need for the signal whistle as most of the fellows were moving before it was blown. The F.M.R.'s came galloping toward us to take up their position on the other side of the road and in the lead, his legs working like pistons, was their diminutive Lieut-Colonel, O.C. of their Regiment. The S.S.R.'s also dashed for their position and the ground fairly shook with the pounding feet.

The cheers of the men from up near the Royal cars broke over the quiet English countryside like a wave and it came closer as the Royal procession rolled slowly along between the lines of soldiers. They came into view, the Queen still smiling that famous smile of hers and waving a gloved hand to the cheering crazy, yelling men and the King by her side waving and occasionally saluting. They passed from view, the wave of noise from thousands of husky young throats following them on their way.

I walked back to my station with mingled feelings, wondering why such a young couple whom should be enjoying life, should be burdened with the rule of a country in such trying times as this but feeling confident that the destiny of the Empire was in capable hands. The King's every bit a man and a soldier, the Queen, a beautiful woman with a beautiful smile and every bit a Queen. Disregarding the Empire and the freedom of the people, they are inspiration enough to fight a man threatening their safety. God bless them both.

MAR. 28, FRI.
The Cameron Sigs are taking over duties at Brigade again. I was ordered up here for a day to show Reg (in charge) the ropes and to alter any technical aspects of the situation including telephone instruments and exchanges. We took over from the F.M.R.'s about 3:30 this afternoon.

MAR. 29, SAT.
Started work very early this morning as we had plenty of work to do before I returned to Delville this afternoon. Reg had a very good start at becoming used to the comparative large volume of traffic as there were plenty of dispatches piled up on the table.

He soon had everything under control by his own efforts and by asking me dozens of questions, then I was able to complete what I really went to Brigade for; that of rewiring the signal office phone line and superimposing a D5 onto a G.P.O. I came back to Delville around three this afternoon and Peters left for Brigade at six where he will stay for duty, until my leave starts.

I worked on a phone cradle until 9:00 this evening which I am designing and making for the D5 at Brigade. We had our first raid alarm for some eight days this evening and the "all clear" sounded at 10:20P.M.

MAR. 30, SUN.
No parade today so spent the morning writing to Marcelle and studying. Letters between Marcelle and I are getting more intimate, I wonder how it will end up.

Did my laundry this afternoon and took the plans for a phone cradle over to Cpl. Budd of the pioneers. Reg came over from Brigade just after supper and fell asleep soon after, where he stayed until nearly eight. While Reg was sleeping, I pressed my good uniform and added some more to Marcelle's letter. At eight Reg and I went down to the NAAFI for something to eat then he went back to Brigade and I returned to finish Marcelle's letter. I asked her for a close up picture of herself. I wonder if I'll get it. I should study some more while I have the chance. This last week seemed to be a very good week for England sea, land and diplomatic forces what with the capture of Keren and Harar in Africa and the Mediterranean fleet's clash with the Italian Navy at last and the Yugoslavian revolution over the signing of the Tripartite pact. There is a rumour around that Mussolini is dead which was discredited in the papers.

MAR. 31, MON.
Made a trip up to Brigade to fix a fullerphone switch and check over the line and to tell Peters that he had to come back and go on the scheme tomorrow as I can't go because I am going on leave on Friday and the scheme doesn't finish until Friday night.

The afternoon I spent in doing last minute repairs on the equipment that will be used on the scheme. Reg came down for awhile this afternoon but didn't stay very long. I was warned for guard duty for tomorrow but managed to get out of it by saying if I went on guard I would be back as a Private the next day. Sgt. Richardson was instrumental in getting me off.

I fixed Corporal Hatch's lighter this evening and postponed my trip to Brigade.

APR. 1, APRIL FOOL'S DAY
Despite the recognized status of the date, the weather wasn't fooling in the least when the battalion was carrying out last minute preparations for the scheme. It was raining fairly heavily this morning which soon turned to exceedingly wet snow but the convoys left on schedule. I accomplished a satisfactory renovation on a couple of D III's which I intended to use for communication between the A.A. lookout tower and the signal office. I was in the process of installing one of the phones in the signal office when we received word that the scheme was postponed due to adverse weather conditions. I immediately suspended my activities and began preparing for my contemplated visit up to Brigade. It's raining again now and am strongly inclined to call it off until tomorrow too.

I went out and made a halfhearted attempt to find the defect in the brigade line but it was too wet to be of any use.

I wrote a letter to Ivy telling her that I expected to be there on Friday afternoon. I hope I can get away alright. She seems worried about just how she should greet me at the station and I am afraid I did not help her make up her mind, very much. Received 300 cigs from Nelle. God bless her.

APR. 2, WED.
We woke up this morning to find it still raining but decided to make concerted effort to locate the break in the Brigade line. I took Crosse with me this time; we started testing a hundred yards from our own signal office. We climbed poles on precariously positioned ladders, we jumped and waded ditches, we climbed fences, we rode bicycles through sticky masses of mud until finally our determination was rewarded by our locating the break

alongside the railroad tracks. Someone had dropped a tie on the line and one of the none-too-good joints had parted under the strain. Communication was soon restored and the wire was soon hot with messages.

We decided to follow the line the rest of the way to Brigade and found a number of joints improperly made which we rectified without breaking contact. We arrived at Brigade and found Mr. Kent and Sgt. Richardson there and we received favourable comment on our work. We installed a buzzer clearing system between signal office and exchange room. Altered the improvised phone cradle and were back at Delville by noon and in time for dinner. I checked over a D5 this afternoon, started answering Rose's letter that I received this afternoon. It had taken over a month and a half as it had to go through the censor office. Mr. Kent phoned and asked me if I could find some way to turn the Bettle radio on and off automatically so spent the rest of the afternoon trying to find a suitable method. He must have great faith in my inventive capabilities. No solution as yet, but still trying.

I received two letters one from Nelle and one from Bobbie, both of them bulky and interesting. How those girls can write letters. I finished Rose's letter this evening which I will probably mail tomorrow. Ken Peters made some coffee this evening and we bought some cakes from the NAAFI canteen. The smell of coffee must have been wafted round as Tully walks in soon followed by MacKenzie who in turn was followed by Harry Guedesse. We had quite sufficient coffee to go around so played hosts to our unexpected guests. Some despairing remarks were uttered about the quality of the coffee but we ignored them completely and successfully changed the subject. Peters, who had prepared the refreshments, made a mistake and put four lumps of sugar in MacKenzie's cup and none in Tully's. One complained of it being too sweet and the other, too bitter. We solved the problem by mixing the two and equally dividing it again. Despite the numerous mistakes in Peter's culinary efforts, it was not bad, totally bad I mean.

APR. 3, THURS.
I checked over a D5 set this morning thus completing a thorough overhaul to all instruments including 14 lamps, 7 D5's and two exchanges.

Occupied this afternoon in packing my kit in readiness for my leave. Managed to wrestle up a new pair of gaiters.

APR. 4, FRI.

Got up at 5:00 A.M. this morning and left camp before seven having passed up breakfast in camp, and caught the 8:11 from Farnborough Main Station. Arrived in London at 9:00 or 8:45 and retired to the Beaver club where I had breakfast and found I had to wait until 4:15 for a train to St. Neots.

I was at King's Cross in plenty of time so sat and read a newspaper for a half hour or so while the crowd consisting of sailors, flyers, soldiers and civilians streamed by. Once in a while the train announcer with the aid of a public address system, would add to the general turmoil, usually present in a large railway station.

Finally our train pulled in and I found myself sharing a compartment with an elderly and high-ranking naval official. Why he was riding third class I never found out. On leaving London we passed through about six tunnels, the first being the longest. At the first stop we were joined by a fat woman and her husband, looking slightly henpecked, and a young married girl. No I didn't ask if she was married but she had two rings on her finger.

At the next stop, the name of which I have forgotten, a Jewish looking foreigner came in and no sooner sat down than he was asleep. Every once in awhile he would wake up with a start and ask for the time and the name of the next stop. The sea official disembarked at Wakefield after bidding me a pleasant good afternoon. The fat lady and her henpecked husband (I was sure of it by this time.) stepped off at the next stop, leaving plenty of room in the compartment which was instantly filled by two R.A.F. men. They were real friendly and I had quite a little talk with them. We pulled into a place called Sandy and as usual the little Jew was asleep but he woke up with the customary questions. The train was ready to start again when he decided that he was at his station. With the combined aid of the Air Force and the Canadian Army he managed to disembark safely with his two straw bags in his hands. I asked the Air Force how far it was to St. Neot's and the young bride gave a little start and looked at me quite directly. We finally reached St. Neot's and the lady told me that this was my station. Very nice of her I thought.

It was six o'clock when I stepped onto the platform but I could not see anyone that looked like Ivy. I decided that she had not received my letter telling her of my purposed visit. I boarded a yellow bus for the St. Neot market square which arrived too late for the bus to Southoc.

As soon as I started walking it started to rain but it turned out to be only a shower. I asked a "Bobby" how to get to Southoc and his directions were typical, "Cross the common until you strike the north road, then down that a "bit" (the "bit" can run from 100 yards to 50 miles) then turn left and you are there. He said it was a four mile walk.

Just after leaving him a red headed youngster on a bike came up beside me and asked me if I was a real Can "i" dian and wanted my badge. He said it was 3 ½ miles to Southoc and also imparted with the astounding information that there was a Miss Doris Turner living next door to him in St. Neot's.

Then a young man fell in beside me and said it was a little less than 2 miles to Southoc. He seemed very proud to tell me that he had just come back from Bedford after taking his medical for enlistment with the Royal Engineers.

A friend of his picked us up just as we were crossing the Ouse River and he told me that it was five miles to Southoc and would give me a ride to Little Paxton. I just stepped out of the car when I heard a young lady say "hello, I am Ivy." She looks a lot prettier than her picture and we walked the rest of the way together with Ivy carrying my pack on the handle bars.

The walk to the Three Horse Shoes did not seem so very long and so came to the conclusion that the policeman, the lad on the bicycle, the young man and the driver of the car must have had different methods of judging distance. During the walk, Ivy had difficulty holding the pack on the handle bars but she was determined that I was not going to carry it any further.

I met Uncle, Louie, Betsy and Ada then had tea. Louie showed me my room and I had quite a time convincing her that it was quite satisfactory.

Time hasn't been sufficient to express my opinions of the folks as yet, and we feel more or less like strangers to each other, which I hope will be rectified in short order. Louie took me over to meet Maggie, Wally's wife and her two boys and Maggie said she would write to Wally and tell him I am here. He may be able to come down on Wednesday. Uncle is ailing and consequently isn't feeling so good.

APR. 5, SAT.

I received a pleasant surprise this morning when Louie brought me a cup of tea in bed. It was the first cup of tea I have had in bed since as far back as I can remember. The last time, I think, was when I had the measles or scarlet fever.

Ivy and Louie are both working; Ivy in St. Neot's and Louie in the village post office. Ada and Betsy keep house and wait on the bar. Uncle was up this morning for awhile but had to go to bed. I spent the entire day sitting in the kitchen talking to Ada and Betsy.

Ada and Betsy went out this evening but Louie, Ivy and I sat around the fireplace in the living room and talked until Ada and Betsy came back and joined in the talk. We finally got to bed around 12 or 12:30.

APR. 6, SUN.

I guess the cup of tea in bed was not an accident yesterday. Lou brought another one in this morning. Everyone was busy house cleaning this morning but myself. They refuse to let me do anything to help.

Lou and I walked into St. Neot's this afternoon but all the stores were closed so the walk there and back again was for nothing. A cold wind did not help to improve the trip back. We spent the evening around the fireplace in the living room and told Ivy something about the Indians and Canada. Ivy would like to pay Canada a visit and we calculated a rough estimate of the cost of the trip. Again it was after midnight before we hit the hay. I am afraid I am not seeing much of Uncle since he had to go to bed. I saw a letter that Dad had written twenty years ago.

APR. 7, MON.

Another cup of tea in bed; I will have to train Peters a little better when I get back. I sat in the kitchen all morning talking to Ada who seems to be holding down the official position of cook. Betsy took me with her on a business trip up to the top of the lane (the village main street) to another pub called the "Bell."

I started to walk to St. Neot's this afternoon but obtained a lift from a chap of short acquaintance called Gordon, who deposited my carcass at the market square. I have come to the conclusion that a Canadian is quite conspicuous in these parts. I bought a couple of bottles of ink and then walked home again.

The Bar was closed this evening so Ada and Betsy went out; Ivy and Louie and I sat around the fireplace and they told me all about Auntie. I wish I could have met her. Ivy ironed and mended my shirt for me and she wanted to do some of my handkerchiefs for me but I refused to let her. I wouldn't wish that job on to anyone let alone Ivy. Ada and Betsy came in and soon after Ivy and Louie went up to bed as they have to go to work in the morning. I got to bed at 12:30 again tonight.

APR. 8, TUES.

Lou is spoiling me, imagine me staying in bed until nine and waiting for a cup of tea when I get back to camp. Blimey, wouldn't the sergeant be riled. Uncle was up today but I think he is far from well. Louie had the afternoon off and Ada and Bets went to Huntington on a shopping tour.

Lou and I went to St. Neot's to meet Ivy at six and the three of us went to the "pictures" (a show in our language). The "alert" sounded while we were there and it was still on when we came out. I got the lowdown on Ivy's raid experience in London, and she has every right to be frightened when the "alert" goes. I haven't seen anything yet compared to what these folks have experienced.

After searching all over Aldershot, Farnborough, London and Cove for an ignition file I had to come to an out of the way place like St. Neot's to find one. I should buy a couple more before I go back and be sure of a supply.

We came out of the "pictures" at 9:00P.M. (2100 hrs) and the girls decided to have supper at home so we walked back at least, Louie and I did. Ivy had her bike so she rode it while I held her arm and pushed her, in the same manner as skating. Ivy has a good singing voice and she sang practically all the way home; it's not the first time I have heard her sing. Auntie must have been a wonderful woman and from what I have heard, she must have been very much like Mrs. Gibson in more ways than one. I am sorry I got here too late, I would very much liked to have met her.

I think Wally will be down tomorrow so I will meet him. Julia and her husband Bill are up at York. Len is with his unit, as is Albert. I hope some day to see them all. By tomorrow I should know the ones I have met and be able to express my opinion of each one. I am ashamed to admit I haven't seen much of Wally's wife and will have to call on them tomorrow.

APR. 9, WED.
This will be my last full day here and I will be sorry to leave. I hope I haven't been too much trouble. Wally doesn't get here until noon.

Ada had to go into St. Neot's to the butcher's and she asked me if I would like to cycle in with her. So I pedaled the three miles to St. Neot's and had a very difficult time keeping up with Ada. I enjoyed the ride and the company. It's queer, but I haven't felt strange with these folks in the least.

I met Wally today and he measures up to all I have heard of him. I would like Nellie to meet him. He only stayed for a little while this afternoon. I spent another afternoon in the kitchen talking with Ada and Betsy, a pastime that is pleasant, at least, to myself. How they put up with it I don't know, they are both OK and good company.

Lou reminds me very much of Nelle, she takes care of Uncle and watches over Ivy and seems to think of everything. She likes to tease me of my Canadian accent. Ivy and I made a visit to Little Castleberry to see Wally and Marguerite and spent a very enjoyable evening. He showed me some very good photos taken during the better years before the war. We came home around ten thirty to find Gordon waiting to find out what time I was leaving so that he could drive me down to the station. Gordon is the milk man, young and a decent sort of a fellow with a slight crush on Ivy. Who can blame him? She is quite a girl.

APR. 10, THURS.

My conscience got the better of me this morning so I got up and took the morning cup of tea down stairs. I did most of my packing this morning as I knew I wouldn't have much time this afternoon.

Thursday is market day in St. Neot's so Ada, Bet and I walked in to do some shopping. We were walking around the square and Bet stopped to buy a pair of those scarce feminine wearing apparel, silk stockings and Ada and I were standing waiting for her. A small gray-haired old man (75 years, I judged) came up and spoke to me. He had lived in Calgary for 30 years, having gone there when the streets were still mud. He had come back to England not long ago and has a house of his own in St. Neot's and is living comfortably on a weekly pension. I had to leave the old gentleman when Bet rejoined us after dickering with the Jewish stocking vendor.

Soon after I parted company with the girls to do some shopping of my own and having bought the desired goods was standing on the corner waiting for Ada and Bet when another old gentleman spoke to me. I judged him to be between 70 and 75 and he had spent 40 years, more or less, in a small town 18 miles north of Brandon. He asked me if the farmers were still finding it hard "sledding" on the prairies. The English accent was totally lacking in both of their speech.

Our return bus came along at 4:35 but it wasn't large enough to accommodate the large crowd so we had to walk back to Southoc. Bet being foot-sore and Ada being leg-weary, they did not enjoy the return walk in the least. By the time we got back, it did not leave a great deal of time before I had to leave for the station.

Gordon called for me at 6:30 and after saying good-bye to Bets, Ada and Uncle, we were soon at the station, having picked up Ivy in St. Neot's. We (Ivy, Louie, Gordon and I) waited until the regular time for the train then we learned that this particular train had a persistent habit of being late. It did finally arrive, fifty minutes later.

During the farewells that followed I experienced one of Ivy's "pen slips" which I usually find at the end of her letters and had the desire to repeat the performance. Louie can sure hand them out too. I hated to leave, but the army refuses to consider sentimentalities.

Not satisfied with being an hour late to start with, the train ran into an air raid zone and had to crawl along at reduced speed and stop at every station on the line, which resulted in my arriving at Kings Cross at 10:30, much too late to catch my train from Waterloo. The tube station at Trafalgar Square was closed as was the one at Waterloo so I walked from Piccadilly Circus to the Beaver Club where I hoped to learn the times of later trains. To Farnborough but it was closed as well. As buses seemed to be as scarce as hen's teeth, I hired a taxi with a very accommodating driver who set me down at Waterloo station for one and nine.

Upon inquiring at the booking office I learned that the next train would be at 5:30 in the morning. This naturally introduced complications as to accommodations for the intervening six hours. A member of the Royal Artillery also missed his train so we set out together to find a place to sleep. We found it right in Waterloo station. On the door is a sign which reads, "Shelter for His Majesty's Forces Only."

The interior of the shelter is shaped like an "L" with the entrance at the end of the horizontal and shorter stroke of the "L." On the right, as you enter, is a Y.M.C.A. refreshment booth which stays open all night, the lady attendants working in hourly relays. A cup of tea and meat pies and cakes cost 2 pence each. The remainder of the short branch of the "L" is lined along both sides with double-decker beds where the men and other members can rest or sleep while waiting for their respective trains. The larger and vertical stroke of the "L" has three or four rows of beds with a toilet conveniently placed. It doesn't cost a penny to stay here.

Every branch of the Forces is represented here including the WAAFS and ATS. Care is taken not to embarrass the gentler sex. It's midnight so will have to start another day.

APR. II, FRI. (3:25 A.M.)

The dull penetrating reverberations of heavy bombing has been steady for the last hour, so I guess London is experiencing another bad raid after 18 days of comparative quiet. My R.A. friend is asleep directly across from me and I have promised to call him in time to catch his train. He told me that he has been bombed out of two houses and burnt out of the third, after which he sent his wife and 9 month old baby boy to live with his sister, four hours' ride up country.

Whether an air raid is an excuse for being late, I can't say, but in any event the worst they can do is to take my stripe away. I think I will be able to dodge the guards and get to my quarters safely without arousing suspicion. The explosions are getting louder and closer together; someone is going through hell this morning.

I roused the R.A. fellow out of bed at 4:30 A.M. and we had a cup of tea and a couple of cakes before going up and locating our trains. Mine was scheduled to leave at 5:40 and he had to go to Victoria station for his, so we shook hands and parted company.

I caught the train alright and in due course arrived in Woking where, for some unknown reason, I had to change trains which was accomplished with seconds to spare. I arrived in camp just in time for breakfast but still one hour and a half late. By careful manipulation of a few important strings and by taking full advantage of a little luck, I managed to get away with it. I barely had time to get my equipment off and hung up before I had to start working on some antiquated phone equipment. However, the job didn't take much time so I slept the rest of the morning.

This afternoon I was placed in charge of a section for a six mile route march which I can't say I enjoyed in the least, in fact, I caught myself sleeping on my feet a few times during the march.

I wrote a letter to Ivy this evening and it's not a very good letter, but it will serve to start the letters coming again. Ivy, a girl that can be described in two words, "The Tops." She is very considerate and generous to others, the kind of a girl one does not want as a cousin or sister. I am lucky to have her as the former. Gordon has a golden opportunity as he sees her very often. I wonder how old he is.

Louie, shows many of the traits found in Ivy and is quite capable of carrying responsibility. She was genuinely concerned about my comfort. She has the pleasing habit of bringing tea to folks in bed the first thing in the morning.

Ada, a very good companion and seems quite capable of taking care of herself in any situation. Very easy to talk to, once you know her and is a good conversationalist.

Bets, small, but I think she is a little package of dynamite when riled. She would make a good friend to anyone who knows her. She seems to know what she wants and will probably get it.

It's impossible for a man especially of my mentality, to understand four women in less than a week so the impressions I have written are those that I got during my short association with them. Personally I think the four of them are OK and I hope to see them again sometime.

APR. 12, SAT.
I didn't do a thing this morning but watch the boys sweep and scrub the floors. I had a call to change the location of the phone in the hospital but it was cancelled before I got started.

I started out for Aldershot this afternoon with the intention of doing a little shopping but finished up by going to see "Maryland" playing at the Rex in Farnborough. When I returned to camp I discovered that Peters had locked the door and taken the key to Reading with him. I had to force my way in by prying the hasp off the door so I will have to repair the damage first thing in the morning.

I wrote a long letter to Nelle this evening in answer to the one I received from her before I went on leave and the one I received this morning. I will write another one to her tomorrow describing my leave.

I bought a fairly good and much needed screwdriver this afternoon, in Farnborough and I am going to make certain it will not be claimed by the army and entered on the signal stores inventory.

There is no raid warning tonight and it's turned 2400hrs. Peters isn't back yet from Reading. I don't want to be awake when he comes in or I'll be awake all night.

APR. 13, SUN.

I almost overslept and nearly missed breakfast this morning. I had to attend church parade and despite the fact that it was Easter Sunday, the service was the same boresome, cut-and-dried type we usually sleep through.

I washed my dirty clothes this morning right after church parade which gave me the entire afternoon and evening to write a short letter to Ada and start a long one to Nelle. I kept writing until 11:00P.M. and still wasn't finished so I decided I had better call it a day and finish the letter tomorrow.

APR. 14, EASTER MONDAY

There is nothing around here that indicates that it is Holiday Monday as everything is going on like any other weekday. Repaired two units in No. 2 exchange this morning, then copied out some wireless notes from Sergeant Richardson's wireless book on No. 18 sets. I wrote a short letter to Bet this evening and one to a friend in London whom I had promised to write to.

Peters scrounged up some genuine ground coffee from somewhere and Stewie bought some cake at the Canteen so we had quite a midnight lunch although the coffee did refuse to boil properly.

Reg called this evening and we discussed the N.C.O. situation of the platoon for some time, both present and future possibilities. Reg threatens to obtain a transfer to the 8th Reconnaissance Battalion as a radio operator and if things happen as we think they will I probably will go with him. He is doing a bang-up job of taking care of the signalling at Brigade H.Q. There is too much Hartney, Manitoba at the top of this platoon and it may cause dissension among the boys if there is any more of it. I wonder if Ivy and Louie have received the letters I wrote the other day; I hope I get an answer back before we go on any long schemes.

I had a piping-hot shower tonight at 11:30 which brightened the outlook on life considerably. At least, it makes one feel clean for awhile. It's twenty minutes to one so I guess I had better turn in.

APR. 15, TUES.

Ken and I had a surprise Anti-tank rifle test this morning which included loading five rounds of ammunition into a magazine three times out of four with fifteen seconds for each magazine. The tests were comparatively simple and we had no trouble in getting a passing mark on it despite the fact that Ken tried to put his first round in the magazine the wrong way. Neither one of us had any instruction on this particular weapon so I think we did alright. We packed up in readiness for a four day scheme, this afternoon and the trucks are all loaded ready to go.

I made a trip to Farnborough this afternoon after four o'clock and I went to see "Duley" starring Anne Southern at the Rex. I made it back to camp just in time to have a cup of coffee that Peters had made. I finished a 21 large paper letter tonight which will have to be mailed early in the morning. Also mailed a letter to Bet and one to Miss Charrington.

The "alert" sounded at 10:30P.M. and we can hear the flights of planes flying overhead.

The bomb and A.A. gun explosions are quite plain tonight so I guess they are after someplace close by. A flight comes over about once every half hour but no doubt half of the planes are our own.

I just heard a bump and a groan and when I turned around there was Ken limping around holding his back. He has a piece of a mattress here on the floor and he tried to do a back flip. The mattress is only two feet square and when he back-flipped he missed the mattress, by a good two feet. He is offended because I laughed at him.

APR. 16, WED.

We started a four day scheme this morning at 10:30 with Peters, Forsythe, Crosse, Cormack and myself riding in the back of the store truck. We passed through some wonderful looking country. One place especially, where we descended a long hill and the valley and surrounding country was very good to look at. The even symmetrical squares of different shades of green, fresh with a young crop, formed a pleasing study in contrast. There was a cool looking stream running down the center of the valley; a well kept farm house nestled on its banks with a white stone stable a hundred yards or so away. A series of hill ranges stretched beyond, seemingly getting higher the further away they were.

We arrived at our overnight stopping place at about 3:00P.M. and had to establish communication between all the companies, First Aid Post and the Battalion H.Q. I did not enjoy the meal that was prepared in the least as by the time I had a chance to eat, the stew was cold and there was no tea.

Reynolds, Susie and myself made our beds in the back of the stores truck but despite the four-ply thickness of the blanket under me, the cold came through from the cold steel floor. We heard no "alerts" but we can hear the planes going over; sometimes we are able to hear the roar from three or four different flights flying overhead. We are about 40 miles south of our camp which may account for the increased air activity. The truck is shaking from the bombing but they are not falling near here.

APR. 17, THURS.

I dragged myself out of the bed into the cold misty, clammy morning just after dawn. After breakfast came the tedious job of repacking the bedrolls which didn't take quite as long as usual. Some of the boys saw some enemy raiders shot down in flames last night but I guess I was asleep at the time. (2:00A.M.) I wish I could have seen it.

We had trouble this morning with earth faults and shorts on the U.C. exchange but there is nothing I can do with it as it's really a lineman's job. Sgt. Rankine and I went hunting for pheasants this morning and although we saw plenty of signs we did not see anything worthwhile. I took another crack at trying to fix the earth shorts in the exchange by changing entire units but gave it up as a bad job. We are supposed to be on the move again by three this afternoon, still going south. Just at present, I am perfectly contented to sit here in the sun and watch the traffic stream by on the nearby highway. Motorcycles, lorries, buses, cars, both civilian and military, stream by in unending procession.

It's a warm sunny day although it did start out cloudy and cool. Birds are busily flitting around picking up scraps of bread that the fellows dropped during the meal hours. There is one in particular that I have been watching closely. He is the size of a sparrow with the red breast of the robin and seems quite unafraid of the crowd.

About twenty feet away is a small partially dried up creek so I had a good shave and wash this afternoon. I have just been informed that we are not pulling out until eight o'clock this evening which means we will have to make a camp in the dark. Our next camp should be closer to the coast so we may see more aerial action than we did last night. I have a new idea for a bed tonight if I can persuade the boys that they don't need their big packs. By arranging these packs properly I should be able to make a comfortable resting place. We just saw two trucks with trailers go by with wreckage of German planes on them. Probably the ones the boys saw shot down last night.

We had supper at five then I spent a couple of hours putting things straight inside of the truck for when the time came to move. Finally we pulled in all stations at nine o'clock and the stores were all ready to roll at 9:45 P.M. Major Law and his batman climbed into our truck which had one too many men in it as it was. Consequently, we were much too crowded for any of us to snatch a few hours sleep. Before pulling out we had to walk half a mile in pitch blackness to draw our rations. It was supposed to do us for breakfast and dinner tomorrow but most of the fellows had eaten theirs before we ever pulled out. I managed to save a small cheese sandwich and a piece of cold meat for tomorrow.

We left the camp grounds about 10:30 and with many stops and starts proceeded on the next phase of this four day scheme. Then we got tangled up in the sweetest little traffic jam I have ever seen. It so happened that four convoys, including our own, met at a cross-roads. It took half an hour to straighten things out.

APR. 18, FRI.

The truck was too crowded and jolting to much to allow us to get any sleep. We travelled until 6:30 this morning before we found ourselves among the South Downs where the main part of the scheme was to take place. We are the reserve force so have been in one spot since our arrival this morning.

These Downs are something worth seeing and under much different circumstances I may like to roam through them. Deep valleys and high hills dotted with sumac trees. A civilian claimed that the coast is quite capable of being seen from the hill in front of us, as the sea is only four miles away, but we are not allowed to go sightseeing while the scheme is in progress.

I finished my rations at noon and it wasn't quite enough to satisfy my appetite. Forsythe opened his can of bully beef (his own rations) so we had something extra to eat after all.

It started to rain this afternoon and word came around that we would be having supper at 4:30 after that no one knows what is going to happen.

We were on our way out of the Downs by 5:45, climbing the precipitous road, over and down high hills, through deep valleys to the next climb which caused the motor to labour and growl on the upgrades and race and whine on the descents until we reached the paved roads again. We had a little delay there for awhile while the trucks were being loaded and allotted to their positions in the convoys. There was a space between the pile of bed rolls and the canvas covering of our truck and we had fourteen men squeezed into a space really meant for six so I utilized the space on top of the blankets and slept through the entire journey back to our old camping grounds of the first night. There was plenty of hot cocoa waiting there for us and it certainly hit the spot. We only had four hours to go before the five o'clock reveille so Sgt. Rankine and I did not bother to unroll our blankets but slept on all the packs with our great coats over us. We only removed our boots.

APR. 19, SAT.

We were up at five after spending a not too uncomfortable night and had breakfast at six. With only six men in the truck this time we were on our way back home by 7:30. We made fairly good time on the return trip and we were back in camp by 10:30A.M.

I had no time to take my equipment off before someone handed me a letter from Ivy which helped tremendously to dispel the tired gloomy feeling one gets when relaxing from a tough scheme. This particular letter pleased me no end and I was particularly glad to get it. Also received 300 cigarettes from my Quebec friends which came during a critical crisis in my smoking situation. They are sending another electric torch to replace the one they had given me and the same one that I had lost during my five day landing leave in London.

I answered Ivy's letter today and mailed it on my way to see Bing Crosby in "Rhythm of the River" at the Rex. After a great deal of trouble I succeeded in obtaining a suitable book for the third volume of this diary, also a book for some wireless notes and diagrams.

It was raining when I came out of the theater but I arrived back in camp just in time to partake of a cup of tea with Cpl. Hatch, L/Cpl Steeds, Cormack and Peters. I found a parcel of cookies waiting for me from Mrs. E. (Janet) Lindstrom which was a very pleasant surprise. I received letters from Louie, Harry, Marcelle and Miss Flo Banks this evening. It's funny how you can get more out of a letter after you have met the writer and have gotten to know them. For instance, Louie's letter this evening I could imagine just how she would say the things she had written and thus enjoyed the letter that much more.

The alert sounded while I was at the show but the "all clear" went about 11:00P.M. The alert just went again a few minutes ago making it two tonight. There is a very low ceiling tonight and it's raining and drizzling miserably. I don't envy the flyers this night.

APR. 20, SUN.

No parades today so wrote letters to Louie and Harry, then copied wireless notes and diagrams for six hours. Feeling tired tonight. Reg came in for awhile this evening; they are turning over B.H. signalling to R.C.C.S. tomorrow. I put my name in for night school for wireless, electricity, short hand, typing and mathematics. I have lots of mail to answer yet and will likely have more tomorrow night. Am feeling intensely dissatisfied with myself tonight. No "alert" as yet; perhaps later.

APR. 21, MON.

I had a busy day checking over phone equipment and finally discovered the secret of renovating worn or seemingly worn out D III field sets.

I received letters from Nellie and Captain Brian Hall of Quebec and enjoyed perusing the contents of both.

I did not seem able to settle down to studying, writing letters or copying notes this evening so Reg, who has returned from duty at Brigade, and I went to see a couple of shows at the Rex Theater. We had lunch at the Toc H club afterwards and got back to camp around 10:30. Although the water was ice cold I had a shower and am ready for bed now. I wonder if Bets and Ada will answer the letters I sent. My letter writing is piling up on me and I will have to start soon and clear it up. I feel disgusted again tonight.

APR. 22, TUES.

Still checking instruments this morning but managed to find time to copy a few more radio notes in between times. I wrote a letter to my Quebec friend at noon today and immediately after dinner paraded Peters before the paymaster. I was notified, this afternoon, to report for firing the anti-tank rifle tomorrow, quite likely another postponement will appear.

Reg and I were supposed to help the manager of the Garrison Theater buy a second hand radio. I was to supply the technical advise and Reg was to try and bring the price down. We went to the gentleman's quarters and he said the set had been sold but he appreciated our good intentions so served us with refreshments and gave us two of the best seats in the house for the evening's performance called "The Ghost Train," a very good three act play. Ignorant wise cracks from the audience nearly ruined the show.

I started a letter to Bobbie tonight but had to discontinue and clean the anti-tank rifle for tomorrow's activities. The "alert" sounded about ten o'clock, followed by two fairly heavy explosions about two miles away, possibly four. There is a rumour going around that 150 paratroops landed in the Downs last night. The rumour was discredited. Sgt. Major Good and a corporal were killed in London Saturday night. Clare Archer was promoted to Transport Sergeant today. He is a good man at convoy work.

APR. 23, WED.

At 8:30 this morning I was sitting in a jolting, bouncing truck with an Anti Tank Rifle in my hand on the way to the ranges. We fired three shots apiece making a good score despite the numerous handicaps. This afternoon was sports day so I wrote a number of letters to people back home. I must get that one away to Louie soon or I will have her pinning my ears back. Wrote letters again tonight and almost finished a letter to Bobbie.

I may have trouble tomorrow explaining why I didn't parade for supper. It's not worrying me very much although I may lose this stripe over it.

The "alert" sounded about 9:30 with the "all clear" following about an hour later.

APR. 24, THURS

I spent the morning thoroughly checking an exchange that has been causing plenty of trouble. I think it will work satisfactorily now. Sgt. Rankine , Peters and I spent a good two hours drawing plans for our stores truck and I believe when we get it fixed the way we want it, it will be a great improvement to the old method of packing.

I received a letter from Nellie this evening, in which she says she received a letter from the R.C.A.F. asking me to report to the nearest recruiting center for enlistment as radio expert or something. They are just about 16 months too late. There are hundreds of men, who tried to join the Air Force at the beginning of the war and were told there was no room for them and who are capable of doing much better work there. Now the Air Force is crying for trained and partially trained radio men.

APR. 25, FRI.

We got up at 0500, breakfast at 0600 and we were on our way by 0700. We travelled by truck convoy through Fleet, Camberley and Odiham, a 23 mile circle and finally reached the scene of the day's forthcoming operation which was only three miles from camp by straight line. Why we took the round about route is still unknown to most of us.

Soon after debarking everyone was in position, including the three units that were attacking us. Our communication was set up in quick order and was so efficient any officer in the forward positions could talk to anyone in England and it was no freak or accident. A signalling officer, acting in the capacity of judge, enjoyed himself thoroughly by cutting our wires every chance he got, but our linemen were right on the job to fix it each time. When the day's activity was finished he said it was the best show of signalling he has seen for some time. The platoon is also regarded as the best trained and proficient signal platoon in the division, which means a lot.

The main idea of the scheme was a strategic withdrawal by the Camerons from a larger mechanized force but when the time came for the withdrawal the Camerons had taken so many "prisoners" the enemy didn't have enough force to attack. The last message to come over the lines was, "Enemy seen retiring in column of route." Hunger finally forced us to withdraw back to "B" Echelon where we had supper at 9:30P.M. We got back into camp at 11:30P.M. and hit the hay immediately.

Dear Nelle:

So ends the second book of my diary. If anything, it's worse than the first one and although I have tried to make it as interesting as I could, I am afraid it fell far short of my expectations. Maybe the next one will be better; I most certainly hope to have more material to write about.

The writing is terrible as some entries were written on speeding trains, heaving boats and other awkward positions. Adios, good luck and lots of Love, Fred.

FRED LODGE DIARY
April 26, 1941 to August 14, 1941

Book No. 3

Daily Diary: F. T. Lodge H19859.
Camerons of Canada (C.A.S.F.)

Please mail to:
Miss N. Lodge
Box 165
Kenora, Ontario,
Canada

APR. 26, SAT.

Peters and I got up just in time for breakfast this morning. Ordered a truck and took Crosse with me out to the scene of our sham battle exercises, yesterday, to retrieve all our cable that we were forced to leave there. Learned that the S.S.R. (*South Saskatchewan Regiment*) had bundled it up into tangled heaps and delivered it to our Quartermaster.

Came back around 11:00AM and found a fatigue party making tea when they should have been mopping the floor. The tea sure tasted good and it hit the spot. The floor wasn't very dirty anyway. Spent the afternoon reading over the preceding book of this diary. Painted numbers on two D5's and a Fullerphone this evening. Received another letter from Marcelle. I started a letter to Nelle and wrote until after eleven, then went and had a shower. Getting late, maybe it's early, fifteen to one.

APR. 27, SUN.

Church parade this morning with the usual procedure despite the fact that we had a new minister. I finished a letter to Marcelle and one to Nelle today job well done because both of them rate lengthy letters. I received a very good letter from Rose today and apparently my letter to Nelle in which I described my five days in London has travelled quite a long way. If they keep on shooting those compliments for my letters across at me I'll get so swell-headed I won't be able to write a decent letter. Perhaps I explain things better than I thought I had, but I can't remember it being anything out of the ordinary.

I enjoyed writing to Marc this evening even though the result was not anywhere near what I wanted it to be. I wonder what is going to happen in the coming three or four years. Will I be in as good shape as when I came over or will I go home a physical wreck; will I go home at all??? Will I be able to find work if I do go home, will Marc be there and the rest of the folks? Foolish things to ask because no one knows the answers, but there is no harm in wondering or is there? It's time for bed; will probably be back to normal in the morning. The future doesn't look so bright disregarding the war angle; probably another post-war depression.

APR. 28, MON.

Engaged with the usual day's activities that of checking and repairing telephone equipment. Regardless of how many instruments I check, there is always one or the other going haywire. I have fifteen signalling lamps, 18 electric torches, eight D5's, 2 Fullerphones, 2 exchanges and 6 D3's to take care of. Soon I will have from 6 to 10 wireless sets (combined receivers and transmitters) to keep in shape as well, so I am looking forward to a busy time. Five o'clock is going to be my quitting time unless it's a dire emergency. Quite a few of the boys came in for coffee this evening and we had a little difficulty finding enough cups. They stayed until almost midnight and the pros and cons of the war situation and other subjects was discussed to great length.

APR. 29, TUES.

Spent another full morning checking and adjusting No. 2 exchange. The darn thing seems unusually sensitive and temperamental. I will have to readjust it again tomorrow. Pay parade today and I received £2 10s.

Finished a letter to Janet and started another to Marcelle. I saw Andy Miller's name mentioned in the Daily Mirror yesterday and I am sending the clipping home. I may go to London this weekend but can't make up my mind. We were informed today that we won't be going on this three-day marching scheme which starts tomorrow. Also informed that I may have to learn to ride a motorcycle. It's eleven forty-five so will have to close shop for the night.

APR. 30, WED.

The battalion started the three-day route march minus Headquarters Company. The four linemen, Peters and I cleaned the Signal Stores building this morning and they made a fairly good job of it. Mr. Kent came in this noon and seemed very enthusiastic about the No. 18 wireless transceiver we are getting soon. He said he would try and get me on a course on maintenance. Four new Fullerphones came in this afternoon to the Quartermaster's and I guess we will have to draw them in the morning.

Reg and I went downtown for supper at the TOC H Club then wandered down Queen's Hotel way. We had quite a talk with the owner of a hardware store. We were inquiring about the price of second-hand bikes. We got back to camp around 8:30 and we both settled down to writing letters. That is how we ended up the evening. It has developed into a contest between Reg and I as to who will do the treating. I lost tonight so Reg paid for the supper. That sounds foolish but it's the truth so-help-me. I finished a letter to Marcelle tonight. I received a letter from Ivy today and there is something about it that I don't like. She sounds like she is afraid I'll come down again.

MAY 1, THURS.

"M" section of the R.C.C.S. called today to check and repair telephone equipment and it so happened that we had just received the four new Fullerphones, two of which were defective so they at least had something to repair. They will be coming around once a month from now on as it's a new idea they are working on.

Reg and I went to see a show called "A Little Bit of Heaven" at the Rex this evening then had a lunch at the Wigwam Hut. We had to wait twenty-five minutes for a cup of coffee. They, like the TOC "H" Club cater to the "Limeys" and a Canadian hasn't much of a look-in. We got into camp at about ten-thirty and I studied for an hour before going to bed. It's getting late (12:15).

MAY 2, FRI.

I had a busy day today, fixing equipment that "M" section had repaired yesterday (that word should be "impaired"). Also had a chance of going to the R.C.O.C. (Royal Canadian Ordinance Corps) as repairman but decided to stay put and try for the Air Force later. Reg and Harry Guedesse came down this evening to write letters but we discussed the war so much we did not achieve a great deal. I managed to make a good start on a letter to Rose. Reg wants to go to Aldershot or Guildford tomorrow so that is where we will probably finish up tomorrow, either one of the two places. It's 11:15 and time I was turning in.

MAY 3, SAT.

I spent the morning repairing an exchange that was supposed to have been checked by the R.C.C.S. the day before yesterday. Reg and I went to Aldershot this afternoon and browsed around the shops when we weren't forcing our way through the dense street crowd. Saw a swell stationery case that would have made a swell birthday gift for Marcelle but it was a little beyond my means. We came back early and wrote letters all evening. I received a telephone call about 10:30 to the effect that Peters was on his way home in a very inebriated condition but I finally went to bed after waiting until 12:30 for him to come in. He was tight alright but he did not cause unusual trouble.

MAY 4, SUN.

Time went ahead an hour at midnight last night and we almost missed church parade. Managed to do some laundry early this afternoon. Reg and I then went out for a walk and ended up at the Rex where we saw "I Stole a Million" starring George Raft. We came out and ran into Sgt.'s Richardson and Rankine so we walked along together. Rankine phoned a friend and made arrangements for three girls so we tossed coins to see who would be the one to miss out. I finally won so I came back to camp. I do not like blind dates, you never know what kind of girl you are getting.

MAY 5, MON.

Maintenance on Fullerphones all day. I was notified that the mathematics class started this evening at the Farnborough Technical College and we, (Peters, Forsythe and myself) were requested to attend. The school itself is a modern constructed affair which reminded me very much of "patio" style of architecture. We all, (beginners and experienced men alike) were placed in classes and the job of deciding where to start took an hour. We start from the beginning. We were leaving on our bikes after the cessation of the class and Forsythe came out of the gate on the right hand side. It would have been all right if an elderly gentleman had not been passing at the time. The old gent became rattled, ran into the curb and fell off of his bike. He suffered no injuries but he ripped his trousers in the accident which failed to help his already badly disrupted dignity. A group of Canadians standing in the school yard gave vent to their amusement in no uncertain terms which failed completely to help in pacifying the aged irate cyclist. I had gone about 100 feet before I could stop and happened to be a few feet from a group of young people who had gathered to watch the incident. A remark one of them made,

made me lose my temper completely. The remark was, "those Canadians get on my nerves, really they do." I got sore and I am afraid gave them an earful, anyway they seemed too surprised to answer back. Perhaps I didn't mean all I said but it was the first time I have lost my temper completely for some time.

MAY 6, TUES.

I was occupied all day with the usual daily maintenance work which I have mentioned all too often already. We received word today that we were starting another scheme tomorrow night late.

Received a letter by airmail from Miss Banks in Quebec. It was the first letter to come back since I started my numbering system. It was number A7 in answer to L7 sent on March 15. It took a little less than two weeks to reach here from the day of mailing until I was reading it. The postage was 30¢ and it travelled by "Clipper" (there is some controversy regarding the exact route it travelled, some say via USA to Lisbon to England and some say they come across on ferried bombers, which is quite likely.) Ken is teaching me the rudiments of mathematics and I should have a fair idea of it by next Monday.

MAY 7, WED.

I had to inspect a faulty G.P.O. telephone this afternoon and found a broken wire in the microphone but I left the actual repairs to the G.P.O. service man when he comes around. I experienced my initial endeavor of riding a motorcycle this afternoon and found it easier than I first thought it would be. We spent the afternoon preparing for the scheme we are starting at 0100 hours tomorrow. We received the cupboards for the store truck and believe they will measure up to all our expectations.

For some unexplainable reason I have been chosen to formulate a suitable epistle to Judy Garland asking her if she would consider being the platoon's official Luck Bringer. The genuine reason is somewhat vague and obscure and I am a little hesitant to start the letter; it would probably not go any farther than her secretary.

MAY 8, THURS.

We left camp on schedule (0100) this morning and travelled for the few remaining dark hours, and everything went along well to a certain point. We travelled through Ashville, through Bagshot Lea, along the Farnum Bypass, over the Hampton Common, Crooksburg Common to the town Elstead. Here we ran into difficulty while entering a place called Pot Common. The draw back was in the form of a long steep and exceedingly sandy hill and it was necessary for one truck at a time to climb the ascent. All went well until it came for our turn to make the effort but for some reason the R.S.M. held us back while six carriers went ahead. We were very fortunate to have a four wheel drive, 1 ½ ton truck and we experienced very little difficulty at climbing the hill. Our trouble started when we reached the top and found ourselves at a junction in the excuse for a road. We had the choice of turning to the left or to the right and according to the tracks on both branches we decided the right way was the right fork, so we proceeded along this road which developed into a steep incline, comparable to the incline we had just climbed. For two miles we kept forging ahead through axle deep sand, passing a small truck here and there, hopelessly stalled in the deep loose sand. No one we encountered seemed to know where the main column had gone. We were not entirely on our own in our dilemma as Dispatch Rider Grant was chugging right along beside us on his motorcycle.

Finally we were stopped by "B" Company who were resting along the side of the road, and they were unable to supply the necessary information, that of the whereabouts of Battalion Headquarters. After a hasty conference we decided that further progress in our present direction was useless and settled down to wait until dawn. Soon we were very much surprised to hear other trucks pulling up behind us and we soon learned that the remaining half of the convoy behind us had followed us down into the heart of Pot Common. We all settled down to wait for the dawn to throw some light on the subject.

At the crack of dawn Sgt. Major Lane appeared out of nowhere to guide us to the H.Q. site. We made a complete right turn and were soon travers-ing Elstead Common through to the golf course situated north of Hankley Common. We soon arrived at Battalion Headquarters and signals soon were busily engaged in establishing communication. After that had been completed to everyone's satisfaction, we had breakfast.

I had very little else to do for the rest of the day but keep my eye on the store truck and its contents. It was a cold bitter day and it was no pleasure to hang around doing nothing. Things remained at a stand-still until eleven in the evening when the real reason for the scheme got underway. The order came to withdraw and in half an hour we had all the wire wound up and in the truck along with the rest of the equipment. We had to wait until one next morning before the actual withdrawal was to start so we waited around for that length of time. While we were waiting we were treated to the experience of seeing a hot anti-air barrage in action from a distance.

MAY 9, FRI.

We started the actual withdrawal at 0110 hours by traversing the deep sandy rutted road back to the main highway where we decreased our speed to a marching pace in order to stay behind the troops. The driver and I were very sleepy as we had not slept a wink since Wednesday morning and the heat of the cab made us very drowsy. The slow pace did not help very much to dispel the drowsiness. I had to stay awake to keep the driver awake. Frequently we would both dose off and would wake up with a start to find the truck grazing the hedge alongside of the road. It took us five hours to travel fifteen miles then we came to "B" Echelon where we had breakfast. We were on our way again soon after, but at a much faster pace and we soon arrived in camp at about 10 am. Needless to say, we spent the rest of the day sleeping.

MAY 10, SAT.

Interior economy this morning. A few of us including Reg and Crosse attended the first session of the electrical course held at Guildford Technical College and by the sample of the teaching it promises to be a very good course. The only disadvantage of the whole thing is it is held every Saturday afternoon.

MAY 11, SUN. MOTHERS' DAY

Only memories prevail for me today. Memories of one person that are held all the more precious because they are so few and erratic. Memories of another mother that are vivid and numerous and almost as precious. We had church parade this morning and I spent the afternoon writing letters and studying, then slept from five pm until 8. Prepared the usual nightly lunch for two dozen ravenous signallers that gather in our room each night.

MON. MAY 12

Sports parade this morning and as per usual didn't indulge in any sports. Amused myself puttering around with an exchange unit. We made some changes in the U.C. 6 line setup this afternoon; mainly putting a Brigade line on the exchange with a Fullerphone superposed on it.

Attended the second class of mathematics this evening but it has developed into a refresher course for fellows who have passed 11th, 12th grades which is not exactly what I need. Perhaps I am ignorant, it's too fast and deep for me. I doubt if I will go back next Monday. We had a little difficulty over bicycles tonight with Lance Corporals Steeds and Mills which I hope can be settled satisfactorily tomorrow. Heard today that Hess, Hitler's right hand man, had been captured in Scotland today. What would Hess be doing over in this country at a time like this? Considerable mystery surrounds the rumors.

MAY 13, TUES.

The Daily Mirror this morning says that Hitler claims that Hess was demented and had committed suicide; other papers claim that he is in custody after landing by parachute in Scotland. The evening papers carried the full story except for his reason for deserting Germany, under the present circumstances. Peters accepted the Regimental Storeman's job which will probably mean two stripes for him. We lose a good storeman, but good luck to him. I don't know who will fill his place here in the signal stores as yet. The abundance of ignorance displayed by certain heads of the signals yesterday and today, pertaining to the installation of certain equipment leads me to believe that I am not as dumb as I thought I was. I just lack the power to express my convictions. A cat can look at a king but he can't argue with him. There are some people that arguing with them is against the powers of a lowly Lance Corporal. However, I have the satisfaction of being able to say, "I told you so" even if I haven't had the chance yet. Reg and I saw a very good vaudeville at the Garrison Theater after which we partook of the nightly late lunch which is now attended by over half of the platoon. I finished a letter to Miss Banks tonight. Mail has not been coming in so good lately, two letters, one from Nelle and the other (airmail) from Miss Banks in the last two batches.

MAY 14, WED.

The order to prepare the stores for a three-day scheme was sprung on me today of all days. Ken started work in the regimental stores this morning which left me practically alone to do the necessary preparing. Ken likes his new job and he will probably go places in it. I had three trouble calls from the kitchen, R.A.P. (Regimental Aid Post) and signal office this afternoon. The bell hammer was broken off the armature in the phone from the kitchen. There was no one around to answer the R.A.P. phone and the Fullerphone at the signal office only required adjusting. By four o'clock I was in a vicious frame of mind but was here to load the stores and I received four letters and a parcel of magazines and papers from Canada, including a Miner and News which I think is Bobbie's doings. I have received four copies now and they are pretty welcome. The mail came just in time as I was beginning to think that all my mail had been lost or the folks at home had gone on strike. I received letters from Nelle, Bobbie, Vera and Olga (Mrs. Gibson), the Miner from Bobbie since the other forms of literature (*were*) from Miss Banks. I have been worrying about the safety of the parcel that Miss Banks says she has sent but I completely neglected to consider that the letter came by airmail and there is no use expecting the parcel until the 22nd of this month at least.

MAY 15, THURS.

We hung around until after 0200 hours (AM) then we were informed that we would have breakfast in camp at 4:30 and leave at 5:30. Nearly everyone divested themselves of their equipment and prepared to obtain a couple of hours sleep before breakfast. I went down to the signal office where it was warm as my blankets and coat were packed away in the stores truck. I spent the two hours reading a very descriptive True Story to pass the time away. We had a breakfast consisting of pancakes with syrup (a little watery) and tea, then we were under way. We stopped in front of the Battalion orderly room and Mr. McMannis our spare signalling officer, who can't read Morse

(Code) yet, came along and kicked me out of my warm place in the cab where I usually ride so I had to climb in the back with the line men. My opinion of officers by that time was hovering around zero and threatening to take an additional plunge. I slept, or rather laid, between Big Fisher from Keewatin and Cormack from Winnipeg.

After leaving Farnborough we passed through Wychette, then Ashwald; over the Hog Back, through Tangham to Seale. We skirted Crooksbury Common and soon were traversing the streets of Elstead, the same town that we passed through on our last scheme. After leaving Elstead behind we came to Milford then across Whitley Common to a place called Thursley. We passed through the Devil's Punchbowl to Hindhead. Leaving Hindhead we passed through or close by to Grayshot to Arford. At this point our course became a trifle complicated but we finally ended up somewhere around Headley, quite close I think if not on Headley Mill Farm.

We had communication set up before breakfast and then everything settled down for our short stay at that particular spot. It proved to be an ideal site for a camp at least from the men's point of view as there were a couple of canteens right handy and one station was close or on Sir Britain's estate. He happened to be there in person and treated the boys to refreshments at the same time inviting them to make use of a fully equipped trailer if they were going to stay all night. Tommy Suttleham had no idea as to who his benefactor was and persisted in calling him "Mac." However, they were never destined to accept the hospitality of the titled gentleman as we received the order to move around three in the afternoon. We had to wait for two or three hours so some of the boys made full use of a wet canteen located about a hundred yards down the road. We finally continued on our way about six or seven in the evening, possibly later. After an hour's travel we came to a high hill where we saw something I never expected to see over here during wartime. I took it to be a revolving aircraft beacon; a very bright light that kept flashing its brilliancy around in a huge circle at ground level. The light itself was broken up into a long flash, a short one, another long one and another short so that every time it flashed by it formed the letter "e." We stayed by the light for nearly an hour so we had ample opportunity to speculate on the reason for the contraption. I slept the rest of the time until we stopped at our next campsite at four in the morning.

MAY 16, FRI.

We had barely stopped rolling when the fellows clambered around the back of the truck for their blankets and one couldn't blame them as it was a bitter cold morning. Soon everyone was curled up getting a couple of hours sleep except the cooks who had to prepare the breakfast. Fisher and I made a bed out of the assortment of packs and laid on them fully clothed as we could see no object in unrolling our blankets for a two hour sleep. It proved a little too cold so I roused myself to walk around until daylight. We had breakfast then Sgt. Rankine and about five others started an argument over the possibilities of the Sgt. lighting a campfire with only one match. He did it all right, using the Boy Scout method. After that we kept the fire going and argued about practically everything we could think of from fishing to the theory of flight until we all fell asleep. We woke up in time for lunch at ten o'clock (AM) and by eleven we were on our way home. To describe the country we passed through adequately is beyond my capabilities except that it was very interesting and there was plenty of it. We arrived back in camp at 4:15pm and soon had supper under our belts. We were too tired to go any place so contented ourselves with just going to bed.

MAY 17, SAT.

We made some big changes on the telephone exchange system and as far as I am concerned very unsatisfactory ones this morning, but have an idea that when put into operation may eliminate most of the disadvantages now apparent. Reg and I stayed in Guildford after the class this afternoon and finally decided that it is just as bad if not worse than Aldershot. We came home early and had supper at the Highway Cafe in Farnborough, after which we sat on a bench by the Clock Tower and watched the crowd and traffic go by. We saw the remains of a German plane go by on a truck and it stopped down the street a ways. It turned out to be the plane that Hess made his comment raising flight in. Despite being charred by fire the Swastika was very plain on the rudder. I obtained a small piece of the covering as a souvenir.

(Fred (second from right) & friends)

MAY 18, SUN.

The whole company had its picture taken this morning instead of going to church. Reg and I went to the Rex this evening after I had spent four hours fixing the platoon's radio. We had supper at the Highway Cafe again then came back to camp where I found a carton of Sweet Caps waiting for me, sent by Nelle. Boy were they welcome and their arrival timely. No other mail. In the last week I have received letters from Jack, two from Nelle, Bobbie, Marcelle, Vera, Mrs. Gibson and from a stranger, Miss Iris Lawrence of Winnipeg. She sent me a card at Christmas on behalf of the Insurance Company so I wrote and thanked her for it. She answered my letter with a very good letter in reply, in which she says that she is sending a parcel. She is a grand letter writing and it's a pleasure to read her handwriting.

MAY 19, MON.

Hooked up two exchanges in parallel this morning and it works okay with a few revisions here and there. The G.P.O. squad came in this morning to lay a subterranean cable which will dispose of a number of poles that we have our lines on. So I have to get a party working tomorrow and change the wires from the poles to the buildings. I finally got started on a letter to Miss Iris Lawrence and wrote until 12:30AM. I will have to finish it tomorrow. I am all alone in the hut as Ken has moved out and the new storeman, Bill Garlick doesn't move in until tomorrow. Sent a telegram to Marcelle today for her birthday.

MAY 20, TUES.

Marcelle's birthday. I hope the telegram reaches her in time. If I remember correctly she is twenty-five today. Comack, Day, Cormack and I managed to complete the line work before 4:30 this afternoon and it proved to be quite a job. Received orders this afternoon that all D3 telephone sets, anti-tank muzzle covers, oil cans and mess tin covers had to be turned in to the Quartermaster. We are going to miss those D3's as they were used in our barrack communication scheme. Reg and I had supper at the TOC H. Club, then went to the Rex and saw Sabu in "The Thief of Baghdad" then had a feed of fish and chips afterwards. Practically certain that Reg will be getting another stripe soon despite certain people who think otherwise, mainly two or three other N.C.O.'s. I would like to be able to read a certain person's mind when he does get it.

MAY 21, WED.

I made a big mistake in yesterday's entry; first of all I had the days and dates mixed up and secondly it's Marcelle's birthday today. The telegram will have plenty of time to get there.

MAY 22, THURS.

Completed the dispersal area telephone this morning thus completing three miles of cabling. I received the parcel from Iris Lawrence and must admit she certainly knows how to pack them. Started trouble shooting on the Rifle Company's line this afternoon but failed completely to locate the trouble. Answered Marcelle's letter tonight and will probably get it away tomorrow. Reg and I went down to the NAAFI around nine this evening for the usual bite to eat then dropped into the exchange room to investigate a report on exchange trouble. Resulted in my working until one in the morning before

I had it repaired. A few fellows had been fooling around it all day and quite likely shorted something which caused excessive drain on the batteries.

MAY 23, FRI.
Slept in this morning which resulted in our missing breakfast. We had a rush call to load all stores onto a truck and transport them in quick time to the dispersal area in a practice air raid precautionary measure. I spent the morning and afternoon looking for the defect in the company's lines and finally cured the complaint by cutting out unused wires and rearranging the entire line. It works okay now. I received a parcel from Nelle today containing all the things I asked for; files, razor blades and writing paper, as well as chocolate bars. There is quite a difference between Canadian and English chocolate. I enjoyed a real hot shower this evening; it's the first time in two weeks that there was hot water available. I received letters from Olga (Mrs. Gibson), Jack, Nelle and a few more.

MAY 24, SAT.
Interior economics this morning so did little else but listen to a three-hour argument between Big Fisher of Keewatin and Sgt. Rankine on professional weightlifting. Received letters from Marc, Bobbie, Bezzie, Doc, etc. Doc has received a commission now and is a Pilot Officer at Trenton, Ontario. They have made an instructor out of him which means he won't be coming over. We attended the electrical class again this afternoon and although the lectures are on familiar stuff, they serve to clear up certain points that I was a little hazy on. I received two Miners and a parcel of papers which were sent by Miss Banks in Quebec. I am afraid the other parcel she sent containing the flash light and maple sugar has been lost. Also received another letter from Marcelle this evening. Reg and I went to see "Wings of the Navy" at the Garrison Theater this evening and the aviation picture and Doc's letters made us feel like kicking ourselves for not joining the air force. There isn't much chance of transferring now.

MAY 25, SUN.
No parades for me this morning as most of the company are at the ranges re-firing their rifle qualifications, so I wrote letters until noon. Reg, Tommy

Bell, Stewie and myself went to the Rex to see the Dead End Kids in "On Dress Parade" this afternoon and enjoyed it a lot despite the fact that I had seen it before. We left camp at 2 in the afternoon and it was after seven when we got back but we had a very good time in a crazy sort of way. I spent the rest of the evening writing letters.

MAY 26, MON.

Nothing unusual happened today, I spent the morning and afternoon working on faulty equipment and the evening in writing letters. I received the parcel from Miss Iris Lawrence and came to the conclusion that she has had plenty of practice at packing them. It sure was a fine job.

MAY 27, TUES.

We had to go through the gas chamber again and found it not too unpleasant. More instrument repairs and more mail. Received the long expected parcel from Miss Banks and it sure was a dandy. It is by far the biggest parcel I have received yet, and it contained another flashlight to replace the other one that was purloined in London. I have received in the last three or four days, two parcels and seventeen letters. Three letters from Nelle (one of them came last week), two from Bobbie (one came last week), two from Marcelle, two from Iris, one from Bezzie, one from Jack, one from Rose, one from Vera, one from Miss Banks, one from Olga, one from dad and the rest from over here. That's quite a lot of mail for one throw and it will take me sometime to answer it all.

MAY 28, WED.

I started the morning off by drawing circuit diagrams of the Fullerphone but Mr. Kent came in and asked me to draw a diagram of the telephone system, including the G.P.O. system here in camp. I managed to finish it before noon. I was supposed to play ball this afternoon but elected to fix the Platoon radio instead. Sgt. Rankine has been offered the Intelligence Sergeant's position and that will mean two promotions for two Lance Jacks, one Corporal and two Privates. I heard on good authority today, that Reg and I will each get another stripe. Sgt. Richardson is leaving on an officer's school soon and Hatch will go to full Sergeant with two more privates getting Lance Jack stripes. Reg is sure of his other stripe but it is a toss-up between Wally Mills and I for the other one. Here's hoping.

MAY 29, THURS.

Some signaling lamps needed repairing and so managed to put in the morning. I am almost certain of getting another promotion soon. We had quite a lot of fun on the miniature rifle range this afternoon where we went to have our rifles zeroed. Mine was already shooting perfect but I managed to confirm my confidence in its accuracy. Wrote letters all evening.

MAY 30, FRI.

The same old stuff for another day; wrote letters until late this evening.

MAY 31, SAT.

Muster parade, M.O.'s inspection and pay parade this morning. The Muster parade did not amount to much and immediately after we were issued with a cup apiece. The M.O. was looking for things unprintable and he did not find the hunting very good; game was scarce. I drew three pounds and as usual, the old problem of how to budget it so that it would stretch over two weeks is still bothering me. We went to school at Guildford this afternoon but the class is getting smaller every Saturday. The fact that it is held on Saturday afternoon may have something to do with it, but I think the stuff that we are taking is becoming a little too complicated for most of the boys who just cannot be bothered using their brains. Reg and I came back to camp and wrote letters.

JUNE 1

The usual church parade this morning which lasted for the usual half hour. Spent the time from ten AM until 2:00 PM writing letters, then Reg and I went into town to the Rex after which we had a lunch at the TOC Club. We didn't feel like coming back to camp so early so we parked ourselves on one of the benches and watched the traffic and people go by. We started back to camp about eight and I sat up until midnight writing letters.

JUNE 2

These Fullerphones and D5's are a nuisance and they are always developing ailments which kept me busy all day. I revised the Fullerphone circuit diagrams which makes thing much more easier to understand. I wrote letters this evening.

JUNE 3

Another Fullerphone to fix first thing this morning, they are getting me down. Mr. Kent and another officer came in this morning and commandeered a D5 to make some experiments with. The idea seemed to be that as soon as anyone tried to use the phone they would unknowingly set off a detonator cap. Just how near they came to being successful I don't know but when the phone was returned, it refused to work. It took me half an hour to get it back into operation again. I spent the rest of the afternoon drawing more diagrams. Then Reg and I went to see a stage show at the Garrison. It was a very good show and afterwards I wrote letters until midnight. A very late hour to get to bed.

JUNE 4, WED.

I learned today that in all probability Sgt. Rankine would refuse the position as Intelligence Sergeant which knocks my expected promotion into a cocked hat. Despite the disappointment at the collapse of my promotional expectations I am very pleased as is a good number of the platoon that he will be remaining with us. There were sports this afternoon and the platoon N.C.O.'s and Officers were to play the men a game of basketball but I had a trouble call from the exchange and it took all afternoon fixing it. I wrote letters until after midnight again tonight. This is getting to be a habit.

JUNE 5, THURS.

We started a two-day first aid course this morning which will have to be abbreviated for it to fit into the short time allotted to it. Reg and I went down to the Rex to see a show and had supper at the TOC H Club as per usual. We are getting to know that place as a Royal Tank Corps hangout. It is always crowded with "Limeys" who never fail to convey the impression that they practically own the place and vulgar Canadians are definitely not welcome although they are tolerated. I wrote letters until midnight again tonight. Rumors are becoming prevalent and as yet there is no real foundation for their existence.

JUNE 6, FRI.

First Aid course all day today. I found out for sure that Sgt. Rankine was definitely not leaving the platoon which naturally eliminates all possibility of my receiving a promotion for quite some time. Sgt. Richardson will be leaving on Monday or Tuesday and it is a foregone conclusion that Reg will step up to Full Corporal. More power to him as he certainly has earned the break.

We received orders this PM that all equipment must be blancoed and dry by Monday. I think there is an inspection by General Odlum sometime this coming week. I at least, made a start at the tedious and unpleasant job by doing my respirator, haversack and sling. Wrote more letters this evening. Bill Garlick, Storeman, came back off leave, lamenting the fact that he had to take full equipment to Glasgow and he was unable to have a good shower for the full nine days. Midnight exactly.

JUNE 7, SAT.

Bill Garlick and I spent the morning cleaning and straightening the stores which had been allowed to go for the last three or four days. We attended electrical class this afternoon and we started into wireless. Reg and I got off at Aldershot on the return trip, where I bought another wireless book, this time on servicing problems. We thought of going to a show but there was a long line before each one and so came back to camp and blancoed our equipment. I wrote letters until midnight.

JUNE 8, SUN.

Church parade today without respirators and steel helmet, the first time we have gone anywhere without these. Reg, Ellison and I went to a show at the Rex, followed by supper at the TOC H Club. It was too nice out to come back to camp so soon so we went for a walk toward North Farnborough Station. It was a very pleasant walk through a very quiet and very pretty neighbourhood. We came back to camp after watching a tennis match between four none-to-good players, and I wrote letters until 11:30PM.

JUNE 9, MON.
Checked over 15 signaling lamps, 1 D5, one exchange and one line. Discovered that there had been an act of sabotage on the dispersal area line; someone had slashed it in six or seven places. I send four linemen out to fix it. I'll have to report the matter to Mr. Kent and let him worry about it. Sports parade was cancelled this afternoon on account of rain. The linemen were unable to get the D.A. line into operation so I will probably have to look it over myself on Wednesday. Started a letter to Marcelle this evening, keeping it on a strictly friendly basis as requested. I agree with her reasons, they are quite sound. I received a letter from Charlotte today as well as one from Nelle and one from Bobbie.

We had to load the stores out on the 1500 pound truck this afternoon, during a heavy rain. We managed to get it all on and still leave room for one man, providing we don't have to load bicycles. I had a talk with Sgt. Rankine this evening, about the talk one hears from certain members of the platoon. It can only be described as subversive and is very dangerous to the morale of the men. One of the worst offenders is a L/cpl. but I don't believe he means most of what he says and doesn't realize the effect it has on the men. Bill said it would have to stop.

JUNE 10, TUES.
We woke up this morning to the rattle of rain on the roof but the contemplated scheme started on schedule with Garlick and I cramped up in the back of the stores truck. It rained all day and the only thing I derived from the day's activities was a cold and a very tired feeling. However, I had enough energy left to scribble a note to Marcelle this evening, then we paid a nightly visit to the "Naffy." It is 10:30 now and I am getting to bed early for once.

JUNE 11, WED.
Interior economy this AM but I managed to check over an exchange before dinner. I was supposed to be on a compulsory sport parade this afternoon

but I missed it somehow so I studied radio theory and watched the various planes flying around. I saw a formation of three "Tomahawks" fly over about 4:15PM. I received a letter from Lil, Aunt Ett's youngest daughter and she wants me to visit them the next time I am in London. I may find the matter of procuring a week's accommodation impossible as I understand that sleeping quarters are scarce since most of the clubs and hostels have closed down. I wrote a letter to Nelle this evening.

Tommy Bell is trying to play Scotch songs on the "crooner" off of a bagpipe and judging from his contortions and very red face, it must be quite a battle to keep sufficient wind entering the instrument. Nevertheless, he is doing a lot better than Grant has done after practicing for a month, but it still sounds terrible. Our paper-man, Mr. Mundy, predicts the end of the war by January, but he says the Canadians will be kept here for a good twelve months after that, because of the shortage of troop ships.

JUNE 12, THURS.

I've decided to try fixing the Dispersal Area line myself this morning; it had previously been cut in six or seven places, presumably by an irate farmer who had lodged a complaint to the Adjutant. I don't think his story of wrecked fences which allowed his best cow to stray onto the highway and to be struck by a truck, was accepted by the military authorities.

I worked all morning trying to find the apparent short then changed 200 yards of bad cable but still the trouble persists. Managed to finish a big laundry this evening and wrote a letter to Bobbie and started another one to Charlotte. I found one shilling and six pence that I didn't know I had and I decided that eats were more desirable than smokes. Tomorrow is payday so I won't be without tobacco very long. There is a nice little controversy raging over who is going to get the next paid stripe when Reg goes up. It looks impossible.

JUNE 13, FRI.

This is the third Friday the thirteenth since I enlisted eighteen months and ten days ago. We left Quebec for Halifax on December 13th, a Friday. Crosse and I spent the entire day painstakingly checking the Area line, using a line

D5 set to call back to the exchange every fifty feet or so. The first of source of trouble we located had fifty feet of line cut out which we soon replaced. The next place had twenty-five feet of line cut out; after that had been replaced the line was in operation again. It may have been done by some farmer wanting wire, but it looked like the work of a man who has had plenty of practice at cutting lines.

We were paid this afternoon and I drew three pounds then lent Reg £1 10s as he is going on leave on Monday. I finished a letter to Charlotte today; then Reg and I went to the Garrison to see a show called, "The Amazing Mr. Williams." I spent from ten o'clock to midnight writing letters.

JUNE 14, SAT.

The truck came around for loading at 10 this morning. We had both cupboards on and loaded when another truck pulled up and told us that we were to have two trucks, which pleased us no end because it is a difficult task to get all the stores on one truck and still leave enough room for two men. So we unloaded one of the cupboards onto the other truck and everything looked fine. Mr. Kent and Transport Sgt. Archer (some people in Kenora might remember him) came along on motorcycles and said one of the other trucks had been disabled and we could only have one truck, which necessitated changing all the equipment from the second truck back to the first. The boys and myself were plenty mad as the cupboard is plenty heavy and it's no fun lifting it around. Finally the stores were loaded and as we are not sure when we start on the scheme and my tools and service equipment is packed away on the truck there is very little I can do this afternoon.

I understand that this is going to be one of the biggest schemes ever attempted, embracing tank corps, medical corps, two squadrons of airplanes and three or four army corps, including all Canadians. As we are the reserve battalion in the reserve brigade which is the reserve brigade in the reserve division of reserve army corps, the chances are we may not leave camp. This won't make us mad as it looks very much like we are going to have our regular scheme rain. We received orders to move at 8:30PM and from then on it was a mad rush to collect all the phones and pack the last minute articles on the truck. Finally we began to roll around nine o'clock but just cleared the gates when we stopped and parked for fifty minutes. I discovered I had a green driver on our truck and the job of reading the route card fell to me. We could only travel fifteen minutes out of the hour and for the remaining forty-five we just parked.

Finally it was decided that the Battalion HQ trucks, including the signals, would forge ahead and set up Battalion Headquarters. So we soon found ourselves roaring along dark winding roads, without lights sometimes doing forty-five and fifty miles an hour, which soon brought us to the site of our overnight camp. I had to wake up Garlick, who had fallen asleep in the back of the truck so that the boys could get their blankets and packs. It wasn't long before quietness reigned over our wheeled community. The truck driver and I decided to sleep in the cramped quarters of the cab as it was nice and warm from the heat of the engine.

JUNE 15, SUN.

The cab was warm for a while but it proved too cramped for comfortable sleeping and after the cold crept in I was glad to see Reveille roll around. I saw the dawn and heard numerous birds of every description warbling their own little greeting to the new day. We had breakfast then proceeded to look around at our surroundings. For once, they had chosen a very pleasant spot for our camp. Trees are plentiful and there are a few small clearings. There are two huge chestnut trees which has been the object of my curiosity since early this morning, so I decided to take a closer look at them. The smaller of the two and the nearest was about fourteen feet in circumference and had plenty of initials and dates carved into its aged bark. There was a large "A" with 1811 under it. Then a large B with 1885 beside it; AC with 1890; RCL & 1893; then WEK with 1901. There are a few more new ones on the ancient trunk such as FT 1941. The bigger of the two trees measured about 18 feet in circumference and we estimated the span of the branches as close to 80 or 90 feet, from the tip of one branch to the tip of the corresponding branch on the opposite side.

It was cloudy this morning and as there seemed very little doing we slept most of the time. A "Limey" General paid our camp a visit and our officers had a chance to tell him how much they thought they knew. By 2:00PM the clouds were breaking up nicely and the increasing appearances of the sun foretold of the heat to come. I watched a kitchen staff of an artillery unit unloading bread and wondered if our food is handled the same way. They were unloading the bread from a ration truck; the man down on the ground was catching the loaves as they were tossed out by twos, at the same counting them as he tossed them onto a piece of none-too-clean canvas. Occasionally he would miss a toss and the bread would land by his feet so he merely kicked it onto the pile. Soon the canvas was covered and piled high with round loaves of bread so he started throwing them onto a camouflage net which is noted for its ability to collect dust and oil. Evidently a Lance Corporal had noticed the man's disregard for cleanliness and proceeded to rectify the situation.

By 2:30 the sun was out full strength so I slept beneath the smaller of the two chestnut trees, until Fisher woke me up to ask me if I wanted a cup of tea as the YMCA tea wagon was dishing out free beverage and biscuits. The climate is very unpredictable, first it was cool, then everyone was moving out of the sun to the cooler shade of the trees. I feel a lot better after a shave and wash down at the nearby small but cool brook. At 6:30 A Company returned after taking part in the actual fighting of the scheme since early this morning. They claim to have captured a whole Brigade of "enemy" parachutists. There is a rumor that the scheme may last until Wednesday. Soon after all our supporting units such as artillery, communication trucks and anti-tank regiment were detached from us and we stood by waiting for orders to move. It was rumored that we were going to reinforce 4th and 5th Brigade. The boys had an attempt at a sing-song which did not turn out very good as they all didn't know songs they were trying to sing.

JUNE 16, MON.

The troop carrying vehicles turned up at 3:00AM, arousing me out of a nap which I was taking in the cab of the stores truck. It wasn't long before we were on our way, at least, until we got to Milford, where we had a long stop. The reason for the delay became apparent when we traveled around the nearest block in Milford, back to the outgoing road again, then began passing our own vehicles going in the opposite direction. Our consternation was complete when we pulled into the spot we had just left and we parked the truck under the same old tree. I had quite a time convincing Mr. McManus and Charlie Longley that we hadn't gone anywhere but that we were back in the same old campsite. Showing Charlie my initials I had carved on the tree failed to convince him so I had to show him where he slept the night before. We got two hours sleep and had breakfast at 7:00AM then slept until noon. I slept for a while this afternoon until I woke up and found myself in the sun and feeling like a stuffed turkey being baked in a very hot oven. God, how it can get hot over here. I had quite a confab with the operator of the wireless truck on Amateur Short wave radio operation, and he remembered hearing VE3ADP, Bert Nilson's station.

We had a good sing song this evening which lasted from 8:00PM until midnight. An elderly lady, a Bristol evacuee, came up and asked us to sing the Maple Leaf. We ended the sing song with Oh Canada.

JUNE 17, TUES.
Reveille came at 7:00AM followed very closely by breakfast. Sgt. Rankine and I went down to the brook for a shave and wash. It is another clear day and hot as blazes.

The boys discovered that there were some land girls on a nearby farm so there was a stream of men going for a walk with the expressed purpose of buying fresh milk. Played cards nearly all afternoon then received orders to have the stores ready by 5:30PM. We had a rush supper and pulled out for camp on schedule arriving here soon after six. After we had unloaded the truck Forsythe and I reinstalled the exchange and phones around camp. I took a good hot shower in the Battalion HQ shower room.

JUNE 18, WED.
We had a late Reveille this morning consequently the morning parades were shortened to such an extent that we had interior economy. I had quite a time trying to keep the boys on the job here in the stores, cleaning windows and mopping the floors. They managed to achieve some order of cleanliness but the windows turned out much dirtier than when they started. It was a very hot day so I let them go.

It was a sports day today and I was in the mood for a good game of softball but a complaint regarding the exchange prevented me from taking part in the game. I had to change the entire exchange to rectify the fault which took me until four o'clock. At five o'clock the engineers made a mess of three lines, including the one to Brigade by running around camp with a raised derrick, which means another full day of troubleshooting and line repair work.

I went down to the signal office to report the matter to Sgt. Rankine and found him talking to a girl on the phone. He informed the young lady that I was an Indian and asked her if she wanted to speak to me. Our conversation was punctuated by an abundance of giggles and expressions of disbelief. She informed me that her father was an Indian also, then in answer to her question I told her that I was a member of the Ojibway tribe. Sgt. Rankine wanted me to go on a swimming date with them next Saturday as she had a girlfriend who needed an escort. I refused mainly because I do not like blind dates and I am a very poor swimmer. I tried to be helpful by suggesting other men better talented for the job but they all have other plans for Saturday. I wrote a letter to Nelle tonight.

JUNE 19, THURS.

Forsythe, Crosse and myself completed most of the repairs on the broken lines this morning so I sent Forsythe out on the Area Line this afternoon and Crosse had to take his motorcycle test this afternoon which left me by myself to complete the work on the camp lines. I worked from two o'clock until five thirty, consequently I missed my supper and the truck to Guildford where we were supposed to have last Saturday's radio instruction but I managed to get the mess untangled. Forsythe came back without finding the trouble in the Area Line, Crosse passed his test. About 6:30PM the exchange man sent up word that he couldn't get through to the kitchen and thought that the bell on the phone wasn't ringing. I ran into R.Q.M.S. McCammon at the kitchen door sweating and fuming because the night cook was nowhere around. He informed me that the phone was ringing okay, but there was no one there to answer it and by the gleam in his eye and his choice of cuss words the missing cook was going to get his ears burnt off.

Sgt. Rankine again brought up the question of my going on a swimming date with "Sandy's girlfriend" but I wouldn't commit myself. I received a surprise today in the form of a letter from Auntie Pat (Fenn) who is living at Southend-on-Sea. She said her daughter Doris is living here in Farnborough at Woodland's Grove. I have often thought it would be nice to have relations close by. I will have to hunt her up on Saturday. I told the Sgt. that that was what I was going to do on Saturday, but he said I could go practical map reading tomorrow afternoon and find her. Doris is the sister of Vi whom Bill used to go with a lot in the last war and who was working in Northern France at the time of that country's capitulation and has not been heard of since. Aunt Pat got my address from her son Harold in the Merchant Navy who received it from cousin Steve in Africa who got it from his family who got it from Rose in the States. Aunt Pat wants me to go down and see her which will mean the necessity of obtaining a special permit to enter the restricted defense area along the coast.

JUNE 20, FRI.

Received a rush order to pack all stores ready for travel before eight after being "Reveilled" at 5:15AM. It was another inspection along the same lines, at the same place as the King and Queen's inspection, but by the Duke of Connaught this time.

And as before we had to establish a miniature signaling scheme to demonstrate the workings of a signaling platoon. It was not a long drawn out affair like our other one and we were back in camp and unloaded by 11:30AM. This afternoon I put Crosse on fixing some bad joints on the kitchen line and sent Forsythe out on the Area Line again; he had better luck this time and found the break where some farmer had cut the wire where it crossed one of his gates. It is happening too frequently to be funny. At three o'clock I set out in search of cousin Doris. It proved exceptionally warm pedaling the bike on the freshly tarred roads, but after asking a couple of "Bobbies" the way to Woodland's Grove I finally found the place in a very pretty section of the town where I haven't been before. The lady who answered the door was small, gray-haired with a kindly expression. She was a little deaf so sent a younger man "Mr. Baxter" by name out to talk to me. He informed me that my cousin Doris was still at work in Woking but she would be home at 6:30 and she was going home tomorrow on a week's holiday and she was redheaded. He was a very obliging and pleasant fellow and suggested I come back between seven and eight and he would tell Doris I was coming.

I wondered what she looked like, whether she was stout, slim or thin; grouchy, snobbish or friendly. I was soon to find out as I arrived at the house for the second time in four hours. This time Mrs. Baxter, the young man's wife, answered the door and immediately called up the stairs for Doris. Doris came down and she was red-headed, about 5 ft. 6 or 7, well proportioned, not fat not thin; she couldn't be classed as exceptionally pretty, but she appeared pleasant. She said, "You're Fred." I said, "Yes and you are Doris." Instead of greeting me like a stranger like other relatives I have so far met, she did it as if I had been away for a few months and was just arriving back again. We spent two hours getting acquainted with each other and telling about our respective families. When I was leaving she rode down to the Farborough Road with me. We are going to a show at the Rex theater the Wednesday after next after she returns from her holiday. The young couple with whom she is staying are very friendly and very nice, and they told me I would be welcome to the house at any time. Mr. Baxter is in the Air Force, stationed at the nearby airfield. They have a little daughter called Margaret who is friendly like her parents. The little old lady was not in evidence on my second visit. Maybe I have found some place to go to once or twice a week.

JUNE 21, SAT.
Another blistering hot day with interior economy this morning and radio school this afternoon. From the college windows we could see the people lining up (or queuing) for a swim in the swimming pool across the street. The line was a block and a half long and two or three deep. Despite the fact that the lesson was very familiar to me I still found it very interesting and I am getting many points cleared up that I wasn't sure of before.

JUNE 22, SUN.
We had the usual church parade this morning after which I set right to answer the five or six letters I had left to answer. It was too nice a day to sit indoors so

I combined sunbathing with letter writing by being on a blanket in the sun dressed in shorts and wrote letters. Jack Tully gave me two packages of cigarettes and a package of tobacco that will help me out a great deal. Comack and Crosse have been chosen for an advance party that leaves Tuesday morning. It looks as though we are finally moving to a different location.

JUNE 23, MON.
We had the Army Act read to us again this morning. I haven't heard a man yet who could make it interesting; and I still can't quote anything from it. Garlick and I spent the remainder of the day taking stock and making out inventories. Had a lesson on motorcycle riding this evening and took my first spill. Sustained a scraped knee.

I finally caught up on all my mail today. Reg just returned off leave and he claims he is not going back to Canada after the war. He must have had a grand time. The night he left to come back to camp he was in a crowded place about closing time when the proprietor asked for silence and said there was a Canadian soldier in the room. Immediately the whole crowd stood up and sang "The Maple Leaf Forever" and as they were leaving the room, they filed past and shook hands with him. He has a good job waiting for him over here when he gets out of the Army, one can't blame him if he stayed. For myself, the future does not look any too bright. I would like to take a six month's course in radio at the Radio College of Canada, but radiomen are going to be a dime a dozen after this war.

JUNE 24, TUE.
The advance party left this morning, destination unknown. We will probably follow in the near future. I am very doubtful when I will see Doris again, she doesn't get back until Sunday night. There is nothing of great importance happened today, except Mr. Kent informed me that we will have to pull down and reel up all lines some day soon. We drew 110 rounds of anti-tank ammunition this afternoon. Reg (he is wearing two hooks now) and I went to see a show called "Seven Sinners" at the Rex. Marlene is a terrible singer.

I received a very swell letter from Marcelle today and one of Nelle's usual interesting books. It made me realize that my letters have been nothing to boast about lately. Mailed letters to Bobbie, Ivy, Lilly, Rosemary, Aunt Pat and Aunt Ett.

There was a dance in the "Naffy" for HQ Company but I wrote a letter or started a letter to Nelle. I had only made a good start when Wally Mills and Harold Steeds came in with two ATS girls to show them our stores. Unfortunately the best half of the equipment was on the truck ready for the scheme tomorrow. I don't suppose the girls were interested in the stores, but it served as a good excuse. Wally stayed for about ten minutes then left Betty in my care while he went down to the dance to find Cpl. Hatch. Thus began my first experience with an ATS girl. Her emotions and affections were very versatile so when Wally left she turned her attentions to me. I came to the conclusion that she was pretty well experienced but the other company in the room cramped her style. However, eleven o'clock soon came and she had to catch her transportation back to her barracks. It was quite a diversion from the rut I have allowed myself to get into although time would have been welcome. The versatility of her affections was demonstrated again just after I left her at the dance. The last I saw of her she was standing in a shadowy corner with another soldier, making full use of the little time she had left.

JUNE 25, WED.

We got up at four this morning and were on our slow way by 6:15. We were behind the troops so could go no faster than a marching pace. It gave us plenty of time to see the scenery and other attractive sights. Bill French, driver of the stores truck, tried repeatedly and desperately to buy a bottle of milk from the girls driving milk wagons but failed completely. At the ten o'clock stop the YMCA tea car hove into sight and received a grand welcome from all personnel. At 11:30 we stopped to eat our haversack lunch consisting of one cheese sandwich and one bologna sandwich which had been given to us at breakfast this morning.

The ration truck caught up to us carrying "B" Company's mail and transports. The fact that they did not have signals and #4 platoon's mail caused the Quartermaster to be the subject of some uncomplimentary conversation. The Y tea car was going back to camp coming back tomorrow afternoon so Sgt. Rankine gave him a chit to pick up our mail and bring it with him. We arrived at our destination, a place called Oak Tree Grove a mile from the village of Fernhurst, at about three in the afternoon after passing through some wonderful looking country. We shaved and washed in a little stream across the road, had supper, then went into the village for an evening's fun. We had two hours before the dance was scheduled to start so five of us, Stewy, MacKenzie, Ellison, Reg and myself caught a bus for Hazelmere, a larger place three miles away. After visiting the places of interest we went to a dance at the Victoria Hall. The five of us were willing to clean the joint out when a civilian was heard to remark that the dance was spoiled when the new strangers arrived. We naturally thought he was referring to our presence, however, he left soon after and as a result of a lot of argument and persuasion on the part of the manager and the girls working there we stayed until we almost missed our last bus.

We got back to Fernhurst and found the dance there going full swing and with a good crowd in attendance. I sat with the drummer for half an hour who was playing under the adoring gaze of his young wife who was sitting beside the saxophone(ist) playing, knitting socks or something. He wouldn't let me take a crack at the drums and use the excuse that he couldn't take a chance on my ability. MacKenzie, Ellison and I piled onto a truck that was already crowded and we left for camp around 12:30. Somehow we managed to squeeze five more fellows in who we met on the road. MacKenzie's hat flew off as we were pretty close to the camp and were traveling at a good pace. We decided to walk back and hunt for it. We were quite unsuccessful because of the darkness so we had to abandon the search until morning. I rolled in with Garlick.

JUNE 26, THURS.

We were roused out of bed at seven this morning and there was plenty of groaning and comments about the size and condition of heads as the pubs evidently did very good business while it lasted. Sgt. Rankine and I set out to find a little lake that was marked on the map and figured that the best way to find the lake was to follow the little "crick." All that remained of the lake was a little pond barely two feet deep. The one time elaborate dam at the bottom end had been allowed to decay and fall apart which was allowing the water to pass too freely. Apparently there had been a water mill just below the dam and the slippery moss covered cement foundation was still much in evidence. When we climbed to the top of the broken dam we met an elderly man with a plump rosy red face but at Sgt. Rankine's polite good morning he turned around and walked up the path. Possibly we were trespassing and he disapproved of our presence. We cut straight across country to our camp but we were late for lunch so had to be content with kippered herrings and cheese washed down by lukewarm tea.

I was awakened soon after from a two hour sleep by the arrival of the tea car and the hot tea and biscuits hit the spot effectively. Mr. Kent arrived with a thousand cigarettes that was sent to the platoon by one of the platoon member's sister. We don't know who the lady is as she didn't send her name. It was suggested that we should write a letter of appreciation to the Free Press in Winnipeg with all our names on it and let them publish it in the paper. I was elected to write the letter.

On the way out yesterday, French and I talked for three hours about rowing. He rowed in the Winnipeg Bantam Eight for a number of years between 1934 and 1938. We beat them in St. Paul in 1937 and they beat us in Fort William the following year.

Mr. Kent brought the good news that we are to turn in all of our signal lamps which will be getting rid of one of the bulkiest part of our equipment, also that we signals will be going home (sacrilegious) tonight instead of tomorrow as we have to have a complete store check tomorrow morning. We are camped in the middle of a grove of 50 foot oak trees which reminds one of the poems and remarks on the quality of the Sturdy Oak. We each donated three pence and we bought enough milk from a nearby farmer for supper.

After supper we packed up and set out to take part in a scheme with the local home guard. It wasn't much of a scheme and the defenders won against the paratroops as usual. The mortar platoon put on a demonstration after the "battle" that wasn't bad and soon after we hit for home, where we arrived at a little after midnight.

JUNE 28, SAT.

We almost had to leave on another scheme this morning at 9:30AM but were taken off of it at eleven thirty. There was a dance in the Sergeant's Mess this evening.

JUNE 29, SUN.

Church parade was cancelled and the boys had to scrub barracks instead. I didn't do much else but get ready for muster parade and inspection which we are having tomorrow. I blancoed my webbing and wrapped up two pictures that I am sending to Nelle.

JUNE 30, MON.

I managed to get on muster parade, looking fairly respectable but missed inspection because I had to show the Signal Corporal of the South Lancashire Regiment the lines. I spent the afternoon taking inventory and packing stores.

Called on Doris this evening and decided to go for a bicycle instead of going to the "pictures" as it would be very hot in the theater. She didn't know the country and neither did I so I am not sure just where we got to but we managed to find our way back again. It was too early to go inside so we went for a walk down to North Camp in search of a tea room but we had very little success. We did enjoy the walk though which resulted in our becoming better acquainted. I heard more about Bill and Ivy and we dwelt for some time on that old argument as to which one of us had the accent. We said goodbye in the lane, in front of a deserted tea room, in fact, we said goodnight twice. I found out that she is working at assembling the machinery I have been studying for quite a while. I hope to see her again sometime; she is quite an interesting person. Did I mention before that she had red hair?

JULY 1, TUES. DOMINION DAY

Canada is 74 years old today and it was supposed to be a holiday but we had to pack stores. We managed, by a lot of hard work, to load all of the stores onto the 15cwt truck but Maj. Law said it was too much so had to store 5 panniers and 4 bicycles in the R.Q.M. stores until next Monday. It was four o'clock before we had everything squared away and I was plenty mad before the truck was loaded to everyone's satisfaction. We went down to the kitchen for supper but decided to eat at the "Naffy" as the kippered herrings and boiled potatoes didn't meet with our approval. I started out for the Rex theater this evening but only got as far as the signal office. I found the heavy uniform much too hot so changed my mind and discarded tunic, Balmoral and respirator and went to the stage show at the Garrison. I had a good shower tonight, probably the last one I will have for some time. We leave at 6:30 in the morning. Reveille at 5:00.

JULY 2, WED.

Reveille was on time as was breakfast but our departure was a little late. Once we got started we made fairly good time despite the size of the convoy. The signal platoon bus broke down just after we passed Dorking but we did not stop. We ate our cheese and tongue sandwiches while we were moving so we didn't waste any time while traveling.

We started getting unmistakable signs of coastal defense about 1:30 this afternoon and I am sure I could smell the sea. Chalk cliffs began to appear more frequently and the convoy slowed down to a crawl. Finally we were met by Comack and Crosse who were to direct us to our billets and working area.

The place we came to did not appear very attractive and was reached by a very rough dusty chalk covered road. The few of us that were here unloaded the stores and we changed the two exchanges and eight phones. The exchange room, signal office, Sergeant's room, etc. is in a fairly large private house with the name UTOPIA tacked on the front door. The stores and sleeping quarters are across the street and a few doors further down the street. The house where the stores are is called "Theresby."

The platoon arrived on a 30cwt truck at about 11:00PM four hours late to take over from the South Lancs. It seems that the bus broke down in the vicinity of a put so a few of the boys took full advantage of the break. I found that the South Lancs #1 platoon is just as crazy and carefree as ours so have come to the conclusion that to be a good signaler a man has to depart from all sane and conventional activities.

(UTOPIA house)

JULY 3, THURS.

Today was spent in getting acquainted with the telephone system and in my case getting the stores straightened around. We tried out the No. 17 wireless sets and they are fairly efficient. The main disadvantage is the weight which is very much for the size of the actual machine. They were built for portability but they are being used as stationary equipment. We are in plain sight of the channel from here so we could see a 24-ship convoy complete with balloons, sailing up the channel. Large numbers of Spitfires streak over this vicinity, daily, on their way to France or Germany. There is no noticeable decrease in the number that come back.

I struck up a friendship with an R.C.C.S. wireless operator named Bud Ray. He seems a very decent sort of chap. We are planning on going to the nearby town to hunt up some radio parts some of these days. We went for a bicycle ride to C Company and back this evening.

JULY 4, FRI.

Reg and Stewie came back a few days ago, from Cove where they were left as a rear party. The rest of the stores came in soon after. I had the usual daily quota of trouble with defective lines today, which kept me busy for a while. I have been working late every night since I got here and it doesn't give me much time for letter writing and it's piling up on me very fast.

JULY 5, SAT.

Bud Ray and I went into town this afternoon with the intention of buying some resistance cord and a magnetic loud speaker. We got tangled up with a radio dealer who claimed the distinction of working with Clifton away back when radio was a baby. He said he started with a crystal set in 1912 and had built up a very good business but since the war he has been unable to procure the necessary spare parts and radio sets and the trade has dropped off. All we could get from him was a pencil advertising his store. Why he continues to advertise is beyond me. He is a reader of the New York Radio & Television Mag. which he gets every month. We dropped into a tea room for some nourishment and cleaned up on a cup of tea apiece and about a dozen cakes. There was little else to do so we came home before five.

JULY 6, SUN.

The usual things today, like repairing minor discrepancies that creep into the telephone system. Bud Ray and I pedaled to a town further on down the coast this evening but it is out of bounds so we didn't stay. I took a spill when my front wheel tangled with Bud's back wheel. I sustained a skinned elbow and knee, nothing serious. We had tea and toast at the radio station. I just got back from the bike ride and Mr. Kent asked me to fix the CO's reading lamp which took me until dark.

JULY 7, MON.

A and D Companies' line was shorted today so we sent a line party to find it and to run lines from the Company's HQ to their battle HQ's. I had too much to do around here during the day so didn't go out with them. They had to go out again after supper; they started from the other end and Crosse and I started from here. We climbed trees, hedges and fences; waded through nettle filled spare lots, crossed railroad, followed a cattle chute affair to the river. We had to climb through a barbed wire entanglement and we weren't sure whether the area inside was mined or not. After we had traversed about fifty feet we were fairly certain that there were no buried explosive traps and consequently felt a lot easier and made faster time. It is not a very nice feeling not knowing whether your next step is going to be the one to set a land mine off. They practically ruin a man for life. However, we reached the River at the same time as did Sgt. Rankine and Mr. Kent on the other side where they found a deliberately-made short in the wire. We finished the job about 10:00PM.

JULY 8, TUES.

We have experienced some aggravation from the weightless cords on the UC 6 line exchange and the operators have been tying bottles, spikes, etc. onto the cords. I had a bunch of lead-covered cable (purloined from various places), so set about making good weights to take the place of the assortment of bottles and other miscellaneous articles. Crosse and Guedesse helped me and we whipped out seven small but heavy weights that served the purpose admirably. Three German airmen were picked up today and No. 9 Platoon were told off to guard them. They were being kept in the local town jail until they are handed over to the British Intelligence. We received five No. 18 sets this afternoon and the way certain people played with them reminded me of the proverbial poppa playing with Junior's train on Christmas morning. We took them out this evening for operating practice and must have drove our neighboring operators wild. They are a sweet little set, if one gets to understand them. The boys are going wireless crazy which will probably last for a week or so then the complaints will start coming in. After the sets are assigned to the Companies I won't get much chance to operate. They would be a swell emergency set for any "ham" station. I worked until after ten again tonight.

JULY 9, WED.

Fullerphone trouble the first thing this morning then I found a broken connector on the HQ No. 17 set which I re-soldered with the aid of a gas-fed water heater. A small electrical soldering iron would be a Godsend on this job. We have one dipole antenna with four makeshift connections, all for the want of a drop of solder. I proceeded to get acquainted with the new No. 18 wireless sets by dismantling the chassis and looking at the innards.

The boys were in again for instruction on the radios and they continued the practice all through the evening in my workshop. As I was unable to write letters I spent two hours washing my dirty laundry. I loaned Bud Ray my book "Foundations of Wireless." I have to go up to the "Wrens Barracks" tomorrow to fix a dipole antenna. Pretty girls and a fifty watt transmitter. I want to take a look at that "power plant," the other fellows can take care of the girls. I received a big but pleasant surprise today when I got a letter from "Murph" also one from Nelle and one from Jack.

JULY 10, THURS.

Had a very aggravating day starting this morning when they decided to alter the arrangement of wire location over at the signal office and to put Fullerphones in at each Company. The first thing that I had to do was check over all the Fullerphones and found two defective from mistreatment. I had to substitute two ruined spring contacts with two old ones then re-solder a small wire connection by using the water heater as a blow torch and my screwdriver as a soldering iron. I'll have to admit my screw driver has a much better temper in it. I had three senior members of the Platoon urging me to do the job in a hurry as they wanted to have everything going by noon. I was ready to do my part at 9:30 but they couldn't agree on the extent of the changes so waited the rest of the morning for them to decide. The line party started working on their part of it and I can't start until they finish so I came down and tried to work in my stores but Mr. Kent, Mr. McMannus and Sgt. Rankine were playing around with the new #18 sets so I gave that up and rectified the phones in the RAP and Transport Office. I may get into Brighton soon as they are starting to issue passes for outside areas now. I am going to try and buy a small soldering iron. I managed to clean up the stores this evening in preparation for Odlum's inspection tomorrow. I had quite a time wrestling the 150 lbs. of "Bully Beef" and 250 lbs. of hardtack, comprising the Platoons iron rations around. Sgt. Rankine and I went down to the preacher's canteen and had a very good cup of tea and some excellent cakes.

There has been large flights of fighters flying over here daily. They come from somewhere west of here, pick up the bombers east of here then go over and bomb the continent. According to the number that go out and the number of times they go by, they must be pounding the target very heavily. I started a letter to Murph tonight.

JULY 11, FRI.
Spent most of the day rearranging the company lines into an omnibus circuit and installing Fullerphones and necessary manual controlled switches. I refused to have anything to do with the No. 18 sets while other certain people insist I needed advice. The "Quarters" and I tried out a set that was stricken with very poor reception and output. I'll have to try and get off by myself tomorrow, away from the "masterminds" and try and fix it.

JULY 12, SAT.
Had no chance to repair the sick 18 set today. I was busy all day trying to do the impossible, that of making Fullerphones and D5s work simultaneously on the same line without superposing. Bud and I took in a show this evening. I take it back, the Fullerphones and D5s work OK.

JULY 13, SUN.
I was too busy to attend church parade, because of a lot of trouble with the exchange not registering. Sgt. Rankine and I went up to the "Wrens" (WRNS) barracks to fix a No. 17 dipole antenna. Had a good look at the 100-watt Naval set there and we talked to two Wrens on duty. I sneaked the defective 18 set away and repaired a loose antenna contact and gave it a thorough cleaning. The set works excellently except for output meter reading. Worked till 12 midnight before locating the short. Bud Ray and I had a good rag chew after midnight, he was using the No. 11 set and I was operating the No. 18. I was using the call "Wahoo" and he was using "Tang." The set works

so good Mr. Kent wants me to fix the rest of them, the same way. Had to change the Coy lines back to the original condition.

JULY 14, MON.
Cleaned the two No. 18 sets and the necessary antenna equipment this morning at HQ. BDE (*Brigade)* sent an electrician down to see what was wrong with the exchange and Fullerphone circuit but located the fault at the BDE end. Pay parade this afternoon so Ray and I took in a show at the Deluxe Theater, then joined Sgt. Rankine and Reg at the Cafe for something to eat. The local community had their first experience with Camerons with money. According to all reports everyone had a good time.

JULY 15, TUES.
Cleaned up the stores a little this morning and did a spot of writing. Tried to continue Murph's letter at noon today but had to go down and fix the C.O.'s lights and the adjutant's phone. Someone had kicked the Leyden jar type of battery over and spilt the acid all over the floor. I did not like the idea of touching it but finished the job without getting too much of the stuff on my hands. The little that did come in contact with my hands burnt a little but not seriously

Everyone able went to the dance this evening but I elected to stay home and finish Harry's letter. I had a little difficulty repairing no. 6 bike this afternoon. I think I will get the D.R. to buy me a few things in the larger town a little further inland.

JULY 16, WED.
Had a tedious morning packing and wiring the auxiliary battery units and checking over wireless spare parts and essentials. I asked Grant to get some resistance cord, fuse wire and a soldering iron this morning. He ordered them and is to pick them up this afternoon. He thought I wanted a plain iron, one that only costs 2/6p so I am getting that one for times when electricity is not available and an electrical one for times such as this.

We are finding out that C.S.M. Orleski is an anti signal advocate and persists in sticking his nose into places where it ought not to be. Someone is liable to change the shape of it if he doesn't stop interfering with communications.

JULY 17, THURS.
I blew my top this morning when Sgt. Rankine informed me that Colonel McPherson was coming to inspect the stores, but I didn't let it deter me from constructing an improvised switching unit for Fullerphones.

I had the Officers' Mess radio in the shop this afternoon with a chronic case of hum and found a filter condenser open circuited. I sent Jarvis down to Lewes this afternoon for a resistance cord, solder and soldering iron but he came back with only solder and the information that I could get the iron on Fri. or Sat. The resistance cord is unobtainable in that locality. I spent a little time this evening trying to make an antiquated magnetic speaker operated from a No. 11 set. Finally gave it up as a bad job. A Naval man wants me to help him put another speaker on an ordinary receiver. It will be quite a job and a little expensive.

Had a service call to the I.O.'s office to repair a bell that refused to ring. Someone had given me a small screw about a month ago saying it was out of one of the phones and this happened to be the phone. I found the screw in my pocket book and I managed to manufacture a washer out of a piece of brass. It worked ok.

Three more days to the twentieth. I am unable to finish Nelle's letter this evening.

JULY 18, FRI.
We spent the entire A.M. preparing the billets and yards for the Odlum visit and as per usual he failed to visit. Installed the switch that I made yesterday but the system isn't working so good. Cross and I experimented with two telescopes this evening but we were unable to ascertain the results

We had a very special lunch this evening consisting of toast, peanut butter, homemade jam and coffee made from real ground coffee, with milk and sugar. Managed to finish Nelle's letter this evening but will have to wait until tomorrow to mail it.

JULY 19, SAT.

We had a little trouble with the O.P. "B" phone and finally traced the defect to the earth pin. Dry hard chalk makes a very poor ground. Sgt. Rankine, Quarters and Sgt. Major Martin and I of course, went fishing down on the breakwater. The style of fishing used is entirely against my principals of active sport. All that is necessary is to obtain a fifty yard line with two or more single hooks attached and baited with lug worms, muscles, periwinkles, silver paper, etc. A large weight is attached to the end of the line and the other end is made fast to some stationary object than the weighted end with the hooks baited is whirled around and thrown out into the sea. Then the fisherman can sleep, read and stroll around until a fish bites which they never do. Periodically the line is pulled in, mostly for curiosity, re-baited and tossed in again.

We spent two of the five hours that we were there digging for Lug Worms. Finding these worms is quite a difficult job. First of all, a little mound of sand has to be detected, it looks something like the results of Junior squeezing Poppa's shaving cream tube too hard. A spade is then vigorously wielded until the worm is exposed, picked up and placed in the bait can. The man on the shovel has to be fast or the worm puts his boring mechanism into high gear and disappears very quickly.

To make a long story short we fished until six o'clock without catching a thing then the tide started coming in and the south wind was kicking the sea up so badly that the spray was climbing the fifty foot wall and drenching us would-be fishermen on the other side. When we saw porpoises in the vicinity we pulled our lines in and retired to a cafe for supper. By this time it was raining and it also was a good excuse for stopping as we had no waterproof clothing with us.

We ordered eggs and chips but we were informed that there just wasn't any eggs; then we ordered sausage and chips and received the information that the chips would not be ready for another twenty minutes. We sat down with a cup of tea apiece and watched the crowd gather or played with the penny slot machines. Finally we received our order and Sgt. Rankine started teasing the pleasant looking waitress with the soft voice. I think when we left the cafe she was quite convinced of our insanity as she made some remark regarding all Canadians being the same. We stopped at the fish and chip store and bought a shilling's worth of chips and four hunks of fried fish to take to our billets.

We soon had a fire going and the boys soon flocked in to share in the lunch which was practically the same as the other night except that we had fish and chips as the primary course.

JULY 20, 1941, V-DAY, SUNDAY
No church parade today so I started a letter to Miss Banks to thank her for the carton of smokes she had sent a while back. The complaints soon started rolling in, the principle one coming from "B" company stating they couldn't ring the exchange. The linemen were unable to find the defect so I went out there this afternoon and found the trouble to be a poor ground.

I was riding No. 7 bike coming back (I had to push it up the long steep hill when I was going) and the darned thing had no back brake and a very poor front one. The hill is long, steep and exceedingly rough consequently it developed into a wild rough ride which resulted in my making the trip in nothing flat. It was no wonder because I bet the wheels only hit the ground twice during the whole return trip. How I managed to turn the corner at the bottom I'll never know and I am not going to try again to find out. Walker was runner the other day and was using the same bike when he started down the hill that went straight ahead to town or to the right to Battalion H.Q. or to the left to Seaford. He said he was going so fast at the bottom of the hill he dared not turn so coasted into town and then pedalled back again.

I fixed it late this afternoon but missed my supper in the progress, resulting in my partaking of four fish paste sandwiches and a cup of tea at the "Naffy." I resisted all temptations to go out tonight and took a hot bath and washed my dirty laundry.

Cross saw the flashing light tonight that a few of the boys claim they have seen. MacGuire said he read a message it sent last night, consequently he was questioned by the intelligence about it this afternoon. Cross said it sent three S's in morse tonight.

JULY 21, MON.

Started the day packing Auxiliary field battery boxes until I had to go up to Naval H.Q. to help in some wireless experiments with antennas . There certainly was a mess of gold braid, red ribbon and other badges of rank floating around. We did not finish the experiment until 2:00 in the afternoon so we had to satisfy our appetites with cheese sandwiches and jam. The experiment was a huge success despite interference from certain "Brass Hats."

Cross and I went back this afternoon to re-erect the antenna in its old place and to make temporary connections and so missed supper.

Sgt. Rankine and I called at Petty Officer Clark's radio station and had a very interesting half hour talking wireless. Left there after borrowing a small soldering outfit and receiving an invite to visit him anytime we wished. He had a real smart set-up which looked really neat and business like. His new rig is built along the same lines as the National HRO receiver; a very neat arrangement and from what I can gather very efficient.

Petty Officer Clark served 26 years in the Navy as a wireless man, serving a number of years at Gibraltar. He was pensioned off a year before war was declared but was called back inside of a year to take the man-sized job of handling and servicing all Naval radio in this district. He is a very obliging fellow who, unlike most radiomen, is quite willing and pleased to talk about radio work and equipment. I would like to work under him.

JULY 22, TUES.

I had to go up to "B" Coy to solder the No. 17 set antenna. I was armed with the usual array of pliers, screwdrivers, wire cutters, etc., and in addition I was reinforced by a small blow torch and a small soldering iron. I suppose it would have been okay but all the windows were broken and the wind kept blowing the torch out until I scrounged a couple of shields to put around it.

It took a lot of wind on my part but after a couple of hours blowing hard through a rubber tube I made a passable job.

Then I had the same job to do up at Naval Headquarters but this time I took my own electric iron along with the borrowed torch and accessories. There was a socket for an outside light close by to where I had to work but found the iron wouldn't heat up when plugged in. So I found a switch which appeared like it might control the outside light but which when pushed up, turned the lights out in the plotting room leaving the two WRNS workers and a man officer floundering around the dark. I couldn't find any other suitable place to plug the iron in so resorted to using the puff-hard blow torch. I had hardly started when the fuel gave out. I was walking around looking for someplace for my iron when Mr. Kent came up. He finally got permission to use one of the sockets in the plotting room. It didn't take long to finish the job after that.

JULY 25, FRI.
Went to Brighton with Mr. Kent for radio parts and enjoyed the trip very much. I saw the Palace Pier and the other intricately decorated pier. Both of them had large sections taken out of the gang plank.

We bought a resistance cord for the radio, a condenser for the Officers' Mess radio, some mucilage, wrenches, etc. Just as we were leaving we saw a very eccentric old lady. We first noticed her across the street, she had mauve colored hair bound with a bright red silk bandanna. She wore a long flowing black dress with red canvas shoes many sizes too big for her. She had a small poodle tucked under each arm and two on leashes held in each hand and she was pushing a baby sulky filled with parcels of all shapes and sizes. It was a sight to stop traffic and believe me, it did.

Immediately after arriving back at our billets I had to put the new condenser in the Officers' radio and the trouble disappeared as expected. Major Thompson, 2 l/c seemed very interested in my trade during peace time.

We had a nice lunch in the signal office later on in the evening.

JULY 26, SAT.

Exchange trouble again this morning which happened to be the Fullerphone switch again which someone had forgotten to switch over after using the instruments. Repaired the Platoon radio this afternoon and finally managed to get it operating satisfactorily. The question of whose room to put it in is the problem of paramount importance and the source of heated arguments. I wrote four letters this evening, one to Janet, one to cousin Edith in Rhodesia, one to Aunt Pat and one to Harry. A queer thing happened today when I received a pair of socks and a letter from Iris Lawrence. The letter contained two clippings one from the Free Press and one from the Tribune telling of the Winnipeg girl who had received a souvenir in the form of a wing covering from Hess" plane from a Cameron in England. The girl happened to be Iris and the Cameron was myself. Iris very wisely refused to allow them to mention any names. The Tribune sent their photographer down to take her picture and the poor gent was totally unsuccessful. I wonder if Nelle received the piece I sent her.

WINNIPEG FREE PRESS. FRIDAY, JUNE 13, 1941

World

e Factories

the last 50 years. He is survived by a daughter, Mary, and three sons, William and Samuel in Winnipeg, and Robert, in Forget, Sask. The funeral will be held Saturday at 4 p.m. from Bardal's funeral home to Riverside cemetery.

Winnipeg Girl Gets Fragment Of Hess Plane

A small triangular-shaped fragment from the plane Hess used on his mysterious flight to England arrived in Winnipeg yesterday.

A Cameron Highlander, stationed in England, happened to be in the right place at the right time when the remains of the enemy-bearing plane was being moved away. The Cameron said he managed to get a three-inch triangular piece from the wing covering as a souvenir, but warned against smelling the paint used on it because of its vileness. The swastika was plainly discernible on the damaged plane, according to the Cameron, and most of the body with rudder still in position was there besides an assortment of pieces from the elevator wings. The soldier clipped off a small corner and sent it to a girl in the Great-West Life war service unit.

Members of the war unit had sent at Christmas time greeting cards to all policy holders in the armed forces. This soldier wrote to the girl who sent him the card and through the correspondence came the prized bit of Hess' plane.

Women·

Travelle

Leaders

A feature of the F session of the 31st council meeting, c Manitoba, Saskatche berta units of the U cial Travellers of An initiation of John M Cook, Nebraska, selor of the Unite Travellers, and W grand counselor of units, into the speci garter of the ladie the U.C.T. of Ameri

Three members grand auxiliary vis counselor, Mrs. R. S.

(Free Press article)

JULY 17, SUN.

Missed church parade again today when I had to convert all Fullerphone keys into Navy type knobs, as ordered by Mr. Kent. We had tea and cheese sandwiches in the signal office late this morning. I went down to dinner and received the usual ration of stew and I couldn't find a place to sit so I dumped the stuff into the garbage can and washed my dishes.

I meant to write letters all afternoon but received a call to fix the exchange which took me until four o'clock. I soldered a DV bell armature this evening then had a bath followed by a lunch. Reg's second stripe has changed him quite a lot. He is coming very close to nagging the boys. Some of them are resenting it although I don't think he realizes it himself.

Young Cormack is leaving for a baker's school tomorrow. The boys are all on edge now and serious arguments are occurring all of the time. Perhaps they are in condition or perhaps this waiting is getting them. In either case, if they ever get a chance to do a real job of work which they have been trained for, it will take something to stop them.

Wrote a letter to Connie this evening. I expect more in tomorrow.

JULY 28, MON.

Wrestled with the two signal office Fullerphones all day and the only results I obtained was a bad headache. My aggravation wasn't alleviated by the sarcastic advice of my superiors which was meant for kidding but I didn't feel just in the mood for it.

The usual lunch was prepared in the signal office and if an uninterested stranger had of walked into the office he would have thought he had stepped into a room full of chronic cases in the local psychopathic institution.

I made a passable ash tray out of an OXO can and a few pieces of tin and now have to make four or five more to give to fellows who covet mine. I wrote a letter to Doc this evening.

JULY 29, TUES.

Took a bus-man's holiday today after fixing an exchange unit early this morning by making a couple more ash-trays. I moved over with Reg this afternoon and told Walker, the new storeman, to move into the stores.

I wrote to Jack tonight which means I am gradually clearing up this mail of mine. I must start a letter to Marc before I go to bed.

JULY 30, WED.

I had Fullerphone troubles again today and with one of the same one I worked on yesterday. Finally I found it necessary to put a D5 armature and screw contacts in the Fullerphone and the parts from the Fullerphones in the D5 then put an extra battery in series, before it would work properly.

I finished the letter to Marcelle this evening. We were all paid this P.M. and most of the boys are wandering back or staggering, depending on the amount of beverage they disposed of and things are getting a trifle noisy.

The rumor of our being relieved is intruding persistently on the serenity of life as we find it but our next destination is never the same one day as it was the day before.

JULY 31, THURS.

We received 22 – 162 volt batteries for the No. 18 sets and 25 tins of chocolate for emergency rations. Also received a new pair of shoes which may have arrived a little too late to prevent my other pair from being condemned by the shoemaker. We had battle station practice today and the results of which I know nothing.

I took a few messages on the Fullerphone today from Brigade and didn't do too badly. I occupied the time this afternoon with small jobs and keeping out of sight generally. Finished letters to Marcelle this evening and wrote one to Nelle which was quite an achievement as I was writing under trying conditions. I wrote through three or four heated arguments that sounded like extracts from the recordings of a hog callers convention, but I wrote "finish" to the letter at 11:15 P.M. a little earlier than usual. Things have quietened down considerably while the Sgt. is consuming the last few crumbs of the fish and chips, and I am ready for bed.

AUG. 1, FRI.

I slept in again this morning and missed the second scrambled egg breakfast in two days. I'll bet if I get up on time tomorrow we will have sausages. We had a battle station stand-to inspection this morning and saw more gold braid and red hat bands in half an hour than I have seen in eighteen months.

I blew my top again today when a few of the fellows dropped a high tension battery on the cement. We weren't sure if the battery was dead or not and were going to try it in operation but the accident decided that. Sgt. Rankine was participating in the little game and he was included in top blowing.

Sgt. Rankine and Reg went out this evening leaving me to take care of the signal office.

I had a few minutes of message taking and am almost back to my old form again. No one felt like making tea this evening so we went to bed without it. I finished a letter to Dad this evening. I also received a new pair of shoes.

AUG. 2, SAT.

I was put in charge of interior economy and managed to get the fellows working long enough to have the billets clean in time for inspection. Had a little trouble with the exchange today but repaired it after a little experimenting. I was left in charge of the signal office again this evening but there was hardly any business at all. I am quite convinced that some of the fellows are beyond "acting" crazy; acting isn't necessary now.

I wrote a letter to Bobby and one to Nelle this evening and started one to Iris. Also finished one to Ivy during the day.

I am gradually answering my mail horde and only have five more to go. A move in the near future with six weeks under canvas at the end of it has developed into a strong rumour.

AUG. 3, SUN.

I took the day off, unofficially and wrote a letter to Iris Lawrence and one to Rosemary. Some of the fellows are betting that we leave here in a few days and there are some who are betting equal amounts that we will remain here for at least another two months.

I heard some Germany propaganda over the radio today comparing living conditions in Holland to those in Russia. According to the questioner (it was staged in the interview method) and the interviewed man, Holland is the Utopia everyone is trying to find and the Dutch are supplying great quantities of foodstuffs to Germany at higher prices. What is the price? A life maybe. One may be inclined to believe it all if it was so obviously exaggerated and ridiculous.

AUG. 4, MON.

Managed to get up in time for breakfast this morning and then made two letter boxes out of tin for the signal office. I had intended going up to "B" and "C" Coy's to check over their equipment but kept putting off for other things until it was too late.

A mist coming in from the channel is steadily getting worse. Visibility is very poor today. I should do some studying but can't seem to settle down to it.

Paid a visit to "B" and "C" companies this afternoon to check over phones and found everything in good shape at both places.

I started a letter to Nelle tonight but broke off for awhile to read a book called "Carrying On after the First hundred Thousand" by Ian Hay, out of which I copied practically the entire portion dealing with signals. It took me until 2 in the morning to complete the little chore. The book is about a Scotch Regiment during the last war and was based on the contents of an officer's diary.

AUG. 5, TUES.

Rumours of a move back to canvas are more persistent than ever much to the unit's annoyance. Even if it is true there is no sense in rubbing the fact in. It is not exactly a fitting reward for six weeks of hard work improving the defense works and lines of communication in this area.

Nelle's letter was duly completed by eight P.M. and the manuscript I completed during the small hours of this morning, was divided into three and placed in three separate envelopes. A letter to Marcelle was started, finished and is waiting for some generous person to donate an envelope. (I have already borrowed nearly a dozen.)

The fish and chip plus cocoa lunch has been disposed of and a trifling argument regarding a few sundry and unimportant matters with Reg has been temporarily suspended for the night.

The whole establishment is settling down to the nightly activity which isn't much except for a little trouble on the Brigade line which seems to have been mixed up with the 6th Field Rgt's exchange. It will probably be straightened out in due course. It's time that all good and conscientious soldiers were in bed (with due apologies to Sgt. Rankine who appears to interested in a book which he will continue perusing for another hour yet, at least) so I'll say goodnight.

AUG. 6, WED.
A trouble free day for the telephone system so I busied myself with the construction of a code practice oscillator. Due to the condition of the valve (tube) I had to raise the specified plate voltage of 22 ½ volts to 162 volts before I obtained satisfactory results. Other than that there was very little doing.

AUG. 7, THURS.
Sgt. Rankine manipulated a deal today that would have done credit to the worst Jew on Main Street back in Winnipeg. It appears that another sergeant found an inoperative discarded radio receiver so he showed it to Sgt. Rankine, who being an enterprising sort of a fellow said we would try repairing it and if we couldn't he, (Sgt. Rankine) would buy it for junk or parts of which there were plenty. We worked on it all afternoon without any encouraging results until around four o'clock when we had decided to proclaim the set hopeless, and I was ready to pull it apart piece by piece and salvage the good

parts. Then we hit the cause of all the trouble, the tubes were all in the wrong sockets which when placed in their proper places produced the desirous results. Remaking a few soldered joints here and there with a little adjusting and we had a good set.

Handing the rig back to the other Sergeant was not entirely agreeable to Sgt. Rankine so he conceived an airtight scheme to gain ownership of the receiver at low cost. He informed the first party that it would cost four pound to fix the thing up properly and if he did not want to pay that much out he (Sgt. Rankine) would buy it off him for ten shilling or so. Sufficient to say that the radio is now reposing in Sgt. Rankine's room emitting very good well toned music.

I received another parcel from Iris containing razor blades, gum, chocolate, cigarettes and socks. So I wrote her a letter tonight. She is beginning to express veiled hints that the friendship could be developed into something bigger.

AUG. 8, FRI.
There was a little exchange trouble this morning which was finally traced to the other end of the line so Crosse had to go out and fix the trouble. It was raining all day in gusts and spurts and the roads were plenty muddy. Things were going pretty smoothly so I ventured to write a letter to Olga this afternoon.

I washed a few dirty clothes this evening, had a bath then wrote a letter to Bezzie.

Sgt. Rankine and Reg do not appreciate my punning endeavours. I pulled one tonight that took them a little time to get; I practically had to draw a picture for them. When they did get it, I nearly got thrown out. It developed into a real friendly scrap with Reg and I throwing shoes at each other and Sgt. Rankine seeking sanctuary from flying foot gear by crouching under the table.

I accomplished something unusual this evening; I wrote a letter to Bezzie and at the same time listened to the interesting dramatization of the "Battle of Britain."

"Skip" alias "Ink" Inskip sustained a bad burn on his hand while making toast this evening. He was using the handle of his mess tin to hold the bread over the hot coals, while holding onto the body of the tin. He had finished toasting a slice of bread and had placed the tin on the table and started buttering the golden brown morsel, when without thinking he grabbed the handle of the mess tin. The handle was still red hot, so Skip is operating the exchange with one hand tonight. Cpl. Peters came in wanting to know why he had to run down to W.T.O. when there were signallers around. He was told forthwith and left the office unconvinced and plenty burnt up.

I had the opportunity of reading my horoscope this evening and it's not so good although complimentary in places.

AUG. 9, SAT.
Started studying this morning until I had to go over and take charge of interior economy. Then I had to fix a super sensitive relay on the exchange that kept on indicating with the least bit of agitation such as dropping a pencil on the table. I salvaged a few radio parts from an old receiver chassis and finished my practice oscillator.

The Lancs advance partly arrived today so I guess our leaving this locality is just a matter of days. I wrote a short letter to Ted this evening and started one to Rose but due to the lack of news was unable to finish it. Studied radio theory for three hours this evening.

According to information received regarding our next destination, visit to Doris will not be at all difficult providing they don't clamp down with a C.B. order.

AUG. 10, SUN.
The platoon's iron rations were turned back in this morning and it is the first indication that we are moving other than the departure of the advance party.

Dirty laundry took up most of the afternoon and after a great deal scrubbing it didn't turn out too bad.

Our civilian neighbour brought down a huge green caterpillar with purple and white stripes he had found while trimming his hedge. It has crawled over every table, phone and book, up and every upright object until we are tired of seeing it undulating along in its groping search that we humans have not the slightest idea. Reg, who claims that it distracts him from his letter writing, went and found a piece of lilac bush for it to gallivant over. Just in case the monstrosity was fussy he chose one with a nice purple bloom on it. We are seriously debating whether or not to liberate the thing.

I wrote a five page letter to Rose this evening but was so dissatisfied with it I tore it up and burnt it.

I ran completely out of cigarettes early this A.M. and I have already borrowed four packages of cigarettes already and I don't like borrowing any more. Reg discovered my plight and came to the rescue with a package.

AUG. 11, MON.

Reg and I missed breakfast this morning but we made some tea and toast from the remnants of last night's lunch. Walker and I were packing panniers this morning until eleven o'clock then Crosse and I went up to "D" and "A" Companies to pick up any surplus equipment that we could pack. I also managed to rouse Charlie Smalley long enough to acquire a haircut, which, I am told by our cynical Sergeant, isn't so good.

By three o'clock this afternoon all was ready for loading all idle equipment for an advance load to our destination. By special request a lug was soldered on his hat badge. All palliases were emptied of straw and turned into the quarters so once again we are sleeping on hard floors. I wonder what a spring mattress would feel like now. Four reluctant individuals were commandeered for loading the truck at seven this evening and in due course we had the vehicle over-flowing with equipment. Garlick was chosen to accompany the truck, tomorrow to act as wet-nurse to the contents, much to Garlick's disgust.

Reg and our fiery Sergeant had a rough and tumble set-to this evening and disrupted the tranquility of this otherwise peaceful office. They play rough when they play around here so I hate to see them go at it seriously; they were only playing tonight; they nearly wrecked the office.

The sergeant has installed his radio in the office and it is a nightly occurrence to call up the girls at different points in town and all the companies then hand the telephone in front of the radio and supply the listening audience with the choicest of musical programs. The other night, the Queen's voice was heard in a number of extra places by this means.

AUG. 12, TUES.

For some reason or other I started a letter to Nelle this morning immediately after breakfast. Then my literary endeavours were interrupted by the need for repairs to a Fullerphone. Reg interrupted this operation by taking me down to the cafe for tea.

It was a busy afternoon what with the many small things that had to be done before turning over to the Lancs. Pressing of uniforms seems to be the order of the day so I pressed mine. Garlick came back today and reports the camp as a h—l of a place with barbed wire all around it. I took a bath this evening and I should pack now.

I read an article on radio location and am now trying to find a buyer for my radio books. Radio men will be dime a dozen after this war.

AUG. 13, WED.

All was a rush this morning to get things done before the Lancs arrived to take over from us. The rain did not help to alleviate the general aggravation of the situation but despite the difficulties encountered the stores truck was loaded by noon and by two o'clock in the afternoon was ready to move. We experience a certain amount of difficulty with the exchanging of equipment which was climaxed by the signed list of goods being carried out of reach by a very strong wind.

Finally our business with the Lancs was concluded and we proceeded to the Drove Hall in New Haven where we were to spend the night. Drove Hall is a barn-like affair with a refreshment booth on the left and water heating department on the right. Simply by stepping through a gate in a railing you come out onto the floor which is used alternately for roller skating and dancing. At the far end is a stage which I imagine is used for seating the orchestra during dancing and skating and speakers and performers on special occasions.

After supper everyone had borrowed or tried to borrow money enough for an evening's entertainment until finally all available cash was fairly well divided up. Sgt. Rankine and I managed to raise a shilling between us. We had no hankering to take in the town for the last time so stayed in with four or five other fellows. We procured one of our two radios from the stores truck and managed to supply ourselves with music for the evening, the same which the girls behind the refreshment booth counter seemed to enjoy also.

All was comfortable until the fellows started coming back then it became too noisy for the radio. The lunch counter closed at ten so we disconnected the set as no one could agree to the proper program. We all finally hit the hay or in this case boards and after teasing Mackenzie about the art of French kissing settled down for the night.

AUG. 14, THURS.

We got on an early start on our trip to our home for the next six weeks and except for being hit in the eye with an apple that had been tossed by a youngster with generous intentions we arrived at our destination. It reminded everyone of Camp Shilo and the same old inconveniences seemed present here.

Walker, the stores and I are all crammed into one half of a small marquee tent but there is a chance of obtaining more suitable accommodation tomorrow. I will be exceedingly glad to roll in tonight. There is no lights allowed so it will be early.

Dear Nelle:

Book No. 3 is finished and for the life of me I can't seem to make this diary interesting in the least. I hope it will give you some idea of the activity we are meeting every day, possibly the future will supply better material.

As always
Fred.

FRED LODGE DIARY
August 15, 1941 to December 22, 1941

Book No. 4

PERSONAL DIARY OF
L/CPL LODGE, F.T. H19859
SIGNALS. Q.O.C.H. of C.

PLEASE MAIL TO
Miss N. Lodge
Box 165
Kenora, Ontario
Canada

AUG. 15, FRI.

We had a very busy time this morning setting up communication between different points in the camp. Mr. Kent received permission to use one of the tin houses across the road for stores so if anyone had of happened along about two or three in the afternoon they would have beheld a stream of signalers moving in an unending chain between our old abode and the new; half of them loaded with an assortment of equipment that go to make up the signal stores. Inside of a half an hour the stores complete were safely reposing in the shelter of the corrugated steel shed. It gets dark early these days so am hitting the hay early.

AUG. 16, SAT.

There was a kit inspection this morning to see if the boys had everything that they were supposed to have and as far as I know they weren't missing much. Some say it was because some dumb cluck had sold a uniform and a pair of rubber boots during a moment of financial weakness. Reg and I walked into Aldershot again this afternoon to do some shopping and found it overrun by Canadians, mostly boys from the Third Div. I bought myself a small vise, a long screwdriver, writing paper, flashlight batteries, steel wool, a new hackle and a few other odds and ends that I needed. The place was much too crowded to be pleasant so we came back early. Walker found some used truck oil in a can this morning so we decided to make a cup of tea by setting the oil alight. It was raining at the time so we brought the improvised source of heat into the store room. By the time we had the tea made we could hardly see one another for the thick black smoke coming from our "stove" and the stench was terrible. Walker promised to have a better arrangement thought up for the next time. We had tea again this evening and Walker kept his promise about the "stove" which this time consisted of a biscuit tin with the appropriate holes cut in the proper places. It worked after a fashion.

AUG. 17, SUN.

Missed church parade in Aldershot this morning as I had to install a buzzer system in the officers' mess. It is too much trouble for the officers to walk ten feet to ask for a drink. I wrote letters all day and went to see "The Road to

Singapore" for the third time that was showing in the YMCA tent. After that came out there was little time left to do anything else besides hit the hay.

AUG. 18, MON.

The fellows were obliged to move their tents this morning from their quiet out-of-the-way position up to within twenty yards of the B.O.R. (*Battalion Orderly Room*); needless to say the fellows protested vigorously with no results. The four linemen were kept busy all day rewinding cable and straightening reels while I was kept busy fixing the exchange and D5s and experimenting with an arc lamp in between times. I had a very nice shower this evening after which we had toast, cheese and tea, prepared on Walker's brainchild, the biscuit tin stove. I finished a letter to Bobbie this evening and Mr. Kent informed me that I would have to read the map on a trip to Chichester where we hoped to purchase a few used G.P.O. (*General Post Office*) telephones.

AUG. 19, TUES.

Got up before breakfast and shaved by the light of the rising sun. We started out for Chichester about nine o'clock with me sitting up in the front seat nursing two maps and Mr. Kent, Capt. Taylor and Charlie Longley in the back. All went well until we hit Hindhead where we ran into complexities regarding the maze of roads around that locality. However, it wasn't long before we were back on the right road again and from there on it was plain sailing into our destination. Here we ran into one of those unexplainable English "quirks" of character. We discovered that the place where the telephones were being sold was about five miles further west, down a twisty, crooked road at a place called the "Pillars" which we almost missed because of the screening trees that partially hid the isolated dwelling. The lady of the house informed us that the gentleman who was selling the phones wasn't at home and would not likely be back until tomorrow. The best we could do was to leave a telephone number in hopes of a future appointment. From there we went to Petersfield, where we once visited before many months ago, on a scheme. Charlie and I walked around town renewing old acquaintances. We stayed in there for a couple of hours then headed for home by a different and much easier route. The map was no good on the return trip because they don't mark roads on the margin of maps. We had to call at Mons Barracks to allow Capt. Taylor to transact some business, then we dropped him off in Aldershot. He was last seen buying a ticket to a show. We arrived back in camp, just ahead of a downpour and just in time for supper. I don't think I did too badly as map reader as one mistake, easily made, isn't exactly a washout. Reg and I went over to the NAAFI for a cup of tea and finished up with a full supper. We just got back to the stores when Rankine comes along and nothing would do but to have tea with him. A table appeared beside the store room hut sometime during the evening. I don't know where it came from or how, but while it is here we may as well use it.

AUG. 20, WED.

Up and shaved again early this morning, had a little trouble finding a wash-basin but finally obtained the use of one by a little application of diplomacy. All I had to do was convince the other guy that he didn't need it. I postponed my leave until such times as Reg and I can go together which may mean the end of September or in October. We are both going to London. It rained again this noon just as dinner was being doled out. Sports half day this after-noon so I indulged in a little letter writing. One letter to Nelle, one to Marc and one to Jack. Received two new shirts from the R.Q.M.S. this morning so I guess that clears up the shirt situation so far as it concerns me. It rained again this late afternoon and evening which may have had some effect on the contents of the letter to Jack. I'm afraid I wasn't very encouraging to his desire to get over here. Rumors are again thick as flies and it's impossible to pick any one of them as the most likely one. Just to illustrate how these rumors start, one of our men expressed the opinion that we may be out of this camp by the end of next week. By seven o'clock this evening it was all over camp that we would be leaving for Scotland next week sometime. It only shows to go you.

AUG. 21, THURS.

Slept a little longer than I intended to this morning so had to forego the shave before breakfast as I have been in the habit of doing recently. The day dawned with little wind and a clear sky and we have hopes that it will remain so just for one day, at least. A wasp caused a minor disturbance in the mess hall this morning and it was interesting to see full grown men frantically dodging the insect until it made the mistake of landing; then they all jumped on the critter and exterminated the little fellow. Nothing exceptional during the day except for a visit to the stores by B Brigade and 3rd Div signal officers accompanied by Mr. Kent. I wrote letters to Bobby and Aunt Pat this evening. Mr. Kent wants me to experiment with Ultra high frequencies and motor demobilizing rays, etc. but my knowledge is far too limited for that sort of stuff. Feeling a little disgusted tonight. We may move down to Fleet for a while.

AUG. 22, FRI.

Nothing seems to be going right today. We discovered that there is 67 Line labels missing from the stores, evidently left at Denton. Mr. Kent has another fancy scheme of keeping track of all the stores which will properly last for a couple of weeks, then die out like all other ideas that have been tried. I am waiting word from Moreau as to his interview with the Brigade Staff Captain in regards to a transfer to the Air Force. If he makes the grade, then I may work along the same lines. Qualified signaler with a speed of 18 words a minute and 1st class shot in Lewis, Bren guns, also rifle should be a good reason for transferring. Time, like in the past endeavours, will tell. Had to check over all No. 18 sets this afternoon before they were taken out. With material purloined from a tent peg mall, I managed with the aid of a classmate, and a discarded mower blade, to fashion a fairly decent handle for my claw hammer. Started a letter to Nelle this evening in answer to one I received from her this afternoon, but failing light forced me to leave it before finishing the mess. I think I am gradually losing the knack of writing letters. Some of the boys are wondering why the barbed wire entanglement appeared around the Colonel's tent. The truth of the matter is an F.M.R. private (French-Canadian) coming home after dark one night, slightly under the influence of alcohol beverages, walked into the Colonel's tent, violently shook that worthy head of the Camerons and asked him to show the way home to his own camp. The Colonel's reaction to being roused out of a sound sleep by a buck private for such a trifling matter, isn't exactly printable. Next day there was a crew erecting a barbed wire fence and the next night a guard was posted at the entrance.

AUG. 23, SAT.

It started raining just as Reveille sounded this morning but only sprinkled for a while. It wasn't raining when I went for a shave at 6:20 AM, but soon after breakfast it started in earnest and it has been pouring all day. The camp and everything not under cover is saturated, the roads are just masses of mud, and everyone is feeling miserable. There are rumors that we are going to move into billets at Fleet; these rumors have practically been substantiated by order that I have received regarding the equipment. I copied ten pages of notes this morning and finished Nelle's letter and wrote another to Doris this afternoon. Mail came in this evening but there was none for me. Just received orders from Mr. Kent that finishes a miserable day off right. All No. 18 sets have to be checked and ready for use on a scheme tomorrow. It is bad enough holding the scheme on a Sunday, it's worse just after a full day's rain and it's climaxed when we are to move on Monday and all the packing to do. Aw nuts, the scheme will probably be canceled anyway, I hope.

AUG. 24, SUN.

I pulled a boner that I never thought I would be ever guilty of. I got up at 6:00 AM thinking it was Reveille and Walker followed suit. We were on our way over for breakfast at seven when one of the guards told us that Reveille had not gone yet, as Reveille would be at seven as per usual. I don't think Walker will ever forgive me for causing him to lose an hour's extra sleep. The truck was loaded with a few necessary signal items we had dinner at eleven and we were on our way by eleven forty-five. We just went through our old stomping grounds Farnborough to a lake on the other side where the "crossing" by assault boat and pontoon bridge was to be made. I stayed behind with the stores truck so have no idea of what took place at the lake. The scheme finished up by four o'clock in the afternoon and we got back in time for supper in camp. I received another Miner and a letter from Nelle this afternoon. Feeling terribly disgusting this evening and made a poor job of a letter to Nelle. Ross got himself in a jam a few month's back; he met a girl while on one of our numerous schemes around the Manitoba countryside and took her out twice. Evidently she fell in love with him and persisted on writing amorous letters to him despite his protests. Finally, in desperation, he wrote her a letter a typewriter to say that he had been killed and to make the document authentic, stamped it with the Battalion stamp. Yesterday, Ross was called before Col. Dudley, who told him that Ottawa had sent the particulars, including the phoney letter, demanding an investigation into the case. Evidently the girl had sent the letter to Ottawa for confirmation. Ross can be charged with a number of things, including the illegal use of a Battalion stamp, forgery and resorting to pretentious means to disillusion someone, just to name three of them. Everyone is watching the matter with interest.

AUG. 25, MON.

The linemen were busy reeling up some of our wire that is strung around camp and Walker, Lang, Bridges and Hill were down at our new billets getting things ready. Everything was packed and ready to load when Mr. Kent wanted an inventory of the stores. Just about the same time a new No. 18 set came in from Brigade, the condition of which didn't meet with my approval in the least. It was supposed to be a new machine but the battery was run down and the storm cover was dirty and there was twigs and grass inside. The tube compliment wasn't right so I wouldn't sign the invoice. Finally everything was straightened out and Mr. Kent evidently saw the folly of demanding an inventory at a time like this. We put the first load on the truck this afternoon, ready for the first trip in the morning. The boys then had to scrub the floorboards of their tents and stack them outside. We managed to smuggle our table, purloined in the first place and which I was using for a workbench in the daytime and a bed at night, onto the truck. I understand we are going to a pretty swell place with plenty of fruit trees in the yard. I received cigarettes and a letter from Flo in Quebec and a card from Marcelle and a letter from Nelle.

AUG. 26, TUES.

Up early this morning in time for a shave before breakfast, after which moving got under way. Two big truck loads of stuff and they still say I only need a 15 cwt (*hundred weight truck*). This is as good a place as any to introduce one "Torchy" Cawson who is in the new class of pupils drawn from the rifle companies. He didn't get that name "Torchy" for nothing, he has a hair trigger temper that goes off unexpectedly and at any time. As the name Torchy also implies, he has red hair. As it happened we were loading up the last of the stores and the men were waiting for transportation at the same time. By coincidence, the stores truck was loaded just as the other trucks came along so Torchy climbed into the front seat of a stores truck which was loaded too much to allow anyone to ride on top. It is a well known fact that I have to go with the same truck as the stores and always ride in the front seat, so I told Torchy that he would have to ride in one of the other trucks. Torchy blew his top in a mild way but I was too busy to argue. From what I have heard of Torchy I suppose I am in his bad books and should be scared but somehow I'm not. Eventually we pulled out of the rain sodden camp and were soon pulling up in front of a mansion-like building which looked a trifle run down and bore signs of previous military occupation. There were packs and kits piled all over the front yard and individuals were pulling these piles apart hunting for their own belongings so that they could lay claim to the choicest bed spaces inside the house. Walker was very mad because they had changed the location of the storeroom. The change wasn't for the better either and after I had been shown the room we were supposed to have had, I was just as sore as Walker. The present storeroom is what I think, was used as the groom's workshop. It about ten feet wide and twelve feet long; there is two small barred windows at one end that are inadequate for lighting up the other end of the room, even in daylight and a flashlight is used whenever we want anything stored there. In the center of the wall on one side is an old English fireplace cook stove, very contrary, that usually sends all heat up the chimney. On the other wall, running full length, is three shelves at present loaded down with all sorts of signaling equipment. The whole interior is white washed; consequently, we have to be careful where we hang our clothes as it is very hard to brush off. The rest of the day until three in the afternoon was spent in arranging the stores so that we would have room for two beds. Finally came to an arrangement where one of the beds had to be dismantled every morning and set up again every night. I scrounged a light globe but spent three hours tracing the line through the maze of corridors and rooms til I found a blown fuse. We had tea and toast for lunch with a can of spaghetti to add flavour.

AUG. 27, WED.

Walker goes on leave today so had to rush to get ready before eleven. I checked over 9 D 5s and two exchanges this morning. Started making a new pair of drumsticks this afternoon but had to discontinue when Sgt. Rankine came in and was raving like a maniac because the boys weren't using the proper procedure on the wireless. I received a letter from Charlotte this afternoon and a note from Felicie. They both write very good letters.

Jeff Reynolds dropped in tonight with all his writing equipment as well as a photo tinting outfit. We both wrote letters for a while then boiled some water, bought some cakes from the "naffy" and had lunch. Sgt. Rankine dropped in and joined us. The talk got around to wood carving and wood-work in general. Sgt. Rankine has done quite a lot of it and his father used to be a woodcarver. Jeff is a wood turner and worked on tables and other articles of furniture. The meeting of three finally broke up and Jeff showed me how to use his photo-tinter and left it here for my use. I took a shower in the dark and found it doesn't work so good.

AUG. 28, THURS.

The morning started out with promises of an easy day but was soon altered by an order for everyone to blanco equipment and be ready for parade by 1:30 pm. Ross, Hill and I were doing ours on the roof where there was plenty of breeze and sunshine to dry it off in a hurry. Ross sat down too hard on the skylight, lost his balance and fell partway through. He looked like pictures of people caught in a barrel with his legs up around his head. I had to help him out before he fell right through which would have meant a two-storey fall down a stairway well. They even pulled men out of the kitchen to blanco their webbing which disrupted the preparations for dinner to such an extent we had bread, cheese and tea only. Quite a few of us finished our dinner in the NAAFI. I think everyone was on parade on time, that was supposed to be on, then followed a series of inspections, starting with Sgt. Rankine making the first one; followed by Mr. Kent doing it again and going one further and holding a rifle inspection. Then came an interlude in the proceeding during which I managed to remove some excess dirt from my firing piece. Major Law held the next inspection accompanied by Lieutenant Rutherford and Sgt. Major Thomson, acting C.S.M. After that it was just a matter of waiting for the Colonel but it started raining and as is usual it poured down in sheets so Major Law told us to release our gas capes for protection. These gas capes are rolled in such a way that when the ripcord is yanked, the cape unrolls, then it is pulled around and fastened at the front by glorified dome fasteners. The capes are voluminous and are made to cover a person carrying full marching order, and they are camouflaged in weird designs so that when a couple of hundred men were draped in these garments they resemble something out of a fairy book. When these capes are being rolled great care has to be taken to make sure they are tied properly or they will not work when the time comes. Tommy Hill made some little mistake when he was rolling his which caused the slip knot to bind on the first jerk. Tommy's next jerk was a little too violent and one of the straps tore loose and the cape came to rest under Tommy's chin, still rolled. The rain persisted so the whole thing was called off until tomorrow at 9 o'clock. But I won't be there as I have to go up to B.H.Q. to get the exchanges working properly.

Mail came in today and I received 300 cigarettes from Nelle and a letter. There was lots of mail but that was the best I could do. I also received a letter from Aunt Pat and one from a second cousin named Peggy, whose last name I don't know.

A charge came in from the Provost Police against Stan Walker for not wearing his respirator and steel helmet while in Fleet last week. He is on leave just now and doesn't know anything about it yet; he may get C.B. out of it.

AUG. 29, FRI.

I went up to B.O.R. and performed two or three minor adjustments on the exchanges and stayed there until 11:30 am and got back after the inspection. Mr. Kent asked me for a detailed report on the stores which kept me busy for the rest of the day and part of the night. He got his report alright, but I am not prepared to say whether it is accurate or not.

We were paid this afternoon but I had to stay in and finish the stores report. When they gave me this stripe and this job they were quite emphatic that all I would have to do was to repair any defective instruments and having nothing at all to so with inventories and indents, etc. They gradually worked around until now the stores are my chief headaches, while the storeman is really only an assistant. I think when Walker comes off leave I'll put him in complete care of the stores like it was first arranged.

I finished the desired report about 11 pm and Sgt. Rankine took it away with him. I am going to try a treatment to get rid of these pimples. They are not serious, but they are an awful nuisance.

AUG. 30, SAT.
Interior economy for most of the fellows today so I tidied up the stores and scrubbed my table white. It's made a vast improvement. I am sending for some soluble Sulphien and boy it better be good because it is costing me £1:10.

I went downtown this afternoon but could not get any of things I wanted so went to a show at the Odeon after which I had a lunch at the YMCA. I was back in billets before dark, very much disgusted and fed up. I felt better when I had written a letter to Nelle. Poor Nelle, she will be wondering what is the matter with me because of the type of letters I have been sending to her recently.

AUG. 31, SUN.
I missed church parade this morning for some reason or other, but managed to finish a murder book by three this afternoon. I made a ring smaller for one of the boys in mortars this afternoon, started a letter to Charlotte this evening.

SEPT. 1, MON.
Why does the time go so fast, I just get used to writing down Aug. when along comes Sept. Installed a Fuller phone at B.O.R. this morning and tried to rig a practice buzzer for the classroom this afternoon.

I should have gone and seen Doris this evening but I decided to go to the show instead. I am trying to trade leaves with Comack so that I will have more money when I go. It will only be a matter of a week or so.

It is a wonderful night outside so peaceful and quiet it is easy to forget that there is a war on.

SEPT. 2, TUES.

A company dental parade this AM for the purpose of forming new dental charts. Everything is okay with me in the molar situation, that is, what's left of them.

I had the use of the PU this afternoon, Jeff driving, to install fuller phones at the companies. The job was finished except for H.Q. Company by four o'clock. Personally I am unable to see the reason for them while we are in this position and it must be Mr. Kent's own little idea. For the trouble they cause there isn't much use putting them in.

I was planning on going to see Doris this evening but my bike had a flat tire, so had to postpone the visit again. I stayed in and perused a Red Book and wrote a letter to Felicie. The boys next door, the mortar platoon, borrowed my kettle so felt obliged to invite me in for lunch, which I accepted.

Reg dropped in this evening and said he had a good mind to go to holding unit and transfer from there. He said he feels like he isn't earning his $1.50 a day at the Sig office and wanted to do a little every day, anyway.

Cross, Day, Forsythe and Ross went canoeing on the Basingstoke Canal this evening and mere paddling became too monotonous so commenced to stage a canoe tipping foray which resulted in the four of them coming in soaking wet. Evidently they enjoyed it while it lasted.

SEPT. 3, WED.

Installed H.Q. fuller phone this morning which necessitated an additional contact on the fuller phone switch at the Sig office. I stayed there all morning so as to escape the spit and polish that usually proceeds a general inspection. Tomorrow is the day I think.

On the way back Cpl. Hatch and I stopped at the Glen Cafe for a lunch and had three tomato sandwiches, one cake and a couple of cups of tea apiece.

I think I have finally located a tailor in town where I can have the neck of my good uniform cut down to fit me. Hatch expressed the opinion that we may never see action and I agreed with him. Schemes, inspections and interior economy seems to be our lot for the duration.

My leave has been set back to the last week of this month again which is far more favourable for me regarding financial position. I haven't heard from Aunt Ett or Lilly for some time now, I wonder if they have moved. There is a strong possibility as their house was badly damaged during last fall's (*air*)raids.

There was a 2 i/c's inspection this afternoon and as it was also sports day I cleared out of the way by using the excuse that I was going to the ball game. Ball games don't interest me in the least so I dropped into the signal office for a while then went for a walk along the Basingstoke Canal, a shallow weed-grown ditch, the primary purpose of which has been long forgotten. Even along here it was impossible to be by oneself. I passed soldiers sleeping in the shade of the thick-foliaged trees, people on bicycles wheeled up and down the narrow path; women sat along the banks writing, reading or knitting.

This evening I went up to the B.O.R. and ran into a hoard of newly arrived Canadians who were swarming the streets. They evidently think they are here to save England and expect everybody to show it. I wonder how many people have stopped to think just how much the Canadian soldier has done in this war compared with similar forces of other countries. Aldershot is like a Canadian Colony now, Canadians everywhere.

The 1ˢᵗ Div have come close to action a couple of time but have never really seen any of it. They were over in France a few days before that country's capitulation; they were equipped and ready to go to Norway and their latest disappointment was when the Russian German war started. They were actually on their way and were seven hours on the North Sea but they turned back and disembarked again. Someone of high position had gone to London, imbibed too freely and talked without discretion, even naming the place where they were going to land.

Napoleon was right, the worst thing for a trained army in war time is idleness. Schemes are just schemes, inspections are distasteful and something to be endured; both are inconveniences and a nuisance. Men in the other units such as artillery, anti-tank, R.C.C.S., engineers, etc. want to transfer to the infantry and men in the infantry want to transfer to the above mentioned units. It doesn't make sense.

I came back from town early and had a shower, started a letter to Marcella, then went to town for lunch before going to bed.

SEPT. 4, THURS.

The inspection was due to start at nine this morning and I'll confess I hadn't an excuse thought up good enough to get out of it. At 8:45 I received a call from the Sig office conveying the welcome news that one exchange was completely dead, so I lost no time in a strategic withdrawal to a better position.

The Brigadier did inspect the Signal office, but after a few questions about batteries he didn't bother me anymore. An officer, not so well liked by all and sundry, lingered after the Brig was gone to draw our attention, in no uncertain manner, to the fact that there was some ashes still in the fireplace, left over from some papers that Reg had burnt.

I stayed at the Sig office until ll:35 so as to miss the inspection at my own billets but it appears that the Old Boy was called back suddenly and will inspect H.Q. company Saturday or Monday. There are rumors of ceremonials tomorrow. We have even got back to those things.

We had our rifles inspected by ordinance this afternoon and despite the fine shooting qualities of my weapon, they condemned it for body wear. I am supposed to receive a new one in the near future. Reg and I went to see Chad Hanna this evening and although the picture itself wasn't too bad, inside the theater was so hot we couldn't enjoy it. I think Reg is thinking the same as myself, two years in the army wasted.

The ride home in the moonlight was the most pleasant experience I have had in many a day. It was perfect but one can't really enjoy it unless he can share it with someone. Walker was in bed when I came in; he had just come off leave this afternoon.

SEPT. 5, FRI.

We spent the morning taking stock with the help of three arguing linemen, Cross, Day and Forsythe. At least we checked everything that we have in stores which isn't a great deal. I was informed that I would not have to go on ceremonials this afternoon which doesn't make me a bit mad.

The boys left for ceremonials practice after I had left for the Sig office. I wasn't taking any chance on them changing their minds. There were five regular signallers on parade, the rest were all on duty or sleeping after being on all night.

I went to Farnborough on a bicycle to see Doris and we went for a very nice walk. I am taking her to a show on Monday evening. It's quite a little jaunt on a bicycle but the roads are all good except for the hills. I also found out 2nd cousin Peggy's last name. It's Kent, so I will have to write to her now. Also found out that she was twenty-one a few days ago. It rained a little tonight, but not enough to worry about.

SEPT. 6, SAT.

We almost were forced to go on the ceremonial parade this morning but there was no definite word saying we were supposed to be on it so we stayed off. The new Brigadier is taking the salute.

Checked over all battle batteries for dates, then finished a letter to Marcella, then wrote one to Aunt Pat.

The boys came off the inspection parade with mixed convictions regarding our new Brigadier. He was supposed to have said in a speech after the inspection that the Canadians were chosen to defend England from a land invasion. This means that we are a glorified Home Guard army. He also remarked that there is a possibility that we will be here all winter with a likely probability that we will be going back to tents during the winter. Tents in the summertime is miserable in this country which we discovered last month, but tents in the winter will be much worse. It isn't a very bright prospect for the Canadian Army Overseas. I think I know why the people over here are so aloof with us Canadians. They still think that Canada is still barbarous and we are a bunch of savages and they are afraid of us. It's getting the fellows down and their regard for Canada has grown beyond all former limits. When we compare the friendliness of Canadian people with that of the English people, we are glad that we are Canadians. I have changed my mind, I am not fighting for England, I will be fighting for Canada. I'll admit there are some of the people over here who are quite like the people in Canada and are quite friendly but they are all too few. In other words, the average Englishman is still thinking along the same lines as the people did centuries ago. Old fashioned, narrow-minded ideas that are outdated by scores of years. One man in B Company always wanted to be referred to as English before he came over. He was born in England and lived most of his young life over here. A few months after we had been here someone asked him how he liked England and he said, "three months over here has made me a damned good Canadian." I am not sure just what the trouble is, but families can live side by side for years and still not know one another. Perhaps they have been crowded on the island for so long that their desire for seclusion has smothered their neighborly instincts completely. They consider it a social crime and an insult if a stranger speaks to them without a proper introduction.

I went down town this afternoon and bought a cheap block plane. I am still looking around for a draftsman's ink compass. Came back to billets before supper and made one of a pair of new drumsticks. Wrote a letter to Peggy; her last name is Kent.

SEPT. 7, SUN.

There was a church parade this morning but L/Cpl. Lodge wasn't there; there was a little work needing attention so I was excused from that little ordeal. I finished a new pair of drumsticks and washed all my dirtys which was of such volume I raised two lovely blisters, one on each hand.

This afternoon I went down along the Basingstoke Canal and found a nice shady spot and read one of the full length novels that Nelle sent. I received a carton of cigarettes which takes care of the leave smoking. Bobby sent both Reg and I a carton. Bobby will never know how Reg appreciates the things she sends him. He can't understand why she sends parcels to a guy she only knows as a friend of mine. I walked up to the Signal office and collected Reg and we went to see Edward G. Robinson in "Doctor Erhlich's Magic Bullet", a very good picture. Reg paid the way this time so I bought the lunch after the show.

We heard strong rumors that we will be moving again soon. It is still rumors because there is nothing official as yet and rumors only agree on the fact that we are moving but differ as to time and destination. A full moon and a clear sky, but just a little chilly. Walker is in bed so I suppose I had better follow suit. Having the light shaded this way reminds me of the nights I used to spend studying at my desk with an old cloth thrown over the lamp. That's how Jack's blue sweater got burnt one night.

SEPT. 8, MON.

Nothing was done in the Maintenance line this morning mainly because all the instruments are in use and seem to be operating satisfactorily, something that is unusual for a change. Received a message from Mr. Kent this morning via the D.R. requesting the deliverance of the handset for our other U.C. exchange. I informed the D.R. to tell Mr. Kent that I had told him on a number of occasions that one D5 had come back from Ordinance minus the handset and that we were forced to use the one out of the exchange on the incomplete telephone, therefore as previously notified, we have no handset for the U.C. available. I left for Farnborough early to keep an appointment with Doris, then we went the Rex Theatre. I had seen the picture before and we were late and only saw the main feature, "Major Barbara" and the newsreel. The newsreel was a new one and it wasn't a total loss. Doris is a nice kid but I will have to be careful she doesn't get any serious ideas or notions. Arrived back at billets at 11:30 and enjoyed the ride in the glow of a full moon.

SEPT. 9, TUES.

Rumors are more persistent and appear partially authentic even to the date of moving, so I guess it's the straight goods this time. The news broke over the radio this morning that Canadians and English troupes, aided by Free Norwegian troops, had taken Spitsbergen in a surprise attack. Spitsbergen is an island about the size of Iceland and noted I believe for its coal and iron mines.

Received 28 new batteries for the No. 18 sets so spent the remainder of the morning checking them off and sorting them out according to the dates.

The linemen were trying to find out why H.Q. company's line failed to register on the exchange all morning and part of the afternoon, then they called me in to fix the exchange. I tried the line on four different units with no success whatsoever. Some months ago I had a similar experience while on a scheme and after trying every unit on the board I finally discovered that one of the judges had disconnected the wire from the ground end. Since then I have found that cause particularly common with that variety of complaint so I asked Forsythe if he or Cross had looked at the grounds and received a reply to the positive. A point was reached where I had done everything I knew to the exchange and the linemen had checked the line over a number of times with still no results, so Cross went to check the ground again just to make sure and he discovered six feet of wire missing from the leads, which all goes to prove that the thingamajig won't work unless the ground wire is intact or something? I had to walk back to Dinorben arriving there just in time for supper and where I found another job waiting for me. The No. 18 sets were being prepared for the scheme tomorrow and batteries were changed and defects noted. On my desk was one of the sets that had a faulty receiver with all indications pointing to the pressel switch in the microphone handle. Upon examination everything appeared in good condition but the battery was a bit low. Changing the battery and cleaning the switch contacts seemed to rectify the trouble satisfactorily.

I've decided to check all of the forty batteries I had in stock while I had the set meter available and I found twelve out of the forty batteries defective; eight absolutely dead and four weak. The unusual part of it was they were nearly all new batteries delivered this morning, but according to the dates they were old and had evidently lost their life from shelf depletion.

SEPT. 10, WED.

All equipment being out there was very little I could do this morning so I started a letter to Nelle. It was sports day today so I managed to finish the letter this afternoon and when finished, I decided it was the craziest letter I had ever written. I got mixed up in a debate as to what relation would one relative be to other relatives if a cousin married a cousin or a second-cousin. The results were amazing, to say the least. Another 28 No. 18 battle batteries came in today and as they were of later dates, all except one were in first class shape. I started a letter to Bobbie this evening and being in the same mood as earlier in the day, I got off to another flying start that promises to be just as foolish as Nelle's letter.

I walked up to the Sig office this evening to get my bike and had something to eat at the YMCA with Reg. Coming home on the bike with the night as black as a coal bin I suddenly saw a man, walking in the center of the road, loom up in front of me. Evidently he was a new man over here and black outs were proving a little difficult for him. He didn't realize that danger from lightless cars and trucks was far greater on the road than lamp posts were on the sidewalk. I had no bell so must have scared him out of a few years' growth when I brushed silently by him. He will learn if he isn't killed or flattened by a truck before. Came back and soaked this carcass of mine in a steaming hot bath followed by a cold shower and I feel fresh as a daisy. I will have to douse the light soon or Walker will be climbing my frame. Foot inspection tomorrow.

SEPT. II, THURS.
The foot inspection took place and was passed without a hitch. Sgt. Rankine and I went up to the B.O.R. soon after, me to get a lock for the stores and Bill for some information. Managed to procure a lock as well as a notepad and reinforcements then came back to billets by eleven o'clock. I told Red that there was no entry of my second year qualifications entered in my pay book, nor as far as I can learn, in the company records. The records of my first qualification was lost and the entry never made, now the same thing is happening here again; it is too much to be coincidental. I paid Joe Forsythe a shilling to press my uniform this afternoon and I soldered another badge for Sgt. Baker.

Called on Doris again this evening and we went to a show at the Rex called, "The Prime Minister" which was about the political life of Disraeli. Made arrangements with Doris to see her again on Monday so that she can give me the latest news from her home where she is going for the weekend. I made myself a cup of tea after a cold, beautiful ride home. At last we know the horrible truth, the reason for the foot inspection this morning. We are going on a twenty-two mile march tomorrow night. Some mad official showing off his temporary authority while the big shot is on leave. I hope he falls down a man hole and breaks his _____ ankle.

SEPT. 12, FRI.
Spent most of the morning writing notes on radio theory. Everything was ready for the scheme by noon and by three o'clock we had the truck loaded, with one cable cupboard, spare batteries, (7), three reels of cable, three telescopes, three binoculars and one empty pannier. A bicycle was added as an afterthought. Supper at four, a haversack lunch was handed out, then we were under way on one of the most senseless schemes I have ever had the misfortune to be on. The first boner (I call them "boners" because that is exactly what they are) was travelling 28 miles by a motor convoy along a circular route and ending up only six miles from the starting point. To some people that may be petrol conservation, but to me it smells like a waste. The second boner was when we had to wait 7 and a half hours from 9 in the evening until 5 in the morning for our part in the scheme. As far as I can gather the sole purpose of the whole idea was to test a pontoon bridge that the R.E.'s had erected across a narrow part of Lake Holly. We crossed the bridge at about 6 am. There was nothing stopping us from going to bed in our billets until four in the morning but instead we had to sit around all night unable to sleep because of the cold.

We arrived back at billets in time for breakfast after which Walker and I turned off the light, rolled the blackout down and went to bed. I got up at eleven, had dinner, washed and shaved and was ready for pay parade at 3:15 this afternoon. Made arrangements with Walker for the loan of two pounds when I go on leave. I drew £1:10 this afternoon. Canadian mail is in, mostly parcels and cigarettes. The mail was sorted about five thirty but there wasn't even so much as a letter for me. I received a letter from Aunt Pat this morning.

Jeff Reynolds and I went to a show tonight at the Odeon called, "Love on the Dole," it was a very good picture. I have been noticing a suggestive trend in these Limey pictures toward bettering the conditions of the ordinary people. Quite a number of pictures lately have been about the common working classes and hardships they have to put up with; the squalor they live in and the need for healthy clean houses to take the place of the slums. Perhaps after this war is over, the old crowded tenement houses will disappear entirely, giving way to the modern sanitary method of housing. The importance of the working class of people has been emphasized like it never has been during peace years; they are the backbone of any nation and if they are dissatisfied and miserable, the whole nation feels it. A dissatisfied nation means resentment which invariably leads to national dissatisfaction. From there on anything can happen; madmen climb to power on the surges of discontent, governments dissolve, new policies appear, some of which are good and some develop into danger for the whole world. Surely there must be a happy medium between the slow cumbersome movements of the large governing party and the selfish, power-mad rule of the individual. Somehow it must be found before permanent world peace is obtainable. Contentment in every nation means a lasting peace.

SEPT. 14, SUN.

Another four hours spent on copying notes this am. I don't know why, perhaps I have a notion that I may go in for amateur operating if I can save enough money from that pick and shovel job I have picked out. Maybe it would be fair to myself to admit my failure and start on another line. With my mental ability, politics would be the thing but my dislike of attracting attention is against it. There is no use fooling myself any longer, radio is out of my reach, away over my head. Perhaps I should try the gambling racket, it doesn't take brains; on second thought, I am too careful for that game. From observations based on nearly two years of service, I think I am in the right place, the Army. I must be, if I had brains I wouldn't be here. Sgt. Rankine got a letter from Doc. He has been grounded for cracking up a bomber while training three students, no one hurt. He also cracked up in another way recently; he is engaged and likes the "beautiful drabness of the bald headed prairie." Sure, a guy in love will like any kind of country if the recipient of his affections lives there.

247

I went to the show this evening, alone as per usual. There was not anything else to do but to come back to this hole of mine and brood. That seems to be the one thing I am good at. Some people might say that I am losing confidence in myself but those same people don't know that I never had any, so I am losing nothing. Perhaps a cup of tea will cheer me up, there is nothing like trying. Maybe I should get myself psycho-analyzed; my personal jinx is working overtime lately. Decided to take a bath at 10 pm; finished about eleven and started a letter to Marcelle while waiting for my hair to dry.

SEPT. 15, MON.

Started checking over an eighteen set this morning but couldn't find anything wrong with it so discontinued and left it for a more thorough when there wasn't such a crowd around. A practice buzzer took up another two hours, it had a short to the permanent magnet. My intentions were first rate this afternoon when I set out for "A" company to repair the eighteen set there but I never got any further than the Signal office.

I received a large parcel from Bobbie this afternoon and I divided it up and took half of it to Reg this evening on my way to Farnborough. Also received a letter from Nelle, one from Marc, and one containing a large bunch of snaps from Bobbie. I took a bar of Canadian chocolate that Bobbie sent up to Doris this evening as I had promised her I would as soon as I got some more. Doris and I went to the Rex again tonight. One of Doris' fellow workers, a Miss Doris Murphy, claims she lived in the big house that Emmy is living in now. This Miss Murphy gave Doris some names to see if I knew them and they included Bill and Tom Hinton and their two sisters, Irene Swanson and the McGikky (not spelt right I am sure) family. I am inclined to think Doris misunderstood her about living in Emmy's big house. It was a bit difficult coming home in the blackout as the night was very dark.

SEPT. 16, TUES.

The day was spent in a very unimportant manner with odd jobs of little consequence. Completed a shade for Ackeley's (Keewatin) reading lamp, the one I refer to as Cross's folly. The sick No. 18 set was thoroughly examined this afternoon and was found to be suffering from a loose top cap connection on the A.R. 8 tube, and a weak battery.

Reg and I went to see "Cheers for Miss Bishop" showing at the Odeon theater. We had lunch at the YMCA afterwards. It was very crowded so didn't stay very long there. I came back to billets intending to finish Marcella's letter but found Sgt. Rankine waiting for me with a bag of fish and chips. We talked until a late hour about sports of all kinds, even discussing the qualities of different kinds of boats. So there was no letter writing tonight.

SEPT. 17, WED.

Checked over another No. 18 set this morning; then we had a medical examination mainly for the purpose of locating any diminutive creatures that make a soldier's life miserable, and I don't mean lice, but as far as I know everyone got a clean sheet. Our immunity from the various forms of insect life that usually feed on the human body, is due, I think, to the simple ablutionary facilities available wherever we go. Much different to what it was in the last war. I finished a letter to Marcella this afternoon and found time to patch one of the bicycle tyres.

I found Doris alone in the house this evening when I got there and we started looking at my collection of snaps. Mr. and Mrs. Baxter came in soon after and joined us around the open fire. They are a very friendly and interesting young couple and very interested in Canada. Mr. Baxter asked the inevitable question, "what do you think of England?" and so we spent a very enjoyable evening talking about everything in general. They, like nearly all the people over here, have no conception of the vastness of Canada and the States and asked, if and how many times I had been to New York. I told them it was in the neighbourhood of two thousand miles from Kenora and couldn't very well finance a trip to that city. They were quite amazed at the distance and immediately asked if I could go from Kenora to New York by train. So I offered the information that not only could we go by train, but also by sleeper or night bus. I wonder if they ever teach Canadian history or geography in the school over here. Nevertheless, I enjoyed the evening immensely and was very sorry it was so short. Mrs. Baxter has a brother in Canada last heard from twelve years ago when he was in Vancouver. I took one of the chocolate bars up to Doris that I received from Janet today. I asked them where Happy Forest was and they claim they never heard of it. Doris thinks it is Epping Forest in Walthamstow, a few minutes walk from where Peggy lives. Perhaps she can help me find the tree. It was a very nice evening and one we don't get the chance to enjoy very much over here. It was misty and dark coming back but I made it with difficulty.

SEPT. 18, THURS.
Doing nothing seemed to be the general pastime this morning and there was a crowd in the stores until noon which, if I had wanted to, would have prevented me even getting me even getting near my bench.

I had to attend an N.C.O. meeting this afternoon during which we were informed that the men were becoming too familiar with the N.C.O.s and officers. It's an old story and no one pays much attention to it. We were issued with more blanco this afternoon and I managed to do the bulk of my webbing; another Brigadier's inspection; they never seem to stop. Reg and I went to see Deanna Durbin in "Nice Girl" showing at the Odeon. Also saw the pictures of the raid on Spitsbergen with not the least jealousy or envy toward the Canadians that took part, my opinion of that raid can be expressed in one word, "child's play." It was a job the boy scouts could have accomplished just as easily. No doubt it was important in itself and the destruction of the coal industry on that island was necessary but is that the kind of action we came four thousand miles to take part in? From the danger point of view, the only peril the army was in was the possibility of seasickness or pneumonia so why all the shouting? Perhaps I have the wrong slant on things and I have no romantic, glorious ideas of this war game; also I have a fairly accurate picture of what an actual battle will be like, with its misery, agony and blood spilling but I did think we would be aiming our rifles at something more than a painted target. I can't see anything glorious about war and the consequent misery, destruction and death that keeps pace with the swing and sweep of battle but waiting for it is far worse than the dread of the actual battle. Although I am proud to be a Canadian I am unable to see anything special to crow over in the Spitsbergen raid, with more apologies to the boys that took part.

I had a steaming hot bath this evening and after soaking fully submerged in water so hot I could hardly stand it, I ran the water to ice cold gradually until I had to get out. I feel like a million bucks now.

SEPT. 19, FRI.
Finished blancoing this morning and was glad to be finished with the dirty messy job. Finished a letter to Peggy this afternoon.

Called for Doris about 7:30 pm and we went to see "Love on the Dole" showing at the Rex. Doris is going to see her brother Jack this weekend so I won't see her again until Monday; I may start my leave on Tuesday.

SEPT. 20, SAT.
I checked over the No. 18 set at the Sig office this am but found it okay. McGuire came in while I was there and confirmed some of the tales I have been hearing of him. He was put in charge of "A" company signals and he is either over zealous or working for a stripe. The other two Signals think he is batty with the responsibility. I have been informed that he has been trying to repair his wireless set himself and made some sort of a mess of it. I hate to jump him for it but I can't afford to take the consequences or responsibility of work done by others.

Wrote a letter to Nelle this afternoon and mailed it just before I received another one. Boy, does she know how to dash off small little gloom chasers. Also received another carton of cigs from Bobbie. Reg dropped in about six or seven thirty and seemed a little worried because he had also received a carton from Bobs. He said he just couldn't allow her to send any more and was going to send a telegram telling her not to as he couldn't send her anything. He greatly appreciates the smokes but thinks it isn't right for her spending her money for things for him.

I went down to the Sig office tonight and Reg and I walked around for a while. We had some fish and chips, then went to the YMCA for tea and cakes. On the way home, in fact I was almost home, just slowing down waiting for the guard to yell "HALT" when the alert sounded. It's a long time since I heard that wail and nearly fell off the bike from surprise.

I was talking to the guards when we heard the lone raider flying comparatively low. All search lights from different directions converged on him which must have scared him a little. We heard him diving to get out of the lights, then he turned and headed back again. He must have unloaded his bombs during his dive because a few seconds later we heard the scream of their descent. They exploded a short distance away and we could feel the concussion quite easily. There was only three comparatively light detonations so we came to the conclusion it was a flight to try out the AA defences. The AA guns wisely kept silent. The all clear has not gone yet. 11:20 pm.

SEPT. 21, SUN.

Voluntary church parade this morning and very few turned out for the parade. Letter writing seemed to be the main occupation before noon. Managed to complete two letters before 2:00pm, one to Bobs and one to Nelle. Started packing my bag for leave which I hope will start Tuesday. May leave on Monday night.

Went up to the B.O.R. to see Reg and obtained the loan of ten shillings. Except for the usual crowd of soldiers pacing up and down the streets there was nothing interesting in town. Heard the news about the lone raider of last night being shot down by AK AK fire. Some fellows think he was forced inland by night fighters and when he got caught in the search lights, unloaded his bombs not knowing or caring where they landed. Official confirmation of the fall of Kiev was in the papers tonight, the same papers are screaming for a speed-up with the aid to Russia.

SEPT. 22, MON.

Started checking over No. 18 sets at the companies this morning. First on the list was "D" company, a good barber, Charlie Smalley, is stationed there and I did need a haircut badly. "A" company this afternoon with the good intentions of making "B" company as well, but "A" company telephone line developed a fault which delayed proceedings to such an extent, the "B" call was postponed until tomorrow morning. As is always the case, the little man wanted an inventory and detailed statement regarding signal stores, which includes the location and serial number of each instrument, before tomorrow afternoon. I am supposed to go on leave tomorrow.

Took Doris to the show again tonight and saw the picture, "Atlantic Ferry." Doris said that cousin Steve and Jack will be in London at the Criterion or Africa House where Steve is going to talk on a broadcast to Africa at 6:00pm. I may get there in time to see them. Making plans to go and see Aunt Pat during the coming weekend. As prearranged, I met Reg at the clock tower just before eleven but his front light had burnt out. However, we started riding with me on the white line hoping we wouldn't meet a policeman. We did, so Reg and I after listening to the reason why riding without lights wasn't allowed, walked until we had passed around the nearest corner. It was misty by this time which didn't help matters in the least but it was a long walk home so took a chance and rode our bikes again. The mist developed into a real fog which limited visibility to a few feet but we managed to get back to billets without much more trouble, at least, none from other patrolling lawmen. It took us over an hour and a half to make it. Two cups of hot chocolate took the dampness out of my system.

SEPT. 23, TUES.

Checked over the last two No. 18 sets this morning and left the inventories and check of stores to Stan. Eric Day, Joe Forsythe, two Canadian Sailor friends of Eric's and myself started leave this afternoon. We got into London at six o'clock and Joe Forsythe was impatient to find the sleeping quarters and get to a dance. We went to the Beaver Club to find out where we could get rooms and were advised to go to the Maple Leaf Club. We were hardly settled there when Joe was dragging us off to a dance at the Covent Gardens on The Strand. The interior of the Gardens was worth the 1/6 admission itself. A big crowd was dancing on the hardwood patterned floor. At one end was the orchestra and at the other a double stairway let up to a wide balcony. Around the sides of the dance floor and in the balcony were thick soft carpets and deep upholstered chairs. The hall itself was richly ornamented with statues of women in silver on a background of gold. Joe and Bill Kirk, one of the sailors, stayed to dance so Eric "Ink" Miles, the other sailor and myself started waking back toward Trafalgar Square with the intention of dropping in on

The Strand House Cafe. We bumped into three girls in the dark so invited them to come along. Their names were Irene, Helen and Kathleen. It was late when we came out of there so we started to take the girls home. The tubes were closed, the buses weren't running, so we had to take a taxi all the way to Highgate where we dismissed the taxi. After saying goodnight to the girls we discovered considerable difficulty finding transportation back to central London. We finally nailed a late cruising taxi which dropped us off in front of the Maple Leaf Club at three in the morning.

SEPT. 24, WED.

We were awakened this morning by a girl from Toronto at nine. We call this girl Queenie now because she claimed that Toronto is the Queen's city. We spent the morning cleaning up and getting oriented. This afternoon I set out for Walthamstow to find Peggy but missed my train from St. Pancreas Station by twenty minutes, so spent three hours shopping on The Strand. Finally found an ink compass that I have been searching for so long. Eric, Ink and I went up to the Paramount Dance Hall on Tottenham Court Road where we were supposed to meet our three girlfriends of last night. We found Kathleen and another girl named Rose. Ink started dancing so the two girls, Eric and I retired to a place across the road for refreshments. We lost the girls in the crowd when the dance folded up so the three of us walked back to the Maple Leaf Club arriving here at two in the morning.

SEPT. 25, THURS.

We were roused out of bed by the nurse of the club at nine again and we had a very good breakfast. We went out for a short walk this morning before dinner up to the Vauxhall Bridge. We found the outgoing tide interesting as it left the bottom of the riverbed exposed for a hundred or so feet on each side. The Thames barges loaded with coal, wheat and other goods, were all squatting in the mud waiting for the high tide and the numerous cranes along both banks were all busy loading or unloading other barges. This afternoon I set out to find Aunt Ett's place by taking a tube train from Victoria Station to Liverpool Street. Soon I was in a district containing names I remembered dad mentioning. Bethnal Green, Shoreditch Parish Church, Dirty Dick's, to mention a few of them. I had a little difficulty finding Ashford Street, but with the willing help of an aged paper vendor it was finally accomplished. Number ten was about half way down a court-like affair. I had knocked three or four times and had received no answer when a lady came running down the street. It was Aunt Ett. She looks an awful lot like dad, both in looks and in manner of talking. The girls Lilly and Ann, were both working so Auntie and I had quite a talk before they came home. Aunt Ett is young yet and very much active, unafraid of bombings and refuses point blank to move out of her damaged house. Lilly came home first and was met at the door by Aunt Ett who told her that she had a soldier waiting to see her. Lilly came into the kitchen (I always managed to get into the kitchen) and just looked at me for quite a while. She finally said she didn't know me, then she realized who I was, she like Aunt Ett seemed very pleased to see me. Then Ann came in, but she saw my Balmoral being on the front room table and knew who I was before she came to the kitchen. They are both very nice looking girls and, like their mother, unafraid of raids. They seemed very disappointed when I told them I wouldn't being staying tonight as I wanted to go down and pay Aunt Pat a flying visit. I am sorry I made that decision now because I think I could enjoy a stay there. Lilly had a date and left soon after six thirty, just after Ann's friend came in with her baby boy. I stayed until it was time for Ann's friend to leave and Ann and the friend showed me the way to the tube station.

I was supposed to change at Bank for an Inner Circle train but at the next stop on the other side of Bank I decided I was going the wrong way so disembarked and went back to Bank and got another train. On arriving at Victoria Station I got mixed up in the blackout and obtained the aid of a policeman to put me on the right track. I lost track of the "Bobby's" directions on the first turning so grabbed me a handful of No. 24 bus. I arrived at the Maple Leaf Club about 9:30 and went down to the dining room for a snack which turned out to be a meal when Jane, one of the girls, asked me if I could eat a steak. I think I have done enough writing tonight so will hit the hay. Eric and "Ink" aren't in yet.

SEPT. 26, FRI.

The nurse woke us up this morning and we had a late breakfast. Eric and Ink were feeling a little tired after their long walk back from Highgate last night so we took a short walk this morning down toward Vauxhall Bridge. The two sailors, "Ink" and Bill dropped into a men's hairdressers (Barber Shop) for hair cuts so Eric and I walked on to the bridge and took a look at the Thames waterfront from that vantage point. There wasn't much activity as the tide was near low ebb and the day was hazy around the embankments.

This afternoon, Eric, "Ink", and I paid a visit to the zoo and had a very interesting two hours. We were back at the Beaver Club soon after four o'clock but were unable to get on the Canadian broadcast. I think every Canadian in the forces, in London on leave, was there all waiting for a chance to talk to folks back home. We came back to the Maple Leaf Club for supper. "Ink," Eric and I started out for the Marble Arch this evening and before the evening was far expended we were up at the Covent Gardens on The Strand. We got back to the club after midnight feeling a little worn out.

SEPT. 27, SAT.

This morning the gang split up, Eric and "Ink" going to Leatherhead, Joe to Brighton, Bill was staying and I to Walthamstow. I thought I was giving myself plenty of leeway to catch the 12:30 train but it pulled out while I was buying my ticket, so had to take the 12:40 from St. Pancras and change at Kentish Town. A young lady willingly told me when to get off at Walthamstow and an obliging young man told me how to reach Mission Grove. It was market day and the High Street was filled with people buying from the stalls lining both sides of the street. It was no difficulty finding No. 9 Mission Grove and Mr. Kent (cousin Bill) answered the door. Mission Grove is a court-like affair very similar to Ashford Street, the only difference was in the design of the houses and Mission Grove has trees along both sides and the end. The usual air raid shelter was present in the middle of the rectangle and a school blocked the other end, thus forming a blind street.

Peggy had just got up (she works nights) so cousin Bill and myself went for a walk along High Street. When we got back Peggy and Eileen were both there preparing a cup of tea. They are both great kids and immediately started making arrangements for the evening. Peggy had to work but it was fairly early so Peggy and I went for a walk in Epping Forest. We had a very nice walk and of course, most of the talk was of Canada. On the way there we dropped into the library and met Muriel, a Canadian-born girl from Vancouver. It was nearly seven when we got back from our walk and Peggy had to rush off to work. Now Fred Croucha, Eileen's future husband was there and after a hasty cup of tea, we set out for the pictures. They wouldn't let me pay for anything. We got back from the pictures around ten thirty and after a lunch of cheese sandwiches, I was shown my room. Before leaving London this morning I sent a cablegram home to Nelle.

SEPT. 28, SUN.

Awakened very early this morning by AA guns firing nearby at a lone stray raider but soon fell asleep again. Woke up at six thirty and laid awake until Peggy came home from work. Eileen and Fred Croucha left early for Southend and cousin Bill, Peggy and myself left at ten. The bus was fairly crowded and we had to stand up for half the way. Peggy was tired after working all night and kept dozing off but the bus was too uncomfortable for her to get any real sleep. Made friends with a fair haired blue eyed youngster across the aisle and he helped to pass the time away to keep Peggy awake. We arrived at Aunt Pat's place around noon and then came the meeting of all the cousins and friends. First of all there was Uncle Jack and Aunt Pat, a better couple couldn't be found. Cousin Steve Hawes from South Africa, a big friendly, red-headed cuss. Then Cousin Jack, his wife Alice, their daughter Jessie. Cousin Jack reminds me very much of brother Jack. Cousin Beattie and her husband John and their two children, John and Marion. Cousins Elsie and Doris. Edith, Harold's wife; cousin Bill, Peggy and Eileen. Fred Croucha and Mr. and Mrs. Croucha completed the group.

After introductions all around, Jack wanted pictures of us all so we posed in every conceivable attitude. He seemed very pleased to have cousins from South Africa and Canada there at the same time. Then we all went out into the vacant lot at the back of the house and played ball until dinner was ready. The dinner would have made dad's mouth water, especially the Yorkshire Pudding. After dinner there was more ball playing until our arms were sore, then someone found a skipping rope and skipping was enjoyed by the few who were young enough to participate, which included everyone except Uncle, Auntie, and Mr. and Mrs. Croucha. Doris was very quiet the whole day until she started playing the piano. We had tea consisting of Cockerals and bread. At six o'clock John and family had to go back to the city as well as Bill, Doris, Eileen, Jessie, Jack and the Croucha's. Peggy and I decided to stay the night so we stayed. The evening was spent in tales of Canada, South Africa and bygone days in London; Aunt Pat, Uncle Jack, Elsie and Beattie supplying the latter. I slept with Steve in the upstairs front room and before going to sleep we compared his country with mine and the two of them with England. They are a grand bunch of people and I am proud to have them as relatives. I would like to meet Steve's family now.

SEPT. 29, MON.

I had intended to leave early for London as I had promised Aunt Ett I would be coming back this morning, but Elsie, Peggy and Beattie wanted to show us two Colonials, the pier at Southend-on-Sea so we changed our plans a little. To say the least, it must have been a lively spot in peace time but now it is all barricaded and guarded. We managed to find a souvenir store open at the bottom of Pier Hill where I obtained some postcards. Peggy bought a souvenir handkerchief for Nelle and asked me to send it to her.

We got back to the house around three in the afternoon, thus knocking my plans back another couple of hours. After promising Aunt Pat again and making arrangements to meet Steve, Elsie, Beattie and Jack at the Liverpool Street Station, Peggy and I caught the 4:10 bus back to Walthamstow. Peggy wanted to come all the way to Liverpool Station with me but the bus was delayed too much for her to do so as she couldn't get back in time to get to work at 7:30pm. However, she would insist in paying my fare, regardless of how much talking I did. She said that she would meet us at Liverpool Station at 12:30 tomorrow too. She is a sweet kid and was a great help to me during the trifly complicated traveling. I arrived in Liverpool Street Station at seven and was at Aunt Ett's before blackout time. There I learned that I had missed seeing Uncle Ted who had come up from Luton. Anne had just taken Sis home who was very disappointed at not seeing me again. Lilly had gone to the pictures with her boyfriend, Charlie. I am sorry I didn't stick to my original plan. Anne came in soon after and we settled down to talking. Lilly and Charlie came in but Charlie didn't stay very long. Aunt Ett confirmed dad's story of the Lord Oliver Lodge murdering his wife and the burning of the family records. We talked until it was too late to catch the tube train to the Maple Leaf Club but after a little rearranging I found myself reposing in a very good bed for the night. Anne is quite a girl, quite good looking. Lilly is good looking in a different way and seems to be the don't give a damn type. Aunt Ett reminds me very much of Mrs. Gibson and of dad, very much. I would like to spend a week with them but due to raids, putting me up would be very difficult. They absolutely refuse to let me pay for my keep. When I was down at Aunt Pat's they wouldn't even let me pay my bus and train fares. Neither Lilly, Anne or Aunt Ett like Uncle Wal so I guess the feeling is mutual.

SEPT. 30, TUES.

Anne had gone to work when I got up but Lilly was still getting ready; she left finally a half hour late. After a shave I went for a walk. Went as far as Wellington's statue on Threadneedle Street, the place of banks. I passed Middlesex Street, sometimes or commonly known as Petticoat Lane with Dirty Dick's on the right hand corner; Primrose and Pindar Streets, the Church of Ethelburga, the Virgin, Lombard and Princess Streets, the Bank of Canada and the Bank of Montreal, as well as the Canadian Bank of Commerce, and the statue of Peabody sitting in a massive chair serenely watching the scurrying traffic. I managed to obtain a wireless valve at a radio store during my early morning wanders and I got back to Aunt Ett's at 11:45am. While I was eating dinner, Aunt Ett told me all about grandmother and how she died. I was fifteen minutes late getting to Liverpool Station where I found Steve, Jack, Elsie and Beattie waiting for me and Peggy. Peggy hadn't arrived by two o'clock so we finally had to leave without her. Jack adopted the role of guide and soon had us on the top deck of an omnibus on our way to Trafalgar Square. He pointed out the Guild Hall, St. Paul's, the Bow Church, which has been badly damaged by bombs. We were introduced to the "Old Lady of Threadneedle Street," the Bank of England. We got off at South Africa House where Steve had some business to attend to. Elsie, Beattie and little Marion waited outside while we went in. When we came out we found the girls feeding the pigeons at the base of Nelson's Column. It wasn't very long before we had pigeons all around us. We boarded another bus for Waterloo Station and again Jack pointed out the places of interest. At Waterloo Station we found out when Steve's train left for Portsmouth and while we were there I inquired about my train. I was informed that the last one left at 9:00pm from Platform No. 10. We had a little more than an hour before Steve left so we went across to the P.S.O. Cafe for something to eat. All this time Jack refused to allow Steve and I to pay for anything but I told him that I was paying for the meal this time. He asked me if I would fight for it and I said, yes, he said "I guess you pay for it then." But he tried to get the better of me by having Beattie leave on some fictitious errand and pay for it as she was going out but I got there first and paid. Steve wanted to pay half but I wouldn't let him.

Steve left at 4:00pm and in all probability we won't be seeing him again as he is going back to home waters where the climate is more agreeable to him. Elsie, Beattie, Jack, Marion and I caught a tube train to Liverpool Station where we were just in time to put the girls on a train for Southend. Jack was supposed to be still on duty as a postman so he walked up to Old Street with me where he caught a train to his office. I arrived back at Aunt Ett's around 5:00pm in time for tea. We spent the remainder of the time to eight o'clock talking around the fireplace. Alfie's future wife, Gladys, came in and time flew too quickly. Anne and Gladys took me to Liverpool Station and saw me onto the right train. I caught the 9:00pm train and was in bed by eleven. The battalion is out on a scheme and won't be back until Friday. I could have stayed at Aunt Ett's another day at least. I had a good time at both family's. I like Anne and Peggy the most, I think, although everyone treated me swell. Anne suggested I go back to their place for Christmas. Jack wants a reunion soon after the war is over, so I guess my leaves will be all taken up for years to come. It is very easy and pleasant to go on leave but distasteful and difficult to come back.

OCT. 1, WED.

Oct. 1st; time slips by with so little to show for personally. The place seemed deserted this morning except for very few fellows who appear very much like optimistic mice in a deserted house. There is nothing to do and worlds of time to do it in. There are letters to be written to Aunt Ett, Aunt Pat,

Peggy, Anne and Nelle, but somehow the ambition is very much lacking. Went to see a show called, "The Prime Minister" for the second time just for something to do. Came home early with the intention of taking a bath but I think I will leave it until tomorrow night.

OCT. 2, THURS.
Awakened by Cpl. Peters, company clerk, at nine o'clock and was informed by that so-and-so to be at the orderly room at 10:45 to take charge of a coal party. The job lasted until 11:00. Eric and "Ink" Miles who is on another six-day leave, and I went to see "Boom Town" at the County Theater; then we had supper at the Glen Cafe. They were going to Aldershot to spend the evening and their money so I got ready and hightailed it to keep a date with Doris. We went to see "Target for Tonight" at the Rex and found the place so crowded we had to sit on the stairs until there was a couple of seats empty. I made arrangements to meet her tomorrow night to let her know if I would be able to go to Jack's place for the weekend. I am afraid it's a little too late to apply for a weekend pass and a little too soon after my seven-day leave for it to be granted. However, one can but try.

OCT. 3, FRI.
Eight-ten this morning saw one L/Cpl Lodge sleepily trudging over to the kitchen with mess tin and cup clanging merrily in his good right hand. Everything was hazy and obscure in the thick clammy early morning mist. It was so clammy, it was dripping off the trees with an unhurried dismal sound but the atmosphere felt fresh and clean and that spells healthy appetite in any man's language. Breakfast just wasn't being served, it was a case of a homey help-yourself proposition, and everyone did, and enjoyed it. This method, of course, is unpractical when the whole company is present and doesn't happen very often, so we made full use of it and still remained in the limits of our rations. This seemed to be an ideal morning to apply for a pass for the weekend and indications are such that I am very optimistic, in fact, it will be a surprise if it isn't granted. The unit's return was postponed until Monday so there is no logical reason why it shouldn't come through. Was summoned before the C.S.M. (a regular fellow) and was detailed to take charge of an escort to 2nd Div. Reception Station to bring back, alive and in

good condition, one prisoner, or rather, a defaulter. Torchy Cawson and Jones comprised the escort and we had to hoof it to the Battalion Orderly room to catch our transportation which consisted of one 30 cwt. truck belonging to the Tenth Field Ambulance Company. According to all reports and tips offered, the "prisoner" was a bad egg of long standing with a crime sheet like a newspaper so we were fully prepared for difficulty after he was signed over to us. We arrived at the Reception Station and when the Sergeant saw us get off the truck, he said, "Only three of you came?" which substantiated our expectations of trouble. The man was duly signed for and handed over to us. As it turned out, someone had misunderstood the name and, instead of a ring tailed hurricane, we found our prisoner to be a quiet, informative chap, with the firm belief that he had been misconstrued or something. However, when we got him home he proved exceptionally helpful as he was the only one who knew where the guard room was located and so acted as a guide. He led us right to the place and was soon taken off of our hands by the Corporal of the Guard. Doris was the object of another call from myself this evening and we went for a little walk to make arrangements about the weekend. We walked for quite a while through the bright moonlit night and were back at the house by nine. For the first time, Doris asked me in for a few minutes, something I think she has been wanting to do but wasn't sure how Mr. and Mrs. Baxter would like it. The news report gave us plenty to talk about for an hour or so, then Mr. Baxter's two female cousins from Boston (England) came in. Two, more fun loving, carefree girls I have never met before. Muriel plied questions about Canada and the States in barrage-like rapidity which I was called upon to answer to the best of my knowledge, and ability. They expressed the wish to go to Canada after the war is over. They are two swell kids and I hope I meet them again sometime. I left Doris with the understanding that we would proceed to Jack's place independently and meet there. The other girl is Sylvia. I realized a long-sought-after minor ambition tonight. I rode nearly all the way back to billets with hands off the handlebars. The last time I tried it, it cost me a pound to have my watch repaired.

OCT. 4, SAT.

A miserable day with a constant threat of rain, my pass is held up until after the Battalion gets here and muster parade is disposed of. It will be a late departure. Evidently they are certain of it being granted because they didn't put me on any guards or pickets and they are short of men. Indulged in a good bath this morning and am all ready to go. No pass yet. In fact, no Battalion yet and it's 1:30 now. I waited until 3:30, then saw the C.S.M. again; he made the pass out then told me I would have to find Lt. Bryce to have it signed. I found him playing billiards at the Poplars. He informed me that there was to be no weekend passes while the Battalion was away, but after second consideration scribbled his John-Henry in the proper place. I high-tailed back to the Battalion Orderly room and had the pass officially stamped and then caught the 4:35 train to Wimbledon. On arriving at that station I asked a tram inspector the way to Quarr Road and was told to catch a 93 bus to Morden Station, then change to a 157 bus, but the conductor couldn't tell me where Quarr Road was and advised me to get off at the next stop. By asking questions, innumerable questions, I finally found Jack's place on Quarr Road at 7:30 in the evening. Doris was already there and, of course, Jack, Alice and Jessie. The dog, Spot, nipped me as I stepped in the door but inside of an hour we were good friends. I met Rose, a cousin of Jack's, had tea, talked for some time, then was shown to my room. I think I am the only Cameron who has a weekend pass this weekend.

OCT. 5, SUN.

I was awake at seven this morning but laid in bed until nine when Alice brought up a cup of tea and cookies and the morning paper. We had breakfast around ten-thirty, then Doris, Jessie and I went down to Morden Station to meet Jack coming home from work. Jack, Jessie and I went down to the railway station to inquire about trains this evening. Having obtained the necessary information, which incidentally was vastly different to what I got last evening, we started for home again. Peggy was supposed to arrive 2:30 this afternoon so Jack took me for a walk around the neighbourhood. We waited at the bus stop for Peggy until Jessie came down, then we left her to wait for a while and we returned to the house. Jessie came in soon after so we gave up hope of Peggy coming and proceeded to do justice to Alice's perfectly cooked dinner. Someone suggested a game of Housy-Housy so we played for ha'pennies until tea time. Just as we were sitting down to tea, along comes Peggy and from there on things livened up considerably. Doris read my cup and by the sounds of it, the near future is going to be pleasant. At eight o'clock Jack, Peggy, Doris and I left for the station. The 9:28 from Waterloo was late and very crowded so decided to catch the 9:46 which besides the possibility of not having so many people on it, gave us more time to talk as well. Jack promised to show me the inner workings of a General Post Office after the war, something I think will be very interesting.

I arrived at Woking and like a hundred or so other people had to wait for the train to Fleet. Finally the train pulled in and everyone piled on. To say that the train was crowded would be a gross injustice to the constructional strength of the coach, it was crammed. I found myself in the corridor midway between two doors and from the conversation of my fellow passengers, I came to the conclusion that I was going to be the first one to reach the desired destination which meant that I would have to squeeze past, through and around the crowd to reach the door. It proved all too true but by squirming, twisting and tripping, managed to disembark at Fleet with very little damage. I found Walker asleep in bed and it won't be long before I will be doing likewise.

It has been a very good ten days, well spent and I have taken a new lease on life, at least, I feel like a million dollars after a welcome change. I would advise Jack and Roy to visit the Cox's, Fenn's and Kent's first, it will make them (Jack and Roy) feel better.

OCT. 6, MON.
Back to the old grind again but in a much better frame of mind. Reg and I went to see Judy Canova in "Scatterbrain" and "The Trial of Mary Dugan" at the County this evening, after which we had a good feed of fish and chips. I wrote letters to Anne, Ivy and Aunt Pat today.

OCT. 7, TUES.
Spent the better part of the morning fixing an 18 Set that had gone haywire during the scheme last week. Also fixed some fuller phones this afternoon. Crosse has been busy making a hitching device for the "baby carriage" so that it can be trailed behind the stores truck instead of on top. The "baby carriage" is a two-wheeled device with wheels similar to those on a motorcycle, with a steel frame and handles and a winding contraption. Its purpose is for laying

and reeling up cable that is to be, or has been laid a long distance. One man pulls or pushes the carriage while another man handles the winding device. It may prove to be a handy device but ease of transportation isn't one of its advantages, so Crosse is making a trailer hitch so that we can drag it behind the truck. I received a carton of cigs from Nelle today and they were very welcome because I have to buy Limey smokes which aren't very good. I went down to see Reg tonight for a while but came home early and took a bath. Started a letter to Nelle today describing my last seven-day leave. Hit the tenth page and am only up to Friday noon, just before we went to the zoo.

OCT. 8, WED.
I made a trip downtown this afternoon especially to buy stationery and went into the Y hut for tea but landed in a middle of a free showing of M of I Shorts for the public and didn't get out again until after four. Reg and I had supper at the snack bar across the street from the theater, then we went down to see the bank play retreat. I came home soon after and finished a letter to Nelle. I forgot to mention that Gordy Robertson of Kenora is in our transport now. He used to be with the "Pats" (*PPCLI*). The advance party is leaving tomorrow morning.

OCT. 9, THURS.
I tried to get a new uniform this morning but they didn't have my size so will have to wait until Tuesday. Peters promised me a matched outfit this time. Received a new rifle in place of my old one which was condemned for body-wear. Sgt. Major Martin brought a battery radio in for me to fix this afternoon and so far my efforts have been useless. I went to a show tonight alone. The picture wasn't too bad but the place was packed and hot. We went through another gas chamber drill today with the usual procedures followed to the letter; it's not very nice.

OCT. 10, FRI.
Walker was busy packing the panniers this morning as we are sending them and most of the rest of the stores tomorrow. Mail came in this afternoon and received six and one postcard. The letters were the thing I needed for a long time; Nelle, Bobbie, Marcella, Iris, Jack and Dad were the letter writers

while Bezzie was the sender of the postcard. I am glad to hear that she got through her operation. Doris seemed to have enjoyed the show at the Rex this evening. I saw Sid Wright at the B.O.R. but I was late for the date with Doris and couldn't talk very long with him. When we were leaving the house Doris and I saw a light actually floating in the sky. There was no sound but it was traveling fast before a stiff breeze. Doris went back to call Mr. and Mrs. Baxter to have a look. I guessed it to be a hydrogen-filled balloon like the kind Meteorologists use for collecting weather data. Mr. Baxter said he would try and find out tomorrow. I battled a head wind all the way home tonight and between that and watching an interesting search light display, I nearly landed in the ditch many times. It's a windy night with low, rain-laden clouds which emphasized the brilliancy of the lights. Got home about 11:30.

OCT. 11, SAT.

The 30 cwt truck was loaded with all the stores not in use and sent down to Lewes with Walker aboard to look after things. The line gang were busy all day reeling up the wire we had strung around Fleet and I wrote letters, one to Marcelle, Nelle, Bobbie and Jack. I received letters from Anne and Aunt Pat and a carton of cigs from Bobbie and a Miner. Crosse brought his parcel down this evening so with Pepsi Colas bought at the NAAFI Canteen we had a very nice little lunch. I had a hot bath. As far as anyone knows there is no particular reason why we are leaving tomorrow as the advance party for the incoming outfit won't be here until Monday but we are going to march three miles to Minly Manor then sleep outside for the night which means two meals will have to be prepared over an impromptu field kitchen and everyone will be miserable. Brains plus. It will probably rain to top things off.

OCT. 12, SUN.

We finished loading the 15 cwt truck which when finally completed resembled a crop picker's wagon, and as a last straw the "Baby Carriage," a two-wheeled cable laying apparatus was hooked on behind. At 3:30 in the afternoon we evacuated our billets and headed for Minly Manor where we were to stay for the night, sleeping in the open. Except for the baby carriage breaking loose, turning a few complete rolls and finishing sitting right side up on the other side of the street, nothing much happened on our short trip to the Manor grounds. After supper we sat around the dying embers of a small fire talking and very occasionally singing until it was time for bed. Then we rolled in.

OCT. 13, MON.

A cold frosty morning with the first glimmer of dawn streaking the sky as we lined up for breakfast. We started for the coast soon afterwards with Crosse and I riding on top of the stores and keeping a watchful eye on "Dolly" the baby Carriage, but she was docile this morning and didn't rebel like she did yesterday. We arrived at our coastal billets at 2:30 and were able to move right in without delay. Everything was under control and soon after we were proceeding smoothly. We were experimenting with a powdered milk this evening in an endeavor to make some hot chocolate but the milk called, "SMA" wasn't very good. I think we were influenced too much by the fact that the description on the can said that it was practically the same as human milk. Anyway, we decided to use just plain water. Grant had received some soda crackers, cheese and onions from home so we had quite the nice lunch. When Walker wasn't looking Sgt. Rankine put some cracker crumbs and onion peel in Walker's bed. Now Rankine is unable to go to bed until Walker discovers the trick because he doesn't want to be hampered by blankets when Walker finds out. We listened to Canadian news tonight and heard a voice vainly trying to copy Ivan, the voice of Russia, but he didn't do so good; he couldn't talk quite fast enough, besides that the few cracks he did get in were out of place and foolish. He didn't sound very convinced about his own propaganda.

OCT. 14, TUES.

The day was spent in getting things straightened around and becoming reacquainted with the complexities of this telephone system. Nothing has changed around here since we left it last August; of course, there is no flowers at this time of year. Phoned Ken Peters about a new uniform, may get it tomorrow. I wrote a letter to Anne and dad.

OCT. 15, WED.

A little work on the exchange this morning kept me busy for a while. We made some alterations in a GPO telephone which I understand is strictly against rules but sometimes we can't wait for the G.P.O. service man to get here, so have to do the work ourselves. Went down to Lewes to see about a new uniform and to help change a telephone. I keep Peters busy for a while trying to find a matched uniform but none of the trousers fitted so Ken is going to fix me up later. Sgt. Rankine and I had a feed of beans and toast before we went to bed. These parcels from home are the real thing, especially the day before payday.

OCT. 16, THURS.

A high wind carrying the occasional rain squall was sweeping in off the Channel this morning and the breakwater was partly obscured by flying spray. I drew 3 pounds on pay parade this afternoon. MacKenzie and I went to a show tonight called, "All This and Heaven Too," after which we prepared a coffee, toast and crab-apple lunch. The German heckler is still making his poor attempt at heckling. He can't seem to get the proper effect.

OCT. 21, TUES.

The last five days were uneventful, except a letter from Rose and the news that transfers were possible to the air force and everyone is excited about it. I went into town on Saturday afternoon but couldn't get what I wanted. On Monday afternoon Sgt. Rankine and I went into Brighton to do some shopping but I only managed to procure some of my favorite writing paper. We caught the last bus back to our billets. We were told the life history of a young woman of 23 who had strayed from the straight and narrow when she was fourteen from the person herself. She is supposed to be reforming now. Nothing much happened today that could be called important. We scrubbed out our room today; Reg is back from leave and the arguing is resumed. The door from the coal bin is strangely missing this afternoon, but it makes a very good bed. We have had a canine visitor around here lately, a good looking pooch, white with black spots and two black ears, so we have been having spots before our eyes for the last few days. He has the habit of monopolizing the nearest bed regardless of the right owner. Just at present he is having nightmares (or whatever dogs have), on my bed and he jerks, barks and growls in his sleep. I wrote a letter to Nelle this evening, and enclosed some lavender seeds, it sure smells nice. The arrival of another convoy of Canadians came in and it was announced this am maybe Jack or Roy is among them. Brigadier's inspection tomorrow; I wonder if he will notice the missing coal bin door and if he will find it.

OCT. 22, WED.

Interior economy with the usual form of exercise but we had completed most of our dirty work yesterday so got off a little easier. The exchange (one of them) chose this particular time to go haywire and it was well into the afternoon before I had it going again. Mail from Canada came in this morning and besides cigarettes from Bobs, I received three letters from Nelle, one from Marc, one from Flo, one from Charlotte. Red, Reg and I went to see Charlie Chan in, "Murder Cruise" at the Deluxe Theater this evening. A funny thing happened while we were there; everyone was interested in the picture when there was a dull report and a flash of flame under a radiator beside Reg. Somehow some film had found its way behind there and the heat from the rad set it alight. No one was excited about the incident and it soon burnt itself out. I found a letter from Iris waiting for me when I got back. I started answering a previous letter from her this evening.

OCT. 23, THURS.

We got up late for breakfast this morning, in fact, it was eight o'clock before I climbed out from between the blankets. Ralston was expected this morning but knowing these celebrities and their habits proceeded to renovate a chair that was in constant use and falling about. Ralston didn't appear. I erected an aerial that Mr. Kent asked for a few days before. I received 1,000 cigarettes from Bobbie this evening which makes it 1,300 I received from her in two days. Reg also received the same amount from her which has him going around in circles. He can't understand why she should send them so regularly to a person she hardly knows. He even said he couldn't let her send any more and was going to send her a telegram. He would be really hard up for smokes if she didn't and does he ever appreciate them, as do I. I wrote a letter to Iris this evening and started one to Marcelle. A little touching up of the adjustment improved the radio quite a lot tonight. French brought down some canned bacon so we had a good feed of toasted bacon sandwiches with real butter, also supplied by French, and tea. I had a horrible thought today. Supposing I get into the air force and get assigned to a barrage balloon crew.

OCT. 24, FRI.
Mr. Kent, Cpl. Hatch, Crosse and myself went down to look at a partly completed alarm system at the Fort but couldn't make any sense out of it so decided to try and get permission to install our own method. Red, Reg and I went to the Deluxe to see "There's Magic in Music" after which we had a feed of fish and chips at the Stish and Fips Chore.

OCT. 25, SAT.
The Sergeant and I scrubbed our floor this morning, then I was informed of some exchange trouble which needed attention. I wrote letters to Charlotte and Nelle today. We had some toasted cheese sandwiches and tea this evening.

OCT. 26, SUN.
The entire day, except for a few hours this morning, when suddenly discovered work prevented me from going on church parade was spent in letter writing. Letter writing also occupied the evening.

OCT. 27, MON.
Exchange trouble was the cause of many busy hours this morning and afternoon. Due to the chilly weather prevailing hereabouts just now, the coal supply at the kitchen is mysteriously and rapidly disappearing. Finished the altering job in the officers' mess about four this afternoon and was rewarded by a cup of tea with cake. Sgt. Rankine prepared a couple of mess tins full of fried onions and french fried toast which certainly hit the spot.

OCT. 28, TUES.
Mr. Kent and I spent the morning tracing wires in the signal office and exchange room. Sgt. Rankine, Mr. Kent and myself went up to the Wrenry on signal business and had a look at the new layout, which is something. Got back to be informed by Reg that we (Reg, Q.M.S. Nicholson, Private Fick and myself were ordered to report to Ordinance H.Q. for an interview on the

30ᵗʰ. I very sincerely hope it something I can refuse without being downright foolish. Wrote a letter to Peggy and one to Iris this evening.

OCT. 29, WED.
We were informed by Wally Mills to the effect that they would be wanting all names of the fellows wishing to apply to the Air Force. Tomorrow is pay day too. Verily, it never rains but it pours. Tomorrow will settle the Ordinance angle one way or another. Snow flurries driven by a strong cold north wind, today. Started a letter, such as it is, to Nelle this evening.

OCT. 30, THURS.
Reg, Fick, Nicholson and myself went to Crowborough for the interview with an Ordinance officer. They want us to transfer to that unit for a course of training in Wireless mechanics. I am very much tempted to try it but I imagine it will be very dull back there, a lot duller than it is here. We put our names in for a transfer to the Air Force but I don't hold much hope of getting in, due to educational difficulties. Pay parade this afternoon and I drew three pounds and squared my debt with Walker by paying him a Pound. Reg and I went to the Deluxe to see George Raft, Humphery Bogart and Anne Sheridan in, "The Road to Frisco."

OCT. 31, FRI. (HALLOWE'EN)
I am ashamed to say I did exactly nothing all day except read and eat. I wrote a letter to Bobbie this evening and finished one to Nelle. Still unable to decide about transferring to the Ordinance.

NOV. 1, SAT.
There was the usual interior economy this morning and a muster parade at eleven. It was a cold wet morning so that the fellows made a rush for the N.A.A.F.I. canteen and a hot tea as soon as they could. Sgt. Rankine left on a weekend pass to keep a rendezvous with his three brothers. Walker went to Brighton for the weekend and Reg succumbed to the temptations of a dance at the Drove Hall this evening so I pretty well have the run of the house.

NOV. 2, SUN.

I took advantage of the day and slept in until after nine this morning. Spent nearly the entire day and evening reading. Reg had a date with a girl he met at the dance last night. Finished the day with a hot bath.

NOV. 3, MON.

I started to unwind an audio transformer this afternoon previous to rewinding. I completed the unwinding of the secondary at four this afternoon. The prospect of rewinding isn't very enticing. I went to see "The Fighting 69th" at the Deluxe this evening, and as usual went alone. I bought a double order of fish and chips on the way home.

NOV. 4, TUES.

The "Exlax" scheme got under way this morning and not wishing to become a mythical casualty, I stuck close to the exchange room for the day, out of sight of the judges. It was a cold wet day and riding around in ambulances, improvised or otherwise, didn't appeal to me, in the least. I finished a short letter to Marcelle and one to Aunt Pat this evening. I can't seem to write a letter anymore without finding myself beefing. Why did I ever raise an ambition? Other fellows seem quite happy living from day to day with very little thought of the future. Just now I haven't the ambition to follow an ambition. There is no doubt as to the attitude of the people in certain parts of the country toward Canadians. Some people regard us as a necessary evil and the others can't see why it's necessary. They want to know when we are going to stop "playing" at war and start earning our rations, and I suppose one can't really blame them. The Canucks themselves don't help alter the situation when they get so damned bored, they break loose and shatter the serenity and century-old customs of these sometimes smug, self-satisfied communities. We have a bad reputation, generally, and I guess none of us are improving it much.

NOV. 5, WED.

There wasn't much doing today. Letter writing and reading helped to pass the time away.

NOV. 6, THURS.
An 18 wireless set was brought into stores for repairs and after a series of tests it was found to have five valves (tubes) burnt out and a bent center arm on the receiver filament potentiometer or voltage control. We, (French and I) went to see a show called, "Danny Boy" and were back in time to catch the canteen open. Wrote a letter to Anne and started one to Nelle before going to bed, one letter from Nelle today.

NOV. 7, FRI.
Piled out of bed pretty late this morning and missed breakfast—again, it's getting to be a habit. We finally received permission to install the alarm system in our own way so work was started this afternoon by tearing down the mess that the "Limeys" had put up. Received a letter from Miss Banks this am and a Miner. I guess the people back home are finding it equally hard to find news. Finished Nelle's letter this evening and started one to Miss Banks. News came around today that our Div. Commander has been promoted to Canadian High Commissioner to Australia.

NOV. 8, SAT.
Began reconstruction of practice oscillator today using a new transformer and was rewarded with a good clear note. This evening was spent in letter writing and arguing politics, religion and human traits which as we all know, is very much against regulations. The argument lasted until the wee hours of the morning so the amount of letter writing completed can well be imagined.

NOV. 9, SUN.
Sgt. Rankine went on leave this morning for seven days. Wally brought a receiver section from an 18 set in for repairs which were postponed until tomorrow. The practice oscillator is all contained in one box, including a tape pulling motor and it works like a charm. Received cigarettes from Bobbie again and a letter from Miss Flo Banks. A good bath and scrubbing of dirty laundry were the main activities this evening.

NOV. 10, MON.

It took six hours of probing and sweating to find the simple fault in the 18 set receiver. Received a letter from Bobbie this evening and started answering it immediately and finished it before eleven. Reg started writing but a sentimental song was played over the radio and he became so blue he had to quit. We heard in the news tonight that a Brigadier Such-and-Such from Kingston is to be our next Div. Commander.

NOV. 11, TUES.

We are celebrating the Armistice Day, today, and poppies are a part of everyone's apparel. On the way up to dinner we were met by a lady with the customary tray of poppies and dangling coin-box. She greeted us with, "Officers Orders, no poppy, no dinner." All I was able to muster was a brass trouser button but she said that that would do so I dropped it into the box and got a poppy in return. MacKenzie and I went to see, "I Wanted Wings" showing at the Deluxe. When we came out it was raining and we only had one ground sheet between us, consequently, we were pretty well soaked before we gained the welcomed warmth of our billets. Did a little studying before our customary late lunch.

NOV. 12, WED.

The "M" section of the R.C.C.S. came down this morning and took our two 6 line W.C. exchange out for an overhaul, leaving a ten line machine in their place. Nothing but trouble. Stayed in this evening and studied.

NOV. 13, THURS.

There was supposed to be an inspection by our new Div. Commander, but the steady drenching rain squashed the idea. Our Christmas dinner, (army style) is the source of much discussion and pessimism. Christmas cards are increasingly hard to obtain, due to this new paper-saving scheme. Maybe it would be a lot easier to send telegrams or something.

NOV. 19, WED.

The last seven days have been practically uneventful. A few days were spent at the waterfront, on the alarm system but I am afraid it will not prove entirely satisfactory. We are having some difficulty with the No. 18 sets, three having come in for repairs. Finished the last one this afternoon after seven hours of probing and tracing. Except for a few English letters there has been no mail for over a week. I had to cancel my seven-day leave, on account of low finances. We had our blankets and palliases sterilized today and fresh straw was provided. The fellows are becoming jumpy and are all too willing to start scrapping over trivialities. To make our lives more miserable, the Colonel has decided to move back again as he can't stand the sound of pigs, in the nearby pig-pen. This was the second time he has moved because of his dislike for noise and each time the NAFFI canteen had to move to make room for him. This time the "Naffy" moved right out of the area so we have to depend on the erratic Oriel Cafe run by a women to whom "customer satisfaction" is secondary to her can't-be-bothered attitude. She opens her store at any hour and closes the same way, just because she doesn't feel like serving any more. From seven to nine in the evening we are able to buy a cup of tea or coffee and a cake at a place called The Glen Roy Room which is run by a minister and his wife. They are very nice people and the food is good but that doesn't alter the fact that the big shot has on two different occasions, caused inconvenience to a good many people by his petty desire for unreasonable quiet. Everyone gets all settled and fix up their respective rooms as home-like as possible, then the old so-and-so finds out that everyone is comfortable then develops a dislike for the sound of pigs. Everyone has to move, rearrange their billets, loose the convenience of the NAFFI entirely. Why is it possible for one man to make it so damned miserable for so many other individuals?

NOV. 26, WED.

Nearly the entire past week was spent in exerting our diligent endeavours to the successful operation of the Fort alarm system, which, to date, refuses to reward our efforts with so much as a healthy tingle, despite the fact that we have over 500 volts applied to it now. Tomorrow is the last day we are going to work on it and if, after a few major changes, it still refuses to operate, I am through, unless a different power source can be found. I received cigarettes from the Overseas Unit of my insurance company (Iris' doing) a carton of tobacco from Nelle and a very welcomed parcel from Janet, during the week. The nights have been mostly spent in writing letters, reading or studying, with the occasional argument thrown in. There has been no further word from either the Air Force or the Ordinance. Today we went to a nearby town to do some shopping and our trip wasn't entirely for nothing. We went to work on the alarm system again this afternoon with little success. I have been trying desperately to obtain a Canadian uniform for the last month or so, but without any results as yet. I started when we were stationed at Fleet but they didn't have my size so was advised to wait for the next shipment. I am determined to get a Canadian outfit for my "Sunday Suit." The new "Limey" suits are anti-gas treated and smell to high heaven when they become damp from rain or perspiration; the odor they give off in a crowded theater or dance is very embarrassing to the wearer and quite unimaginable. Perhaps I will be lucky in the next couple of weeks or so.

NOV. 27, THURS.

We finally had to give up the alarm system as impractical with this kind of material so Kutch went down with a few line-men and collected all the batteries. Managed to alter two telephone installations this afternoon. I received a very nice parcel from Flo this evening which was greatly enjoyed by all. Had a craving for a good feed of my favorite "Kashu" nuts appeased as a result. Evidently she is sending a number of them as well as 1,000 cigarettes and a parcel from Eatons. She told me to expect them in the near future. I don't know how I will ever repay her for her generosity. Had a good feed of nuts, toasted meat sandwiches, fruit cake, cookies and coffee, before going to bed.

NOV. 28, FRI.

Repaired a D5 buzzer unit this morning and changed the location of the Adjutant's telephone this afternoon. No Canadian mail this evening but some tomorrow. Reg very mysteriously informed me to expect an invitation to a house party in the near future and not to turn it down or else. I don't feel like house parties these days, especially among strangers. Wrote to Flo thanking her for the parcel and one to Aunt Pat telling her I would not be able to spend Xmas with her.

DEC. 5, FRI.

Nothing of any importance has happened during this last week. Sgt. Rankine, Bill French and I went into Hove to see the "49ᵗʰ Parallel." There were some changes made in the allocation of personnel and I don't like the present setup. Rankine and I went to the Deluxe to see Bing Crosby, Bob Hope and Dorothy Lamour in "The Road to Zanzibar." We dropped into the fish and chips joint for something to eat. The proprietor had heard something about the French-Canadians and locked his doors early. They have a tough reputation to live down in this town. I have almost decided to accept a transfer to the Ordinance Corps when and if they ask us again.

DEC. 13, SAT.

The Xmas mail is pouring in now and grub is plentiful and good. Marcelle, Nelle, Connie, Bobbie and Emmie, Flo Banks, Iris and Janet have all sent parcels. We had pay parade yesterday and I drew three pounds. Received word that the Adjutant wanted to see me at 9:30 but stayed until I got paid and arrived at the Adjutant's office at 10:10. Ordinance wanted CQMS Nicholson and myself to transfer as soon as possible but the decision was entirely up to us. I told the Adjutant that I would go. In the afternoon I went down to see the Quarters and he said that he was going to take the transfer. After having time to think it over I could find plenty of excuses and reasons why I didn't want to transfer. I don't think I would feel so good if I had to sit at a workbench and read about what the fellows were doing on some hot front-line position. I guess I couldn't bring myself to leave the gang. Before going to bed I had made up my mind to see the Adjutant early this morning. I then learned that we were supposed to leave by noon tomorrow and work was already going through on our transfers but the Adjutant agreed to give me until four in the afternoon to think it over and work on my transfer was suspended for that time. I phoned the Quarters and told him that I might not be going but I would let him know how I decided. So I phoned the Adjutant at 11:30AM and told him to cancel my transfer as I had decided to stay. The Quarters thinks I am crazy for turning it down but I don't think that I will regret too much. Some fellows think I am foolish but they are not in a position to know the facts. I feel kind of relieved now that I have finally decided.

DEC. 14, SUN.

We slept in until eleven this morning and played Crib in the afternoon. The Quarters left for Camp Borden at noon today. We had a great feed of bacon sandwiches and coffee this evening. I have received parcels from Connie, Nelle, Bobbie, Marcelle; I have 1,300 cigarettes from Flo Banks as well as a parcel; 300 cigs from Harry and Bezzie; ½ pound tin of tobacco from Bobbie; ½ pound tin from Marcelle and a pound from Nelle. Bobbie sent files and screwdrivers and loads of other stuff dear to the appetite of a soldier. Marcelle sent a swell wallet and many other things. Nelle's and Connie's parcels contained a good variety of eatables as well as towels, underwear, gloves, etc. We won't be short of food at Christmas. I have also received 300 cigs from the Ladies' Auxiliary.

DEC. 15, MON.

Trouble developed on the exchange just as I was ready to go down and draw my new Canadian uniform that I had waited two months for. Reg, MacKenzie and I went to see Stan Laurel and Oliver Hardy in "The Flying Deuces." We had bacon and chips at the Mikado Cafe afterwards.

DEC. 18, THURS.

There hasn't been very much doing this last three days, except we have been eating kind of high since the Xmas mail arrived. We have been treated (?) to Christmas Caroling by two young schoolboys. They come here every night and sing a couple of Carols and then leave a few shillings richer. Some of the fellows think it might be a good racket for raising beer money for Christmas. I wrote a letter to Marcelle and one to Jack. The Sergeant and I took a beating at Crib today.

DEC. 22, MON.

Nothing of any importance worth mentioning in the last four days. I met one of the fellows' friend the other night and have received an invitation for "tea" on Xmas night and a house party on Saturday night. My new uniform is ready to wear so I am not refusing. I finished sewing the flags and Canada badges on my tunic this evening. Received a letter from Nelle, a Miner and cards from Aunt Pat and Uncle Jack and Cousin Beattie and John. I wrote to a person I never thought I would write to again. Perhaps my conscience was bothering me a little. The last time I wrote to them was May 29. I wish I could get these diaries home, I don't like carrying them around.

Finis.

Book No. 4

Material is getting scarce, Nelle, perhaps the new year will be a better provider.

FRED LODGE DIARY
December 24, 1941 to August 1, 1942

Book No. 5

Diary: L/Cpl. Lodge F.T. H19859.
Camerons of Canada (C.A.S.F.)

Please mail to:
Miss N. Lodge
Box 165
Kenora, Ontario,
Canada

DEC. 24, WED.

Tried desperately to buy a good pair of drumsticks but it appears as if musical instrument stores just ain't in this particular neighbourhood. I met Reg and Ellen in front of the show and although I tried to refuse going in, using a new cold as an excuse, they wouldn't take no for an answer. We caught the last bus home and I left them at the Denton Corners. The whole Canadian Army seems to be celebrating in the usual Xmas Eve style and the noise is terrific.

DEC. 25, THURS. CHRISTMAS

The cold is decidedly worse today, but Reg and Ellen still don't know the meaning of the word "no," so I dolled up in my Sunday best and accompanied by Sgt. Rankine, we kept our tea appointment with the Page family. Mr. and Mrs. Page are real old typical English folks and they made us at home. There was three young ladies there, ranging in age from fifteen to seventeen years. (I guess.) We had a very good evening and had lots of fun. By the time it was polite to leave, my cold was bad and my chest felt like it was ripping wide open every time I coughed, which was frequent. All I can find are two aspirins. We didn't have no turkey today as "A" coy, to which we are attached is duty company this week. So we will have our turkey dinner on New Years if the birds will keep that long.

DEC. 26, FRI.

Every blanket I could muster (six) was utilized last night, aided by my great-coat, a sweatshirt and a sweater, to raise a sweat. It helped quite a lot in loosening the cold but my chest is still feeling raw inside. The drugstores are all closed today, but the Sgt. procured some very good medicine from somewhere and I hope to break this cold before tomorrow night's party; failing that, I won't go. We made inroads on Mac's preserved chicken this morning. Since I got this "medicine" a lot of fellows have developed impromptu colds; I think they are just thirsty.

DEC. 27, SAT.

The day was spent in pressing my uniform, etc., for the party tonight, which, I had looked forward to with a great deal of apprehension. Sgt. Rankine had to decline the invitation at the last moment because there had to be at least one N.C.O. in billets and Hatch and Mills also were going out. Reg and I started out about six PM, a little early perhaps but we dropped into the Bridge and thus killed a little time. Even at that we were the first two to arrive, but it wasn't long before the rest of the guests started arriving by two's and four's. In about an hour the house was full of people; Ellen, Yvonne, Jean, Joan, Joyce, Rolly, Maizy, Cathy, Ronnie, Sonny, Ray, Burny, Rod, Mrs. & Mr. Page, Reg, myself and a few more I can't remember. Refreshments were plentiful and frequent and the games full of fun. We played "Whispering," "Dumb Orchestra," "Forfeits," "Murder" and lots of others. Of them all, I liked "Murder" the best because there were no embarrassing forfeits attached to it. It proved very pleasant to find myself alone in a dark cold room with an unknown young lady who wasn't quite sure if she was more cold than scared, as both called for consolation. The better hidden the "suspects" the longer it took the "detective" to round them up, so the longer you enjoyed the pleasure of offering comfort to the unknown lady. "Post Office" was also played with vim and vigor. Surprising for such an ancient and childish game. During the course of the evening, I received another invitation to a party next Saturday night and an invitation to the Club of one of the guests. The party wound up around two AM and Reg and I got home about an hour later. They are pretty nice people and we have an open invitation to visit them any time.

DEC. 31, WED.

This is the last day of 1941, in another four hours another year will be ushered in with people wishing and confident of peace and victory. The last year has seen many changes, both in locality and I think nature and habits. Some of the latter aren't so enviable to some people. I have met 75% of our English relatives and have seen plenty of this country, but I am looking forward to the new year to bring greater activity and better times.

JAN. 1, 1942, THURS.

Missed breakfast this AM and according to the more ambitious fellows, really missed something. We had a very excellent turkey dinner, well prepared and served by the Sgt.'s, which added to the flavour of the meal.

JAN. 5, MON.

Except for the party on Saturday, nothing else has happened worth recording, unless it's the fact that Frank England owes me ten dollars by his getting married to Iris. The party on Saturday was very much like the other one, except that we didn't have quite so much fun. The Sgt. almost missed this one too, but by his own fault. He was all ready to go when two fellows started wrestling upstairs. Red went up to stop them, (so he claims) but they grabbed him, took his clothes off and smeared him with brilliantine, a very odorous hair lotion. He even had it in his mustache and was almost refusing to go, but finally cleared up sufficiently to pass the non-too sensitive snozzles and we got there about 45 minutes late. We got back again around 2:30 AM. I have heard twice from Ted and once from Roy. Ted says he will be down here some time on a 48 hour pass, to see me.

JAN. 6, TUES.

Manage to get up almost before breakfast and had the floor swept before 8. Waited around for inspection which never happened and wrote to Bobbie this afternoon. Went down to the Mikado for supper with Reg. Then I went to a show while Reg kept another appointment. Got back early.

JAN. 12, MON.

The last six days of activity has been varied and of little consequence. Last Thursday, Reg came over around nine in the morning and told me to get ready for a lesson in truck driving. I didn't do too badly, considering it was my first time behind the wheel of a motor vehicle. I did better in the afternoon. Eventually I am to take my driver's test and get my standing orders *(military driver's licence)*. The motorcycle comes next. Reg and I are taking fourteen days' leave on the fifteenth, which made answering all Canadian letters a necessity before we went. Started fixing the Officers' Mess radio set on Saturday morning and had it working by supper time. Rankine, Beck, Comack and myself went to the Deluxe to see Bob Hope in "Caught in the Draft." Afterward we had double orders of sausage meat and chips at the Mikado Cafe. Today was spent in the pursuit of serial numbers of all instruments required by the C.Q.S. *(Company Quartermaster Sgt.)*, a haircut, and a pair of braces; except this AM when the officer's radio had to be adapted with cable dial drive instead of walking pulley method. It worked satisfactorily. Had a bath; then spent the rest of the evening getting ready for leave. Blancoing gaiters and respirator, last minute laundry, etc. We should be able to get away by four in the afternoon tomorrow. I received two cartons of cigs. this PM, one from Nelle and one from Olga.

JAN. 13, TUES.

Had a difficult time getting ready for leave this morning. There was too many "guests" whom always seem to be in the way. However, by pay parade at 1:00 PM I was all packed and except for changing my uniform, ready to go. We decided that we would catch the 2:30 train from New Haven which left us a little short of time owing to the time taken by pay parade. I left in a hurry, piled everything into Jeff's truck and caught the train. The rush was so great, I managed to forget my lighter (a very important piece of machinery these days), my address book (another absolute necessity) and a few other minor details. There was snow on the ground when we left and more falling and by the time we arrived at Victoria Station, it was damp and chilly out. Disliking the idea of struggling in and out of buses with our rifles and kit, we obtained a taxi to take us to the Maple Leaf Club, where owing to it being mid-week we felt sure we could get a decent room, but "Queenie" opened the door with bad news, they were all filled up. But Queenie, always obliging and willing to help poor homeless Canadians in distress, obtained the last double room at the Gordon Club, only a block down Vauxhall Bridge Road. Two and six a night and breakfast or one and nine for bed only. The Club used to be the Gordon Infants Hospital, very spacious and well managed (the bath tubs are a little small and you practically have to bath one half at a time.) We washed and shaved, then hit the Beaver Club for supper. After which we ventured forth onto that famous thorough affair where money goes fast and not very far, Piccadilly. The street known the world over for its wild night life, which although hard to find by the inexperienced, progresses on every corner and every second doorway. Famous too are the Piccadilly Ladies, nearly always recognizable by the little tunes they hum. The price is high, but considered worthwhile by some, which is far above the ordinary man's income. The "Bobbie" is regarded as somewhat of a hawk in a chicken coop, he is very popular as he strolls along on his rounds. It was there we struck up an acquaintance with Molly, a square shooter, exceedingly wise in the ways of the world, especially Piccadilly. By eleven we had seen everything possible to see in a blackout so we came back to the Club. Piccadilly Circus at night, in a blackout is an experience extraordinary. The roar and twinkling lights of the motored traffic, the hiss and shuffle of pedestrians, the occasional grunt and subsequent apology as two moving bodies come into contact. The voices of the paper vendors coming out of the darkness with fog-horn-like volume calling their wares to the shadowing, shifting masses streaming by. The theatre crowd coming out from the final show blinded by the dazzling lights inside, unable to see anything outside, sweep along the sidewalk like a stampede, sweeping everything with them or aside. Piccadilly, the Indecent, Piccadilly the Great; it's one of the first places a colonial soldier hears about and one of the first places a majority visit, but very few partake of what it has to offer for a price.

JAN. 14., WED.

We were up in time this morning to obtain a free ticket to a variety show up on Tottenham Court Road, which we used in the afternoon. It was still daylight when it came out so we wandered down along the Strand and some of its side streets. We decided to go and see a stage show called the Glamour Serenade, but were unable to find the theater in time for the last performance, so made the rounds of the various night life spots of Piccadilly. During last night's wanderings we were stopped by a Royal Marine and a girl and asked if we would be witness to their wedding the next morning, so at nine-thirty this AM we were at the Marylebone Town Hall. We were just in time for the ceremony but the couple had plenty of witnesses as he had asked no less than ten people to officiate in that capacity. Reg witnessed while I was elected to find a taxi and have it at the side door as the happy company had to catch a train to Scotland. How I actually obtained the desired means of transportation is amusing if not typical of attitude of those serving the public. I had tried to stop a few taxi's but they were occupied and I was just beginning to think that the newly wedded couple would have to start their honeymoon on a bus when I saw a taxi stop for a red traffic light. It had a soldier for a fare, but the driver evidently decided that it was more important to carry a wedding party than a lone soldier who was trying to catch a train he had already missed so that unfortunate person was politely asked to disembark and get a bus. The taxi drew up at the door just in time to receive the exuberant wedding party before its mad dash to catch the northbound train.

JAN. 15, THURS.

We slept in kind of late this morning despite our good intentions of having our pictures took, so that it was nearly eleven before we arrived at the studio that we had chosen for the event, only to find the place crowded. We kept a luncheon engagement with Reg's aunt at twelve, choosing the High Hat in Strand Palais for the mastication of high class eatables. Perhaps we felt a little self-conscious at the spaciousness and glitter of the dining room, but outwardly I am sure, we appeared used to that sort of living. The meal wasn't very expensive, but the real charge came to three shillings apiece. Reg tipped the waitress a shilling and by some misunderstanding we both paid for checking our coats besides which the check-man received two shillings in tips. We walked out of the place as if we owned the joint. Overheard on the street: two cockney girls "blimey, these Canadians go posh, don't they?" We left Reg's aunt on the Strand and tried the photographers again, but there was a bigger crowd this time so postponed our mugging until the morning. We saw a very good variety show, free, this afternoon, then went to see "Sergeant York" showing at the Warner Theater. Can't make up my mind when I should start visiting relatives.

JAN. 16, FRI.

We were down at the Beaver Club early for passes to the Broadcast but so were two hundred other men. We were all jammed into a resting saloon where the passes were to be distributed at ten o'clock. Time came for the distribution and the mob just crowded up to the table en mass. When they were asked to form two lines, they refused to move. It was the worst display of ignorance and stupidity I have seen among soldiers and I have seen lots. Reg and I finally became disgusted and left with the intention of trying again next Friday. We went to the photographers called "Polyfoto" and were lucky enough to be first there. This Polyfoto idea seems to be the real thing and is very popular. The initial price is two and six; the lady operating the machine plants the subjects in a swivel chair. She then tells you to look at various pictures on the three walls, every time you look somewhere different she turns a handle on the camera. The finished products after developing is 48 small photos taken at different angles. If you want enlargements made of any one shot, simply send the necessary money, the number of the snap and the quantity required and they make them and mail them to you. We went to another free variety show this afternoon after which we went to see "A Yank in the RAF."

JAN. 17, SAT.

Reg lost his glove last night, believed left in the Gordon Club canteen, so we set out to find steal or buy another pair. Coupons seemed to be the only way to buy them and we did our best to find a black market; even having the nerve to ask a Bobbie if he knew any black markets where gloves could be obtained coupon free. He claimed he didn't know of any but advised us to go up to Petticoat Lane (Middlesex Street) and try there. We did but everything was locked up, it being Saturday afternoon. Our quest of gloves then took us down to Sloane Square and Sloane Street, to the Chevrons Club, which Reg joined before going back to Piccadilly. On Piccadilly, coupons were again demanded in all stores we found open and we started cruising the back streets until we came to a second hand store hard by to Cambridge Square. Here Reg paid an exorbitant price, four shillings and six, for a second hand pair of gloves. In all the day's wanderings we were snapped twice by a Candid Camera, once coming out of the Strand tube station and again on Piccadilly Circus. Both times we were given a card bearing the number and instructions as to how, by enclosing a certain amount we could obtain three by mail. We may experiment and follow directions. The Beaver Club was packed today with fellows coming in with weekend passes so we decided to find ourselves a quiet little cafe for supper. It proved next to impossible as all establishments off the main streets were packed with the Saturday theater crowds and the ones on the main streets were overflowing. We then came to the conclusion to venture farther afield but after pounding pavement for over an hour that most of the out of the way places closed down on Saturday so when we found a disreputable tea room open, we took the opportunity to partake of coffee (not bad) and ham sandwiches (very rare). We retired to a bright spot on the Strand for the evening. About ten o'clock we decided to view Piccadilly on a Saturday night and found the crowd so dense, navigation in any direction was exceedingly difficult. We met Molly and her friend again and she asked us up to her place for an hour or so to get out of the crowd. I wonder what it cost per "critter for beef on the hoof?" The subways were crowded on the way home and on our last lap on our way home which we walked, was traversed very joltingly; people just seemed to loom suddenly out of nowhere and collisions were frequent and painful. There is a big crowd of men on leave and there is no accommodation left so I guess some of them will be spending the night in chairs or air raid shelters.

JAN. 18, SUN.

Reg left early to keep an appointment with his aunt; he is going up to Bedford for the day. I stayed at the Club for dinner "which was terrible" then caught a tube to Morden with the intentions of calling on cousin Jack but the bus routes from Morden have been changed and no one seems to know the number of the bus I should have taken. It was growing late so caught another tube train back to the Strand. I spent a couple of hours in the writing room of the Beaver Club. Returned to the Gordon Club for supper and a shave then back to the Beaver Club where I hoped to meet Reg. Hung around until ten then returned to the Gordon where I had a bath before settling to reading the paper. I don't expect Reg in tonight; he is probably staying with his aunt.

JAN. 19, MON.

Reg came in this AM before I was up. We spent the rest of the morning shopping for books (technical) and other minor articles such as hair grease and ointment for a rash I have on my legs. I don't expect the ointment will do much good. We also bought a cheap flashlight apiece which will alleviate the annoyance of tripping over curbs in the black out, not to mention inconsiderate obstacles such as lamp and sign posts which have a persistent habit of appearing in front of one when one is not yet accustomed to the darkness after coming out of a brilliantly lighted room. They are detrimental to a person's dignity and personal comfort. We met another Canadian in the company of an Irish war worker, who it appears, was trying to find a room for the night before setting out on an evening's fun which they were hoping to start at the Paramount Dance Hall on Tottenham Court Road. We were invited to reinforce the party and thus it was we spent a good four hours hob-nobbing with the higher classes, such as is found in the Russel and Empire Hotels. We found or discovered, a girl from Winnipeg working in the Russel Hotel and if she could have had her way, the place was ours. Here we were joined by a Canadian sergeant and now being five strong we made our way to the Empire Hotel where our Irish friend was more fortunate by securing a room for the mere price of fifteen shillings. Here Reg, the sergeant and myself were separated from the other two so we spent the remainder of the evening arguing with the girl behind the refreshment bar in the cellar, about the type of stuffed fish reposing in glass cases around the walls. The odd hotel guest joined in the debate and a good time was had by all until it was closing time. Reg and I left the sergeant on the front steps to make our way to Piccadilly Circus, the first leg of our regular journey to our billets. We stopped off at the Circus to visit one of our favorite haunts then on to Victoria Station and thus to the Gordon Club. We had such a good time this evening we decided to stay another day before going our different ways to our respective relatives. I have been here a week now and haven't so much as made a visit on Aunt Ett.

JAN. 20, TUES.

We got up this morning to find the streets messy with wet slush caused by a rather heavy snow storm last night. We went to the Beaver Club and obtained a free ticket to a stage show called The Broadway Gaeities, at the Phoenix. We had bacon and chips at a little snack bar then in order to conserve our rapidly dwindling cash reserve which equals about four pounds apiece. We bought ourselves a couple of novels and came back to the Gordon Club to spend the evening doing some quiet reading. It has been a very dull evening, not helped an awful lot by the flock of reserve Limey soldiers on the premises. We are practically decided on the matter of going relative hunting and looks as if Reg and I will be separating tomorrow morning. I think I will go up to Ett's for a few days so that I will be able to try for the broadcast again on Friday although I don't expect it to be any different than last time.

JAN. 21, WED.

Reg and I booked out of the Gordon Club this morning and separated at Charing Cross after making arrangements to meet again on Tuesday morning.

Arrived at Aunt Ett's around 10:30 just in time to go shopping in Hoxton with her. I spent the afternoon hunting for tools which took me over plenty of ground; managed to buy a poorly made pair of long-nosed pliers. Spent the evening around the fireplace talking to the girls and Aunt Ett. At ten o'clock we went around to the Lion and Lamb for a pint and heard some very good singing rendered by the innkeeper's daughter. We stayed up until two, after we returned, talking around the fireplace.

JAN. 22, THURS.

It was very cold last night and cool sheets weren't exactly an asset. Slept in until eleven this morning, then had a big breakfast, followed an hour later with a bigger dinner. Obtaining coal seems to be very difficult due to the icy roads, consequently it isn't a warm as it could be. Went to the Beaver Club for a shave and a wash up, bought some more matches and a small socket wrench set. I am worried about this rash I have; it looks like scabies. I should see the doctor at the Beaver Club. I was delayed when returning to Aunt Ett's so failed to reach there before 5:30 and the two girls were home from work. Ann and I went around to see Sis and her husband and left at about 10:30. Had a great time with their little son, Terry, also met Sis's brother-in-law Jim, who has spent the last two years in Iceland. We spent until 1:30 AM talking around the fireplace.

JAN. 23, FRI.

Birthday today; left early to try to get on the broadcast but they have changed the time for handing out the passes, it is one o'clock PM instead of 10:00 AM. I had promised Aunt Ett that I would be back for dinner so I didn't wait. I went for a walk around Old Street and City Road this afternoon and bought a new strap for my watch. It was raining pretty hard so I didn't stay out very late. A fellow by the name of George Cox came over from Highgate. (He is some distant relation on the Cox's side and is a sergeant in the Home Guard) and Auntie, George and myself retired to the Lion and Lamb for refreshments. Ann joined us just as George was leaving. The people have a good time in this pub and one can always be sure of hearing a good sing-song. The barkeeper's daughter is quite a good singer and an amplified system has been set up for her use. Everyone knows everyone else and Auntie says there are people there who used to know dad quite well. It is a good place to spend the odd hour and the beverages are not strong enough to cause any harm. As far as I can ascertain there is no age limit for patrons and one can see people of all ages standing around doing a bit of mild indulging. As per usual, we sat around the fireplace talking until two in the morning. I have caught another cold, but the rash seems to be clearing up.

JAN. 24, SAT.

Ann and Lil had to go in this morning and I stayed in bed until eleven again. This afternoon Ann took me down to a place called the "Waste" on Kingsland Road where junk or second hand tools and equipment is sold in booths along the sidewalks. It all looked like junk to me; I even saw a set of false teeth for sale and lying among an assortment of odd sized and rusty wrenches. We did a lot of walking, taking in Dalston, Hackney, etc. We walked through a number of Woolworth stores, but didn't see very much worth buying. We were glad to get home and stretch out before the fire again. George's wife Rose and their daughter came over and later on in the evening Rose (Sr.) and Auntie and myself spent an hour in the local on the corner. Auntie says that dad should remember the Lion and Lamb. We sat up until three this morning and Anne heated some grapefruit juice with three aspirins for my cold.

JAN. 25, SUN.

I ought to be ashamed of myself; I laid in until one this afternoon. We didn't feel like going anywhere and Ann says she isn't fussy about going to the pictures. Ann and I sat in the front room and talked until after dark. Ann claims that she isn't going to get married as it's too one sided in favour of the man. Perhaps she is right; I don't know because I haven't been married. Lily, Auntie and I spent a half hour in the place on the corner but we didn't stay very long. Later when we were sitting around the fireplace again, Lily was asking me questions about Canada and I was surprised to learn that she still thinks Canada is wild, undeveloped and a dangerous country to live in. I was surprised to hear Ann say that her and Alf had always wanted to go there. I was surprised because she never mentioned it before. Ann gave me another grapefruit juice and aspirin for my cold and then I went to bed at 1:30AM. I am hearing some home truths about our money grabbing uncle, these days.

JAN. 26, MON.

I didn't do very much today, except walk around. I exchanged the socket set for a new one, then walked up Old Street to Clerkenwell Road; up that to St. John Street until I found myself among the meat and food wharves. I eventually found my way back to Old Street; then I walked down Great Eastern Street to Bishopsgates. Up one side and down the other to Old Street again, then back to Pitfield and thus to Ashford. Ann and I called on Sissie and George Craig but little Terry was asleep so didn't see him. George was trying to convince Ann that she should get married, but he didn't do so well. His illustrations were contrary to his argument. On the way home we helped a blind man find St. John Church so that it was nearly twelve when we finally arrive home. We had tea and ate some of Sissie's wedding cake that she had given us. I made a five shilling bet with Ann that she will be married before me. I enjoyed these talks around the fireplace during the evening. Ann is quite determined not to get married.

JAN. 27, TUES.

Cold again today with the sink and lavatory frozen once more. Spent the morning packing my things. I said goodbye to Ann and Lily at noon and dragged myself away just after three. Auntie refused to take anything for keeping me for the past week. They are expecting Alf home again some time in July, and my next leave will be due then or thereabouts. I met Reg at the Beaver Club then after a cup of coffee we went to a news theater on the Strand for an hour. It was raining heavily when we came out so we decided to catch the 6:45 train back to New Haven. We arrived here and I discovered that they had moved about half of my stuff over to the room that Reg has above the Sig. Office, so before I could go to bed I had to move the other half. I think we came back at the wrong time as there is going to be an inspection by the Corps Commander tomorrow morning. Had a good hot bath before I went to bed.

JAN. 28, WED.

Hectic rush to bring order out of chaos before the Commander came around. By throwing unnecessary articles out of sight until such time as I could sort them out we were ready for His Nibs in plenty of time. As we expected, he didn't show up so the inspection was canceled just after dinner. Sorted all of my belongings out and everything is back in its place again. I wrote a letter to Ann this afternoon as per promise. I received six telegrams, two air-graph letters, four letter via ordinary means, one parcel from Bob's 1,000 cigs from Brian Hall, 300 from Rose and a bunch of papers. Reg and I went down to the Mikado for a bacon and chip supper but were back again before dark. Rumors are flying thick and fast now and the latest and perhaps the most foolish is that we are going to Australia. Others are more possible and not so pleasant.

JAN. 29, THURS.

At last I have all my things in order and am quite settled in my new quarters with Reg. Repaired a telephone this morning and checked one of three No. 17 sets brought in for an overhaul. Listened to the wireless scheme for a while and was almost tempted to crash in on the proceedings but restrained the desire. Managed to do some more washing this evening and wrote letters to Ann, Rusty, Aunt Pat and Cousin Jack.

JAN. 30, FRI.

Did nothing of any great importance today except agree to go to Brighton to hear and see Vera Lynn at the Hypodrome where she was appearing in person. Sgt. Rankine reserved 3 seats going for 3/6 apiece. We caught the 4:41 bus and secured our tickets before the half hour limit was up. We read, Reg and myself, had a sandwich and a cup of tea before the show in a cafe directly across the street. The show, a variety, was very good and Vera Lynn and her singing was worth the price we had paid for our seats. We came out of the show and had a supper in the cafe across the street, then caught the bus home again. By the time we had reached our destination we were hungry again so we had another supper. From there we came straight back to billets. Reg had a bath and I started a letter to Iris.

JAN. 31, SAT.

General clean up day today so that is what we spent the morning at. I received a letter from Roy at noon, and I guess he is pretty busy. That's what he gets for being a sergeant. Finished the letter to Iris and wrote another one to

Charlotte this evening. Managed to get the gas water heater working well enough to take a hot bath. I went to the M.O. yesterday about this rash on my leg and he confirmed my belief that it is clothes burn caused by excessive walking. I wonder if Iris received that pen I sent her or did the blame thing sink?

FEB. 1, SUN.

Slept in until pretty late this morning. Reg went out for dinner at the Page's and said before he left that I had an invite to tea but I didn't feel like going so went downtown and browsed around on my own, dropping into a few places once in a while looking for excitement and as I had expected I couldn't find any, so came home about ten thirty.

FEB. 2, MON.

Worked on the exchange all day today and wrote letters this evening.

FEB. 3, TUES.

Continued the work and finished the exchange job this afternoon. Then went to the DeLuxe this evening, alone. Had bacon and chips and coffee at the Mikado Cafe, still by myself. A three day communication scheme started this evening and Reg is tearing his hair already. Lost my precious lighter in the show this evening.

FEB. 4, WED.

Nothing of any importance today, except a few minor repairs on the exchange and three buzzer-like units. Finished a letter to Nelle this evening and read a book called "Trailing."

FEB. 5, THURS.

Reg was put in charge of the store job today and he is welcome to the worry it causes. I may have to take charge of the line gang when Cpl. Hatch goes on leave; not certain yet. Received letters from

Ann, Peggy and Rose this morning as well as a carton of cigs from Bobbie. Fixed another buzzer unit this AM. Made a good start on a letter to Peggy this evening which I will probably finish tomorrow.

FEB.10, TUES.

There hasn't been much doing during the past week except I went to the M.O. with a rash on my leg and found out it was clothes burn and a few applications of Whitfield's ointment soon fixed it up. Reg was put in charge of stores which relieves me of the responsibility. We moved the stores from across the street into the front room of this house. I received a parcel from Bezzie and Harry and a letter from Nelle and one from Bezzie and Junie. Also letters from Peggy, Ann and Aunt Pat. Cigarettes and a letter from Rose. Today I received a birthday parcel from Iris containing a very well needed sweater, a pen light, etc. Yesterday I received (not nearly as pleasant) an inoculation but by working on No. 18 sets, I think I prevented the usual soreness and discomfort generally connected with these necessary evils. I finished checking No. 18 sets this morning, then tested all battle batteries. They are playing a song on the radio which might well be our theme song, "I Am Fed Up and Far From Home." I have been writing like mad, trying to answer all my present mail before more arrives, but it looks hopeless. It is starting to come again, but they can't make me mad.

FEB. 15, SUN.

Events of the past week were varied, if of little importance. During the middle of the week we received three new No. 18 sets which required unpacking and checking. On Friday I had to maintain wireless communications with "A" Company who were engaged in a small-time scheme of their own. The job was monotonous and very boring. I received a Valentine from Iris during the afternoon. Yesterday I was again operating an 18 set, this time acting as control station between the artillery and "B" Company. In the afternoon Reg left on a weekend pass and I did some more work on my toolbox. Started taking Suline, a blood purifier in the afternoon. I received a carton of cigs from Flo in the afternoon. Today was spent between writing letters and doing my laundry. Reg should be back this evening. During the week the channel battle took place but we are too far away to see any of it. It is reported today that Singapore has been taken. The news this week hasn't been so good.

FEB. 19, THURS.

The last four days was marked by a visit from Ted. He came Monday noon and left Tuesday afternoon. There wasn't very much time to do a great deal but we caught up on the events of the last couple of years, at least. He told me that Rod was stationed a few miles from here but was posted to a station on Sunday. It is too bad I didn't know before because I could have made the trip in short time and visited him. Ted hasn't changed much, unless it's in his manner and disposition. I am sorry to say he paid for practically everything while he was here as I was and am financially embarrassed. Work on the toolbox has progressed favorably despite the scarcity of suitable material. It's understood, of course, that my ideas don't coincide with other associates on its design. I received a letter from Olga. The letter came the same afternoon as Ted and it contained a swell indoor group snap and an outdoor scene which will help me to explain Canada to certain people over here. Also received a carton of cigs from Bobby as did Reg, a letter from Nelle, one from Bobs, one from Flo, one from Rose and an air-graph from Iris who announces the safe arrival of the pen. I received a letter from a Mrs. Manning of Folkestone who invites me up there for my next leave. She is Holly's former landlady and I appreciate her generosity but I still have relatives I haven't seen yet. Started taking Suline to purify the blood. Answered Olga letter this evening.

FEB. 20, WED.

I worked on the toolbox again today for a while. Reg and Mr. Richardson enjoyed themselves communicating with "B" Company by C.W. on the 18 sets this afternoon while I tried to figure out another practical use for Fullerphones. Finished Bobbie's letter this evening, then had a bath.

FEB. 21, SAT.

Decided that if we allowed the dust to become much thicker on the floor, we would have to scrape the mud off our shoes when we walked across the floor, so it was scrubbed vigorously this morning. Work on the toolbox is nearing completion and is partly in use. A few metal clips for pliers and screwdrivers, a handle, a little sandpapering and painting will finish the job, then I can throw that old signal satchel into a corner. Reg became sufficiently interested to buck a motorcycle about ten miles in a snow storm to buy me some screws. Work was suspended at ten this evening, principally because Reg made tea. He is having quite a time tracing all the stores that seem to disappear so mysteriously.

FEB. 22, SUN.
Spent most of the day working on my tool-box and it progressed a long way toward completion. Spent the evening writing a letter to Nelle and taking a bath. Reg and I opened a can of beans and had beans on toast for lunch before we go to bed. They were canned in this country and hadn't the flavor of those we get back home. A can of Hedlunds baked beans would taste good right now.

FEB. 23, MON.
Another two dozen screws and some sandpaper had to be obtained this morning before I could do any work on the toolbox. Some plastic wood was very much desired for filling screw nail holes but was unable to obtain any, so mixed some sanding sawdust and glue which will serve the same purpose, I hope. If it does, painting will take place tomorrow sometime. Wrote a short letter to Rose and answer to Mrs. Canning's letter this evening. We had soup made from the soup powder that Bobbie sent over in her last parcel. It wasn't bad but we couldn't wait for it to boil for the designated hour and some of the ingredients were still a little hard when it came to chewing them. It tasted alright, however, and we finished the lunch with cheese on toast and a cup of tea. We were issued with a full suit of overalls this afternoon which will probably only serve to take up room in my kit bags. They support the old army slogan, "first class suits in two sizes, too large and too small." The only difficulty in this case is that most of the pants are too small and all of the jackets are too big. I have one air-graph from Iris to answer yet, then I will be all caught up on my mail again. It should be about time for some more to come in.

FEB. 24, TUES.

This morning saw my tool-box take on its first coat of enamel, but the handle and lock is yet to be obtained from somewhere. Sent a birthday letter to Aunt Ett this morning and hope it meets with her approval. The afternoon was spent in making some battery connectors for the exchange, to replace the old wire jumper method. I think it will be an improvement as it will speed up the changing burnt out cells while the exchange is in operation. Started a letter to Iris at noon today in answer to her last air-graph. "A" Company line going dead interrupted, temporarily, all ambitions in that direction so had to continue the letter this evening. Some more Canadian mail came in this PM and I received a carton of cigs from Nelle. Also received a letter from Aunt Pat, but it is very short. Reg received a parcel this afternoon so once again we have a supply of tea bags, sugar, etc. to last us for a while. I think I will try and get the other 3 volumes of my diaries back home before it is too late. A whole week without going out to a show is getting very boring. I will have to break out on pay day, I guess, and go and see "South of Suez."

FEB. 27, FRI.

Nothing of any great importance has taken place during the last three days. Checking DV telephones served to occupy most of the "working" hours and letter writing in the evenings took up most of the time. Mrs. Page and Ellen brought up a swell shepherd's pie which soon disappeared in no uncertain manner, despite the fact that we had supper only half an hour before. We were paid this morning so spent most of the afternoon shopping in Seaford for a handle and lock for my toolbox. We went down in a P.U. consequently we had to leave for camp earlier than I wanted so as to get back at four. Went to see "South of Suez" at the Deluxe this evening, then had bacon and chips at the Mikado. Reg wanted some chips so I dropped in at the fish and chip joint and got him a sixpence worth and then ate half of them for him. Started to answer a letter from Marcella that I got today, but I guess I am not in the mood for writing letters. The Canadian wanted for the murder of a police sergeant and the wounding of a civilian was caught this evening. Bob Budd (Cpl.) told me today that he was going back to Canada as an instructor soon, so I may give him the three volumes of this diary to take back with him. I will have to write to Marc tomorrow, maybe I need a good night's sleep.

FEB. 28, SAT.

Worked on DVs again this morning and soldered two new lugs on a Canada badge for one of the band. Reg went to a town further west of here and came back around twelve with two pads of Airmail writing paper. I went in the other direction to another town, bought another handle for my toolbox and a chest lock which I decided not to use because it would weaken the box too much. Had supper in a restaurant then bought 2 large writing tablets, then came home around six. We have four writing and two packages of envelopes, now that should do us for a while. Finished my laundry early this evening then wrote a letter to Marcelle.

MAR. 1, SUN.

Started the second fourteen day treatment for these pimples this morning and it looks like it might work. Traced down a wall socket circuit and changed a wall socket for one that was broken and got the electric heater working again. Wrote a letter to Bobbie and one to Doc this afternoon and evening. Fish was the main and almost only item on the menu for supper so I went down to the corner store for tea and cakes. I have to have a bath this evening before I go to bed. Started a letter to Rosemary but couldn't finish it.

MAR. 2, MON.

Spent the morning working on a static battery and this afternoon on DVs. Went to see a show called "The Woman from God's Country" and welcomed the snow scenes and the display of rough, pine covered landscape. It is the moonlight night with a thick mist, obscuring visibility and feeling like a cold damp hand on one's face, leaving little drops of glistening drops of moisture on the nap of coats and gloves. It's an ideal night for foul deeds and for ghosts.

MAR. 3, TUES.

DVs again today, but they will soon be all cleared up for a while. Tried to write a letter to Nelle but didn't make a very good job of it.

MAR. 4, WED.

One more DV to go and it will be all cleared up. Had a little difficulty with the Rap unit on the exchange this afternoon. Bought a six penny ticket for the hockey pool also. Took Jack Tully's place on the exchange this evening while he attended the hockey game. Cameron's lost 5-4. The final game will be played next Wednesday. Some more Yanks have landed in Northern Ireland.

MAR. 6, FRI.

I was duly informed this morning of the scheme tomorrow and have charge of what personnel that is left to take care of ordinary duties. There will be six men and myself; why six I don't know, five would do just as well. Sat before an eighteen set all afternoon and held a listening watch while the rest of the stations were getting netted together. Wrote a letter to Nelle this evening. A bunch of fellows left for Canada this morning and they are considered very lucky by a majority of those left. It all depends on how the situation is viewed by the individual.

MAR. 7, SAT.

Hectic times this morning while everyone was getting ready for the scheme. Just before they pulled out Hatch said my name was on the list for the next Canada-bound soldiers. This disconcerting news was received with disbelief, so much so that I bet ten shillings that it wasn't. Now I am not so sure. Set up communication by wireless this after noon which was maintained until a wireless silence was imposed around six o'clock. They started to move off around eight and due to the silent imposition I was unable to keep contact with them as we had planned. Maj. Thomson came in soon after, accompanied by his driver and wireless operator (Bridge) and stayed until nine-thirty at which time he left to catch up with the convoy. We prepared a lunch in the exchange room and I soon found myself working on a couple of exchange units that wasn't working properly and I was still working on them at half past midnight.

MAR. 8, SUN.

Slept in this morning and missed a good breakfast of Corn Flakes, fried egg, sausage, toast and cocoa. I made up for the deficiency by having toast and tea prepared on our little electric heater. Cleaned up my room and then went to dinner. I saw Cpl. Budd in the kitchen and he said he wasn't sure if he would be going home or not. The cook then informed me that I was on the list for the next bunch, as this was a new and uninterested source of info, I am forced to suspect that there is some truth to the story although I can't see myself as an instructor. I will have to do a little personal investigation and find out for sure. I also strongly suspect that I have a case of scabies so I am preparing to go to a hospital for 24 hours and I am going on sick parade tomorrow. We are expecting the battalion back in a few hours so my search for enlightenment will get underway some time today; in the meantime, I will have to get ready for any event when I consult the M.O. in the morning. Wrote letters this PM until the battalion came back then put the exchange back into operation. Wrote letters to Vera and Em this evening. Sgt. Rankine and Reg tell me that this rash I have is hives and not scabies and that I should wait a few days to see if they go away before going to the M.O. I have one of this hives right on my knee cap and my pants irritate it until it itches. I will give it another day anyway.

MAR. 9, MON.

The exchanges demanded plenty of time today as trouble seemed to be the order of the day with them. It started with Brigade coming in on all lines and they would answer no matter who was being called. But I had experienced this trouble before and had it rectified in a few minutes. It happened to be a good time to fix all units that weren't working properly, such as dim lights, lights not staying on and dirty contacts and relays needing adjustment, so the day soon went. Reg and I pulled the gas water-heater apart this evening and found out much and improved the operation of the gadget enough to enable us to have a good bath apiece. I stayed in the tub for an hour and a half and it's one thirty now.

MAR. 10, TUES.

Checked over five eighteen sets today and did a soldering job on Red's lighter. Received a letter from Aunt Ett this afternoon and wrote letters to Aunt Pat and Doris this evening. Our new O.C. is presenting new and complex problems in that he insists that his set should be control station. I guess he doesn't realize what headaches the control station operator has, but will have to learn the hard way. He is a very determined man and insists on doing everything his way, regardless of the soundness of his ideas. I have a hunch I should prepare my belongings for a sudden move, I think we will be getting one soon. Confirmation of the fall of Java and Rangoon came through today. Nothing new on the back to Canada rumor as yet.

MAR. 11, WED.

Nothing much of anything was done this morning except the painting of the brass on my equipment. Took another crack at "D" Company's eighteen set and managed to get it working properly. Reg and I tested all eighteen set batteries this afternoon. Did a little experimenting with my oscillator this evening but am dissatisfied with the results, so far. Started a letter to Rod at noon and meant to finish it this evening but took a bath instead. Our hockey team won the Canadian Corps Championship this evening by whipping the Medical Corps 5 to 4. Received another letter from Mrs. Canning, I presume she is going to write once a week but I can't say that she will get as many answers.

MAR. 12, THURS.

Checked and cleaned another eighteen set. Nothing much doing for the rest of the day. Reg went to a dance this evening and Red came back from a field sketching class around nine. Finished answering my English mail this evening. Then washed clothes until 1:30 ackemma (am in the morning), a poor time to be doing laundry but it had to be done. We ate the can of sausages that Em sent over and found them too good to last. Reg claims that I am going to a dance at the Drove Hall next Saturday, but I am just as determined that I am not going. This damned skin trouble is giving me no end of worry; I will have to go to the M.O. soon and take the chance of going to the Holding Unit.

MAR. 13, FRI.

Friday, the thirteenth for two consecutive months. Reg left on the half day scheme this am in a high rage because he didn't know he was going until the last minute and he had all his gear apart after painting it the other day. The scheme lasted until noon and nothing usual took place in the day's signaling business. Pay parade this afternoon and I drew two pounds-ten.

MAR. 14, SAT.

Except for checking over an eighteen set, the morning was uneventful. Reg and I went to the next town to do a little shopping during which the course of which I managed to spend a 10 shilling note and brought back an HL2 valve for my oscillator, two batteries for my pen light and a book of stamps. We then went to the local cinema and saw a picture called, "Ice Capades" which wasn't exceptionally good. We had supper at the Mikado before coming "home" to write letters. Soon after our arrival we received a report that the signaler at "A" Company had left his duty so Reg took over for the night. Inskip came in and got into Reg's bed, apparently for the night, and I wrote a letter, or at least started a letter to Iris. Rankine and I had toasted bully beef sandwiches for lunch.

MAR. 15, SUN.

Inskip had left and Reg was occupying the bed when I got up at eleven this morning. Reg got up for dinner and then I tried to adapt the new tube to my oscillator, with little success. Reg left for a date after supper and I finished Iris' letter, and started one to Bobbie. I took a creoline bath tonight and with the aid of a little laundry soap, emerged quite a bit cleaner than when I stepped into it. Reg is in bed and has his face to the wall so I guess I had better retire too.

MAR. 16, MON.

The day seemed to pass with little effort and except for a small repair job on one of the exchanges, maintenance had an easy day of it. Reg and I took tea at the Glen Roy this evening and I was told that the paved roads on this hill would be an everlasting monument to the Canadians' stay here. I heard also the history of the mile of road from here to town from the minister's elderly wife. It used to be just a track before the last war, but Conscientious-objectors were put to work on it during the war and present road was the result. Nothing to do now but go to bed, seeing as I have finished Bobbie's letter. One to Nelle and one to Jack and I will be all caught up again.

MAR. 19, THURS.

The usual routine for the last two days with little to write about. This morning and afternoon there was the usual bustling before the scheme. I am staying behind to take care of the signal office and exchange skeleton staff. We had a busy time of it on the exchanges and Fullerphones during the early hours of the evening, but it quietened down to a reasonable level when the scheme got underway. It's pretty late so I guess I had better get some shut-eye. George Wilson told me today that Cpl. Budd isn't going after all.

MAR. 20, FRI.

I got up for breakfast this morning for the first time in months and found the early rising had its rewards as I got a breakfast of corn flakes, milk and sugar, sausages, toast, jam and well-made cocoa. Saw Cpl. Budd there and he confirmed what Wilson told me yesterday so I will have to find other means of getting these things home. We received news this morning that Archer is in the hospital with a compound fracture of the skull and pelvis and lacerations to the face and is in a very critical condition. He had a crack-up on his motorcycle while riding convoy last night; it was exceptionally dark last night. He joined up the same time as I did along with Taffi Loverage who went to training center before we left Shilo. If he pulls through this, it will be a long time before he will be in circulation again. I made a poor show at taking a Fullerphone message this morning, but managed to get it through eventually. Received word later on this morning that Claire Archer had died soon after being admitted to hospital. The gang pulled in this afternoon around six and there wasn't much time to blanco equipment so the mad goose cancelled tomorrow's activities which met with unanimous agreement. The dispatches had been piling up all day so I had to send Stewie out to deliver them. I guess he was pretty tired after riding on the scheme, but he was the only one available. But he did it cheerfully.

MAR. 21, SAT.

Of all times to shove a new man into the sig office, as operator and signal clerk, and "Toffi" the unfortunate individual could stand a little more operational training. The signal register was a little screwy which multiplied his perplexities substantially. Finally had to take Garrett off the exchange to straighten the office up while "Toffi" teamed up with Jack Tully on the exchange. Everything was fixed up pretty well in the signal office and business was soon proceeding as usual. We have decided to hit the hay early this evening because we have been getting up early and keeping pretty late hours.

MAR. 22, SUN.

I think nearly everyone slept in this morning and except for the occasional buzz or ring from the exchange room things were pretty quiet all day. Another scheme starts at an early hour tomorrow morning and so again we have decided an early blanket fatigue would be appropriate.

MAR. 23, MON.

Five o'clock AM saw nearly everyone astir and the outfit pulled out around seven again, leaving four exchange operators and myself behind. It was a swell day and we spent most of it sitting out in front where we had an excellent view of the harbor and sea across the valley. It was while we were enjoying this exceptionally warm day that the tranquility of early evening was rudely shattered by a small number of enemy planes dropping bombs in the harbor. Very little damage was cause by the four bombs they dropped but it served to break the monotony of waiting. The battalion came back soon after and the boys were peevishly disappointed at having missed the show. One of the planes was shot down by anti-aircraft fire. If the Spitfires and Hurricanes returning from their daylight sweep over enemy territory had of come along a few minutes early, we may have seen a dogfight. But they came in just after the raiders had disappeared. It's two AM now and there is another scheme tomorrow. Maj. Law came into the exchange room during the evening, waxed very sarcastic about not answering the calls on the exchange, but cooled down when we found that the batteries had shorted and burnt out, thus the exchanges wouldn't indicate the calls. He told us that the enemy raiders were expected back tomorrow.

MAR. 24, TUES.

I had to get up before six so as to rouse two D.R.s (*motorcycle Dispatch Riders*), Cross and Stewart because there was five special messages to delivered before seven-thirty. There was a stand-too order from 08:00 hours until 12:30, then the battalion started today's scheme which only lasted until around 3-30 or four. Due to the bombing incident yesterday, an increase of A.A. (*anti-air-craft*) activity is noticeable. As was expected, three enemy planes came back this afternoon; dropped three bombs into the sea and made off again. It was a swell day again, perhaps a little warmer than yesterday. Ross was kept here as signal clerk and local op. so I went on the exchange with Miller until five. I went to the show this evening and saw Bumstead picture and the feature "The Man Behind the Mask." It is a bright clear night, not too cold. Tried to start a letter to Nelle but couldn't make much headway.

MAR. 25, WED.
Another swell day with bright sunshine and a clear sky. Went down to take a look at the adjutant's phone but found it all right at that end so told the Exchange Officer to phone G.P.O. (*General Post Office*) and report the defect. The Brigade line went out about three this afternoon so I borrowed "A" Company's P5 and checked the line as far as Blackcap hill and found it okay to our exchange, so as it was nearly suppertime I came back and left the rest of it to Brigade. I had a bath early this evening and afterwards didn't feel like writing letters so I am sorry to say nearly the entire evening was wasted.

MAR. 26, THURS.
Exchange operating took practically all of my time as Garrett was working all three of them by himself. Mac left yesterday for a commando course. MacGuire went on it yesterday but soon after when he had plenty of time to ask a few questions, he claimed he had sore feet. Some of the fellows think he is suffering of severe frostbite to the feet. He came back a few hours after he had left and MacKenzie has gone out. I wrote a letter to Nelle tonight.

MAR. 27, FRI.
Nothing much of any importance today in the line of daily work. Rankine may go to the commandos later on; Beck went this afternoon. Also heard today that four signals N.C.O.s were recommended for O.C.T.U. (*Officer Candidate Training Unit*) which means I would probably jump up to sergeant but later on this evening it was changed to two names being handed in; Reg being advised to get some experience as a sergeant first, the fourth person

wasn't consulted at all, and I doubt very much if he even heard about the original plan. However, if the two, whose names have or are going to be submitted, pass their preliminary examinations, it means that Reg will go up to sergeant and two full fledged corporals will be made. Who knows, if this war lasts long enough, I might even get a chance at O.C.T.U. some day. Started a letter to Bobby this evening.

MAR. 28, SAT.

The day started with Garrett bringing the good news that one of the exchanges was on the fritz, long before I intended to get up. New batteries was all that was needed; strongly suspect the night alarm of shorting the batteries. A new pin in Eric Moore's lighter was the next job and that only took a few minutes. Took Bridge's place on the exchange for an hour this noon while he went down to get paid. Patched some bicycle tyres this afternoon and otherwise got two bikes in running order. Finished Bobbie's letter this evening and heard the King speak over the radio. We heard aircraft cannon fire this afternoon, away out over the Channel, but the planes (two) were too far away to ascertain if it was a "bona fide" dogfight or target practice. Made two decisions this evening: (1) learn to ride motorbike, regardless of consequences; (2) enroll for a radio engineer's course next week, despite the fact that I don't think it will do much good. Rankine asked me if I would like to go "down the river" as a signal sergeant.

MAR. 29, SUN.

I missed an egg (2) and sausage (2) breakfast this morning, plus corn flakes by sleeping in, but managed to be there for dinner. Some of the boys were taking snaps this afternoon so I will have to get some of them and send them home. Rankine and I went out on the motorcycles this afternoon, me as a pupil and Red as instructor. My machine started by jumping ahead like a bronco, climbing the side of the road, whereas I rode a couple of hundred feet over very rough ground between the road and a mined ditch; it was a toss-up whether it would return to the road or take the final plunge into the ditch in which case I might not have been interested in future events. However, I persuaded the temperamental "critter" to get back onto the road where the riding was much easier. I managed one way or another to get her

A Quiet Man's Journey Through Hell

into high gear and things sort of settled down for the next four or five miles until Red pulled ahead and stopped me to tell me that I was doing 45 miles an hour. I thought the machine was just starting to warm up. Red took the lead from there on and started hunting for rough, hilly roads and pretty well succeeded. One especially that I had thought wasn't meant for motored traffic but we managed to navigate it all right. We ended up down at headquarters company where we picked up the platoon's mail, then a fast run along the coastal road back to our billets. This is my first real lesson on riding motor bikes. Wrote a letter to Anne tonight and received another two from Nelle, one from Marc, and one from Bezzie.

MAR. 30, MON.

The day dawned dull and threatening mist limiting visibility to short distances. Nothing of any importance today except I had to make another aerial mounting for the other station wagon. Went out on Tide Mills line this evening and had to go right to the end where I found five feet of wire cut out of the ground wire. Someone probably wanted a piece of wire to tie his bedroll. Returned to barracks around ten-thirty after hoisting the bike over two gates going and coming. No letter writing this evening.

MAR. 31, TUES.

Hundreds of silent prayers were answered when we woke up to find it raining pretty hard, consequently the inspection and route march was postponed for the second time. Everyone is hoping the "mad goose" will get discouraged and discard the idea entirely. There is a couple of radio sets on the work bench but there isn't a great deal I can do without the proper tube replacements. Went down to the Deluxe this evening and saw James Cagney in "The Strawberry Blonde." Dropped into the Mikado for bacon and chips and ran into Smith so we came home together. Walked into the exchange room this evening and found Hill on duty; he started "beefing" as soon as he saw me so I left him to it.

APR. 1, WED.

We were up early this morning and the outfit left on the scheme pretty early. Busby and Ross were supposed to be on the exchange but I let Ross be local operator and signal clerk and I went on the exchange. At three Hill and Walker came on so I took over the signal office. The unit came off the scheme just after six and business started to pick up again. Ross and Busby weren't warned for the 2200 hr shift and Ross went to a town some distance away and didn't get back so I was on the exchange all night.

APR. 2, THURS.

Came off the exchange at eight but going to bed was useless as there were too many people running in and out. Hill had to see the M.O. for a boil treatment at ten so took over until noon. Worked on "A" Company No. 18 set this afternoon. The meter needle was sticking and although I pulled the delicate mechanism apart, I failed to find the cause. Tomorrow I will have to pull the sender filament rheostat apart and readjust the rotating arm. Sgt. Rankine and I had a can of chili con carne and a can of fresh strawberries for lunch this evening. I am feeling awfully sleepy this evening so may hit the hay early. Received a carton of cigs from Bobby today as did Reg.

APR. 3, FRI.

Nothing very important today, except a little No. 18 repair work. Garrett and I went into the next town east of here and saw James Cagney in a picture called, "Jeannie." We caught the last bus home.

APR. 4, SAT.

Repaired an 18 set this morning and changed the telephone in "A" Company transport this afternoon. All my superiors went out this afternoon leaving me in charge. Played a couple of games of crib with Miller this afternoon while operating the exchange and got whipped in both games. A flock of messages came in this evening and we had a pretty busy time for a while. Worked until 1 am entering dockets for the first thing in the morning. A special dispatch is scheduled for first thing in the morning which means that I will have to be up early.

APR. 5, SUN.

Up for breakfast and got the special away in plenty of time. Worked all day as signal clerk, Fullerphone operator with a dash of exchange operation thrown in for good measure. Played Miller another game of crib and was beaten again; I will have to learn that game. The possibility of getting a promotion is hanging in a balance and it is doubtful when and if, Sgt. Rankine goes to O.C.T.U. if it will come my way. I am not worrying an awful lot about it. Hatch didn't get by the Colonel's interview so it is a foregone conclusion that he will be Signal Sergeant if Rankine goes. No one seems fussy about him being Sergeant. I forgot to mention yesterday that Johnny Smith walked in on me last night. He is with an artillery unit stationed near here. He is looking very good. He told me that Jack Owen is over here as a Lieutenant, too, but I haven't seen him. Had a hard time finishing a letter to Marcelle this evening. It smells as if something is about to happen soon. I hope I don't miss it through this pain in my right side which I suspect as being appendicitis. It isn't bad yet, but it's there.

APR. 6, MON.

In the Signal Office today as signal clerk and a local operator. Brigade put a new metallic line in today and as far as Fullerphone goes, I don't like it very well; line noise nearly drowns out the signal and makes reading exceptionally hard. Cross and I went to the Deluxe and saw two pictures, Jane Withers in "45 Fathers" and another film called "Hudson's Bay." The queue was five deep and up the street when we arrived but we managed to get two 1/6 seats. The Mikado was closed when we came out so we had to be contented with fish and chips.

APR. 7, TUES.

Worked all morning in the signal office then Ross came back at one o'clock. Walker was away to the hospital this afternoon so I went on the exchange from two-thirty until five. Took part in a game of cards this evening but had to leave to operate a Fullerphone and take a 78 group message from Brigade. I will have to go back into the signal office again tomorrow because the battalion will be away on a route march leaving exchange men, two D.R.s and myself to perform signal duties around here.

APR. 8, WED.

The battalion left early for the inspection this morning and business wasn't much slacker in the signal office. Took a number of Fullerphone messages, including a 60 group headache. Business slackened off around two this afternoon and the battalion was back from their route march around five. Reg was pretty tired, especially in the feet. We had tea at the Glen Roy Tea Room. As Fullerphone operator, I had to stay on duty until ten, but nothing came over all evening. We received a phone call this afternoon and were informed that there was a 50 gallon can of petrol or spirits and a bale of rubber washed up on the shore and if we could fish it out, ready for loading. There would be a couple of pounds in it for us. We couldn't go because we were on duty so we relayed the information to the B.O.R. (*Battalion Orderly Room*). In no time the wires were hot between here and H.Q. company and everyone had ideas of their own about earning the promised cash. If all went down to fish the goods out of the water, who said they were, there was enough there to eat the stuff and two pounds wouldn't go around very well.

APR. 9, THURS.

Things were back to normal again this morning with Ross in the signal office and me back on maintenance, with the two U.C. 6 line exchanges as the first patients.

APR. 13, MON.

The last four days have been mainly uneventful except that there is a probability that Rankine may not make O.C.T.U., which means that there will be no promotions for a while yet and Rankine will be like a bear with a sore head. The battalion is leaving on another scheme this evening and will have to walk forty miles before it is over. Once again I am here in charge of things, at least until the unit gets back tomorrow.

APR. 14, TUES.

Didn't get to bed until late last night so I had a lay-in this morning and missed my breakfast. Reg came in off the scheme this morning in case I wanted to go on leave this afternoon. Am having a very difficult time getting ready and will have to leave two eighteen sets in need of repairs as I haven't time to fix them.

Took Bridge and Garrett down to the paymaster for our pay, and those two worthies were soon on their way to a good time. Still not ready for my leave which started at four this afternoon.

APR. 15

I didn't get away until eleven-thirty this morning, consequently it was after one-thirty before I got to Victoria Station. A lad from the Toronto Scottish and I got a taxi to the Beaver Club where I had lunch and dashed off a short note to Ann. I caught the four o'clock train to Southend from Fanchurch Street Station after making an attempt to find cousin Jack. This line runs nearly all the way along the shore of the Thames Estuary so I some wonderful views of the waterfront life. I got out at Southend and by asking a lot of questions which were answered in the usual vague manner, I eventually found myself standing waiting for a bus just opposite to the L.N.E.R. Station. I was only there a few minutes when a lady informed me that I had just missed the bus and would have to wait thirty minutes unless I accepted a lift from them in their car, so I sat in the front seat with my kit bag and rifle between my knees. It was a good car and they were swell people so in an amazing short space of time I recognized Aunt Pat's house. Aunt Pat met me at the door and I was soon very comfortably resting my tired dogs in front of the fireplace. Aunt Pat made tea, (sausages and chips, etc.) for me and it wasn't long before I was feeling right at home. Elsie had a picture date with Edie so Uncle Jack and I played Crib and with the able help of Aunt Pat, I beat him five games out of six. We stayed up until after midnight talking. I get a great kick out of listening to Aunt Pat and Uncle Jack recalling bygone events especially when they disagree to dates and places and sometimes people.

APR. 16, THURS.

Did little else but sit around the fire place this morning talking to Uncle Jack. Beattie came in with Marion and we (Beattie, Marion, Elsie and myself) went to the pictures in Southend this afternoon. Beattie and I tossed a coin to see who was going to pay and Beattie won. Elsie and I saw Beattie to her bus queue, then we went and caught our own bus at the garage. Edie, Harold's wife, came in this evening for a while and we made arrangements to go to the pictures tomorrow night. I beat Uncle four games out of six at Crib again this evening. I guess I am lucky and I think Aunt Pat loves to see Uncle Jack beaten. She is no mean player herself.

APR. 17, FRI.

I got up about nine this morning and played with Nigger, the dog, in the backyard for a while. Had a bath about eleven o'clock, followed closely with a shave. We sat outside and watched the planes flying around this afternoon. Elsie and I caught the six ten bus to Southend and met Edie at Victoria Square. Then we proceeded to the Astoria and saw "Hold That Ghost" and "That Feminine Touch." I finally was allowed to pay for something, having insisted before we started that the treat was mine. Auntie received a letter from Violet this afternoon. I guess I had better write to her like I promised. Peggy also wrote saying that she would be down early in the morning, and enclosed a little note for me. We at least I, am going to bed early this evening as I am feeling awfully sleepy.

APR. 18, SAT.

Peggy evidently didn't catch the early bus from Walthamstow because it is noon now and she isn't here yet. Edie was here for a while this morning but has left. Elsie and I have to catch the twelve twenty bus to go down to Beat's for a while. Edie wasn't waiting at the Bell when Elsie and I got there and it was near one when we finally caught a No. 8 bus for Seveyne Ave. only this particular No. 8 didn't go near Seveyne Ave., but we got back at Nursery Corners and walked to Beattie's place. Marion is still shy but not Mrs. Pat's little girl Jennifer who seemed to elect me as official walking stick. We stayed at Beattie's until 2:30 then caught No. 8 back to the Bell again where Edie left us. Elsie and I were just turning in at the gate when Peggy got off the bus with a boxful of little chicks and a huge shopping bag. The chickens squeaked from the time they were brought into the house until I went to bed at twelve-thirty. I spent a couple of hours converting a coal box into a chicken coup this evening but I am afraid the job was no credit to my capabilities as a carpenter. Doris came home around seven or eight and we spent the rest of the evening around the fireplace. Peggy is quite a tease. Doris plays the piano by ear and plays all the latest songs real well.

APR. 19, SUN.

We got up this morning to find that five of the chicks had died during the night and four more were in a very bad way. Peggy did most of the nursing until it was time for us to leave for Beattie's again, at eleven-ten. We were stopped and asked for our identification cards on the way down and Peggy had left her card behind; consequently she was presented with a summons to report to the police station at Rayleigh within two days. We met Edie at the bus stop at the Bell and we caught No. 8 (the right one this time), which dropped us off at Beattie's door. Again, little Jennifer, Pat elected Edie and I to take her for a walk around the yard. We left there with John, Beattie, young John and Marion around two thirty and we changed buses at the Bell. Spent the afternoon grass fighting with Eileen, Fred Goucha, Reg Goucha, Peggy, young John and little Marion. Marion finally broke down and became quite friendly. I gave Doris my three diaries to take care of until after the war. Peggy and I had to meet Elsie in Southend; Beattie and John and family were going home. Doris, Eileen, the Groucha bros. were returning to Walthamstow, so we were all at the bus stop together. There was some pretty long faces among the crowd. We were stopped again for our identities again and pass through okay this time. As we had suspected, we were too late to meet Elsie so we caught the next bus home. John, Beattie and family got on the bus at the Bell; they had been waiting there all that time. Elsie was home when we got there. At nine o'clock, Elsie, Peggy and I walked down to the Kent Elm bus stop with Edie. She chased me in and out of some air raid shelters while we were waiting and enjoyed ourselves a little. She gave me Harold's address and asked me to write to him. We spent the rest of the evening listening to Aunt Pat and Uncle Jack disagreeing about times, places and people and teasing each other. Four more chicks died today.

APR. 20, MON.

Peggy and I caught a bus for Rayleigh where Peggy had to report to the police for being without her registration card. We found the Police Station eventually and Peggy got off with nothing more than a calling down and a warning not to let it happen again. Rayleigh is a quiet typical English village where strangers are easily spotted by the inhabitants, consequently we were conscious of being the recipients of many questioning stares. Aunt Pat had dinner waiting for us when we got back, and as the time for departure drew close, I wanted less to leave. Peggy broke down and cried, but Aunt Pat told me it was the usual thing when she was going home after visiting them. We left Aunt Pat's around one-thirty or two and caught a bus to the L.N.E.R. Station (*London North East Railway*). The bus conductor must have felt sorry for us too, because she only charged us for one fare to Victoria Square. We checked our luggage at the station, then walked down to see Elsie. A little black dog gave us some anxious moments when he kept getting between our feet. After seeing Elsie and saying goodbye for a second time, we returned to the station and caught the three-thirty-three to Liverpool. Peggy, I think, was on the verge of tears all the way up to London and I did my best to keep her mind occupied with commonplace conversation. We got into Liverpool Station just after four and Peggy left for Walthamstow on the next train. She is a great kid and I like her a lot. I will have to write to her as soon as I get back. Her goodbye was abrupt and I think she was close to crying again. She is a staunch and firm believer in Communism and predicts an industrial revolution in this country after the war. Far be it from me to hold any political or religious belief against a person of Peggy's calibre. Aunt Ett was standing by the door when I turned into Ashford Street and I was soon inside and relieved of my hat, rifle, respirator, kit bag, etc. Tony Hobdell was here. He is Joe Hobdell's son. Later on in the evening Sissy and Terry came in, followed by Tony's mother Annie, and later still Tommy Hobdell and his wife Mary. There was a little family spat between Tommy and his wife which didn't amount to much and which I tried not to notice. Later on in the evening Ann and I took Sis and Terry home where we ran into another family quarrel as soon as we saw George, Sissy's husband. Ann and I tried to ignore that one too. Young Terry finally decided that he knew me and we had a little ballgame together. I met Sissy's brother and his family and Ann and I left early. Ann, Lilly and I played Rummy until pretty late. It is two-thirty o'clock in the am now.

APR. 21, TUES.

I got up at eleven this morning, much past the time I intended to, as I wanted to do a lot today. Aunt Ett gave me a breakfast of haddock followed barely an hour later by a big dinner. I went down to Victoria Station this afternoon to see about trains and was told that the last one tonight was at 8:45, much too early for my purposes and the first one in the morning was at 5:20. I decided to take the morning train which means I'll have to get up at four. Even a cousin can't cause that much inconvenience for their relatives, so I booked a room at the Maple Leaf Club. Then I went in search for the West Central Post Office in hopes of seeing Cousin Jack, but by the time I found the place, I had paced about three miles of very hard pavement, only to be informed that Jack had gone home fifteen minutes before I got there. A person can travel mighty far by bus or tube train in fifteen minutes so I gave up that intention and caught a bus on the Strand which took me to Liverpool Street. I window shopped along Bishopsgate and finally arrived back at Aunt Ett's just in time to meet Aunt Sue's two daughters, Esther and Rose who were just leaving. I don't know their married names, but they belong to the Bill Smith family. Uncle Bill is dead. That's another family I have to see before I go home. Ann and I went over to Sissy's again tonight and as usual I preferred to play with little Terry than to listen to George air his pet grievances. George is a Communist, but one of the speech making kind who believe in down with everything. We came away at ten and I watched Aunt and Lilly play a couple of games of Rummy. Aunt Ett has a Rummy playing technique that is peculiar but effective. She never bothers to sort her hand out but merely picks up every card of one suit and usually ends up with a seven card run, much to Lilly's disgust. Ann walked down to Old Street tube station with me and there I saw the last of my relatives for this leave. The journey down here by tube was uneventful. My roommate proves to be a member of the Dutch army with a variety of insignia's on his arm. Princess Irene Regiment, then a cloth shield affair with Netherlands across the top, the whole of which is just above a USA insignia, below which is a large gold maple leaf. I can't make up my mind just where he belongs. He told me that he had just had his Canadian type respirator stolen and like the average soldier, he had obtained another one by the same manner. We talked until midnight. Then he went to bed and was soon snoring. I won't be long behind him.

APR. 22, WED.
The night porter came and woke me at four and after a wash and shave, I was on my way to the station. As I was leaving the Maple Leaf Club the night

porter called me into his room and gave me a cup of tea which certainly was welcomed because there are few canteens open at that hour of the morning. There were approximately twenty-five soldiers, two sailors and one lone nurse waiting for the 5:20A.M. train, which surprised us all by pulling out on time. We changed trains at East Croydon and continued our slow way southward. The train was one of those that stops at every little and large station. I was sharing a compartment with one other soldier and the nurse. It wasn't long before we were on talking terms and time didn't seem so dragging after that. The other soldier got off first which left the nurse and I with the compartment to ourselves. During the course of conversation she said she was supposed to have been in last night, but if she could get in for duty at 7:30 she would be all right. We reached her station, Hayward's Heath, at seven. She said she needed a taxi to make it on time. I hope she did. Eventually, we pulled into Brighton where I had to change for Lewes. The workers on their way to work crowded the train pretty thoroughly but I managed to get into a seat just before the train pulled out. I had to change again at Lewes and there the crowd of workers thinned a little. We pulled into my station around eight and by eight-thirty I was entering my billets. There was some good news waiting for me here as Sgt. Rankine had left word with the corporal of the relieving signals that I was to remain here and lend aid if anything unusual happened to the signal system, which it very often does; there were also five other signalers left behind so Bridge decided to stay as well. There was very little we had to do except answer the odd question once in a while so Garret and I went to a show at Seaford called, "The Parachute Battalion." Afterwards we had steak and chips at the Dorothy Cafe.

APR. 23, THURS.

Today is a repetition of yesterday, except for the train journey; in its place I slept in until ten this morning. Garret and Bridge went to Seaford on bicycles and were supposed to be back at four-thirty, then Garret and I were going to see a show called, "Dangerous Moonlight" but they weren't back at that time so I started out by myself. After the show I had another supper of steak and chips at the Dorothy, then went up to the Church Army Canteen for some matches. I met Bridge and Garret at the bus station and we came home.

APR. 24, FRI.

The unit came back late this afternoon, preceded by Rankine and four or five signalers in the PM who were followed by Reg on a motorcycle. Reg looked like he had a hard time of it and stories of the scheme soon were being related. Evidently the 2nd Div. stole the whole show. Sergeant Rankine brought a timid little black dog back with him because she seems to be a great rabbit catcher, an asset to any man's platoon. They call her "Lady" for obvious reasons. By nine this evening we had taken over from the relieving regiment and had all of our exchange equipment back in place again. The two regiments doubled up on the billets tonight to avoid another night's bivouac.

APR. 25, SAT.

I worked in the signal office all day and had some busy moments taking Fullerphone and phonogram messages. The Intelligence telephone line was torn down by a lorry about four-thirty so I had to make a temporary job on it, then changed my shoes then hightailed it to the show called "The Tower of Terror" at the Deluxe. I met Bud Ray so we went together, afterwards having a supper of bacon and chips at the Mikado. From then until ten-thirty we spent at the Tamplin Hotel, feeding our faces with sausage sandwiches and beverages to match.

APR. 26, SUN.

Fergie was in the Sig office today so I didn't have very much to do, so spent the day writing letters and took a bath during the afternoon. Ross leaves for the R.C.C.S. (*Royal Canadian Corps of Signals*) holding unit tomorrow and most of us move to new billets. Worked out a new signal diagram this evening. Whether they follow it or not doesn't worry me at all. It is as how I think it ought to be done for the minimum expenditure of wire.

APR. 27, MON.

Cross and I were moved down here to our new billets first thing this morning. The billets are the best we have had but they are a little too far away from town. The neighbourhood seems to be a residential section and this particular part of it is built in a sort of a square. The road makes a complete circle with only one way in and out. The center of the circle formed by the road is green turf with two air raid shelters in the center. The houses are recently erected, possibly just before the war, so they are comparatively new and modern. They are what is known as council houses, or houses built for the not-so-well-off people in the poorer sections of the big cities. A family can come into one of these houses, pay a pound a month rent, which goes toward paying for the house and eventually the family owns the place. These houses are built along modern lines and plenty of large windows and fairly large rooms appear to be the key note of the design. Reg and I have a front room on the ground floor with windows about seven feet by five feet, overlooking the square. It is a very secluded spot and I dare say, there isn't an officer within a half a mile from here. Tommy Cawson, Tommy Hill and I swept and mopped the place from top to bottom this afternoon, then we started straightening up the front yard with its two years of matted grass. We tried burning it off, but it was too thick and we didn't have a rake to loosen it up. A neighbour promised to lend us a pair of shears tomorrow which will help a lot. Most of our civilian neighbours are old folks so the place is pretty quiet. Reg and I were settled in our room early this evening; Wally Mills and Tommy Cawson were out somewhere so "Smitty," Tommy Hill, Reg and I went down to the cafe and had potato chips and beans as an evening lunch. I wrote a letter to cousin Jack after we came back and started one to Violet, then we played cards until midnight. Reg has finished his reading in bed for tonight so I guess it's time I was rolling in myself. I have a busy day ahead of me as I have to check all No. 18 sets for the scheme on Wednesday.

MAY 3, SAT.

The last six days have been busy with small things taking place. I was on my first scheme in a year or almost a year, when I had to go on an all night one the other night. But I didn't mind it at all as it was a swell night, if a little chilly. We came off that at three in the morning and I slept until eleven, only getting up in time for dinner. I have been receiving mail from home and from this country pretty regular, but repair work has prevented me from doing as much writing as I would like to do. During the six days the Quartermaster Sergeant came in and took some of my blankets because I had six when I was supposed to have four, but that situation was soon rectified because when Walker left for Signal holding unit, along with Hill, Cawson, Thorn, Jackson and Busby, he left me four extra blankets that he had plus one that he had brought from home. His blankets were much better than mine so I discarded two of mine and kept his four. I am using his personal blanket as a pillow. I also traded palliases with him because his was a square one and mine was tapered, so I gained all around. No. 18 sets are causing me some bad headaches these days and complaints from the exchanges are numerous for some reason or other. Rankine was in Brighton for a few days trying his final for O.T.C.U. I hope he makes it, although I can see an eruption if Hatch goes up to Sergeant. Reg is leaving for a special signaling instructors course in the near future, so I guess Hartney will have practically a free reign. Mills and Hatch both come from Hartney and I have a slinking suspicion that Mills will go up to full corporal despite the fact that I am senior lance corporal. Seven qualified signalers were brought in from holding unit to take the places of six unqualified that left. The old gang is gradually disappearing and the platoon is losing some of the spirit it used to have. It's just another signal platoon. We had an inspection ceremonial and march past this morning and because it was the first one I had been on for ages, I had to be company right marker. However, things went off without serious hitches taking place, but we almost froze our hands during the inspection. I went to Denton this afternoon for a visit and MacKenzie and Beck came to the show with me. Those two are in training for the Commandos and will soon cease to be Camerons. They appear to like the change and say they wouldn't come back to the unit for any price. After the show we met Guedesse and Ellison and we retired to the Mikado for supper. I guess we were hungrier than we thought because we had double orders of everything. I wrote to Alf this evening after I got home.

MAY 8, FRI.

We were roused out of bed at 5:00 this morning and we had quite a time getting ready for this seven day scheme. We had breakfast at six, then until nine we were busy storing what equipment we wouldn't be using on the scheme. We were under way by 09:45 with Grant, Jarves, Toffi Chambers and I in the back of the stores truck, packed between two large cupboards, front and rear. Except for a minor one-night scheme a few days ago, this is the first for me since last June or July and the experience is a little interesting. We eventually pulled into a grove of elms and as the scheme proper wasn't supposed to start until Saturday night or Sunday morning, we busied ourselves taking as much comfort as nature had to offer, by making beds out of bracken and devising effective windbreaks. Lines were strung out to the companies and an exchange put into operation with very little difficulty. Some of the fellows played ball this afternoon, but I spent nearly all of the afternoon gathering material for a makeshift bed. We had no blankets with us and we had to makeshift with great coats, tarpaulins and camouflage nets for comfort and warmth. We spent the remainder of the evening lying around a small fire until the fire had to be extinguished to conform with blackout regulations. Then Sergeant Rankine and I tried to get some sleep in our improvised shelter. It's twelve o'clock now and it's cold and getting colder; Reg is snoring.

MAY 9, SAT.

What a miserable night that was; only a very few got any decent sleep, as far as I can find out. We were up well in advance of Reveille and had a fire going as soon as blackout regulations permitted. It was misty, cheerless and decidedly cold and it took a few hours of hot sun to return it to favorable conditions. We played penny-ante all afternoon, at least, until it was time to get ready for the next move in this scheme. The Battalion H.Q. pulled out just after supper leaving Forsythe, Chambers, Middleton, Peel and myself to take up the lines. The truck came back for us around nine thirty, then we moved to our new position two miles away. We repaired the brigade line which we found broken, arrived at this place just after dark. It feels as if it will be colder than last night. I am bedding down in a shallow dry ditch, where I hope I will be out of the wind. No hot drinks this evening.

MAY 10, SUN.

We were awakened around four this morning and after finding Toffi Chambers and reeling the lines up again, we were on our way for the next place and phase in this scheme. We had hardly stopped at this new position before we had a fire going and were heating water for tea. They started bringing in "prisoners" this morning, including the booty, such as three trucks and a number of carriers. We sent some kids for some bread. It started to rain this afternoon so some of us retired to the equipment laden truck, where I slept for two hours on top of one of the cupboards. I had to get out later on to relieve my cramped legs and Bill occupied the cupboard bed until suppertime. We are hearing little bits of news of a naval battle in the Pacific but papers are scarce away out here in the sticks and there is no definite word about it. Well, we are already for another move tonight and I think I will sleep in the truck in case the order to move comes during the night. I am back on the cupboard again.

MAY 11, MON.

We woke up late for breakfast but managed to scrounge a dozen or so sausages from the cook as well as many meat and jam sandwiches. There is a withdrawal scheduled for this morning so we turned the truck around, ready to slip into the convoy as it goes by. The convoys were going up to the "front-line" all night, so there will be plenty to come back. Finally it came hell-whooping down the road and we managed to slip in behind the W/T truck. We crossed a bridge built by the engineers at four this morning and eventually pulled into a field and parked again. Around eleven we made a fire brewed some tea and had a passable lunch. The day is clearing up fine and the sun is shining most of the time now. All we have to do now is wait for the next move, which will probably be around four this afternoon. By the looks of things now, supper isn't forthcoming this evening until pretty late, if at all. Guedesse came down around seven pm and picked up Hatch, to go on a recce somewhere. He came back soon after and said he had made a mistake and said I was the chosen one, so I clambered aboard behind "Guedie" and was whisked to B.H.Q. where Hatch gave me his equipment. I still think there was some buck passing connected with the whole idea. Hatch is a past master at that game. Twenty minutes later we were on our way to Brigade Headquarters to receive final instructions. We had a fairly long wait there but finally were tearing over the quiet English countryside toward a south coast resort town. On the way we saw an aerial battle of short duration, anti-aircraft guns vs two German raiders, one of which crashed into the sea. We arrived at our destination, stopped a minute or two, received absolutely no instructions, then proceeded to a small village where we were to meet our respective platoons and guide them to the new battle area. We were dropped into the solemn solitude of the village life without ceremony, comment or supper.

Nourishment was our first thought with sleeping facilities running a close second, so we canvassed the town for food. Ale and potato chips seemed to be the only thing available at that time of night and it wasn't at all satisfactory. Somehow or other I fell in with Lieutenants McGill and Johnson, Corporal Riley and Bateman Major in their semi-organized search for nutrition. We tried a quiet house first, but they already had 13 soldiers inside and couldn't handle any more. We decided that our only chance was to try a tea room long since closed for the night. We met with little success with our persuading until McGill said that we hadn't eaten in sixteen hours, then the good lady took us in and we had all the bread, butter, jam, cookies and tea we could eat, for only eight pence apiece. Five more fellows came in just as we finished and they had a similar story and when last seen they were occupying the chairs around the table we had just vacated. Before we left we had permission to sleep on the floor in the front room which would have been a lot better than sleeping under some hedge. We had to attend a conference at the top of the hill after which seven of us, including the two officers, returned to our beds in the front room of the tea room.

MAY 12, TUES.

The recce last night turned out to be somewhat of a flop as far as we guides are concerned. We had just settled down for a few hours' sleep when the runner came in to inform us that our stores were outside and we had to take them to their new positions. Then started a four-hour rambling in and among the streets and roads of the coast town looking for positions which hadn't been shown to us. Every time we saw a policeman or two, we stopped and asked them for directions but we had the usual difficulty in following them in the blackout. At four in the morning we found H.Q. Company and decided to stay there for the night. There was nothing to see riding around in a blackout anyway. French, Hatch and I crawled under a big tarpaulin and didn't wake up until an hour after breakfast. That little deficiency was rectified when the Intelligence Sergeant waltzed in with a couple dozen cakes around ten this morning. "A" Company line was torn down by an omnibus at one of the road crossings, then later when the company moved again, there was a joint that wasn't making contact. About the same time "B" Company line was ripped down by another bus, but it wasn't long before we had them both going again. Communication with "D" Company was solely by No. 18 set and set trouble developed late this afternoon. We found 10 valves blown in two sets before we got a combination that worked half satisfactorily. It rained all afternoon and is still coming down. We played a little penny-ante this evening but had to break it up because there was too many officers coming in all of the time. It's eleven-thirty now and high time I was rolling in. We are very fortunate to be billeted in a building this night. It is the Beresford House, boarding and day school for girls and kindergarten, junior and senior, at least that is how the sign reads on the gate.

MAY 13, WED.

We were up for stand-to at five this morning, the same same which lasted for an hour. I had to take the 15 cwt truck up to "D" Company to look at their wireless set and found all it needed was a little readjustment. We got back just in time for breakfast. The R.A.P. (*Regimental Aid Post)* line went out this morning but it was just outside the door and easily fixed. I think this scheme will soon be over, probably in a few hours. We finally arrived back here and as is usual after a hard scheme, I have been relaxing for the last 4 or 5 hours so I think I will hit the hay soon. There is some disquieting rumors going around about another move into the interior.

MAY 14, THURS.

This particular rumor materialized quite rapidly this time as we have been packing stores all day. We move tomorrow. Did some unfinished business during the afternoon.

MAY. 15, FRI.

We were up at 05:00 hours this morning and had breakfast at 06:00. The troops pulled out, marching, at 08:30 and the transport at 09:30. French hadn't returned for the last load of stores by that time so it was closer to eleven when we left for a new home. We finally arrived at Denne Park at 11:50 just in time for dinner. The first impression of the camp was of squat corrugated steel huts, not unlike huge steel drums cut lengthwise and the halves being placed on foundations to form half round affairs, which were scattered helter-skelter over a wide area of once beautiful park, beneath high leafy elm trees. We were confined to barracks immediately and just after supper we had to parade for a speech by the C.O. This was the first we knew that we were going to participate in something out of the ordinary. I don't think anyone was really excited about the news but it wasn't long before the rumors were circulating the camp thicker than ever. The advance party leaves tomorrow morning. It might not be action, but it will be the next thing to it.

MAY 16, SAT.

We spent the day orienting ourselves and sorting out the "buckshee" stuff from the signal stores. Pay parade was at one thirty this afternoon so, as was expected, the little town of Horsham was over run during the evening and I think a good time was had by most. I bought a 20 shilling money order to send to Mrs. Winters for the radio we had rented from her at Seaford. I managed to get back to barracks before the tattoo roll call was handed in.

MAY 17, SUN.

We had an open air church parade this morning, during which I think I dozed most of the time, so I don't know much about what the good man talked about. Owing to this coming move, all necessary stores had to be checked and packed which took up most of the afternoon. At last, we have received a consignment of valves to replace some of those that have been blown in the No. 18 sets. If Ordinance could loosen up that much the importance of our future activities is apparent. We have been trying to get a new lot of tubes for months now. Some of the boys went into town tonight but the majority stayed to get their kits ready.

MAY 18, MON.

A day marked almost solely by frequent trips to the C.Q.M.S. (*Company Quartermaster Sergeant*) stores to make up shortages in our kits. After I had packed my kit a number of times, I still wonder if I did right by putting cigarettes where my winter underwear should have gone. No less than five times the trip to the C.Q.M. Stores was made in hopes of replacing some worn out or lost article, each time only to receive the same negative answer from a very weary Quartermaster Sergeant. I managed to purchase a clasp knife which strangely enough was sharp when I got it. Also drew out 70 free issue Canadian chocolate bars (2 per man) which have been donated by some friend back in Canada. Stayed in tonight and wrote letters and took a shower, probably the last one for some time, also sewed buttons on my denim uniform.

MAY 19, TUES.

From five-thirty this AM until 08:00 we were kept busy changing our packs to conform with rapid frequent changes issued every few minutes. Eventually we were all set to go and were lined up in front of the company orderly room, relieving the weight of our packs by propping our rifles under them. Then came the order to move and start of a long march through town to the railroad station. We passed one unfortunate who had his foot caught in a square hole in the road, originally for some part of a tank barrier. We were halted a block from the station while the paymaster's muster roll was called. Then we proceeded to the station where we boarded the train. At noon we were still jolting southward so we ate our haversack lunch of eggs, cheese sandwiches and fruit pies, washed down with water from our water bottles. About one-thirty we came to a large and widely known seaport where we had to wait 45 minutes for a boat. Southampton. It was only a short trip across the water but we passed sea craft of every size and shape as well as some sentried island forts. After we had landed we had to march 4 ½ miles to our camp area, stopping only once to eat the remainder of our lunch. (Isle of Wight) Evidently, we were regarded with amusement and interest by the natives possibly because we were the first lot of Canadians stationed in these parts. It wasn't long before we were assigned to our canvas homes and soon everyone was improvising means of making their home life as easy as possible. After supper we were assembled in a little clearing and given a fairly good idea of what to expect. During our course of training by the O.C. we started erecting camp communications but had to discontinue on account of darkness.

MAY 20, WED.

I think everyone spent a somewhat miserable night, last night, as it rained all night and the ground was damp. There was very little to do today except habilitate ourselves; complete the telephone system and make ourselves as much at home as possible. Passes were issued tonight until 10 o'clock so most of us went down to Ryden, Isle of Wight, where we landed yesterday. Rankine and I went together and after eating supper of eggs on toast and cakes, we walked down along the esplanade. We found our way into one of those amusement arcades, filled with slot machines of every variety. This particular gyp joint had a .22 rifle range and naturally we made a bee-line for it. We shot for 2/6 and I took five bob away from Bill before he said "quits." We walked around until eight o'clock then headed for the bus station where we caught a bus for our camp. While we were away orders were issued that there were to be no fires around the tents so I guess we will have to shave in cold water from now on. It isn't exactly meeting with the approval of the fellows, especially when they can't see any apparent reason for the order. I had to check over all No. 18 sets before I could go to town, but it didn't take very long and I found only two which need major repairs.

MAY 21, THURS.

I was elected duty N.C.O. today, so missed all of the marching and introductions to our sea craft that we are going to use in our training. I slept all morning and did very little this afternoon. They asked for the names of all swimmers and I put mine down as poor. I don't know what will come of it, but my name is in, anyway.

MAY 22, FRI.

Up early this morning and on our way by seven o'clock, starting with a four mile march to the pier where we boarded a queer shaped motor craft. We were taken to a beach a few miles down the coast where we practiced landing. When we jumped off the boats we found ourselves surrounded by icy cold Atlantic up to our waist. We had to wade ashore a few hundred yards away and by the time we got there our legs were numb from cold. It wasn't exactly finished with that however, as we had to wade again from shore to boats. We came back to camp for lunch and we were served hot tea and we changed into dry clothing. The dry clothing didn't do very much because we went for a route march this afternoon, marching two hours out and then came back inside of an hour. We were soaked with sweat so I changed my clothes again. We had a supper tonight that really should go down in history. It consisted of tomato soup, corned beef and cabbage, fruit, tea, bread and butter. I have a blister on my heel tonight and I feel too tired to go into town as I had planned. All N.C.O.'s and officers were given a lecture by an R.A.F. officer but we got there a little late and missed some of it.

MAY 23, SAT.

We received word late last night that we were to stay in this morning and clean weapons and as I only have a rifle to take care of, the D.V.s received some unexpected attention as well. The boys are out on No. 18 set practice and I am expecting some poor reports from at least two of them. The N.C.O.s were supposed to go to a training picture just before lunch but by the time those on No. 18 set work were recalled, we had missed the truck. We started on the afternoon's activity by marching 4 ½ miles to the pier, then boarded our little sea-craft again to practice a landing at the same beach we were on yesterday. However, it was high tide this time and we merely got our feet a little wet, when we jumped off the boats. It started to rain when we were coming back in the boats so we put our gas capes on when we got to the pier. We looked like a troop of camouflaged ghosts striding through the rain. We were soaked from the knees down when we got back to camp. We had a good supper. There are rumors of a night march tonight.

MAY 24, SUN.

We had our night march all right, being roused out of bed 02:00 hrs and getting back at 05:30 hrs. The rest of the day was a holiday so everyone heated water and washed clothes. We went on a bath parade to a place which, according to the C.S.M. (*Company Sergeant Major*) was only half a mile away. He was pretty close in his guessing as it was only a mile and a half. What's a mere mile in a soldier's life?

Passes were issued this afternoon and we had to draw to see who would stay behind as duty N.C.O. and I as usual stayed in camp. In the evening I took a chance and went out until twenty after nine getting back on the job in time for tattoo roll call.

MAY 25, MON.

Every day it rains and we are having a difficult time drying our clothes out. We went over the assault course this morning and it was the toughest bit of work I have done in two and a half years. Running a muddy, greasy hundred yard path through scrub, crossing a ravine on two ropes, sliding down a fifteen foot rope, crawling through a debris choked culvert, climbing a muddy slope, scaling a ten foot wall, running uphill, crawling through a barbed wire tunnel, jumping off of a raised platform, through fire into a pit, climbing through barbed wire entanglements, bayoneting dummies placed in awkward places and firing laying down, standing up and from the hip while a Bren gun fired over our heads, all on the double. How I made the last hill and fired the fifteen final rounds baffles me yet. The blister was much worse this morning, so I was more than thankful when the trucks picked us up and brought us back to camp. Stan Jarvis wrenched his knee again this morning when he jumped off the platform on the assault course. He hurt his knee some time ago in a motorcycle accident and he is unable to walk tonight, so they are sending him back to hospital. Won a little pin money at cards tonight. I didn't like the M.O.'s method of treating a sore blister, so I doctored it myself using the needle idea.

MAY 26, TUES.

We fell in at 08:30 this morning for a cross-country march which means anything can happen and probably will. It was decided that I would stay behind and sort batteries but minds were changed at the last minute so I went along. Through bush, bramble and bog, over fields, roads and fences steadily pushed on. We ended up in a chalk quarry with steep cliffs, up and down which men were swarming, some with the aid of ropes and some without. Others were practicing unarmed combat, while still others were jumping over a cement wall four feet wide and eight feet high. The whole thing looked amusing, to say the least. It was a quite long time before we had our turn at the activity and it was much easier than the assault despite the running, climbing and jumping we had to do. It started raining again just when we started homeward, and it rained right up until 5:00 in the afternoon. I applied for a pass until 22:00 hrs. and encountered numerous set-backs before getting it. We spent the remainder of the evening at the Sloop Inn.

MAY 27, WED.

The morning was a little difficult as we had to do a ten mile run and walk to a beach where we submerged ourselves in ice-cold Atlantic. It was too cold to stay in very long, but the short dip was refreshing and as we learned when we started back, a little stiffening too. Inskip, Suttlehan and I laid the floorboards in the exchange and stores tent which took most of the afternoon. There is a scheme on this evening which starts around nine o'clock and lasting all night.

MAY 28, THURS.

Last night was pretty hard slugging, including a very cold ride on a tossing motorboat in a blinding rain storm. When we landed, we found an old storage shed full of tents, etc., and we crowded seven into the remaining space. The scheme eventually wound up around two in the morning. We walked home from the beach and eventually arrived back in camp at three in the morning. Suttlehan was lying on my bed passing a message to all companies, so he merely vacated the premises and I took off my shoes and tunic and turned in. We were up again at six. Cliff climbing was scheduled for today but just as I was grabbing previous to my usual mad dash for parade, Sergeant Rankine stuck his flaming head in the tent and told me to stay back and check No. 18 sets. These sets were recently checked and supposedly repaired by Brigade Maintenance, but evidently they didn't respond to the overhaul. Anyway, I worked on seven of them today. Pay parade was called for this evening at six but it was nine-thirty before our company managed to get paid, so that going out for the evening was impractical. The boys are plenty sore about the whole thing because we had all planned on going somewhere for the evening. I received another letter from Dawn, one from Jack and two from Nelle, this afternoon.

MAY 29, FRI.

All N.C.O.'s were called together this morning and while the men went on a swim parade we were taken to a bombed area and taught how to clear houses and villages of the enemy. I found this type of work interesting, if a little blood-thirsty. Street fighting was also included. Everything found in the houses is exterminated or else driven out into a street where machine guns are sweeping the thoroughfare from numerous advantage positions.

Nothing is allowed to live in the street, regardless of species, sex, or uniform. They are drastic measures but very necessary. We found some onions in one garden which very mysteriously disappeared during the morning; the smell of onion followed us right back to camp. We went out on the boats again this afternoon for firing practice and had quite a lot of fun. Inskip nearly clipped Sergeant Major Moody acting C.S.M. of Headquarters Company when the boat lurched just as he pulled the trigger. Some of the fellows think the boat didn't quite lurch far enough. I found I did better shooting from the hip than when I aimed. Hatch and I went down to the Sloop for an hour with Sergeant Rankine.

MAY 30, SAT.

The first thing this AM was a six mile route march to the chalk cliffs where we spent the morning scaling cliffs, walls, barriers, etc. The cliffs are climbed simply by pulling oneself up by a rope, hand-over-hand, then to descend, the rope is straddled and passed over one thigh, in front of the body, over the opposite shoulder, then by manipulating the slack by the hands, descent is possible in a series of stiff legged hops. From the cliffs we marched a good four miles to the assault course. We had a very short rest, then went over the course for a second time. It seemed a little easier this time, perhaps because we knew when to run and when not to. The imperial commandos went over the course yesterday and they said it was one of the toughest they have been on. We had dinner during a pelting rain storm; then we marched the six and a half miles back to camp. Hatch and I went into Ryde this evening where I bought this new pen. Hatch bought a cigarette holder in a store on the Esplanade for one & six there. He saw the very same kind in another store for a shilling. We went into the Arcade while waiting for our bus and did some shooting in rifle range for sixpences. I made two & six out of the doings. We caught our bus okay.

MAY 31, SUN.

Except for an N.C.O.'s meeting this morning, and a bath parade this afternoon, it was a parade free day. I went into Ryde again this evening and met Wally Mills and Tommy Suttleham getting off the bus. We stayed in Ryde until nine-twenty, then caught the Canada Special to Fishhorne Lane. We call it "Canada Special" because it is an extra bus put into service to alleviate the crowding caused by we Canadians. It only comes as far as the camp; then turns around and goes back. There was a poker game in progress in the exchange tent which was soon moved to wider and more open spaces. I have to go with "C" Company tomorrow as No. 18 set operator with Grant. It is the first time that I have been assigned to a Company since they decorated my arm with this measly stripe.

JUNE 1, MON.

The scheme started early by riding in buses or troop carriers for seven miles. We disembarked near an aircraft factory and commenced to get on with the scheme. Grant was carrying and operating the set on his own volition. Over fences, hedges and fields, through fields, brambles, rose bushes, swamps, Grant and I wrestled the set. At noon, the first stage of the scheme was over and we were more than willing to put the set aside and eat our lunch. During the morning, at one instance, we stopped at one heavy A.A. battery and while taking a brief respite from the battle of the brambles, the battery received a battle station order. For a while we thought we were going to have a ring side seat at some A.A. action but the "all clear" came before they could get going. After dinner we had to march three miles to some bombed houses for some street fighting. After the thunder flashes and Bren guns had lapsed into silence, we sigs rejoined our own platoon for a long hard route march to a place where we were to do some field firing. I think it was one of the toughest marches I have ever been on but after the firing we were transported back to camp by truck. After the firing, which was very interesting if a little danger-ous, everyone was practically dead on their feet and we still had to march to the road for the trucks. It seems to be a characteristic of the foot soldier that when progress seems almost impossible, someone will start to sing and in a few minutes everything is OK again. In that manner, we navigated the rough valley, singing as hard as we could and swinging toward the road.

JUNE 2, TUES.

We started the day by marching six miles to the cliffs where we loosened up by running up and down cliffs, with and without the aid of ropes. Then we threw each other around in unarmed combat for an hour. Then, H.Q.

Company N.C.O.'s proceeded to the "Tommy Gun" range where we were introduced and initiated to the deadly little weapon. Grenade throwing came next, after a three hour wait during which we ate a too dry sandwich haversack lunch. Except for the occasional base-plug, the grenade throwing was uneventful, if a trifle noisy. We had another two hour lay-down before we were taken in trucks to the assault course. We finished that around five-fifteen. The route march home was a hot dusty, wearying affair, but a good supper had us back to normal again soon after. The Colonel isn't exactly popular with the men these days, his nickname, the "Mad Goose" is accepted as the only one for him.

JUNE 3, WED.

We had a fairly quiet day today, starting with P.T. followed with bayonet fighting. This afternoon we went for a swim in the Atlantic again and enjoyed it thoroughly. I played cards for a while this evening, finally ended up by going down to the Sloop for an hour with Tommy Dean and two other R.C.C.S. men. Dean is well known for his lies and it wasn't unusual to hear him plastering it on with his two pals.

JUNE 4, THURS.

The Colonel has ideas of converting an eighteen set into a mine detector and I can have all the time I wish to experiment, so it was I stayed off parade today and did some experimenting. The brigade signaling officer caught me red handed with the set all apart and a mess of wires connected here and there besides two probes. I thought he was going to blow up and give me the works, but after trying the arrangement, he merely gave me some suggestions as to how it might work. At noon I laid aside the work and relaxed in a game of cards in which I didn't do so good. There will be no sleeping tonight except in the cramped interior of the boats. We will be in them all night followed by an all day cruise around the coast. Right now it is getting dark and fellows are running around getting ready. I guess I had better go too.

JUNE 5, FRI.

We fell in about eleven-thirty last night, Hatch carrying the set and myself toting the pack carrying equipment for both of us. I don't know what was wrong, but it so seemed more like twelve miles than four and a half to the pier. After a little difficulty in finding our proper boat, we finally clambered aboard and set out for the all night cruise. It was without a doubt the most miserable night I have ever spent in a boat. The cold sweaty undergarments made sleep impossible. At approximately four-thirty we got the order "prepare to land." Luckily the tide was in and it was dry jumping. We stayed ashore for about an hour, had breakfast, then boarded our boats again, then started on the cruise around the coast. The scenery was exceptionally beautiful after the sun had swept away the heavy sea mist of early morning and the shore stood out in the clear, new sunshine like the product of a master artist's brush. I was one of the few who forced myself to stay awake and see it. During the morning the flotilla leader, or whatever he is called, put on a demonstration of maneuvers that went off like clockwork. The white towering cliffs, green fields and cozy little towns slid by as we progressed on our way along the south coast. Two Spitfires seemed to be following us around and offered a diversion with their aero-antics over the fleet of speeding boats. It was a beautiful day which matched and formed an appropriate setting for the beautiful island only a half mile away. The sea was calm, blue and vast, stretching away as far as the eye could see and our little boats were big and fast enough to churn the quiet serene sea into a heavy white fury of boiling water. We rounded The Needles at 10:45 and headed north again until we came to a place where we were scheduled to make a landing and scale a cliff. We were a little early for our show so we watched another unit embark through a heavy smoke screen. At last our turn came and the boats started heading for the beach in groups of five to discharge their human cargo. I don't know the reactions of the other fellows, but jumping into the cold sea and trying to climb the slimy muddy cliff was like a mild nightmare to me. We finally reached the top wet, muddy and tired. We had dinner then boarded the boats again to resume our cruise. The Colonel made a spectacle of himself over dirty rifles during dinner and I am afraid he slipped a little more in the estimation of the men. Forty-five minutes after boarding the boats again, we landed at our swimming beach not far from camp. Some of the fellows ahead of us had to jump in waist deep but the skipper of our craft chose his place well, refused to use the mud hook as a brake and consequently we landed on dry sand when our turn came to land. Hatch, Suttleham and I spent a quiet hour at the Sloop this evening, but I was too drowsy to stay longer. I bet I sleep tonight.

JUNE 6, SAT.

The platoon went out for a demolition demonstration this morning, but I had to stay in and check No. 18 sets. This afternoon we were transported to the scene of scheme "Winnipeg" one which went off fairly well and which terminated in our obtaining transportation home; something which surprised the fellows so much they forgot to air their pet grievances as is usually the custom. This evening was spent at the Sloop with Hatch, Wally Mills and the Hartney boys. We returned to camp at about ten o'clock. I noticed that the two white swans which have become a permanent fixture of Wooton Pond have had four little blessed events in the form of four downy signets.

JUNE 7, SUN.

We heard that all the officers are confined to billets for a week because of the dirty rifles last Friday. I think the "Mad Goose" is much more unpopular with the officers than he is with the men, and that is plenty. We had a stiff inspection of arms this morning which was very detrimental to the attendance to the voluntary church parade called for this morning. At last I finished some laundry this afternoon and was assailed by the idea of whittling a pipe from a hawthorn root. I am not at all sure that the idea will work out but I have one big blister from manipulating the knife already. I didn't do much else today except on the advisability of writing a letter to Nelle as I am not sure if it would pass the censor safely. I think a chap named Rosen deserves mentioning in the lowly essay. He is a Jewish lad from one of the rifle companies and seems to be getting a kick out of life. The other night he pulled out his pigskin tobacco pouch and made some remark about his mother not knowing about it when she sent it to him for his birthday. He also claims that the amount of bacon he gets for breakfast doesn't even give him a guilty conscience.

JUNE 8, MON.

For some reason we have been excluded from this new battle drill training but the platoon has been operating No. 18 sets all day while Corporal Hatch has been getting the exchange fixed. I amused myself with No. 18 set repairs and experimenting with the mine locator. Nil results on the locator. I wrote a letter to Nelle this evening and received letters from Anne and Rod Gibson. I had to go out on a phone repair job this evening and was surprised to find the man capable of a little human feeling. We discussed trembley bells and magnetizing and demagnetizing of metals. I got back to my tent just in time for a lunch of chili con carne, bread and butter, and tea.

JUNE 9, TUES.
Maintenance today while the rest of the fellows were out on No. 18 set operating. They had me riding a bicycle, going from set to set, checking the odd minor fault. Late this afternoon found me visibly digging the earth away from the roots of a hawthorn tree looking for a suitably shaped portion from to fashion a pipe. The rest of the day and evening was spent in whittling and digging the bowl and burning a hole in the stem. Finally had my first smoke from the semi-finished article, minus the mouthpiece. I worked until dark on the homemade fumigator.

JUNE 10, WED.
The day was mostly spent in preparing for the scheme tomorrow which promises to be miserably tough. Finished putting a mouthpiece on my pipe this afternoon. We had to attend a lecture by the R.C.C.S. Colonel during which we were given a fairly accurate description of the forthcoming scheme as it will affect the signals. Around nine brigade phoned up to say they would be down tonight to net their 18 sets, so I guess I won't get to bed as soon as I expected.

JUNE 11, THURS.
Brigade didn't come down until midnight; they fooled around nearly an hour before they decided to go home again. Talk about your unwelcome visitors. However, they weren't the only ones to be bothering me last night; the Adjutant phoned up around two in the morning, wanting Sgt. King on the line which caused me to search at least a half an hour before I had to ask for help from Bert Pope, duty fireman and between the two of us and a flashlight we managed to locate that unfortunate individual. Then the same Adjutant

wanted to speak to Stewie, our D.R.; then the orderly officer came in and the idea of sleep was forgotten for another hour. So it was I settled down for a few hours' sleep around three-thirty or four in the morning. Reveille was at five and it took me until breakfast to crawl out of my blankets. Then it was only hunger that prompted. Preparations went on for the scheme, such as drawing grenades, plus detonators, etc. We didn't leave camp until after five this evening, traveling by truck to the pier where we waited two hours or more for the boats. I found a little brass anchor, lying on the pier walk which was added to my little collection of souvenirs. At eight o'clock we were all loaded and on our way, heading out into the choppy Channel. Later, it became rough and we tossed around like a cork. Somehow we managed to get "C" Company's blankets on our boat, besides our own, so someone will have to sleep shivering tonight.

JUNE 12, THURS.

How our skipper kept track of the course and the convoy is beyond me, because when I stuck my head through the hatch around two in the morning, all I could see was a black void, broken once in a while by a white cap. Evidently there were other boats around because we bumped twice with other craft. To make matters worse it was raining and blowing pretty hard. The sea became decidedly rougher in the next couple of hours and the cramped quarters of our small craft were far from comfortable. We heard later that even some of the sailors were seasick. However, there were only two on our boat who were violently ill, Sgt. King and Mr. Wilson. Perhaps that is the reason they waited so long before giving permission to serve breakfast which we were carrying in thermos containers. It wasn't until we were in sight of our landing point that the permission to eat came through but even at that it was slightly mixed with the order to prepare to land. King started serving the beans out but became sick again at the sight of them and Sgt. Rothne took over. I managed to eat two mess tins full of beans which were cold and sour before we had to land. Some of the fellows couldn't look at them. Our craft grounded on a pebbly beach, thus affording us with a dry landing. I had to help unload the 3" mortar before rejoining Hatch and our wireless set. By that time, the clearing of the beach was in full swing. Some fellows were struggling mightily with bicycles loaded with mortar bombs, the wheels sinking in a good ten inches into the loose pebbles. Some of the fellows who were sick on the boat were sick again from the exertions. Other men were scaling the cliff face with the aid of ropes let down from the cliffs above. We soon discovered that our course lay along the beach for a couple hundred yards then through a steel tank barrier and through a mine field which had been dealt with by the engineers; over a few barbed wire fences, finally emerging on a secondary hard-surfaced road, a good mile inland. It was hard going for those of us who weren't seasick during the night so I guess it must have been hell for those who took the sea journey the hard way. Hatch was not feeling any too good when we hit the road but picked up after we had gone a few miles. Hatch and I, being cursed with the spare No. 18 set, could see no reason why we should try to keep up with the head of the column, so it wasn't long before we found ourselves traveling with the M.O. and his R.A.P. (*Regimental Aid Post*) staff. We were directly behind the bicycle squad which had passed us on the road and when we cut across country we had to wait at every obstacle for them to get through. We helped them navigate three deep, heavily wooded ravines but eventually pulled ahead and passed the sweating cyclists at the first of a series of long steep hills and set out to overtake the head of the column a good three-quarters of a mile ahead of us. We stopped for a breather at the top of the first hill before descending into another deep valley which was only a prelude to another steep slippery climb. We had gained the top of the second hill which was marked by an old ruined house and a very welcomed road, when Hatch discovered that he had left his steel helmet on the last hilltop. So while he went back for it, I took the set and kept going down into the next valley, to the foot of the next climb where I sat down to wait for Hatch. Eventually we caught up to B.H.Q. (*Battalion Headquarters*) and thereafter found the going much easier. Onward we plodded past a farmhouse around a corner until we came to a junction in the road which we had supposedly captured. As far as I could find out, the scheme was progressing according to well laid plans, leaving little room for complaints from the higher priced help. At the road junction we put the spare set into operation as rear H.Q. and we had no trouble in joining the net. From there we were ferried to our next stop in a truck captured from the "enemy" and were set down within easy sight of our final objective, a little village about six miles from the point where we had landed. The village was momentarily captured by our forces but a strong counter attack proved to be a signal for a withdrawal. It had started to rain so in a drenching downpour we speed marched to our embarkation beach where the boats were waiting to take us off. We were herded efficiently and hurriedly onto L.A.C. (*Army Landing Craft*) and taken to one of the larger troop ships which were standing a mile off shore for that purpose. The warmth and hot tea were comparative luxury to our trip in the little "R" boats last night. We were told to shed our equipment and make ourselves comfortable and we would be served with a hot meal from the ship's galley. We had visions of a good hot meal and a good night's sleep but it was jeopardized by the return of the Essex Scottish who had used the boat last night. Eventually we were served with a very good meal of liver, fried potatoes, beans, fresh ship's bread, butter, rice and tea. Needless to say, after a liberal second helping of everything we were more disposed to view the situation with a more optimistic point of view. The system of feeding is a big difference and a vast improvement to the army method and it seems to work pretty well. The tea, sugar, milk, butter and bread is drawn by one member of the table and has to last twenty-four hours but there is plenty for that and tea in between meals. Then at seven-thirty or eight there was a lunch of bully beef and vinegared beets. We ate chocolate bars purchased at the ship's canteen to sort of fill in the gap. After the evening lunch we sat in the passageways while the question of sleeping accommodation was thrashed out. The boat was built to handle just so many men and with the Essex, some F.M.R. (*Fusiliers Mont Royal*) and us on board, the problem was really acute. At one time the Essex were all on deck waiting to leave the ship but a last minute hitch caused them to return to the staterooms. About ten in the evening Wally and I read a message to the ship from the shore to the effect that the Essex would be landed at once and the Camerons would stay on board for the night along with the few F.M.R's. Needless to say, we lost no time in spreading the glad tidings to our own fellows. The cries of protest from the Essex were deafening but they were soon on their way. It wasn't long after they had left than we hoisted ourselves into the seaman's hammocks. I have always wanted to sleep in a seaman's hammock and at last the ambition is going to be realized.

JUNE 13, SAT.

We were roused out of a deep and much appreciated sleep at six this morning and after a breakfast of tomatoes and bacon, we were ready for anything the day had to offer. We left the ship by A.L.C.'s around ten in the morning and were taken ashore where motored transport was waiting to carry us to our camp. The rest of the day was spent in cleaning weapons and equipment that had become rusty and corroded from contact with the salty Atlantic. All in all, the past few days' activities have been an interesting experience and despite the difficulties and hardships encountered, I think I enjoyed it all. We sent Harry Guedesse over to the kitchen for lunch and all he could get was a bowl full of sugarless cocoa; quite a difference to that aboard ship. Why should there be such a difference?

JUNE 14, SUN.

Reveille at seven, breakfast at eight, bath parade at 9:30, dinner at one, armor's inspection at 1:30; No. 18 set cleaning at 2:00 and supper at 5:00, all on our day off. We heard tonight that signalers may be issued with pistols in place of the rifles. There is a possibility that we may get Sten Guns which will be just as much a nuisance as the rifles.

JUNE 15, MON.

Today has been occupied mostly with No. 18 set maintenance. There has been little else of any importance except that H.Q. Company was paid first this afternoon, for the first time in ages.

JUNE 16, TUES.

The mine detector experiments took up most of the day and I stayed in this evening.

JUNE 17, WED.

We were taken to N------ this morning to see "Next of Kin" and as a propaganda film it proved very enlightening especially for some officers. I stayed in town to try and find some material for the mine detector. All I could get was a half a pound No. 28 D.C.C. copper wire. I got me a haircut, but found I needed another when I saw my reflection in a mirror in a cafe, so I had another before returning to camp. I caught a 69 truck back to camp, thus saving car fare. Guedesse and I left for Ryde soon after supper where we saw a show called, "The Man Who Came Back." We had lunch at the W.V.S. Canteen then caught the last bus back to camp.

JUNE 18, THURS.
Spent most of the day working on the mine detector with very little success. Stayed in this evening and wrote to Peggy.

JUNE 19, FRI.
Had to take all the equipment used in the detector experiments up to the Colonel's tent but he was too busy to look at it. We repeated the performance again this afternoon but he was still too busy to look at it. Stayed in this evening and finished Peggy's letter.

JUNE 20, SAT.
We heard that all junior officers had to hand their pistols in this afternoon for redistribution to the signals. Some of them are mighty slow in complying with the order. Hatch and I went into Ryde to see "Hot Spot" showing at the Scala. We had beans on toast before going to bed tonight.

JUNE 21, SUN.
Missed church parade with the excuse that I had to make a new "feeler" for the mine detector. The Colonel said I could have all the time off I wanted to experiment and church parade is as good as any to miss, especially when it means walking eight miles. We went for a bath parade this afternoon which is developing into a Sunday ritual. Quite evidently the neighbors in the vicinity must be getting used to seeing nude Canadians strolling on the lawn and entering the shower house. None of the fellows think twice of disrobing outside in plain view of a dozen houses which form a square around three sides of the shower location.

JUNE 22, MON.
We were issued with pistols this morning and I happened to be fortunate in getting a fairly new one in good condition. We pulled out of camp on the

first stage of the scheme and were loaded onto side-wheelers. Our craft was ancient, dirty and odorous but after a skimpy supper of kippered herrings and cheese washed down with cocoa, Hatch and I spread our two blankets beside the pounding engine for the night.

JUNE 23, TUES.

We were roused out of a light sleep and ate our breakfast in the dark, then we boarded the smaller landing craft and went ashore. Things went along fairly well and we were back on the smaller craft again inside of five hours. I enjoyed watching the "Mad Goose" getting his feet wet when he was climbing into the boats. Hatch and I made it a point of boarding the same boat as his nibs because we would be sure of getting on the best side-wheeler. It was much larger and cleaner than our craft of last night. Eventually we arrived off Cowes, where we read a lamp message from shore to the effect that we would be on board all night. This failed utterly to meet with mutual approval as everyone wanted to get back to camp tonight. I am afraid I insulted (unknowingly) a few sailors by calling their honourable tub a mud scow. I didn't know they were standing behind me until I heard their mumbled protest. However, their disagreement failed to alter my opinion that their floating barn was a mud scow in disguise. Finally we pulled out for Ryde where we were landed at the pier. There we met the trucks which brought us to camp so we will have a good night's sleep after all.

JUNE 24, WED.

Reveille at 07:30 today with breakfast at 08:30. I didn't do very much besides clean my rifle and pistol. We will soon be handing our rifles in. For the first time since coming here were issued with a pass starting at 2 in the afternoon so Hatch and I went into Ryde to see "Dive Bomber." It was a pretty good show and we managed to catch the "Canada only" bus home.

JUNE 25, THURS.

Spent the morning cleaning the tent up (it was just as untidy in a few minutes) and cleaning my weapons. About noon someone of authority decided that we should have boat loading practice this afternoon so it wasn't long before we were on trucks heading for the pier. When we arrived at the pier there was only five boats available which "B" Company was using so the rest of us returned to camp. Tully, Stewie and I went into Ryde to see "Wild Geese Calling." We went into a little snack bar and had scrambled eggs on toast and coffee. We met a very nice girl there and although we did get talking to her we didn't have much of a chance to get better acquainted before the last bus came by.

JUNE 26, FRI.
We had boat loading practice at Cowes which consisted mainly of climbing aboard small craft, riding around in circles then boarding the side-wheelers by means of rope ladders. After staying aboard these very unpopular craft for a few minutes, we got into the small craft again and rode a few more circles, then went ashore. We were back in camp before noon. I saw my first submarine this morning. We cleaned all the No. 18 sets this afternoon for the signal scheme tomorrow.

JUNE 27, SAT.
The boys went out on a signal scheme which lasted until almost noon. This afternoon there was passes starting at four as per usual. Guedie and I went into a show and almost didn't make the last bus.

JUNE 28, SUN.
The usual Sunday bath parade didn't take place until 2:30pm, but it was just as effective as a morning bath. Ellison, Day, Inskip, Criss Cross and myself went to the Scala to see "You Can't Have Everything" staring Alice Faye and Don Ameche. We had lunch at the W.V.S. canteen then caught the last bus home.

JUNE 29, MON.
On special request from a certain Sergeant, I gave all No. 18 sets a good check over, which took me all day. The unit was down at Ryde for sports day, so we had the camp to ourselves. Hatch and I went to the Royal to see "Weekend in Havana." According to all reports our next scheme should be interesting. This doesn't happen to be a rumor, it is the straight goods, at last. This is verified almost to a surety because very few know about it and it hasn't

reached the men yet. Everyone thinks it is just another scheme terminating in our going back to our old positions. It's a great deal more than that, this will be what we have been waiting for. The only reason I know about it is because I have to do some special work in connection with it. As far as I know Hatch doesn't even suspect yet. It's a hard secret to keep when everyone is speculating as to our next move.

JUNE 30, TUES.

More No. 18 set work today and even missed a very important parade as a consequence. As far as I can determine the good news hasn't leaked out yet, which is something of a miracle. Guedie and I went to the Commodor to see "Wolfman" and "Men of Timberland." Lon Chaney stared in the first one and Andy Devine had a leading role in the second. All the news reels are showing men like Cripps, Beaverbrook, etc., advocating the immediate opening of the second front. A majority of the boys are skeptical, some are hopeful, but none are sure. I wonder if we will be spearhead for that do.

JULY 1, WED.

This day was announced as a holiday by the top men, but I worked all day repairing an 18 set. The rest of the fellows were on No. 18 set operating so some idea of the army holiday is conceivable. Things are shaping up for this scheme starting tomorrow. It's a wonder the fellows aren't wise to it because everything seems pretty obvious to me. Wrote a number of letters this evening, just in case. I believe it is going to be a warm affair while it lasts because Fritzie has been nervous recently and reinforced all coastal positions. When the fellows start planning their next leave I feel like telling them to wait until after the scheme, because some of us may not be in any position to carry any plans out.

July 2-8 on board first Dieppe attempt.

JULY 10, FRI.

The first six days from the second to the eighth were the most trying days I think I have ever spent in the army. For six days and six nights we were living below decks of a small coastal on tables, on benches, in companionways, in the engine rooms, and some were even in the washrooms. Equipment was piled in every little nook and corner and all personnel were crowded but pleased because they were going to get a crack at something more than an imaginary enemy. Enthusiasm was high on the morning of the next day because the actual do was to commence early next morning. All day we cleaned and oiled our weapons, studied detailed maps and plans of attack until we knew it all by heart. Late in the afternoon we experienced our initial disappointment when the plan was postponed because of unfavorable weather conditions. However, we had hopes for the next three days and all we had to do was endure the inconvenience of the limited quarters for another 24 hours. During this time, we sailed from New Haven to Southampton where we took on more fuel oil. On Sunday (July 5th) we were taken ashore for exercise and fresh air and we learned the plan was postponed for another 24 hours because of bad weather. Low visibility would have deprived us of our air support. The next day we changed boats because the one we were on was too slow. We traded with an outfit that was scheduled to land some time after us. We returned to New Haven where we remained at anchor until Tuesday night. Each time the plan was postponed for 24 hours cut 1 hour off our operating time we would have on shore, as the tide plays an important part in the landing and evacuation of troops and equipment. On Tuesday (July 7th) the new shortened plan was explained and we had to do some more studying. Everyone was ready and confident for the next morning and spirits were high. It wasn't until eight-thirty on Tuesday night that the Colonel called us together and told us that the weather reports were very unfavorable and the tide too low for our purpose, so the whole thing was called off indefinitely. Every man was keenly disappointed. It was like rain on a picnic holiday. Late that night we sailed from New Haven back to Cowes, Isle of Wight and next morning (July 8th) moved to the West Beach where we went ashore in landing craft. This is the closest we have been to action and we are not feeling any too happy about it being called off. That day, Wednesday (July 8th) in the afternoon General Roberts (*Commander 2nd Canadian Division*) came down and gave us a little speech designed to cheer us up but I don't think it went over very well. Yesterday, Thursday (July 9th) we spent in packing stores and otherwise preparing for return to the mainland, to resume our old existence of the last three years. Bert Bridge and I went to see a show called "The Gay

Falcon." (July 10, Fri.) It has been raining all day and it has been generally miserable. The order to move tomorrow, came through today and in view of the fact that we have had our chance for some time the news was welcome. The desire for leave seems utmost in everyone's mind.

(small diary from July 10-July 29 missing) Return to Horsham, leave recorded in it.

JULY 29, WED.

We were up pretty early this AM at 5 to be exact and we were all packed and under way in a couple of hours. Riding the stores truck again, with Sgt. Rankine and Joe Forsythe. Had a good book to read so didn't pay much attention where we were going, probably missed some interesting sights but even the book was abandoned when we started the long twisting climb to our bivouac. Within a few minutes of arriving here we were busy improvising a canvas shelter out of the truck tarp and building a small fire merely for comfort sake. Two lines and an exchange were then put in and my book was finished before supper. Some of the boys have gone to the nearby town this evening, it will probably be their last chance for awhile. The camp is settling down and it looks as though we have been here for days instead of for hours. I guess I had better pick a spot for my bed before the hoard returns; there is only a limited number of men able to get under this shelter of ours.

JULY 30, THURS.

We were sort of rushed for time this AM as we had to make an early start for this scheme rehearsal. After a few perfunctory starts, Joe Forsythe and I found ourselves with the 2/I.C. (*Battalion second in command*) set and sitting in a "Jeep" waiting for the worse. A ride in a fast moving jeep and trying to operate an eighteen set over the South Downs is quite a job. After the scheme had barely got under way I discovered I had a lemon of a set, one of those that were supposedly repaired by Brigade Maintenance. To make matters worse, I had to take control of the net and me with a set that kept changing frequency so fast as I could press the pressel switch. It finally became so bad I had to turn over control to another station; after that it was just a matter of finding a soft spot to read in. According to all reports, none of the sets worked the way they should have, so after returning to camp this afternoon, we spent a good three hours and a half trying to get a good net. It finished up with one set going completely out of action with 5 burnt out valves. Criss Cross had to make a trip to our future camp for replacements. He isn't back yet and the sets are all apart waiting for the parts. We had a pleasant time around the fire this evening, eating toasted cheese sandwiches made from material scrounged by various men from various places, and drinking sugarless tea (2 men somehow managed to obtain a can of milk apiece, so the lunch was entirely passable.)

JULY 31, FRI.
Except for sliding down the hill once in a while we had a fairly good night. Up before breakfast this morning and before nine ready to carry out the real purpose of this scheme. I was assigned to the R.A.P. as a wireless operator along with Willie Behune, I worked on my set until away after dark last night and it seems to be working good this morning. However, one of the company sets was acting up so traded sets. There wasn't much wrong with the company set as I had it perking in a few minutes. The most interesting part of the whole day was when a barrage was laid ahead of our advancing troops by the artillery. When the ceasefire came through we were soon on our way to our new camping grounds. We in the R.A.P. truck, had ample opportunity to enjoy the scenery of the valley stretching for miles on either side of the high ridge we were traversing. On the right we could look over the rolling Downs to the sea in the distance; on the left stretched multi-coloured fields, orchards, towns as far as we could see until it was lost in a blue haze on the horizon. Our camp for the night was on a high hill, not far from Brighton, in fact some of the fellows have gone in there for a few hours this evening. Rankine, Beck and I went for a walk in the little village nearby, bought a bottle of beverage and drank it sitting on the village green. When we returned to camp we found some of the fellow cooking bacon, ribs and chips over a small kerosene fire. So when MacKenzie came back with fish and chips the cooking victuals fell to us and they happened to be good. I think I will throw my bed roll under the yon holly bush and lay claim to the spot.

The Battle of Dieppe

Sapper C. W. Barnes
B25330, 2nd FD. COY. RCE
Toronto.

It was the eighteenth day of August in nineteen forty two,
    We sailed away from England and no one knew where to;
We had received no orders, no friend to see us leave,
    The Canadian Second Division with the blue patch on the sleeve.

    . . . .

Early next morning when everything was still,
    We saw the tracer bullets coming at us from the hill;
But we kept right on sailing and no man will forget
    The morning that we landed on the beach, there at Dieppe.

    . . . .

The enemy were waiting and had taken up their posts,
    We met a hail of bullets as we landed on the coast.
But every man there landed, or at least he tried,
    Though many men were wounded, many more men died.

    . . . .

It was early in the morning when we started into fight,
    The mortor bombs came at us from the left and from the right;
They shelled us from the cliffs and they bombed us from the air,
    But the Second Canadian Division was not so easy to scare.

    . . . .

We fought there for eight hours, from six A.M. till two,
    Our losses were terrific but there was nothing we could do;
The navy came to help us but their boats they could not land.
    So we had to surrender, at Dieppe, there on the sand.

    . . . .

What is left of us are prisoners beneath a foreign flag;
    Here in the heart of Germany at camp eight B Stalag.
Many of our comrades fell but we never will forget,
    They gave their lives, there fighting in the battle of Dieppe.

. . . .

When this war is over and once again we are free,
　To our Homeland we will be sailing, to the Land of Liberty;
Though many have a battle scar, no man will forget,
　The morning that we landed on the French coast at Dieppe.

⁻ . . . . ⁻

What Price Dieppe

Did you ever hear of Dieppe, boys,
　It's a little town in France;
The "Brass-hats" sent us in there
　To make the Jerrys dance.

. . . .

It was our first taste of action
　As we waded in and fought,
But "Jerry" was expecting us
　And our fighting counted not.

. . . .

We kept right on a-going;
　The blood and limbs flew high;
We saw our comrades falling
　And we had to let them die.

. . . .

There must have been a reason
　For a slaughter such as this;
Surely someone will account for
　The faces that we miss.

. . . .

So much for Dieppe, boys,
  For our plans that hit a snag,
While we wait for the armistice
  In a lonely old Stalag.

     ‾ . . . . ‾

PTE. George Oliphant, H19294
Q.O.C.H.
P.O.W. No. 26207

(Preparing to assault beach at Pourville)

(Cameron Highlanders boarding landing craft)

FRED LODGE DIARY
August 19, 1942 to December 31, 1944

Daily Diary: H19859, F. T. Lodge,
Camerons of Canada (C.A.S.F.) Canada

Book. No. 6

AUG. 19

Captured, which would seem unbelievable if it wasn't for the black bread, herb tea, the debris littered floor we have to sleep on and the "newly graduated Hitler youth" stationed at the door with a rifle and bayonet always ready for use. The battle itself and the events immediately preceding are far too confused at present to try and describe it coherently so will have to wait until a later date. It is sufficient to say now that we met with unexpected resistance, the Germans being prepared for the attempt since Aug 15. Ross Findlay and I are trying to cheer each other up. We were given ½ a loaf of black bread and herb tea if we had containers. All I had was a 4oz. Chocolate tin and the cook tried to pour a quart ladle of tea in it with the result that three quarters of the hot liquid was poured on my hand.

AUG. 20

Spent a miserable night on broken bricks. We were given another loaf of bread this morning to last 24 hours. It's practically uneatable being very sour and vile tasting stuff. Singled out for questioning and taken across the road to a farm house. Was very glad to see Eric Day; I thought he was dead. While waiting for interrogation we were given French bread, butter, jam, fruit, ginger ale and wine by two French women. I answered all questions with "I don't know" and so left the officer with the impression that for a soldier I was exceedingly ignorant of current affairs. We began the march to the station at 7:00P.M. Eric had lost his shoes and finds walking difficult. Every time they tried to take pictures of the column everyone held their hands up in the victory "V" sign.

AUG. 21

We arrived at this French prison camp near Vierville (*Vierville-sur-Mer*), thirsty, tired and hungry, some without wounds properly dressed. A sorry looking crowd we are.

AUG. 22

Spent an unbearable night in a hut crammed with over 300 others; the doors and windows were locked. The heat was terrific, the smell sickening and we were lying on top of one another trying to sleep. Some stood up all night.

We were questioned, searched and cataloged then moved into another compound where living conditions weren't much better.

SEPT. I

Spent approx. a week in the Vierville camp during which time I saw so called civilized people revert to the dictates of primitive instinct. Due to a few ill-mannered glutinous, greedy individuals it was virtually a battle to obtain one's rations and a constant vigilance to prevent being robbed before they were consumed.

The Germans tried to rouse ill-feeling between the French Canadians and the rest of us by showering them with cakes, fruit, biscuits, sardines, chocolate and cigs but the Frenchmen were wise to the idea and shared their good fortune with the rest of us. Cigarettes were few and far between and a smoke usually consisted of butts thrown away by German officers and re-rolled in any kind of paper available. A cigarette thus made would usually be shared among as many as twelve men each taking a "shallow" drag apiece. The minute remains would be zealously preserved until sufficient material was again collected for another fag. Toilet paper was nil, grass being utilized when necessary which wasn't often as everyone was constipated. We entrained again at Vierville on the 27th of August. When we were waiting to be loaded into the "hobo pulmans" we stopped near a group of Frenchmen and women loading grapes into a box-car. The presence of the Germans prevented the French from openly giving us grapes but they didn't object too much when we "pinched" some. They were the sweetest grapes I think I ever tasted. When two German guards helped themselves as well the civilians complained to the Commander and the two guards were placed on charge. The two unfortunates later confided that they would probably be sent to the Russian front as punishment, an ever present dread of all German soldiery. After a great deal of Teutonic yelling, shoving and swearing we were finally loaded into the cars. 40 men to a car, with 40 loaves of black bread, 20 cans of stewed meat (believed horseflesh) a few pounds of margarine, two pails of drinking water and a latrine box with bucket; food and latrine piled indiscriminately in the center of the straw strewn floor. Ventilation was confined to two small wire covered openings near the roof at either end and on opposite sides of the car. Four days and five nights spent in this manner with one or two stops for latrine clearing proved to be an extremely hot, miserable, smelly ride. We arrived at Lamsdorf station September 1, Tuesday, dirty, tired, hungry, covered with two week's growth of beard and thoroughly disgusted. We had a rude shock when we saw raggedly dressed prisoners unloading a car of ammunition under the supervision of a mean looking individual with a vicious looking bull-whip. They looked utterly dejected and subjected consequently we were assailed with grim apprehension. We later discovered that these men were Russian prisoners from a nearby camp not under the protection of the Red Cross. After a lot more yelling (favourite mode of German conversation regardless of topic) we were again searched then marched into camp (Stalag VIII B) amid a shower of cigarettes from the men captured at Dunkirk, Crete, Greece and St. Nazaire. Immediately upon arrival the International Red Cross commenced to alleviate our deplorable condition by giving us a feed of beans and bully beef stew, followed in rapid succession by a food parcel between four, soap, herb tea and cigarettes. The stew was eaten with our fingers from tin cans taken from the neighbouring compound dump and thrown over the fence to us. An Air Force fellow gave me two towels, six bars of soap, two razor blades and a razor. It was a great relief to get the brush off. The following five days were spent in getting settled, making eating and cooking utensils out of tin cans, being deloused and registered. The fellows who were supposed to be repatriated a short time ago are in this camp and looking forward to another chance. Would like writing material, sewing kit, a couple of note books and a text book on wireless. May enroll for German language when the school starts on Monday. Eric Day, Charlie Norris, Bern Bender and I share in R.C. parcels. We were registered with the Red Cross yesterday. I may volunteer for bush whacking this winter if I am outfitted with suitable clothing.

Lamsdorf O.9.

(Stalag VIIIB, Lamsdorf)

SEPT. 7

The school starts today. Want to take electrical engineering, engineering maths but there doesn't seem to be any efforts of organizing the people who want to go. We had free run of the camp yesterday for three hours. I understand it is the usual Sunday custom. Read a book called "The House of Violence" and didn't think much of it. A guard fired a warning shot at one of the FMRs who was inside of the warning wire peeling bark from one of the main fence posts. Fuel for cooking is scarce and cooking our meals is becoming increasingly difficult. Bed-boards are gradually dwindling and the German head is becoming grayer and grayer trying to stop us burning them. The water situation has been terrible but was relieved somewhat last night when it started running again, in fact we couldn't stop it so it poured forth all night. Also rained last night, it's pretty wet out this A.M. Day and I did our little bit of laundry today then Day had to go to the hospital as the result of a medical inspection yesterday. I hope he doesn't stay long. Norris is pretty sick today and off his food. Eric came back from hospital at 2:30 P.M. as hungry as a bear and the food we saved for him soon vanished. We were issued with jam and bully beef this afternoon. The Red Cross rations and parcels are a Godsend. Kitchen came back from school today full of information. Apparently radio courses are strictly forbidden by the Germans and the nearest to it is electrical engineering. I won't bother about school until after clothing parade at least.

SEPT. 8, TUES.

Missed the school parade this morning because we thought there would be clothing parade today. Tried to get out of the compound this afternoon to enroll for school by falling in behind a clothing parade but were discovered and turned back, thus missing the first class in German. We are going to try sick parade in the morning. Made a handle for our bread knife this afternoon. A lot of the fellows are going to the hospital with a complaint very similar to dysentery. We wrote our first letters home from this camp and my request for stuff was pretty long. Received our third Red Cross parcel this P.M. and had a good supper. Took our usual evening exercise around the compound and borrowed cigarette papers from Bill Robertson. I will have to try and get some camp money soon as we will need it for school supplies. Ate our chocolate bar this evening. Norris is feeling a lot better and is eating again.

SEPT. 9, WED.

Managed to get out and enroll for school by falling in behind sick parade this morning. Enrolled for electrical engineering, eng. maths, intermediate arithmetic and German language. For some reason we were refused when we tried to get out for math class, went to German class this afternoon. Eric was sick last night and isn't feeling well today. An English chap gave me a "mark" this evening but the cigarettes were all gone by the time I got up to the canteen, so bought two pkgs. of cig papers. Am reading the "Vicar of Wakefield" now.

SEPT. 10, THURS.

Eric, Norris and I went to the arith. class this morning. We had a good dinner made from Red Cross rations. We missed the German class but Eric and I went to electrical engineering only to find that it was too advanced for us to enter it, so we withdrew our names until a new one starts, also withdrew from eng. Maths. We had a medical this afternoon presumably for working parties this winter. We had a big supper this evening finished off with a steamed pudding received in our R.C. parcel. We are completely out of smokes and it appears to be ditto for the next few days. Finished the "Vicar of Wakefield" this evening.

SEPT. 11, FRI.

We spent the morning in minutely scanning the compound area for cigarette butts, but evidently other people have been doing the same as our search was practically fruitless. I saw Bill Robinson who loaned me three player cigarettes with which we made six cigs simply by breaking them in two and re-rolling them; at least we have one apiece for our after dinner smoke. The medical parades are continuing today and were finished by noon. We were refused exit from our compound when we tried to go to German class for some unknown reason which we will learn at 2:30. Most of the boys are getting discouraged with school by missing so many classes and are gradually quitting. Bender has a headache today. All compound gates are open but ours today. Spent the afternoon trying to remodel a couple of exercise books into a diary volume. We were issued with a R.C. food parcel as well as a sugar ration, this afternoon. Stood in a queue for an hour this evening for cigarettes and managed to get 15 for 50 pfennings. Bern and Charlie attended the band concert and Day and I strolled around the camp. Our gate was open this evening. Eric happened to ask an English fellow for a light for a re-roll cigarette and this chap asked how we were fixed for cigarettes. Eric truthfully informed him that we were picking them up. We were immediately invited to this fellow's quarters where we were given a handful of cigarettes apiece. Some of these fellows are quite all right. We ate our bar this evening. This camp, the largest of its kind in Germany has a no. of very good dance bands, a military dance band, and a symphony orchestra; as well as a theatrical troupe. I have heard the brass band and could find little room for a layman's criticism. I have yet to hear of the other bands in action. Meal times in this compound would be an interesting spectacle to the folks back home. A good number of the fellows have fashioned tin stoves from tin cans; the shapes are varied and interesting demonstrating the respective makers' ideas of how Stalag stoves should be made. Wood is exceedingly difficult to obtain therefore, every shaving, twig and carton is painstakingly gathered and saved. One third of a fair sized bed-board cooks one meal so bed board are gradually being sacrificed to the cause much to the worry of German. They threaten dire penalties which are usually ignored. We were issued with a spoon today as a direct result of the camp commandant making a tour of inspection during one of our meal hours. He was very much impressed with the improvising ability of the Canucks in making cooking and eating implements from practically nothing. The water situation has slipped again and we have formed a habit of making our breakfast tea from German mint tea that is supplied every morning. It actually is nothing more than hot water anyway.

SEPT. 12, SAT.

We received bulk rations today from the Red Cross which included nearly a pound of cheese, a pound of butter and thirty-eight large biscuits, very similar to soda crackers on a larger scale, besides the regular camp issue. Eric and I went down to the library this morning for a little private study in our individual trade interests. We prepared a good supper of fried spuds, cheese on toast, jam on biscuits and coffee. A brief but violent storm arose just after we had finished cleaning up the supper things, putting the slower people to complete route. There was hasty grabbing of boxes and cans containing their partly prepared meals and a mad dash for shelter. Eric was fortunate in obtaining a penful of ink from one of the English lads. We received paper for another letter this afternoon, this one is to go via airmail. Bothered with piles this evening and slight constipation; a laxative is indicated.

SEPT. 13, SUN.

There was a slight change in our roll-call procedure this A.M. which didn't amount to much. It interrupted our breakfast a little but failed to spoil it entirely. Wood was scarce at noon so we had a semi-cold dinner finished off with buttered cabbage. This afternoon Eric and I went down to the boxing matches in the Staff Compound and stayed until four. Another bed-board and a wooden shoe were sacrificed for supper tonight but specially prepared fried hardtack served with stewed raisins plus potatoes and sausage washed down with good coffee is well worth the result of the missing shoe and bed-board. Eric left it too late to hand his letter in today so he will have to wait until next week. Some more buckshee goods were drawn for this evening and I got a wash cloth of all things. I obtained some laxative from the First Aid station this evening; piles are a little better tonight. I hope Reg goes through my kit before the Q.M. gets his hands on it and takes care of my diary. Bern Bender isn't feeling well today.

SEPT. 14

The laxative worked like a charm and I am feeling much better today. Eric and I went for a walk down to the library and did a little more self-inspired studying. Our bulk rations consisted of four cans of boiled beef, consequently we had a very good dinner. Bern couldn't eat very much today. We went for another walk this afternoon and collected a Canadian Red Cross bulk box I asked for a few days ago. We plan to make a couple of boxes for our personal belongings. We had scalloped potatoes, boiled beef, toasted bread with honey and coffee. We received 20 cigarettes apiece. Eric, Charlie and I walked around until dark making plans to get together after the war for a party. We are also planning a trip through England, Scotland and Ireland before going home. The silence of the German wireless leads us to believe that all is not well with the Germans on the various fronts. Despite the strict censorship imposed the news eventually leaks in. The next compound to us shelters the disabled boys from the various fronts, the same fellows who were supposed to be repatriated last year. There is talk of another endeavour coming up. I hope they make it this time.

SEPT. 15

Nothing much doing today. We got another parcel from the Red Cross this afternoon and had a good supper. We were on clothing parade today and were issued with two shirts, two pairs of socks, two ties, two pairs of long underwear (pants), two handkerchiefs, a pair of sabots (wooden shoes) and a service cap. My old uniform was in bad condition so got an exchange for it. I was so busy changing my uniform I forgot to try my hat on; result my hat doesn't fit. We walked around as usual this evening then came back and ate our bar.

SEPT. 16

Eric and I started our barrack room box this morning and finished it this afternoon. Smoking situation is so bad it takes very careful control to make what we do get last a week. Tried to get my hat exchanged today with nil results. The fellows are volunteering for work parties today. We are going to wait for awhile as Bender has to take treatment for trench mouth. Went for our usual evening walk this evening. Planning our meals so that our food issues will last seems to be our only and main occupation. I think we could do better on a working party. There would be more rations, better billets, besides a greatcoat and a blanket. Hate to think of spending winter in this camp. Churchill's last speech has caused hopes to go soaring and general optimism isn't misplaced. I have an idea for embroidering a Cameron Cap badge, if I can obtain the necessary thread.

SEPT. 20

Except for a few odd incidences life continued as much as usual for the past four days. Being in possession of a Royal Canadian Engineer's hat badge, a rare scarcity hereabouts, I have been searching around for a suitable trade offer. To date we have obtained offers of 45 cigarettes from one engineer and an offer of seven fags from an Indian. Needless to say, the latter offer is receiving no considering in the least. We are sure we can do better than 45 fags if we could contact the right person. Perhaps the most prominent member of the German element as far as we are concerned is a poor mistreated compound focker of uncertain rank whom we refer to as Herman the German. The poor fellow has a very trying time and at times makes things pretty trying for us so I guess the score is just about even. The burning of bed-boards is his pet worry. Due to the shortage of fuel the burning of these boards becomes practically a necessity; so Herman strolls leisurely between the foursomes at meal times looking for this particular kind of wood. If he catches an unfortunate cook unawares he berates him in his most violent German manner, confiscates the wood, kicks the stove over, leaving the cook with a cold supper. We have been fortunate of late so far as we managed to obtain a wooden Red Cross box, which was big enough to make a barrack room box and still leave us with fuel for four or five days. The barrack box may be sacrificed in the near future, especially since it is fast becoming a nuisance at the foot of my all too short bed. The preparation of meals uses up most of our time and to make our rations go a long way. Dishes such as puddings are becoming increasingly favoured. Hardtack is soaked for at least three hours then cooked with prunes or raisins then served with a sauce made from powdered milk and sugar. The result isn't at all displeasing, in fact, we have always discovered that a second helping is desirable but unobtainable. Fried or scalloped potatoes as well as stews and hash are common and appreciated. Corn beef, cabbage and potatoes is well accepted.

Traded the engineer's badge for 50 cigs, 1/8 lb of tobacco, a small scrub brush, a can of tooth powder and a stick of shaving soap. Bender was trying to drum up a trade for some cigarettes, specifying a towel and toothbrush. Eventually he obtained one towel and a handle-less shaving brush for nothing. The question of work parties seems to be the main topic of conversation these days and it is generally believed that we will be going out to pick sugar beets in the near future. Some of the fellows are doing odd jobs around camp. There is a small party outside here today digging a drainage ditch. There is about 700 N.C.O.'s being moved to another camp as some of us may be moved to the compound they vacated. Playing with the idea of making a tooth brush from the scrub brush I got yesterday. I wrote a letter to Peggy yesterday because I figured the folks in England will be wondering where we disappeared to.

SEPT. 22, TUES.
Breakfast this morning was helped quite a lot by the prune jam we made last night from six prunes and the last of our sugar. For the first time we managed to save four slices of bread for dinner. We usually eat it all for breakfast. Herman the German is plenty peeved over the disappearance of two wooden doormats from the latrine doorways; evidently they have gone the way of the bed-boards. Wooden shoes are fast disappearing now, adding to Herman's worries. We had a fast supper this evening as Eric and I wanted to see a show called "Murder in Vaudeville" put on by the local theatrical troupe. Two good hours of first rate entertainment. It was after eight when we got out and Herman had locked the gate so not wishing to spend the night in the road, we simply lifted the gate off its hinges, replacing it after everyone was in. We may be moved to a different compound this week; there is a lot of men going out on working parties and to other camps.

SEPT. 23, WED.
Herman the German is becoming desperate regarding the burning of bed-boards; he threatened to lock the compound gates regardless of schools and concerts if there is any more similar wanton destruction, as he calls it. I don't think he has the mental ability to grasp the fact that if he would allow us to gather wood in the nearby brush, there wouldn't be any necessity for burning our beds. Perhaps the wood situation will improve when we move to another compound. We received definite word that we would be moving to another compound in the morning. Noticed the Czech mountains to the south for

the first time this evening; they are a good fifty miles away. We had fried corned beef, German sausage and potatoes followed by a pudding made from prunes, hardtack, sugar and water served with sauce made from powdered milk and honey. Finished packing our stuff before going for our evening walk. Need another laxative.

SEPT. 24, THURS.

We had an early breakfast of bread, butter, German honey-butter and tea, then evacuated our billets and lined up on the square. It was nearly eleven before we were moved to the new compound and I am sorry to say we were unfortunate to draw four lower bunks, minus bed-boards and palaises. Facilities for cooking our meals are decidedly worse, as is the water situation there being none at all in this compound. We are overcrowded a fair number being entirely without a bunk, consequently are forced to sleep on the tables or floors. The living and cooking facilities may improve in time and working parties should be thinning our rank in the near future. Nevertheless, we are going to take a crack at cooking outdoors this evening even if it is against compound principles. (*three lines of blocked out text in original diary*) The English, Australians, New Zealanders and even the Indians co-operate splendidly among themselves and with everyone else with a result that their lives are run along smooth regulated plane, whereas the (*three more lines of blocked out text*) Perhaps it's their individualism showing itself. The only solution is a working party or go live with the Limeys.

SEPT. 25, FRI.

Spent most of the morning getting our palaises filled. Soup came up at the unearthly hour of ten; at noon we had a spot of tea and some biscuits. Porridge gruel came in around two and we had our supper at 3:30, this is due primarily to the cooking utilities being overcrowded and have to be used according to a schedule. Made a new bread knife this afternoon which I think even Bender can operate half decently. They called out the first work party today, totalling 40. They leave on Tuesday; there will be another party of over two hundred in a week or so. At last I found sufficient time in between trips to the latrine to sew buttons on my trousers. The more I see of this mess the more I think a working party would be an improvement. This new cooking arrangement is a nuisance as it seems we are either eating soup or cooking meals.

SEPT. 26, SAT.

Today there was an issue of 15 cigarettes per man and the main interest of the day was the trading and selling thereof. We also received a quarter pound bar of chocolate. Obtained 10 cigarettes for 6 squares of choc. Ten Players sell for five marks and 6 French fags costs 20 phennigs so actually we get 150 French for 10 Players. A half bar of chocolate usually sells for 15 cigarettes. On rare occasions a heavy smoker will give a full bar for 10 fags. Cigarettes are also used for stakes in card games instead of money but the game usually dies an early death because the participants consume the stakes in due course then they resort to a milder game for pfennigs. Wrote to Iris today. The latrine still claims a great deal of my time. Enrolled for the new course in electrical engineering which starts on Monday.

SEPT. 27, SUN.

I missed church this morning due to latrine difficulty which hasn't improved in the least. I am afraid that some fellows see me so often up there that they will be thinking I own the joint or at least pay rent for one of the positions. It is the reason for much hurrying first thing in the A.M. and a slow retreat late in the evening. During the night the night latrine is paid hurried visits on the average of five times between 9:30P.M. and 5:30A.M. Did my laundry this afternoon in preparation for the bath parade tomorrow. Also had to send my shoes in for repair which means I will have to wear my wooden shoes. The daily culinary routine is becoming complicated; Bread, jam and tea for breakfast; German soup and spuds at 10:30. A typical evening meal consists of stew, tomatoes, German sausage, a few isolated spuds, broken crackers, etc. We finish up with a pudding of stewed prunes, soaked hardtack, powdered goat's milk served cold with thick sweetening "KLIM" sauce. Around six we have a cup of tea with a piece of bread spread with jam, cheese or meat roll. On Saturday we had a raisin duff with chocolate sauce.

SEPT. 28, MON.

The art of wearing sabots is one which takes long painful practice, as well I know. Having the usual latrine runs today. Went down for a bath today after which I attended the first class of the new electrical engineering class.

OCT. 1, THURS.

Miserable with a complaint very similar to diarrhea. The fact that I have to wear these wooden shoes isn't exactly improving my disposition. Finally forced to report sick, castor oil capsules (6 of them) and charcoal tablets prescribed. May have META-DYSENTRY caused by a bug; an active laxative only remedy. We received a package of porridge the other morning so we have had porridge for breakfast ever since. The gathering of thread for my badge isn't exactly successful to date. Saw Irwin at the hospital this morning. There was a few more names called for working parties on evening roll call. Kitchen, nicknamed "the Professor" by some of the more sarcastic people, was among them which pleased everyone in the hut. Kitchen has enrolled for nearly thirteen classes at the school. However he managed to get out of the work party somehow and all the fellows are wondering how he accomplished it. It was simple, he merely made himself a Stalag Corporal and got away with it. Feel a lot better this evening so much so, went to the football match with Eric, even view the sabots with a little more tolerance tonight.

OCT. 2, FRI.

Had a long talk with Cpl Good on the opportunities in wireless and electricity after the war. Parcel day again. We may hit the next working party. The organic disorder came back worse than ever today; am beginning to think it's here indefinitely.

OCT. 3, SUN.

Got my shoes back yesterday and lost no time in putting them on. Our source of news and rumours seems to be divided in opinion as the two seldom correspond. Our news source is decidedly not the German radio the integrity of which is well-know; nor is it the weekly paper "Camp" which is German controlled, so the only other means is by recently shot down Air force men. Apparently these gentlemen don't read newspapers because their news stories differ to a great extent. However, the chaff is eventually separated from the grain, actual news from rumour and we finally obtain fairly accurate ideas of world events. Eric made another pudding this evening which we will test when we have our evening tea. Wrote a letter to Nelle this afternoon and no matter how I try I can't help asking for something.

OCT. 6, TUES.
Yesterday was nothing out of the ordinary; went to electrical engineering class in the afternoon, the rest of the time was spent in preparing meals. This morning we experienced the famous German retaliation technique, when the issue of all Red Cross rations was cut off because they say the German prisoners in England and Canada are being mistreated. The older prisoners say that this has happened before; one time the ban lasted a month and again for only a few days. We all know it's deliberate lies and the ideas for the real reasons are numerous. Due to the silence of the radio today, the most favoured opinion is he is meeting reverses on one of the many fronts and seeing as he is taking it out on us it is probably Libya or Western Europe. Another opinion is that he figures we are becoming a might too cocky and is showing us who is boss around here. Besides the cutting of of Red Cross issue the compound gates are being kept locked; the only ones allowed out are the sanitators for the daily German issue of rations.

Last night I decided to do something drastic about the latrine trouble so traded tin Player cigs for twenty French, then gave Eric and Bender two Players apiece for their share of the cheese and Charlie took my share of chocolate for his share. I ate over half the tin last night and the rest this morning. The visits are fewer today but still too many.

OCT. 10
Last Wednesday, the ban on the Red Cross rations was lifted temporarily but on the 8th we, "all Dieppe personnel" were moved back to our old compound, lined up and informed of the bad news. We were to experience the German's famous reprisal methods again; this time in a more severe manner. Because of the mistreatment of Germans taken prisoners at the Channel Islands and elsewhere (as the excuse goes) we are to have our hands tied until

such times as satisfactory apologies and promises are forthcoming from the British Government. Evidently they expected us to resist because we were surrounded by German soldiers armed with machine and Tommy guns. The first day we were tied from twelve noon to 2A.M. and found such activities as preparing and eating meals, rolling smokes, going to the latrine seriously difficult. We weren't allowed to sing whistle or any other form of music and we couldn't go outside our rooms except to the latrine then only in groups of ten and under guard. At 2A.M. Thursday the Germans came in and released our hands until eight A.M. All the Red Cross issue is of course stopped again and the sensible use of what we have on hand is our first consideration. Tomorrow we are going to make jam out of some dried apples and raisins. Our hands are released from nine P.M. to 8:00A.M. and again from 11:00A.M. to 12 noon. Today some of the Air Force in the next compound were similarly bound. The Red Cross issue has of course been stopped for the whole camp while this "punishment" or retaliation is in force.

OCT. 12, MON.

We are still going around with our hands tied and able to find something humorous about it all to laugh at. Yesterday we had a double ration of spuds so by using our last can of bacon we had a fairly good meal of bacon and spuds, also made some jam of sorts from dried apples and raisins which helps a lot. Went on sick parade yesterday for a skin irritation and got myself smeared with mustard ointment. There is a rumour going around that the Channel Islands are in British hands, also the Russians have broken through on a 600 kilometer front. We can't afford to believe these kind of rumours just now, it's too hard on morale when and if they are proved wrong. We heard today that our Red Cross bulk rations are going to the kitchen to be put into the soup, etc.; I wish it wasn't because we may lose it altogether.

It is amusing to watch the fellows trying to pick a German who ties loosely, and when after we are tied there is the usual comparing of bindings. During the tying up everyone tenses his wrists so as to obtain a little slack when relaxed. We heard a rumour today that the ropes may come off today; I hope so because if they do we will go back to our old compound where the living conditions should be better than these. Eric and I are sleeping together on the floor because there isn't enough beds to go around.

OCT. 15, THURS.

Our hands are still tied from eight to eleven and from twelve noon to 9P.M. but we have become so accustomed to them it doesn't bother us very much now. Some of the fellows have rope burns and are being treated by the M.O. when he makes his daily visit to the compound. Went on sick parade yesterday and the M.O. put my complaint down as scabies; consequently I was called out for treatment just at eleven. Altogether I had my hands free from about 10:20A.M. until 1:30P.M., starting with the bath parade, only getting back again in time to go for a sulfur bath which lasted until 1P.M. then we were allowed a free half hour to re-heat our soup, and eat our dinner.

The "scabies" treatment is a queer mixture of misery and pleasure. First of all we disrobe completely, wrap our belongings in a bundle which is sterilized with steam while we stand around in the "altogether," pretty nigh blue with cold. Then we have a hot shower with tar soap, scrubbing ourselves thoroughly, then liquid sulfur is smeared all over. This stuff is ice cold and the shock of it after a hot shower is terrific; then we stand around and shiver until the sulfur is dry. Then we put on our steam-heated clothing again. We were allowed another half hour for dinner when we got back from our treatment today. Eric, Don and I walked up and down the compound this evening; the Hun is letting us out for exercise now.

OCT. 16, FRI.

The sunrise was really something worth watching this morning. The Germans who do the tying seemed different this morning. The usual drill and show-off methods were missing and they sauntered out, tying at random. We heard another version why we are tied; Germany informed England that she was tying so many prisoners as a retaliation. England replied that she would do the same with German prisoners; Germany doubled the number, England did the same, so there the matter rests while we have our hands tied. Today is the eighth day.

OCT. 19, MON.

Two months since we landed at Dieppe; it has been getting colder daily, so we are expecting the first snowfall anytime now. We could see snow on the Czech hills this morning; we had a west wind and rain. We are not properly clothed for winter yet, we only have the uniform and one blanket. We still have our hands tied which hinders any movement to get warm during the day; there is no fires to speak of except when someone warms up a few spuds, using mattress straw for fuel. Eric and I are still bunking together on the floor and find it chilly at night. There is no sign of this hand-tying business being discontinued as yet. It looks like a hard winter. I try to pass the time studying electricity but I am stumped by the mathematics involved; besides it's damned cold sitting still. Wrote a card to Aunt Pat and one to Marc yesterday; I must send the next letter to Bobbie. Hope the mail starts coming in soon. There is a rumour that the second front has started.

OCT. 21, WED.

Yesterday was a red letter day; we received a bulk issue of Red Cross rations which included cheese, crackers, dried fruit, sugar and chocolate. Besides that it was supposed to be a short bread day (seven on a loaf) but it was the usual five instead. We also received porridge from the kitchen this evening. The sharing of rations went on until late in the evening and trading was rife. Issued with greatcoats the day before yesterday; nights have been very chilly recently. I wonder what Nelle would say if she could see me eating cold spuds? We aren't allowed fires of any kind now. Cooking grease on bread with a little salt is part of every meal. The grease is synthetic, the bread 33% sawdust. The German mind works in queer channels; they allowed bulk rations to come through but refused permission to have fires for cooking purposes. Just struck with a brilliant idea; I am going to set aside a week after I get home just for the purpose of eating the things I crave now. That's besides the regular home-cooked meals. How I am going to enjoy that! All relatives and friends will contribute to the success of the week.

OCT. 22, THURS.

Since the restrictions on all fires our meals consist of the following: Breakfast, two pieces of bread (one with grease and jam and one with German jam if we have it); dinner, hot stew prepared from Red Cross bulk at the kitchen and delivered in large metal containers, one slice of bread and grease; also boiled spuds half of which is sliced into the stew. Supper, the other half of our spud sliced and sprinkled with salt, one slice of bread with grease and salt, or cheese if we have it with hot English tea, prepared at the kitchen from R.C. bulk. Going to bed lunch (9:30) one piece of bread and jam; the jam Eric made from our dried fruit rations. Eric and I are eating together and Charlie and Bern are mucking in together. We separated because there was a divided opinion as to how to prepare our meals. Eric and I were doing all the work while the other two were enjoying life. Bern is going to hospital tomorrow for ulcerated tonsils. He will at least get out of this hand tying business for awhile and be warm and well fed for a few days anyway. Everyone is sitting around waiting for nine o'clock to roll around when our hands are untied. Some are reading the few available books or playing "SORRY" or "SNAKES & LADDERS" or "CRIB," a few are pacing the floor. I spend my time studying electricity or copying Service's "Songs of Sourdough." It's almost time now and the boys are getting restless; pretty soon forbidden fires will be going as the few heat up their spud rations prior to hitting the hay. Forbidden electric water heaters are making their appearance too; these usually blow the fuse every five or ten minutes. This is usually greeted by a storm of deprecating remarks from the rest of the fellows.

OCT. 27, TUES.

Five days during which eating and drawing of rations played prominent parts. Hands are still tied, except for half a day Saturday afternoon when we were left free to clean the billets and cooking utensils. The midday soup had developed into a thick stew since they have taken to dumping R.C. bulk into it. Yesterday we were issued with 1½ lb. of cheese, 25 cigarettes, a can of honey, and thirty-two crackers per man. Some of the fellows drank their honey straight and were out behind the latrine a few minutes later, exceedingly uncomfortable. Others ate all their biscuits and cheese at one sitting; one fellow traded a can of honey for 1½ lb. of cheese, then ate the cheese straight. Eric and I try to make ours go over four or five days because we never know when the next issue is coming in. This afternoon we had stewed fruit from the kitchen instead of the usual porridge gruel we get on Tuesday and Friday. This was our day for "seconds" so we had plenty of fruit, the second being larger than the first. Then a "buckshee" issue of prune juice and bread came in which was cut for by sections; our section was one of the four that won so Eric and I had for supper 2/3 of our potato ration (cold with salt) two slices of bread and butter, a piece of cheese, an extra large helping of stewed fruit and a goodly portion of prune juice and bread. We were issued with a pound of sugar, ½ lb. of butter, ½ a bar (4 oz.) of chocolate.

It is noticed that the young guards have all practically disappeared being replaced by soldiers classed on par with the Home Guard in England. The young bucks are scheduled for the Russian front and every one of them do their darnedest to get out of it. Some low down rat is pinching rations again; if caught it will mean the "latrine cure." It looks like we may be picked for work parties soon.

OCT. 31, SAT. (HALLOWEEN)

Eric and I are making our rations go a long way these days; we are on our last ½ lb. of cheese, our first can of honey, we have enough butter for three or four days and I won an extra ration of sugar last night in a raffle. We ate our last few crackers for lunch last night with a revision in the bread consumption to two slices for breakfast, one for dinner and two for supper; tomorrow we will have one slice for supper. We received 25 cigarettes from the R.C. yesterday. Three men escaped the other evening and weren't missed until the middle of the afternoon yesterday. If they had of taken a little time to erase their tracks going through the double fence they would have had more time as their absence was being covered up on roll calls. The Stalag watch discovered the holes in the fences during their regular rounds.

We had a little trouble at "tie-up" when the Jerries claimed there were five ropes missing and threatened to "chain" two men out of every ten and the rest would stand out until the missing rope was found. Four were found or manufactured in no time at all and the Hun gave us to eleven to produce the other one. Eric and I were hooked for carrying coal while we were taking our morning walk; we didn't mind because we had our hands free for an extra hour. Making plans for after the war; we have plenty of time to do the thinking these days. We got some pretty reliable news that the Libyan campaign is coming along, with the Yanks coming in behind Rommel from the south. This news came in via a long grapevine and if true it certainly is good news. I wonder if Reg has my diary I left in my kit back in camp. Also my radio books and tools. News from home is very desirous these days; in the line of parcels, chocolate and notebooks come first with cigarettes running a close second. Fairly well fixed for clothes now; were issued with a pair of gloves and a pullover sweater yesterday.

NOV. 3, TUES.

There hasn't been much doing for the past three days; Eric and I have been taking our morning walks and afternoon strolls pretty regularly and playing four handed crib to pass the time away. Time has been set back an hour because of the late sunrise. Yesterday we were issued with a Red Cross bulk ration of 30 biscuits and a tin of jam per man, and 10 lbs. of sugar per section (1 lb. per man). Eric and I heated our spuds after nine, mixed with a Yorkshire pudding batter; we saved the powder from our last food parcel. They turned out pretty good, something similar to scalloped potatoes. Today we received the remainder of the week's Red Cross issue; 1 lb. of butter between two men, ¾ lb. of cheese for one man and a bar of laundry soap. The cheese was in varying state of decomposition; we salvaged about ¼ lb. out of 1 ½ lbs.; it will do to cook with our spuds. The first mail came in for some Dieppe personnel; mostly all from England. It was written mostly on Oct. 6. We might start receiving mail from Canada in two or three weeks. We have been hearing rumours of the war in Libya, especially while on bath parade. The Allies have taken 75,000 prisoners recently and Rommel is governor of occupied France, supposedly to prepare it for a possible second front. I spoke to the Padre today for a Bible. We are on 26th day of having our hands tied.

NOV. 7, SAT.

Besides being exceedingly miserable with damp, dreary weather, matters are made worse by the return of diarrhea. Frequently there are warnings of General's inspection which means cleaning of barrack rooms, especially the floor (cement) which requires repeated sweeping with a willow broom. These brooms soon wear down beyond common efficiency and sweeping becomes a chore no one cares to undertake. Our section is on duty once in every fifteen days. A water pipe burst in No. 38 hut the other day, consequently we have been without water for three days. Drinking water is hauled in soup kűbels and doesn't last very long. We managed to hit a delousing parade yesterday and so obtained a bath, although it meant standing around in the nude shivering, while our clothes were being deloused. There are strong rumours that the ropes are coming off for good this afternoon and work parties are going out next week; I would like to get to a bush party to get away from these reprisal ideas the Germans get periodically. A good demonstration of pigs dining can be seen at noonday soup time. Everything goes along in a fairly orderly fashion by section but as soon as the section scheduled for "seconds" is through there is a mad rush by about ten men all armed with spoons, trying to scrape the insides of the kűbels. When we received Limey tea, the rush for tea leaves is something the folks back home should see. The lucky individuals who are successful in obtaining these leafs use them for brewing more tea, simply by adding water and boiling briskly over a fire. Some fellows merely add sugar and eat them; both would make Nelle shudder with repulsion while the latter habit would start with Dad telling the story about the girl who chewed tea leaves in a tea factory. Eric and I refuse to join in this custom and satisfy ourselves with fried spuds, flavoured sometimes with a little meat.

NOV. 10, TUES.

The price of a lowly soda cracker has skyrocketed to dazzling heights in early P.O.W.'s estimation and greatly surpasses its lowly position it occupied on cafe tables in pre-war or pre-capture days. The issue per man per week is 30. One biscuit is as satisfying as two slices of German black bread which doesn't speak well of the food-value of said bread. In any compound one lone biscuit will bring 2 English player cigarettes. Their present value can be readily realized in view of the fact that we only receive five cigarettes a day, not counting the re-rolls on the butts. Raffles of every description are always in swing, for instance this A.M. one biscuit or two cigarettes will buy one chance on two 2-ounce cans of English tobacco. Other raffled articles include mitts, towels, razor blades, bread rations, sugar rations, etc. Eric and I were extravagant and sacrificed one precious biscuit for a chance on the tobacco; using Eric's number.

Went to the M.O. yesterday and received a 2 ounce dose of Epsom's salts, followed four hours later by a spoonful of white paste to counteract the salts. Except for slight cramps I don't feel too bad today. It is rumoured that the Libyan campaign is over and the Russians are making headway again; 500 plane raids over the French coast seem to be everyday occurrences now. Ropes may come off soon and a 500 man work-party sent out.

George Lyons from Fairview, Manitoba discovered a German guard who has a brother in that town; after a lot of talking, both orally and sign, George decided he used to live next door. The guards are beginning to talk to us now but they keep a wary eye open for the "Unteroffizier." The weather has been exceedingly miserable lately but if it helps our war effort I guess we can stand it alright. Have arrived at the conclusion that the German race is exceedingly stupid or possess a twisted sense of humour. For instance; he issues us with raw sausage grease, and potatoes then says fires of all sorts are strictly "verboten." Then he raises hell about cleaning our billets, orders floors and bunks scrubbed then turns off the water. Every other morning he keeps us standing outside for a couple of hours because he claims there are one or two ropes missing and we stand until they are produced. The said German never reasons how we are to produce the missing rope while standing outside under the muzzles of a dozen or so "Tommy guns."

NOV. 12, THURS.

Yesterday was a busy day as we received the order to pack for an inter-compound move immediately after roll call, consequently we had to rush through our breakfast before packing. The move proved to be only from our original compound to the one we occupied prior to being tied. We had just moved into our new quarters and were wondering where to pitch our bed rolls when at a prearranged signal (two long whistles) we all stood at attention for two minutes and for once that I can remember, complete silence reigned, even the clumping of the guard's jackboots was stilled; whether or not our "host" recognized the occasion for their own dead I am not prepared to say.

The problem of what to do about bunk was finally solved by trading a honey tin full of sugar for two bed-boards then trading a burlap mattress for a canvas one. We split the boards in two, inserted them in the ends of the palaisses, then stretching them across the frames of two upper bunks then nailing the ends to the tail boards of the frame. This makes a fairly comfortable bed; the only disadvantage is they may let the sleeper down without warning anytime during the night. We soon had a cupboard erected for our grub (it being high enough and conspicuous enough to discourage any ration thieves) so by eight o'clock we had made ourselves as much at home as is possible in the present circumstances. Another touch of dysentery; this complaint is caused by a bug of some sort and Epsom salts is the best way of getting rid of it. Took 2½ ounces of salts today. The padre autographed the Bible he gave me and offered some advice as how to get the most benefit out of it.

According to rumours the war is going favourably for the Allies; all West Africa including Port Darwin and the French fleet have been captured.. For once the Germans have given us some edible cheese.

NOV. 14, SAT.

The droning monotone of the Bingo dealer's voice beats monotonously on the eardrums as I write this day's entry. The price of a chance is one precious cigarette a card; the reward for the lucky participant who fills the card first is 15 or 16 aforementioned "coffin-nails." I am wearing sabots again but this time it's because they are much warmer in this damp low-temperature weather. Our hands are still being tied twice daily and there are no indications how long it will last. The last of the three escapists who crawled through a hole in the fence in plain view of the corner guards was brought back the other day after getting as far as Hungary, a distance of 1000 kilometers. The other two only reached a point 200 kilometers before they were recaptured. It is a bad time of year for making breaks but spring ought to see an increase in business.

There are some very persistent rumours going around that the Yanks are in possession of French Morocco and the French Fleet with Admiral Darlan captive. Also heard on roll-call that the British have taken Sicily and are making progress against Italy. Arguments center around how long we will be kept in convalescence when we get back to England and if our personal belongings will be returned to us; whether we will return to Canada as convalescents or we will rejoin our regiments, etc. etc. The Battle of Dieppe and its reasons also come in for some heated debate. I had an argument with Kitchen on the various methods of consuming our meager rations; Kitchen favours the one big meal while I support the spreading out theory; others just eat them as they come. It's just a matter of opinion, I guess. I wrote a post card each to Rusty and Rose this evening. I have read as far as the first ten chapters of the Book of Leviticus in the Bible. Yesterday we had to take our leather boots out for inspection at role call; many think it is merely a nuisance idea. Tonight we had to produce our spoons for inspection. Imagine twelve hundred full grown men standing five deep in the four-thirty dusk, with soft snow sifting down, holding up their spoons of varying brightness while the Unteroffizier made a poor pretense of inspecting them. The spoons had to be held at arm's length, if possible while the German skimmed by. The Bingo-dealer's voice drones on: I-16, B-23, N-39 and so on into the evening. Toast and melted cheese or ketchup, crackers with honeyed peanut butter and plenty of tea like only Nelle can make, what a thought to while away the evening with.

NOV. 15, SUN.

Our culinary and ration procedure is undergoing drastic alterations recently, in that, instead of eating our day's rations of spuds sliced cold, we peel them at noon, cut them in half, place them in a klim can with a little grease, then put them in the heat chamber of the stove. They come out five hours later baked to a turn and steaming hot. The old system of filling the sections' spud boxes is changed after today, because as it was no one in particular seemed to be in charge and any Tom, Dick or Harry would do the job. It has been the practice of a few to gather up the broken bits left in the wooden carrying box; sometimes obtaining the equivalent to several large spuds. Lately they have taken to deliberately smashing spuds just to make a few more crumbs. Two sanitators will be in charge of filling the boxes from now on. Soups, including German and Red Cross issues, are being placed on a more systematic basis so that we know what is coming up each day. On the whole I think the whole arrangement is a big improvement. Bulk rations such as sugar, butter, jam, biscuits, etc. will be issued on Tuesday and Wednesday instead of Monday and Tuesday. Cigarettes will be issued on Monday and Friday, 25 per man each day, 50 a week. Had to pay 20 cigs and a bar of face soap for a note book and an indelible pencil. It is interesting to note the increased value of certain articles since we left England. 2 cigs for one measly soda-cracker; 25 cigs for five thin slices of German black bread. Reg Weir, Cliff Dawson and I were discussing how we are going to enjoy and take advantage of the privilege of eating what and when we like after the war. A fellow beside me is deeply interested in a book called "Rip Van Winkle," a book he would not have given a passing glance a few months ago. Others are planning the future, some are going to build new homes, others are going to stay in the army and others are just going on a tear until they are broke and are forced to find work. I have planned and re-planned my radio shack a half dozen times; and have made the decision to take advantage of the soldier's rehabilitation scheme and try to take an 8 month radio servicing course sponsored by the government at the Radio College of Canada. It is a queer world when viewed from a barb-wire fence guarded by armed green clad German soldiers, a person's sense of perspective and value of certain things undergo unbelievable changes.

NOV. 16, MON.

We had a fairly good midday meal today, despite the fact that it was a disjointed, spasmodic affair. First of all we received mashed spuds instead of the customary soup. Tie-up interfered but the Germans in one of their occasional generous gestures told us to finish our dinner. Then we were issued with 2½ pork sausages from the Red Cross; Eric and I ate ours with the last of our crackers we received last Monday. Then just before the second whistle sounded for afternoon tie-up, a half a kübel of thick sweetened porridge arrived. There was only four or five spoonfuls per man but Lord did it ever taste good. Far be it from me to ever turn up my nose at porridge again. Speaking of rations reminds me of a compound housing all staff personnel such as men who work in offices (administration, quartermasters, etc.) cook, Red Cross workers and a lot more. Extra rations can be obtained by other inmates only by paying fantastic prices. All variety of rations can be had for English cigarettes, gold rings, good watches, fountain pens, badges, jackknives, etc. For instance a half a loaf of black bread for forty cigarettes, a piece of German sausage for 20; a Red Cross box full of raw spuds for 25. For my wrist watch I could easily get five loaves of bread, 100 cigarettes and one complete Red Cross box just as it is sent from England. A pound of German coffee is obtainable for anywhere from 25 to 40 cigarettes. When the Red Cross M & N was first added to the noonday soup we got something resembling good thick stew; lately it has mysteriously grown thinner. It's a well known fact that soup, porridge, etc, going to the racket compound at noon is practically all bulk and thick; the porridge besides being thick is also sweetened; we have to add sugar to ours. Other forms of rackets such as boots, clothing, etc. are also in constant practice. If you are not in with the right crowd you will find that the only exchange for worn out boots is a repaired German shoe with wooden soles but certain people always are able to get a new uniform and a good pair of new shoes. The mail racket is the lowest of all. There are some Air Force personnel who claim to have definite proof that their mail has been deliberately detained and in some cases destroyed. The letters destroyed were in most cases mentioning the dispatch of personnel parcels. It is assumed that the racketeers wait for the parcel and it disappears and never reaches the addressee. It is asserted that most of the staff personnel will be facing charges when they get back to England and therefore are not over anxious for this war to end.

A rumour found its way into camp, to the effect that confirmation of the Libyan success is in the German papers and that is the reason for German army in Vichy, France. There is no inkling as yet when our ropes will be coming off. Paid ten cigs and a bar of soap for a note book this afternoon and lost the remaining ten at Bingo this evening. The clothing parade was postponed indefinitely and the work party rumour is revived. It is widespread opinion that the war will end in late winter or early spring. Bulk rations will be coming in tomorrow as well as biscuits and jam. Today is the 41st day of tie-up.

NOV. 17, TUES.

We received our bulk rations of soda crackers, honey and sugar, so we are practically set for another week. It's been a miserable day with a northwest wind bringing rain. Another racket I forgot to mention: any hut can get an extra ration of coal for 100 cigarettes from certain Germans. The cigarettes are collected from each man in the hut. We had a fair decent supper of roast spuds, two slices of bread and a mess of stewed prunes and apricots. Tonight for lunch we will have one slice of bread, two biscuits each. Drew some plans for my radio shack this afternoon. We are expecting mail from home daily. I while away a lot of time reading the Bible; have reached the 23rd chapter of the Book of Deuteronomy.

NOV. 18, WED.

There was a bath parade this afternoon and we nearly froze while waiting for "Jerry" to untie us. Issued with half a tin of butter and a bar of laundry soap this afternoon. The "Jerry" issue of dry rations came at the same time as our evening tea and somewhat spoiled our supper. The ration thief or thieves have been busy again. Almost cornered him (or them) when a fellow lost a tin of honey and claimed he could recognize the can, but the rats had enough time to empty and throw the can in the garbage box. We were also the victims of another spasm of Teutonic stupidity when they ordered a blanket inspection for roll-call. It was so dark they could hardly count us let alone see blankets. We have on successive nights carried our mess tins, spoons, identity discs, and blankets out for inspection. Confirmation of the Yanks being in Morocco, the British advance in Libya, and the German entrance into Vichy, France was in the Camp paper this week.

NOV. 19, THURS.

Three months from Dieppe; besides being an anniversary, we received good news today. It was more or less confirmation of a number of rumours that have been going around camp; to wit: a naval convoy of 500 troop transports and 300 escorting vessels had landed at four or five different points on the North African coast. The entire French Fleet along with Admiral Darlan surrendered to British; Benghazi and Derna taken; Tobruk fell with entire panzer division and the airdrome complete. 150,000 prisoners were taken, 90,000 German. Rommel's army is trapped in northern Africa. Very good news if true. I think the end is definitely in sight. Second front can't start until Africa is cleaned up; maybe in March or April. Tonight we were given permission to lie in our beds from 5 o'clock (P.M.) on. We also heard that Germany has withdrawn from the Caucasus. The French fleet will be a big help if it is usable. Darlan must have seen writing on the wall. Up to the Book of Samuel in my Bible reading. No snow to speak of yet, and weather fairly warm to what we were given to expect by the "Limey" element of our fair community. Mail has started arriving from England; expect one from Peggy soon.

NOV. 20, FRI.

We received 25 cigarettes today and I lost 15 at Bingo. Eric received 2 letters from home today; I wonder when I will get one. Reached the 8th chapter of the 2nd Book of Samuel tonight, also started reading a book of prose called "Dante;" it is very heavy reading. It is rumoured that we will be free for half a day tomorrow to do our laundry and such. Going to make a pair of slippers out of an old tunic to wear in my sabots to prevent my socks from wearing out. Hope I get a letter from Nelle tomorrow. Our section is on duty; Eric and I drew latrine duty for tomorrow.

NOV. 22, SUN.

Eric and I were up early yesterday and performed our unpleasant task. We were left free in the P.M. and I washed a pair of underwear, a shirt and a pair of socks. The boys have found a way of visiting the rackets compound after dark and such things as pens, badges, watches and cigarettes are finding their way into the racketeers' wealth bags. One hundred cigarettes for a loaf of bread also a Cameron hat badge; watches and pens bring more than that depending on the made and condition. It is generally believed in honest circles that that is the reason we received five strictly German soups last week. Today it is bitter cold out with a N.W. wind driving fine stinging snow before it. Another miserable roll-call this evening, probably. Went to church this A.M. Almost completely out of smokes.

NOV. 23, MON.

This has been quite a day as far as issuing of and trading of rations is concerned. We were willing for awhile to believe that the "Rackets" weren't dealing in Red Cross goods but altered our opinion when we saw a French-Canadian with unpunched cans of butter and honey. If the cans are not punched it means they have not passed the German censor. Cans of Red Cross corned beef are coming in for exchange for rings, etc. One hungry individual received four loaves of bread, two 2lb. Cans of "lieberwurst" and

400 cigarettes for his watch yesterday. We held a vote tonight whether or not we wanted ½ a parcel one week and bulk to the equivalent of ½ a parcel the following week and we voted unanimously for it. Another vote was taken whether or not we wanted it sent to the kitchen or have it issued direct. Of course, we voted for direct issue; hoping to keep it out of the racketeer's hands. As one fellow so aptly put it, "we haven't enough cigarettes to buy it back again, if it goes to the kitchen."

Today we received an issue of ¼ lb of chocolate, ¼ lb margarine and 25 cigarettes each; this has to last a week. Plans are afoot for Xmas concerts and pantomimes commencing on the 28ᵗʰ of December. We may get a full parcel for Xmas if as the Jerry says, "we are good boys, and behave ourselves." Mail came in but none for me.

NOV. 24, TUES.
Enough snow was on the ground this A.M. to allow some of the more active members to make foot slides while we were waiting to be tied, much to the amusement of the German guards. We received ½ can of bully beef this A.M. also mashed spuds, instead of soup, it was followed by semolina pudding an hour or so later. Stewed prunes came in just at roll-call so we had roast spuds, bully beef, stewed prunes and two slices of bread for supper. Biscuits came in this afternoon, 30 to a man and to prevent the ration thieves from getting them, ate the lot in short order. No mail for me today. We were told the compound was solid for ½ parcel or equivalent in bulk issued direct. Was forced to go over to 19B and borrow some salt off of Bill Robinson and Rod Grump. Finished designing my desktop and sides; the frame comes next.

NOV. 26, THURS.
Yesterday was clear and frosty and we took advantage of it to go for a walk around the compound while the hut was being cleaned. Started embroidering a Cameron badge but encountering difficulties in obtaining suitable thread. Darned a pair of socks with my hands tied, something the folks back home have never done. We are having some rip-snorting' arguments about this racket situation. A few of us maintain that the persons dealing with the racketeers are merely buying their own rations. The price of a loaf of bread

has soared to 150 cigarettes. Some enterprising individual is corralling all Stalag money with the idea that it will be redeemable after the war. A loaf of bread can also be had for one 18 karat signet ring. No mail today. Am predicting the end of the war in March, England in June, leave in July on our way home in September. We heard that Duncan, Cpl. Budd and Bert Bridge made it back to England. Plans for Christmas are going ahead despite the shortage of material for decorations, and the fact that our hands are tied.

NOV. 27, FRI.

Much warmer today with rain this A.M. Manufactured a strap for my watch out of an old shoe and made a passable job despite the hindrance of ropes. We are expecting to receive Red Cross food parcels in a few days if the consent of the "Jerries" can be obtained. The supper rush from roll-call is becoming more hectic every day. If anyone should fall between the fence the lamp post and hut 22A he would probably be lucky to get into the hut along with a few antiquated and foreign records and a box of third or fourth hand needles. It is having difficulty making itself heard above the usual bedlam of a crap game and a bingo game. My left hand is starting to swell from chilblains; if these ropes continue our hands will be ruined with rheumatism.

It is rumoured that the Russians have driven the Germans back across the Don River. Some of the guards claim that it will be over this winter in favour of the Allies. There was a little mail today, but none for me. Heard that Cpl. Sammy MacLeod got back to England but died of wounds. The dealers of rackets were caught climbing the fence this evening, consequently the business is poor tonight.

NOV. 28, SAT.

We have to vacate the premises every morning while the place is being cleaned up and keeping the hands warm, tied like this almost impossible. It was pretty crowded outside this morning and we were forced to follow the crowd to avoid collisions with other moving bodies. There were four or five different circuits according to individual inclinations. Route I: Around the parade square where we have roll-call, much in the same manner as skating in the old rink back home. This type of "circuitists" don't care much for change of scenery. Route II around the basketball pitch in front of the latrine; same as Route I but in a different part of the compound; these people don't seem to mind the latrine stench. Route III: up and down the straight piece of road running down one side of the compound; the road is abruptly terminated at each end by a very businesslike barbed wire fence; no scope for imagination. Route IV: around the outside of the huts; very hard walking, especially in sabots; then there is the old trouble of congestion at the corner by the gate. Route V: a favourite with Eric and I which supplies the greatest variety of scenery and distance per circuit. Once around the basketball pitch, down the straight piece of road to the parade square where we join the crowd there for one complete round, then back to the road and thus back to our starting point. The maximum number of people are walked with and met in this way and we can always think we were never diverted from our course by a fence. Then there is a few who stand around the doors of the hut gradually freezing and too lazy to walk.

NOV. 29, SUN.

Attended church parade this A.M. then started making a pair of mitts from an old pair of underwear "britches." The guard commander claimed he was fifty ropes short this A.M and threatened a dire penalty if they weren't produced. At nine he had fifty too many and being a trusting soul demanded another roll-call to see if we were all tied. Funny people these Germans. A strong cold north west wind has been howling all day making outside parades miserable.

Someone stole all the tea, sugar and milk from the kitchen last night so we had German herb tea for breakfast. We were informed this evening that we would be getting a special packed Xmas parcel at Xmas so we are going to try and get filled up. Wrote cards to Reg and Connie this evening. Good news from Russia and North Africa today; hope it continues.

DEC. 1

The first day of the last month. A few of the French-Canadians have under-taken the making of Xmas decorations and the results are a credit to their initiative and ingenuity. Cigarette packages, cellophane from biscuits and red string from blanket ends are the principle material used. Biscuit cartons are transformed into glittering wreaths with and without candles; stars and streamers are being turned out by the dozens. Santa Claus, complete with laden sleigh is one hut's masterpiece while 19B have a stable complete with manger, Baby and all the characters. One fellow used the sailor head circles of Player cigarette packs to make a merry Xmas sign about seven feet long. The weather continues mild in comparison with Canadian winters but the damp cold is far worse than 40° below back home. Common comment is, "this is as bad as English weather." Made a small crib board complete with peg compartment today, also made a fresh start on a Cameron hat badge; thread supply is pretty meager just now. Eric made a pudding for lunch this evening out of four biscuits, a slice of bread and a few spoonfuls of stewed fruit we received from the kitchen this afternoon. I have to put a cuff on my mitts, make a housewife, a winter cap and finish my badge; my thumb and first finger is tender from so much sewing. No mail yet.

DEC. 2, WED.

May get the remainder of this week's bulk ration today; it is rumoured that it will consist of jam or honey, chocolate, dried fruit and sugar. It's a fairly mild day, rained for awhile then changed to snow. A confirmed report states that the remainder of the German African army is surrounded and cut off from all supplies and it has the choice of starving or surrendering; Crete has been evacuated by the enemy and Russians advance on all fronts. One of our camp prophets predicts peace by Xmas. We had our heaviest fall of snow to date; about 3 inches. Received bulk ration this P.M. (jam & sugar). The jam was cut in half this week and there is talk of a further cut in other commodities. We were shackled with handcuffs and chains this noon; a big improvement over the ropes as we have nearly fourteen inches of chain to play with. Sewing, washing, writing and card playing no trick at all now. Within five minutes every man knew how to pick the locks and were making a suitable tool for the purpose. Eric and I decided to drink our tea as it comes from now on and save our sugar to put on bread when Jam, honey, etc. are scarce. A new system for the issue of German honey-butter was started today. Instead of each hut receiving a portion of the compound ration each day, each hut takes its turn in taking the full day's rations. Received a little salt today, a God send or German ration, because spuds no matter how they are cooked don't taste so good without it.

A report just overheard states that Rommel is missing and is believe dead; also three German troop ships were sunk while trying to leave Africa loaded with troops. Eric and I fixed our beds today. Finished the housewife and made good headway on my badge this afternoon. Cigarette ration is to be cut in half next week. Most war "news" is supposed to be received by "verbot-ten" radio sets somewhere in the camp, made from tediously gathered parts. Periodical searches by Jerry has failed to locate them.

Rumours and reports are coming in thick and fast; another is that certain places in England are being made ready for the convalescence of war prison-ers. No mail yet. The theory that the war will be over by February is gaining ground rapidly; I still say March or early April.

DEC. 4

Snow covers the ground these days; the entire compound is slippery from countless pacing feet. It is miserably cold and undershirts are greatly desired. Obtained some blue thread from one fellow's pajama cloth towel, for my badge. Today was miserable, starting when the guard commander demanded a roll-call early this afternoon for a chain check. Then at 2:20P.M. we were chased out again because the Germans thought our billets weren't clean enough; we stood out on the parade square for an hour and three quarters, and the clacking of heels was the loudest I have heard them yet, but still our feet got cold. Then the order came around that we had to wear our leather boots on five o'clock roll-call and they had to be polished. An officer inspected them with a flashlight and found a dirty pair, consequently we have to parade again at 9:30 A.M. tomorrow.

We heard yesterday that one of our fellows escaped from Dieppe and by way of Spain, reached England in sixteen days and was immediately given £50 bonus, 14 days' leave and was promoted to a full Cpl. It is rumoured around that a German newspaper asserts that when the Libyan campaign is cleared up the war will end. Also heard that the contents of the Xmas parcel will be 1lb of cooked meat, 1lb. Fruit cake, 1lb. Xmas pudding, 1 can of turkey or chicken, two small sized chocolate bars, sauce for the pudding, 1 can of condensed sweetened milk, sugar and tea; each man is supposed to receive one parcel. I am hoping for a parcel from home as well. Today is the third anniversary of my enlistment; I had been so impatient to join up. Getting through this winter and combating the German petty meanness is our main difficulty. It has finally been decided that a daily routine is necessary for a start. 6:00A.M., reveille; 7:00, morning roll-call; 8:30-9:30 everyone outside until clean-up is completed; 11:00 to 12:00 dinner; 12:30 to 1P.M. outside again while the room is aired and cleaned; 5:00 P.M. evening roll-call; 6:30P.M. third and last room cleaning; 8P.M. unchaining time. I hope they make it stick because it will counteract many of the silly German orders. It's cold in here tonight but perhaps lunch will warm us up.

DEC. 5, SAT.

Eureka! It came at last, my first letter and as I had been expecting, it was from Peggy. She tells me that Jack has finally landed in England and was down at Southend for leave; I bet he enjoyed himself there. She is going to try and send some embroidery thread in her next letter; I don't think she will be very successful in that direction. I have been pulling threads out of towels, handkerchiefs, pajamas and even old braces. I am getting so interested in the art I almost forgot to get unchained at noon so that we could do our laundry (in ice cold water in a blizzard-swept room). My hands nearly froze before I finished. Peggy speaks of a get-together after the war and I can't see myself disappointing her. Wrote a letter to Peggy and sent an Xmas card to Nelle.

DEC. 6, SUN.

Everything went wrong today, starting when I stood in the rear column at roll-call and had to stand out an extra ten minutes because the late arrivals didn't cover off in time. Then they were five chains short and we had to stand out again while they checked up and found them. The noon soup was thin and we had to use our spud ration to make it up. Thus depriving ourselves of our usual hot spud supper. German stewed fruit came in later in the afternoon but it was thin and tasteless and we were forced to use some precious biscuits to thicken it for supper. Our section failed to receive our German meat ration today so we had to use some of our dwindling sugar supply. The sanitator usually makes sixteen piles of rations, one for each section of 10 men; it is a debatable point whether he only made fifteen piles or someone or one section took the sixteenth pile. The fact remains, however, that our section didn't get any meat today.

Work on the badge didn't progress very favourably today, I couldn't find any red thread for the thistles and background and my green thread keeps breaking. Besides that, they decided to change the cooking arrangements which knocked our eating schedule into a cocked hat. Official announcement of the Xmas parcel contents was made tonight. One can of steak and tomato, one can of steak and macaroni, 1 can of sweets (candy), 4 oz. of chocolate, one can of chocolate biscuits, 3 oz. Of tea, sugar, 1 can of condensed sweetened milk (½ size), cheese, butter, 1 fruit cake (1 lb.) and probably a pudding.

DEC. 7, MON.

Two more fellows escaped last night, consequently we had quite a long session on the parade square this morning. One of them was Staff Sergeant Rod Grump. We had just time to have breakfast and be tied up when another roll-call was called for. They were missing alright but I don't think they will get very far at this time of year before hunger and cold will force them to give themselves up.

We were duty section today and quite a difficult time of cleaning up. It's a mild night following a mild day and all the snow is gone again. Heard a disconcerting rumour today to the effect that we are to be moved to a special "reprisal camp" by the sixteenth or immediately after Xmas. A reprisal camp is a place where, if someone kicks a German P.O.W. in the pants in England, ten of us would be kicked twice in the pants over here. The rumour was soon "squashed" by the person who was alleged to have started it. Another rumour says there will be a large Canadian work party going out immediately after Xmas. Still another but in war news line, the Yanks have evacuated Tunis; and the Russians have pushed the Germans back past Kharkov.

Worked on my badge today and my mitts this evening. I am getting the thread for my mitts from the hem stitching on the ends of my blankets. No mail at all today. I wonder how Jack is making out in England. My left hand is swollen from chilblains. Morris spent the day in the guard room with his toes against the wall and his hands tied behind his back for moving around during roll-call this morning. Pea soup for dinner tomorrow. Our cigarette ration cut to 25 a week today; may as well quit entirely.

DEC. 8, TUES.

Parades all morning which were very tiresome although the weather was fairly mild. Eric and I had a fairly good supper this evening considering the available material. A Klim can full of roasted spuds, three thick slices of bread, and we mixed five and a half soda biscuits in each of our stewed prune ration this afternoon which made a fair pudding. We got the German honey-butter today so the problem of bread spread is solved for another few days.; it was approaching a crisis stage. Tomorrow we get ½ tin of bully beef and mashed spuds, semolina pudding with raisins for dinner, which will leave a full ration of spuds for supper; sugar is also on the Red Cross ration list for tomorrow. On Thursday we get ½ tin of jam and 3 oz. of cheese per man. My badge is rapidly approaching completion, obtained some bright red thread for a background from Weir's blanket.

DEC. 10, THURS.

Taking a hot can of spuds and bully beef out of the oven this evening, a French-Canadian narrowly missed having his face scalded. Warm today with a balmy breeze from the Czech hills. Had another extra roll-call this afternoon for a chain check; evidently the check tallied alright the first time. Understand that this present guard is going to the front, being replaced by an older bunch of men unfit for front line duties. The Xmas week bulk ration is a subject of much discussion and the semi-verified version is: 64 soda crackers, a can of jam or honey, a can of butter, cheese, a can of dried bananas, a package of dried fruit, sugar, 1½ lb. of chocolate. On Xmas day, so the story goes, we will receive porridge and tea for breakfast, mashed spuds, pork and beans for dinner, with a marmalade pudding for supper, besides the already mentioned parcels. Some say they saw the list and others claim there is no authenticity to the rumour. Am having a miserable time making these 25 cigarettes last a week. Finished my badge today; a wash improved it 100%

Eric and I were planning a big feed of tin crackers and cheese each tonight so were disappointed when the cheese and jam didn't come in.

We had a section leaders' meeting (I'm one of those) yesterday about the seconds on soups and tea and decided on two nominal roles being adopted. Also cooking arrangements altered again and a new method for issuing of daily dry rations.

As for the war news. Stalin is supposed to have stated that they will be fighting on German soil in sixty days; at present they are reported at or near the Polish border. Undertook to draw two Cameron badge on cloth for Thomson and Holiday, for eight cigarettes. No mail for me since the first letter from Peggy; can't understand why there is no mail from home. We will be starting the 67th day of having our hands tied, tomorrow.

DEC. 11, FRI.

Received 3oz. can of cheese and a can of jam from the Red Cross today. Eric and I cut an ace and took the can of strawberry jam. We had two extra roll-calls today for chain count but the weather has been comparatively mild recently. Nine chains are still missing and "Jerry" threatens to cancel all Xmas privileges if there are any more losses.

The rumour summary is as follows: chains coming off for good on Monday; a working party of 500 going out after Xmas; Dieppe personnel is being moved to another camp 40 kilometres from here; we will receive ½ R.C. parcel next week and all bulk in the soup, etc.; tea in morning and evening will cease; Germany sustained heavy losses around the Mediterranean; Russia doing well.

Eric and I had a supper of roasted spuds, bully beef, 1 ½ slices of bread, and five cheese and cracker sandwiches. Put my badge on my cap this afternoon. Stumbled during evening roll-call and caused quite a tangle; lucky I didn't get up with a broken neck or something. Eric held the crowd back until I regained my feet.

DEC. 13, SUN.

A new system inaugurated for chains which may eliminate the reason for reprisals and threats by the Germans. Each barrack room commander has signed and is responsible for the chains allotted to his room. If any go astray the room in question is alone punished. Yesterday was a day of rumours, conflicting contradictory, senseless and otherwise. Waste of paper to repeat them all here. Received Red Cross food parcel today for the first time since being tied on October 8. They will be issued as one parcel per four men twice a week. Eric and I cut cards with Morris and Parker to see who would take the first parcel; we lost so we have to wait until Thursday. The rumour that we will be moving to another camp is gaining headway steadily. I hope we don't move until after Xmas.

We hear that Smolensk and Minsk are being bombed by the Germans which mean, if true, that the Russians have recaptured the towns. Rumours of 75 divisions of Germans being cut off by the Russians are also sifting in via returning working parties. No bulk in the soups this week because of the parcel issue but tea, morning and night, and stewed fruit on Tuesday continue. We will receive bulk and parcels next week. Almost finished my mitts, although the days remain clear, mild and snow-free; January and February will probably be dirty weather. I hope we receive clothes, smokes and chocolate parcels from home soon. Reached the tenth Psalm in the Book of Psalms in my Bible reading this evening. Drew two Cameron badges for cigs yesterday but the desired smokes aren't forthcoming until Monday. Twelve days to Xmas.

DEC. 14, MON.

Big things are shaping up today; three hundred and sixty-six men moving out of this compound. We think it is because there is an International Red Cross commission due to arrive soon and it wouldn't do to let them find us overcrowded, and sleeping on floors and tables. We are left with 100 men in a room with no one sleeping in bottom bunk or on the floor. Eric and I escaped the axe, are still together and slated to remain as is.

Heard today that Tunis and Tripoli are cleaned up and a "keeper" fresh from the Russian front says the Russians are driving ahead and will end that part of the world conflict inside of a month. A wild rumour is circulating this evening, that Singapore has been retaken. Evidently we receive ¼ of a parcel tomorrow, after the Red Cross representative argued long and loud with German authority. Of course, there are certain stipulations the Jerry insists upon, such as, he will allow them to be issued direct, if all cans are immediately emptied and handed in for scrap metal; and if the stuff does not require re-heating (he wanted all cook-able contents to go to the kitchen), so we will have to eat cold meals for awhile until he gradually forgets about it, as is usually the case with all of his silly orders. Eric and I plan on eating all of our spuds in our hot soup at noon. We get hot fruit stew in the afternoon tomorrow, and bread soup on Fridays, hot "Limey" tea at 2P.M. on Saturdays and Sundays. There is a possibility that we won't be chained tomorrow.

Worked on my mitts today. We should be cooking again by the end of the week and in the meantime we are accumulating coal for Xmas day. We think Jerry is trying to put the "Fritz" on our receiving Xmas parcels.

DEC. 16

Living conditions have improved considerably since the move yesterday. We have ten sections of 10 men each now and a table for each section which eliminates the reason for the mad supper rush at evening roll-call. We had two fairly good suppers yesterday and today. Yesterday we had baked spuds spread with German fish paste, two slices of bread and meat roll and a pudding made from stewed fruit, biscuits and cocoa. Today we had sliced potatoes with bean and tomato sauce, another pudding we made yesterday, two slices of bread and tea.

The inquiries prompted by the manufacture of a pair of drumsticks are numerous. One fellow in particular asked me what I was doing and when I said, "making wood soup," he said "Oh" in a most satisfied tone of voice and walked away. I almost had them finished when Cpl. Ward asked me what I was going to do with them, he seemed peeved when I told him I was going to eat rue with them.

Rumours are coming in thick and fast today, mostly with some Naval men who were captured at Dieppe and were staying at a camp near Bremen.

800,000 prisoners taken in Africa with a loss of 80,000 men, Berlin bombed for 31 hours; Rome, Naples, Genoa bombed heavily, Russians advancing all along the line taking Rostov on Don; Singapore and Hong Kong retaken. Other rumours are the entire Royal family of Italy killed in plane crash while escaping from the bombing of Rome; war ended today at 2:30P.M. A typical example of rumours that sometimes spread through camp and the amount of sifting required to separate the grain from the chaff.

We were informed today that we would be chain-free over Xmas. The Germans gave each hut a real live Christmas tree; there is a ten gallon keg of beer in the house and we get bulk and Xmas parcels next week. Clothing parcels stipulations were read out tonight; any towels, gloves, etc., cannot be handed out until they have been marked on our clothing list as issued by the Germans. All leather goods will be confiscated and returned to us after the war.

DEC. 17
Rumour today: starting the Xmas bulk rations on Saturday and half a parcel on Monday besides the Xmas parcel. Actual facts: another ten gallon keg of beer came in today. Our supper of spuds, yeatex, galantine (*gelatine?*) meat, bread, jam and tea very satisfying tonight. We were called out on parade this afternoon and made to stand until someone returned two missing doors for one of the stoves; they were produced after a few minutes. Eight more days until Xmas; time is slipping by pretty fast. Consensus of opinion is that we will be home for next Xmas; I hope to be home before then, say October.

DEC. 18, FRI.
A very nice day with bright sunshine. School starts again on the 28th so I enrolled for electrical engineering and engineering maths. Had a passable supper this evening of canned beef stew, dumplings and carrots, a ration of spuds, two slices of bread, jam and cocoa. We won the buckshee bread soup this evening and by the time we downed that we were plenty full. Rumours today deal mostly on Xmas ration issue. We are duty section tomorrow.

DEC. 20, SUN.

A day of great disappointment brought about when the week's rations were officially announced. Absolutely no bulk; Xmas parcel only on Thursday, 25 cigarettes tomorrow; bread soup on Monday and Thursday (1000 men to a kübel. Everyone was anticipating a big feed on Xmas day but there will be little of the parcel left by then. The Germans have finally decided to investigate the rackets, probably because the bread magazine was robbed recently. They found a store of bread in the racket compound. Whether or not this will effect our Xmas plans is difficult to say. When I think of the German prisoners in Canada sitting down to complete turkey dinners on Xmas as they probably will be doing I have an overwhelming desire to place my best food violently against the nearest Teutonic posterior. The Germans are omitting the noon day soup and giving us a few extra spuds which will come off on the next day's ration. New year's week will be just as good as we are getting the bulk ration we were expecting this week.

The French-Canadians have done a very credible job of decorating the otherwise depressing interior of the hut, thereby producing the only Xmas spirit visible herein; even the lowly Canadian salmon (a pure luxury of no mean value in here) has contributed to the festooning of our quarters in that the red labels from the cans are used for decorative streamers. One has only to raise one's eyes to see "No. 1 grade salmon" advertised on the links of a streamer chain spanning the space between two rafters in swooping scallops. The tree decorations are multiplying daily under the nimble fingers of the enterprising Frenchmen. Snow is conspicuous because of its absence but we don't mind that because every warm day now makes one less cold on this winter. Lord how I wish I was home for Xmas.

Longing for hot buttered toast made from white bread, liberally covered with Ontario mild cheese with a generous helping of strawberry jam on top. Would like a good feed of nuts, any kind of nuts with "Kashu" and peanuts preferred. For the last two nights, Eric and I have made tea in the recognized manner. Saving old tea leaves and boiling them again. After the suppers are all cooked, cards are cut for turns at the fire for making tea. Last night we were fifth and tonight we are 22nd. Everyone puts a dixie of water in the oven to warm up while waiting their turn to "brew up." Sometimes if a person is 32 or so on the list the water is hot enough for cocoa or shaving. Evidently some people are unable to recognize their own pots because ours was gone when our turn came up. We still had our tea however, by simply taking someone else's pot. The old army style of replacing stolen goods. We had the tea safely consumed when the irate pot owner came and claimed his depleted property. Wrote a letter card to Nelle and cards to Bezzie and Em this evening. Am reading David Copperfield and have read the 65 Psalm in the Book of Psalms in my Bible reading. Conversation, thoughts, dreams, post-war intentions all center around food. Everyone planning what they are going to eat when they get back. Still figuring the war will be over by April.

DEC. 21, MON.

500 of us, complete with shackles were allowed to attend the band concert in the theatre this afternoon. Nearly froze from the knees down. The first hour was taken up by the Brass band breezing through "The Sons of the Brave," "Sea Shanty Medley," "La Traviata," "Goldie Locks & the Three Bears Fantasy," "Three Dull Dances," and "Merry England." I wish Nelle could have heard it; perhaps she will as this band is booked for a tour after the war. The last hour was taken by a Dance Orchestra who also met with approval from the appreciative audience. We got back in time to divide the day's rations before roll-call.

The Germans were all excited this evening warning us that anyone seen outside the huts after seven would be shot; then they rushed in and collected the chain in a flurry of excitement. A postern said that Hitler was making a speech and they all had to listen to it. Rumours have it that the Germans are making a comeback in Africa; and Turkey has opened the Dardanelles to the British.

We used the last of our Nestles condensed milk this evening and as our sugar ran out pre-expectedly we will have to take our tea straight tomorrow night. We received 25 cigarettes this morning. Feel more optimistic for Xmas day. May get the biscuit issue tomorrow instead of New Years week, which will help until our Xmas parcel comes. Weather remains good and clear with a full moon tonight. Drummed a little to Wilcox's fiddling this evening. The shortest day of the year is over. I have given up hope of receiving mail from home before Xmas. We receive 25 cigarettes on Thursday and ten extra on Xmas. We received four kübels of bread soup for the compound this afternoon instead of eight. It was thick with bread this time. The bread investigation is still on which may account for the thicker soup; we were certainly getting robbed before. They found a supply of bread in the racket compound that couldn't be satisfactorily explained.

DEC. 25, XMAS DAY

Right now I feel decidedly uncomfortable for the second time today (I guess I shouldn't have eaten those last three slices of cake and drank that tea); Eric apparently has been violently ill judging by the pallor of his face. Beyond a doubt we over-ate, a thing I thought impossible in a place like this.

We began the day by attending the special church service at 9:30A.M. The church was decorated with pine and cedar boughs very simply but effective. Congregational singing of "Come All Ye Faithful" opened the service, followed by the Padre leading in prayer; a rendition of "Noel" by the male choir was followed by more prayers, then "Good Christian" by the choir. The first lesson reading was from the 6th verse of the 9th chapter of the Book of Isiah, followed by congregational singing of "Peace on Earth." The second lesson reading was from the 2nd chapter of the Gospel according to St. Luke. The sermon was on the following theme, "At the heart of the universe all is well for at the heart of the universe is God." "Hark the Herald Angels Sing" concluded the service.

We paid a number of visits to the other compounds, overate a great deal, sampled some German beer, which I thought tasted much worse than other beer I have tasted and now I am afraid to go to bed. The three preceding days were merely build up preliminaries for today. We received our Xmas parcel on Wednesday and that same night by mixing four squares of sweet chocolate, 1 tablespoon butter, ½ spoon of Nestles condensed sweetened milk and a little sugar and boiling the works over a slow heat, we made a pretty smooth tasting icing for one of our cakes. On Thursday we used up a can of beef stead and tomato pudding for our supper. On Xmas Eve we walked into a concert in 20B and thought it pretty good, especially the skit of two P.O.W.'s drawing their back pay after two years of enforced confinement.

Xmas morning (I couldn't finish this last night) we had a dish of soda cracker mush followed by bread and marmalade and tea for breakfast.

For dinner we had two pieces of bread liberally spread with cheese and jam (a special treat we have been looking forward to) one soda cracker apiece with cheese and jam, one package of chocolate coated biscuits, and a healthy slice of our iced cake with tea. We went visiting in the afternoon and got a line on some salt. Walked into the racketeers' hut and saw the tables set for supper. Each table was decorated with Xmas finery, complete with porcelain plates and silver eating utensils, and occupying the centre of each table was a large round Christmas cake made in the local kitchens. We came back and put our dinner in the oven, consisting of two Klim cans of steak and macaroni and spuds, one Klim can full of just spuds, a canned plum pudding and a dixie of water. We visited Charlie Norris in convalescent compound (he went to hospital some time with meta-dysentry) and arranged the salt deal. We had supper at 6:30 and were greatly disappointed when it was greasy and non too warm. Eric just barely finished his first piece of cake and ½ his tea when he had to quit. I managed to finish three pieces of cake and my tea but in five minutes I was pretty uncomfortable. We had to lie down for two hours to relieve the strain. Beer was dished out at 8:30 and a sing song started but everyone was too full to fancy the beer or muster a song. I made a cup of tea at eleven after supper, so I went to bed hoping nothing would happen before morning. Eric gave me a present yesterday morning, a caramel candy from the can in his R.C. parcel. He was violently sick last night.

DEC. 26, SAT.

We had our usual breakfast of two slices of bread and tea. We both felt better after yesterday eating fest. We had mashed spuds and semolina for dinner, then we went to the Carol singing. Am drawing two more Cameron badges for ten cigs. Charlie Norris is trying to get us salt at the Convalescent Canteen. Bill Robinson will give us two French cigs for 1 player. We had a supper of baked spuds spread with German fish paste, two slices of bread and a piece of cake apiece. We went out for another walk this evening then came back and had a lunch of cocoa, a slice of bread and marmalade and a piece of cake.

DEC. 27, SUN.

There was supposed to be 15 chains missing this morning and the gates were supposed to be locked and remain that way until they were found. They were open when we came back from church so I guess the missing links were located. Finished drawing the two badges. We visited Charlie but the salt deal is hanging fire pending a fresh supply. We confined ourselves to German cabbage soup for dinner and prepared our supper and saw it placed in the oven. Every day at noon the oven is packed tight with a miscellaneous gathering of Klim cans, dixies, butter tines and mess tins containing dinners, then a fire is kept going until after evening roll call, at which time the respective owners sit down to suppers of varying degrees of temperature, depending on the position they occupied in the oven.

We went through the Air Force huts today looking for a friend of Eric's but failed to find him. A new form of trading has materialized now that the rackets are treading so softly. The Indians will give an old greatcoat and a can of meat for a new one; some of the fellows are coming back with some pretty fuzzy looking garments and a can of steak and macaroni. I'll keep my own coat and go hungry if need be. Discovered the loss of my fountain pen this A.M. so I guess someone has been eating pretty good lately. The ration issue for this week has been read out and promises to be pretty good, starting with 25 cigs, 1/10 tub of tobacco and a tin of margarine per man. Tuesday, sugar and 1 tin of salmon; Wednesday ¼ of a parcel; Thursday, ¼ of a parcel, 25 cigs; Friday, ½ tin of bully; Saturday, ½ tin of jam and 3 oz. of cheese. Tonight we had a Klim can full of potatoes and steak and tomato pudding, slice of bread and half a plum pudding each. We were fifth in the tea brewing line so had it with our supper. For lunch we had a slice of bread and the rest of our marmalade, a piece of cake and a cup of cocoa, each. We are planning a good "scoff" on New Years day; we are going to make a couple of puddings if we get a Canadian parcel on Wednesday.

We hear rumours of Germans evacuating North Africa. According to said rumours the Germans managed to load their evacuation craft but 21 or 27 were sunk when they tried to leave. German news-papers are supposed to have admitted that they have withdrawn 150 kilometers in Russia. Still trying to get a line on a pipe and a spoon. There is no snow yet but it is quite cold today. Still reading "David Copperfield." Most people here think that the Canadians in England won't see action unless the war lasts another year. Given my pen up as stolen or "lost." Mail will soon be coming in again; perhaps I will be more fortunate this time. One fellow heard from a relative in England that Canada House has sent 2000 comfort parcels for Dieppe Canadians.

DEC. 29, TUES.
Bumming ink off of Ernie Kitchen. Attended electrical engineering class for a second good start. On our return found the entire compound personnel standing outside as punishment because 22B refused to obey one of "Spitfire's" orders. He had to draw his revolver to get them out there. Apparently he figured we were not worthy of the punishment and motioned us to our huts. They stood out there for a full hour and were only allowed in because stewed fruit and bread soup came in. The Red Cross issue for this week has been altered slightly; instead of two ¼ parcels we got ½ on Thursday and in addition to what was mentioned before will get 15 soda crackers each. Yesterday we traded 20 Player cigs for 40 French, hoping to build up a supply for trading purposes. Thought I had a math class today and didn't realize my mistake until I burnt my mouth with hot soup and rushed down to the school. Potatoes, soup, and bulk rations came in between 10:30 and 11:00A.M. We had a salmon and potato hash for supper tonight. Eric met Charlie at school and came back with a cake tin of salt, four pkgs. of cig. papers and a package of German breakfast cereal. We will use the cereal for thickening our puddings; we saved our stewed fruit on Monday for these puddings. Tonight we traded a can of salmon and six biscuits for a can of steak and macaroni which we wanted for our New Years' dinner. If we are lucky in our parcels we may have four or five puddings this week. Trouble was encountered in the tea brewing business when there wasn't enough cards to go around, consequently, a new system was inaugurated in that each section is allowed to boil three dixies of water; which means that there were 33 dixies to boil and only about half got through before the fire died.

There was a verse tacked up in front of the stove, composed by our chief decoration maker. "May this Christmas lead you through the Gateway of

Happiness into the Sunshine of all your hopes." Another little motto, "Morning knoweth not what the night will bring." War rumours are scarce these last few days except for vague whisperings that we have won a naval battle someplace. Weather decidedly cold, no snow. Some of the fellows are sinking pretty low in their dealings with the Indians. Deprived of feminine company they are resorting to other means. I wonder what is wrong with my mail.

DEC. 31, THURS.

The chains came off at noon today and will remain off until Saturday morning, leaving our hands free for New Years. We received dried apples in our parcel today which, mixed with prunes and biscuits, will make a fair addition to New Years dinner. Copied out a logarithm table last night and today so now I have to find some rules to go with it. The camp commandant wished us all a Happy New Year and said we are soldiers and prisoners together and not enjoying the situation in the least. Also we should all be home by this time next year as he is sure the war will be over in favour of the Germans of course. He also said the chains aren't a political idea but is direct punishment for atrocities committed at Dieppe.

War news is scarce at present as is the mail. New Year's Eve in a Stalag Barrackroom (20A, block VI. The Xmas decorations are still up, diminishing the usually not too brilliant illumination, which is decreased still more by smoke from innumerable cigarettes. Blackout blinds, torn, ragged, haphazardly put up, hang askew at the windows. The tree in the center of the north wall looks strangely forlorn, seemingly forgotten and out of season. At the ten or so tables there are groups of men in various pursuits and all with a pall of smoke-haze hovering over their heads. Some are having their evening cup of tea, rattling their cheap, rusting German spoon in biscuit-tin cups or spreading jam or Nestles sweetened milk on soggy, margarined German black bread. Others are finding a quiet game of crib or bridge, complete with "kibitzers" absorbingly interested. A few are reading. Others are studying or copying notes after attending day's session of school classes (closed now until Monday.) A noisy crap game at No. 10 table is claiming the interest of the gambling element; while a group sits around the stove reminiscing or discussing the potentialities of the future. Every once in a while a bellow from the fireman for another pot of water breaks above the general hum and buzz of the room. "One more pot from No. 10 section and hurry it up." Someone will move to comply. Two fellows are earnestly arguing about how hungry a person has to be before he is starving, another is extolling the quality and flavour of a freshly made cup of cocoa; making a neighbour very curious why that particular brew warrants such high-flowing praise and desiring a sample. So the cup passes across the table at frequent intervals. Above everything and always audible is the unintelligible jargon of the French Canadians, who hold their own arguments and discussions on identical topics; eight of them are sitting around and singing French songs, but not very loud. Some are wandering around unable or not willing to find something to pass the time; while the commando corporal with the squeaky voice is trying desperately to convince a fellow the period of peace between this and the next war. Arguments spring up suddenly and without warning and usually center around the question of food, although it being parcel day no one is in the least hungry. I could almost paint a mental picture of this New Year's back home but next year we will actually be taking part in it and impatiently waiting for the roast goose to come out of the oven. Just now a cup of cocoa and a slice of black bread with gooseberry jam is looming deliciously. A fifth of a loaf of bread doesn't go very far and every mouthful practically becomes a ritual, to be enjoyed to the full. Oh, for the day when we can eat all the white bread we want, when we want and with who we want.

Trading is still in progress; one fellow, evidently wishing to appear a big shot is bellowing his deals in everyone's ears. He rarely makes a profit, trading a ration of sugar for a ration of bread, the bread goes for ½ can of jam, which in turn is traded for 12 biscuits which probably will be traded for a ration of sugar. The most frequently heard phrase this evening is, "remember a year ago tonight we were eating so-and-so." I venture to say that meals and food, past, present and future monopolize 99% of the conversation among the voracious appetited Canadians.

JAN. 1, 1943, FRI.

Gates have been open all day. Eric and I went for a walk this afternoon then came back and made two Klim cans full of Stalag puddings for supper. We traded ten Limey cigs for 20 French, then went down to the racket compound and sold two packages of Limey for ten marks.

Rumours have it that the Russians have advanced 200 miles further this winter than they did last and have cut off another 90,000 in the Caucaus and the Germans are feeding them by air. Rumours of a more local nature have the "Repats" and "Sans" going to a new camp in Italy, while the Air Force is supposed to be taking over this camp. We are supposed to go out on working parties about the middle of this month. Canadian comfort parcel and some Canadian mail reported arrived. Eric and I are fully convinced that we will be home in time to eat pumpkin pie, apples and Halloween candy this year, that's including time spent in leaves and convalescence in England, etc.

We have been warned against the spreading propaganda among the German soldiers and population which leads us to believe that the German authorities are trying to withhold true facts from their armies and public.

I feel pretty drowsy after eating so much; I guess our stomachs have shrunk in the last four months. Our New Year's dinner consisted of a Klim tin-full of spuds, steak and macaroni, a Klim tin stalag pudding, a slice of bread and fish paste and a cup of tea. For lunch we had a slice of bread and crab and anchovy paste and another slice of bread and jam with cocoa.

JAN. 3, SUN.

They chained us for half a day yesterday. Eric and I spent Saturday morning in the private study room of the library; he studied building construction and I, log tables. Arriving at our compound gate we were refused admission but the S.C.P. fixed it up okay. We attend church in 19B this morning and I read a book called "Mystery in the Channel" by Mill Croft. The wind veered around to the northwest which brought a driving snow; roll-call miserable affair this evening. Fellows are talking about being in England by next summer.

The British have taken French Somali-land and Corsica without much opposition and the Mediterranean is free to British shipping; the Russians are supposed to be on the old Polish border. Rations from Red Cross this week: ½ tin of jam, 1 tin of salmon, 16 soda crackers, 1 chocolate bar per man on Tuesday; 25 cigarettes, 1/10 tin of tobacco on Monday; 1 can of cheese, 1 package raisins, 1/3 lb. of sugar, 1 can of meat and vegetables per man on Friday. Sending my shoes in for repairs tomorrow. They say there is lots of Canadian mail which will start to appear this coming week.

They marched a Lance Corporal into the hut this evening and made him stand on a bench while the sergeant major told us how he was caught stealing someone else's supper out of the stove. Besides being branded a thief before 900 men, he has to do latrine duty for a month. He belongs to the Essex Scottish Regiment.

Imagine trying to heat a room 120 by 60 feet with one small central fire. The floor is cement and feels like ice to the feet; the place would make an ideal refrigerating plant. We all have chilblains of the hands and feet.

JAN. 5, TUES.

We spent yesterday morning down at the reference library studying in our own time. Spent the evening drawing another desk top design and bringing my notes up-to-date. We had a medical for lice and nearly froze running around divested of protective garments. Sewed buttons on my uniform this evening while Eric was at school. We made a couple of Stalag puddings out of 12 biscuits, two slices of bread and our fruit issue. Blanket inspection on roll-call this evening. Jerry is on the rampage again because someone was caught burning bed frames; Red Cross cut off as punishment. I hope it is lifted before Friday when we are supposed to receive the other half of this week's R.C. rations. It is going around that Spitfire's wife and child has been killed in an air-raid thereby explaining his attitude of late.

It is rumoured that Berlin was subjected to a severe bombing on New Year's day and is continuing. There is a heated debate in progress around the stove as to whether we will be paid after the war and whether we are subjected to army discipline while we are here. The person arguing "no" to both questions has shown a surprising lack of intelligence on many former occasions and to even listen to him argue is bad enough, let alone trying to convince him of anything. Stubbornness is his shining characteristic. Some of the fellows are doing plenty of beefing because they had to take "seconds" on bread soup. Another half hour to supper.

JAN. 7, THURS.

Attended math class yesterday but missed the electrical class because of a check roll-call which lasted from 2:30 to 4:30; there was no 5:00 o'clock roll-call because of the lateness of the check-up. Rumours prevailing are: Spain has asked U.S.A. to take over. Today the rumour gathered ground and had U.S.A. troops in Spain. All hog-wash, I think. Another rumour going around is that the British ambassador to Germany at the time of the Munich farce has been shot in the Tower of London for treason and Lady Astor was arrested on the same charge. Sounds like another brand of hog-wash. Still another rumour (strong) is going around that the chains will come off for good tomorrow night. We have heard this so often no one takes it seriously anymore. In fact, anytime we hear a rumour we don't believe we merely say "the chains are coming off for good, too."

Went down to the school early this morning to study but had to return for a camp-wide general check roll-call; thereby making up for the one we missed last night. It's been cold all day and it's practically impossible to find a warm place to thaw out; our huts certainly don't come near meeting these requirements. Everyone will be exceedingly glad to see spring roll around; this continual cold is getting hard to take. We received New Year's greeting cards to send out today so I sent mine to Iris; I had already sent one to Nelle. Iris will get this one with the first spring thaw.

JAN. 9, SAT.

It's very miserable in these huts these days and it's the usual procedure for most to put on a greatcoat as soon as they get up and take it off only to spread over them at night. There is usually a daily 8:30 stampede to the school private study library, the warmest place we have admittance to. Eric and I have sat there studying the whole A.M. just because it is not as cold as our own barrack room. Yet, this winter isn't near as severe as Canadian winters; it's the lack of nutrition and warm quarters. This is the only compound where roll-call is held outside regardless of weather. Bulk ration yesterday was 2 oz. Tin of cheese, package of raisins and 2/3 lb. of sugar per man; we were supposed to receive M. & W. too, but Jerry said it required cooking which meant bed-boards would be burnt and so refused permission to issue it. We received a tin of meat-roll today instead. The size of the spud ration is dwindling daily; more and more spuds are showing signs of frost bite. Good and rotten spuds alike are all boiled in the same copper. It's a fact that Eric and I had five puddings, (five days in a row) 2 apricot, 2 dried apple and one raisin; we will be having stewed raisins for supper tomorrow night. It's a fact that the only time we feel anywhere near warm is when we are in bed sleeping.

Rumours and news reports are plentiful; among the former are: The Russians have broken through into Poland in two places; the Germans are forcing the Poles to join the German army. The hospitals of Germany and some occupied countries are filled to capacity with German wounded from the Russian front. The Ruhr Valley is taking a terrible pounding from the R.A.F. We received cards bearing Xmas greetings from the Canadian people today and at the bottom was the sentence: "Christmas parcels following." It will probably be many weeks before we see the parcels. There was five cards to ten men; I got one by cutting the eight of clubs. Another persistent rumour is that we will be moving from this camp soon. Last night one of the fellows lost his shackles during roll-call so this morning he was forced to go over the whole parade square and vicinity with a rake in an effort to find them; a Jerry with pea-shooter supervised his labours. Jerry may cut off Red Cross issue next week; I don't think the reason, good, poor or otherwise, has been thought up yet. God, these people encourage other people to hate them.

JAN. 11

Very cold today; estimated personally as 6 or 6 below zero (F); felt the need of underwear vests greatly. Had two outside roll-calls this A.M. and another long check parade at noon, also outside, then our five o'clock parade. The huts are like ice-boxes so have been nearly frozen all day. Hands are swollen from chilblains and they itch at night. Gates were closed all day because one man couldn't be located. May hit clothing parade tomorrow; going to try and get a new uniform and still keep my old tunic for a vest; it's a tricky business but it has been done. I have to get some extra clothing somehow.

Rumours for today and yesterday are: the Russians have retaken Rostov; they are in Old Poland. A working party that has been in a coal mine in Poland for two years has been brought back, bringing reports that there is a morale uplift among Polish people. The African campaign is definitely finished; Canadians have landed in Alexandria. We may get half a parcel if Jerry sanctions the issue. He wants all foodstuffs such as requiring re-heating to go to the kitchen; in this way he could cut his supply of rations considerably. Wrote letters to Aunt Ett and Marcelle yesterday. I hope this country is subjected to a January thaw like Canada is; it would break up this cold spell. This cold has one advantage; the snow isn't tracked in so much and the floor is fairly dry. Studying algebra and trig. No mail from home yet; Anne says Roy is training for a promotion (OCTU I take it) also Jack has been to see them.

JAN. 13, WED.

Last night Eric and I decided to go see the pantomime "Aladdin" so ate our spuds and meat-roll at four. The show was good but we all, including the performers, almost froze. Cliff Dawson had tea ready for us when we got back so we had bread, salmon, German honey butter with tea before going to bed. Jerry refused to let us have the ½ parcel this week, demanding that all meats and milk go to the kitchen. We received a can of salmon, a can of biscuits, a can of margarine and approximately ¼ lb. of dates last night. Went on clothing parade yesterday, received a new uniform, a pair of puttees and a pair of shoe laces. Managed to get away with my old tunic, which serving as a vest, makes quite a difference. Worked on algebra and electrical notes all evening. Sent away for three books on algebra, mathematics and trigonometry and one book on shorthand. Windy this A.M. but decidedly warmer this P.M. Thermometer sank to 16° below zero yesterday morning.

JAN. 14, THURS.

It's queer weather we are having; we woke up to melting snow and a stiff cold breeze. By late afternoon the wind increased to gale proportions but the snow was still soft. Eric and I joined the milling mob on the basketball grounds this morning; this daily mass of penned humanity shuffle or stroll around a circle, reminding me very much of a herd of cattle. Evidently Jerry places more importance on the possibility of the water pipes freezing up than he does on the prisoners freezing to death, because he has given orders that the door to the washroom must be kept open day and night so that what warm air there is in the hut can circulate into the washroom; ignoring or neglecting to recognize the fact that we have all we can do now to keep ourselves warm. Lack of sugar or milk necessitates the drinking of our tea in the raw or straight. Here is a little philosophic piece which I think holds great meaning: "Death triumphs over all men—the strong, the weak, the noble and the humble—even glorious deeds of war count for naught. Virtue and virtue alone lasts through all eternity."

JAN. 16, SAT.

The weather has been mild these last two days, so much so that the snow has almost disappeared again. Finished "David Copperfield" yesterday. Started work on a pair of moccasin slippers. Got a fairly interesting book from the lending library called "Romance of the Movies." A few of us started a discussion on what we are going to eat when we get back and as a result we all became hungry. There are so many delectable dishes I crave to sample just now, that it isn't funny. The chain situation has become more or less a joke now; in the morning at 8 at the call of "Chains" one man can go up and get a whole handful of them and more or less delivers them among his friends. During the day we put on and take off our great coats at will, taking our chains off when necessary with small tools made from can-keys, nails, etc. At night the chains are collected by anyone going up near the waiting postern and his box. We were "free" for half a day, today. Received a letter from Alf today, still no word from home. We hear that meats of all kinds are no longer rationed in England.

JAN. 18, MON.

Studied logs, anti-logs, and a little trig today. The ration corporal came in this evening and announced that we would receive ½ parcel on Tuesday minus M. & N. which the Jerries insist goes to the kitchen for re-heating. War rumours are prevalent, one regarding the Russian front has the situation pretty complicated with a large body of Germans in the center, surrounded by Russians, who in turn are surrounded by Germans with another ring of Russians around them. One German is supposed to have said that if the Germans fail to break out they are finished but if they do break the ring the war will last indefinitely.

Some of the fellows went down for their first personal parcels from home this morning coming back with heavy winter garments. One fellow got three 1 lb bars of Canadian chocolate and is the envy of us all. It is some consolation to know that parcels from home are in, although I haven't received any mail from home, myself, yet. The German issue of rations is becoming smaller day by day, one man's ration of spuds barely half filling a Klim can. The noon day soup is nothing more than discoloured water which sometimes comes in under the honoured name of pea soup. Corporal Sims was one of the lucky ones to receive a personal parcel today and he traded his last five-cent chocolate bar for a bread ration. A copy of a recent B.B.C. news broadcast has found its way into camp and is going the rounds; it's all good news. The 50¢ a day raise for Canucks overseas seems to be partially confirmed, also rumour going around that we are to receive 25¢ a day as hardship compensation while we are chained.

JAN. 21, THURS.

Nothing much happened during the last 3 days except that we received ½ a Red Cross parcel each on Tuesday. Personal parcels are coming in from Canada, the number per day per hut averaging 3. Had a smoke of Canadian tobacco rolled in a Vogue paper that Scotty Law gave me. There is a persistent rumour that Italy is in a bad way and has even capitulated which is being accepted with a large grain of salt. Another rumour is that Berlin is being bombed incessantly by daylight. Pre-Xmas news was more or less confirmed when a Sgt. Major came through just before roll-call and read it out. It included items such as the fall of Tobruk and a giant pincer movement by Br. and the Caucuses. 25,000 prisoners taken in Africa. Heavy bombing of Italy, especially Genoa. Everyone is hopefully looking to spring. The camp paper mentions a Canadian contingent landing in North Africa, thereby confirming a rumour previously mentioned. Weather is fairly warm; rained and froze yesterday. Fellows returning from parcel parades claim the post office is packed with parcels waiting to be sorted. As far as we have noticed almost everything is coming through without much trouble. The post office has been notified that parcels mentioned on cards from the people of Canada are on their way from Geneva. No letters from home yet. Today is Connie's and Nelle's birthday; Janet's tomorrow, mine the next day.

JAN. 23, SAT.

What a place to have a birthday in, especially a 30th birthday. Since the reading of the news the other day rumours are scarce; genuine news is sure cure for rumours. Laundered my clothes today and nearly froze my hands. Received a letter from Rusty today in which she said Jack was trying for leave on the 23rd Dec. so that he could spend Xmas at Southend; the lucky stiff. Apparently he didn't go to Africa after all. Wrote to Anne, Peggy and Alf today. It has been warm and muddy out these days. Kitchen and Guy still go to bed fully dressed as they have been doing all winter. No one can remember seeing them washing clothes this winter. The only time they have taken their trousers off is when we go on bath parade (once in two weeks if we are lucky) or medical (louse hunt) inspection once a month. Having extreme difficulty following trig and algebra at school.

We received a printed letter to send to next of kin, listing articles on the "verboten" list such as radio sets, radiators, firearms, ammunition, blank paper, potatoes, etc. This goes into effect on March 1st. Used the last of our milk and sugar for supper tonight so will have to drink our tea straight for a few days. Eric was summoned before the German M.O. yesterday in connection with war wounds; they must have been some mistake because he was not wounded on the raid. The possibility of our being taken out of here by air after the war is coming in for considerable discussion recently. Now that I am thirty years old, three whole years being wasted in the army, I can't afford to waste any time when I get home.

JAN. 26, TUES.

Cold yesterday and today. War news appears to be all good these days; the Russians do a real job on the eastern front; 6th army corps taking part.

General Rommel has been captured in Africa (am inclined to disbelieve this.) The parcel situation and the method of distribution is undergoing drastic changes since the incoming Canadian parcel swelled the influx. News of the Canadian Xmas comfort parcels is good too, the Sgt. Major announcing that they would be issued next week sometime. Eric has gone to concert in 21B so I have to prepare a German soup powder and put two puddings in the oven. We traded one of our cans of jam for a meat roll today. The boys are really hugging the stove tonight; it's very frosty with a south-west wind. Five or six personal parcel chits today. I thought he said Lodge for the first one but turned out to be White. Where the resemblance between the two names is, I don't know.

JAN. 28, THURS.

The Hun took us by surprise this morning when we had to stand out from roll call 9:00A.M. (2 hours and ten minutes) while a fairly extensive search was conducted for secreted radios, tunnels, etc. Our tea was almost cold by the time they had searched to their satisfaction. They failed to find anything. The M. & N. soup was postponed until Saturday because there wasn't time to prepare it. The Canadian comfort parcels are a topic of numerous controversial discussions, contents and issuing being the salient points. They are said to contain a roll-neck sweater, 3 pairs of socks, 10 pkg. gum, 300 cigs, a shaving kit, toothbrush and powder. It is rumoured or wishfully thought that they also contain a towel and some chocolate. They are evidently holding up the sorting and censoring of personal parcels. I hope someone thought to put plenty of chocolate in my personal parcel. Eric and I want to try Scotch haggis and black pudding in Scotland before we go home.

The news from the Russian front remains good. Weather variable; frost night before last, snow yesterday, rain last night, thawing tonight with a threat of rain. "Spitfire" is back. Rumoured that 1,000 Germans killed in riots in Marseilles.

JAN. 30, SAT.

M. & N. for dinner today. Everyone is wondering who forgot to turn the water off and where the M.& N. came in. Probably we will be able to buy a can or so later on, from the rackets. Chains off for half a day, today. Rumoured today that British and American forces have sailed through the Dardanelles into the Black Sea. Also that British troops have landed at four points on the French coast. Hitler and Ribbentrop reported to have made speeches. Comfort parcel issuing postponed until Monday. Rumoured that we get Canadian Red Cross food parcels next week instead of bulk. To make it more unbelievable we are supposed to receive a full parcel per man. It will probably be bulk again and in less quantity than last week. It is believed that we are supposed to receive a full parcel or its equivalent in bulk every week.

The method of cooking is becoming extremely complicated these days. The main cooking is done in two shifts from 2:00P.M. to roll-call and from roll-call to 6:30P.M. This is for reheating of spuds, meats, puddings, etc., in which the oven is used, a fireman or two being appointed to keep the fire going. At one time it was strictly taboo, in the interest of hot suppers, to boil pots in the fire-box, but now it is done by sections, using the three-pot-a-section idea. Then someone started making toast in the afternoon so that too is done in sections, each man being allowed to toast 2 slices of bread.

With the arrival of Canadian cigarette parcels a loaf of bread has jumped to 500 cigarettes; one man's day ration is 50. Finished "Oliver Twist" today and am reading "Ye Olde Curiosity Shoppe." The weather remains fairly warm, consequently there is plenty of mud outside and inside. Arguing goes on unabated all day and evening, around the stove.

FEB. 1

A day of good news and rumours. Stanford Cripps is supposed to have said that the war will be over before some people think. Another interesting item, true or not, is that an American naval force encountered and sunk nearly all of a large Japanese naval force (supposed to be B.B.C. news). The rumours are equally good, such as Italy is asking for peace and is being bombed heavily. Eight British landings from Narvik to Dieppe. Dieppe bombed for 15 hours. Hitler putting out peace feelers and threatens to use gas in Russia. The Russians are half way across Finland and going strong. The fact that both news and rumours, no matter how far-fetched, is all good these days, plenty of reason for optimism. There is a decided change in the attitude of our German guards; they are less inclined to treat us rough and they try to be friendly. Reports coming in from "outside" say the civilians are saying, "Deutschland Kaput." Most of us received our comfort parcel which contained 1 turtle-necked sweater, 3 pairs of heavy socks, 1 pair gloves, 3 hankies, a Gillette razor with ten blades, a shaving brush, one toothbrush and one small can of Idol tooth powder, 300 cigs, 2 bars of face soap, ten small pkgs of Beechnut Chiclets, one hold-all bag and last but not least a roll of toilette paper. It was announced today that we would receive ¼ British R.C. food parcel on Tuesday, and ¼ Canadian R.C. parcel on Friday. Failing the Friday parcel we would receive bulk equivalent of ¼ parcel. It is very difficult to cut a parcel four ways so Eric and I cut cards with Dawson and Bartlett for Tuesday's parcel. They won so we have to wait until Friday for our ½ parcel. Cliff Dawson has written home on four different occasions telling them not to send parcels but he was the only one to receive a personal parcel notice this evening. We received a pretty fair German issue of rations today beginning with thick pea soup at noon, followed by liverwurst, marg., salt and treacle (made from sugar-beets we hope.) There is no doubt that the German attitude is steadily changing, I think they are beginning to see the way of things.

FEB. 2, TUES.

Eric and I have to get along on German rations until Friday and are we getting hungry. The other ¼ of a parcel may come in on Thursday instead of Friday (we hope). Dawson gave me a piece of Canadian chocolate and I didn't realize Canadian chocolate tasted so good. There was only two parcel chits in this P.M. but quite a few letters. May get something sooner or later. Would like a good newsy letter from home. Eric received a letter from the platoon and they sent all his snaps home for him. I hope someone is taking care of mine. Rusty says that Jack spent Xmas with Aunt Pat and apparently enjoyed himself. Roy is gone or is going back to Canada for special training; I hope he makes it okay.

Rumours tonight: German occupational troops in Greece and Crete all prepared to evacuate. The Russians are so far into Finland the country is disorganized. The German women and young women are going up to the Russian front to take care of the wounded. There is a report going around tonight that 14 guards went A.W.O. "loss" today. A guard caught me taking my chains off tonight and thought it a great joke. There is only six weeks for my March 17th prediction to come true, so come on Russians. Scotty Law received his second cig. Parcel notice this evening; some have received their third. I wonder if the folks back home are writing.

FEB. 3, WED.

The blight of our present existence today was "Spitfire" our Mongolian looking diminutive compound "fuehrer." He has been stamping, raving and threatening all day long until everyone fervently wishes him sent to the most active part of the Russian front.

The coal ration was cut in half today, probably because it has been mild recently. Rumours are coming in so fast it is almost impossible to keep track of them. Those for tonight are: Finland has quit; Hungary has refused to fight anymore and the 11th German army is in a precarious position around Rostov, their lines of communication have been cut; half a million casualties at Stalingrad; Churchill is in Turkey. That last one is a little hard to consider. Have read "Oliver Twist" and "Treasure Island" in the last couple of days and am reading the "Jovial Ghosts," a Topper series. Breakfast will be 1 slice of bread with grease and salt and a cup of "Limey" tea from the kitchen. We will have fish for Friday supper, anyway. The air force have started the ball rolling toward cleaning up some of these rackets; it's getting bad when we have to buy our own rations. Disorder in the mail department resulted in no mail today.

FEB. 4, THURS.

The grease and bread breakfast wasn't so good this morning. It's been a day of good news and good rumours, beginning with a hot one this P.M., to the effect that the Red Cross issue tomorrow would be a parcel to two men and tonight it was officially announced by the ration corporal so Eric and I receive ¾ of a parcel (Cdn.) apiece. After barely existing on German rations for four days this is really going to be a treat. We also received 15 extra Turkish cigs. This evening. Handed my name in because I hadn't heard from home yet.

They are investigating all such cases to make sure the next of kin have been properly informed.

The Air Force sure blew the lid off when they started inquiries into Red Cross personnel activities. It was learned today that this is the only camp in Germany that hasn't received a full parcel per week per man. A rumour came around today that Turkey had entered the war at ten this morning and British and American troops are already in that country ready for a push north. By six this evening it was reported as confirmed, but later some fellows came back from the rackets and said it wasn't sure news but the rumour is plenty strong. Needless to say, we all hope it's true. Hitler is supposed to have ordered his S.S. troops to shoot anyone talking for capitulation. Everyone thinks the war will be over by June. It is going to be a good day for rations tomorrow. Besides our regular issue of spuds we will get a ration of mashed spuds instead of soup, followed closely by porridge or semolina with bread soup around 4 o'clock besides ¾ of a food parcel each.

FEB. 6, SAT.

Yesterday was parcel day; after many anxious hours we finally were issued with the long looked for grub. We were supposed to get them immediately following a special blanket inspection parade at nine but the issue was unexplainably cancelled; then we were supposed to get them at 11 o'clock and this time the boys were actually in the Red Cross premises when they were again cancelled, with no excuse given. By this time most of us had a few more gray hairs. Three o'clock was then set for the time so when I returned from my electrical class at 3:45, I was just in time to split the third parcel, Eric and I receiving 1½ parcels. Apparently there is some mix-up regarding the issuing of parcels to working parties. From what I understand parcels have been sent to these parties and word has come back that they haven't arrived; some are inclined to think they have been rerouted to the Russian front. Also heard that there is 17½ parcels per man unaccounted for this winter. They are still coming to us but where are they? Perhaps certain Red Cross personnel could enlighten us. Also understand that parcels have been pilfered off of the truck between the station and the camp.

This is my lucky day, I received 2 letters from Rusty, 2 from Rose and 1 from Aunt Pat. None from home yet. Eric and I had a swell supper last night. A tin of mashed spuds, ½ can of salmon, ½ slice of bread and butter, 2 slices of bread and cheese, 1 ½ big Canadian hardtack biscuits and jam, ½ chocolate bar and a cup of coffee. This evening we had a tin of mashed spuds, ½ roll of "Spork," a pudding of raisins and biscuits with thick Klim sauce, 1 slice bread and butter, two slices bread and jam, and a cup of tea. It was announced this evening that we will receive ¾ parcel each next week. We are to be allowed to attend the proper church tomorrow for the first time since we were tied.

FEB. 7, SUN.

Started work on the carving of a pencil box today and whiled away a few hours. Eric received a parcel chit this afternoon which he goes down for tomorrow morning. He says he will give me the harmonica if he gets one. He also said he would give me a towel if he got two and some chocolate if he got any. I will, of course return the kindness if and when my parcel comes. Because of the short time we are allowed to make a brew, a new method for coffee has to be found so I am experimenting by soaking three spoonfuls of coffee so that the grounds will be soft before we start boiling them. We brew tea by using two tea bags for two brews each, then boiling the leaves for the third brew. The klim we get in the C.R.C. parcels make swell thick cream for our Stalag puddings besides for our tea and coffee. Eric and I won the German issue of sausage. The issue is supposed to be for ten men but wouldn't be considered sufficient for one man under other conditions.

The B.B.C. news is being read out in one of the huts, it dates back 20 days or so and includes: Russians closing in on Kharkow or Karkov; the landing of a German force in Tunisia in an endeavour to stem the retreat there; complete recapture of New Guinea. Heard yesterday that the German population expects the war to be over by June with Germany "kaput". The ration corporal announced tonight that there will be ¼ parcel per man on Friday and ½ Canadian parcel on Tuesday. This will be the issue per week for the next four weeks. Wrote a letter to Nelle this evening. Four months tomorrow since we were tied.

FEB. 8, MON.

Somewhat of a hectic day. Eric received a very nice parcel in which was included a patent can-opener, he turned the opener and the mouth-organ over to me. Can openers have a disconcerting habit of disappearing around here. We had a fairly good supper of buttered mashed spuds, flavoured with German sausage, a big Stalag pudding served with sauce made from klim mixed with German treacle and plum jam, a piece of bread and butter, 1 slice of bread and jam and a cup of tea. Received my first letter from home, it being the fourth one Nelle had written; the whereabouts of the first three is a big mystery. Received another one from Rusty again today. Expecting to hit a parcel soon. The ration corporal came in and announced the issue for this week will be 1¼ parcels per man, one on Tuesday and a ¼ on Friday. Also forty cigarettes on Saturday. Evidently we are to receive the extra ¼ parcel per week until we have received those that we were supposed to have received during the past months. We will eventually settle down to a steady issue per week, but while this present situation exists we will be eating pretty good. We will be having bigger and better Stalag puddings and we will get ahead on our tea, butter, etc. The only difficulty now seems to be the fuel shortage. The coal ration has been cut in half with the expressed possibility of it being stopped entirely on March 1ˢᵗ.

FEB. 11, THURS.

Three days during which I have received letters from Anne, Rusty, Harry and Bezzie and another from Nelle, evidently her third. According to this letter, the old house is undergoing repairs and renovation. According to other news received, Red Rankine couldn't have got back; Roy was married at the end of January and they are expecting him home soon. Apparently Murph is away from home, whether working or in the army isn't clear. Can't place cousin Reg, mentioned in all letters, either. Rusty hasn't arrived yet. Giving up expecting a parcel from home as Nelle didn't mention it in either of her letters. Should be receiving a letter from Reg soon in which I hope to hear about the rest of the fellows who came on the raid.

War rumours today include the recapture of Rostov and Kharkov and Brynsk, with the Russians still pushing ahead. Reported opinions of posterns hereabouts and elsewhere is that the war will be over by March and that we will be home some five months later. I hope they are right. More local news is that all bully beef will be extracted from the Canadian parcels, by German order. We are of the opinion that it's a move on certain fellow prisoners in responsible positions part to account for a deficiency of this commodity in the store records. Had an accident this morning; change of grub probably.

Tomorrow we get ¾ parcel apiece minus the bully beef; ¾ ounce of good Canadian chocolate to chew on. I had a Sweet Marie bar yesterday. Had a fairly good supper of mashed spuds and salmon with a hefty slice of bread and German fish-cheese, followed by a swell prune pudding liberally doused with klim milk and raspberry jam sauce. This was followed an hour later by ½ slice of bread and jam and tea. We have a pudding with klim sauce every night now.

Due to coal shortage it has been found necessary to cut the section's tea brewing down to 2 pots for ten men and we had a little difficulty re-arranging things so that it would be fair to all. We divided the section up into five sub sections of two men each, one group drops out each brew, leaving 8 men for the two pots. When three pots are allowed, four men (determined by cutting cards) go on one pot and three men for each of the other two. Finished the first half of my pencil box today.

FEB. 13, SAT.

Yesterday was parcel day with the usual hustle and bustle usually connected with this event, and to add to the bedlam, bread soup and porridge came up just about the same time, near roll-call. We received ¾ of a 5oz. Lowney's pure milk chocolate before roll-call. We received ¾ of a parcel minus the bully beef, consequently, I had one ration of porridge, one of bread soup (eaten in between the dividing of the klim and tea), ¾ of a 5oz. Lowney's pure milk chocolate before roll-call. Immediately after roll-call, as per usual, there was a tinful of mashed spuds and bully beef, ½ a klim tinful of Stalag pudding, 1 thick slice of bread and butter, followed ½ hour later with 2 slices of bread and jam and a cup of tea.

The excuse for extracting the bully beef from yesterday's parcels was given that it was a German order, but general belief is it was to make up a shortage in the R.C. books. In fact a rumour of the rations for next week tends to confirm this belief as we are receiving the parcels with bully beef intact. Each Canadian food parcel has a card in them which is supposed to be filled in and signed by the person receiving it, remarking on the condition of the contents. So we filled our cards out to the effect that there was a can of bully beef extracted. Whether the cards were sent to the Canadian Red Cross we have no way of knowing, but we have grave doubts.

The Jerries freed us for the afternoon and opened the compound gates besides so Eric and I went visiting over to 7-10 compound. The full parcel and bully beef rumour is strong tonight. "Spitfire", in a streak of mysterious generosity, said we could have as many fires as we liked so long as we didn't burn bedboards. (My kingdom for some glue.)

A queer thing happened today when a German guard saw his brother as a prisoner-of-war in the Air Force compound. The prisoner was a parachutist taken during a raid on Genoa. It's said around gossip circles that the commandant has a son in the British Navy.

It is rumoured this evening that Count Ciana and the royal Italian family are in England pending the capitulation of Italy. I wonder if "Spitfire" will notice his depleted coal bin in the morning. There was no guards on today and when Spitfire left the compound on business, our coal supply mysteriously grew in the next half an hour. There is no doubt that the Jerry attitude is becoming gentle and in some cases actually friendly. One gentle old hard boiled Sgt. Major used to bellow and banish his revolver at the least excuse but lately he has been all smiles and soft words. No mail for the last two days.

FEB. 15, MON.

The main Red Cross stores are being moved outside of camp; the camp being issued with supplies in the same manner as any other working party or group. In this way we won't have to go short if there is any mistakes in the quantity, like we have been doing, viz: the bully beef. We have been having quite a time with check parades, etc. but were consoled with the realization that tomorrow is parcel day again, ½ parcel per man.

The war rumours are plentiful today and include: Turkey entered the war on the 8th for certain; Rostov and Kharkov was as disastrous as Stalingrad to the Germans; Churchill tendered ultimatum to Hitler for unconditional surrender; Franco of Spain was at the Casa Blanca conference; 3,000 plane bombing raids made on German cities, nightly, and Britain and America can finish this war in three weeks if they have to. This news was supposed to have been brought in by a new bunch of Air Force fellows. Mail isn't coming in so good these days. Have been trying to imagine the changes Dad has made on the old kitchen but all I can see is a wall-boarded interior. Still waiting for letters from Bobbie, Reg, Jack, Iris, Marc and a few others. Have been trying to buy a pipe for cigarettes but the fellows receiving them in clothing parcels are hanging on to them. Since the arrival of Canadian cig. parcels the price per loaf of bread has jumped to 300 and 500 cigarettes, one man's ration for 80; 150 cigs. for a can of bully; 20 for a 2oz. can of cheese; 5oz. bar of Canadian chocolate for 80 cigs. Ernie Jones from Keewatin received a clothing parcel from home the other day.

FEB. 18, THURS.

Rumours regarding the fall of Rostov still strong; may be something in it after all. Was informed on returning from school at noon, that I was wanted by the "Limey" M.O. for a medical examination and began wondering if I was "looking" sick. Major MacLeod, head of the hospital had received a letter from Geneva asking him to inquire into my health as someone was making inquiries into why I hadn't received an embroidery parcel. After a few pointed questions regarding my health and letter writing habits he said he would inform Geneva that I was in good health but had not received the parcel as yet. Very little mail this last week; none at all for me. This evening there were about fifteen parcel notices came in but none for me.

A recently shot down airman, who claims he was in Canada three weeks ago, asserts that the (our) next of kin have been advised not to send any more parcels to men overseas or P.O.W.'s after March. And the British have a pursuit plane with a top speed of 700 miles an hour and a cruising speed

419

of 500. Instead of parcels next week we are getting bulk supposedly equivalent to a parcel in weight, per man. So far the bulk weight has always been considerably less than parcel weight. Eric and I are trading one of our bars of chocolate to Ernie Jones for his bully. Fairly busy day today, put a new handle on my mess tin, drew a Cameron badge for Eric and did my laundry (nearly froze).

Cripps is supposed to be in Switzerland at a peace conference; 3,500 British troops are supposed to have landed in Norway, and Germany has evacuated Holland.

FEB. 21, SUN.

Rumours have been coming in in great style recently and include the fall of Kiev and the Polish border being reached. The Norway rumour is dying down but we are still hopeful. Received two pleasant surprises in the mail yesterday; one from Iris (it's good to see her perfect handwriting again) and a 25 line card from Violet here in Germany. Iris said that Nelle had written to her and sent a copy of my first letter to reach home. The post office is swamped with Canadian mail and the mail staff seems incapable of coping with the situation. Yesterday they handed 500 cigarette parcels alone to Canadians, mostly 1,000 cig. Cartons. There is also 1,500 more comfort parcels in from Canada house and the possible contents is thought to be: (1) 1,000 cigs, (2) pajamas, pullover, socks, handkerchiefs, etc., and (3) the same as our last parcels. Whatever is in them they are supposed to be issued this coming week. Yesterday, to foil the Germans order to send all bully beef to the kitchen next week, we were issued with a can apiece.

Some of the fellows have received four personal parcels in a row while others, like myself, haven't even received a mention of one. Also received another letter from Peggy the day before yesterday. Eric is sitting across from me now, stoning and cutting up prunes for tomorrow's Stalag pudding and the usual hum and noise of the room continues unabated. Eric and I finally arrived at the conclusion that a haircut was essential so on the pretense of going to church we managed to get out of the compound, took our chains off and found ourselves a barber in the "Repat" compound. Then we rejoined the homing church parade and had no trouble getting back in again. Tried to manufacture a pair of small hinges out of band iron for my pencil box but the material was too heavy for the tools, a jack knife and a piece of iron bar. Have read "Conflict," "The Death Ship," "Traplines North," (a very good book) and am reading "Tiger Snake" and another one called "Murder at Swathling Court," with another one waiting called "North of The Stars" by Stoddard. Will be answering Nelle's two letters this evening. New rumour this evening: 30,000 troops made a landing in Norway, fairly heavy casualties, reinforced and Union Jack raised. (Hard to believe.)

FEB. 23, TUES.

Yesterday we were issued with 50 cigarettes and 1/10 tin of tobacco per man. A very nice day something like late spring back home and the same today. Issued with 1 tin of jam, 1 tin of marg., 32 soda biscuits, 6 oz. of sugar per man today. The ration corporal announced that there would be 1 British Red Cross per man next week. The contents of the 1,500 comfort parcels are one bath towel, 1 suit of underwear, 1 chocolate bar, 1 muffler, 3 pr. of socks, 1 roll neck sweater, 1 pr. of gloves and a Red Cross grab bag, similar to the one in the other parcel and a suit of pajamas. Canadian senior officer suggest that 125 men volunteer their parcels to Canadian Airmen who failed to receive a parcel last time. Unsettled as yet. It's being suggested that each section volunteer one parcel and the other nine men make it up to him.

Rumours tonight are that Churchill is ill. There is a report going around that one darn fool Canadian gave 1,200 cigarettes for a loaf of bread. Put the hinges on my pencil box which seem to interest a German postern very much. Eric almost finished his badge today. Received a letter from Jack Fisher and learned that Bill Rankine, Kutch, Tully and Stewie didn't get back. It surprises me that Comack and Skip got back. Bobby Grant got back although he was badly wounded, but is doing well. Reg is getting himself hooked to a blonde; I presume it is Ellen.

FEB. 27, SAT.

The last four days have been filled with great events and marked with good news and rumours. On Wednesday evening I received the long awaited clothing parcel notice and it wasn't until late Thursday afternoon that it was settled if it was the embroidery parcel or a next of kin parcel. It was the personal parcel, however, and contained two suits of winter combinations, a blue cable knit sweater, a sleeveless roll neck sweater, two pr. of socks, two sticks shaving soap, 15 razor blades, 1 lb can of Red Rose Coffee, a quantity of sugar was an unexpected pleasant surprise, probably one of the first lot of coffee and sugar to be received in personal parcels. The lighter was "verboten" and confiscated and the flints being useless without the lighter, so the Jerry reasoned were also kept. The underwear is something worth having. Thus, I had a good feed of nuts and chocolate, thus satisfying a craving for nuts I have been holding in check for months. Shared the gum and chocolate with Eric and got our fill of it, too for a few hours. The 1 lb. bar of Fry's we thought was cooking chocolate but on Friday we tried making a drink out of it, failed miserably so ate the rest of it like any other chocolate bar. I don't know how many bars was in the parcel as the censor broke everyone into two or more pieces. The sugar and coffee filled a beverage vacancy in our grub box and the edibles were duly divided 50-50 between us. On Thurs. evening I received two notices for cigarette parcels, one a thousand Sweet Caps from Nelle and 300 Exports from Harry. So I am taking my smoking off of the self-imposed ration list. There is a semi-confirmed rumour going around that there is ten lb. food parcels from Eaton's and a 2 lb. box of Laura Secord chocolate coming in for every Canadian.

The new batch of comfort parcels are in but the Germans say that each man will go down and take out what he really needs. The pullovers, socks, etc. will go to the quarter stores. Everyone will take all they can such as pajamas, towels, razors, eatables, etc. Again we think the Limey's are behind all the trouble. If I can find a soap dish I will get a metal Cameron badge made. Eric got three more cig. parcel notices this evening. Received letters from Jack Fisher containing first news of Bill Kutch, Stewie and Tully, also a letter from Messel who says he is taking care of all my personal stuff.

The Norway affair is supposed to be confirmed as is Churchill's illness and Eden acting Prime Minister. Today the Russians are reported 80 km. west of Kiev. The camp is swamped with Canadian cigs. now and their value as a trading medium has dropped considerably; 100 for a can of jam; 250 or 275 for a can of bully; one man reported to have given 1,200 cigs. for a loaf of black bread. My math, instructor advised me to apply for personal instruction in algebra.

Next week we get an English Red Cross parcel apiece, with no mention as yet about the M.N. coming out. Softball equipment is arriving in increasing volume now and plans for teams and leagues are getting underway. We had a swell cup of coffee this evening from the Red Rose supply; there is no comparison with ground coffee from the parcels which lose its flavour en route.

MARCH 1, MON.
There was over 3,000 cig. notices handed out on Saturday, to be collected this morning. 22B had to stand out an hour yesterday morning because they refused to carry the chains to the guard room Saturday noon. There were so many going down for cig. parcels this A.M. they were forced to close the school. M. & N. will be taken out of the parcels this week and sent to the kitchen. Eric received 310 cigs and a lb. of fine cut. A Red Cross representative is investigating the comforts parcel situation. An idea is circulating that if we refused to accept the depleted parcels they will be returned to Geneva, thus starting an investigation from that end. The Eaton food parcel and Secord chocolates are said to be at base post office waiting for room in the camp post office. Apparently our next of kin can send food parcels now, I hope Nelle is wise to the fact, although the coffee and sugar in the last one indicates that she is. Bobby Bartholomew loaned me a corn cob pipe (slightly used) until I could find one.

MARCH 3, WED.
We were issued with a British R.C. food parcel yesterday between 2 men; the other 1/2 comes Thursday. The second comforts parcel is hanging fire temporarily. There is a rumour that the rumoured food parcels will go to the hospital. Applied for personal tuition in Algebra and start tomorrow morning. We had quite a time with "Spitfire" and mess tin inspection, this evening. Some of the fellows thought they could get away with not having the articles in question on parade; consequently, they stood out for an hour. The nickname "Spitfire" fits him like a glove. Made a six inch ruler for my pencil-box. Received letters from Nelle and one from Peggy this evening;

Nelle's was dated October 19 and November 20. News therefore being irregular and spasmodic, more disjointed. Peggy has sent the embroidering parcel and is asking me to state any other articles I want. Algebra and trig text books are the present pressing requirements. There is a lull in the way rumours and news which usually means something big will break soon. Real March winds with a smattering of snow. Went for a shower yesterday afternoon and donned my new underwear. Very nice.

MARCH 5, FRI.
We received the other 1/2 of the parcel yesterday; we hit it lucky by getting 3 tins of meat. Received another 300 cigs. from Nelle this morning. Bought a good pipe for 150 cigs. yesterday from a fellow in Convalescent. Nearly got a book on Algebra as well but my negotiator was too late. Bill Robertson brought my metal Cameron badge around to me yesterday; it will have a high souvenir value after the war being made from two Polish coat buttons and a bowl of a spoon we were using in the French Camp at Vernville. Made a potato masher today. School was closed again today because of the issuing of personal cig. parcels. Received two more letters from Nelle this afternoon. Apparently the kitchen has undergone great changes recently.

MARCH 7, SUN.
It is rumoured that we may receive our Canada House comforts parcels on Tuesday, minus a few articles. The missing articles is causing many heated debates. The towel, pajamas, and chocolate is all I really need. A new game was introduced last night called "horse racing" with cigs. as stakes. It requires four tables to accommodate the game.

It is rumoured around that Tunis (consequently the African Campaign) is definitely cleared up with 160,000 German prisoners, 60,000 Italian and 25 Generals. Today we had another cigarette collection for recently shot down airmen who claim or verify the landing at Odessa and the fall of Kiev. Finished the pencil box yesterday and started a photo frame. Finished reading "Tiger Snake" and am reading two books called, "The Blood Eagle" and "Little Red Foot."

There is supposed to have been an 80 hour bombing of the French coast and northern Germany. 80 hours seems to be a long time for one bombing spree. Some impossible members of our little community; those who whistle and sing while washing clothes in ice cold water in a frigid room; those who think they can play the accordion and trumpet and persist in demonstrating; those who eat their rations as they come, then wander around at meal-times watching other people eat with a longing hungry look; Beer, the barrack room nit-wit; Rocky who tries to be witty, comical and serious all at one time; the "Brains Trust", a body of brighter minded people (or so they thing) who when not losing their cigs at craps or poker, are arguing about something none of them know anything about and settling nothing; Little, the person everyone agrees is slightly "teched" which incidentally dates further back than the battle of Dieppe. ("Tea at the gate" is the yell, so guess I had better get lunch ready.)

LATER: A rumour going around that Allied troops are landing by thousands at Dieppe. This is supposed to have been confidentially imparted to a veteran P.O.W. by a German officer.

A Canadian "flat-foot" came into the hut today claiming that the Canadian senior officer received a letter stating that a ten pound Eaton food parcel and 3 lb. Laura Secord chocolates have been sent to each Canadian. Also rumoured that C.H. comfort parcels will be issued tomorrow. Wrote to Iris this evening.

MARCH 9, TUES.
Caught cold yesterday; am feeling tough today. Consoled by receiving six letters, one from Marcelle (the first) and the rest from Nelle. Nelle's dated all the way from October 10 to December and contained a fair quantity of news. For instance, I know for sure what happened to Rod, and that Bill, Kutch, Stewie and Tully failed to return; Reg is sporting 3 hooks; Dawn is over the St. Vitus Dance; young Murph is in the army; the kitchen is remodeled and papered, with cream woodwork and furniture. Doug, Roy and Jack have seen one another. Marce felt pretty bad about my being missing which only increases my egotism. No mail for me today. "Spitfire" is back and raising a new brand of hell but with a smile on his Mongolian paw.

We were issued with 2oz. of cheese, a package of raisins, 4oz. of damp sugar and a can of salmon from the Red Cross today. Russians are reported to be still advancing; the inter-compound move is finally completed with no changes in hut personnel. Tomorrow we draw what is left of the comforts parcels including about 2 1/2 lb. of chocolate. Ran out of milk today and will have to drink our beverages straight until we are issued with more on Friday. Wrestling with the problem of how to obtain the jam and bread ration necessary for having a Balmoral crocheted. Finished the "Blood Eagle."

MARCH 12, FRI.

We drew our depleted Canada House parcels, the remaining contents included 1 suit of pajamas, a bath towel, one face towel, a balaclava, 1 scarf, a hod-all bag containing 1 razor, 1 toothbrush, 1 shaving brush, 1 hair brush, 1 comb, three hankies, a face cloth, 1 can of tooth powder, 1 stick of shaving soap, 2 bars of face soap, 12 pkgs. of Chiclets and 1/2 lb. bar of chocolate. Received another letter each from Harry and Rose and two from Nelle this evening. I should sort them all out according to dates mailed. Went to the medical orderly for cold remedy but he said all they had was aspirins and they were right out. It is rumoured that Munich is leveled by a 24 hour machine gun and bombing raid. The German papers are yelling Barbarians, murders, etc. Essen and Nuremberg also hard hit. Men from Polish working parties say 6 weeks; I hope they are right.

MARCH 15, MON.

The weekend was very quiet and both in local events and war rumours. Mail from home has fallen off considerably. Parcels this week again. I am dickering with Eanis Jones for a trade for 1/2 a bar for his bread ration so that I can get a Balmoral made. Received two more letters dated Dec. 12 and 15 from Nelle; one contained quite a lot of news and the other three swell snaps of Murph and the Four Steps. Surprised at the way Murph has grown.

A new batch of captured airmen came in today and claim that the Russians are still doing well and the second front is expected to start in a few weeks. They say the British bombing raids are continuing unabated. Went for a bath today; we had to take our own chains off because the guard room was locked up. Tip Holland wanted to send a fruit cake and cigarettes. Evenings spent in wrestling with the mysteries of Algebra and am gaining a small degree of success.

MARCH 18, THURS.

Well the 17th has come and gone and the war continues. I have received letters from Nelle, Jack, Olga, Harry, Peggy and Rusty. Have received 12 snaps from Nelle, to date. Have framed the one of the "Four Steps," Dad, Harry and Holly and one of Holly herself. See great change in all of them. Also received a letter from Iris, she is sending a snap in her next letter.

This being parcel day the rumours are plentiful and a little wild. The Russians are being pushed back; the Russians have taken Karkov again, 17,000 Germans have landed in England, mostly dead, the second front has started, so considering them all, there are rumours for the pessimist and optimist alike. regarding the second front rumour, there seems to be a general opinion that there is some truth in it. It is supposed to have started in Holland; the numerous fighter planes that have been splitting the breeze thereabouts presumably have moved to some active front. A German postern is supposed to have said that the war will be over by the end of this month with Germany "kaput." On Sunday the convalescent, camp police, medical men will be allowed outside the camp for exercise and a change of scenery. Next week we are supposed to start compulsory P.T. and route marches outside the camp. Incoming work-parties say the 2nd front has started in Holland. We have been hearing vague rumours of large troop movements in England all week.

Rusty says that Vi may be going home soon; she didn't say if it was a repatriation scheme or not. Sold a 1/2 bar of chocolate for a bread ration and had a Balmoral made. Our guards have dwindled from two well-armed able-bodied soldiers we had at first in each hut to one old banged up has-been with a rifle of uncertain vintage for two compounds. Chains come off and on just whenever we really feel like it. I personally believe that the war is entering its final stages.

MARCH 21, SUN.

First day of spring. Received letters from Aunt Pat and Rusty yesterday; didn't do much else but study Algebra and reviewing my electrical notes. Rusty and Aunt Pat are justly excited at the prospect of Vi going home. Some of the fellows are receiving their 2nd personal parcels that were mailed in January; I wonder if mine are here yet. Made a passable ruler out of a piece of oak found in the shaving box. Finished reading "Little Red Foot," and "The King's Enemies." Started the "Traitors Gate." Wrote to Nelle this evening and answered 19 letters. Missed my hour of personal Algebra instruction and math class Friday morning because of delousing parade. 20A (our hut) whipped 20B in softball this afternoon by a score of 24-5. No news or rumours these days; people back home seem to favour June as the month of armistice. I have stopped predicting. Sinclair went to the hospital with a sore throat and a fever, being replaced in the section by an F.M.R. named Ladauceur. God, I would like to sit down to eat with an unlimited supply in front of me. The necessity of saving a slice of bread and a lump of sugar for my next meal is getting me down. Oh! for the day when we can go where, when and how we please. It looks like I will have to look around for another book for this diary.

MARCH 26, FRI.

There isn't much to write about recently; the old war rumours and the fact that I have received three smoke parcels in four days. 1,000 from Bob and Harry Gibson, 300 from Cameron's Women Auxiliary and 1lb. of fine cut from Dad. Dad's came today, Bob's and Harry's the day before yesterday and the auxiliary's the day before that. Trading value of cigs. continues to decrease slowly but steadily. Framed Dad's photo in the existing Stalag manner, Murph's and Holly's in a circular wooden frame. Have been studying Algebra so much lately I hopelessly despair of even bringing order out of the general chaos in my mind; y's, x's, x~, etc. are jumbled up hopelessly.

The rumours are, on the whole, repetition of previous ones such as Kharkov being in Russian hands, Kharkov surrounded and Tunis cleaned up for the third or fourth time. On the whole, consensus of opinion in our little barb-wire community is perhaps just a trifle more pessimistic these days than formerly. Popular estimation for the end of the war is 18 months; I still expect to spend this coming Xmas at home. Saw a fellow received a Canadian Legion course through the mail, the lucky stiff. I hope the books I sent for will soon arrive. The personal Algebra tuition sessions are becoming embarrassing and emphasize my Algebraic ignorance and the math class is just a bi-weekly nightmare. (Am holding my own in electrical engineering.) although a couple or three good books would be a God-send. Finished reading the "King's Enemies" and the "Traitor's Gate" and am wading through the "Man Who didn't Answer." Looking around for a pkg. pipe tobacco.

MARCH 28, SUN.

It's been pretty quiet in the rumour line these last few days despite the fact that another batch of "winged" airmen came in besides a large group of men from a camp near Munich. Finished reading "The Man Who Didn't Answer" and started "The Crimson Clown" and started and finished a book called "Unlawful Range" this morning. Carved a wooden identity disc for Cliff Dawson today. Eric received letters yesterday informing him that his brother is in England and that his 2nd personal parcel has been sent, which means it is probably here. Quitting personal tuition in Algebra.

Our guards are even taken to playing musical instruments when they come in now. They coolly lean their arm against a convenient bed, then torture unfamiliar tunes from the various instruments. One is here now arguing with a would-be Canadian musician about the origin and composer of "Silent Night." We had a spring shower last night and the garden's not in yet. Our compound fuehrer, taking Spitfire's place for the weekend, is a young blue-eyed, fair-haired Unteroffizier with a mutilated right hand. He doesn't waste any time with petty bickering like "Spitfire, consequently the roll-calls are much shorter. Mail hasn't been so plentiful lately as the German staff are out on a firing course. Hope they finish their patriotic activities soon and do something useful in the post-office.

MARCH 30, TUES.

Rumours are pretty good for past few days. Turkey is in the war again; the 5th, 9th and 12th armies are in Bulgaria. A party from Munich said that moral of the civilian population in that district is very low and "Hitler Kaput" heard on all sides. They believe that Germany and England will soon be fighting together against the Russian Red menace.

Received 300 cigarettes from George Holland this morning and got another chit for another lot for tomorrow. Went on bath parade today and we came back and washed our clothes in hot water for the first time in 7 months; they came out surprisingly white. Our next change of clothing will be into summer gear and our winter things will be packed away. Received 1/2 a Red Cross parcel today with the other half coming on Thursday.

APRIL 4, SUN.

Weather miserable for last few days. Strong northwest wind and driving rain which makes the huts damp and cold. I "discovered" a good book on Electricity in the camp reference library which has quite a bit on wireless and television in it. Must take some notes on the cathode rag tube and photo-electric cell. Received another lb. of tobacco from Budd the other day and 3 letters from Rose and one from Rusty during the last four days. Also received notice from the Red Cross that a book called "Mathematics for Engineers" was sent on the 11th of February; it hasn't arrived yet. On Friday, for no expressed reason, they took 30 men from each room and gave them new uniforms whether they needed them or not. This is very unusual as they have been telling us to take care of our clothes as they are hard to replace. Speculation is rife; working parties is the first guess and Germany losing the war is the second. Yesterday, we departed from daily routine when the chains came off at four and we had roll-call at seven; apparently, it is only for the weekend while the Germans had a banquet last night and sports today. For some unknown reason we were without lights last night; I guess the bloke who controls the switch pushed it up and dashed off to the banquet and the switch dropped again. There was plenty of paper burnt for other reasons besides boiling tea water, mostly to produce illumination to allow them to cook their late suppers. Eric and I managed after a little difficulty and inconvenience, to brew, cook and consume a pot of porridge and a pot of tea. We are hoping for lights this evening, however. The weather has moderated a little with the sun shining and the wind less boisterous. Managed to drive two holes in my badge with a drill made out of a nail. Besides the completed badge, I am sporting a couple of luscious blisters from manipulating the drill. I am experimenting with wet tobacco as a wood stain now. Finished reading "Kidnap Island" and am reading "Death at Dyke's Corner." with "Singing Guns" next in line. Except for the R.A.F. bombing activities and Tunis being almost cleaned up, there are no new war rumours. Sold 60 cigarettes for 15 marks Lagergilt yesterday.

APRIL 6, TUES.

Nothing much doing right now or for the last few days except that I received 300 Sweet Caps from 202 Main yesterday. Coming back we were walking behind the Spud wagon which was taking a load of raw spuds to the kitchen and I think every man along the route filled his pockets with spuds. In the course of their petty looking, they dropped spuds along the road; by the time I had reached our compound gate, I had picked up a good pocketful of spuds. We had them mashed and covered with fried egg powder for supper. We received a can of milk, and hardtack biscuits and 6oz. of sugar today from the Red Cross. The weather was fairly nice yesterday and early today but the wind changed to northwest and brought rain. This is the rainy season and we will be glad when summer comes so that we can get rid of these chilblains, kidney colds, etc. Received a letter from Nelle in which she says she received my letter of August 24th, written during our ten day stay in the camp in France. Also received a letter from Harry, both were fairly newsy in comparison with others I have received previously. I think I have a chronic case of spring fever or something. Coal is cut off for the summer and so begins the fuel problem for our meal presentation.

APRIL 9, FRI.

Nothing very important in the line of war news or rumours. Received 8 letters from Nelle, one from Harry, one from Wally, one from Rusty, also 300 cigarettes today but didn't have a chance to see who they were from. Received 3 more snaps of Dad, two of them show him cutting our spacious lawn. Nelle says she has sent a second clothing parcel with more clothing than I will need; she also ordered a book parcel of notebooks, etc., from Eaton's, I presume. Was informed that Sid Sutton has been posted as killed in action. I didn't see him at all during the raid.

Still plugging away at Trig, Algebra and Electrical Engineering; can't see where I am getting ahead much. Battle in Tunis in full swing; we hope it's the straight goods this time. Russian front stagnant, both sides apparently preparing for spring offensive. Miserable weather this last week, northwest winds, driving rains, snow-flurries and frost. Eric is making a Stalag prune pudding which we intend to eat tomorrow night with a sauce made from a German fruit soup powder. Prefer parcel week to bulk week.

APRIL 12, MON.

Received a letter from Peggy today and 3 from Nelle on Saturday. We had no fuel yesterday; consequently, our suppers were eaten cold. Today, believing the coal was cut off for the summer, we revised our eating program and ate our spuds for dinner; had two pieces of bread and jam before roll-call, then two pieces of bread and meat roll and a currant pudding with our evening brew of tea. Coal came in unexpectedly this afternoon so we will revise the revision and go back to former methods, just so long as the coal lasts.

We traded an apple pudding for a currant pudding this P.M. because currant pudding sliced, buttered and eaten cold tasted just like cake. We received 1/2 a parcel each today so traded 2oz. pkg. of tea for a can of cocoa.

News is exceptionally good today; it is supposed to be announced over the German radio that the Tunisian campaign is cleared up with the fall of the capital, Tunis. News via "Raf" states that 11 ships being used for evacuating German troops from Africa, were sunk by bombing raids. News yesterday was that the Russians have started their spring drive and are advancing. Archy Pettigrew, one time sanitator of this hut, returned from a work party yesterday. When he left he was fairly dripping pessimism, claiming convincingly that the war would last another 3 years. Now he says he expects it to end any day. He says the German people are ready to call it quits and a few more raids like the one on Munich would be the last couple of straws; also there is strong feeling gaining headway among the civilians against the Nazi party. Here's hoping.

Listened to a lecture by a fellow who was captured in Tunisia on February 26 and learned how the French fleet surrendered to the British. Optimism is exceptionally high tonight, even the most chronic pessimist is a little more cheerful. For the next two months we will be receiving a parcel a week per man, instead of 1 parcel one week and bulk the next; nearly everyone prefers parcels to bulk. I am looking for an old pen now; I have a glass nib I think I can use.

APRIL 15, THURS.

Accomplished what I always thought was a hopeless job on Tuesday, the renovation of a patent can opener by putting a crescent shaped shim in the bearing. The shim is made from a flattened nail, filed to fit with a nail file (it works). Germany is reported to have taken over Italy as an occupied country. Tunis is almost cleaned up. The Renault works in Paris received another terrific bombing as did a large factory at Essex covering 62 acres.

We had a long felt wish fulfilled today when one of the planes training in this area nosed into the ground from a few hundred feet. Ate good yesterday, with two soup rations at noon, 2 bread soup rations and one apricot ration at four; a klim can full of spuds and tomato, 2 slices of bread and jam and a cup of tea after roll-call, and two slices of bread and pilchards and a marmalade pudding and cocoa tonight.

Here is the B.B.C. news bulletin of April 8 to 10. 1st and 8th armies advanced at great speed on Tunis. 1st army took Sakhota and 2,500 Italian prisoners. 8th army advanced and took Maharis and Sfap, Lusa and Blanca also 2,400 Italian prisoners. The Germans always leave Italians to fight rearguard and take all the transport for themselves. Many Italians want to change over to our side and fight the Germans. At one place an Italian General, 17 officers and thousands of men marched out to surrender to a Scottish Division. 1st and 8th armies meet at Hairous. The enemy are boxed in a small area (Beserta-Cairaun-Lusai) and are being bombed day and night. 11 transport ships were sunk while trying to leave Beserta. Barges cannot set out at all. The motto of our troops is "Remember Dunkirk" with a vengeance. The De Gaulist troops along with N.F. 7th army Div., 51 Div., and New Zealand Div. praised by General Montgomery. They advanced 80 miles in 3 days and captured 1/2 enemy division and destroyed the rest. General states, "nothing can stop us now." Beserta is watched day and night. In recent air battles 16 Junkers shot down with a loss of 8 British fighters. General Rosario, cousin to Mussolini is captured. 27 Junkers carrying troops shot down. The best photographs of the war taken of the Renault works in Paris, Kruppe works at Essex, and steel works at Daishoro. Kruppe was bombed on Sunday, Tuesday and Wednesday last week and works severely damaged. 2 new models of Spitfire in production, they were christened by Princess Margaret Rose. Three German tankers sunk off Norway. Russians have captured a rail-head in the Donetz basin. Russians say German attacks losing strength. Seven Jap transports sunk and 16 planes destroyed. American navy sunk 2 Jap cruisers off New Guinea. (By now the Tunis affair should be finished.)

Our diminutive compound commander is credited with the assertion that we would do well to take all the P.T. we can as we will be in England in two months. Apparently he is completely fed up with the war.

APRIL 19, MON.

The last four days which embraces a weekend, have been very quiet in regards to war news and rumours. School is closed to all classes because of the examinations in progress. A test in engineering maths is coming up from 3 to 4 on Thursday and one on electricity from 6 to 8 Wednesday evening. Spent the weekend copying notes on cathode ray tubes and photo -electric cells. For the first time in months we got mint tea from the kitchen, we made cocoa out of it yesterday, but declined to waste the precious commodity today so used the mint tea to wash our eating utensils. However, we all handed our tea in today from the parcels so we should get the good stuff again tomorrow. Eric and I did more trading than usual after receiving our parcels today. Eric did the trading; the apple pudding for a Devon pudding; a can of cheese for a large can of tomatoes, then the small can of tomatoes for a can of cheese, then a partially used can of mint seasoning for another can of cheese, then two service biscuits for two rations of jam. Pretty good for an amateur. Cigarettes are going up in value again; for instance, an Indian came in trying to sell a can of oatmeal for 200 cigs. inside of half an hour it dropped to 150 cigarettes and still he couldn't make a sale. By the end of the week the prices should be back in reasonable limits.

Meldrum and Rocky were out behind the latrine to settle a difference of opinion this evening but neither of them look much the worse for wear. The mail has dropped off lately, probably accounting for the rising value of cigs. Spitfire is supposed to have said that the war will be over in two months; a fellow in 22A is willing to bet 50 pounds with all necessary papers that the war will be over by the end of June.

APRIL 21, WED.

Apparently we are on strafe again because a couple of a hundred guys have traded identities, which is about the only way of making an escape. Trading of identity is usually done with someone scheduled for a working party, then the escape is made from there. With the coming spring and ideal escape weather, a lot of Canadians barred from work parties have been trading with men from the working compound; such trades have been increasing in numbers and have finally come to the attention of the Germans; consequently the R.A.F. and this compound are locked up, pending a portrait check-up. As a punishment, the gates will remain locked for 14 days, thus I miss two exams. Eric and I traded a can of cheese and a can of egg powder for two bread rations. R.C. parcels tomorrow.

Civilians on the French coast have been warned to evacuate immediately and the Belgian's have supposedly been told they will be free by May 5th. A few minutes ago the rumour came in that the second front has actually started. The new men from Munich claim the Bavarian's are openly voicing their desire for the downfall of the Nazi party. A work party from Poland claim that 60,000 Russians starved to death this last winter. Made a frying pan out of an old dixie this P.M. I am taking a rest from studying this week. The fuel situation has reached a crisis and various parts of beds are going up in smoke.

The rumour about the 2nd front has been met with a variety of opinion; some greeted it with open and sometimes violent skepticism; others maintain anything is possible now; others greeted it with I-hope-so attitude while a few are firmly convinced it's true. The month of August seems to be the favoured month for the cessation of hostilities now. The chains are more or less of a joke these days, each man collects a chain in the morning, throws it on his bed where it usually remains until collecting time in the evening. Have read "The Case of the Caretaker's Cat." "Peril at End House," "To the Last Bullet" and am reading "The Tragedy of X."

APRIL 23

Good Friday and a longing for Hot Cross Buns, toasted with jam or thick butter. Our would-be preacher gave a preliminary Easter speech on the parade square this morning and didn't do too badly, if he knew what he was talking about himself. The 14-day strafe continues with an extra guard employed. Two sanitators had to stand at the wire this morning because they left the compound last night. They protested loud and long but failed to move Spitfire in the least. I think I will join the happy throng of sun worshipers tomorrow by getting my hair clipped off and make a pair of shorts.

Vague rumours about landings in Norway and France. Nearly everyone thinks August will be the month, I certainly hope so; nevertheless, I am keeping good care of my winter clothing. A German came into the hut last night selling bread; he had quite a time in the dealing. Two violins, a guitar and a banjo, plus a dozen or so lusty voices, slightly toneless, and the clumping of sabots on the cement floor all go to fill the shack with plenty of noise this evening. Some Frenchmen are demonstrating their idea of a square dance Frolic. The general bedlam is interspersed with wild cowboy yells from our "Western" element. Personally, I don't believe most of them have ever been further west than North Main in Winnipeg.

APRIL 24, SAT.

Tomorrow is Easter and all the ladies who are able will be doing their last minute shopping in preparation for the Easter parade tomorrow morning. Imagination needs no stretching to visualize the decorated shop windows with their white and pink icing trimmed chocolate eggs, chickens and bunnies. Decidedly no hot cross buns for us yesterday so will have to wait until next year for them. We were very fortunate in obtaining two spud rations for 1/2 slice of bread today so we had a can of sausage and a mess of fried spuds, bread, lemon curd and jam, finished off with a cup of Rowntree's cocoa. The scene here is a far cry from that I remember back home. A French Canadian is cooking his supper in the fire-box in the center of the room while Meldrum is preparing his over a tin creation brought into existence by the combined effort of Pratt and Mahoney. Grey is trying to shave at one of the windows by the feeble light from the storm darkened western sky. The faint rumble of thunder can be heard above the hum of many conversations. Most of the fellows are next door listening to a lecture on Finland and Russia. We traded a can of egg powder for Bill Morris' tomorrow bread ration. We are going to have quite a time making our curd, cheese, butter, etc. last over to Tuesday when we get 1/2 a parcel. These Limey's are more or less fanatical in recognizing various holidays. The 1/2 parcel is usually due on Monday but the Red Cross workers insist on recognizing Easter Monday by taking a holiday. We are confronted with a fuel shortage so anything burnable such as can labels, cig. cartons, etc. is zealously saved for cooking and brewing. We have enough for our cocoa tonight but tomorrow will be a problem. We hear that Tokyo has been heavily bombed; consequently, the Jap and German papers are hollering, Murders, Barbarians, etc. We got spinach soup this noon but it was inedible because it was loaded with gravel. A fellow from one of the other huts swears he found a rat skin in his turnip soup yesterday. Recopied notes all day today.

I see some of the fellows are sporting bright and no doubt painful sunburns these days. Shorts seem to be the favourite lounging suits these sunny days. I think laundry is the sport for the day. We can't depend on the water being on these days. August is still the favoured month.

APRIL 25, SUN.
Easter. We wouldn't know it if we didn't keep homemade calendars. No painted eggs or the last few Hot Cross buns left over from Friday. A piece of black bread and cheese and a cup of tea for breakfast; with sauerkraut soup and spuds for dinner. A slice of bread and lemon curd with afternoon tea and four slices of bread with meat roll and the last of the lemon curd with cocoa for supper. Tomorrow will be a bad day with no spread for our bread or fuel to heat our supper.

The German racketeer came in again last night and sold his bread in no time and departed via the window with his treasure of cigs, tea and cocoa. I used to take pride in thinking the average Canadian was endowed with a little more than his share of brains but after watching the dealings tonight I am forced to change my mind. Some of them were giving the German 300 cigarettes for a loaf of bread which could have been bought for 150 or even 100. Greed, I think, routes any dealing sense they might have possessed; the fear that the next fellow might get there first actuates their business deals. A few seconds after one proud Canuck got a loaf for 200 cigs, another brainy individual offered 300 for a similar loaf. We suspect everyone from the Guard Commander to the lowest postern are in on the racket. Finished reading a book called, "The Frightened Lady" by Edgar Wallace. Two genuine eggs were fried on the homemade stove this evening and the curious flocked from all corners of the hut to see what frying eggs looked like.

APRIL 28, WED.

Rumours have been plentiful and perhaps a little wild these past four days. It started when the news came out that there were forty men including a submarine crew being kept in the old stables outside of the camp. The concluded reason for keeping them there is because they know too much to have it spread around camp. One of the party is supposed to have wandered away from the barn and hollered at a camp "citizen, "It's on" before he was reclaimed by the guard. So the rumour spread around that the second front has definitely started, with three point attacks in France to divert the attention from the main thrust in Holland where the Allies have established a 100 mile front. Landings are supposed to have been effected in southern France, Italy, Sicily, Greece, etc. and the Germans are gradually being pushed out of Tunis. Personally I can't bring myself to believe that landings would be attempted on Sicily and Greece while Tunis remains a dangerous question. One German Unteroffizier is credited with the statement that the war will be over inside of a month.

The Russians are reported to have been pushed back 400 kilos only to close in behind the attackers with their consequent annihilation. The Russians are said to be visiting Gibraltar on a tour of inspection by the German newspapers. the rumours sound pretty good but the authenticity of such reports is very questionable. There are whisperings that in some parts of the country, the people have gone pro-British and are protesting the removal of British P.O.W.'s from certain sectors. Undoubtedly the attitude of the Germans around camp has undergone a big change in the last 8 months. We were warned against signing the "Parole paper" the Germans were bringing around. This is a printed statement that the signee won't try to escape from a working party. Immediately a prisoner affixes his signature to such a document he forfeits all his pay, allowances, etc. and is liable to court marshal and 3 years imprisonment when he gets back. Besides that if he escapes and gets back he will be returned to prison life by British Army authorities. It sounds far fetched to me but there it is. Bought a German made pen for 300 cigs from a lad from Munich. The ink question is becoming monotonous and exasperating. I line up a Jerry guard to get me some then he is replaced by someone else. I am bound to hit it lucky one of these days. We had a barn dance last night but have a feeling some of the musicians didn't think much of my drumming; the feeling is mutual in a way because I thought some of their pieces sounded terrible. Received a letter from Sergeant R.G. Langston today in which he says he has all my books and tools, etc. but no diary, also only one purse. Am worried now.

MAY 1, SAT.

A German finally got me some ink which cost me the comparatively trifling sum of 40 cigarettes and a bar of soap. The 2nd front rumour was officially squashed yesterday but the news that Jerry is still holding 150 mile front in Tunis; 8 troop ships (German) have been sunk; 100 and some troop carrying planes were shot down; the booty taken in Africa so far exceeds what the British lost in Dunkirk; Cunningham has divided the Mediterranean in two with a formidable array of front line "battle-wagons," sort of compensates for the letdown. On the strength of the 2nd front rumour being so ruthlessly squashed, I had all my hair clipped off, feeling certain it would be grown in again in plenty of time.

Little tin stoves are appearing rapidly these days; one "battery" consists of three of these "masterpieces in tin" with three cocoa-can chimneys converging in a tri-directional manner into a larger biscuit tin which in turn is connected to the main chimney by another cocoa can. It is surprising the number of suppers and brews that are made on them after the evening roll-call. There are two more single efforts in the washroom, one more at the front of the main stove with its chimney poked into the fire-box. Sometimes it gets kind of smokey, especially if green wood is burnt but that is a trifle as long as the suppers are cooked okay. Finished "The Case of the Curious Bride" and have started "Border Breed." We have 3 more days of strafe to go yet.

MAY 4, TUES.
The bread loaves are larger now so we are 7 on a loaf; spinach soup which very few eat has become tri-weekly or quad-weekly event now; still plenty of gravel mixed with it. Parcel day yesterday and my choice met with Eric's evident disapproval. Apparently I am considered a part of the Old Time Dance Orchestra as I have "rattled" the sticks at four dances in five nights. Need a pair of good sticks so hit up R.S.M. Beesely; he promised to do his best with no visible success to date. The strafe finished today at ten thirty when the gates were officially opened. Softball leagues get underway again tomorrow. Repaired our can opener once again. Word came in that Wigness, one of the three who made a break last fall from No. 2 block, tried another break from a working party and was shot while riding a train; he was found on the tracks with a bullet wound near his heart and both legs cut off by the train. Wigness used to go to the same classes and slept in this room before he went on the working party. His one idea was to escape somehow.

MAY 7, FRI.
Mickey MacManus is trying to get a pair of drumsticks made at the carpenter shop for me. It's a little early to expect any results as yet. Copped the fish-cheese box yesterday for a drum but it is dead; besides it stinks to high heaven. We have 3 guitars, one banjo and 2 violins in the band now and may include a mandolin. Wilcox and Wheeler are the fiddlers and Ferris and MacLeod the guitarists. I don't know the banjoist's name. We played for a dance in 21A last night and there is hardly anything left of my sticks. The Jerry was in, selling bread again this evening and raised quite a row when he missed 1/2 a loaf. Some of the fellows have been giving him cans of sand in

place of cocoa. This place could very aptly be named the Lamsdorf dust bowl if the dust storm this evening is any criterion, and we had a blanket inspection at the height of the storm. Four fellows were chained with their hands behind their backs because they were caught without their chains on. The Aces beat the Buckaroos 6-5 this afternoon. I guess most of us are living for the day when we can drop the word "ration"(past, present and future tense) from our vocabularies. "Spitfire" orders us to have all our palaises washed by Monday but failed to forward any idea as to what we could use for water. How 900 men are going to wash palaises with the water situation as it is, constitutes a major mystery.

MAY 9, SUN.

We played at dances in 21A on Friday night and 19A last night. We were supposed to take part in an open air dance and concert last night but rain prevented outdoor performing. The gates have been locked on and off all day yesterday, finally reaching a climax when we had a portrait identity parade in the afternoon. I have decided to take a crack at journalism which starts on Tuesday. Finished my lanyard by making a fastener from chain from an old Rosary. Pulsifer is back from a working party. Heard a good reason why we are chained up; the Germans figure we are specially trained for guerrilla warfare and escaping so they think they aren't taking any chances. It's of little consequence if we are able to remove said chains whenever we wish. They are always worrying about us obtaining anything that could be used as a weapon, yet they put the finest weapon a man could wish for, the chains and handcuffs.

Our grub box is as depleted as I have ever seen it for many months, having used the last of our jam, syrup, cheese, bacon, milk and sugar this evening. However, it's parcel day tomorrow so lack of vittles isn't exactly a pressing problem. Hope to get my new sticks tomorrow. Heard a repeat on a transmission rumour to the effect that German papers are supposed to have said that the evacuation of that front is almost completed. Their excuse is that they are evacuating because they have no further use for Africa and don't see any sense in wasting life and material needlessly. The Russians are supposed to be advancing in the southern sector of that front.

Three fellows came in, after being captured while making a break from a work-party and they were forced to stay a night in a Russian prison camp. They claim the conditions there were a disgrace to any so-called civilized country. Russian men and women all sleep in the same room with a latrine bucket in the center, which is emptied once a day. They have no beds palaises or blankets and the place is crawling with bed-bugs and lice. They only get two soups a day made from unpeeled, unwashed potatoes; cold in the morning and hot at night. Sticks, straws and filth float on top and the bottom is filled with silt, sand and stones. They are dressed in any old rags they are fortunate to have and bare spots are wrapped in paper if they are lucky. No one goes outside the hut except the men who empty the latrine bucket, then they double for fear of being shot for dawdling. We have periodical collection of old clothes, soap and cigarettes which is delivered by mysterious means by the TOCH. Thousands die of hunger and disease every winter.

Received a letter from Reg the other day otherwise mail is very skimpy. Some of the fellows are making a pretense of washing their bed boards.

MAY 13, THURS.
Received a pair of drumsticks from the carpenter shop for 100 cigarettes; with a few minor alterations they will do alright. The math instructor whispered in my ear that I was his most promising pupil. Held a dance in 22A night before last and one in here last night. Square dance and old time music getting very monotonous.

The BBC news as read out last night: 2 German armies captured or destroyed in Africa; 8th British army proclaimed the greatest in British history and will have the honour of opening the second front. Large force of Germans surrounded at Kuban bridgehead including the famous Goering Panzer division; ultimatum extended to Italy to withdraw from war; they have three days to make their reply. Germany reported to have closed the Hungary-Turkish border because Turkey has allowed the entry of British troops. England has launched 3 million tons of shipping over what the Germans have sunk; America has launched 33 merchant ships in 3 days; 93 German planes shot down on the Russian front in 2 days. America claims to have received from a reliable source that Germany is planning on using gas on the Russian front and has been duly warned by Britain and America.

Parcels are just about due to come in so must clear the decks for action. In another ten minutes the place will be like an auctioneer's nightmare with fellows trying to trade off things they don't like for something more to their tastes.

MAY 14, FRI.

Still battling with trig. problems and apparently getting nowhere. Very warm today. Nineteen men were missing from roll-call this evening which had "Spitfire" pretty worried for awhile. The wood party was too great a temptation for two escape minded airmen, consequently, the party was held up at the main gate. Spitfire was greatly relieved to find his missing sheep standing there while a search for two airmen was carried out. This will probably queer the wood parties for awhile so a fuel shortage is expected soon.

Rumours going around today that Turkey is in the war <u>again</u>, and that Germany is agreeable to peace with Britain if she is allowed to fight the Russians unmolested. Eric received a parcel this afternoon from Geneva, containing four bottles of ink, six or eight pen holders, a box of nibs, a three-cornered ruler and a straight edge. He doesn't know who they are from. Played in 20B last night.

MAY 16, SUN.

What a day. 8 hours of standing outside while the Gestapo search us and our beds and kits. No one knows for sure what they were hunting for as all they confiscated was one homemade tin stove, 2 old dixies, a broken fire grate, one cardboard box and a few raw spuds. Being forewarned, everyone disposed or hid matter best kept out of unfriendly hands. I hid this diary in my palaise this morning but later decided it was in danger so navigated two washrooms via three windows, retrieved the article mentioned, returned the same way, under the very nose of the postern supposedly guarding against such actions Finally managed to put it in a safe place until after the danger had receded.

Eric received another book parcel yesterday but hasn't been able to go down to the post office because of Gestapo activities. Half a New Zealand parcel and bulk equivalent to half a parcel next week. Spitfire caught us with three homemade stoves going the other night and confiscated the works. Fuel is getting scarce again. It is rumoured that Il Duce has ordered his 1st army to capitulate. Wrote cards to Nelle and Rusty this evening.

MAY 19, WED.

Nine months today since we were captured. The gates are still locked following the Gestapo search on Sunday. The New Zealand parcels met with general approval despite the absence of milk and biscuits. the German papers are supposed to say that the last round has been fired in Africa and now that that front has served its purpose, there is no need of wasting any more German lives. Churchill is supposed to have made a speech in which he stated that the Allies don't care if the war lasts until 1946. I don't think Churchill would make such a statement public.

Received a parcel presumably from the Red Cross in England, containing embroidery silks and cottons in balls and skeins in a variety of colours, burlap and tooled leather for belts, numerous brightly coloured buttons; a complete amateur book binding course with paste, glue, etc., 3 pencils, 1 foot ruler, two paint brushes for paste, a queer shaped knife, a good pair of scissors, rolls of pink and white tape, balls of different coloured yarns, etc. All because I asked Peggy to send enough thread to embroider a Cameron hat badge. She even sent special needles and a bunch of used razor blades.

MAY 20, THURS.

Received a biscuit and jam bulk issue today. My Chinese sound block is nearing completion; I received my book binding instructions from the censors today. We had an inoculation for Tetanus this afternoon; arm is a little sore this evening. Perhaps gates will be open soon as the school is scheduled to re-open Monday.

News this evening: Sicily has capitulated; Rome has been bombed and there has been commando raids in Italy someplace. The Ruhr Valley is flooded due to some very accurate bombing of dams; thousands drowned; industry hard hit. the Jews are being accused of giving the necessary information to the British.

I broke another tooth out of my plate this morning while eating bread; that makes three. Was a chain short in my section this evening and after lots of searching and arguing, found it in my own tunic pocket. Did I feel foolish.

MAY 22, SAT.
Finished my Chinese block yesterday and christened it by playing in 20B last night. There was no lights on last night and a large Alsatian caused quite a little excitement and amusement in the compound. It is supposed to be authentic that Sicily has capitulated after 5 hours. According to the BBC news, 2/3 of the Ruhr Valley is under water and 200,000 bodies have already been recovered. Churchill is supposed to have told the Home Guard that the zero hour is very near for the second front. the American Navy has withdrawn from the Mediterranean and is concentrating all her force in the Pacific against Japan. Tried my hand at book binding. the gates are open today and school is opening tomorrow. Finished reading "The Devil to Pay."

MAY 24, MON.
Worked on altering a suit of pajamas into underwear shorts yesterday and after a few false starts, finally accomplished 1 pair. Felt unusually homesick last night for some unaccountable reason.

The Red Cross issue this week is coming in for camp-wide criticism. As it stands now, it's 1/2 English parcel on Monday, plus 50 cigarettes, 4oz. of soap, 4oz. butter, 8oz. of biscuits, 4oz. of sugar on Wednesday and Thursday, 4oz. of sausage, 4oz. chocolate on Saturday. The cause for the howl is that the bulk issue is supposed to equal 1/2 parcel in weight and is 16oz. of M&V per man from the kitchen which we don't. One Sergeant sanitator is going around trying to gain support in a racket breaking scheme but his idea sounds fishy and he is not getting many recruits. The guard commander <u>asked</u> the R.S.M. to tell the boys if some of us would wear chains, just for appearances sake, he could over-look a lot. One of the guards came in this evening, sat down talked to some of the boys while others were examining his rifle. Finished reading "Enter a Murder" and "The Man from Scotland Yard."

BBC news tonight didn't mention the fall of Sicily but did say it was being bombed continually. Besides the large force put out of action in Africa, the booty was tremendous. 17 high army official including a Commander-in-Chief (not Rommel) were captured. Italy is being bombed unmercifully. Western Germany being pounded continuously, night and day. Russia continues pressure around Kuban bridgehead. Sea-warfare undergoing change, 17 U-boats being sunk by new boats. 56 laden Italian troopships knocked out during evacuation from Africa. Wrote to Reg last night, asking about my diary and purses. Must see the M.O. about having the teeth reset in my plate.

MAY 27, THURS.

Russia has outlawed international communism and now calls her policy "social democracy." Thus she has taken Germany's excuse for the war in Russia away from her. Germany can't say she is fighting communism now. There is persistent rumours that Italy has capitulated but we are disinclined to believe it. The protests over the bulk issue grew to such proportions that the issue was changed from bulk to 1/2 a New Zealand parcel. The complaint that the bulk ration assigned to the camp was forwarded to Geneva. Lavatorial conditions in this camp are chronic anti-sanitary; our latrine is overflowing and a separate hole had to be dug before the night latrine buckets could be emptied. Dangerous business now that warm weather is here. Went on dental parade yesterday but walked away after waiting all morning. Some of the fellows are still waiting from three or four days ago. Put a new handle in our can opener. Drummed at a dance in 19A night before last. Received a letter from Nelle yesterday morning.

MAY 31, MON.

We are finally obtaining a good idea of Red Cross issues and stores now that we have a hut representative (Mickey McManus was elected.) Quite a lot of excitement just now; a fellow from 20B decided to take a bath in the tea copper. He calmly continues his bath with his knees tucked under his chin, grinning idiotically at the ring of indignant men voicing deprecating remarks at his conduct. This week we get 1/2 English and 1/2 New Zealand parcels; probably bulk next week. No mail recently. Have to write up the Saturday night lecture for the Journalist class.

446

The BBC news was read out this A.M. 900,000 enemy killed, 600,000 captured besides unstated amount of equipment. The dams that were bombed in the Ruhr Valley flooded 54 towns and caused hundreds of thousands of casualties. Anthony Eden said in a speech recently that everything is nearly ready for the second front.

JUNE 2, WED.
Embroidering a Cameron pennant for the ball team which has to be finished for the opening game on the 19th. Sent my shoes to the shoemakers and am wearing a borrowed pair that are killing me. Heard today that Britain has given Italy 14 days to think it over. German papers are still yelling about the Ruhr Valley episode. No mail.

JUNE 6, SUN.
Getting short on sugar and milk in fact, we are completely out again. We used honey in our tea this afternoon. We may get bulk this week and bulk never comes up to a parcel in weight. Spitfire confiscated our dixie yesterday when he caught Eric boiling water for tea in one of the stoves. Lack of hoops is holding up work on the pennant. We heard rumours that Italy had capitulated but the Germans were still in the country. It doesn't make sense. Missed Electrical Engineering and Math classes on Friday. Played at a dance in 20B Friday evening. Wrote a letter to Bezzie and Budd this afternoon.

JUNE 13
Witticism: seven days is a long time to let a diary go but other matters have been taking up time. the Germans made another step forward the other day in keeping check on chains and maybe forestalling souvenir addicts in the future. Each man had to put a label with his name and number on a set of chains so that if any are lost or broken, the blame can be placed on one man instead of the whole hut. The Journalist class is starting a weekly paper called "STIMMT" and I am assigned to cover softball in general. Here is a perfect example of the gambling spirit of the Canucks. A "Diepper" was caught with his chains off by an officer and sentenced to stand facing the wire with his hands chained behind his back, with strafe chains. He pulled a coin out of his pocket and offered to match with the officer if he would stand for double

the time or not at all. The officer agreed, the coin was tossed and the Canuck got off without his punishment. The officer thought it was a good joke and walked away smiling. One of the M.O.'s is willing to bet 100 pounds that the war will be over in two months. There are rumours of trouble in the German army around the Kuban bridgehead and there are riots in Bulgaria. Rommel is supposed to have died from malaria or something. Italy's little Gibraltar between Sicily and Tunis has fallen (Pantelleria.) Dusseldorf and Wilhelmshaven severely bombed.

The Whitsun track meet scheduled for yesterday had to be postponed until today because of rain. The exhibition game between the "Canadians" and the "Americans" will be played at 9:30 Monday (instead of yesterday). No afternoon roll-call today or tomorrow, possibly no chains as well. What is this prison coming to? Received a book on maths from England the other day through the Bodlien Library in England. Swamped with work, pennant taking up all my time. Played the sticks at a dance in 20B last night.

JUNE 20, SUN.

The past week has been extremely hectic in regards to rumours and news. Rumour No. 1 is that there are 1,600 dress uniforms coming in for the Canadians and the Limey Q.M. wants us to share them with the rest of the camp. How we get dress uniforms here when we couldn't get them in England is a mystery. As for us sharing them with the other members of the camp I vote decidedly "no." The Canadians are running around with worn out clothes and are told it's impossible to get anything else but patched replacements, yet every "Limey" I have seen can sport two brand new uniforms or one new one and another in good condition. They seem able to get new uniforms anytime they want. Boots is another source of contention. The "Clarion" reports 9,000 pair of new shoes in a new shipment immediately after, all the Limey's who know the right people are sporting new foot-gear. We have our shoes condemned by the shoemaker only after the leather is so rotten it won't hold any more. Then we get shoes with wooden soles and patched uppers. Share our dress uniforms, why should we?

German soldiery is being cut to a minimum around the camp; the male mail censors have been replaced with female workers. The Russians have been reported breaking through in many sectors; the Kuban bridgehead is in Russian hands now; Sicily is being pounded continually with heavy bombs; Pantelleria and a companion island in British hands, probably stepping stones to Italy. The German radio announced that there is a commando raid on Italy and Musso is mustering all available troops to meet the threat. Sixteen or so German officers were walking around camp the other day and some one in the RAF compound asked them if they were refugees from Stalingrad and asked them where Rommel was. The hut in question had to stand out for an hour as punishment. There was a time in the not so far distant past when the whole hut would have been machine gunned for less.

Trucks and dump carts have been assembled from the kitchen corner to the baseball field; they are going to build a water reservoir in case of fires or a swimming pool for propaganda purposes. Finished the ball pennant on Friday night; a poor job compared with the FMR product. Assigned to cover the show "Square Crooks" Friday night. the first edition of the "STIMMT" rolled off the press or struggled out of the typewriter on Tuesday, quite a paper. Two of my articles were selected for it but one was slashed to one measly line and the other failed to appear at all; lack of space is the reason. Trig coming along fine and becoming interesting. Painted hankies are becoming a demand for souvenir value. Cadeaux is doing some and they really are something.

JUNE 22, TUES.

Three more German trainer planes crashed yesterday. These accidents are becoming almost daily occurrences. Heard tonight that Turkey had occupied some Italian Islands. My deer story may make space in this week's "STIMMT." Assigned to interview the librarian this week. Material for "brews" was becoming downright scanty this evening but we were saved by my receiving two clothing parcel notices which means coffee, tea, and sugar. Apparently it will be the second and third parcels. A more opportune time couldn't be imagined.

The Canadians lost to the Bulldogs in football this evening, 8-0. I can go to bed tonight happy in the anticipation of a good feed tomorrow.

JUNE 28, MON.

Received two clothing parcels on Wednesday; the sugar, tea and nuts were missing from the January parcel although there were traces through all the clothing. apparently the parcel was damaged by the time it reached Geneva and was repacked as the chocolate and small items were in a box stamped with "made in Switzerland." The sugar bag in the April parcel was split but the German censor salvaged most of it for me. However, the parcels were exceedingly welcome besides the good chocolate, clothes, etc., they break the monotony and are a link with home.

Another worry was taken off my mind this morning when I received three blank record books, two erasers, six pencils. I was fortunate in having an Englishman to censor my parcel and I got the books out of the post office with no undue trouble. Blank paper is strictly against regulations imposed by the German authorities.

Some misunderstanding regarding arbeits (*work tasks*) from this compound reached a crisis this morning when the gates were locked while R.S.M. Beesely, the Block fuehrer and the Commandant, had a conference in an endeavour to straighten things out. We were under the impression that just the garden party and the reservoir party would be picked from this compound but recently they have been coming in demanding more and more men each day. Finally the fellows refused point blank to go to work. The outcome of it all is an explanation from the Camp to the effect that he thought the Canadians would welcome the chance for some exercise thus the working parties, then Beesely explained how the Canadians didn't like the uncertainty of posterns coming in all hours of the day picking men to go to work all over the camp. An agreement was finally reached where this compound would supply so many men daily for the reservoir and garden jobs. The Commandant then apologized for the gates being locked, explaining that it was a mistake and was sorry if it caused any inconvenience. the new "Feldwebel" came in a couple of days ago between 5 and 5:30 in the morning and roused everyone out of bed as Beesely lodged a complaint which resulted in the mad Feldwebel receiving several varieties of Hades from the commandant and orders to leave this compound alone. the guard commander has been instructed to look the other way when he sees men without their chains on.

Obtained a 12" banjo head for a drum but am having a hard time tuning it to the string instruments. I interviewed the librarian and obtained a line on a shipment of Canadian Legion correspondence courses that were addressed to the Senior Canadian officer and then turned over to the reference library for camp use. Some Canucks resent the fact that they weren't given to the Canadians, apparently unable to comprehend that if they were put at the disposal of the Canucks only a few would derive any benefit from them. Kitchen is one of the principle objectors. Am trying to get one of my white hankies painted but the artist ran out of paint.

A new phase entered our prison life last night when it was announced that the room doors would remain open continually instead of being locked every night at nine. Of course, we were warned that anyone seen outside of the huts after ten would be shot.

Went to sleep last night to the tune of "My Mammy Don' Tol' Me" emitting from a portable music box accompanied by the usual scratching and distortion caused by old needles. Woke up an hour and a half later to the same tune and apparently the same needle. I had a horrible momentary suspicion that the darn thing was continuous.

JUNE 29, TUES.

Two rumours late last night, an accident this afternoon and a strong rumour this afternoon merits special entry and the use of valuable paper. We heard last night that Sicily had definitely fallen and the Russians had broken through all along the line. Goebbels made a speech last night in which he pleaded with the German people not to get panicky at the critical moment because if they did how could they face the thousands of soldiers, who are bravely fighting and dying in the fight for the cause, when they met them in heaven. There is a strong rumour circulating that the camp police will be taking over inside the camp and bugle calls will again enter into our daily routine. Also we will be allowed to go anywhere north of gates 3 and 2 with shirt sleeves and without puttees. Also a vague rumour that all Red Cross food except chocolate will go to the kitchen and we will be served with 3 square meals a day. No one believes this last one. If all this does come true it will be a sure indication of the beginning of the final act.

A Limey softball enthusiast met with a very embarrassing and odorous accident while playing ball this afternoon. He was backing up very intent on catching a fly ball when he backed right into the sump hole of the latrine. He crawled out, left his clothes in a heap and went in search of an adequate water supply. His associates and team-mates are arguing whether or not he caught the ball before he took his plunge. We threaten petty thieves with a similar fate but I don't think anyone would have the heart to subject even a ration thief to such an ordeal.

JULY 1
Dad's birthday. The bugle blared forth Reveille this morning and the cursing and grumbling which greeted it reminded me of other days. They may be trying to get us back to a military frame of mind again. The man behind the noise bungled the first four or five notes pretty badly; apparently he is out of practice.

Cologne received a terrific pounding the other night according to the latest rumour. 3 more British POW's were shot to death while trying to escape recently; evidently the Germans are determined to stop escape attempts. Three of my humble journalism efforts got into the "STIMMT" this week. Received 1,000 cigarettes from a Hilda K. Collins, 220 4th St. N., Kenora, unable to place the lady. Also received 330 from Mrs. Bodger a few days ago. The chains are merely a symbol of our punishment now; no one, not even the Germans, take them seriously. They come in the morning at 8, lay under the blankets all day until collected in the evening. Some of the boys are making miniature sets as souvenirs. The noodle soup arriving in the parcels is just tops; it is coming in hand when German soups are inedible which is often. Have been assigned to cover basketball this week. Received four letters from Rose in two days.

JULY 5, MON.
Rumours are plentiful and sensational these days. Hitler has resigned and the army is in control. Sicily and Crete definitely taken and there is fighting in Greece. Corsica successfully raided and first time Union Jack has flown there. 3,500 to 5,000 planes in bombing raids over Germany. Landing in

France; Naples bombed heavily. Here is something which indicates how slack the guarding is getting; Shelly was acting guard commander this morning. the bugle blows at Reveille, quarter hour dress, time signal at twelve noon, compound lockup and ten o'clock. Received 1 lb. of tobacco from Dad, one lb. from Harry and 300 cigarettes from Bud Brown today. Camp once more swamped with Canadian cigarettes but boys are remaining pretty canny in their dealings. Obtained a complete report on Basketball for STIMMT. Am making a pack-sack out of an extra shirt and a suit of pajamas as "lantern" is almost finished and may have to move in a hurry. Trig is getting interesting. Crete, Greece, Sicily and Corsica rumours very strong tonight. Lloyds of London is supposed to be laying odds that the war will be over in three months. Men from working parties claim civilian moral very low. Demonstrations taking place at stations when troops leave for the Russian front. These troops include nearly all very young men or elderly men. The milk has been skimmed too often.

In the last two days, I have received 1,200 cigarettes and 2lb. of tobacco, today I received 300 from Iris, 300 from Dawn and 300 from the Ladies' Auxiliary. The Canadians are showing some sense this time as they have formed a committee to control or set prices for each article in terms of cigarettes. This places a set value on these articles; for instance, if a chocolate is down as 40 cigarettes and a can of jam as 40, then the tins can be traded without any difference. If one article is valued at 40 and the other at 60, then the difference of 20 cigarettes must be made up, either in cigarettes or some article worth 20 smokes such as 3oz. of cheese. Have been working on the pack-sack for the last couple of days.

War rumours are unbelievable as ever. There is a honey going around there is a proposal undergoing consideration back home to give all Dieppe personnel wearing chains £1,000 bonus for the hardships of last winter, especially. No one expects anything to come of it; the government will probably want to give us an acre or two of rocky ground and an old cow.

Am assigned to cover a show called "Little Nelle" and the wrestling this week. Iris wrote a letter in which she informed me that she was engaged to a fellow she calls Gib.

JULY 12, MON.

Last Saturday there was a rumour to the effect that Britain had sent an ultimatum to Germany for an unconditional surrender by the 25th of August or receive the full force of her naval, air and land forces. Posterns around here say Germany can't last much longer. Germans have admitted that the largest airborne attack ever attempted in this war was made on Sicily by British and American forces. Sicily is supposed to have fallen. Large scale activity in Orel and Kerseh area; Russians continue to make good showing. Received 1,000 cigarettes from Dad and 300 from Nelle today. Altogether I have 4,100 cigarettes and 2 lbs. of tobacco this mail already. Finished my pack yesterday. Decided to quit journalist class as it takes up too much time.

A Cameron by the name of Chura died in hospital (Lazaret) this P.M. from ingrown boils in the nose. French Canadian Sergeant Major who has seen action in the Red Revolution, the Spanish revolution, etc. died of appendicitis in the Lazaret, in the morning of the same day. My math teacher expressed a desire to teach me calculus. If he only knew how hazy I am on the simple trigonometrical ratios and formulae he wouldn't think of it. Received letters from Nelle and one from Budd on Saturday.

There are quite a number of flu cases in camp and it threatens to develop into an epidemic; wet miserable weather isn't helping the fight against it.

JULY 16, FRI

Quite a lot of excitement around the camp today and yesterday. We were supposed to receive Red Cross parcels yesterday but it was a German half holiday. But I am afraid the Hun didn't enjoy it very much as two men were missing from the work compound, then the trouble began. We had 3 rollcalls in three hours; the last one from 6:15 to 8:30, during which time we stood out on the parade square while the camp was being searched. They even looked in the partially completed reservoir and dump-carts. Dogs were introduced into the search but proved useless as they had no idea where the trail started. Finally with the usual warning to remain in our huts after ten or be shot, we were dismissed and allowed to return to our billets where we resumed preparations for our evening meal.

This morning the search continues. Red Cross rations are cut off also water is exceedingly scarce today and it is thought the situation will last until the missing men are found. There is a story going around that one of the dogs disappeared during the search last night and it was found in the Red Cross compound dead. Anyhow, there is a company of Germans in that compound carrying out a detailed search of all the huts, for the missing persons. They may retaliate on the rest of us with further methods than cutting the Red Cross rations off. Ernie Jones has a touch of the flu.

There is a rumour that forces in Sicily made a landing on Italian soil and are 90 miles inland. A correction on the dog story, the pooch was found in a Red Cross crate with six pups. Am taking the story with a large grain of salt. It was announced that we would get our parcels at 9:00A.M. tomorrow.

We hear that the greatest battle in history is raging on the Russian front. The Russians brought in 80-some fresh divisions. Another reason for the search last night was that a Postern thought he heard a radio in the Red Cross stores and reported it. They had to remove two months' supply of rations to search it properly.

JULY 18, SUN.

News of a Canadian spearhead attack in Sicily came through yesterday; 3/5 of the island taken; the Italians and Germans have taken to the hills, with all main cities but two have been taken. Yanks have taken 8,000 prisoners, Canadians 1,000 and British paratroops none. A force of 30,000 with tanks have made a landing on the heel of Italy. Cologne was heavily bombed the other night.

It has been customary to maintain two months' supply of Red Cross rations in the camp at all times, but since it took nearly 100 Jerries all day to search for a radio, the irate commander has issued orders that no more than a week's supply can be kept at any one time. The Red Cross officials are trying to have the order changed to at least 2 weeks' supply. Incidentally, they worked for nothing as their search disclosed everything was shipshape.

JULY 20, TUES.

BBC news read out last night, dealing mostly with Sicily. V sign for victory found wherever the troops go on the Island. Anti-Fascist groups welcomed the Allied invasion and helped wherever they could. It's also believed that Anti-Fascist groups are willing to aid occupation of Italy when and if the occasion arises. People of Italy are blaming Mussolini for the bombings. The civilian population in Sicily welcomed Allied troops. General Alexandria appointed governor of Sicily. A body of specially trained men are being trained in Africa to take over the governing of occupied countries as they are taken. Churchill is supposed to have asked Mussolini why he didn't give in and Musso is alleged to have answered that the German's wouldn't let him. All planes encountered in Sicily are Italian, no German planes present. A German N.C.O. is supposed to have said that the Russians have broken through in several places and consolidated; the Germans are being pushed back relentlessly. Aforementioned N.C.O. said Germany is finished and can't last much longer.

The guard and officer marched into the compound during roll-call this morning and carried out a 2-hour search for a radio or something. One sergeant with a brain storm even procured a ladder to inspect the roof and look down the chimneys. The flower bed was a convenient place for my purposes. They didn't bother the lantern. Everyone thinks the Germans are trying to curb the news coming into camp.

JULY 23, FRI.

Rumours of a landing in Norway at Trondheim was circulating yesterday. According to Jerry papers the attempt was repulsed. No further news of Sicily. Heavy fighting on the Russian front. I carry my diary on parade every morning now; no telling when a search may be made. School is closing from the 28th to August 9 for examinations and alterations. We are having a trig test immediately after reopening. Bucking the Germans all the way, we managed to obtain enough whitewash to cover the interior of the hut and wash tube. The lower four feet along the walls is done in grey made from cement. Men engaged in the decorating were covered liberally with the stuff but eventually we got it finished. The Wash tube is whitewashed, with black trimmings of creosote around the basin and copper. Then to give it a finishing touch two French-Canadian lads stenciled red, green and yellow maple leaves along the top of the gray border. All the huts in this compound are doing similar jobs and the notion is spreading to other compounds. "Spitfire" bucked the idea at first, then refused to co-operate but is tickled with the results. Jig-saw puzzles have been assembled and pasted on cardboard and add a homey touch to it all; a clock we bought at one time for six cigarettes each gives it a finishing touch and is the envy of the rest of the compound, even if it does gain 20 minutes every twelve hours. BBC July 24 news broadcast: Sicily finished all but 2 positions; Rome bombed heavily; 6-engine bomber causing great concern to Germans; new plane flew from Cairo to London in 4½ hours. New Mosquito plane armed with cannons, causing great damage to rail transport in France, claim an average of 150 trains a month each. Germany admits heavy losses in Russia; Russians broken through at 7 points; consolidated around Orel. Churchill claims the downfall of the enemy will start by autumn. Still fighting in Norway. Rumours: one town in Italy fallen; Norway raid repulsed at first attack; 48 hours later attacked again, gained a foothold and were reinforced.

JULY 27

A small area at the eastern tip of Sicily remains in enemy hands. Russians still pounding away at German lines. Word came in yesterday that Mussolini had fled and half the country taken by Allies. Hitler claims that as long as there is Germans in Italy, Italy will fight. The fact that something happened to Musso was confirmed in German papers but claim he was forced to resign because of ill health; later he said Musso had betrayed the German people. Another rumour has Goering in jail after caught trying to flee the country.

Another plane crashed this afternoon but the pilot parachuted to safety. Received a E.U.P. book on Mathematics today. Italy is said to be under martial law. Hamburg heavily bombed again. Germans hereabouts think Germany may possibly last another three months; they give Italy a week after Sicily is finished. Over half of the Solomon Island in American hands. The Red Cross issue is good this week, ½ English parcel on Monday, approximately 1 lb. of bulk sugar and ¼ lb. of cocoa Wednesday and ½ Canadian parcel Thursday.

Delousing parades have started today. Fleas attacking continually; counter-offensive is being planned.

If the rumours keep coming in like they are now, I will have to start hourly entries. Rumours tonight: Italy capitulated; Germans using gas.

JULY 28, TUES.

Almost definitely confirmed that Italy capitulated after Mussolini turned over to King Emanuel who asked for capitulation to forestall a revolution. If Italy capitulated that means that Albania and possibly Greece is free, and Italians on Russian front may be effected. The Germans themselves are inclined to confirm Goering affair claiming he was dismissed because of inefficiency; Himmler is said to have his position. Placards are supposedly appearing in all large cities in Germany with "Finish this war" printed on them. Hamburg called the "City of the Dead" in German newspapers. Russians advancing along a 1,500 mile front. Pamphlets reportedly found in this district advising the Russians to "be prepared; the day is near." This is believed to be the reason for the extra machine gun and grenade supply in all sentry block houses around the camp. It's a debatable question if the extra precautions were prompted by fear of a mass break-out or to prevent arms and things coming in. Some think it may be for our own protection against enraged civilians. The "Little Man" told some fellows in 19B that they would be home soon. Germans around the main gate very quiet and glum looking. All Posterns refuse to discuss current affairs with prisoners, as they used to do. Went on delousing parade today. Received a letter from Nelle and one from Rusty, this morning.

JULY 30

Two more training planes met an untimely end yesterday when they crashed head on in mid-air. Italian delegates reported attending peace conference at Cairo. The Germans searched Block II the other day, where the pin-pointed maps are on display; they confiscated the Russian map showing the Russian line according to German newspapers. They left the maps of Sicily, and the far east. Betting is prevalent as to when we will get back. There are three books I am going to ask Nelle to get and keep for me. "They Landed at

Dawn," "Dieppe" and Quinton Reynolds' "Dress Rehearsal." The last one is a bestseller in America.

We received a book called "The War Log" through the Canadian YMCA as a gift from the Canadian people. In it there is blank paper for diary or journal or other matter such as portraits, etc. A space for a snapshot album and stickers and spaces for souvenirs at the back. It's a nice looking book and will make a dandy souvenir. Every Canadian is supposed to get one. the binding is of rough cloth with a maple leaf embossed in red on the front with the title, "A Wartime Log" in half inch red letters below. The first page repeats the title, followed by a sort of dedication, "A Remembrance From Home through The Canadian YMCA." Then follows a page headed by a Maple Leaf, then a few blank lines headed, "this Book belongs to" with the YMCA symbol at the bottom. The next page is a ruled blank page headed,"Contents" and "page." Page No. 1 has a head of a line of red maple leaves with the figure "1" in the center. Seventy-two blank pages follow, then nineteen snapshot pages, then 78 more blank pages. The last page has six small cellophane envelopes for souvenirs.

I haven't said much about the physical features of the camp in this journal so far so some day in the near future I will take a crack at it. Another feature of the camp or rather the inmates is McClusky's gang. The school could very well stand a little space as well as the Theatre. Not to mention the Toy factory, the post office procedure. I may try drawing a plan of the camp if I can obtain near enough figures of lengths and such.

AUG. 1, SUN.
The arts and crafts exhibition opened yesterday with a display of entries that would do full credit to talent where material and tools were conveniently at hand. Pencil copies of photographs perfect in every detail and expression; paintings and sketches of prison life in all its phases. Wood carvings of all types, statues, onlay and inlay, etc. Needlework that would make a woman envious. Miniature models of aircraft, sailing vessels, destroyers, racing cars, etc., complete with interior detail. Hand worked rugs, mats, clothing, etc. Sport shields, regimental badges, reliefs, picture frames carved in minute detail in wood. It's too bad the whole display can't be sent on a tour to show

the people the ability of the artists. Not only the fact that material is difficult to obtain and the tools in a majority of cases, were razor blades and pen-knives, that many of the exhibits were perfect in detail and craftsmanship.

The water reservoir, alias swimming pool, experienced its first bunch of bathers early this morning, the water being only a foot deep. At 7:30 this evening it was three feet. It is of queer construction for a swimming pool; square, about 12 feet deep with steep sloping sides; once a person gets in, he has to have top side aid in the form of an extended walking stick, belt or towel, to get out of the hole, again.

News and rumours have dropped off this last day or two, nothing coming in about Sicily or Italy. They do say however, that the German papers are yelling, murders, killers of women and children, etc. following the damaging raids on Hamburg. The Germans didn't think of women and children when they were bombing London or wasn't it Germany who said back in the first years of the war, that every woman, child and babe was a potential enemy?

The Camerons downed the Air Force in softball this afternoon to the tune of 13-2.

AUG. 3, TUES.
Rumours: Japan has declared war on Russia, something I think the Russians have been expecting and preparing for. I don't think the Japs surprised the Russians very much. A large German force is trapped in the Orel district with the Russians on three sides and the Dniester River at their back. The fiercest fighting the German army has ever experienced is in progress in this area. The German army is ill-clothed, no distinguishing marks between officers and men. There is still fighting in eastern Sicily; and Badoglio claims that the Italian war aims and intentions remain as before, despite governmental changes. He fails to mention the execution of those intentions, however.

The swimming pool was in use the day before yesterday, while a German photographer took some pictures of the boys cavorting in a foot or so of water. Today there is a guard on the pool, stopping everyone from so much as touching the water. The photographer was taking snaps of the track-meet yesterday so it is expected that the folks back home will be seeing propaganda photos of our swimming hole and sports meet. What a laugh, they fail to mention that the water in the pool is stagnant and that the chains weren't taken off on Saturday afternoon because we would have our hands free yesterday. The fact that we haven't had water in this compound for 36 hours, and they demand a clean floor and washroom for inspection every morning. Prior to yesterday morning, if a person wanted to have a bath or do his laundry, he had to get up at 4 in the morning because the water is shut off between 5:30 and 6:00. Water for tea has to be carried in kűbels from the "rackets" or "repats."

The fashion for summer attire a-la-POW took a revolutionary turn last night when "Chicago" Hickman appeared for the first time dressed in only a handkerchief and a piece of shoe lace. Argumentary matter ranges all the way from the weight of a bag of cement in Canada to that time mellowed riddle about the man and the photograph ("That man's father is my father's son"). Is a girdle the same thing as a griddle? Am drawing a plan of the compound in detail with a plan of the interior of 20A shown, to scale for my War Log Book. Talented persons are painting sketching and drawing prison scenes in their books; I envy these people their talent. Others are just getting autographs of everyone in the room. I am collecting P.O.W. poems.

Being of a curious nature and wondering what all the noise was that was coming from the reservoir (alias swimming hole) I decided to investigate. Try and imagine about 100 men, all different shades of tan, trying to dive and swim in a pool 15 by 15 ft. Honestly believe that the neatest diver was a one-legged chap who appeared to encounter no difficulty in climbing out of the hole, where his two-legged companions needed the aid of the spectators.

Heard a rumour this evening that 5,000 Germans were captured by the Russians at Orel.

AUG. 5, THURS.
We have been hearing so many contradictory rumours lately it is practically impossible to separate them in any sensible sequence. For instance, the Italian government has changed again, Badoglia being unable to fulfill his political obligations. They say Orel has fallen with German casualty estimation in the

vicinity of 600,000, fierce fighting at the Kuban bridgehead. The British and American Air Force continue to bomb Hamburg and other German cities with devastating effect. Germany is supposed to have been warned to evacuate women and children from Berlin by the 8th; there was 500 tons of bombs dropped on fortifications in the Brenner pass.

Jerries around here have the wind up about something as they have doubled the night guard twice inside of a week. A Postern came in yesterday and asked for numbers of the men not wearing their chains. Some of the answers he received would have been excuse enough to shoot a few of us a few months ago; he finally became discouraged and followed by various deprecating remarks made his exit from the hut via the wash-tub door.

Received 2 letters from Nelle this morning, one dated Dec. 3 in which she answered my air mail letter of Sept. 12. The other one is April 12; in both letters she mentions that my letters have been put in the "Miner." Perhaps the notoriety may come in useful later on. Once again, I find myself an envious spectator while associates enjoy themselves at "aqua-antics."

Then there is the Czechoslovakian Jew who joined the Palestinian army, assumed Grecian citizenship when that country went under, was transported to Poland to work for Jerry; noticed the way the British P.O.W.'s were living, disclosed his army standing to the Germans, transported to this camp by way of Hamburg and Berlin. Claims that people of Hamburg and Berlin sleep in the surrounding country and woods at night. Both places somewhat messed up.

AUG. 7

War news taken from German papers is "that Orel, being of no further military value, was successfully evacuated, according to plan." (They forgot to mention whose plan, theirs or the Russians') We also heard a rumour that the German civilian rationing system has broken down, especially in areas subjected to heavy bombing. Also heard another rumour to the effect that Turkey is allowing the passage of Allied troops through to Hungary.

Am spending considerable time collecting the desired information for War Log book; am working on a diagram of the camp now. The whole difficulty is, as soon as anything is done that looks half decent, so many want it done in their books and swear they are incapable of doing it themselves.

AUG. 9, MON.

Thought we were going to have to stand outside for awhile this morning but the doings scheduled for last night were postponed indefinitely. The fact that 3,000 veteran P.O.W.s are due in camp this evening or tomorrow morning is giving rise to many rumours. They are prisoners from camps in Italy; they are from danger zones in Poland or around Berlin, etc. This is the day the bombing of Berlin is rumoured to start. Churchill is supposed to have sent a message to Berlin warning them to evacuate Berlin and that the cities of Germany will be systematically destroyed. Hitler is supposed to have answered that if Berlin is bombed on the ninth he will shoot one out of every ten P.O.W.s and if they bomb the next night he will shoot one out of five, and if the bombing continues he will dispose of all of us. A nice topic of conversation, the fellows are deciding to cut cards or take it by sections. By tomorrow noon we are expecting 54 more men in the hut, so the re-arrangement of kits is indicated. The Camerons got licked 16-0 by the Bulldogs yesterday. According to recent information leaking into camp by mysterious means, German troops are heading toward France and according to general belief, both German and British P.O.W.s, Germany is probably planning on taking one last crack at invading England. There is also expressed belief in certain quarters that Germany is going to pull a surprise in Russia soon. This may be a little more medicine from Goebbels' department to bolster flagging civilian moral. Sicily is reported definitely finished tonight.

AUG. 10, TUES.

According to the latest BBC news report (2 days old), 8 Italian divisions refused to fight against the Allies and laid down their arms; this leaves the Germans holding a small area of Sicily. Badoglio is in Berlin conferring with Hitler. The German casualties during the battle of Orel is the heaviest they have sustained in any one battle. Stimson of U.S.A. is in Turkey, also Allied troops and a state of war practically exists between Turkey and Germany. Roosevelt is in Sicily inspecting American troops there. The reason for the devastating raid on Hamburg was given as: the civilians in that area lynched

65 British airmen, thereby conducting themselves as participants in combat therefore, they were treated as combatants. Hitler has asked the people to hang on for another 6 weeks. There are long queues of people trying to get trains out of Berlin. Rome heavily bombed by 1,500 bombers; people are practically living in cellars and shelters. It is rumoured that Hitler has warned the Italian people that if any town, village or city shows the least indications of revolting their ration will be cut off. Heard also today that seven million Russians and 4½ million Germans have lost their lives on the Russian front.

3,040 British P.O.W.s arrived from Italy today straining the camp accommodation to breaking point. We have 54 more men in here. Each hut in this compound took up a collection of cigarettes for the newcomers, the fellows in our hut received approximately 40 apiece. They received ½ parcel each soon after and 40 issue cigarettes. They are getting their palaises and blankets now. The fact that these men were moved so hurriedly to an already crowded camp, may indicate the uncertainty in which the Germans consider Italy at the moment. These lads were all decorated with bright red patches on their backs, greatcoat, shirt and tunics, and a red patch on the right leg of their trousers. Incidentally the patches are disappearing rapidly. Of course, comparing of experiences as fighting men and prisoners, scenes seen, places visited, battles witnessed, is in full swing. They believe Italy is done and they will be home by Xmas. They are even billeted in the school, the camp is that crowded.

AUG. 13, FRI.

The day and date momentous events as far as some of us in the Camerons are concerned. In regards to the couple of thousand more prisoners coming in from Italy goes, except for a little more inconvenience they are fairly well settled in the floor bunks and making themselves at home. Other huts in other compounds are finding it more difficult as they have so much kit they found it impossible to get it off the floor, the new fellows are sleeping on the floors around the walls. We had roll-call inside last Tuesday night for the first time since we were tied last October 8. Even Spitfire didn't have the heart to make us stand outside in the pouring rain.

Rumours are coming in that Britain is protesting against the transfer of prisoners from Italy to Germany. More are expected soon. We had trouble during roll-call yesterday. On the day after the new men came in "Jerry" didn't bother with the chains so yesterday they decided to have a chain check. The five o'clock roll-call was supposed to be followed by this check-up but difficulty was encountered across the road in the A.F. compound, so we were dismissed. Then we were in the middle of preparing our supper when we were again called out. One of the "repats" who had climbed over the fence to get in had to climb back out again and the Unteroffizier saw him; he ordered him to stop but the fellow kept going. The Jerry pulled his revolver and as eye-witnesses claim, pulled the trigger but the gun misfired.

It was rumoured last night that there is hand-to-hand fighting in Minsk, following the fall of Orel. the Russians are reported to be within 40 kilos of the old Russian frontier. Germans are pouring troops and supplies into Italy. Fighting in the Sicilian Straits.

Received a food parcel today in which the fruit was rotten, the tea, chocolate and sugar moldy and highly contaminated. Have to try and get it changed. Later: Tried to have the parcel changed but only managed the fruit, the tea and half the chocolate. Almost caught reading a book on parade this evening by the Feldwebel. He was across the road in the R.A.F compound and saw us reading; he yelled something at Spitfire then mounted his trusty bicycle and came over. He parked his vehicle against a convenient fence post (there's plenty around here), looked at me and said in his best broken English, "Where's the book?" I looked dumb (almost natural) looked down the line away from the irate Hun and very innocently said "He wants the books." Apparently thinking I was a hopeless case, (an opinion probably shared by many khaki clad people as well), he strutted down the three columns and collected seven or eight books.

AUG. 14

Three men caught reading and smoking on Parade last night received 14 days' strafe, 2 of them for smoking and one for reading. The two "brainy" individuals who queered the wood parties by trying to escape from it the other day came back from serving 3 days' strafe. They were totally unprepared for the

465

attempt and were picked up a few hours later 10 miles away. They offered the excuse that they had been separated from the main body of wood gatherers and were lost. The Jerries who picked them up decided that as long as they walked 10 miles for wood it would be a shame to return empty handed so they had to carry a load that would have made ten men perspire freely, back to camp.

There was a little excitement this afternoon when a Russian was noticed sitting on the outside of our fence, pretty badly shot up. Apparently he had tried to escape and was shot through the hand and chest as a consequence. He was still very much alive and was finally removed by a cart which was sent out to pick him up. According to the way the Russians are treated, his life isn't worth two cents.

We are hearing rumours of a big naval encounter in the Black Sea between German and British small craft. There have been 5 raids simultaneously at different points of Italy; Genoa specially mentioned.

AUG. 16, MON.

Drew a set of chains in my log book with an inspirational V behind them; I notice a few copies appearing today. Watched the partial eclipse of the moon last night; local meteorologists set the time for it a week or so previous. Rumours of large working parties leaving in the near future are prevalent also that large groups of prisoners will be replacing them from Italy. The water situation has reached a chronic condition again; getting out of bed in the wee hours of the morning is the only time and method of accomplishing one's laundry or obtaining a bath. Very poor bulk this week but I guess we will live through it until parcel day next week. Heard tonight that Sicily was officially finished on Saturday; this is about the sixth report of similar import on this front. Russians are supposed to be still advancing.

AUG. 19, THURS.

A year as a prisoner; we have seen big changes since the heat of the battle of Dieppe. Is it only a year ago; it's more like ten. We have outlived the chain situation to such an extent that they come in the morning, remain in obscurity until the Jerries come for them at night. The principle use for them now is modeling or symbolic drawings for War Log Books. Dieppe has been re-fought over again today; the stories being added to where necessary to impress our visitors from Italy. Speculation for the end of the war ranges from two months from the more optimistic element to one year from the pessimists.

Received 1,000 cigs from Dad last Friday, a letter from Janet the other day, one from Peggy this morning and an air mail from Nelle this morning, containing the list of articles in the July parcel. Have been doing some sharp dealing recently; bought a German pipe, carved with deer, etc. for 250 cigs. Then bummed a comb off of Shurvell, cut it down to a barber's comb, traded it for a Royal Marine badge; bought three new text books on engineering for 650 cigs, sold one for 150. A year ago today, I had only what I crawled out of the ocean with; now I have a pack sack full of clothes, enough cigs and tobacco to last four months, writing material wholly sufficient for some time and a few text books which include Mathematics, Shorter Geometry, School Geometry and Trigonometry, Elementary Engineering Science, Mathematics for Engineers, Technical Electricity, etc.

Rumours: Hand to hand fighting in Minsk; Russians still advancing; one million people evacuated from Berlin; Rome being bombed, Pope wants to proclaim it an open city and advocates peace at any price. Sicily finished for sure. Eating too heavy these days; fattest I have ever been.

According to the BBC news read out this evening, the Russians are advancing in a u-shaped formation, Kharkov, Kiev, Smolensk and Bryansk being mentioned. The figures of casualties and prisoners taken at Sicily was also given, as far as I can recollect they are 180,000, dead, wounded and prisoners. Finland is groping for peace terms. The Chief-of-Police of Oslo has been executed. The president of Denmark handed in his resignation but it was refused, later he was arrested.

It is rumoured that Stalin has made good his promise that Germany would not realize the Ukraine grain crop; he burned them with incendiaries. News of a more local nature include the construction of slit trenches all around the camp. The purposes of these is a topic of contention. Some say it is a protective measure for the Stalag watch and guard in case of air-raids; others think it is a protective measure against Russian parachutists; still others think it is in case the civilian population gets out of hand and storms the camp. The latter seems more feasible.

AUG. 21, SAT.

Blistering hot these last few days and water is scarce in this compound. If a person is lucky and has a helper with good lungs, he may obtain a cupful of water from the pipes when his co-worker blows in another outlet. Sometimes all the puffing and blowing of two men won't produce a drop. All I can think of these days is a tent, a canoe and necessary accouterments for a fishing trip, as some quiet pine surrounded spot on the old lake back home. Maybe my imagination and memory are playing me tricks; but what could be more pleasant than a tent snuggled in pines close to the blue rippling lake, the whispering pines, as a gentle breeze plays among their boughs and harmonizing with the gentle lapping of wavelets on the rocky shore and the variety of songs, twitterings, etc. of the wildlife in the bush, punctuated now and again by the splash of a fish after an unwary or venturesome fly. The smell of bacon and coffee rising on the fresh morning air, pine needles in everything, adding that special flavour only acquired and enjoyed out in the open. Even sitting on the old well, refusing to heed the follies of civilization and listening to the carefree chattering and laughter of the "Four Steps" in play; the slamming of the screen door as Nelle comes out for a pail of water, the radio adding its share to the homey atmosphere with the Happy Gang bursting forth with musical efforts. Dad sitting in his old rocker puffing contentedly on his oldest Brier, planning the garden harvest, etc., Connie calling the kids from inside the porch; myriads of other sounds connected with home. Back to earth and existing conditions, "Spud boxes up" is the cry so starts another splurge of dividing and issuing of rations; "fed up and far from home" is the only phrase that fits.

With the arrival of the spuds comes the remembrance that there are a couple of rumours that should be recorded, to the effect that the Russians have captured another town; that Churchill is supposed to have told those towns in German that have so far escaped attention not to worry as their turn was coming. Hitler hasn't been mentioned or heard of since Nov. 6.

According to the story going around camp, an Aussie working party was stoned by some civilians which led to a general melee, in which three Aussies became hospital cases. The Aussies claim they routed the civvies with many civilian casualties.

Rumour from a German source claims that there is large scale allied landings in Norway and France, Dunkirk specially mentioned.

AUG. 22, SUN.

We have been warned not to drink un-boiled water, to cover our food from flies, to wash our hands at every opportunity and to keep our cooking and eating utensils clean. There are three positive and one suspected cases of typhoid fever in the camp. If an epidemic ever gains a good start, crowded as we are, I venture to say that 50% of us won't see England or Canada again. The camp is overcrowded now and still they bring more in. Weather remains scorching, windy and dusty with no improvement in the water situation.

Wrote letters to Nelle, Rose, Harry and Bezzie, Janet and Bobby and cards to Anne and Ted Cox, Peggy and Rusty today. McCowan, the poet, gave me extra letter cards and cards yesterday. Noticed the Germans came on duty with their white summer dress today. All working parties have been cancelled for awhile and not from the typhoid scare either. There is a mass band concert with three male choirs in Block 2 this evening. It's too hot to stand out there.

AUG. 25, WED.

The typhoid scare still exists although it is thought to be under control. The drinking water supply is proclaimed safe but the M.O. (Major De Olive Lowe) has issued a warning to keep all our cooking and eating utensils clean and to wash all vegetables thoroughly as human manure is used on the fields as fertilizer. The district is also crowded with refugees from bombed areas and their knowledge of safeguards against disease is restricted. The reservoir is believed badly infected with typhoid germs. So far as we know there has been no more cases reported outside of the three probables and one possible.

The razor gang threatened bodily harm to the bath attendant (Sailor Wilmot) the other day because he refused to let them bathe out of their turn and whenever they wanted to. When one of them produced a razor Wilmot threw him out. This is the same gang that attacked and seriously wounded an Indian in Block 2 during Whitsun week.

The store in Block 2 is going over big and is having difficult time handling the business that two more have opened, one in 9A and one at 32A. I have started a very expensive and difficult hobby, that of collecting genuine cap badges. The new fellows from Italy are being "ticked" off for working parties, 1,000 going out during the following week. This won't relieve the strain accommodation, however, because there are more coming in. It has been rumoured around that some working parties have been stoned by the civilians recently. One party went out, were moved from place to place, no one seeming to know where they were supposed to go; finally they came back. One of them said while they were changing trains at Breslau they were talking openly to groups of refugees from the bombed areas and were told that as far as Britain and Germany were concerned, the war was over between them.

Rumours: Commando raid on Toulon, France; Sweden has declared war on Germany; American Air Force dropped 5,000lbs of bombs into Mount Vesuvius crater, but they failed to explode, people are fleeing the district. There are persistent reports of placards seen in neighbouring towns with a British soldier neatly dressed, marching smartly along with his rifle at the slope; and a Russian soldier, brutal, dirty, crushing women and kids under his hob-nailed boots. It is captioned with "which one would you rather have?"

Supposedly BBC news: five landings in Italy, 4 are successful; Hitler has asked for peace conference to be held in Sweden; Goebbels stated in speech that unless Britain and America joined Germany, Russia would overrun Europe, as Germany was unable to hold them any longer. American and Canadian troops have attacked and taken an island in the Aleutian group. Russians are 75 kilos west of Kharkov and 75 kilos from Kiev.

One fellow said tonight that a friend of his swears that he heard over the radio that there are large demonstration parades in all large German cities for peace, and that a peace conference is due for August 28. No one here is taking all these rumours and so-called genuine news reports seriously. Some of the fellows think we will be in England for Xmas, others think we may see it in a year's time. I think the end is overdue and may come anytime and we probably will be fighting Russia in 10 to 15 years. Russia had the same intentions toward ruling the world as Germany and Italy, only their methods were different. Despite the recent change of political titles, I think their intentions are the same. Whether called Communism or Social-Democracy their ambitions, though delayed by war with Germany, still remain.

AUG. 26, THURS.

The gates were locked all day because 22B has mislaid 2 sets of chains; by evening roll-call there was still one set missing so the gates remain locked. This sort of thing is a perfect example of childishness and stupidity, forever showing itself in the actions of the German race. The chains have become a toy and is utilized to shorten the tedious roll-calls. It's a favourite pastime to try and hook one handcuff by the key hole unto the prong of the other handcuff in the same manner as cup-ball. It's not an unusual sight to see hundreds of "chained" prisoners indulging in this pastime. Rumours this evening are: the British 12th army has landed in Sicily without loss; Kiev has been taken by the Russians.

Have one of the moods on this past few days; everything gets on my nerves, especially the perpetual haggling and arguing; subjected to the urge to either smash something or write poetry to relieve my feelings. I can't write poetry worth a damn and smashing something just isn't done, not even in prison circles, so the feeling is suppressed and smolders. Ambition is gone by the board and past occupations fore me no end. Although I continue to record them as they come, I refuse to believe them in the least, even so called BBC news fails to strike a responsive cord. In fact I am walking around boiling inside but still capable of speaking to associates with a certain degree of civility. Perhaps I am suffering from an acute case of homesickness.

AUG. 27, FRI.

A windy dusty day. Camerons beat the Royals 4-3; they still have a chance for a play-off berth. Beer got three days in the digger for breaking his chains. The gates were open today with a chain still missing. Rumours tonight aren't much different to yesterday's. Anthony Eden is conferring with German officials in Sweden; Swedish papers claim war will be over in two weeks; Kiev and Minsk are supposed to have fallen.

Received a letter from Peggy yesterday; a little worried about her.

Here are some extracts from letters received by some fellows from home, printed in STIMMT: "I went to a dance with an American airman, purely platonic, my dear." "They say travel broadens the mind, you lucky man." "I will be glad when you can come home and earn some money again." "Please don't frequent those beer gardens too much, dear." "Glad to hear that you are getting plenty of tennis and swimming."

Just finished reading a book called, "The Shadow Before" definitely not recommended for prayer meetings or Sunday schools. The M.O. has pointed the forbidden finger at dances in the camp. Received 300 cigs. from Eric this morning.

AUG. 29, SUN.
Rumours not very plentiful this evening except one coming from the "repats" that all D.U.s (definitely unfit) and prisoners with 3 years' standing will start going on Sept. 5th; this rumour was refuted by STIMMT at the first of the week, but has since been renewed and is going strong. Eric is busy these days studying a building book he received lately. Our table is becoming quite studious. Jones is learning Morse Code; Engbert, auto-engineering, Dawson, shorthand, Bauer, German, Eric, building and myself, electricity.

Raining today and there is an international cricket match on. They have been playing since early this A.M. and seem not the least discouraged despite the rain. Some of the new fellows are going out on working parties this coming week. Red Cross issue for this week will probably be 1 English parcel and coming the week will be 72oz. of bulk and 1/2 a Canadian parcel.

AUG. 31, TUES.
Yesterday morning the German who drives the gravel wagon for the reservoir construction, came to work bubbling with happiness and had everyone guessing the reason for his sudden jubilation. At last, Mickey, MacTyre, interpreter, ask him why he was so happy. The Teamster replied that he thought

his son was numbered among the dead as he hadn't heard from him for years; the day before yesterday he received a letter from his son, who is a P.O.W. in England.

Four members of the 1st Canadian Division came into camp this morning among 50 or so others from Sicily. From their information it sounds like the Canadians led a spearhead attack across the island with no reinforcements. This particular informant believes their losses were very heavy. He also figures that most of the Canadians had left England. I have received 1,000 cigs from Nelle today. It has been a big cigarette day for the Canadians and bedlam and confusion ruled at the post office.

BBC News broadcast for August 28: The Russians have advanced 673 miles in the last few months (weeks?); they are fighting on a 300 mile front and are storming the approaches to Kiev and are advancing on Odessa. At Charkow the Germans threw in 3 divisions of their best troops and as a counteracting measure, the Russians did the same. The resulting battle was fierce and heavy but after 7 hours the Russian army continued their advance.

Excellent co-operation between New Zealand, Australian, American and British troops in Burma resulted in the Japanese being driven south until they occupy only a very small sector, and the Burma Road to China is once more carrying war supplies to China. Sweden continues to maintain a strict neutrality policy by confiscating 3 German troop ships and interning 3,000 German personnel. Units of British Mediterranean fleet heavily shelled Turanto and Naples harbours. British naval forces have free run of the Mediterranean, a large convoy steamed up the Adriatic unmolested. Italy has been told that she will experience 2,000-plane bombing raids a day. Nuremberg has had two terror bombing raids and is in nearly the same conditions as Hamburg.

Churchill in a speech, stated that the time has arrived for the subjected peoples of Europe to make trouble and cause so much damage as possible as the deciding factor of the war will take place in the next two months. He said he was sorry he couldn't promise definitely that the war would end by Christmas, but he believed it would be over early in 1944.

The rumour that Italy had capitulated is circulating again, but no one will actually believe it until verified by the Germans or BBC.

It is becoming a daily habit now to make the rounds of the stores to see if any bargains are going.

Forgot to mention the Japs losing the Solomon Islands; this increases the difficulties of supplying her outlying positions. All in all the news is very good.

SEPT. 3, FRI.

Four years of war today; three years and nine months tomorrow since I signed on the dotted line. Wednesday was the anniversary of our arrival in camp; I hope we don't see another. Due to the recent German order to clear out the room where the bulk rations are stored, our issue this week was a confusing mix-up; ⅓ of the camp received parcels and ⅔ received bulk. The bulk, all from Argentina, was of ample gross weight but very low in quality. The bedlam started at eleven this morning and was still in full swing this afternoon at one. 25 men to a bag of powdered goat's milk (undissovable and strong to taste) 14 men to a block of cheese (dry, old and strong) four men to a pound of jam (dry, tasteless which we cut like pie) 9 men to six packets of biscuits, 10 men to four 1 lb. cans of butter and 1 pkg. of margarine (the latter is rancid, smells like old stale lard and inedible). 2 men to a can of lamb & beans, sixteen ounces of sugar per man, 1oz of tea per man; 2oz. of Arg. Cocoa per man (bitter, muddy stuff against which extravagant use of sugar is unavailing). The worst of it is we get a similar load on Monday. They say the reason for clearing the stores out is to make room for the Christmas parcels. The Agriculture Society refuse to make plans for spring cultivation because they figure they won't be here by then.

A little controversy is raging in the Air Force compound these days because of the interpreter trying to run the compound. He engineered the removal of the Dieppe personnel back to 7 to 10 and the return of Air Force personnel back to his compound over Joe's head and against the wishes of both parties. Four irate 7 to tenners nailed him this morning and held him over a latrine sump hole. He is a badly frightened man just now but still capable of getting a court of inquiry underway. We are hearing tales of heroic action on 1st Div.'s part in Sicily from our latest members. One of these gentlemen said that a good number of people in England and at home think we gave in without trying at Dieppe. If that is true, I wish those people had of been there. To feel the clinging sand dragging on their feet while trying to run with an eighteen set strapped to their backs and weighed down by ammunition while Ack-Ack tracers, machine gun and rifle fire snapped past their ears and kicked up sand around their feet. I'd like to have seen them trying to climb over a barbed wire capped sea wall in the face of a deadly crossfire. Men hanging helpless on the cruel barbs riddled with bullets, their blood dripping on the shoulders and upturned faces of their comrades. I wish they had been in the streets of Pourville, crawling over rough cobble stones while the deadly accurate four-inch German mortars in inaccessible hill positions, showered them with accurately placed bombs. I would have liked to seen them crossing the ridge under a crackling barrage of machine gun fire from strong indiscernible pill boxes across the valley and dodging across a grain field with only one or two stooks of grain for shelter from penetrating, searching hail of lead; to see their associates pitch, scream and thrash around on the ground with a fatal burst of machine gun slugs in their vitals. I wish they had been there when we met a solid front of entrenched troops supported by tanks against which our puny rifles and bayonets had no effect; then the retreat to the beach, in blistering noon day heat, through mortar, machine gun, rifle and grenade fire only to find the tide out and the boats unable to land. I wish they had been there.

Some leaflets that were dropped on Berlin and translated into English and brought here by some unknown manner, were read out tonight. According to them Italy is finished. It is rumoured around that one German paper in its last publication stated that Germany had lost the war but Britain and America had lost the peace.

SEPT. 4, SAT.
Rumours are coming in fast again but there is no way of estimating their accuracy. Some of the fellows who understand German say it came over the loudspeakers today that Allied forces made a landing in a place called Reggio in Italy and that German and Italian forces were putting up a heroic struggle. This evening a rumour is going around that there has been five landings.

The Russians are supposed to have Kiev on three sides and are pounding at Odessa. Later the report that Kiev, Minsk and Odessa had fallen. British and American bombers are reported to be bombing the Romanian oil-fields. Men coming in off working parties from the vicinity of Berlin say that there were 121 raids, two in daylight each lasting five or six hours. Refugees from Hamburg, Nuremberg and Berlin are flocking to this part of the country, especially Breslau. More cases of civilian animosity toward British P.O.W.s are circulating, spitting and stoning reported prevalent "outside." Probably it was this civilian disposition that caused the "latern" project to be abandoned.

Lavatorial conditions are reaching a critical stage; three or more outside lavatories being locked as the inadequate disposal equipment is unable to cope with the situation. The typhoid scare is abating but still present, no new cases being reported. School may open again next week. Eric and I are reading "Gone With The Wind," taking turns at perusing this famous story. I received a pound of line cut tobacco and papers on Friday morning from Buddo. This is the first time I didn't have the papers confiscated by the Germans. The Essex Scottish and the Windsor Bulldogs are playing off for the Regimental Championship now, best two games out of three. The 'Dogs took the first game. Favourite subject of discussion these days is how we will go home, how long will be the period of quarantine and convalescence, how long will we remain here after the war is over? Questions of paramount importance to us.

SEPT. 6, MON.

Rumours are floating about Italy now. Prisoners taken there are arriving in camp; a couple the other day were captured 6 days ago and flown here. One of them belonging to the R.C.R. said the coasts of Italy were severely smashed by bombs and when they landed the transports were warped to piers and then "MARCHED" ashore. Since then other prisoners have arrived still wearing their steel helmets and respirators. Tonight the word went around that there was a group of prisoners outside the gates, and some airmen with them who were captured only 40 hours ago. There is a rumour going around that the "Pats" have taken an awful beating down there. This doesn't mean that they were licked but that their casualty list is very high. Aside from that, there is no more. About 300 of the I-tie prisoners left the compound this afternoon for working parties.

Meditating on potential post-war problems these days; wondering, in the first place, if all these fellows who have left good jobs will get them back and if they do are they prepared to hold them or will their knowledge be too obsolete. Or will we be treated like the return soldier of the last war. They were complimented and praised for putting up a good fight but were considered inadequate for daily work. In my case (pre-war) my mental and physical equipment was sorrowfully deficient for climbing the ladder to security and the initial boost, so necessary at the start, was also missing. The question is, am I any better equipped for the climb after the war; will I have an opportunity to acquire the necessary knowledge; would I be wise to change my ambitious plans (radio) for something requiring less mental training; will I find myself with the all-too-familiar shovel handle in my hands???? I don't like the idea of just drifting as some of these fellows will probably do and actually I have nothing to use as an anchor. Matrimonial inclinations are growing weaker each day, principally because I refuse myself the dubious pleasures of wedlock when I have no security to offer. This I do know, I am quite determined that I or any family I might have, will never go hungry again. If I can't or am not permitted to earn life's necessities, I will acquire them somehow. To my way of thinking, every man or person who has seen active service has earned the right to a full stomach and if I am unable to buy it, I'll acquire it by other means.

SEPT. 7, TUES.

Rumours and news galore today. BBC news is supposed to be: Advance continuing in Italy, aided by anti-Fascist groups. People appear pleased to see Allied troops. Large groups of Italians are giving themselves up and the prisoner of war situation has developed into a problem. As fast as they surrender, they are disarmed and sent to their homes; this method was also adopted in Sicily. The Italian police force is helping the British M.P.'s direct traffic, etc. The Americans attacked and captured Athens in Greece. The Russians took 150 towns in one day and the fall of Kiev is expected hourly. King Boris is dead, presumably assassinated by Nazis. Open fighting between Dutch and German troops in Denmark. Fifty tons of bombs a minute dropped on Berlin the night before last. News of more local nature reveals the "Repats" in the lime light again. They are supposed to be waiting for transportation back to England now. the Sanitators held a meeting recently and they were asked to supply 200 volunteers to remain behind, 75 of them are required to accompany the "Repats" on their home bound trip. Everyone hopes it is the real thing this time. If the rest of us are in England by spring we will consider ourselves exceedingly lucky. Churchill is supposed to have said that "the second front will start in a couple of weeks and will be opened at five or six points at the same time so that the Germans won't know where to send their troops." Apparently, every nation in the world realizes Germany is finished but Germany. Personally I think she knows she is licked but is fighting on because they are afraid the Russians will carry out reprisals if she gives in now, and is hoping America and England will get here first to forestall Russian retaliation.

The hut team just got whipped by hut 21 by about 24 to 11 or thereabouts so the noise resulting from "friendly" discussion and verbal replays is somewhat above a stage whisper. Sometimes I wonder how these fellows are going to hold their voice down to a reasonable level when they get back home. I guess my nerves are all shot or I have a terrific case of homesickness.

SEPT. 8, WED.

Seven to ten caused Jerry a little trouble this morning when three huts refused to wear their chains. In no time at all a squad of steel-helmeted, jack-booted Germans with loaded and bayoneted rifles was on hand and in accordance with a gesticulating officer's shouted orders were rousing the culprits out onto the parade square. A fair sized crowd was accumulating on the road and in adjoining compounds to watch the proceedings. the Germans decided to disperse these curious onlookers and thereby caused an amusing incident. B.S.M. Sabey of 'STIMMT' fame was one of the most interested speculators and when told to vamoose, replied that he was only trying to collect news to take home with him. The irate Hun on receiving a similar reply to his second request, placed Sabey under arrest and marched him before the camp commandant. As a result this former journalist was sentenced to stand for four hours with his face to the wall to meditate on the trials and tribulations of the transgressor in much the same manner as an erring school-boy. The men who refused to wear their chains were given 24 hours to think things over or take the consequences whatever they might be.

The repatriation rumour is stronger than ever, although there is no perceptible activity toward that end as yet. The water situation is extremely acute. Kiev is reported tonight to have fallen again. According to German news reports the Allies are still advancing in Italy and north west. Germany is being bombed. Lorne Engbert is raving mad this evening over the manner in which his best shoes were repaired this week. It's queer how leather half soles, heels, and tats appear for sale in the Stalag markets for fifty cigarettes a throw and shoes sent in for repairs come back with wooden soles put on with wooden pegs. Mail is scarce these days to such an extent as to be almost nil. I understand a letter, notifying the Int. Red Cross in Geneva of mail censoring, water shortage, overcrowding and sanitary conditions, has been sent. Whether or not it will bear fruit is questionable.

This Stalag can be aptly described as a huge accumulation of stinks. Refuge from the latrines is dumped on the surrounding fields and this stench combined with that of six or seven overflowing latrines and various dumps is terrific. I think we are all resigned to another Xmas here.

SEPT. 9, THURS.
(10:30) A semi-verified rumour came in this morning to the effect that the Italian army had capitulated at nine last night. The rumour is becoming stronger as the morning progresses and it looks as if it might be something to it. Most groups seen in conference today are talking about the Italian rumour or the repatriation news. Regarding this last, they asked for 300 volunteers to remain behind (sanitators) and so far they only have 50. Scotty Law just said the Italian capitulation was announced on the German radio so it must be definite.

(2:00P.M.) German radio announced that the German armies will continue to fight in northern Italy, Southern France and so to Deutschland. Badoglio is also supposed to have said that Italians in Northern Italy will continue the struggle. We are led to believe that only the Southern Italian armies have given up. "STIMMT" carried a statement by one of the men taken in Sicily that an Italian Officer in Italy had asked him when the British were coming to help them.

(7:00P.M.) The Italian's so called capitulation has been put forward in so many different versions it is practically impossible to record the true state of affairs at this early date. Lyons & Edwards came back from the garden arbeit and claimed they heard the German news on the radio at the Casino and it said it was complete capitulation; yet Dennis says he heard it over the broadcast systems and it was only the Italian armies in the south that have capitulated. So we will just have to wait until we get hold of something definite.

Am doing some sharp dealing with cigs and chocolate bars in an endeavour to obtain a very obtainable hat badge. Bill Robinson came in and gave me a Polish Army hat badge this morning. According to some of our hosts the war will be over in two months; some of the higher ranks give it six weeks.

According to the German news announcement for yesterday; the battle for the Donetz basin continues undiminished in ferocity and in order to shorten the front, the city of Stalino was evacuated according to plan. Strong Soviet attacks on the city of Karkow were repulsed after bitter battles. The German and Italian forces in Italy are unable to stop the northward march of Allied troops.

It's been a wild day for rumours and news but it all will gradually straighten itself out. The bad-boys who refused the chains yesterday in No. 3 compound decided to take them today but the gates are still locked, apparently as punishment for yesterday's affairs.

The news about the late afternoon German announcement regarding the troops in Northern Italy still fighting has turned out to be a misrepresentation by a few fellows who went off half cocked. The complete capitulation statement takes the biscuit. The only thing we can't seem to get straight is the time of the momentous event. I first heard that it took place at nine P.M. last night, since then it has been seven, eight and eleven; even four o'clock in the morning. General opinion is that the war will be over inside of three months and we will be on our way back by late winter or early spring; this is the calculations of Germans and prisoners alike. According to a few letters that are included in our meagre delivery, there is a rumour going in England that Canadian P.O.W.s will return direct to Canada without returning to England. Peggy mentioned that possibility in her last letter. Like the majority of Canadians here, I sincerely hope not as there is a number of things I want to do, people and places to see before I go home. I doubt very much if I can conduct a return trip once I get home. Two more shooting fatalities on a work party; one Australian and one Englishman.

SEPT. 10, FRI.

A late rumour last night has 2 million De Gaulist troops landing in Toulon in Southern France. If that is the case, the German intention of evacuating Italy through Southern France is frustrated. Later in the morning it was practically verified that British and Free French forces had landed in Toulon and Marseilles; at the same time there was a diverting pass made at Dieppe again. Later on the Dieppe rumour increased to, the raid had been carried out successfully and they met practically no opposition. The latest is that Allied forces are 80 kilometres from Paris. As I said before it is practically impossible to separate the wheat from the chaff, especially when we don't know which is which. Predictions for the end of the war ranges from 3 weeks to 5 months. All the Posterns believe Britain and America will eventually join forces with them and fight against the Russians. There is a possibility that in view of every German's dread of the Russians gaining a free hand in this country, that the German army may try and get the British and American forces here before the Russians. I think the majority of Germans realize they have lost the war and are only fighting a losing battle because they are afraid of Russian reprisals if they give in. Some big official in the States is supposed to have said that if Germany doesn't give up by the 16th of this month she will experience a detailed campaign many times worse than the one in Italy. According to men coming in from working parties, the civilians outside are quite ready to admit defeat and the end of the war.

Obtained the address of a fellow from Yorkshire who sleeps below me and he says if I call on him after we get back to England, he will give me a souvenir he picked up just before or at Dunkirk. With the recent war news, I notice everyone trying to sell things for Lager geld; it is redeemable after the war, they think. One mark is worth or will be worth approximately one shilling (or two-bits Cdn.) so watches, originally worth five dollars are selling for 400 marks which figures out to 100 dollars. There is no sense to it.

The latest is, "Blackhammer" has been bombed and it is necessary to move 5,000 British P.O.W.s out to safe zones. There definitely is fighting in France. This, my informant tells me is strictly "STIMMT." This is a phrase in Stalag lingo meaning it is straight goods.

SEPT. 11, SAT.
Received 1,000 cigs from the 16th Med. Battery Ladies Auxiliary today and discovered a little about Hilda K. Collins, who sent another thousand some time ago. Received a letter and snap from Nelle, a letter and 3 snaps from Marc and at last, a letter from Bobby. One of the fellows received a letter from a girl in England informing him that he was the father of a six-month old baby and asking for money consignment toward its keep.

The first time since the war started there is no German war communiques in the daily papers. The view is prevalent among jubilant P.O.W.'s that this is significant. The same papers claim that there is heavy fighting in the Brenner Pass; also there are 54 divisions of Allied troops in France. These papers are also carrying what they call the true version of Mussolini's disappearance. Musso was just finishing a two-hour conference with King Emanuel prior to his abdicating when General Badoglio turned up with an armed guard, arrested Musso, tied him to a stretcher and gave him a one way ride to prison in an ambulance. Any day now, some of us are expecting to hear of a similar governmental collapse here in Germany.

A group of Air Force fellows here went into conference and debated the problem of cleaning the prisoners out of Germany to England after the war. The result was they decided that rail transportation will be disrupted so that method would be a slow tedious affair. They finally concluded that the easiest and quickest way was by air. A few of us have had that idea for some time; with the size range and speed of Britain's modern bomber planes, it would be no trick at all to land at Lamsdorf Airport and load prisoners from there. Similar airports that are convenient could be utilized in clearing other camps.

News according to German newspapers of Sept. 9/43, headed:

SIX POINTS OF DESTRUCTION
THE CONSEQUENCES OF THE BETRAYAL OF ITALY

The unconditional capitulation of Italy has been the foundation of the destruction of Italy's imperialism, so it has been said in the headquarters of the western powers. Six points have been laid down for the future formation of Italy.

1. *Complete abolition of the army and fleet*
2. *Deportation of the previous fascists to the working camps of North Africa*
3. *Setting up of an international police*
4. *Internationalization of Rome as the traditional centre of imperial idea*
5. *Distribution of the former Italian colonies among the western powers*
6. *Annexation of Sicily by England. The setting up of an administration, similar to that of Malta.*

BADOGLIA'S COWARDLY BETRAYAL

The official British news service has given out from the headquarters of General Eisenhower that the Italian Government has offered the unconditional surrender of the Italian fighting forces. Eisenhower has accepted the capitulation and Italy has guaranteed an armistice, which was signed by a representative and deputy of Marshal Badoglio. With the signing, the armistice is in force immediately.

In the meantime Badoglio and the King himself have refuted all such thoughts as slander, but yet on the 18th September the capitulation was confirmed in a broadcast over the Rome Radio. He approached Eisenhower with the view to an armistice. In face the signing took place on the 3rd of September. The Italian fighting forces were to discontinue all hostile activities against the British-American forces.

Since the criminal stroke upon the Duce on the 25th of July and that with the English American revolutionary outbreak for the removal of the faithful members of the Fascist government, the German leadership was prepared for this open betrayal of the Italian Government and have taken all necessary military measures. The treacherous stroke against the defender of Europe will fail in the end just as similar undertakings.____

German naval forces and shipped parts of a Grenadier Regiment attacked the Allied base at Spitsbergen on the 8th of September. The object of the undertaking was the destruction of the extensive military depots and large stores of munitions and incendiaries as also the radio and weather stations, which for the operations of the sea and air forces of the Allies is especially important.

It is said that the coalmines under excavation and the military buildings which form a real part of the base were put out of action.

Despite the heavy artillery fire and bitter resistance of the military occupants on land, the task was completed with the collaboration of Naval forces and landed Grenadiers. The Allied base was completely destroyed. The Allies suffered heavy losses. Besides a large number of prisoners taken. The German losses on board ship and on land were slight. The German troops have returned to their base.

BERLIN. SEPTEMBER 9, 1943

In the Donetz Basin the Soviets threw new troops into the battle which suffered particular high losses . South and West of Charkow many enemy attacks failed. In the middle frontal sector the Soviets attacked only in the sector west of Charkow with heavy forces. On the other fronts Soviet attacks were weaker than in former days. A Soviet group which was surrounded in our defensive battle was destroyed, German and Romanian flyers supported our troops yesterday in several engagements. Ober-Lieutenant NOWOTNY leader of the fighter squadron scored his 196 to 200 air victory. 208 tanks were put out of action on the Eastern front yesterday.

In the Gulf of Finland marine batteries of the Island of Tutters shelled a Soviet fleet of mine-sweepers. It sank one minesweeper and damaged 2 others. In bitter battles west of Charkow the Panzer Grenadier division, "Great Germany" "The Hess II," "Lower Saxony 19" and the "Rhine 34 Infantry" have especially distinguished themselves.

In South France, in Italy and in the Balkans where German and Italian troops formerly fought together, all changes are being made which was made necessary by the betrayal of the Badoglio government. They are being completed as expected on the west coast of Calabria, German bombers attacked landing craft in the Bay of Euphemia, sank 1 transport and damaged 4 large ships among which one was a cruiser. British, N. American bombers in attacks on Western occupied countries and over the Atlantic lost 11 planes.

Fast German bombers attacked military targets in Southern and Middle England last night.

Evidently the Germans are pretty sore about Italy giving in and leaving them precariously situated. It's a parallel case to the British predicament when France and Belgium threw in the sponge.

Some more rumours and hearsay came in this morning. The most important rumour is that of British and American troops sailing through the Dardanells and landing at Odessa in an endeavour to link up with the south extremity of Russian forces. The hearsay is very optimistic and reputed to have come from German sources. One individual is betting 50 pounds English money that the war will be finished by Xmas and he is feeling safe in saying only a month more. German officers are credited with the statement that they are unable to understand the reasons for Germany to continue fighting as they undoubtedly have lost the war and further fighting is merely a needless waste of lives. Also 90% of the civilian population is held down by the remaining 10% and a revolution is just a matter of days. Hitler spoke for ten minutes after a six month silence and his address didn't receive the welcome his former speeches enjoyed. Goebbels refused to make speeches in public and there is some opinion that he has been done away with. One German says Germany can only last 26 days at the most before the people take a hand.

Learned today that the German officers don't like the Canadians a little bit. They say we are not soldiers, we don't fight fair because we use knives and we are always causing trouble. apparently we have been one big headache to the German authorities since we were taken at Dieppe. That's why I think the Germans were disappointed when we submitted to being tied without putting up any resistance, he was waiting for an excuse to exterminate a few of us, and recalling the arsenal in the hands of the guards on that occasion he could have wiped us out in a matter of minutes.

SEPT. 13

Another German version of the activity and situation in Italy came out today, painting a much rosier picture from a German point of view than the one the other day, accordingly persons with a resilient disposition are changing their views and adding a few more months on their predictions. They don't seem to realize that the German version might be especially painted for the benefit of the hard pressed civilian population. All German hopes depend on the already flagging civilian moral. The Italian affair, together with news from the Russian front is very liable to be the last straw.

SEPT. 14, TUES.

Yesterday the gates were locked because there was a chain missing; they stayed locked all day, consequently the fence behind the latrine caught hell. This morning there was two chains short so the gates remained closed. Eventually the chains were found (or two more sets purchased), then Jerry found the mutilated fence so immediately posted a guard on it and said the gates would be locked for a month.

The repatriation rumour ceases to be a rumour and is a fact, STIMMT carried the story when it hit the bulletin boards, hot off the press. It seems that they are having a little difficulty deciding what protective personnel (sanitators) are going to accompany them. The exact day of their departure is unknown as yet. Incidentally it will leave almost two compounds empty, which should relieve the overcrowdedness.

We had a little excitement on roll-call this evening when a fellow by the name of Lovell was caught without a hat. One thing led to another until Lovell practically dared Spitfire to draw his gun. As a result, the gun was drawn and Lovell submitted to being escorted from the parade square. An argument raged for hours in the hut here on whether or not Spitfire would have shot if Lovell insisted on being stubborn. Three British P.O.W.'s lost their lives on a working party just recently when one smart individual started shoving a postern around in front of some civilians. The postern pulled his gun and started firing. Some fellows pick the wrong time to be smart.

Started embroidering a school crest on a hankie today.

SEPT. 15, WED.
The gates were opened today with the stipulation that no one would climb over or go through the fence. On roll-call this evening we were all lined up ready for the count when a smug looking officer came along and ordered us back to the huts to put on full battle dress, including sidehats, putties and army boots.

According to the German news, their armies in Italy are advancing on all fronts with the able help of Italians who are disregarding the capitulation. News from Russia is scarce but rumours sneaking in are the Russians are driving the Germans back all along the line especially in the south. The "repats," despite their disappointment about two years ago are becoming a little excited over the possibility of getting home again, and who can blame them.

Managed to get a bath before the water went off again this evening.

It is supposed to be straight goods that Kiev is fallen and German troops in the Crimea are nearly cut off. The Russians have crossed the Knuper in three places and are only 50 miles from the old Polish border.

SEPT. 16,
Worked a great deal on the school crest and despite all precautions and efforts it is going a little screwy. We were supposed to go on roll-call parade properly dressed and with our shoes polished tonight but a deluge happened along about 4 o'clock so for the second time in a year we had roll-call inside.

The BBC news (a few days stale) was read out this evening and including such items as a brief summary of the situation in Italy, the number of craft of the Italian fleet taken over; 3/4 of the Allied Mediterranean Fleet has gone to the Pacific to add to Japanese worries. the Serbs have taken 30 miles of coastline (there is a rumour that British paratroops were dropped to help them; Calais, Dunkirk and another town on the North French coast being bombed continually. On the Russian Front the fall of Novorossiysk is imminent and Germans are evacuating Crimea. (The Germans have since announced the evacuation of Novorossiysk and another town according to plan.)

This is supposed to be the deadline for the rumoured American ultimatum to Germany, previously recorded in this book. They say the Germans down below are all going around with long sad faces. They changed their ideas a trifle about Canadians or they have clarified their former opinions. They say the Canadians are good fighters but no damn good for arbeit, they cause too much trouble on working parties. The only way we can get on working parties now is to change identities with English or Australians slated for working parties. I believe the average German knows there isn't a hope of them winning the war now. but they are holding on hoping to get the best possible peace terms and to forestall capitulation. A German doctor was recently executed for speaking defeatist propaganda. Most of the news published in German papers is on the Italian situation, the disarming of Badoglio's forces and the recapture of Mussolini on the Island of Rhodes. It is believed that most of it is to encourage the people to hang on a little longer. We are given to understand that the occupied countries are starting to add to the Nazi high commands headaches.

SEPT. 17, FRI.

Nothing much new today, at least nothing to get excited about. Churchill is supposed to have stated in a recent speech that the French people could prepare to greet the British and American troops that very soon will be marching through France. This is supposed to be part of the latest BBC news broadcast which also includes the fact the largest ship of the Italian fleet, the "Roma," was sunk by Germans while steaming toward Malta with the rest of the fleet to surrender to the British. There are long queues of Italians in

British held Italy for clothes and food but until the Germans are driven from the country, these people will have to wait.

Received letters from Nelle, Rose, Harold Moreau and Wally yesterday and today. Received 300 cigarettes from the Cameron Auxiliary this morning. Trading and trading mediums are undergoing revolutionary changes. Tea has soared to 150 cigarettes due to Canadian Red Cross parcel containing only coffee. Most of the goods are for sale for marks only; this is probably due to the war news and the fact that Lager geld is redeemable after the war. We were also informed on parade this morning that Canadians, if they wished, could receive the equivalent in lager-geld to six dollars a month which would be taken off their pay after the war. I don't think anyone wanted to take advantage of the proposal because actually we haven't any use for money here, unless its for gambling purposes.

SEPT. 18, SAT.

I considered it necessary to carry this book out on roll-call this morning. A squad of Germans, including officers, Unteroffiziers, "Feldwebels," and privates, (first, second and third class), marched into the huts at six this morning, roused us out of bed, and refused to let us wash or visit the latrine. We lined up for roll-call while some of our keepers made certain there was no one but the sick in the huts. After the usual roll-call routine each and everyone of us were scrutinized closely and our features compared with a photo in the hands of our old friend "Herman the German" sporting a pro-motion. Three men were picked out and coincidentally they all belong to our hut, Shurvel, Millwater and Edwards. We were eventually dismissed while the three men were taken down to the office. Shurvel was only dismissed after they had compared finger prints; the other two had no trouble clearing them-selves. Apparently, they are still looking for the two men who disappeared some time ago. We have the same reputation here as we had in England: if anything goes wrong or there is trouble in the camp, the Canadians are the first under suspicion. Spitfire is credited with the statement that he wouldn't trade his Canadian compound for any other in the camp because if he tells us to not to go through the fence, the boys queue up for their turn through the hole; if they are told they will be shot for going through the fence, they still queue up. He said he thinks there is about 50% of the Canadians married and with families but it doesn't make any difference, they still queue up. He claims that if you want the Canadians to do something, tell them not to and they usually do it. It's a pretty safe estimate that 90% of the Germans' headaches are attributable directly to the Canadians.

Sugar and lumbering has become almost a losing proposition during this last year.

There was no roll-call this evening and we were told to prepare for an influx of 51 more men from Italy. Apparently these men are at the gate and include over a hundred officers. Among them is a Major-General. These prisoners were in a camp near Genoa when Italy capitulated and thought they would be seeing the khaki-clad Tommies come marching in. The R.S.M. of the camp is supposed to have issued orders that no man was to leave the camp with a court-marshal as a consequence for anyone so inclined. They waited and in walked the Germans; now the prisoners are awaiting entrance to Stalag VIIIB.

According to BBC news of Monday, the 13,[th] the Germans are still holding Rome and a line running through Genoa, Rome, Trieste, etc. allied spearheads are still advancing but the Americans are in a bad way, having met Rommel's armoured forces; the Free French are being rushed in to help them. The German Air Force did sink the Roma before she reached Malta with the rest of the Italian fleet which included over 49 submarines. The air is black with planes and the sea black with ships in the Mediterranean around Italy. Troops have landed in Albania, the Greeks have revolted and fierce fighting is taking place. the Yugoslavian outlaw army has cleared 15 miles of Dalmatian coast and are being armed by parachute. In Russia the town of Novorossiysk has been evacuated by the Germans "according to plan." The advance on Kiev and Odessa continues. The Russians are 300 miles from Odessa. The Russians have advanced on the average of 8 miles a day for the summer months. Coastal towns in France (west and south), have been heavily bombed. 6,000 bombers were engaged on one raid without meeting a single German plane. A large scale offensive has begun in Burma.

The German communiques mention most of this news especially the sinking of the "Roma" and the plight of the American troops in Italy. They fail to mention Albania, Greece or the Dalmatian coast.

Worked on my school crest today, finished my laundry and resumed trig. studies, solving seven questions this evening.

As an after recollection of the BBC news, the fall of the Crimean Peninsula is expected this week. Central Italy is mentioned for the first time in German communiques.

SEPT. 19, SUN.
The new fellows from Italy came in this morning so once again, we are filled to capacity. According to some of the stories, one Australian was shot for sticking his head out of the train window. Quite a few apparently departed for parts unknown en route. They are old prisoners alright and were "repatriated" in pretty much of a hurry. Somewhat discouraged with the electrical studies; not getting anywhere.

"STIMMT" 14 Sept. 1943
Official German statement that repatriation for men who have been passed by a mixed international commission, together with protected personnel has been agreed to by both powers means that there will be a big clearance of this camp. This will come in the nature of distinct relief to authority, apart from the sentimental angle. Almost two entire compounds will be at its disposal for this coming winter. Further, since almost every phase of camp life and its institutions will be affected, including orchestras, theatre and school, many avenues will now be open to newcomers, or comparative newcomers to the Stalag. At least we can anticipate "the old order" changing, yielding place to new. The clean sweep which this camp has long needed must be introduced in all sections. Confirmed ranks must yield positions to those of lower standing. Jobs must be found for those men who otherwise have to work outside these gates. Fortunately there is a hardening tendency in the camp against those people whose minds turn to outside occupation when they could be taking advantage of the rank they have won in their regiments. Already a move has come from the main kitchen, where recently joined members

of C.S.M. Osborne's staff were displaced. Four of these men incautiously approached and threatened a certain N.C.O who is known to the camp as "Joe" and threatened him with violence because of statements he had made on these grounds. Their names have been handed to the camp authorities for action. There can be no evasion of the question of N.C.O.'s recognized and paid by their respective governments failing to stand down in preference to privates. The move is tardy, but essential.

FOOD PRICES IN STALAG

Undoubtedly, the open markets which have sprung up like mushrooms are helping to regulate prices through competition. Cpl. G. Holden, the originator of the markets scheme here states, "that food is a far more valuable commodity to a P.O.W. than cigarettes. We know by experience that there is a far larger surplus of cigarettes than of food in the camp." He says that "if the price of an article is lowered from 50 to 30 cigarettes, the value of food is lowered and the value of cigarettes increased. He maintains that this should not be so and if the smoker feels that he should part with his food, then by all means, let him get fair value for it."

TAKING THE BUN-G

That honey bucket wagon of ours, the one with "Beer is best" inscribed on its rear portion, met with an accident in Block 4 recently. En Passant the bung became detached. The Fuehrer of the wagon hastily descended. His mistake was to attempt re-insertion of the bung from the normal standing position. In a few seconds he was drenched with the contents. After some thought, he ascended the barrel and cunningly inserted the bung from his superior position. By this time three quarters of the contents were on the ground. In spite of advice from interested spectators, he insisted on driving the cart out of the compound, returning for another load an hour later.

CRITICISM OF A CRITICISM

A letter has been received bearing the signature of a number of men in this camp complaining that in a recently published statement R.S.M. Lowe reminds us that Red Cross parcels are gifts to the P.O.W.'s by the public of the British Empire and should be accepted gratefully. Also the parcels are intended to supplement and not to replace entirely the military rations. the letter asks whether the Red Cross would not welcome constructive criticism from the recipients of these parcels. It points out that the Red Cross and St. John is subscribed to in many cases by P.O.W.'s to feed not only themselves but less fortunate comrades and wonders if Mr. Lowe considers that because they are P.O.W.'s they forfeit their right to criticize the spending of money to which they have contributed which has been wasted on unsmokeable tobaccos and unreliable and unrecognizable brands of foodstuffs. Does Mr. Lowe imagine that these commodities come from the goodness of the manufacturer's hearts?

SCHOOL BELLS

If present plans are adhered to the two thousand odd scholars in this Stalag will await next Monday with particular interest. It is now almost certain that the school will re-open. It was closed down on July 24th for a fortnight, but fate and a hundred "Italian" P.O.W.'s stepped in and have only just begun to step out.

GROUPING OF PROTECTED PERSONNEL

A letter from the German High Command states that protected personnel lists should be divided into two groups. Group (A)-Australians, N.Z.s, South Africans, Palestinians and Indians. (B)group-British Isles and Canadians.

UNSELFISH SERVICE

At a meeting of "TOC-H" last week warm tribute was paid to the work done by "Job" Masters in the collection of material for distribution to the needy. The present Job Master, "Shorty" Lloyd said that the ground work organization and success went to the credit of a New Zealander, Don Caumeron who started the work some six months ago. Since then amazing amounts have been distributed in various ways. Chairman Cyril Tomas said he regretted that figures could not be published but records could be inspected by any interested, in which every single cigarette and article of clothing subscribed could be accounted for. He said there was still a demand for toilet soap, razors and blades, which present stocks could not meet.

LETTER GO GIRLS

The recent improvement last week of letters issued to the camp numbered at 54,000 compared with 24,000 the previous six days, was the direct result of complaints made by Mr. Sheriff. the circumstances surrounding the acceleration are not known. Asked how much mail was in the censor's office, the camp leader stated there was a large quantity, but he was not sure just how much. The authorities kept it locked up. Last week's personal parcel issue was 5,590 to the Lager and 9,411 to Kommandos, making a total issue of 15,001. Mr. Sheriff stated that he did not think that many parcels were lost in transit; private tobacco and cigarette parcels come direct from business firms, and as in peace time, went through the usual international postal authorities. Clothing parcels, however, were sent through the Red Cross. "Many P.O.W.'s" he said, complained of not receiving their personal parcels, but often it proved that on inquiry the next-of-kin had failed to dispatch them. Red Cross issue labels and clothing coupons were given to the next-of-kin but were not issued further in some cases until proof was given that the letter had been used for the purpose intended.

SEPT. 20, MON.

Blustery and dusty this afternoon until a thunder storm blew up with enough rain to hold the dust down. The German war communiques are gently telling the German people that they are retreating on all fronts in a roundabout way. They are evacuating places for three main reasons: to shorten their front, because the places are of no further military value or according to a previously defined plan. Of course, they have sunk the British Navy again in the Mediterranean around Italy and shot down a half of our Air Force for the fourth or fifth time.

There is supposed to be some BBC news in camp that states that the Russians took Smolensk ten days ago also they bypassed Kiev and are a few kilometers from Odessa, in fact, there is fighting in the suburbs. The Crimea is supposed to be cut off. Strategy in Italy is supposed to have resulted in 38,000 Germans being cut off. Apparently the 5th and 8th armies landed on the east and west coasts with the Americans bringing up the centre. The Americans drew the Germans down and then the two flanking arms made a drive towards the center, thus cutting the Germans off.

The Barn Dance season is opening up now, with the first dance of the season scheduled for tomorrow night in 20B. Received 2 letters from Nelle this afternoon dated May 3 and 10.

SEPT. 21, TUES.

What with daily German communiques, so-called BBC newscasts, intermingled with a flock of rumours that eventually come true if given plenty of time, getting things in sensible sequence is almost an impossibility. Bill R. told me this morning that according to a German news item, the Germans have evacuated seven towns in Russia, successfully according to plan because they were of no further military value. The news item ends up with, "Regardless of what the Soviets do they are unable to halt our retreat." We have become so skeptical of rumours and even news of unknown origin that we wouldn't believe Mahoney this morning when he told us about dissension between the Swiss and Germans over some pass, and the arrest of the Pope in Rome. The general disbelief in regards to Mahoney isn't exactly misplaced because he is a rumour raiser from away back.

However, there appeared on the wall this afternoon a piece of paper alleged to be the latest BBC news. The Germans demand the use of the Swiss-Italian R.R. Tunnel and threaten force if their request is not granted. Swiss refuse on neutral grounds and counter with a threat to blow up the tunnel being assured of full support of Sweden, if necessary. Free French have occupied Corsica and British-American forces forcing Germans to evacuate Greece. Operation directed by Greek general assisted by British Intelligence Officer.

Bulgarian people undecided on stand in their case. Romanian people taking any stand on war questions are immediately executed. Russians steadily advancing in all sectors. First, Fifth and Eight Armies joined forces and continue advance northward through Italy.

How much of this is true and whether or not it is BBC news is difficult to say; the whole thing is very possible. The arresting of the Pope would result in Catholics all over the world (Germany not excluded) to rise up on their hind legs and howl. I don't think even the Germans are willing to take the consequences of such an action. The Swiss tunnel affair, especially Sweden sticking her oar in, seem a little incredible until one considers Germany's big problem, how to get a large army out of Italy besides using the Brenner Pass which is sure to be bombed severely.

Another version of BBC news was read out this evening and practically corroborated the above in many points; the Pope angle and the tunnel affair weren't mentioned in this later report. The Germans admit the evacuation of Sardinia. The American 5th Army is closing in on Rome. The fighting in Greece is under a General Jones, a British officer. The Russians are quite a distance west of Smolensk and 24 miles from Kiev. They have taken the last port next to the entrance to the Crimean Peninsula. Mosquito planes bombed Berlin and other districts without loss.

Apparently the Germans are like a bull in a ring and dashing madly about in an ever narrowing circle.

We had the first real barn dance of the season this evening in 20B with some accordion playing and singing thrown in for good measure.

The school, church and hoosegow is filled to capacity with the arrival of these new men from Italy. They are being deloused and registered now. We took up a collection of cigs. for the ones in this hut and another collection for the hundred odd officers who left for an Offlag this morning. Received a letter from Rusty today, and she says the news is very good.

Heard a discussion on post Canada today among a few of the boys and honestly believe that the young fellows of this war supported by the return soldiers of the last war may make themselves heard in such things as the type of immigrants allowed in the country and the development of Canada's natural wealth. One thing is certain, they are going to demand a drastic change after this war.

SEPT. 23, THURS.
Received 300 British Consols from Eric yesterday. Eric (Day) received a book parcel containing two books on Building Construction this afternoon. While drinking tea yesterday afternoon Ed, the sanitator, informed me that someone wished to see me in the "bunky" (C.S.M.'s room). It was an English speaking

German who claims to have spent some time in Montreal, Quebec and New York and was hoping to meet some of his friends made there. During our confab he asked about chains, mail situation, his experience in New York, etc. He claimed he had a friend in the censor office who gave him my name because I get letters from the States, etc. He said he knew a Scotch lady in Breslau whom he had met in Canada; she returned to Scotland, got married and ended up here. She was crazy for Canadian cigarettes and he would get me anything within reason for cigarettes. He tried, in a roundabout way, to learn where I came from and his knowledge of my affairs seemed meagre for an intelligent officer as I and other fellows believe he is. He said he would come back some night with some lighter fluids and a longer talk. Everyone, including myself thinks he is a gestapo agent of some sort, after some particular kind of information. He will undoubtedly bear very close watching; he strikes me as a person used to a higher rank than he is shown now.

Eric received an Ellis School Building construction course this morning. Received letters from Bobby and Rusty yesterday and one from Peggy today. All cheerful. Becoming very chilly at nights now and I noticed that the crows are starting to gather in autumn flocks. The new men were registered yesterday and I think they will soon be going out in working parties, indicating the changing times and Teutonic attitude, we weren't called out on five o'clock parade this evening.

It was rumoured last night that 50,000 Allied troops have landed in Greece; it just makes us wonder where our friends are. Rusty said she has seen Murph in England; I never thought he would be there in time. The old time band is going to town in one corner of the hut minus the drumsticks. There is a new instrument being tried tonight; a double necked mandolin or ukulele . Our new convert to Christianity, Smitty (Smudger) is trying another argument on Gordie Waters. This "Smudger" gets himself into some deep arguments he finds difficult to and more often impossible to talk himself out of. So far there is no news coming in. There is a rumour going around that the chains are coming off on Sunday since we will be going out on working parties.

SEPT. 24, FRI.

Gates were locked all day today for some unknown reason that is very compound. "Bobbie" came again at noon today with four capsules of lighter fluid. I sicced Jerry Johnson onto him but he evidently did live in New York for awhile but I am still suspicious of his motives. Can't understand why he singled out me. However, if he is looking for information he is wasting his time. As long as I can obtain a few things I want from him, I can tolerate talking to him occasionally. Am going to try getting a draftsman's drawing set off him.

Roll-call was a two hour stand out, seemingly all over camp. Apparently they are still looking for those two missing men. Heard today that there is 1,400 more men waiting to come into camp. There's a rumour going around that they moved the post office to make more room.

SEPT. 25, SAT.

The BBC news from the 1st of August until a couple of days ago was read out this morning and covered the taking of Sicily, the campaign in Italy, the bombing of the French coast and Berlin. The Japanese situation was mentioned as progressing favourably. The steady advance of the Russians and the Yugoslavian outlaw army also was dealt with. In the news was an estimate of prisoners and booty taken in Sicily. This included 130,000 prisoners. The Canadian losses in Sicily including dead, wounded and prisoners numbered 1,809, a little less than the number taken prisoner at Dieppe. Generally speaking it was all good news for the last month and a half. News of more local nature includes the arrival of more prisoners from Italy and they say there is still more coming. Before very long they think we will have 200 men in this hut which was originally intended for 100. There is a blanket shortage in camp, some of the fellows in this hut being issued with overcoats instead. After the coats were issued it was discovered that they were lousy so had to be recalled. A Lt. Col. and another man have escaped and so far they haven't been caught yet.

We heard today that the German papers admit the fall of Smolensk and fighting all along the Knuper River. Thirty five men, (old people) were picked to have a group photograph taken today. Eric, Dawson, Bartlett, Grey and Jones were among those picked. Jones didn't want to be bothered so I took his place. Shined my shoes extra specially, borrowed a pair of pants and puttees and was getting a line on a glengarry when it was all postponed. By paying a mark and five Pfennigs, we will receive 3 copies each. They will make a good souvenir. Have made a half-hearted attempt to review trigonometry but my ambition seems to have taken a temporary slump. Supposed to play at a dance in 19A this evening but nothing seems to be moving as yet. Mahoney, our erstwhile rumour monger, had a good one this morning; the camp commandant is supposed to have phoned Berlin for orders and Joe Stalin answered the phone. Have finally decided I had better wash my uniform tomorrow if the water is on and the sun is shining.

SEPT. 27, MON.

Yesterday morning someone put a dead mouse in Mahoney's pocket without him knowing it. The look on Jim's face when he found it was worth walking miles to see. Claude Norman has been making some enquiries regarding Bobby, the English speaking Hun and found that he is visiting other compounds pretty regularly and the topic of conversation invariably swings around to the news and methods of obtaining thereof. That explains his reason for singling me out; I am registered here as a radio serviceman and mention of it has been made of it in various letters and requests for books.

We had a good do in 20B last night; sort of Barn Dance and concert combined. The soloists were Riley, Wallace and Potts. The latter put over "the Martins & the Corp" in good style. An impersonator did a good job of his performance and received a big hand. A fellow got up to recite and struggled through two poems. Quote: Oh little fly upon the wall, haven't you any coat at all? Aren't you cold, hmm? Unquote. The other was just as silly and was about spring and birds. A sing song wound up the affair with "Home On The Range" the final number.

Some of the new men were warned for working parties; they go tomorrow. The chains have been off since Friday night and some of the fellows from 7 to 10 say they saw them packed up and taken away. Perhaps we will be going out to work soon.

The rumours say that the Germans are in full retreat in Russia and the German High Command is issuing hourly bulletins to the people.

We played in No. 3 compound, 8A, this evening but a big percentage of the hut refused to cooperate in making room for the square dances.

BBC news was read out this evening, the highlights of which were: 1st and 8th armies a little more than halfway into Italy. American fifth army fighting in the hills around Rome. The Yugoslavian outlaw army capture a number of towns from the Germans. Russians have taken Smolensk, the battle being a bigger and more bitter defeat to the Germans than Stalingrad. Russians have crossed the Knuper in seven places and are 80 miles from Odessa and are fast approaching the entrance to the Crimea. Spain is warned by Britain that if she continues to send volunteers to the Russian front it will have to be war between Spain and the Allies. The Allies lost 90 planes in a raid on Hamburg. Australians have 1,000 yards to go before the entire New Guinea will be taken. The 1st and 8th armies in Italy are advancing northward on an average of 20 miles a day. There is a revolt at the head of the Adriatic entailing Venice, Trieste and Filiume. Rhodes Island and another close by, were taken by the Allies.

Rumours: Russians advancing steadily. Germans unable to stem the tide. Issuing hourly bulletins. Greece is in Allied hands.

Washed my tunic today and as expected, it rained.

Heard an idea today about why the Germans are bringing in so many British prisoners from Italy. They want as many Allied British troops in Germany as possible hoping that it will serve as a check on Russian reprisals, they fear will take place following the final crash.

There was quite a parade through camp today. Some General was visiting and they rode through camp in two automobiles loaded with high ranking officers and a horse drawn carriage with footmen fore and aft, smiling and saluting at the men encountered on the road.

SEPT. 29, WED.

We held another concert in 22A night before last which although not as good as the one in 20B, went over pretty good. While we were away, Churchill's latest speech was read out and from what the fellows who heard it say, it was quite a speech. The highlights were that Italy was not the second front but when this long talked of and awaited event takes place, the men, supplies and material crossing the Channel will be the largest in history. Another item which was of special interest to us was the statement that the P.O.W.s in Germany will be evacuated as soon as possible after peace is declared or hostilities cease. The second front reference has only one meaning that it will take place in France and unless launched in the next few weeks will have to wait until spring. Rumours are still coming in and include the periodic variety such as there are 40 Russian divisions in Poland. Another is that 20 German divisions are encircled in Italy. Heard yesterday that in the bombed cities of Germany the death toll is so great, the dead are piled in the street and the civilians won't go near them because the Black Plague has broken out. The authorities are recalling the Pioneer Corps from occupied countries to handle the situation and bury the dead.

Eleven men left this room for working parties and there are eleven more coming in soon. All the bed space is filled and one corner of the room, ordinarily used for tables has to be utilized for the overflow. The "repats" haven't gone yet and the latest reports are that only 300 sanitators out of 3,000 are going and the B2 category group are remaining behind. There is a fairly large group of D.U. men just arrived from camps in Italy. The Germans want sanitators of their own from England to take care of civilian casualties which are mounting steadily. Churchill said that we have 50% air superiority over the Germans and it is increasing rapidly. Production is 4 times as great as German production. The U-Boat menace is practically non-existent, although Germany is building a new type of submarine but the Allied Naval authorities think they can counteract it effectively.

It's been raining, drizzling and thoroughly miserable for the last five days and the present bad weather may be a prelude to a hard, long winter.

A copy of the Rehabilitation Scheme for Return Soldiers has made its appearance and according to some discussion overheard on the subject, some of it could be improved. Most men express their intention of taking advantage of the educational privileges when they get back. Possibly about 2% will carry out those intentions.

Received a letter from Lieut. R. P. Murphy the other day, also a letter from Rusty containing three snaps. Letters from Rusty come in pretty regularly; she writes every week. Received a letter from Marc some time ago with 3 snaps that she had taken while on her holidays. Jeez! This is a dark miserable hole; nearly all the windows are gone and the empty spaces are filled in with tin. It's hardly any better at night because two globes burnt out and haven't been replaced yet. Trying to study trig these days but making a poor job of it. I guess we can resign ourselves for another winter here.

OCT. 2, SAT.
News and even rumours are not so plentiful this weekend. There was a few such as fighting going on in the outskirts of Odessa and Minsk. Recruiting for active service is no more in Canada and England and men signing on now are for post-war services. Production of war material is suspended and is being transformed for civilian products again. They supposed to have enough men and material to finish the war. In the German papers yesterday they claim to have sunk a flock of ships both naval and mercantile, apparently this is the sixth or seventh half of Britain's floating strength which has been sunk three or four times before.

We had a good time in 6A, block 2 Thursday evening playing all known and unknown Scottish, Irish and Barn Dance pieces. At half time we were served with tea, biscuits, cheese and jam. The gates were locked by the time we finished so we had to come home by the way of the hole in the back fence. Some four or five hundred more prisoners were brought in from Italy, some of them stretcher cases. A good few of them have only been prisoners a matter of three weeks.

Had another musical session down at 12B ("Repats") last night and had a fairly good time. Jerry Johnston told Wilcox to organize the band into a stage act with a few soloist, dancers, etc. and he would try and get a performance in the Gaiety. I overheard last night that some of our fans think we have Jimmie Howe beat a variety of ways. Washed my pants this afternoon and found it quite a chore. Also finished manufacturing two Red Cross string beds this afternoon after raising a handful of luscious blisters. Eric and I are going to assemble them tomorrow. Borrowed a pair of pants, a glengarry and a pair of puttees this afternoon and we went down, 35 strong to have our picture taken. If we ever get the results they will be quite a souvenir. Scotty Law has been chosen as the most prominent athlete of the camp and will be presented with a watch in the near future.

The rainy weather finally cleared up after five days of miserable dampness; it has served to remind us that winter is coming and to prepare for a few cold months. Eric and I are thinking of hoarding a portion of our weekly Red Cross rations for future use; we expect things to get decidedly worse toward the end and to have something to fall back on wouldn't be a bad idea. I read a newspaper printed in English yesterday, called the Tripoli Times. It carried the story of the landing of the 8th Army in Italy at the beginning of the present campaign. I guess the school will be closed for the duration now. Caught a cold yesterday. I have been giving so many cigarettes away lately my supply has dwindled alarmingly.

CAMERONS of CANADA

STALAG 344

LAMSDORF GERMANY

DEC. 11, 1943

1ST ROW, L TO R.	MORRIS, W.J. WINNIPEG.	RENNIE, A, CARBERRY.
SCAMMELL, B. RATHWELL.	LAW, H.J. W. KILDONAN.	4TH ROW.
LECKIE, LL. WINNIPEG	KILFOYLE, F.M. McGREGOR	DORY, H.W. ASHURN.
BAIN, J.A. WINNIPEG.	HORNAL, G FLIN FLON	ROSS, H.C. NOKOMIS, SASK.
PIKE, D.A. STONEWALL	LINDSAY, A WESTON.	RUSSEL, C.H. WINNIPEG.
HODGERT, A WESTON.	SORENSON, O. MATHER, MAN.	HOLLIDAY, C.H. McGREGOR.
WARREN, E.B. ISABELLA, MAN.	3RD ROW	JANZON, A. WINNIPEG.
SIMS, F. McGREGOR	NORRIE, C. ISABELLA.	HUNTER, W. NEEPAWA.
FINLAY, R.M.	DOWSON, C. MAFEKING.	WEARE, R.E. RIDING MOUNTN.
PERRY, A. KAMSACK	OLIPHANT, G.H.C. WINNIPEG.	MACDONALD, W. WINNIPEG.
DUBRAY, C. SWAN RIVER	ANGUS, A.A., ANGUSVILLE	MACHUK, J. WINNIPEG
2ND ROW.	KNIBBS, L.G. HOLLAND.	KALININ, G WINNIPEG
RIGGS, D.T. WINNIPEG.	RATTRAY, U.G. WOODNORTH.	FRAME, L.A. LENORE, MAN.
HICKMAN, H CHICAGO, ILL.	ZAPATOCHNEY, J. ST. CLAUDE.	AITKEN, N.N. ROLAND
PETTETT, E.J. WINNIPEG.	BAUER, L.A. WINNIPEG	WOLESHYN, A, NEEPAWA.
MORRISON, C.M. STEINBACH.	WILCOX, E.J. FRANKLIN.	SMITH, A.J. WINNIPEG.
MACMILLAN, A. QUEBEC.	WILMOT, J. FT. FRANCIS.	WOOD, E. WINNIPEG.
LODGE, F.T. KENORA, ONT.	HOPKINS, W. FORGET, SASK.	LITTLE, A. CALLENDER, ONT.

(POWs-Fred Lodge, second row centre)

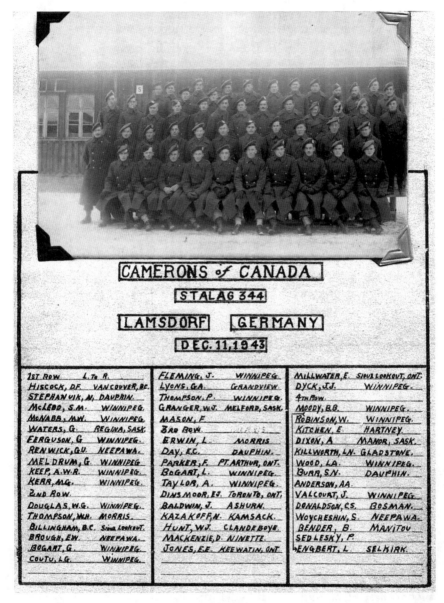

CAMERONS of CANADA

STALAG 344

LAMSDORF GERMANY

DEC. 11, 1943

1ST ROW L. To R.	FLEMING, J. WINNIPEG.	MILLWATER, E. SIOUX LOOKOUT, ONT.
HISCOCK, D.F. VANCOUVER, B.C.	LYONS, G.A. GRANDVIEW.	DYCK, J.J. WINNIPEG.
STEPHANVIK, N. DAUPHIN.	THOMPSON, P. WINNIPEG.	4TH ROW.
McLEOD, S.M. WINNIPEG.	GRANGER, W.J. MELFORD, SASK.	MOODY, B.B. WINNIPEG.
McNABB, M.W. WINNIPEG.	MASON, F.	ROBINSON, W. WINNIPEG.
WATERS, G. REGINA, SASK.	3RD ROW.	KITCHEN, E. HARTNEY.
FERGUSON, G WINNIPEG.	ERWIN, L. MORRIS	DIXON, A MANOR, SASK.
RENWICK, G.U. NEEPAWA.	DAY, E.C. DAUPHIN.	KILLWORTH, L.N. GLADSTONE.
MELDRUM, G. WINNIPEG	PARKER, F. PT. ARTHUR, ONT.	WOOD, L.A. WINNIPEG.
KEEP, A.W.R. WINNIPEG.	BOGART, L. WINNIPEG.	BURR, S.N. DAUPHIN.
KERR, M.G. WINNIPEG.	TAYLOR, A. WINNIPEG.	ANDERSON, A.A.
2ND ROW.	DINSMOOR, E.J. TORONTO, ONT.	VALCOURT, J. WINNIPEG
DOUGLAS, W.G. WINNIPEG.	BALDWIN, J. ASHURN.	DONALDSON, C.S. BOSMAN.
THOMPSON, W.H. MORRIS.	KAZAKOFF, N. KAMSACK.	WOYCHESHIN, S. NEEPAWA.
BILLINGHAM, B.C. Sioux Lookout.	HUNT, W.J. CLANDEBOYE.	BENDER, B. MANITOU
BROUGH, E.W. NEEPAWA.	MACKENZIE, D. NINETTE.	SEDLESKY, P.
BOGART, G. WINNIPEG.	JONES, E.E. KEEWATIN, ONT.	ENGBERT, L. SELKIRK.
COUTU, L.G. WINNIPEG.		

(More Cameron POWs)

OCT. 4, MON.

With the washing of our palaises my heavy laundry is finished. It's a fine day today so my pants finally dried. Put Eric's and my name in for Red Cross packing paper the other day and the C.S.M. was under the impression that I had spoken for it sometime ago. Far be it from me to disillusion the poor man so we got the palaise filler today. With the completion of our Red Cross string spring, a clean palaise filled with clean shredded paper, our sleeping facilities should be all set for the winter.

I noticed that the reservoirs are being used for washing clothes and are rapidly being covered with a slimy soap scum. Blower stoves are becoming a common cooking utility throughout the camp and are appearing in a variety of shapes and designs.

Played at 27B last night after a little mixup in the booking. Scheduled to play at two places at the same time and finally chose 27B as they asked first. We may play in 5A this evening. May get a regulation pair of sticks and maybe a drum soon.

Rumours that Bulgaria and Romania, in accordance with an Allied warning, have stopped sending men to the Russian front is circulating today. Also the one about the Black Plague running wild in German cities is going strong again.

Scotty Law was awarded a wrist watch yesterday for being the most prominent athlete of the camp. Received 300 cigs. From the P.O.W. Relations Association this morning. Wrote to Roy yesterday.

OCT. 5, TUES.

Our beds are a huge success and merits praise worthy of the Perfect Rest Mattresses back home. We had a very good barn dance session down at 8A, Block 3 last night with Scotch and Irish tunes in between sets. Acquired two new books this afternoon, titled "Electrical Engineering Arithmetic" and "Electrical Wiring and Contacting." What with Bauer studying German, Eric building construction, Lorne Engbert automotive engineering and myself electrical engineering, our table is pretty studious during the day.

We played in 5B, Block 2 this evening and judging from the applause following each number and the speech by the room commander when we signed off, I might go so far as to say our efforts were appreciated a little. As far as I know, we have no engagement for tomorrow night—yet. Things seem to be moving down at the "Repats" today and tonight; they were checked again for names and numbers again this afternoon and tonight all men requiring dressings were warned to be attended to tonight. It is expected they will be gone before morning. They have been waiting for a long time and everyone hopes they make it this time. There will be a few Canadians included in this attempt including Geoffrey Pasquil, sanitator.

Two new light globes do wonders to dispel the murkiness of the hut. If I do say so myself, this hut and others in the compound are the cleanest and brightest in the camp.

OCT. 7, THURS.

The "Repats" are still having check parades but the actual date of their departure remains unknown. They, at least those who were fooled last time, are crossing their fingers and won't believe it until it happens. Musical instruments are hitting the markets in increasing numbers due to the possibility of their leaving; nearly every musical group in the camp will be affected. I obtained a kettle drum and stand yesterday and we tried it out tonight in the wash room, thoroughly disgusted and determined to rid myself of the drum and stick to my lowly sound block. Received four books today. "Teach Yourself Algebra & Trig" and Pitman's Shorthand" and key. I'm so doggone disgusted with the whole thing I may get rid of my books as well. Practically no news recently except German war bulletins. The veracity of which is well known.

OCT. 9, SAT.

Yesterday was the anniversary of our being tied; it is rumoured around that the chains came off because of this repatriation scheme and as soon as the Repats leave we will get them back again. It is thought that the Germans want a good report to go back with the Repats then they will crack down on us again. Tried the drum out Thursday evening and disappointed to discover it fails to harmonize with the band. Our melody section is much too weak. We went down to 7A last night to take part in a concert. Incidentally, first grade corn on the cob was a feature of the program. We were announced as Jock McKearny's Canadian Band; Jock is a diminutive Scotsman with a strong accent who plays the accordion. His musical accomplishments are confined mostly to Highland tunes, *Tipperary*, *Take Me Back to Dear Old Blighty*, and *Run Rabbit Run*.

A bunch of fellows, including Eric, received their fourth personal parcel this morning. There's a possibility I may be among the lucky ones next week. Am receiving letters from Nelle that were posted in April and May.

The West whipped the East in an all-Canadian Rugby match this afternoon. The event was dressed up in true college fashion with cheering sections, mascots, etc. On hand was a group of cowboys signifying the West and a bunch of Redskins representing the East. Half-time was their cue and they put on a side splitting comedy in the middle of the field, which was fully appreciated by the large crowd. The game was marked by the steady stream of casualties trooping out of the scrimmages. This hut appears to have become the mecca for players with sore stiff and injured limbs this evening, and of course, the game is being re-hashed in the inevitable postmortem.

News and rumours remain scarce these days for some reason or other but we are expecting a BBC news report any time now. There's a suspicion of winter in the air now especially at night and in the early hours of the morning.

A commando fellow of 21A went off the deep end last night, believed to be brought on by trying to figure a system of bridge that would beat Culbertson's system. I hear they are trying to get young Coll on the Repat scheme as a TB case. "Brew up" time to eat again.

OCT. 12, THURS.
Received 1 lb. of fine cut from Nelle yesterday and the 4th personal parcel today. The coffee was broken and messed up the pajamas, underwear a little, but otherwise it was in good shape.

The "Repats" are still waiting for word to move as all work here is completed now and orders from the High Command is slow in coming. Aside from daily German bulletins there has been little news coming in. (Supposedly BBC news for Friday states that: the 5ᵗʰ Army is 25 kilometers on the other side (north) of Naples, but are held up by bad weather. The 1ˢᵗ Army is north of Rome and closing in; the 8ᵗʰ Army is pushing steadily ahead. All airfields in Southern Italy are in British hands, from these fields the Air Force have raided Athens, Salonika and towns in Germany. There was a commando raid on St. Nazaire on Thursday which was a success.

Stafford Cripps in a speech, said that Italy is only the third front and that the 2ⁿᵈ front will come when they deem it necessary. Russians are on the old Polish border. Fifty troop carriers, loaded with troops, were shot down while trying to leave the Caucus. Cripps stated that the war will be over by Easter.) This news met with a little skepticism, especially the last statement credited to Cripps. No man in his position can afford to make predictions like that. However, the Germans have admitted the evacuation of the Kuban Bridgehead area (successfully and according to plan, of course.)

The commando, Mills, who went off his rocker trying to figure out a bridge system, was taken away to the New Lazaret in a straight jacket and lodged in a padded cell.

It was rumoured around today that Russia has signed a non-aggression pact with Japan and Turkey has signed one with Russia. Some fellow received a letter yesterday from one of the fellows in the old outfit and we are led to believe that they are in Italy or Sicily now.

We are thinking there must be quite a racket in this book parcel situation. If our people are sending the money to the book firms, the firms certainly are getting rid of all their unsaleable books. Imagine book such as "A Sunshine Sketch of a Village," "How to Play Poker," etc. Some fellows go down to the post office with a book parcel chit, stand around for two hours waiting to get in, then receive a pocket book entitled, "Little Women" or a cribbage board.

I understand that there are over 350 applicants in camp that have filed for divorce. Imagine receiving a letter saying "I am going to adopt a baby; I <u>hope</u>

it's a boy." One fellow's wife has been running around with four or five different fellows since he has been here; her latest is a black man in the American
army. At least that is one worry I haven't got.

Algebra is taking up a lot of time these days. It's exceedingly frosty these days;
the pajamas will come in handy at nights now. I think everyone except the
Repats are resigned to spending another winter here.

OCT. 15, FRI.

The last few days have seen big changes in camp personnel and rumours and
news. The biggest news item of special local interest was the long talked of
and prepared for departure of the "Repats" and sanitators. We (the band)
held a farewell session down in 13(b) on Wednesday night and by eleven
next morning the first repats were on the move. The strain and suspense
of the last three weeks has been terrific and as a consequence some of the
fellows' nerves have broken down. A few have been taking fits for the last few
days, but they are on the way now and we all hope they go all the way this
time. The Sanitators and remainder of the Repats left this afternoon. They
are going by way of Stettin and Sweden. The B2 group will stop in Sweden.
Geof Pasquill left this afternoon as a sanitator. It is rumoured around that the
B.E.F. (Dunkirk boys) will be next. There is a case of number of N.C.O.'s in
this present bunch which will be interesting telling later on.

The news of the last few days includes such items as the 48 hour bombing
of Danzig, 18 hours of this there was a bomb a minute dropped. The Allies'
long expected push has begun in Italy. Italy has a declared war on Germany.
Germans have successfully evacuated the Crimea. Russians have taken all of
Estonia and one town in Latvia (unverified BBC). Kiev is in flames still in
German hands with the actual fighting west of the city. Rumours that the
three remaining German pocket battleships, the Scharnhorst, Gneisenau
and Prinz Eugen, met an enemy submarine force of Sweden. Results: one
ship torpedoed and sunk, the other two retired to Swedish waters and were
scuttled. Neither German papers or BBC mentions this event.

Made a stand for my two sound blocks yesterday and put a strap on my
watch today. May obtain a crocheted woolen blanket on Monday. Received

1 lb of tobacco from Nelle on the 11,[th] 4th P.P. from Dad on the 12th, 1,000 cigarettes from 16th Battery Ladies' Auxiliary and 300 from Carn. Aux. on the 14th. Received letters from Rusty, Anne, Bobby and Aunt Pat today. Aunt Pat's included a snap of Vi and a company of her fellow internees. Perhaps she has been repatriated by now.

OCT. 18, MON.
The last of the New Zealand repats and sanitators left this morning, and the day was further commemorated by the fact that the chains have come back after being absent since Sept. 24. It corroborates the theory that they were taken off so as the repats would report the abolishing of the shackles when they got home. As a consequence of this repatriation move, rumours are coming in thick and fast. One of them is that there will be another bunch leaving on the 28th of this month. Also it is rumoured that negotiations are in progress for the repatriation of 45,000 able-bodied men. This would if true account for a large number of the B.E.F. taken at the time of Dunkirk. It's a foregone conclusion that we Canadians will be practically the last to leave this camp even after the war.

It is rumoured tonight that the Russians are 80 miles west of Kiev and there has been another large scale landing in Italy. Typhoid is supposed to have broken out in Hamburg and Danzig. Feeling low this evening; I have hit a snag in Algebra which looks insurmountable to me just now. A bad cold is making me cranky and a sore tooth doesn't improve matters a great deal.

OCT. 20, WED.
The news for the past two days has been more or less good. BBC items include, an air battle over the Brenner Pass which resulted in a victory for the Allies. The Germans claim their defeat was due to the Allies using young reckless pilots who used unorthodox methods of air fighting. The recapture of Rhodes Island with its entire German staff. The steady advance of the Allies in Italy. Danzig or Hamburg machine-gunned recently. Heavy raid on Hanover the other night. The bombing of Breslau (30 miles north of here) last Thursday. The sinking of the Tirpitz in Norwegian waters. Russians advance 120 kilos (75 miles) near the Dniester Bend. Some big U.S.A. statesmen

announced that the American Air Force in England will be trebled in the next five weeks? (months)

The chains are a bigger farce than ever since they came back. The only time we see the guard is when they bring them in in the morning and call for them at night. A general made a tour of the camp recently, accompanied by the Commandant and the guard commander. A chap, (Musgrove) saw them coming and snapped his chains on. They came up to where he was standing in the door of 22A and told him to take his chains off. Musgrove said he couldn't. The General told him not to be stupid and to take them off. Musgrove said he had no key so the General pulled out his pocket knife, opened the corkscrew and handed it to Musgrove, who informed the General that it was not suitable. The General then opened the blade and Musgrove took off the shackles. "You fellows are not fooling us any, you know," remarked the General and continued his tour of inspection.

We had a very poor show in 22A on Tuesday evening. Lack of cooperation among the inmates got us off to a very bad start. Failure of some of the performers to put in an appearance didn't help much. The M.C. persisted in telling corny, antiquated jokes and soon had the indifferent audience against him wholeheartedly. This very nearly ended in a melee when he lost his temper and called the Canadians a bunch of poor sports and heels. Our contribution wasn't anything to boast about; stumbling into the starts, hitting discords through the pieces and finally trailing off and stopping individually. It was an exceedingly poor show and we concluded the performance and left the hut amid deep silence. We don't know if the silence was from mass disapproval or if they were ashamed of their apparent lack of cooperation and weren't sure how to redeem themselves. However, we should have a good do in 20B this evening, organized by Sgt. Ferguson. It is going to be a sort of musical and quiz program combined. Apparently the band members are not going to be exempt from displaying their intelligence (ignorance in my case). Another big show is being organized for Saturday night by 19A.

OCT. 23, SAT.
Last Wednesday night the entire camp was suddenly plunged into darkness at approximately 9:30P.M. It is general belief that there must have been an

air raid close by and dousing all lights from the main switch was the quickest means to eliminate the tell-tale glow of the camp. There is some vague international regulation that the lights are supposed to be kept on for identification purposes but regulations, especially international ones, don't worry Jerry over-much. Two lighted camps about a mile apart would be an excellent landmark for any raiders attacking a target within a good number of miles radius of us.

Fellows who have found it necessary to visit the "Paketausgabe" recently report the appearance of some propaganda posters on that popular office wall. From various descriptions these posters are pictures of rows and rows of dead women and children, supposedly killed in one city by the Royal Air Force. The description is in English and one in particular states that British bombers flying low, on a very clear day, bombed a school where children were playing in the grounds. One picture is of a row of women and children, five in width and stretching into the distance beyond the camera's range. Perhaps the showing of these pictures is a prelude and preparative to more reprisals. We had a very good time in 20B on Thursday night with the Quiz and musical program and I think the whole band was thankful that we didn't have to answer any questions. There was a pretty good show in 19A this evening at which I was supposed to appear with the rest of the band but owing to the time of commencement and our usual supper schedule clashing, I had to miss the performance. These days I am struggling with a piece of toothbrush handle, trying to make one of those colourful Stalag rings. Apparently it's quite a job getting it into a perfect, or near perfect, circle. So far I haven't been anywhere near successful.

I never thought we would be asked to elect by poll-voting and candidates for executive positions, but this afternoon we all trooped to the poles to elect a Canadian Cpl. Hussey to the position of Sports Chairman. The election went along in fine style until one fellow was caught voting twice. This was what the Limeys were waiting for, they called the election crooked and refused to accept the verdict. Consequently, we are curious as to the outcome of the heated argument which resulted. For the first time since my last leave in England, I ate a meal off of a porcelain plate (crockery). The last bunch of prisoners from Italy were issued with these plates so when they were called out for a working party recently two fellows, Williams and Rumney, sold us their plates; they seem to improve the meals somehow. Incidentally we hoped that the strained accommodations would be relieved a little by the exodus of these arbeit commandos, but apparently it's not to be, because the 360 Dieppers that left us last winter are coming back tomorrow.

According to a whispered word this evening, tomorrow morning's roll-call parade may be a long, tedious affair; however I am armed with a couple of good books so am prepared for a long outing, providing it doesn't rain. Spitfire seems to have the aid of a second-in-command now, who is fast becoming a familiar figure around the compound. This new chap is badly crippled and word went around that he ran over a land mine on a motorcycle. If he did, he is extremely fortunate to be alive. With no intention of ridiculing this fellow and in accordance with the Canadian habit of assigning nick-names, "Hop-along" seems to be his handle now. Thinking seriously of taking up pipe band drumming.

OCT. 24, SUN.
The German staff seemed to be in quite a turmoil this morning when they discovered 8 prisoners missing. However, they caught two, or at least picked them up, on the railway station just before nine last night. The gates were locked all day and a roll-call was called at a little before four which lasted until 5:30 with officers and dogs in attendance. It looks as if they failed entirely to pick up the trail of the 6 still absent escapists. Just how this break will affect the R.C. issue tomorrow, we haven't as yet been informed.

It was announced by the room commander (Groves) this evening that there were 1,900 more prisoners coming in from some other camp, and that 280 Dieppers would be moving into this compound tomorrow. This will put us back to capacity again, if not a little bit more. Mail has been scarce this week. Scarcer than usual, that is.

OCT. 26, TUES.
The Dieppers from 7 to 10 moved in yesterday afternoon (officially); they had all their stuff moved before noon despite all German efforts to stop them. Roll-call at three-thirty while the prodigals were being allotted to the

respective rooms. Two German officers showed a poor example when they climbed over the fence in full view of this and the Air Force compounds. Preparing for the coming winter seems to be the main pastime just now. We have all broken panes in the window filled with tin, every little piece of glass is pressed into use and is set in the tin to obtain the maximum of light possible. Electric light extensions are appearing now, there being three in this hut already, with a fourth likely to appear tomorrow. This will give us 4 extra lights. I have come to the conclusion that everything is procurable in here if the right person is approached and if the price is right.

Apparently the fellows have grown tired of playing with their chains on roll-call (only a few still carry them out now) and a new time waster has taken the place of that sport. The latest requires four or more men; one turns his back to the rest then one of the others hits him on the shoulder; the fall guy turns around and tries to guess who it is. The game isn't as gentle as it sounds; I have seen men knocked clean off their feet in the course of a game. Another pastime on roll-call is "star-gazing" and in broad daylight. We actually saw a star this morning but we couldn't convince anyone that it was visible; they wouldn't look because they thought there was a catch to it.

I notice the swimming pools alias "reservoirs" are being used as a large laundry tub. With water as scarce as it is, it's becoming a common sight to see P.O.W.s kneeling on the edge of the pools like a bunch of birds on a drinking trough, gently massaging their clothing on this concrete side of the pool. Received a letter from Marc. today. Have a cold and a headache tonight.

OCT. 29, FRI.
News and rumours of the past few days have been so mixed-up and in such quantity as to be practically impossible to differentiate the genuine from rumour. Germany has admitted, however, that the number of people who have lost everything as a result of the bombing raids is up in the millions. After a certain raid on Berlin there were 73,000 additional applicants applying to food relief centers. There is also a rumour in this connection that there has occurred food riots in different parts of Germany and all food stores have been moved to areas used for training areas by military troops to safeguard against the possibility of mass looting. The potato crop has failed and farmers

are receiving the usual ration per day as the ordinary citizen. According to BBC the advance still continues in Italy but owing to the difficult terrain, only at the rate of six miles a day. The Russians seem to be concentrating on the south end of the line and 250,000 Germans are cut off in the Crimea. At one part of the front the Germans are in a complete rout, while Kiev threatens to be more expensive to the Germans than Stalingrad. Germany is having trouble in Poland, keeping the civilian population in check. We also heard that the "Repats" have reached England alright and received a royal welcome. There were plenty of "pints" and cigs. At the ports and each one was issued with a pamphlet stating that they were special guests of the people, also a cablegram form to notify their families of their return. In the latest BBC announcement it was divulged that the repats claimed that it was possible to buy any German soldier with a package of cigarettes. This is virtually true and it will be more so in the near future because soldiers who were getting 5 cigs. a day, have been cut to 3 while civilians can't get any at all now.

A hot rumour came in today that Japan has experienced the worst earthquake in history. Eighteen million casualties is estimated. They applied for aid to the International Red Cross and another relief organization and then stopped fighting. If this is true, it leaves Germany fighting the world by herself.

After planning, conniving and dickering I finally obtained an extra blanket from a departing repat. Today the racket-buster came in and made an appeal for blankets for some of the latest prisoners in block three so sucker or not, I "loaned" them my extra blanket. It's hard to forget the time we had last fall. He made quite a haul in here so I guess other fellows have good memories too. Received a letter from Iris and one from Nelle today.

NOV. 1, MON.

A keen feeling of winter in the air these mornings which is a prelude to colder weather to come; happily we are in better condition and more suitably equipped this year. Mail is seeping through maddeningly slow and in spasmodic spurts. Apparently the band as we knew it before is no more, since it was included in 19A concert. They borrowed a set of trap drums which included the drummer, added a few accordions and ambitiously tackled modern dance music. Being out of a musical job once more, Algebra, reading and jig-saw puzzles occupy most of my time. Received a book parcel from the Hudson Bay Co. containing three jig-saw puzzles and four fiction novels. If this was the parcel that was supposed to contain cross-word puzzle books, I guess the Bay thought cross words were too much of a strain on prisoner of war mentality.

No real news but a couple of sizzling hot rumours are going around these days. In one of those numerous speeches of his, Churchill is credited with the statement that if war isn't over by the end of December, they will start the new year with 20,000 plane bombing raids. The other rumour is that the war has been over for 6 days but the fact is being kept a secret. Anybody want to buy a drum?

NOV. 2, TUES.

The first inkling we had that there was something unusual in the wind was when our tea (1/2 ration) from the kitchen came in before and we were warned that it would last for three or more hours. However, we had our usual , conducted by our diminutive, mean-minded "Spitfire", then we were dismissed until 8:30. This time we were lined up in groups of 500 and marched out of camp to the field outside the west gate. We were counted going out and coming back in. Half the camp went through this operation first, and on our return the other half went out. The purpose for this strange move came in for a lot of speculation but I think the majority of us decided that there has been so many prisoners escaped unnoticed and noticed, change overs, etc. that the authorities did not know for certain how many men they had in camp. The small ration of free air that was enjoyed outside the gates was greatly appreciated by most.

When we got back to our huts we discovered the three electric light extensions (procured through hard dickering and work) had been torn down and taken away. Evidently the move has disrupted the camp's daily routine as there has been no Jerry soup, bread, etc. today. Word came around late this afternoon so adjusted the meal preparation schedule to suit. At 5:10 Spitfire changed his mind and the parade was called. We just got lined up and covered off when the little man told the R.S.M. to dismiss the parade again. If all the curses directed at him came true, Spitfire would have a pretty hot time. I wonder how many they found missing in the big tally today. Received letter and snaps from Harry day before yesterday; also received our group snap taken some weeks ago. Anybody want to buy a drum?

NOV. 4, THURS.

The latest BBC news report read out last night stated that the Germans are in disorderly retreat on the southern flank of the Russian front and despite heavy reinforcements are unable to stem the Russian advance. This rapid advance has resulted in a large German force being cut off in the Crimea. Instead of withdrawing what troops Hitler had on the peninsula he kept reinforcing them to the tune of 50 divisions and it is estimated that there is a million men involved. The last point on the Dnieper fell into Russian hands in one big attack. Large scale fighting has broken out in Yugoslavia under supervision of Allied military authorities; the forces being armed and rein-forced by air. The advance of the Allies in Italy continues slowly but surely; the slowness is due to the difficult terrain and adverse weather conditions. A plane factory near Vienna was successfully bombed by the R.A.F. operat-ing from bases in Southern Italy. The U.S. Marines have recaptured another island in the Solomon Group. (apparently the Japanese earthquake rumour was just that.) The H.M.S. "Ramillies" was torpedoed and casualties believed high. Of course, Northwestern Germany and Occupied countries are being bombed persistently. A large shipment of food has landed in Britain from Canada including 15,000 (50,000?) tons of fresh apples, a large quantity of turkeys and other fowl.

The rumours today are a little wild but nevertheless received with gravity. First, there is supposed to be a group of fellows in Barrack 38 that will take all bets from a pound to 200 pounds that the war is over or at least hostilities have ceased. Then there is the story of an inmate of this compound who tried to get out on a working party. He applied to the working compound commander and when he stated his desire to get on a working party under his own name the fellow in charge said it was impossible for anyone from this compound to get out to work under his own name and the only thing to do was to swap over with someone else. Then he advised the applicant not to be in too much of a hurry to change his residence as there were some large scale changes due around here in the near future.

A warning was issued today by the German office that when a warning was heard coming over the public address system, in English, possibly accompanied by a bugle alarm, everyone was to get out of sight in the nearest barrack room and remain there until further orders. Anyone not heeding the warning in a reasonable time will be shot. This statement has given rise to numerous speculation, ranging from air-raid expectations by the Germans, to possible attack from civilians and by some, a Russian attack. The preparation of slit trenches is still going on around the camp and the cutting of the pine trees, adjacent to this compound which started today is leading to more speculation. The purpose is to obtain heavy timber for air-raid shelters and for breast work. Also to form a sufficient clear space on this side of the camp to frustrate a surprise attack on the camp.

The Germans have finally found a use for the millions of tin cans they have been collecting for months (it has been stated that due to the fact that these cans are insoluble, they have been used for roads). The cans are now being hung on and between the double wire outer fence to act as alarm givers if anyone tries to force exit or entrance illegally from and to the camp.

There is also a rumour that these fellows from "7 to 10" will be moving back as soon as the new fellows down there leave on a working party. I hope they take their bed bugs back with them.

Wills, the commando who tried to perfect the unbeatable bridge system and had to be removed to the New Lazaret in a straight jacket, died the other day. They believe it was due to a blood clot or something.

Also, word has been received of a chemical explosion in which two British P.O.W.'s, seven Germans, five Frenchmen and two Poles were killed on one of the numerous working parties. Population of the camp in between 15,000 and 20,000 now; twice that many are out on working parties from here. Nobody wants to buy a drum? (Guaranteed a genuine white elephant to the present owner.)

NOV. 6, SAT.

The latest rumour which is greeted with general and open skepticism is that hostilities ceased sometime yesterday or the day before. News has been meager for the last few days but another BBC news report is expected hourly. According to the propaganda sheet "Camp." the iniquity of Piccadilly has reached staggering proportions and Hyde Park stinks to high heaven and both have been mentioned in a parliamentary debate.

The BBC news was just read out and included items such as: The 5th and 8th Armies are continuing their slow hard fought advance. The Russian victory of the lower Dnieper almost complete. As a result of the Moscow conference five European countries have been promised their independence after the war, France, Italy, Poland, Czechoslovakia, Austria and Yugoslavia. A new plane built in the States has twice the range and capacity of the flying Fortress. Punishment for all German atrocities in occupied countries will be handled by the countries concerned. (This will cook many a German goose in such countries as Poland, Czechoslovakia, Yugoslavia, etc.) Cordal Hull is meeting Anthony Eden in Cairo for a conference. Widespread riots in Bulgaria. Bulgaria refused Germany use of boats to evacuate the troops cut off in the Crimea. Marauders carried out attacks on targets in France. The German Bight bombed with special attention to Wilhelmshaven and Dusseldorf. Received five letters today, 3 from Nelle (two with snaps) 1 from Bobbie and one from Buddo.

Amusements promise to be plentiful this winter, Bingo, quiz contests, spelling matches and amateur shows held almost nightly. There are plenty of instruments and talent in the compound so we should see some pretty good performances during the cold months. Sgt. Ferguson is endeavoring to organize an all Canadian show next door. Algebra is still giving me headaches. Started manufacture of a kidney belt in an effort to decrease nightly forays to the latrine to a minimum.

NOV. 8, MON.

A couple of wild rumours have been circulating yesterday and today. One in connection with Hitler's speech scheduled for sometime today. Hitler is supposed to make a speech in which he promises to astound the whole world.

Late this afternoon a rumour came around that he had abdicated in favour of Goering. Significant is the story of more local nature. Forty-two court-marshal cases against prisoners were supposed to go before the German authorities today, among them a case of sabotage and one of illegal intercourse with a German girl. The first case was estimated to be good for five to ten years penal servitude, the latter case, five to ten years and in extreme cases, death. All forty-two cases were dismissed and charges withdrawn.

BBC news dating from Oct. 21ˢᵗ was exceptionally good tonight and besides a few new items, was a resume of the scraps of BBC filtering in from day to day. There was supposed to be a general inspection today to investigate the over crowded conditions of the camp, but like all general inspections, whether army or prison camp, it just petered out.

Announcement was made on parade this evening that anyone wishing to join a compound dance band report to so-and-so in barrack room such-and-such. This will probably lie the death knell of the mediocre band recently formed that knocked the old time band out of circulation. According to recent sentiments heard in this immediate locality, the Old Time Dance Band may reform stronger than ever as a consequence.

Unbelievable as it may seem, two of the lads were decidedly inebriated this evening, presumably from overindulgence of hard stuff smuggled into camp. It's the first sight of this kind we have seen for over 13 months.

We tried a new culinary recipe this evening, canned Pilchards boiled in milk mixed from powdered klim. Not bad at all, a decided welcome change in the preparation of abundant canned fish being received in parcels recently. Received 300 cigs from Iris today.

NOV. 10, WED.

Rumours of Hitler's speech have been circulating yesterday and today. The first one had him announcing that he was abdicating in favour of Dr. Ley. The second said he stated that if the German nation worked and fought harder, their efforts would end in victory, even if it took ten years. Another rumour this evening has it that he stated that every stone and brick knocked down by the R.A.F. in Germany will be replaced by P.O.W.'s before they leave the country. Rumours of more local nature are that we are to move to another camp, VII C, in a few days; that 59,000 P.O.W.s will be repatriated soon.

The construction of a road through the pine grove just outside this compound is causing apprehension for a number of inmates.

The highlight of last night's BBC news report as far as we are concerned was the Allies promise to Germany of bigger and longer air raids, especially on areas that have experienced the bomb tremor, such as Poland, Saxony, etc. The latter is this neck o' the woods. Targets are plentiful around here: Breslau, Niesse, Tamsdorf, not to mention ammo dumps in the all too near vicinity. 5th and 8th Armies still slowly advancing in Italy. Big offensive expected against Japan in the next month or so, launched simultaneously from five main jumping places, Alaska, Hawaiian Islands, New Guinea, India and China. (this is not BBC)

Received letter from Rose today and 300 cigs. from Harry yesterday.

NOV. 13, SAT.

The news for the past few days continues good and includes such items as the capture of three towns in Italy by the 8th Army, the fall of Kiev and the Russian advance 100 kilometers westward. Mention was made again of the large German force cut off in the Crimea. Roosevelt and Churchill both gave speeches in which it was stated that the invasion of the continent will take place early in 1944. Roosevelt says the first stop will be Berlin. Hitler in a speech lasting over 2 hours, reviewed the Nazi party activities and said the Germans would be victorious, even if it took ten years, providing the people and soldiers would work and fight a little harder. 8,000 tons of bombs were dropped on Dusseldorf in 27 minutes the other night. Stalin is supposed to have said that there wouldn't be a German remaining on Russian soil by the New Year. A big move is rumoured around which is supposed to affect German personnel as well as P.O.W.s. One story has it that the R.A.F. and Dieppe personnel accompanied with a staff of Germans will be moving to VII C, 100 km. from here. Another version is that Canadians, R.A.F., "Repats" and British N.C.O.s will be staying while everyone eligible for arbiet will be moving. This latter rumour is more likely as it is much easier to move 3,000 men than it is to move 9,000.

One of the posterns on the garden party is just a young fellow hardly in his twenties. He was wounded just before his 18th birthday and has had both feet and one hand badly frozen on the Russian front; he has almost lost the sight of one eye. He, like "Hop-a-long," who ran over a land mine on a motorcycle, has no use for the glory of war.

Records have become in such a mess since the girls have been working in the "Kart," the German authorities are at their wits ends trying to make sense out of it. Need is recognized, of ousting of the girls and the return of prisoners in executive offices to straighten things out. Due to the number of increasing escape endeavours, the Germans have arrived at the conclusion that they are forcing their way through 2 four-inch barbed wire meshes and three rows of spiral wire; consequently, Eaton's and Maple Leaf butter cans, etc. are adorning the spiral wire, acting as alarms if anyone tries to cut the wire. Beer was wondering why he wasn't hearing from his brother; the other day he received word that he was captured in Sicily and is a prisoner at IV C.

NOV. 16, TUES.
Heard a story yesterday of Royal Regiment of Canada C.S.M. who has beaten up two "repats." He is now in custody and we hope he gets the limit.

A controversy of major importance to us is being heatedly debated here. Roll-call parades have come to such a state that they seldom last less than 45 minutes, sometimes an hour and a half. With cold weather in the offing, drastic alterations are indicated. Opinions to the cause are varied; some believe that the R.S.M. and "Spitfire" are conducting a private feud; (incidentally R.S.M. Murray is unable to handle the parade." Others believe the fault lies with the men themselves, by tardiness getting on parade and the perpetual childish activities on or off parade. Personally I believe it is the ultimate result of a number of things, (1) Spitfire's belief that we are always trying to put something over on him; (2) Inability of Murray to handle the parade and the general dislike with which he is held; (3) The "Spitfire-Murray feud is no dream; (4) Tardiness of assembling for the parades; and (5) The indulgence in childish games by a majority of men (all full grown) while on parade. Put them all together and we have 60 to 80 minute roll-call parade.

Unable to understand what criterion is used in the manufacture of English (Lusty's) meat roll, that comes in English parcels (R.C.) Couldn't eat anymore after the first taste last night at supper. Buck Lindsay is collecting a mark/ten pfennigs for a battalion group picture on Dec. 11. The road beside the camp is progressing slowly and certain people are breathing much easier as a consequence. Engbert has finally arrived at the same conclusion that I did some time ago. Any form of engineering studying is impossibly useless without a working knowledge of maths Algebra, Trig. and Geometry.

We woke up this morning to find the landscape bearing a mantle of white. It was a perfect study in black and white. The sun broke through during the morning and thawing commenced. Mud was the keynote by five o'clock. Have no wooden shoes this winter so am anticipating plenty of cold feet with the resultant chilblains.

Played bingo this evening but failed to repeat my win of 200 cigs of the other session. All profits from the 2 cigs a card fee go to buy extra coal, wood, food prizes and four sorely needed benches. The stores around camp, following "Demi-God" Goodies assertion that he is endeavouring to place a ban on the sale of foodstuffs and clothes have formed a storekeepers union and advocate all spare clothing being placed at the disposal of the Welfare Society.

Perhaps a word about the German canteen in the Stalag which people back home seem to think is a big thing, wouldn't be amiss. On the average it comes in about once every ten days and usually consists of a box of inferior German matches per man at 5 pfennigs a box, sometimes razor blades that won't fit our razors, soup powders that tasted like lye, fruit powders that taste like the soup powders, flea powder and the occasional soap dish, (these last usually sell fast because they make passable replicas of badges and rings).

NOV. 18, THURS.
Entered a crib tournament yesterday but was beaten out by Eric by two straight games. Went down for a bath in the afternoon and put my shorts on again after wearing long light underwear for the past few weeks. In view of the

fact that I already had a bad cold this procedure was perhaps a little foolish. It is still damp, muddy and chilly out with a few traces of snow remaining.

We heard last night that the post office was broken into and 16 personal and a good number of cigarette parcels were stolen. Due to the large quantity taken it is hard to believe that prisoners alone are responsible; the post office is near the administrative building, a taboo area for P.O.W.s after hours unless they were aided and abetted by German personnel. The first hint we had that something unusual was afoot today was when an officer and a number of other ranks appeared during roll-call. After being counted twice, we were herded out of the compound and locked <u>out</u>. A few minutes later a squad of Germans arrived armed with sledge hammers, picks, shovels, etc. and their object was no longer in doubt; it was the tunnel in 19B.

The manner in which they proceeded directly to the inside entrance under one of the bunks in 19B indicated without a doubt that someone had squealed. They spent some time trying to find the outside exit before two venturesome Germans crawled through until they were stopped by the trap door loaded with earth placed there by the road building gang. The two Germans yelled until they were heard by posterns, who unable to understand the sound of voices coming from the ground, placed themselves around the spot with bayonets held in readiness. Queer as it may seem, the Germans reaction to the discovery of the tunnel was one of admiration for a well done job and a well kept secret and a totally unexpected display of good humour. Perhaps the latter was a result of having so many escape cases over a period of six months successfully solved. They are always ready to acknowledge and appreciate work of this kind. The tunnel was started last spring and has been in use for the past six months, the earth being removed in small boxes and spread in inconspicuous places around the compound. The ladder which disappeared from the vicinity of the tea kitchen some time ago was recovered; also, many lengths of drain pipes from the corners of a number of barrack buildings around camp, the pipe was used for ventilation. The cribbing consisted of mainly bed-boards and other pieces and bits of lumber found around camp. This is the second tunneling job attempted, the first which was discovered before it could be used was dug by British N.C.O.s when they occupied this compound.

This one was a howling success and everyone who knew of its existence was surprised it escaped notice for so long. It paved the way for the escaped six officers on one occasion, a Lt. Col. on another and a number of other ranks. No one could use the tunnel unless they had at least a fifty-fifty chance of making good their escape from the country. Borkoff, 2 i/c (*second in command*) of the camp, when leaving the compound was heard to remark with a good-natured smile, "Prima Prima, Gute Arbiet." No reprisals are forthcoming as yet and out gates are open, parcels were issued a little late, but without trouble. Prisoners are coming from all over camp to look at the gaping hole uncovered in 19B. One fellow slept in a bunk directly above the hole for months without realizing it was there.

I have a splitting headache tonight and the corny band picks this room for a practice session. It was announced last night that 8,000 cigs. collected for the Welfare fund were converted into marks and used for the purchase of medical supplies; also some thousand more similarly converted went for much needed dental equipment.

NOV. 21, SUN.

Apparently the German authorities do not feel disposed to retaliate for the engineering feat disclosed by the discovery of the tunnel. We did hear that the report that went to Berlin stated that the tunnel had been dug last week and wasn't finished long enough for anyone to escape. The camp authorities, of course, know different but wonder how they are going to explain the mysterious absence of about 128 men who have started an unofficial trip back to freedom and haven't been apprehended to date. An account written in true German style was composed by "Tennessee" Kline and was typical of news bulletins found in the D.A.Z. It will either appear later on in this book or in my Log Book.

Jerry Johnson told me this morning that one of the Repats wrote from England to a friend here and advised the friend to pick a soft centre bunk and prepare for another five years. Quite a cheerful letter for a prisoner to receive. Also heard that two escapists who utilized the tunnel have written from Sweden; they were there when the Repats went through. Also that Greece had fallen into British hands after 68 hours of resistance. A vague rumour is going around tonight to the effect that Germany has lost close to a million men in the Crimea.

Took part in a whist drive this evening and although I was far from the highest score I was an equal distance from the booby prize. The contents of the Xmas parcels were read out this evening and except for the addition of bacon and salmon and the omission of candy, they are the same as last year. Mail (incoming) is exceedingly slow now and cigs are getting low again. Weather remains pretty fair for this time of year, chilly but not unbearable, with mist and occasional rain. Spitfire is gone again, "Hoppy" taking his place; how long he will remain away is pretty hard to say; forever, we hope. Sent a snap to Nelle today, doubt very much if she will get it.

NOV. 22, MON.

Well it's happened for sure this time. It was announced after roll-call this evening that the chains were taken away for good and work parties would be made up soon. This means that existence here becomes as uncertain as the weather and we won't know when we will find ourselves in another part of Germany. This morning the new Commandant held a meeting of Barrack room commanders and informed them that all men will be off the floor and cleared out of the school by Christmas. He told them he would do everything possible to increase the comfort of the prisoners but we would have to cooperate. He said he hoped this would become the best camp in Germany. Apparently getting rid of the Canadians is the first necessity. I guess a kit overhaul wouldn't be a bad idea. Nothing new in the line of news except a few impossible rumours not worth repeating. It is not known if these work parties start before Christmas or not. I have a hunch that they will be starting soon.

NOV. 23, TUES.

Future decidedly uncertain now. There is a persistent rumour going around that there will be a fairly large working party going out soon. The number constituting the party is open for debate, however, 250 is one guess, which jumped to 650 an hour later and the last I heard it was up to 750. Played bingo tonight without any luck. Corporal and higher ranks, of course, are not forced to go to work unless they so desire and as I have grave doubts whether this diary would get by the search usually made on an outgoing party, I think it would be wise to leave it with someone of that rank for safekeeping. We were warned on parade tonight that if anyone is caught in possession or using a stalag stove in the huts, the culprit will be made to destroy his own handiwork, then he will be reported and probably have to "stand at the wire" for five hours. This is the first and probably second step of making our stay here as comfortable as possible. The Commandant claims to have been a prisoner of war himself sometime and realizes all the drawbacks of being in that category; perhaps conditions at the place where he was held were different to this.

In the lengthy BBC news report today, Churchill in a recent speech is supposed to have given his first promise to the people; he promises the end of the war in 1944. He repeated the statement that Italy wasn't the second front but it would be starting soon and possibly a fourth front as well. In his speech he thanked the Japs for fighting to the last man in New Guinea as it is the means of ridding the world of much cheap labour. He said there were 250,000 prisoners in Japanese hands, that haven't been registered and reported. Their fate is unknown and their safety feared for. One prisoner who escaped was so mutilated he was unable to give an adequate report. The Russians are still coming along good and the Allied forces in Italy are advancing slowly. An Island in the Mediterranean was captured by Germans. The outlaw army in Yugoslavia was keeping 75 German divisions fully occupied; this army is operating under Allied generals and is reinforced and armed by air. Another interesting item of the report was that the Allied countries would adopt the metric system of measure and weight after the war. It will sound odd to say that Winnipeg is 225 kilometers from Kenora, and how will a person ask for a two by four in metric language? Received a letter from Nelle today in answer to my letter of July 4.

NOV. 24, WED.
Our fears of working parties have more or less been annulled today by three main items of interest. First of all the R.S.M. was asked when working parties would be starting; the answer they got was that the only mention of such

parties that he has heard is among the men themselves. Secondly, the R.S.M. for the working compound said when asked that he has not heard of any such party going out, and that he had a compound full of men waiting to go out now. Thirdly Sgt. Ferguson (C. of C.) believed the rumours and took it upon himself to go around and get the names of fifty Camerons who would volunteer for work, with him in charge of the party. He went down to submit the 51 names to Borkoff who told him that Canadians were banned from going to work; he didn't know why the ban was on but it has been for some time and hasn't been rescinded as yet. Fergy came back, I think, feeling relieved and sort of like a pricked balloon.

The stove was lit with coal yesterday and the oven used for cooking for the first time this winter. As a result of the bingo games, we have been able to accumulate a small amount of coal ahead and buy a few other little conveniences as well. The only official news of a move in near future is one effecting 100 men, B3 category who are going to another camp some time early in December. The only place a working party can go now, according to official reports, is the Sudetenland and this will only affect Blocks 1 and 3. Received a letter today from Ellen Zanetti, the lady who gave us such a good Christmas in New Haven. She says she still has my Poly-Photos. It took a little while to remember how she came by them. She wants to know if I want them sent here or home.

Churchill is supposed to have promised a big drive at the end of this month or early next month and he thinks the war will be over in six months. Berlin was bombed very heavily last Monday night.

NOV. 25, THURS.
Every day there are about 85 men called out for grading and according to the numbers, they are starting from the lowest numbers. The Germans say this doesn't mean that we will be going out to work but is merely to get an idea of the different categories.

News of unreliable sources and by grapevine telegraph states that the German prisoners repatriated from Canada have all reported the good treatment received in Canada that the Germans here feel obligated to return the favour, so we can expect a change or changes for the better as a consequence; this was supposed to have come from a German Sgt.-Major.

Also heard via the grapevine this evening that after a severe incendiary and H.E. raid on Berlin, the biggest fires in history are raging there. They are so fierce it is impossible to fight it. In the German communique this evening this was confirmed in a mild way. The same source of news disclosed that there is a large naval battle raging in the Pacific between American and Japanese forces. Large numbers of boats are being lost on both sides with the Japs the bigger loser by 3 to 2. Another group of repats is rumoured to be leaving on December 10, but there is no official confirmation or signs of confirmation as yet.

A queer tale, the truth of which I am not in the position to doubt, came in this evening supposedly from new arrivals taken in the fighting in Southern Italy. They were kept at 7A before they came here and kept in separate cells. They were taken individually before a German official and were propositioned. They were asked to join "The Legion of St. George," and were told that if they joined they would be given civilian clothes and fourteen days leave in Berlin which meant wine, women, song and otherwise a good time. All they had to do was sign a paper stating that they were 100% British, hated the Bolsheviks and Bolshevism and would fight on the Russian front against the Russians. They were told that they would be under British officers and a British Lt. Col. If they signed the paper they had access to a room with comfortable furniture, plenty of cigs. and recreation. The officers were also tempted but showed only contempt for the idea. The Germans claim some of them did sign but everyone doubts that assertion very much. If they refused, they were placed in cells again and remained in solitary from ten days to 3 weeks. Quite a scheme, the purpose of which is to cause dissension between British and Russian people and thereby drive a wedge in the alliance.

Played Whist tonight with much the same result as last time; too low for first prize and too high for Booby.

Also heard tonight that 55% of the repats to reach England had TB.

NOV. 26, FRI.

The grading of the cattle continues; heard today that only 19 out of 84 men were passed with A1 category, the rest came out as B2, B3 and even B4. Rumours supposedly from a German source states that Berlin is still in flames. It is supposed to have had a 48 hour continuous bombing, 7,500 planes taking part. At regular intervals during the raid, BBC kept asking the German authorities if they had enough and promised Munich a similar visit. The raid, as rumour goes, was only a few minutes old when BBC asked Berlin where her air raid defenses were. Casualties are said to be close to a million and just as many homeless. We understand that "Black Hammer" a P.O.W. working party camp, engaged in the construction of a chemical factory, is subjected to bombing. The number of prisoners employed there must be in the thousands. Heard also today that four Canadian divisions have made a successful landing in northern Italy, behind the German front lines, placing the main German army in that country in a very unenviable position. Personally, the rumours are getting so wild that it would be foolish to believe a fraction of them.

The Berlin affair is gaining momentum and mass. According to the latest, all communication is cut off from and to the city, sewage is disrupted and water supply cut off. A Swedish newspaper is supposed to have reported the city flattened and casualties and damage inestimable. Hitler is supposed to have said it is the greatest catastrophe ever visited upon a civilized people. As far as that goes, these raids Germany is experiencing is Hitler's own idea, which he intended for London and other democratic cities, but it back-fired because he hadn't the air force to carry it out first. After the raid, maps and pamphlets were dropped on Munich and Black Hammer; the maps showing Berlin as a blank spot and arrows pointing to Munich as the next target and Black Hammer next in line after that. The Swedish newspapers say that 17,000 planes were over Germany that night and 1,900 were shot down.

A little while ago a certain quantity of eating and cooking equipment came in from some Canadian source and because it was inadequate to supply even this compound, it was given to the River Hospital which appreciated them very much. This action met with general approval among the Canadians, at least until tonight but three Canadians (possibly Americans) came through trying to incite discontent by claiming we should have had a vote on it, besides these three over-generous Canucks think that the sick weren't in need of the equipment at all. They believe the frying pan (one to each hut if the stuff was distributed among the huts) could hang on the stove for the use of 165 men to cook their meals on.

NOV. 28, SUN.

Nothing new since Friday except a few slightly different versions of the Berlin bombing; the essential facts remain practically the same. New rumours of a move coming up is heard at regular intervals, the latest being that after this grading business is finished, all 1 and 2 grades will be moved to three and two compounds, and all B3 and 4 grades will go to the Repat and convalescent compounds. This compound will be filled with N.C.O.s. If this comes about it will mean that the Canadians will be scattered all over camp and subjected to working parties in the near future. Of course, there are so many rumours going around it is difficult to believe a few of them. Presuming the truth of the move, I think it is a poor way of showing appreciation for the good treatment of German prisoners while they were in Canada.

The grub box belonging to Kitchen and Vowles, which customarily perches precariously on the clothes beam fell twice today. This seems to be a daily occurrence and at such times the scattered contents are patiently restored to its wobbly, insecure position. Vowles, one of the partners, is the object of many sad head shakes and visible annoyance from and to the rest of the hut. Granted, he has a cold but is that any reason for wearing heavy underwear, sweaters, shirt, uniform balaclava and a woolen helmet to bed and covering himself with two blankets, an overcoat-blanket and a great-coat? Not only does this take place at night but it lasts all day as well. It will be remembered that these two streaks of misery slept in their uniforms all last winter. The weather now is exceptionally mild for this time of year. Apparently a cold was too much for Vowles' high-pitched voice as it has soared completely beyond the audible spectrum (or is it a plane?) After all, I guess it really isn't none of my business what this apparently unhappy individual deems fit to do, unless it endangers other people's health; we aren't so sure if that isn't the case.

NOV. 30, TUES.

Nothing of very much importance these days going on. Categorical grading has been temporarily discontinued for some reason or other and rumours are just as thick as ever. Mahoney voiced a good one last night. He said there would soon be an 81,300 able bodied men separated soon and in the Geneva pact signed in 1935 there is a clause to the effect that any prisoner subjected to reprisals of any shape or form at the hands of the holding power will be among the first of able bodied men to go. No one is foolish enough to believe it, of course.

According to Goebel's speech the bombing is having its effect on the German people and the authorities consider it wise to try and pacify them with glowing promises of retribution. Bremen and Stuttgart were the targets the other night. Started on Geometry today. Received a cig. chit this evening.

DEC. 2, THURS.

Heavy snow flurries today and mild, clearing off this evening, temperature dropping. Freezing this evening. Arbiet rumours dying down due to the discontinuance of grading parades. There is a little activity around No. 3 compound these days and it is believed that the privates down there will be going out on working parties. There is also much talk of all N.C.O.s being concentrated in one compound.

Understand that there is another shipment of Canadian mail in. Received a letter from Marc today and 300 cigarettes from the Ladies' Auxiliary (C of C) yesterday. When getting up this morning I sustained a kink in the neck which has been troublesome all day. Played whist tonight with the usual run of luck. Engbert, our pessimist of last year is betting that the second front will be starting in 10 days or less. BBC news remains good. Berlin is seriously battered; BBC says that the balcony where Hitler used to speak to the public has been demolished, also the museum which used to shelter the railroad carriage of Versailles treaty of the last war; chemical, rubber and ammunition factories in and around the city are seriously damaged. The Americans have advanced another 5 miles in Italy. General Montgomery has promised to take Rome by Xmas. Russians are coming ahead steadily.

A fairly large tent has been erected beside the Lending Library as a gym. The new Commandant expressed the wish to see an indoor boxing tournament before Xmas. We have been exceedingly fortunate in the weather this year. It is rumoured that Germany is obstructing further negotiations for repatriation because the papers in England quoted one repatriated prisoner as saying that we can buy Munich with a can of cocoa.

DEC. 3

A fine clear day; the warm sun drew the night's frost from the ground and mud was plentiful. The new Commandant has a disconcerting habit of strolling around the camp unattended by the usual number of "yes men" and dropping in unexpectedly, on any barrack that takes his fancy. It is a singular honour that in a recent camp issue of daily orders he mentioned this compound as the cleanest in the camp. He came through again this morning and expressed pleasure at the neatness. However, we were warned tonight that he intends to make frequent and unannounced visits in the evening as well. Most of the fellows expressed their regrets in no uncertain terms. Every day we are interested spectators of an aerial ground strafing demonstration by the Luftwaffe, consisting of four fighter training planes. They skim dive and swoop in the vicinity of and over the camp daily. We always know when the show is over by the leader waggling his wings. There hasn't been an accident for some time now and the boys are patiently waiting, determined to be eyewitnesses.

School opened again today and I attended Electrical Engineering class once again. A new teacher, a long closed period and new pupils decided a new start from scratch. It is not certain how long it will stay open this time.

Mort, the Steinbach wonder, thought a homicidal maniac was loose last night when he woke up to find his neighbour trying to throttle him to death. With a supreme effort he threw his attacker into the aisle. The fellow woke up under the rough treatment and said he was dreaming he was choking someone. Mort didn't think it much of a dream and said he thought it was a Comanche raid. He said his neighbour just jumped up, leveled for action.

It was announced this evening that this camp is no longer STALAG VIII B but has been changed to STALAG No. 344. Reason unknown. There still has to be big changes if everyone is going to be off the floor by Xmas.

DEC. 4

This is the anniversary of my enlistment, four years ago. The events of that day are still crystal clear, but what a change has taken place since then. I have travelled halfway around the earth and penetrated far into enemy territory. The last 16 months won't soon be forgotten, the big question, chewed and pulled to rags in many arguments, is how much longer before familiar scenes unroll on either side of the homeward bound train. Before I step off the train in Kenora I will view the passing scenery of Germany, possibly Belgium, France, England, possibly Scotland and Ireland, the tossing foaming surface of the Big Pond, Nova Scotia, New Brunswick, Quebec and nearly all of Ontario. Quite a little journey but a pleasant one because I will be going home. What a value that word has now.

It was entirely by coincidence that today of all days, I accomplished something I have been planning for two years, not so much planning as intending. I made arrangements for assigning an additional five dollars home to Dad.

Temperatures hovered below freezing point during the last twenty-four hours and surprisingly enough, found it much more bearable than the former damp, chilly weather.

Mail is scarce these days. Rumours are stronger than ever that there is a move of some sort in the offing soon.

Another milestone has been reached in the hut administration in that instead of a different section performing the cleaning duties in rotation, ten volunteers will do the job permanently or as long as we are here. This calls for cooperation on everyone's part and in a family this size it's of utmost importance; nevertheless, it is found that there are a few who refuse to cooperate and there is no way of forcing them to fall in line. Of course, among 160 men there is bound to be a few who live by the rule of selfishness.

The BBC news continues good. The Allied Air Force claim another record when over 300 four thousand pound bombs were dropped on Berlin in twenty minutes, almost 2/3 of the tonnage dropped on England during 11 months of war. A daylight raid following this raid was carried out by Canadian and Australian crews. The 8th and 5th Armies are continuing their slow sure advance in Italy. The Russians are celebrating another key town capture and still advancing. The German government has evacuated Berlin.

DEC. 5, SUN.
Weather remaining frosty and fairly dry. New system of barrack appeared to go off pretty good for the first day. The rest of the BBC news was read out today and the most interesting item was that of some neutral paper which stated that after one of the recent heavy raids on Berlin, the Berlin police were looking for the person or persons, who wrote, "Fuehrer, we thank you" on one of the walls in chalk. Berlin had nine successive nights of heavy bombing. Chilblains on the feet is my present pet worry.

Due to the scarcity of cigarettes in camp, the numerous stores in camp are cutting the food prices practically in half. English cheese will drop to 15, chocolate bars to 20, biscuits to 30 a tin, etc. These stores have been the means of cutting down of rackets to a low level. They are unionized now and prices are rigidly controlled. Wrote to Ellen Zanette, Peggy and Rusty.

Played in a whist tournament this evening but still fell short of the prize limit, scoring 151 when the highest score was over 180.

DEC. 8, WED.
The Electrical Engineering class at the school is so large the school authorities deem it necessary to split the class in two. I am contented to learn that, as one of the veterans of the class, I am included in "A" class with times of tri-weekly sessions unchanged. Someday, if hostilities last long enough, I will finish this particular class; three starts so far and three instructors. Uncertain whether the number of tutors is mere coincidence or if we are wearing them out. Would like to take in the Applied Maths class as well, including slide-rule instruction but the times are a little inconvenient. All my mathematical

endeavours are at present, centered on clearing up the mysteries of simultaneous quadratics. It's quite a mental struggle for my capabilities.

Had another bath today, probably our last before Xmas. Thinking seriously of sending my laundry out this week. It is inevitable that in a community this size, that stores and laundries are the first business enterprises to loom or spring into existence; a community must eat and keep one's raiment presentable. So the laundry or rather laundries have raised our standard of living a little. The medium of trade is of course, cigarettes and the charges, to the best of my recollection, are 15 cigs. for pajamas, 8 for heavy underwear, 4 for light, 4 for a pair of socks, 8 for a large towel, 4 for a small one, 50 for a complete battle dress. Washing winter clothing in cold water in this weather isn't very efficient and is extremely miserable so the prices are well worth the work.

Since we were informed that this hell hole is now known as camp 344, we also learned that the new camp at a place called Faschie? (*Teschen*) will henceforth be designated by the VIII B. Apparently some of the citizens here will be following the VIII B soon.

With four days of freezing weather and the presence of 100 pairs of "clamp-on" skates in the sports stores, I suppose it is natural that Canadian thoughts persist in lingering on the possibilities of ice making. The idea however was destined to an early death, as when an enthusiastic representative gained the audience of our camp Commandant for purpose of obtaining permission to make a rink, he was told that we may as well forget the idea because the weather in these parts isn't favourable to good ice making and the duration of said ice wasn't worth the labour it would require.

The mail is exceedingly scarce recently, at least as far as I am concerned, nary a letter for days and days.

Despite the below freezing climate of late, this year's coal ration is far below that of last year. In fact, last Monday a crisis in culinary efforts and brewing activities was reached when no coal or wood was discovered in the fuel reserve. However, by a dint of commendable effort, buckshee fuel was purchased from the proceeds of Bingo. Since then fuel peddlers have been beating a path to our door and the fuel containers are bulging.

Yesterday, the Commandant sent word around that he had obtained six or eight heaters (details of construction and means not forthcoming), and said that the said heaters would be allotted to the three neatest compounds and to the two neatest rooms in these compounds. He would be the sole judge and presenter of the awards. If they are coal burning gadgets, we or the winners could use them as refrigerators; if electrically operated they might make good toasters, but only after five in the evening because the lights are controlled from down below.

DEC. 10, FRI.
At this moment this war is ten hours older than the last war, thereby proving all prophets who claimed that this little tiff would last no longer than the last one, decidedly wrong.

We were greeted by a mantle of pure white this morning which covered and subdued the harsh ugliness of the locality from tired eyes. The only aspect of this place that is interesting to a person from the bush country is the stand of stalwart pines just outside of the east fence. Tall tapering and stately, covered with a fine sparkling cloak of snow, they stirred pleasant memories this morning.

The abundance of snowball material and restless spirits lent plenty of vim to a snowball fight between this compound and the Air Force across the road. All day the battle waged with plenty of innocent bystanders casualties. The battle sprung into being during roll-call this morning with a heavy artillery duel. A brief quiet spell was recognized for breakfast, then shifting to the vicinity of the compound gates developed into patrol activities from both sides with frequent attacks and counter attacks. The battle dwindled to local insignificant activities during noon but immediately blazed forth stronger than ever in the afternoon. There are men on both sides nursing black eyes and sore arms tonight. Pratt fractured his arm throwing this afternoon, a thing never heard of before. This evening word came around that the "rackets" compound was challenging this and the Air Force compounds to a snowball fight. Of course, volunteers were many but when the warriors went forth to do battle, there was no sign of the challengers. Even now that it is dark, anyone going on business trips taking them outside can't be sure when they will receive a snowball in the ear.

Rumours these last two days have been many, varied and all wild, such as Rommel giving a speech from London, America, Canada (take your choice); the enemy surrendering in Italy and the Russians are marching down the Warsaw highway in Poland, etc., etc.

Received 1,000 cigs from Dad this morning and they came just in time. When I was waiting for my name to be called out a German officer came in rummaged through the empty cartons. Finally selecting a sturdy British Consul box, he turned to us and with a half apologetic smile, offered the explanation that he was sending a Christmas parcel home to his family.

Dieppe is being fought again tonight for the unknownth time and every time it happens, it grows. Anyone listening to the stories would naturally think it was a major engagement lasting at least a couple months and on which the fate of the democratic world depended instead of a nine hour blunder which is probably long forgotten in the outside world. No doubt, our little quibble is long lost in the shadow of Tunis, Sicily and Italy accomplishments.

Received a letter from Nelle this afternoon.

DEC. 12, SUN.

The last two days have been suspiciously rumour and news free. A rumour going around for awhile yesterday said that the Allies have given Germany 14 days to sign on the dotted line or else the bombing will be redoubled. The latrine is full again and the Germans don't supply boats. The Commandant issued a statement to the effect that a field kitchen will supply hot water to every compound in turn, to be used for scrubbing all fixtures and wood work in the rooms. He also was successful in obtaining a number of empty wooden cases which are being stored for fuel for Christmas week.

Undertook a chore which I dislike very much in this weather and managed to launder a suit of pajamas, two towels and 3 hankies before the cold forced me to quit. First of all, for a job of this sort, it is essential that the water is running (usually it goes off as soon as I get everything wet) as it did this time, then after soaping as thoroughly as possible a hair brush is vigourously applied; by this time there is no feeling in the hands and only by sight does the worker know he has a brush in his hands. Then comes the rinsing; this is done by using a few drops of water that bubbles up from a short pipe in the floor. It is inevitable that as soon as a person starts rinsing his laundry by the simple method of wrapping it around the pipe and squashing it on the cement floor, every man and his brother comes in to wash pots, wash, clean teeth, etc. and tea leaves, soup, coffee grounds and the remains of German noon day soup is dumped around the fairly clean laundry so still having a suit of heavy underwear, a shirt and two pairs of socks to wash, I have decided to forego the pleasure of frozen hands, frayed temper, etc. and let the laundry man in 18B earn a few smokes. Still cold out and no sign of a let up.

Bought a large bottle of ink this evening for 60 cigs; the gent wanted 100 but finally settled for my offer.

DEC. 14, TUES.
Lately I have been doing a lot of thinking regards personal post war plans inasmuch as it affects marriage. (I have yet to find a girl foolish enough to accompany me on such a venture.) As it looks, and considering everything it will be at least 5 years <u>after</u> the war before I am in a position to marry, providing no set-backs are encountered, one year for training and at least 4 years to place a business on a substantial paying basis.

Eric and I took in the show, "Philadelphia Story" last night. This sounds a simple procedure if said fast, but it necessitates eating supper at four o'clock, a mad breathtaking dash from roll-call to the theater door, a long wait in the cold, a slim chance of securing a front seat, which we didn't. We were about 10 from the front and the view of the stage ceiling and the occasional actor's head was about all we could see when sitting upright. People in front folded their coats and sat on them, consequently we all had to do it, so nobody gained anything. They say it is the best show put on here but it can't be proven by me. It was like listening to a radio play, all sound and nothing else.

Another case of waiting this morning when I with about 100 other fellows had to go down for grading. A long wait at the gate and a much longer wait at the hospital. Not sure if I got A1 or B2; have three teeth broken out of my plate, which may have resulted in a secondary grade. There is quite a lot of talk that it is for working parties soon. Rumours going around that there will be a big exchange of prisoners in January, which includes men over 40 and B2 categories. I don't believe it.

There is a story going around that an Air Force chap was bitten on a very tender spot by a rat, while performing his duty in the latrine. Latest reports say that gangrene has set in and the fellow may cash-in. The Commandant seems very concerned over the incident and may organize a camp-wide rat hunt. I think it would be better if the latrines were cleaned out so that everything would be out of reach of the rats.

Played Bingo with no luck tonight. With continuance of good ice-making conditions the work on the rink is progressing somewhat. It should be almost ready for its first flooding soon. Expect warm weather about that time too.

A couple of loads of English R.C. parcels relieved the parcel situation just in time; received them today. Understand that personal Xmas parcels were sent by Canadian people.

DEC. 17
The latest BBC news mentioned that a Canadian force distinguished themselves at the crossing of the Sangro River in Italy.

Due to the recent rat menace a drive has been organized by the Camp Comforts Committee and is called "Rat Week." Two cigarettes per tail is the reward with 50 cigs for the best bag during the week. Nearly every latrine is overflowing, the disposal equipment being totally inadequate to cope with the situation. A few breakdowns have been disastrous in this respect. The new Camp Commandant is at least trying to fulfill his promise of better conditions, his most recent contribution being a field water heater visiting a different compound each day to supply hot water for scrubbing room fixtures. It may be our turn tomorrow. This compound, by the way, is one of the cleanest in the camp. Today another step was taken in this direction when all tables and doors were scrubbed clean and the "dining room" whitewashed again. We are liable to hit delousing parade tomorrow or Monday.

There is a rumour going around that the camp Commandant will make an announcement at Xmas which will be welcomed by some and not by others. We are of the opinion that he will say for sure if the Canadians will be sent on working parties or not. Either way, some will like it and some won't.

After many difficulties, the rink received its first flooding yesterday and the second tonight. The facilities for the job depend primarily on the disposition of German officers. The rest of the hockey equipment arrived today including enough to equip two teams. George Waters in charge of the rink construction hopes everything will be ready for a game on New Year's Day.

I think the electrical teacher is under the impression that I am cheating in my homework. Another student here copies my solutions, figure for figure, mistakes included, consequently, when the teacher comes to correct two papers identical in mistakes, etc. there is only one conclusion he can come to. Hereafter, my fellow student will have to calculate his own solutions. Mail is very scarce.

DEC. 20, MON.
Rumours regarding the Canadians here are still plentiful and wild. We are supposed to be repatriated next month; the Canadian government is negotiating for an exchange of prisoners; we are going to a propaganda camp where we will have single beds, white sheets, knife, fork and spoon, a white plate and cup, etc.; we are going out on working parties, to (1) work in coal-mines, (2) clean up in bombed cities, and so it goes, on and on.

Recognition is at last given to the fact that merely pumping the latrine out is futile; they have reached the stage where they have to be emptied by shovel. It was announced recently that the necessary equipment for doing this will soon be available and in use.

For Xmas week we receive 1/2 N. Z. food parcel tomorrow and an Xmas parcel on Friday. There is no mention of New Year's week. Unlike last year, there isn't a piece of decoration up in this hut and although Xmas is only four days away there is, as far as I know, not a piece made yet. Perhaps there will be a last minute rush.

We were told the other day that another "flu epidemic" is sweeping through the States, Canada, England and Europe and is just as bad as the one in 1918. We were asked to sleep head to foot to help prevent it starting in here. Also there are two suspected cases of Typhus in Lager 2 and a sharp lookout for lice be kept.

Have acquired another suitcase much larger than my old one which I hope will serve my purpose better. We are scheduled for delousing tomorrow which is a periodic attack on any lice that happen to find their way in. Last Saturday we removed every detachable object outside and gave the hut a thorough cleaning. I think it should be done oftener. The whitewashing has been completed and the walls are done in a two tone effect. The top part is plain white with four feet of illusive blue at the bottom (ink & whitewash). The border is decorated with brown doodads (cocoa, powdered milk and whitewash). The cold spell cracked last night; consequently, a rain and thaw has made it muddy out. This is tracked in on our feet so the floors are gradually taking on a semblance to the foot path outside.

Hockey equipment has arrived, including everything but how are we to use it? Anyhow because of their arrival we expect there will be personal parcels in soon.

In the news bulletin this evening mention was made that there was 1,000,000 reported cases of flu in the States and to show how rumours grow, a few minutes later a person was heard telling the fellow next door that there was 1,000,000 <u>deaths</u> from flu in the States. It's funny how a former optimist will adopt the attitude of a chronic pessimist when things don't turn out the way he predicted.

They say that Goody, the man who expressed his ulterior intentions toward the Canadians, has gone into protective custody until this Rat Drive is over. There is the case of the Canuck who had to go to Breslau recently and needed a pair of pants. Goody refused to look at them or give permission for the fellow to draw a pair; consequently, the would-be traveler had to make his journey with the seat out of his trousers. I think this situation is going to stink pretty soon because the Canadian government is paying for our clothing here and we can only get patched second-hand articles cast off by Limeys. Second hand boots, old Air Force pants, worn out tunics. A showdown is indicated and is a necessity.

DEC. 21, TUES.

We received 1/2 a New Zealand food parcel this morning. Delousing is over with as far as most of this hut is concerned and as part of the process I had the best shower bath I have had for over a year, one man to a shower and plenty of hot water. The dressing and waiting rooms were unusually comfortable today. a belated effort is being conducted to produce a little Xmas spirit into the appearance of the hut. Johnnie Neame is painting a scene on the wall to the left of the clock. It constitutes the usual Very Merry Xmas with a circle of holly leaves and a smattering of evergreen trees. Other huts in the compound have practically all their walls painted with scenes. I must make the rounds sometime and take a look.

A very persistent rumour is going around that all men who were subjected to reprisals are going to a neutral country. One fellow even goes so far as to say he saw the letter stating this. I heard down at the delouser today that it will be sick, reprisals, and B & F. However, the camp Commandant is expected to make a very important announcement over the camp loudspeaker system, through Goody. Perhaps it will clear the situation up a little. Cigarettes are getting scarce again.

DEC. 25, XMAS

With wild rumours, German and BBC news bulletins and hockey talk drumming our sense of comprehension to a standstill, another Xmas; the fourth away from home is practically over. If this compound came close to winning the biscuit for best decorated huts last year, it has undoubtedly won that distinction this time. This hut, although clean, is the poorest decorated hut in the compound and it still maintains a position in front of the rest of the camp. The best hut I think is 22B and shows an astounding improvement since its administration was taken over by five privates. Our meals today were more suited to our shrunken capacity than last year, discretion being the keynote in everyone's culinary endeavours. We had the usual breakfast, then four of us amalgamated for dinner which consisted of two cans of steak & kidney with macaroni, a half pudding with a klim & honey sauce, then we had stewed fruit, cake, biscuits and coffee at nine this evening. Other combines confined themselves to similar proportions.

There is a persistent rumour going around that we are to go to a neutral country but so far there is no official announcement, as yet. The working party rumour is still lingering and causing considerable uneasiness. The news is such that German and English versions are so contradictory it is almost a waste of time listening to it.

Foot slides are quite a popular amusement in other parts of the compound and I heard today that a fellow fell on one and broke his neck. He is reported to have died since. Work was started on the new rink the other day and if this chilly weather continues we may see a hockey game on New Year's Day. Water has to be hauled nearly half a mile in barrels, etc.

The German contribution to our Xmas was a double ration of coal and spuds, a buckshee issue of wood, gates open to 10 P.M., lights on till midnight and many good wishes.

Mail, of course, is cut off until the New Year and as a result, cigarettes are becoming scarce.

Decorations this year are running to painted pictures on whitewashed walls. 22A inclined to sports, 22B to cowboys, etc. Both these huts had curtains at the windows, woodwork painted, jigsaw puzzles pasted on cardboard, nailed on the wall and frames painted around them appeared in every hut.

DEC. 28, TUES.
Things are almost back to normal now. An argument issued today regarding C in C of the spud issue; no one would volunteer. The common inhabitant thought it was a sanitator duty while those indispensable people claimed they had too much to do as it was. It was finally settled and tempers cooled off when two fellows of the cleaning section volunteered.

News of the last three days discloses that Berlin was bombed the day before Xmas (unconfirmed rumours say that 3,000 bombers took part). From a German source came the astounding admission that the "Scharnhorst" was sunk in a naval encounter with the Allied Navy. General McNaughton, Commander of Canadian Forces in England for the past four years has resigned and Eisenhower has been appointed Commander of all Allied invasion troops in England. According to the Germans, unsuccessful Commando raids were attempted on some points on the French coast just before Xmas.

Rumours of our moving seem to be settled on our going to Teschen on the 15th of January. There are a few stating that we are going to a neutral country (Lisbon or Sweden).

Work on the rink seems to be hitting unexpected snags, persistently. Suitable conveyors of water are hard to obtain. The inmates, perhaps labouring under a false impression that they are helping things along, use the rink as a night latrine. Now comes mild weather during which all work is suspended and what little ice there is slowly returns to its former liquid state. Permission has been granted for 25 hockey players to go out and play a game of hockey on a slough or a pond outside. They seem to be having difficulty selecting the 25 men.

Have been doing a lot of work in my Log Book lately. A trickle of new mail was noticed today, especially when a fortunate few received their 5th clothing parcel. Mail, letters and parcels inclusive, has been surprisingly free of my name recently, but there is always hope for tomorrow. Obtained a crossword puzzle book today, second hand of course, but a little diligent use of an eraser soon obliterates the former owner's efforts.

According to some of the more recent letters received from home by some of the fellows, great hopes are being entertained by the writers, of seeing us home soon. I am sorry that I am unable to share in their optimism. Now the problem of how to smuggle these diaries out if we do move, is one of my more pressing problems.

DEC. 30

Rumours and news all good these days. According to letters received by some fellows, general opinion is Reprisals will either be fully repatriated or transferred to a neutral country, but no one dares to believe in it; the best we can hope for is a move to a better camp. Mild weather has sent hockey aspirations glimmering; the rink is just a placid pool of water now. It looks like the hockey season is over.

Deana Durbin, Nelson Eddy, Paul Robson and many other favourites such as Kenny Baker, Frank Parker, etc., heard over the camp loudspeaker system these days. Records sent by the Y and R.C. are played each day from 10 to 12.

We heard that Mills, MacGuire and a few others got through the O.C.T.U. alright. Remarks regarding MacGuire aren't very complimentary. Steeds is married, according to latest reports.

The fellow mentioned a few days ago who is supposed to have died from injuries sustained while foot sliding is recovering satisfactorily. Flu held in check so far.

We have been hearing rumours recently of doings in France but no confirmation as yet.

The Germans do admit however, raids on Berlin and other cities recently, the sinking of the Scharnhorst and a naval entanglement in the Bay of Biscay. Also, there are reports of appointments and change in command in the Mediterranean and England. Also, there were 275,000 Canadians in England and 50,000 in action in Italy. Russians were delayed in starting their winter offensive until Xmas Eve because of mild weather. Raid on one of the Channel Islands (Narz or Nars) and according to German reports was unsuccessful.

The mud here is terrific. May sell my drum yet. Prospective buyer inquiring this evening.

Wondering what it would be like to use a civilized cup and hear it rattle on a saucer. Received Xmas card from the Days yesterday; also letters from Nelle and Rusty. Parcel mail is slow.

DEC. 31

Gates locked today because man missing from "Digger." He was found about one o'clock in the "Digger." Gates may be open until midnight tonight; if so lights might be on all night. Watch service in church at 23:59. This hut won keg of beer on cutting today. Some of the fellows bought some German liquor and are afraid to drink it. They have tried it in lighters with huge success; subjected it to the varnish removing test with dubious results and have decided it is pure anti-freeze solution. One fellow is drinking it and is higher than a kite already.

Weather cold again with fine snow. It's better than the mud. There are more rumours of raids on Berlin and landings in France. Churchill (according to STIMMT) has ordered all lights repaired throughout England for the great day. He said there will be two orders, "Cease Fire" and "Lights Up Tennessee." Claims that the Russians will be here by August 15th. Dieppe being fought again.

JAN. 2, 1944, SUN.

Gates open until midnight New Year's Eve. Pipes were played all over camp. Many were plastered on smuggled drink. During a dinner for Shoemakers & Taylor at the theatre the razor gang went into action again; one of the victims was a McKenzie, boxing instructor. New Year's Day was quiet as far as I was concerned; read all day. Some of the fellows secured some German liquor but few could or would drink. Played hearts all evening. Dawson, Bartlett, Eric and I joined forces for New Year's dinner which consisted of a can of steak and kidney, a can of steak Rissoles and mashed spuds, toast, tea, Xmas pudding with marmalade klim sauce.

Weather changed to mild again; consequently, mud is almost ankle deep everywhere. Heard today that a group of irate men went around camp today warning the members of the "razor gang" that if there is another incident in this camp, they (the razor gang) had better take a chance of climbing through the fence; it would be much safer than waiting for the "vigilantes" to attend to matters.

Rumours of our moving are prevalent again but the destination is more or less unknown. Some say there will be 600 going to Stalag VIII B at Teschen some time this week for staff purposes. The best yet is the one Johnny LaBatt divulged last night. He said the new Canada House parcels are in and contain a blue suit, as we can't wear uniforms in a neutral country.

Perhaps some genuine news would be welcome. News of the arrival of 150 prisoners from the fighting in Italy came around this afternoon. Mostly American and Canadians, 59 of them are in hospital with wounds. There are 14 Canadians all together, 2 S.S.R., 2 Van Doos or F.M.R. for sure. Among them is an American bomber crew consisting of 1 officer and 3 other ranks shot down 2 days ago. They say the Russians are in Northern Poland, while the Allies in Italy are just seen to be playing around, while the Germans have amassed 17 divisions on the north side of the Po River. A collection of towels, clothing, toilet articles, cigarettes, tobacco, etc. was made for them by four Canadians to make sure these fellows received them. Goods kept out of our second Canada House parcel last year, ostensibly for purposes such as this, disappeared from storage in a short time and British old timers in rackets were sporting Canadian sweaters, shirts, etc., therefore our suspicions of the good intentions of various welfare organizations hereabouts is not exactly misplaced.

A pretty good farcical news report was read out this evening, probably written by some humour over-laden Stalag wit.

JAN. 4, TUES.

Muddy and snow today. Received 1,000 cigarettes from Nelle this morning; also from Jack, Rusty, Nelle and Marcelle. The latter delivered somewhat of a body blow when she imparted the info that she was marrying the Limey airman in October. Quite resigned to a life of a bachelor now, not that I was planning on getting married after the war.

Two English speaking Germans came through the huts immediately after role call and asked for names of Canadians belonging to the 6th Recce (*Reconnaissance Regiment*) and 14th Tank (*Regiment*). One, claiming to be a repatriated prisoner from Canada told us not to worry as we would all eventually be "signed up." Apparently he had a fair idea for the reasons for taking the names but as he wasn't sure, he merely said we were to be taken away from here in the near future. He told 19A that it was not working parties. Of course, this started the rumours circulating and the fact the change overs were called into the R.S.M.'s room, accelerated them. Rumours of a summer resort in the Bavarian Alps, IV B and IV C (Dresden & Berlin), a neutral country (Portugal, Sweden; even Turkey) Southern France, and even complete repatriation are buzzing around this evening.

A touch of dysentery is causing a little worry but it isn't bad yet. Latrine is overflowing again; this is becoming a tri-weekly occurrence.

JAN. 5, WED.
Eric received a personal parcel this A.M. which was messed up a little by OXO and sugar. We had a bath parade this afternoon but the fact that both delousers were also in operation caused a serious water shortage in the showers. It was so crowded under what showers that were working, McCavan, our amateur poet of "Stalag Mystery" fame, said he lathered 3 pair of legs and they all walked away on him.

Ten pound chocolate parcels are coming in for we Canucks from Canada, so far there are 158 parcels in which means about 10oz per Canadian. A few fellows have received individually addressed comforts parcels from Canada. I received letters from Nelle and Rusty.

Plenty of snow last night and wind and frost today. Kerr received a letter today that a letter from this camp was read out at a P.O.W. relations Ass. meeting in Grace Church in Winnipeg and it stated that owing to the water shortage here we all had skin diseases; it added that the C.R.C. were investigating.

JAN. 6, THURS.
Very frosty, personally estimated it at 0°F. Latrine unusable.

The lights went out suddenly last night at 9:25, catching the majority with unmade beds. We heard this morning that two air raid warnings came through, one at 9:25 and another at two this morning. Raids believed in the vicinity of Breslau. Each compound was ordered to form R.A.P. squads consisting of 50 fire-fighters and one N.C.O. as the German squad would not be able to cope with fires if the camp was bombed by mistake some night. also some compounds have had to form pickets to guard burnable material such as latrine peat covers, etc. When on duty these squads are armed with clubs and everyone was warned that anyone caught appropriating said articles can only expect medical treatment, at least.

Some of the Canadian chocolate was issued today and when divided among everyone in the room, came to about 12½oz. per man. There may be more later.

Rumours: that we are going to a new camp before January 12; all Canadians are being returned from working parties. Undoubtedly there is something in the wind.

JAN. 7
Received 1,000 cigarettes from 16th Med. Aux. Germans supposed to have admitted over camp wireless that Russians have broken over old Polish border in one place.

JAN. 9, SUN.
Rumours of a busy week voiced around tonight: delousing parades Monday and Tuesday; identification parades Wednesday and Thursday; clothing parades Friday and Saturday.

JAN. 10, MON.
Delousing parade rumour squashed today; no parades. Eric received another personal parcel this A.M. Another issue of Canadian chocolate today amounting to 1½-5oz. bars per man.

Due to mud and water old tunnel settled, thereby trapping an out-bound honey-wagon; it is still there. Heard that there is some good BBC news in camp. Sent congrats to Marc today; perhaps she won't like the letter.

JAN. 12
Received 1,000 cigarettes from Bob & Harry Gibson.

JAN. 13

Received 300 cigarettes from Mrs. Bodger. Mrs. Day said in a letter to Eric that she saw an extract from one of my letters in Red Cross Bulletin. I received 2 letters from Nelle and 1 from Rusty.

Rumours of raids on Central, Northern and Western Germany coming in. Raids must be big as reported that 300 British planes shot down. (later: 140 odd shot down-German fighters) Also French coast ports heavily bombed.

JAN. 14, FRI.

Jack Ward is back from working party. Nelle said in letters yesterday that Wally had met Morgan Whitte, Alan McMurphy and Keith Affleck. No mail for me today.

Many B2 men reported in England as repatriated are still in camp; German news contradictory.

JAN. 15, SAT.

Received 1lb tobacco from Dad and a letter from Nelle. Letter mail old stuff; mailed in August and September. Muddy today, ankle deep all over camp.

EXTRACTS FROM "STIMMT" JAN. 11/44

The contents of recent mail and verification by the camp Kommandant has shown that a regrettable state of affairs exists regarding those men classified by medical commission as B2 repatriates. A number of these B2 repats have on hand information that their next of kin were notified by the war office that they were being repatriated last October, yet they are still in this camp. A letter brought to the notice of "STIMMT" and an invitation to this paper's representative to visit the repats so concerned, revealed some strange facts. When the Kommandant visited Block 8 on Friday, a BII man told him of this information received. The Kommandant then admitted that, "There had been a gross mistake made by this camp alone." He then assured the men that they would head the list when the next exchange takes place. Nicely smoothed over, one might say, but little satisfaction to men who now know that BII personnel from other camps were included in the repatriation whilst they themselves were just "left behind."

Whatever did happen to bring about this state of affairs is not at the moment defined but the fact remains that many sons, fathers and husbands have not been restored to those who eagerly await their homecoming, and how eagerly they waited.--Here are some extracts taken from letters by our reporter. -Nov. 7: "I have not written for three weeks because we expected you home. We were notified by the War Office that you were to be repatriated but as you have not turned up, I thought you must still be in Stalag." -Nov. 3rd: "Had a letter from the War Office to say that you were coming home." -Nov. 8th: "Both the War Office and Red Cross replied to my letter that they have no more news either, but you might be with the "Barcelona" lot. -Nov. 4th: "News from R.C. headquarters on Monday that you had arrived this side." -Nov. 8th: "Shant count so much next time on the notice of the War Office." -Oct. 28th: "Letter from the War Office saying you were in the last repatriation ----. One man still in the Stalag had his photo printed in a newspaper showing him as one of the recently repatriated men. Letter after letter read by "STIMMT," show what a bitter blow had been dealt by fate; one might well ask-by fate and who else? No prisoner can fail to realize the disappointment to both our repat friends and their people. When the next exchange takes place, the German authorities should make it their duty to see that there is no "gross mistake' in this camp, again.

SLASHERS BEWARE: An investigation committee consisting of C.S.M McNaughton, P.S.M. Rankin and Sgt. L. Robb, has been established with full sanction of the British authorities to investigate all assaults and razor slashings and to clear the names of Scotsmen not concerned. An appeal is made on behalf of this committee to all P.O.W.s, especially those assaulted to report the names, ranks and numbers of, or to give the description of, any Scotsman who has been seen using or attempting to use a razor maliciously in the Stalag.

The committee would like to point out that while admitting the guilt of some Scotsmen, it is unjust to condemn all Scots in the camp. All know the record of the Scots in the field and much good work has been performed by them, both in the Stalag and outside. The camp may rest assured that the culprits will be severely punished, and if this Stalag's cooperation is forthcoming, there will be no further trouble of this kind.

TRIAL BY FIRE To be bombed is not at any time pleasing, but to be bombed by one's own planes whilst locked in cattle trucks was the nerve-racking experience of the P.O.W.s who recently arrived in this Stalag.

When the station yard at Aquila in Italy was raided by 27 British bombers one morning last month, 400 British prisoners on a prison train sandwiched between a petrol and an ammunition train, underwent a severe trial. 84 were killed and 150 wounded, some of which have since died. The concussion blasted open most of the trucks and enabled the occupants to disperse, but burning petrol and exploding ammunition caused many casualties. The station and yards were completely demolished.

PATIENCE GENTLEMEN, PLEASE The S.B.M.O. Major de Clive Lowe, wished it known that he has no knowledge of any repat details at present. But as soon as any news of this kind comes to hand, he will make it known. Please, gentlemen as the medical officer and hospital staff are very busy, do not worry them unnecessarily.

(end of quote)

Heard another story about people waiting for the unrepatriated repats this afternoon. One of the men received a letter from his wife, in which she said that she had cleaned and pressed all his clothes, then she and their little daughter waited for him all night in a railway station.

Lots of "citizens" believe that there was dirty work in connection with this event, and the fault isn't all entirely the Germans'.

JAN. 19, WED.
A sudden announcement to the effect that all Canadian privates will be going out on working parties in the next two weeks. And volunteers for the first 400 were asked for; to go to Stargard and to farms from there. Although the response wasn't bad, they were still 100 or so short of the required number. Arguments aplenty for and against volunteering and destination; the latter embraces places like Stargard, Stuttgart, Strasbourg, etc., which every way, it means a long miserable train ride in cattle cars. All we are sure of is that we are leaving this camp.

Received 1 lb. tobacco from Dad on the 15th, Saturday, also a letter from Nelle dated September 13. On January 16 the gates were all locked and nervous guards and dogs patrolled the streets as a result of some seven-to-tenners climbing over the fence, they were seen and shot at and dogs were soon hot on the trail. It was rumoured one was found by dogs up to his waist in mud.

On January 18 I received 300 cigs from Off. Mess. 2nd Batt. We had a long roll-call that morning as they were looking for missing men inside the camp. Johnny Neame received a letter from his father saying that we will probably receive 4 medals after the war. The Victory, the Overseas, the Service and the Volunteer Service. This last is a new one and is two inches (?) long. Some wit said they are considering adding another inch and make a necktie. Red Cross parcels were issued yesterday instead of today.

JAN. 20, THURS.
This might be the last entry here for some time as due to the uncertain future a plan to safeguard the contents might have to be executed without notice; therefore making this book unobtainable.

It was announced again today that 800 Canadians will be going out soon and if there wasn't enough Canucks, Limey Dieppe personnel would be included. Two parties of 400 each are leaving in the next two weeks and to a place near Stettin. No N.C.O.s are going therefore I am inclined to think that the camp is already staffed and therefore by Limeys. Rumours are plentiful and wild. We are going to reclaim land in the swamps of the Oder River; we will be living on farms, etc., etc.

JAN. 21
Nelle's and Con's birthdays. No further news of any kind re move but what we have is sufficient.

JAN. 22
Janet's birthday. Received letters from Rusty and Rose. Ted P. decided that this was a golden chance of slipping from under the care of our wonderful N.C.O.s so made it his business to find out as much as he could about the

move. D2 is the camp and is 20 km. east from Stettin, 51 km. from the sea, 150 km. northeast of Berlin. The town Stargard has 33,000 population with two gates; steel mills, textile and sugar beets the main industries. Ted advocated all C. of C. privates going together on the first party which was on the whole enthusiastically received by said privates. Eric and I decided to join the first party so we leave for our new home on Wednesday. A change of scenery and the trip might be just what a lot of us need. It is rumoured around that this is an effort on Germany's part to compensate for the reprisals last year and they intend to give us preferential treatment. That remains to be seen.

Bart was informed that he couldn't go because he is down as a Cpl. I don't think he is much disappointed. This book has been buried for two days and now is about to go into temporary seclusion for awhile.

JAN. 23, SUN.

My birthday: second one in captivity. Tomorrow we move down to the working compound for a day or so. Some of the fellows are expecting to have only a 24 hr. trip; the place is about 500 km. from here.

From a number of stories I hear repeated, the Canadians will be missed around here. One Aussie said that when we leave the guts will drop out of the camp. An Englishman was heard to say that he would be glad to see us go because ever since we came they haven't known the smooth peacefulness of '40 and '41; (we cause too much stink over little things I guess, such as rackets). Today is a hectic affair in this compound; everyone is going over their kit for the fourth and fifth time and each time a few more articles are thrown out or given away. As much as they complain, I think everyone is glad they are moving; the unknown is beckoning again and is welcome with all its uncertainties. I am doing my best to get this diary through. There is work to do so I had better get at it.

SEPT. 23, SUN.

Since the last entry, January 23, my birthday, I have been keeping a temporary account in a smaller book. The hiding place of this diary consisting of two volumes was adequate enough for ordinary searches as given when moving from one camp to another or from camp to Kommando, but when Gestapo search was hinted at in our present location, another place was indicated. Since then they have been buried for 2 weeks, under the floor for 3 and another place for 1. The following entries will be taken out of the small temporary book starting from my birthday last year.

JAN. 23, SUN.

Spent day repairing suitcase and sorting kit. Clothing parades start tomorrow. Wrote to Nelle. We are going to a place called Stargard, 20 km. from Stettin, 150 km. northeast from Berlin, near the Odor River; country said to be swampy thereabouts. BBC good.

JAN. 24, MON.

Rec'd 300 cigarettes from Cam. Aux. (Mrs. Troup). Weather mild, drying up fine. A young fellow disappeared from 19B. He had stomach trouble and is believed drowned in latrine sump; probing operations underway. Packing nearly completed; there are rumours of a thorough search and travel by coaches. Something decidedly fishy about this move. Germans making sure no one leaves party or joins it who isn't qualified (qualification: a Canadian).

JAN. 25

Second lap of trip completed, 1st removal of beds and blankets to 26B. 2nd identity parade and move into 26B. Came through in groups of 100, well guarded. Rumoured that there are 16 coaches waiting at the station. Tonight will be last; leaving at 1P.M. tomorrow. Bart (Cpl.) made us a brew and lunch before leaving our old compound. Rest of privates following in a week. So far we have been treated politely and with reasonable consideration. Most have high hopes for this trip. Rest of camp believe we are going to Sweden or England. Treatment of this party very unusual, thereby giving rumours fertile ground to grow. Understand Essex lad still missing; they have decided to drain the latrine completely.

JAN. 26

Orders to be ready by eleven o'clock, three days travelling rations issued. Bingo last night. Many stories going around. Quotations supposedly from Feldwebels: no satisfaction to inquiries made by Goody and Sheriff. General paid us a visit, called us soldiers and gentlemen, wished us God-speed and a good time. One more meal in this camp and we are ready to go.

JAN. 29, SAT.

After a very miserable train trip during which latrine facilities were totally lacking and the last half with 50 to a car, we arrived at this camp II D. We entrained at Annahau, after a fiery search, at 4 o'clock on the 26th and detrained at Stargard at approximately 10:10P.M. last night. This morning we discovered that there are Russians, French, Serbs and Ities here. We are the first British P.O.W.s to arrive in this camp, consequently R.C. was something vaguely heard of but little known. During the day we had the usual regulations read to us but by an unexpected piece of cooperation on roll-call, we made a good impression on our keepers and certain concessions have already been granted. American R.C. parcels were issued today; found them pretty good parcels. Apparently cooperation and discipline is the only way to get along with these people in this part of the country. The Germans insist we salute all German soldiers; we insist we only salute officers, so there is a deadlock. The Commandant says the method of half clenching our hands when standing at attention is a communistic symbol and we must hold our fingers extended; we insist we were taught that way in the army and so another point of contention. For a bunch of privates, organizing has been rapid and fairly efficient unlike other efforts under superiors. 370 more privates are expected Monday. In the next compound there is an eleven year old Serbian lad, captured with his dad. In another compound is a bunch of Ities who have volunteered for the Russian front and only waiting until a full company is formed. Everyone, including the Germans, despises the Ities.

JAN. 30, SUN.

Things are running surprisingly smooth, probably due to cooperation. Apparently our compound and hut leaders took the authorities by storm and demanded more privileges, cleaning equipment, shelves, better blankets, etc. When they asked for a bath per week for each man, the authorities said they hadn't sufficient soap but the wind was taken out of his sails when he was told that we would supply the necessary. The snap and vim of parade this morning pleased the German no end and is paving the way to better concessions.

Racketeering and even conversing with our neighbours is strictly taboo. We are heading for a little executive trouble I think. Delousing starts tomorrow. Air raid tonight from a little after eight until 20 past nine. We heard ack-ack and bombs but couldn't see anything. The lights went out.

JAN. 31, MON.

The blanket exchange and delousing parades hit unexpected snags today. Muster roll-call this afternoon. Elected to collect money for beer for the concert tonight; pulled in 200 marks; concert not so hot. International situation becoming quite a problem here. A statement made by Kingston during the concert causing very heated argument. Appointed canteen rep for the hut. Fell back on the old card cutting method. More equipment came in this P.M. including dixies and coat hangers. Since we have been here we have organized a Red Cross staff, various duty sections, such as compound and hut cleaners, ration carriers, library, etc. Letters have been sent to VIII B asking for sports equipment, school supplies, uniforms, boots, leather, etc. Ted Pettitt has lost his voice.

FEB. 1ST, TUES.

A very hectic morning. First on delousing parade, the posten took us by the back way past Russian compound. The boys threw cigs and soap over the wire. We arrived at the delouser and were turned back because we didn't have all our kit with us. On the way back the storm broke; the posten got seven varieties of hell for not shooting us when we threw stuff over the fence. An irate Unteroffizier wanted to put us all in strafe. While the storm raged we saw a dead Russian lying on the floor of a nearby hut; soon after we saw a group of Russians hauling another stiff through the gate. Eventually things quietened down and in due course reappeared at the delouser. After undressing and arranging our clothes on the hangers, we proceeded to be deloused. Apparently the first operation is the complete shearing of the head by an enormous electric shears. Ted in charge of the parade said, "No;" the German Feldwebel said, "Ya;" Ted said, "No;" the Feldwebel said "Ya;" and something unprintable, so we had our hair cut off. Russians in the delouser were very friendly. Oliphant got hell for clenching his fist; the Feldwebel thought he was giving the Communist salute. Eventually got through the delousing and left the Russians with plenty of soap, cigarettes and clothing we didn't need. The second hundred were treated in a similar manner but the hair clipping order was cancelled before the third bunch would go. Such is prison life and the cost of experience.

A French Canadian who spent his first three days in the bunker says they shot an Itie three times in the stomach because he wouldn't stand to attention, then they walked away and waited for him to die.

The mail delivery procedure especially cigarettes and personal parcels. These are opened at the post office and then delivered; some are refusing to accept them. Dissension is in the ranks so I was elected to list the complaints, a very thankless job. Some privates want L/Cpls. to form an overseeing committee but situation and men's dispositions too critical to interfere with.

FEB. 2, WED.
It was announced today that working parties start Friday, 40 from this room and 30 from C2B. Eric and I are waiting. Compulsory sports parade this afternoon during which the German Compound Commander tried to direct activities. He finally gave up in disgust; we refused to obey his militaristic orders. Hopkins on interpreting the U.O. orders got himself in a bad light. The huts here are on the same principle as VIII B variety, perhaps loftier and a trifle larger. Compound arrangements leads to the conclusion that this was originally intended for a military camp. The latrines are 150% improvement over the VIII B type inasmuch as these have facilities for flushing. A new order came through that as punishment for not saluting we must salute the two Dolmetjers, the Posten on duty, the Unteroffizier and the Feldwebel every time we pass them. Everyone says "nix." First party of 40 formed and others in the process.

FEB. 3, THURS.
The Unteroffizier came through the hut three times this morning before roll-call getting madder each time; consequently, we were warned that if we didn't get up at 6 tomorrow, reveille would be an hour earlier next day, etc. Eventually there won't be any use in going to bed. I received the clothing parcel from home which was mailed Oct. 2 containing blanket and knife,

etc. It was intact and in good condition. Pen excellent writer. The work party Eric and I were on dispersed so I guess we will be last to go. Collected 1,517 cigs for Serbs this evening.

FEB. 4,

Rest of Canadian privates pulled in just before daybreak this morning. There was no N.C.O. or Red Cross reps among them. Held a concert in here last night and 357 litres of beer lasted no time.

FEB. 5

Got busy today and formed a 35 man party out of remaining old fellows and some of the new arrivals, thereby assuring ourselves of going out with fellows we know. Orders for parties all filled which will give us time to make out clothing cards. A search for 1 man apparently visiting neighbours caused quite a lot of amusement tonight. Raid last night; we could hear the bombs plainly.

FEB. 8, TUES.

Busy all day yesterday organizing party. There's a lot of badges and medals coming in as souvenirs. On the lookout for a barbers outfit for the party. Seven or eight parties left today, destinations generally unknown. What with delousing parade, etc. we had a pretty meagre roll-call this evening. Rec'd N.Z. food parcels today. C14 moved into this hut tonight full up again. Hope our party leaves this week. No. "800" sheets to be made out yet. Ten or twelve bags of mail in this evening.

FEB. 9, WED.

Weather turned cold today, wind from east with snow. Rec'd 600 cigs from Overseas League tonight.

FEB. 10, THURS.

3 inches of snow this morning. Am embroidering Canada badges. Have obtained barber outfit for party. Our host is having difficulty keeping track of men. A hole in the fence was discovered. Kingston wanted me to add 15 men to our party but finally allotted us a 30-man group. Had difficulty in

cutting off five men. Ward, a good kid, was among them. Finally allotted party No. 2276 may leave Tuesday. We are hearing rumours of parties that left last week, don't sound so good.

FEB. 12
Discovered we had same no. as another party, our party organized, recognized, but no number as yet. Germans had difficulty obtaining names of men not on parties. Kitchen is in the office forming an index card filing system. Reports from some parties not so good.

Christmas gifts from Canada in today, miscellaneous pots, kettles, pans, saucepans, forks, spoons, can openers, towels, dish clothes, etc., quantities of lifesavers and gum, also 1440 records but no machine. I wonder if they forgot the napkins and lace doilies. Eric reprimanded for not saluting an officer. Party may leave Tuesday. Finished Canada badges today. Trying to get Russian made ring. Ran into the wall in the dark last night.

FRI. 13, SUN.
22 new arrivals came in this morning, mostly men taken in Italy. Among them Beers' brother. Apparently they are taking Canadians from other camps as these fellows say they asked for fellows born in Canada. Ed Vivien finally in the office but dissension still remains.

The 2 i/c of the camp read out at roll-call that German prisoners in Canada are better treated than in any other country; therefore Canadians were to be given preferential treatment. Apparently this is official but why don't they inform the Germans in charge of working parties? We received individual Xmas gifts today consisting of one billy can (1914 vintage), a 34oz pudding, toothbrush, powder and shaving stick. We are not sure about going out Tuesday yet.

FEB. 15, TUES.
Rec'd 2 letters from Rusty and one from Bezzie yesterday. New R.S.M. took over parade this A.M. Common belief that he may have been born in Canada but must have gone to England before he was dry behind the ears. Limeys are not welcome here.

A political controversy raged this P.M. when Maitland started campaigning to oust Kingston and put Vivien in. It turned out later that they both were in and getting along famously. Apparently the campaigner was trying to better himself. We were asked on parade if we wanted to send the Woodbine Willies back where they came from and there was an emphatic yes. I guess they are not popular since VIII B days. Eric received a book parcel which contained "Singin' Guns & "My sister, Eileen," more proof of the book racket back home. Kingston and Vivien came through the huts shortly after roll-call and announced that a letter with our name enclosed had reached Geneva and that this camp would be recognized as a separate Stalag as from March 1st. all supplies from that date would come direct (Limeys in clothing stores 344 will lose lucrative business). Also word from Berlin that a lorry would be supplied to carry supplies to parties once a month. Two parties left today, Hardmires and Tourgets; ours may leave Thursday.

FEB. 16, WED.
Lights went out 8:20 last night followed shortly by raid alert. No bombing near here but heavy explosions and ack-ack heard from direction of Berlin. Visitors to Berlin claim the stench is noticeable before city comes into sight. Preferential treatment not so hot; gates of compound locked and guarded ostensibly to protect us from contamination from our neighbours. Dispatching parties slackening off; as yet only one party scheduled for Friday, another party knocked off entirely, another loses its number. Ours changed from No. 250 to 147.

60 more Canadians expected tomorrow from some other camp. Believed that in time all Canadians will be here or working out of here. Finished reading Irwin Cobbs' "Humorous Stories." We were threatened with 3 day's strafe (bunker) if anyone is caught outside of gates without authority. No diminishing of gatecrashers noticeable this evening.

FEB. 17, THURS.
40 more men expected this P.M., 18 came in last night, among them Wilkie from Kenora. A little trouble with a demand for 100 men to work in Stargard freight sheds. An argument as to its permanence caused misunderstanding.

Six or seven from our party went but it won't affect the party any. Heard in latrine No. 4 that 147 is good party, possible departure next week. Cold and snow persists; wicker work overshoes for night postens fashionable.

FEB. 18, FRI.

Latrine 4 was a refuge for about 25 men when Germans couldn't find 100 men for freight shed party this morning. Knowles party left this morning. Pretty quiet in here this morning.

FEB. 19, SAT.

More trouble this A.M. with Stargard party. This P.M. Germans said additional 30 men needed for Monday. Reveille threatened for 5:30. Ted Pettitt resigned as room commander, refused position. Some men on our party wanted to change to Stargard party but their ambitions were blocked by Germans. Rumours are that there are no more farm parties going out; also 480 more Canucks coming next week.

FEB. 20, SUN.

No roll-calls. Finished reading "How Green was My Valley," "The Spanish Cape Mystery" and "Laughing Waters" since Thursday. Steve elected room commander; getting extremely bored here for some reason.

FEB. 21, MON.

The usual difficulty obtaining 100 men for Stargard party and 30 extra for special job; missed both of them. The 30 came back between 9 and 10, having refused to work because it was war material. Got hooked with 24 others for spreading cinders on road just outside of camp. School kids playing football in field asked for time in English but had to answer in German before he could get it. He said he had been learning English in school for 3 years.

We had another speech by Camp Commandant.; if this is preferential treatment, give me 344 and the chains.

FEB. 22, TUES.

Role call at 6:30 this morning. Eric and Lorne got hooked for Stargard arbeit this morning. Jones and I hooked for road work; finished job about 20 to 10. Fixed jack knife. Ordered to take off our hats when Feldwebel came through; nothing happened. Ryan's party (106) leaving tomorrow; Ennoy's Thursday. Hopkins quit his job. 8 volunteers asked for from this hut for work at station presumably unloading Red Cross. It turned out to be 2 cars of cinders which are called "Geneva cinders" now. Couldn't convince civvies of our large cig. stores.

FEB. 23, WED.

Picked for a couple of hours of work; finished unloading cinders at 12 noon. Ten men wanted this P.M.; had difficulty getting back for dinner. 3 of us went back to station to clean up cinder situation; spent rest of afternoon pretending to work around a hospital warehouse while "dealing" was in process. Dealing amusing, especially when they can't speak English and we can't speak much German. Air raid while in Stargard, people lost no time in clearing streets.

Was informed that party will leave sometime Friday for Mutzelburg near Kossin by Pyritz. Rec'd 2 letters from Nelle and one from Em.

FEB. 24, THURS.

Party exempt from Stargard arbeit today, delousing. Went for a buckshee shower this A.M.

Air raid at about 2:50 this P.M.; the roar of planes passing overhead could be heard for 15 or 20 minutes; a short time later we heard the dull thud of bombs. Bruno the dolm. (*dolmetscher-interpreter*) stood shivering, saying he wasn't ready to die. It does a guy good to hear these planes. Party is leaving tomorrow about noon. Learned that Stettin was the target this afternoon. Talked the German into letting party remain in this hut in view of fact that we will be leaving tomorrow. 480 men expected soon.

FEB. 25, FRI.

All baggage loaded (R.C. & Kitchen utilities), then orders changed. Trailer and tractor instead of train. Rec'd word that transport not available, departure probably not before Monday.

Stargard working parties having trouble. Sinclair threw two sacks of spuds at civvy yesterday; some refused to lift 200 lb. sugar sacks today; also reports from outside parties indicates difficulties. N.C.O.s had riot act read to them last night for refusing to work yesterday.

Big show of brass hats today, including R.C. rep. Hope they heard full gamut of beefs which have been accumulating.

FEB. 26, SAT.

Trouble on parade this morning. Two gangs of 10 and one of 27 picked out but one of the tens went astray (ours). We were found after another roll-call and went to work on a new fence. Stewart was lining up the posts and the results are amusing. We quit at 20 to 11 and returned to compound. Moved to C2B this morning but we still use this hut for eating and reading.

Trouble down on the mill and warehouse jobs this P.M. Both parties refused to work as Saturday afternoon is considered a half holiday in all good stalags. The guards said they had orders to use their rifle butts but the fellows told them to go ahead and start something.

Believe "Tennessee" one of the best dealers I have ever seen in action, Unteroffizier no less. We had a good feed of white bread this evening. He is getting some things lined up for party. New men expected in this evening or early morning. The Germans want 120 men for Monday morning and there are only 107 available.

FEB. 27, SUN.

Our N.C.O.s from 344 came in at noon and the huts are filled again. Apparently there has been a shakeup in the administration; Kingston's heel clicking and kowtowing to Germans finished after hours of arguments. Hall, Lacroix also out, in fact, nearly all former "officers" will be on Stargard party tomorrow. Our party leaves tomorrow I hope. With administration in proper hands we feel more secure of proper treatment from this end. Understand that Kingston is still fighting to stay in power.

FEB. 28, MON.
Party departure cancelled again because billets weren't ready. Germans not agreeable to Lescom taking over; they want "yes-man" Kingston. Men want R.S.M. because of a more substantial administration. Kingston heading for court-martial after the war. He told S.M. to keep quiet on N.C.O. parade today. Obtained Geneva convention information for first time from S.M. Lescom. O.S.M. Cordner (R.C.), Ted Pettitt and Brown parties had dirty deal. Ted blames Kingston and wasn't backward in speaking his mind to him. Everyone of opinion that K. is crazy or pro-German.

FEB. 29, TUES.
We were given ten minutes to be on inspection parade. Arrived Pyritz at 12:45 having waited in Stargard platform for over an hour and changing platforms twice. Rode in coach first time in this country. Left Pyritz at 1:00 riding on three large rubber tired wagons drawn by 3 horses each. Arrived Kosin 2 hours later. Met farm inspector and German Hauptman who promised to make things as easy as he could for us. Rode another 3 km to Mützelburg, accompanied by fairly good looking German girl and youth, picked up older woman on way. No modesty whatsoever, in fact, indecent according to our standards. Billets okay I guess, size about 40x40x12 with 3 barred windows, 1 door, 2 long tables and 1 short one, a typical German stove and one iron heater. There is a lean-to kitchen. Compound small and barbed wire enclosed on two sides and top; barn forms one side and the kitchen the other. Conditions not bad but some improvements are needed. Stocks is cook, Kline dolm. and myself excused outside arbeit, maybe more later. Lots of Poles and Serbs working here, mostly women. Opened 3 cases of cooking and eating utensils, plenty for everyone.

MARCH 4
I think another week will see us settled but still asking for improvements. We had 20 or 18 men on pea threshing, 2 milkers, 2 on wood, 2 on beet root hauling, 1 dolm., 1 cook and 2 on bags.

We had a visit from a Feldwebel and Unteroffizier on Friday; they left a few orders and implied they would return on Mon. The estate owner and wife came in as if they owned the joint. Later learned that even he is not allowed in our billets unless with a competent army man. Kline cut a pretty picture when he obtained a horse of many winters to haul the latrine out. He carried an iron bar in one hand and the horse with the other; when he wanted to turn he first pointed the bar then he and the horse followed. Later he had quite a time acting as peacemaker between two fighting ganders. Dixon and I started a flagstone walk from door to gate yesterday. May acquire a rd. soon. Twenty-five fags for a plane, two chisels, two screwdrivers, pliers. Everyone studying German. Rec'd letters from Roy and Rusty.

MARCH 7
Very heavy bombing in southwest in direction of Berlin. Work on washroom was started today; this requires driving old Peter out of his suspension bedroom which he has occupied for 20 or so years; he is pretty peeved. Ober Gef. seems determined to acquire enough wood for a trunk from or through us. He wanted a piece of lumber we had acquired for a coat cupboard and failing that a wooden N.Z. parcel crate; we refused him both.

MARCH 8
Heard today that Berlin received a pasting yesterday; German papers claim 80 planes shot down. A fellow just back from visit says it's levelled now. Date started a coat cupboard this morning but I don't like the design. Date, Hill and Bater going sick tomorrow. "Little Wetzel Milquentoast," otherwise C. Breiter, ex-photographer, likes nothing else better than a game of rummy with anyone who will play with him. A horse fell this morning, raised him by the simple manner of unhitching other two horses and lashing him until he got up.

MARCH 9
Polish women work like men here. Cobbling of yard finished. Log peeling finished. We saw vapor trails of bombers raiding Berlin this afternoon; the raid lasted nearly all afternoon. "Dead-eye" gravely shook his head and whispered "B. kaput." German orders regarding R.C. liquor distilling

and drinking and mail situation causing me considerable worry. Going to Stargard tomorrow. We are expecting another raid this evening and Friday. Received a near depleted medical cupboard this evening. Putting Engbert on cupboard tomorrow.

MARCH 10

Went to Stargard today with Bater and Date, both with sinus. Poor "Wetzel" tired and sleepy got hell wherever he went. Not much satisfaction on trip; came back with Chinese checkers, a volley ball, crib board, a deck of cards and a game of Can-U-Move. Kingston wants me to take a job of district confidence man for Pyritz. Refused it of course, because I don't figure him as sufficient authority. Signed a statement to the effect that Kingston was not as far as I know, elected by the men. Although a tiresome journey, it is interesting to meet P.O.W.s of every nationality, French, Poles, Serbs, Czechs, Ukrainians, Russians, etc. and a significant fact was that all had ready smiles and handshakes; Germans on the whole quiet and thoughtful.

MARCH 11

Was supposed to go to Pyritz for a load of Red Cross but "Dead-eye" said it was too cold and miserable, then went himself. No mail yet. Engbert finished the coat rack, a shoe bench and a couple of table benches.

MARCH 12

Had a little argument with "Dead-eye" regarding the issuing of R.C. cigarettes. Arguing second hand not very effective. Ended up by him holding 400 cigarettes for men away and me with the responsibility of issuing 5,600 cigs to 50 per man per week.

"Tennessee" decided to investigate the Fraulein situation of Kosin after lock-up this evening, intending to return before nine o'clock. It is a black wet night and he lost his way and didn't get back until eleven. In the meantime, "Dead-eye" experienced some true Canadian ignorance of existing facts, namely "Tennessee" missing and no one knowing how, when or where. The fellows are all pretty sore as we are liable to lose five privileges we now have. If he was making a "break" he would have our willing cooperation and assistance, but just to go girling, nix. I think the hazing the fellows gave Tennessee altered Dead-eye's intention to report it.

MARCH 13
Raining and snowing this A.M. Boys didn't arbeit until after ten. Visit by the Baron this morning; twice is twice too much. Ober-Feldwebel and Unteroffizier came this afternoon, treated Tennessee's escapade as a joke; promised us new blankets, uniforms and boots and seemed disappointed when we couldn't think of anything else to ask for. This whole set-up is fishy, not a harsh word since last year.

MARCH 15
The 28 year old horse ran away from Tennessee this morning; all work stopped to watch the fun. The old nag had to be lifted to his feet this morning before they could harness him. They disappeared over the hill, both walking, to appear an hour later on very friendly terms.

MARCH 16
Went to IID with Gray this morning. Gray for dentist and to help carry 26 blankets for exchange. Had trouble leaving camp; finally had to stay all night. Bummed food off of Shurvell and Warren. Bater and Date coming back with us.

MARCH 17
Left camp 8:30 A.M.; train left Stargard Station 11:30. Wetzel not taking any chances. Arrived Pyritz about noon and had to wait until 20 to 3 for regular train to Kosin, where wagon and team picked us up. Local train so crowded we had to ride platform. Talked to some German kids who are learning English in school. Wetzel disgusted with everything.

MARCH 18
Had argument about fellows working in the rain so Dead-eye called boot inspection for tomorrow at ten, later changed to eleven.

MARCH 19, SUN.
Another argument with "one-eye". He is labouring under the impression that the Germans are clothing us and wanted us to hand in our underwear for new stuff. He couldn't believe that except for uniforms and boots, clothing is privately owned. Am completely fed up and thoroughly disgusted. It is one perpetual argument. Dead-eye wants me to learn German so that we can talk without an interpreter; the use of one usually ends up with a misunderstanding on both sides.

MARCH 21, TUES.
Fireworks this morning over N.Z. packing cases. Dead-eye claimed he had to hand them in to the company and we said we had to use them for building material as the Germans wouldn't supply us with nails and lumber. The fight waxed hot and furious until compromise was reached whereas he kept the boxes until we received permission to keep them. Incidentally he seems to have lost interest in them now. Tennessee driving an ox is Tennessee driving a horse, only worse.

MARCH 22
Looked at Ice-cream Pants' telephone this afternoon and decided trouble either in the line or at Kosin. A little line work some of these days.

Our pants have been taken away at 8:30 each night since Monday. That night resulted in another argument which continued long after the doors were locked. Lost my temper and said somethings not nice. Plenty of snow and wind yesterday and today.

MARCH 24, FRI.
Another trip to Stargard today with Price and Gray, escorted by the wandering Wetzel. On these trips we have to watch our guard; he is inclined to get lost, miss trains or go astray.

MARCH 25, SAT.
Dead-eye told me to use packing cases if I wanted to. Had another argument this evening regarding hours of sport. Dead-eye said he had orders to the

effect that we were only allowed 2 hours each Sunday. It was still unsettled at lock-up time. Have three men in with no boots. Worked on telephone line this afternoon accompanied by Tennessee and "White Pants." The latter wanted to follow the line across ploughed fields instead of following the road to the bush where I figure the trouble was. By the time we got to the bush, White Pants was pretty tired. We found two poles down and the wire snapped in the bush. Made temporary repairs. New poles on Monday.

MARCH 26, SUN.
Snow all day; gates open from 11 to 12 and from 1 to 5. Had a "debate" tonight regarding shoes. Dombrowski stays in tomorrow while Steward, Hill and Bates putter around in the barn (scraping manure off of the oxen.)

MARCH 29
Made a wrecking bar today. Dead-eye says we are always making weapons and thinks we are a bunch of crooks. Another argument with him, rations this time.

MARCH 30
Went to Stargard; took Engbert and Pithouse to the dentist. Shoe situation bad. A fellow in the camp said his folks had seen a group photo of P.O.W.s in R.C. magazine, sent in by a woman from Kenora; it might be Nelle. Wetzel got lost twice today; we have to watch him. Had an amusing incident in Pyritz with a girl on train. Wetzel bought beer in Kosin. Barman spent five years as prisoner in England last war.

MARCH 31
Started to make an oven today out of tin cans. Germans are past masters at stalling and passing the buck. Dead-eye bought 30 pairs of wooden shoes today. Every time he speaks it means another headache. Had an argument with White Pants, alias "Kartoffel Belly;" Howes, Donaldson and Higgins on "dinglemittel flingin" today; Howes came in almost blind. Demanded goggles be supplied; only two pair available so only two men went out. Angus almost hit White Pants with a potato. "W.P." angry at spud waste; Angus disappointed in results. N. Z. R.C. parcels today also cigs and writing material.

Parcels in poor condition. Bought four fowls this week. Had quite a time getting cackle berries into Stalag yesterday. Potato grading today.

APRIL 4

Never a dull moment. Having difficulties with oven manufacture. Nil eventful April Fools Day. Wetzel had his feelings hurt when Stewart bawled him out for being inquisitive about a laundry deal with Johnnie's mother. Today is first time he has been in to sit since.

Had interesting visitors yesterday morning; the Baroness (much more pleasant when not with Baron), a Lt. Col. and a Red Cross nurse who have just come back from 3 years on the Russian front and a youngster. They were very civil and satisfied with everything. Today seemed to be a day for demonstrating cruelty to dumb animals. Moving a couple of cows from one barn to the other, their tails were broken. One mad beast charged a stone wall it didn't see because of a blindfold; it was out for quite awhile. Out in the fields the oxen went through a similar ordeal from the Chef. The oxen were beaten until blood showed, then he grabbed one by the nostrils, then gouged his eye with his fingers, then pounded it with the end of a stick. Then rammed sticks in between its legs. To finish the day off, the barn boss happened to get in the way of oxen horns so he grabbed it by the nostrils and gouged its eyes until they bled. A large number of the horses are blind from being pounded over the head with pitch forks. Dead-eye thought he had caught Tennessee dealing with civvies today but had to back down when Kline told him to bring the Captain out and prove it. Dead-eye couldn't chance it.

Another shipment of Red Cross parcels (120) and 6,000 cigs came in today. That takes care of the month of May. One chocolate bar missing from a Canadian parcel which will have to be reported to Cordner.

APRIL 6, THURS.

Made a trip to Stargard with Engbert and Lapierre. Wetzel in a bad mood. Annie and Freda went to Pyritz. Anna met us at Kosin and won a bark from the meek but smoldering Wetzel. A new Posten was waiting when we got back and Wetzel had to return to the company. He spent his last evening dealing fountain pens and nail files. While we were away "Cream Pants," "Dead-eye,"

Grandpa Snazzie and the Unteroffizier raised hell with the fellow coming in for brews. Grandpappy just peeved because our fellows won't remove their hats to him, like other people do.

APRIL 7, GOOD FRIDAY
Holiday today; thinking of fresh hot cross buns. Red Cross issue as usual. Serbs came today, borrowed records.

APRIL 8, SAT.
Langsam arbeit today; finished at 4:30

APRIL 9, EASTER SUNDAY
Gates were open nearly all day today. People here celebrate in much same manner as at home. Coloured eggs, new clothes and lilies. Girls are getting bolder now; they come up to the corner instead of staying in their back yards. Our side got licked 41 to 7 today at softball. Serbs noted for hand shakes came again today with records and the gramophone. Sick of this job of confidence man; can't give it away.

APRIL 12, WED.
Big doings today at noon; a flight of 150 or so Allied planes flew over. A mystery raid on Pyritz, 18 km away; believed to be leaflets or tinfoil strips. One-Eye and Sheriff claim British planes shot down two Germans; then Ack-Ack got two British. We think we saw the smoke from two of them when they crashed. Sounds of bombing plain today; also heard a dog-fight; clouds too heavy to see it. Dead-eye took me potting crows but Wetzel failed to keep 22 clean; consequently, my first shot resulted in the bullet lodging in the barrel about two inches from the end. Dead-eye and the boys are at loggerheads over prices; D.E. claims prices are too high.

APRIL 13, THURS.
Had an argument with Dead-eye over clothing cards this evening during which I lost my temper. Being ably supported by Fellows and Kline, I think I won a point. Fraulein warned not to talk to us and we are warned not to talk to Frau's.

APRIL 15, SAT.

Was informed that we would have to arbeit tomorrow morning; the whole gang refused. Dead-eye asked me to appeal to boys to go to work and save trouble.

APRIL 16

Everyone refused to go out to work. Captain, a sergeant and two corporals came out about ten with automatic rifles and merely said 5 minutes or else. It's a tough bluff to call especially when there's one up the spout and a finger on the trigger. Baroness worried, made special trip up to make sure no one was hurt. No work on Sundays until harvest time.

APRIL 17

Went to Stargard with Engbert and Lapierre, changed records and obtained a copy of Geneva Conventions 1929. One article says that P.O.W. must be given 24 consecutive hours' rest a week which doesn't mean a thing to this country. Large flights of Allied planes on the 12th, dropped pamphlets. Heard another version of Pyritz raid by flak. One of a crew of a British plane shot through chest and arms; died 3 hours later. This was partly confirmed by Captain on Sunday. "Banjo-eyes" took us into a beer garden and bought the drinks.

APRIL 18

Great day; numerous flights of bombers seen passing over at various heights, target south west of here. German thinks bombing of cities no good now; it was alright in 1940 when London was getting it. We were ordered to salute Unteroffiziers and such but refused. Kranz accused us of signalling to British planes at 1:30 one night. One-eye wouldn't believe him.

APRIL 19

Unteroffizier came this morning and had an argument with German woman about chocolate. Apparently some mothers are beefing because their kids aren't getting as much chocolate as others. Dead-eye tried to stop us from giving it away but the kids still get it. Feldwebel came this afternoon and said he had obtained 1,000 bricks from Berlin, picked up in the street no doubt.

The cement for the wash is in Pyritz; the blacksmith is coming to put tap and shower fixtures in wash room. Trying to get improvement in kitchen; removal of copper to wash room, an oven built in its place and the hotplate enlarged. Feldwebel said we must have cellar for perishable goods with us holding the key. He spoke to White Pants about it. Dead-eye is bringing seeds for our garden. Can't understand these square-heads; they can't do enough for us now. Hitler's birthday tomorrow (55th). French say Allies promised raids on Berlin and Stettin as present.

APRIL 20

Water put into wash room. Dead-eye mad because fellows refused to get up at noon hour to receive foot clothes; he picks poor times for business. This evening he brought clothing sheets to be signed, more arguing; then at nine-thirty he wanted a list of uniform sizes to be ready for 6:30A.M. Finally convinced him that sizes don't mean a thing. Gave Emile (barn boss) two headache pills for upset stomach, action drastic but effective, as bad as putting cough syrup on a cut finger (also German patient); Dixon's mistake. The old twenty-niner, "Max," almost died again this morning; he was working again at 3:00P.M. Evidently bombing not in this area today although concussions noticeable.

APRIL 24

Sent my shoes in for repairs today. Working on a map of the Russian front. Received 3 letters from Nelle, also three snaps of Murph, Alex, Margarite and Rose. How time changes people. Jack is home. Letters made me a little homesick today.

APRIL 29, SAT.

An uneventful week this week. Second front hasn't started although Germans doing their best to help it along. Believe Germans might like Allies in here to check Russian reprisals when they do fold. Get a daily laugh from Tennessee and the Ox. the other day the ox was stubborn, refusing to move when Tennessee wanted him to; so Kline hid a small stick behind his back and approached the stubborn brute with patience and optimism and told the inert mass of potential soup bones that he would give him three guesses what he had behind his back. The ox somberly shook his head. Spud planting started today. Received letter from Nelle and one from Bobbie, also official acknowledgment of increase sent to Dad.

APRIL 30

Ganzegallers (us) beat the Langsam arbeiters 24-16 this afternoon. Life of the party is supplied by Bertrand, White and Demercy; when these three get going the skies the limit. All these European nationalities still remain "Hunkies" to my notion.

MAY 4

Phillips and Engbert kept in to help clean the billets and it sure was dusty. It rained this afternoon so field hands came in, apparently the women followed and an argument resulted between Kranz and White Pants. The General arrived at 6 and found everything here alright; then went up to the guard-room, where evidently he found Dead-eye in possession of Canadian cigs, chocolate, etc.

MAY 5

Dead-eye in a stew this morning because he expects the controller out for a more thorough search. He says he will get 14 days strafe or replaced for sure.

Boys from Maitland's party say they watched two American planes ground strafe the airport near them. They said the planes came so close at times they could see the pilots. Winters' entire party returned to Stargard. BBC says that Russians are preparing big offensive to coincide with 2nd front. a Serb said Kosin talk is that all Canadians are going away soon. Also radio announcement that 2nd front will come this month. Engbert has been working on a borrowed gramophone for three days; main spring, inter cogs, governors. The owner wants us to pay for the use of it; we are going to charge him for repairs. Made a string broom. Miserable weather for 3 days; high wind and showers.

MAY 8, MON.

Dead-eye went to Pyritz today after expecting the controller daily since last Wednesday. He is preparing to leave tonight. He is carrying out some delayed deals.

MAY 9

By noon Dead-eye was ready to leave and put over a few last minute deals. He wished us good luck and said he hoped to see us again. New fellows came yesterday, a Gefreiter and two Postens, "Squint-eye," "Handlebar" because of a full mustache, and "Dusty." New bat from Serbs.

MAY 10

Feldwebel came and seemed peeved about something, left a flock of haywire orders which we don't intend to obey or the guards to enforce. Am having trouble with a couple of swallows who persist in building a nest above the table, but due to public opinion and the ever-present danger of aerial activity during meals, I had to tear the nest down. The birds were mad for sometime. Placed old nest in a corner and everything okay for a time until Mrs. tried to force Mr. out and pulled nest over. Then they decided to rebuild above the table again, but discouraged that by packing rags and tin around the spot. Birds again mad. A strange male came in this morning and formed the well-known triangle. Mr. fought him to a standstill and the intruder had to leave. A state of temporary truce exists between them and myself until they decide on a new site.

MAY 13, SAT.

Four men scheduled to return to Stalag, Price, Date, Perry and Bertrand, as per order from Stargard to cut strength of Party. New guards coming around gradually but terribly scared of rackets. It was a couple of days before the Gefreiter would accept a cigarette. A great day, we saw a flight of 120 to 180 Allied bombers today directly overhead; looked like four motored. One plane had a smoking motor but seemed to be maintaining speed. Another plane looked to be crippled and lagging behind but had a 7-plane fighter protection. It is hard to realize that their crews will be eating supper in England tonight. Germans seem to watch us instead of the planes, probably to see how the sight of them will affect us.

The war with the swallows continues and has reached the stage where they are desperate to build and I am equally determined they take their activities elsewhere, partly because they make an awful mess and partly because some of the fellows have expressed the intention of wringing the necks. I have stopped them from building in four different places, but still they insist.

MAY 15

In the aerial demonstration the other day some of the fellows claim that the last plane was a 6-engine bomber; some counted 180 bombers overhead. A Ukrainian woman found some tinfoil that was dropped. The reason for spreading the stuff is probably to confuse radio locating and radio range finding apparatus; that's my personal belief. Guard commanders changed again today. This one is an Ober Gefreiter and is starting out in a three ganz egal (*I don't care*) fashion. Three guards are 46, 50 and 52 years respectively. New man says war will be over soon and is talking of taking us swimming. Swallows have given up the struggle and evidently found an outside location.

MAY 18, THURS.

New Ober-Gefreiter pretty lazy so far but says rackets not worth the penalty if he is caught. Went to Stargard with McDonald on Tuesday. Hill still in hospital. BBC news items for May 13: French coast bombed and shelled from Denmark to Spain for 48 hours. All railways out of order for 100 miles inland. The Germans officially announced the evacuation of Crimea on May 13. The planes we saw on the 13th bombed Stettin; 26 French P.O.W.s killed in a factory. Bombs dropped near a factory 2km from Stargard. Got back to find Pithouse in bed; he took a dive into the barn drainage pool, smelly pastime! Shurvell got the run around; he thought he was coming here to take over but ended up away north with a French Canadian party near Labes. Don't think four men scheduled for Stalag will go now. Seeding nearly all finished, times are getting slack a little. Dombrowski hopeless. Started making a baseball catcher's mask; too dangerous without. Bill Rattray received foul tip on nose, I have a black eye and two broken fingers. Have a pin pointed map of Russian front. The line as we know it now: Ackermann, Tirospol, Jassy, Harlau, Deketyn, Brody, Kowel, around Pinsk, east of Minsk, Ostrow, Pleskau, Hungerd.

MAY 20, SAT.
Heavy Bombing someplace, probably Stettin . Sound of planes continuous. Witnessed a part of a manhunt this evening when a number of civvie guards came by with shotguns; some Canadians say Russians on the loose.

MAY 21, SUN.
Stettin and Berlin bombed today. Sore fingers forced me to forego softball this evening. Mask works after a fashion, but not perfect.

MAY 23, TUES.
Went to Pyritz with Kline for Red Cross shipment. Rode 42km in rain. Brought back 1 month's supply of R.C. food and cigarettes, with a quantity of soap, etc., also 20 pairs of pants, 5 tunics, 20 pairs of boots, 10 shirts and 20 pairs of socks. "Loudmouth" refused me permission to go to Stargard with Mac and Rowat. He is getting hostile about talking to the Poles and Serbs.

MAY 24, WED.
Controller came today; said latest order is for Stalag to be locked all day. "Loudmouth" said after controller had gone that he meant the doors were to be locked which would mean Charlie being locked in the kitchen and me in here. We raised such a holler and they heard so many home truths, a compromise was reached. He said from today everyone, French, Pole, Serbs and Russians as well would be similarly locked up. Either this is another lie, another display of childishness, of square head intellect or to prevent riots or the second front has started or is expected. Miserable weather. Heard planes again today. Rowat says they had four alarms in Stargard yesterday. Mac in revere for five days.

MAY 29
Holiday today. Kline had another and a more heated argument with "Loudmouth" about Frenchman who was turned back again today. Hard things were said on both sides.

MAY 30, TUES.
Went to Stargard today with Rowat. Took pants and boots in for exchange. McDonald is staying for another seven days. Hill staying indefinitely. Got back to find Loudmouth and Kline at loggerheads over Red Cross issue. Apparently orders have come in that all cans are to be opened, Kline objected, (over) evidently drunk; result: a heated argument again. Managed to get the Red Cross out with only puncturing.

MAY 31
Bertrand, Perry and Kline warned for Stargard this evening. Kline has no time to pack this evening.

JUNE 1
Lots of excitement this morning when Kline wasn't ready to move by 6:30. Loudmouth went mad and forced them out at the point of a loaded rifle. It was a dangerous moment. Kline grabbed what things he could but forgot his tunic, which I got for him. I think "Loudmouth" is subjected to periodic insanity spells or is a dope fiend. I guess we can be thankful no one was hurt. Fellows are feeling pretty sore about the whole thing. Loudmouth then decided that everyone had to help peel spuds after working hours and issued a number of orders to that effect. The man is mad.

JUNE 2, SUN.
Received letter from Canadian at party near French city also Toronto Globe and Mail. Lea has gramophone he is willing to lend us. C. Masterton, Winnipeg. Monthly Red Cross reports a headache. Dick smuggled in 20 bread (white). Gray 44 cackle berries. Change to 11 hours tomorrow. Heavy bombing this evening probably Stettin. German people asking where their fighters are, and why the Allied Air Force is walking all over them. Goebbels said in speech that war will be over in two months, win or lose.

JUNE 4

Loudmouth said Rome reported evacuated over the radio; he seemed peeved when I refused to pin-point it.

JUNE 6, TUES.

Radio news is that the second front has started. "Loudmouth" and Dusty said at 4:30 that it started at 1A.M. Large forces taken part from La Havre to Cherbourg. The Poles here say it was only a raid which is all over now with large no. of P.O.W.s taken. Also, a rumour that they are fighting north of Rome. Things are breaking. Paul cursing. Man, what's the difference. Eric is suffering from boils and has been since Friday. One on his elbow started from scratch but I think it is infection because of the poison streak from his elbow to his armpit. Drew poison out with soap and sugar poultices. No papers until Friday, a sure sign something is breaking. Wrestling with monthly R.C. reports.

JUNE 7, WED.

Went to Stargard with Jones today. Heard all news of 2nd front including the dropping of 70,000 parachutists. Rome declared an open city; fighting north of it now. Heavy fighting northwest of Jassy. Canadians leading landings and spearheads in France. Loudmouth nearly happy. Consensus of German opinion was over by August and we (Canadians) home by Xmas. Felt uneasy travelling today, curious and hostile stares all the way, especially when waiting for trains on station platform. 500 Russians dead from typhus in the Stalag. A Serb repatriation scheme getting underway also. Heard a story of a number of Air Force lads who escaped from VIIIB. They reached Stettin in ten days but had to hole up there until means of further travel could be found. One night the R.A.F. bombed their hideout and had to find shelter in an air raid shelter. They were nearly mobbed when a hysterical woman started crying on one fellow's shoulder and the owner said in English "Don't tell me your troubles lady, I'm no Deutchie." The army arrived in time to save them.

JUNE 10, SAT.

Rain and more rain. Drew a map of the fighting front in Italy. The line ran off the old one. Also drew a map of the France front. Managed to get a line from Volognes and Caan according to German papers. Very little news and no letters this week.

JUNE 18, SUN.
C.S.M. Martin, new chief confidence man paid us a visit. Gates still locked but C.S.M. is going to see the General about it. Germans claim new secret weapon causing panic in England.

JUNE 20, TUES.
Boys saw raid on Stettin; still burning this evening. C.S.M. Cordner and crew brought shipment of R.C. parcels. Had "Loudmouth" going around in circles. He was pretty meek when they left.

JUNE 21, WED.
Saw thousands of Allied planes this morning. Inspector with field glasses calculated about 6,000. Quite a sight. It was a clear day but vapor trails formed clouds. "Pit" Pithouse and Bater, dentist, possibly appendicitis and boils respectively. Planes yesterday were raiding Potsdam and Berlin. Johnson, back from propaganda tour of Berlin, says no German civvies but 23 million French there. Advancing on all fronts. 3rd Division in France, 1st in Italy, Canadians in spearheads, Russians broke Mannheim line and took Viipuri. In Italy Canadians and Indian troops took Perrugia. In France Canadians fighting around Caen. Churchill says war could be over in 3 months, if not terrible high price to Germans. Germans claim London burning day and night. Big battle for Cherburg. Local news Polish Anna and Leo's wife had a set to. Anna vanquished, squealed to Germans about Mantilda singing anti-German song. M.A. fined 25 marks. Sheriff shot near young kid the other day, maybe the kid is still running. Gates still locked. Have received Volunteer Service ribbon with Active Service leaf. A story of the French Canadian marching through villages. Also another party changing pictures. Put Churchill in place of Hitler and changed the caption to Heil Churchill. Am, expecting Gestapo search; must hide this diary again.

JULY 8, SUN.
Ober-Feldwebel came today, called a parade and had me read out a recent order to the effect that due to the uncertainty of civilian disposition the safety of P.O.W. could not be guaranteed if said P.O.W. wandered off by themselves.

JULY 13
Went to Stargard, a 16 hour trip now. People not very hostile; they are inclined to talk more freely of things they can't get.

JULY 14
Threshing of räpes started this morning. Bater came in at 11 with an ugly gash from mower knife used for cutting sheaf cord.

JULY 15
Bater sent to Stargard for medical treatment.

JULY 25
Retrieved diaries from hiding place. In the interim guards have to carry bayonets on their rifles while on duty, presumably for our protection. Heinz fell out of a tree and is pretty well banged up, civvies useless, cried, bawled, yelled and argued while Hassell, Dixon, Price and myself did what we could; he was taken to hospital this evening. Latest BBC by grapevine: Lublin, Lemburg, Bust, Litocosk, Pleskau, Ostrow fallen. All French prisoners or not, must walk on roads without hats. Any German person talking defeatist will be shot. A big news item of past week was the assassination attempt on Hitler, which was unsuccessful. There is something fishy about it; think it might be a set-up by Hitler. Another was the resignation of Jap minister Tojo.

Working hours fluctuating, ranging from ten hours to 9. Today they started working 11 hours threshing rye. Lorne is having quite a time with a cuckoo clock. Personal cigarettes kept in R.C. stores as per German order.

JULY 31, MON.
Another week gone by. Harold and Vi arrived home according to Rusty. Nothing much doing on Mützelburg front. Went to Stargard on Friday; no

news, especially. Russians advancing rapidly; should be in Warsaw in a day or two. Americans made a push toward Coutances. Canadians catching all varieties of hell around Caen. Germans nervous over new Mosquito plane, has warned nation. A 15 year old Russian kid shot by guard without warning in Stalag. He was accepting a present from a Canadian at the time. We are getting short of R.C. parcels, 2 short for next issue. Tired of this job. Sgt. Ferguson in charge of a party and is working. Going to Pyritz tomorrow for R.C. heavy arbeit.

AUG. 1

Went to Pyritz for Red Cross shipment and it rained both ways. We travelled by team and wagon from Kosin to Pyritz and back. Converted French Postern very nervous.

AUG. 12

Lots of girls ages from 14 to 17 called up for work in East Prussia. Americans going ahead in France.

AUG. 19

Anniversary (2nd), will there be a third one behind wire? Americans made drive toward the middle Seine passing Chartiers and Orleans. Orleans evacuated. Another landing this time in Southern France, between Toulon and Nice. Many rumours floating around. General opinion is we will be in England for Xmas. 2 German youngsters shot at Noylin; mistaken for escaping Canadians, sometime during the last two weeks.

SEPT. 14

Padre Flood came this afternoon. He is quite a man's man. 25 years ago he taught school in Dimont, 13 miles from Wobegon. During discussion before a brief sermon, one of Gray's bottles of wine blew a cork. The Padre was telling us not to do anything that would get us shot just as the cork came out. I don't know if he realized what caused the detonation, but am inclined to think he had a fair idea.

Have learned that preparations for our evacuation are complete. Next month or early November.

SEPT. 19

Went to Stargard with Engbert, Donaldson, Jones and LaPierre; "Flannelfoot" as guard. LaPierre stayed in the Revier. The rest of us missed the 1:20 train out of Stargard, consequently, in preference to waiting six or seven hours in Pyritz, we walked the 17 km and got back here before dark.

SEPT. 20

Three men sick today. Jones on light duty with eczema, Phillips and Angus with grippe.

SEPT. 21

Day of events. Another man Hill, sick with grippe, making four. "Over" told Dusty that Engbert would have to go to the field and Jones do the outside Lager work. Lost my temper and blew my top at Dusty, the poor guy wasn't to blame. In the afternoon a German lieutenant and a Gefreiter and 3 Frenchmen pulled in with a talking picture machine. The "over" came back from Pyritz with a bunch of haywire orders, including one that the three men with grippe had to go to Stargard. Flannelfoot brought the order down and I blew my top again in front of the officer who speaks good English. I guess he heard some very uncomplimentary remarks about the "Over", although he didn't say anything. Suddenly decided to let the three men go to Stargard; it's about time he learned a lesson. LaPierre got a good go out of the visit the other day. Also got White on the list.

The show which started at 8:20 was "Representing Lilly Mars," a Judy Garland picture. Both the Chef and the Inspector were present. It is the first show I have seen since we were at Horsham. "Over" still sulking and refusing to speak.

SEPT. 22, FRI.

Four men left for Stargard this morning. "Over" still not talking; he told Dusty not to give us the paper anymore. The cheap childish little rat. He received a jolt this afternoon when three men came back from Stargard with 14 days light arbeit. White stayed in Revier. Kitchen joined party today. "Over" suddenly changed and became very friendly. I just can't figure the man.

SEPT. 26
Five men came from No. III, Noylin, which broke up to make room for refugees from the east front.

SEPT. 27
Spencer new man from Noylin told Kranz and the Sherrif to get down on their knees and arbeit, as it was good for big stomachs. The Over is gradually getting snooty again. Why or over what, I don't know; it's just one of his spells.

OCT. 3
Demeray and I went to Pyritz for Red Cross today while Price went to Stargard. Bater and Dombrowski came back with him. Arrived Kosin on return trip transferred parcels to wagon drawn by Max the old twenty-niner. We had to push all of it, including Max up the long hill.

OCT. 4
Five Noylin men and Junior Date transferred to Kraazin. Found out today that some "ganz egaller" Germans not so "ganz egal" after all, namely the "Over." Apparently he is two faced. I never heard of a three faced man but if there is such a thing he is it. Received 1,000 cigs. from Nelle and 300 from George Holland.

OCT. 5
The "Over" is getting "snootie." He won't speak to any of us now and issues his orders through "Dusty" or "Slew-foot." I don't think he would be wise to linger to say good-bye after the war is over.

OCT. 6

"Over" issued orders that all sick must go to Pyritz. We had a good view of numerous flights of Allied planes today at noon when the airport at Klützow was raided. Silver paper strips and wrappings floated down all afternoon. We could go for lots of that kind of music.

OCT. 7

We saw more planes than we did yesterday, apparently hitting the same vicinity; the aerial torpedo factory, just outside of Stargard hit badly. Saw one of the planes shot down, rumour says four others also knocked down. "Over" really has a snoot on this evening; perhaps because I told him there would be work tomorrow before he was notified.

OCT. 8

"Over" still nursing his grudge we hear he refers to us as "verflucte scheisen Kanadiens." Steward, Bater going to Pyritz tomorrow.

OCT. 9, MON.

Stewart goes to Lazaret at Stargard and Bater had a carbuncle lanced; goes back to Pyritz for dressing on Wednesday. The doctor at Pyritz raised hell for taking them to him so the "Over" loses again. Heard today that the "Over" will soon be changed by special request.

OCT. 11

Went to Stargard with Stewart, Bater, Price and Philips. On the way in passed the airport, scene of recent raid. Plenty of damage to runway, parked planes and buildings, only a few near misses. Flannelfoot so excited he didn't see his rifle fall off the train. He turned us over to another Postern while he went back for his rifle. Nothing new in camp. We met Flannelfoot on Stargard station on way back. Minch!

OCT. 13, FRI.

"Over" went to Pyritz today and came back with 5 days' leave. Everyone hopes he goes for good. No mail today.

OCT. 17, TUES.

Heavy mail today. 600 cigs from Aux., 300 from Harry. Peaceful days these days; Dusty and Flannelfoot two best guards we ever had.

OCT. 20

Five days of peace ended when the "Over" came back this morning. Very little mail this morning. Two Russians were brought here this evening. Apparently they were making a break and while laying over in one of our barns were seen by a Pole who squealed to Dusty. These Poles are on the same level as the Ities, they would squeal on their own mother. Obtained a quivering needle from the visitors; they claimed it was no good; the needle kept going around in circle. They had a pretty decent feed in the kitchen where they spent the night. They got plenty of cigs which they didn't want to take as they would be confiscated when they reached the Stalag.

OCT. 21

Russians left this morning after expressing the opinion that Germans are more to be trusted than Poles. My sentiments exactly for the past six months. Found a Grosbeak today apparently suffering from disease or cold or both. It died this evening.

NOV. 2, WED.

Turbulent times for the past week or so. Finally scraped up enough material for a new stove which Alvoet said he could make, but after inspecting a few of his jobs around the farm decided he was all wind and voice. Engbert took on the job with Alvoet as helper. Alvoet is a nerve racking person at anytime and soon had Engbert and Charlie biting their finger nails. It came to a climax when Engbert clipped Charlie after a heated argument.

NOV. 3, THURS.

Stove eventually completed with bad feelings between all three people in the kitchen.

NOV. 4, FRI.

Charlie gave notice that he was leaving the kitchen and going to the field. I don't intend to coax him to stay so I guess Price will take over tomorrow. Lorne cornered the "Over" and asked to be sent to Stargard, which doesn't make much difference to me either. Am seriously considering taking a change myself and turning this job over to some other sucker. Tired of taking the dirt from two directions, from the Germans and our own fellows.

NOV. 7, TUES.

Went to Stargard and due to recent arrival of 50 new Canadian P.O.W.s, found things a little confused. Heard that Jerry Johnston was shot and killed at Brudenburg for being on the wrong side of the wire after nine; he leaves a widowed mother in New York. A smattering of news from these new fellows includes such items as the Americans being in Köln (Cologne); Canadians have large losses; C.R.A. and R.C.A.C. changed to front line troops. Eisenhower says December 16; Monty the 26th. Canadians flown from place to place as spearhead troops. Left McDonald, Dombrowski and Engbert in the Revier. Bater is to return next week for operation. Repats are rumoured as leaving around the 19th. May be no Red Cross food next months.

NOV. 9

Quite a long blank; have been too busy to think of making entries. Things have happened in the meantime. The Allies have swept through France and part of Belgium, two capitols falling in the drive; the German evacuation of N. France; the revolution in Romania; the Bulgarian armistice; the fall of Finland; the general tightening of the circle around Germany. Stettin totally out of commission; the vibration of heavy air raids felt for miles around. Norrie's escape blocked by last big raid on that city. We had a visit from a Mr. Christian Christianson, Y.M.C.A. rep, a Dane from Copenhagen, Denmark. He was accompanied by two Hauptmen and an Unteroffizier. Everyone here is betting on the armistice anywhere from 3 weeks to 3 months. I think it has to be finished by the first week in November or it will last all winter. Germany is in a bad way internally. Canadians always in newspaper headlines. The German engineer claims we will be here this time next year.

NOV. 12

Price is doing pretty good in the kitchen. Nothing much doing.

NOV. 17

Old guards say they are leaving soon. Slim left today. The Over told Hassell and Stocks they had better take a few days off while he is here.

NOV. 19

Old guards leaving tomorrow. The Over doesn't want to go and Dusty feels particularly bad, he shook hands twice before he finally went out.

NOV. 20

The Sheriff is on guard today with no sign of the new guard.

NOV. 21, TUES.

Sheriff still on guard; the guard from next farm came over. Received Red Cross without a hitch this morning. The visiting guard objected to my drawing cigarettes but the Sheriff over-ruled his objections and I got them alright. The new guard came at 4 this afternoon, one Feldwebel and a Private, neither one so bright.

NOV. 22

Things going on much the same as usual; the Feldwebel doesn't seem to worry about pants so much.

NOV. 24, FRI.

Went to Stargard with Bater, Angus and Donaldson. Donaldson and Bater stayed. Couldn't get any information re request for signatures of all men who thought they could walk 25 kilometers a day. We will be running out of parcels on the 12th or 15th of next month. There is a rumour that the Germans may take all personal cigarettes to Pyritz, leaving us 500 each. Got R.C. issue of parcels okay.

NOV. 25

Both guards went to Pyritz leaving the engineer on guard. He thought it quite a joke to be on guard without a firearm.

NOV. 26, SUN.

Not bothered at all today; drew cigs without any trouble.

NOV. 27

Nothing doing much. Gray racketeered 2 new light bulbs, 80 and 50 watts. We have been short of lights for some time. News is good; Americans in Strasburg; French took Millhausen and reached the Rhine. Russians advancing in Hungary.

DEC. 4

Anniversary of enlistment. Went to Stargard with Stewart and Alvoet. Alvoet stayed with arthritis. Brought Dombrowski and Phillips back out.

DEC. 12

Last complete issue of Red Cross; all is left is 4 invalid parcels. There is no more supplies in Stargard. Mac, Bater and Donaldson came back today. Lebeouf and Mallard called into Stargard.

DEC. 15

Drew out the four invalid parcels; split them up between 24 men and the kitchen the best I could, saving the tea for Xmas. Might have a slim Xmas dinner.

DEC. 18

Went into Stargard with Dombrowski. We had to carry 27 blankets; blew my top at Tony in Pyritz station. Missed the early train and didn't reach Stargard until after three in the afternoon. Dombrowski stayed for operation. Brought Newman back. Missed last train from Pyritz to Kosin and had to walk 17 kilometers; plenty burnt up; blisters on both heels.

DEC. 20

Lining up a pretty fair Xmas dinner if we can keep the guard outside while we are cooking it. Price is baking cakes, pies and tarts in the ash pit of the stove.

DEC. 22

Received a fair chunk of meat and a basket of apples from Kosin. Also bought four chickens so we shouldn't do too badly.

DEC. 25

Up early to help Price. Got the job of icing the two cakes. Made it out of cocoa, sweet condensed milk, margarine and sugar. Finally ended up with a fudge-like concoction trimmed with banana icing. Boiled the chickens and meat, then fried them. Supper was two hours late but consisted of fried chicken and meat, mashed spuds, turnips and gravy, followed by pumpkin pies, pumpkin and lemon tarts and cake. The cake was like pudding but good eating. Still Sunday work and we are getting tired of it.

DEC. 28

Went into Stargard with Howes and Jones, both for dentist. No sign of Red Cross yet. Caught all trains okay, but had a little trouble getting through search room with Kitchen's cigarettes. Brought Lincoln out with us; party 29 now.

DEC. 30

Managed to buy 4 chickens for New Years so far with 3 more coming soon. Layer cakes and pies this time. I watched heavy raid Stargard direction the other night.

DEC. 31

More chickens coming in tomorrow. Heavy blizzard blowing. I hope it dies down for tomorrow so that some of the fellows can go skating and keep the guard outside

FRED LODGE DIARY
January 1 to Jun 30, 1945

Book No. 7

Daily Diary: H19859, F. T. Lodge,
Camerons of Canada (C.A.S.F.)

JAN. 1

Fine day, managed to get the supper cooked while guard was guarding the skaters. Very good supper but with ersatz (substitute) instead of tea.

JAN. 3

No rations for some reason, probably roads blocked by snow. We are eating dry toast, potatoes & turnips and straight ersatz coffee. Decided to finish oven that I started last summer. Raised a stink about the mail. Tony said, Chef wouldn't loan him horse and wagon, so Stewart asked Chef at noon, then the lid blew off. Apparently Tony was lying again and he got hell from the Chef and the Feldwebel (Sergeant). Chef says horse and wagon always available for mail and that we must get the mail. We got it.

JAN. 4

Raised another stink about rations, apparently they are at Köslin forgotten and will be here tomorrow for sure. Working on the oven.

JAN. 5

Rations arrived badly smeared so raised hell again. No marmalade and margarine short. Rec'd word that R.C. is on the way from Geneva.

JAN. 6

Busy day, first the chimney sweeps came and condemned barracks stove, closely followed by Control Feldwebel who promised to report the stoves to the company, then the Chef who promised to speak to the inspector for material. This is about the sixth time we have been after new stoves and it will probably go the old circle and peter out. Worked on oven in between interruptions. A price war in progress now, white bread isn't white, all prices to be cut.

JAN. 7

Bought 4 chickens for today's supper and Price whipped up a couple of deep apple pies served with diluted sugar beet syrup.

JAN. 8

Went to Stargard with Howes & Morrie & Stocks. Took Kitchen's kit and cigs in. What a time we had getting in. They took all our cigarettes away from us. I couldn't get near the Red Cross stores to do business. Finally ended up before some officer with Kitchen's pack. I refused to open it until Kitchen came down. Kitchen finally came and had everything fixed okay. Stocks, Morrie and Howes didn't get their cigs back. Alvoet came back with us much against our wishes. Got in, in time for supper, but the lights were out.

JAN. 9

Lights were out for breakfast this morning, an inconvenience we are getting used to. Price and I gave the Polish Posten an earful this morning. Almost pulled a boner today when he negotiated and completed an egg deal out in the open. Probably hell will be raised tomorrow. Lights were out again for supper tonight. There is quite a lot of cussing because nothing can be done until they go on around 8:00.

JAN. 10

We decided to boil some sugar beet into syrup as we don't get any more marmalade from the Germans. Kranz and civvies raising hell over the egg deal yesterday. Kranz swears he is writing to the company about our dealing. They can't seem to realize that if they would feed us better there would be no need for dealing. Lights were out again tonight and the fellows are becoming disgusted. Scraped us a 75 kilo bag of sugar beet today. Probably boil them tomorrow if we get them prepared in time.

JAN. 11

Finished washing and scraping the sugar beet today, boiling for sure tomorrow. Lights were out again tonight, it's gone by a joke and we never miss an opportunity to let the Germans know what we think of it. Everything pretty quiet on the war front these days.

JAN. 12

What a day and what a mess. Boiled sugar beet all day. We borrowed a press from the Poles but it wasn't much good. We ended up with about 20%

syrup which has to be boiled again tomorrow. Kranz and Tony have finally made the borrowing of the gramophone from Leo "verbotten." We had it for awhile tonight but the "Feldwebel" came over and got it again. Everything gone haywire around here. Oven making is coming along very slow. Russian winter offensive started today and apparently making rapid progress.

JAN. 13

Nothing much doing today except arguing with Tony about the gramophone. Sherriff going to try for a machine for us. Finished boiling the sugar beet down. Not much left. Much better to buy it from the Poles at 200 crip a pail.

JAN. 14

Nothing of any importance except working on the off oven. Russians skipping right along.

JAN. 15

Playing lot of Poker these nights. That is all German money is good for.

JAN. 16

Understand that the Red Cross has been received in Stargard. May be getting them here soon. Hope so because German rations are pretty meager, although we have managed to have a chicken dinner every Sunday since Christmas.

JAN. 17

Worked on the oven, not much headway. Sick parades are getting out of hand. Some want a list made out so that everyone will get a chance to have a day off. Chilblains and colds prevalent.

JAN. 18

Should be getting word of Red Cross soon. Fellows are starting to draw out their cigarettes now.

JAN. 19

Friday. Received word that Red Cross had been sent to Pyritz. Good news. Padre called again today and we had a little service, later followed by communion for those who wanted. He couldn't stay long as he had to spend the night at Köslin. Repats have gone. Russians coming faster and faster. Some Germans actually believe that they will still win the war. Americans, English and Canadians having trouble with the west defenses.

JAN. 20
Oven making mostly and trying to convince the guards that we have to go to Pyritz on Friday.

JAN. 21
Nelle's and Connie's birthday. I guess I spend another birthday here. Russians coming pretty fast, can hardly keep the map pin-pointed.

JAN. 22
Janet's birthday & I haven't heard from her for a long time.

JAN. 23
My birthday and what a day. Tried to get into Pyritz for parcels but Guards said no. Fellows mad and told Ice Cream. He ordered guards to get parcels, Tony the goat again. Demeray and I went. Cold riding on the wagon. Big call up of "Volkssturm" (*People's Militia*) this morning. Kranz, Paul and the engineer from here and Sherriff and 14 others from Köslin. Stayed in French barracks for 2 hrs while Tony ran around town. Late start getting back had to leave parcels at Köslin.

JAN. 24
Parcels came up with milk wagon. "Feldwebel" wanted to issue only 5 parcels, I wanted 15, we got 15. All meats going to kitchen. Russians reported past Posen and Bromberg which puts them about 180 kilos from here. Must repack my stampede pack again. Things look as if they might become critical again.

JAN. 25
Hear that Kranz is coming back again being too old for the front line and a bad case of asthma. Russians or a move expected daily if they maintain

their present speed. Bater changes his prediction date with the new, latest change from April to Feb. 13. Russians at Schneidemühl, 50 or 60 kilos to the Southeast. For the last few days lights off at 7A.M. until midnight, reason given is conservation of coal but everyone thinks it is to cut off news broadcast from the danger area. They can't tell people around here that the Russians are being pushed back. Overhauled the gramophone today so we had music tonight. Tony didn't like it because he was instrumental in our losing the use of Leo's. Refused to sew Tony's braces for him, he nearly cried when I said I didn't have time.

JAN. 26
Cold today, more trouble with Tony. He is sore at me for not fixing his braces yesterday. We practically set our watches with lights out now. They go just at news time. Newspaper becoming sporadic may stop entirely next week. Tony seemed very anxious to have Newman go to Pyritz for his foot (fork puncture) but Jack left him breathless when he said he couldn't walk. "Ice Cream" and Max may be called next up which means Kranz will be in charge. Between Tony and Kranz they might manage to make it really miserable, if the "Feldwebel" goes. No lights again tonight, using a makeshift affair using shoe oil mixed with ersatz benzine. No paper tonight so don't know where the Russians are. Allies attacking in the West but not coming very fast.

JAN. 27
Dixon and Tony had a set to this afternoon. Dix is sick. Tony's loud voice woke him up and Dix ordered him out. Tony blew his top, reaching for his gun. I told Dix to not say anything. Tony threatened to call Controlle and have Dixon put in "Strafe." Apparently, Tony went to the field immediately afterwards and gave the fellows there hell for walking around between loads to keep warm. When I was going for cigarettes Tony told me in confidence that Dixon ordering him around "Gehts Nicht" but he wouldn't phone if I gave him hell. I said I did so Tony was happy.

JAN. 28
Ice Cream and others left at midnight. Civvies (sic) all packed and nervous, Russians getting closer, breaking through everywhere. Boys are sewing and

packing essentials. Lights out this A.M. for awhile. Russians crossed Oder in some places, heading for Berlin, 40 or 50 kilos from here. (12 noon) no word of moving yet. Can't see advantage of doing so unless to Stargard. Stampede kits already issued. Issued all new clothing this morning. (2 P.M.) Tony is scared, first of advancing Russians, secondly that we might tell Controlle he was sleeping on duty this A.M. Sheep men 45 minutes late for work. Big supper this evening cooked all food on hand just in case. Tony asked Newman if he could walk 40 or 50 kilos but no official word of moving yet. We can hear the rumble from SW when everything is quiet. Kranz came back. NW blizzard roaring outside.

JAN. 29

Kranz had all boys out putting canvas on all wagons. Heavy NW blizzard still blowing, hard on evacuees. Heard that there is a train at Köslin, on the road for 18 days, kids freezing to death, bodies thrown out beside the road. 300 kids froze to death when Berlinchen children's hospital evacuated. Very severe weather for riding around in farm wagons. Kranz has killed all his hens and cooked all his pork to take with him.

JAN. 30

Ice Cream back, pretty mad about wagons covered, accused Kranz of spreading panic. He said Russians driven back but Americans coming fast, says war will be over in two weeks. Max says if R. advances as fast again war will be over in 5 days. A few thousand prisoners being evacuated have reached Köslin after marching 100 kilos, 150 Cdns supposed to be among them. No food or clothing; some just falling in the ditches. 1000 may come here for the nite. Just received word that Köslin can accommodate them all. Everyone sewing or cutting down their kits. Have a hunch tomorrow is the day.

JAN. 31

Got up at 6:30 to find the door locked and Bill was standing by the stove when he should have been in the barn. He was sent back to the billets when firing was heard close by. Finally got the door open and breakfast underway. Guards very nervous especially Tony. After breakfast men went to sheep barn and oxen stall to feed the stock. The order to evacuate came at 8:10. What a mess, we drew all Red Cross parcels and personal cigarettes and couldn't find room for it all in our packs so they were scattered from hell to breakfast. All other stuff was left. We got a wagon at the last moment but it was too late to pack the rest of the stuff. The community grub box was just dumped on the wagon with a big bag of cigs and Red Cross parcels. Civvies all down to see us off and crying, whether because we were leaving or because Russians were coming I don't know. "Auf Wiedersehen" was prevalent. We pulled out at 9:05 headed for Kössin and carrying our packs. Pepper twisted his knee, a bad start on the wagon. Heavy walking; Kössin was disorganized. A tank had taken a shot at the church and shoved the telephone poles over. With packs on the wagon, we started evacuating in earnest. Road icy; walking tough; hard on the groins. Civvies from Lindenbuch and points beyond said Panzers only 5 kilo behind and whipped their sweating tired horses more. We helped two old women get their wagon back on the road. Turned down the Arnswald road and headed east for Lüblow. Passed party of Russian POW with 3 Postens also a party of French and Poles cleaning snow off the road. Changed direction NE and kept slugging, passing broken down wagons, abandoned. Stopped to help a woman put a wheel on her wagon. We cut east again across country for Sallentin which we reached at 12:30. Groin playing hell. Obtained hot water from the Serbs, then Albert wanted to return home. We bought him off with cigarettes and grub, partly, then the Feldwebel ordered him to come. We left Sallentin at 1:30, walking still tough. Passed through a place called Klemmen at 2:14; snow covered ice made walking hard and painful. Passed through Warnitz at 3:30 without stopping and headed for Klützow.

It was just a matter of picking them up and putting them down with tense muscles against slipping. We reached and passed Lützow at 4:35, having only 4 kilometers to Stargard. Somewhere along the road we were joined by two girls who put their packs on the wagon. It was a long 4 kilos and walking more or less automatic. Two more women put their luggage on the wagon. Air Force evacuating the airport in lorries and trailers. Finally reached outskirts at 5:30 when another argument with Albert took place which he lost again. It took us an hour to pass through Stargard, reaching the camp at 6:30. There was no search coming in. Soon we were allotted beds, issued with blankets and had ½ dozen belts under our butts. We were the first party in. Other parties apparently evacuated with civvies. Sore groins and blistered feet prevalent, having walked 40 kilos in 8 ½ hours. Glad to get here.

FEB. 01

Rumors and activity aplenty. Russians closing in on Stettin thereby cutting this province off which means we might see some hot times yet. Russians 60 miles from Berlin. Military convoys travelling west along Stettin Road. Eric and Bates and I eating with Eddie Warren, Dave Cochrane & Andy Rennie. Excitement high tonight. Americans treated pretty badly here made to march with frozen feet legs and hands.

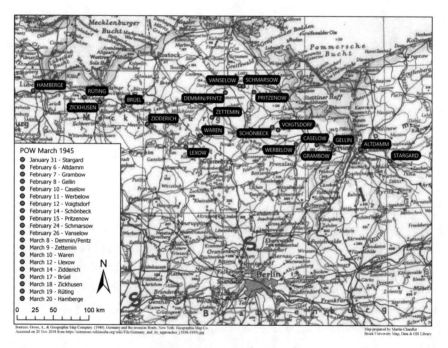

POW March 1945
- January 31 - Stargard
- February 6 - Altdamm
- February 7 - Grambow
- February 8 - Gellin
- February 10 - Caselow
- February 11 - Werbelow
- February 12 - Voigtsdorf
- February 14 - Schönbeck
- February 15 - Pritzenow
- February 24 - Schmarsow
- February 26 - Vanselow
- March 8 - Demmin/Pentz
- March 9 - Zettemin
- March 10 - Waren
- March 12 - Llexow
- March 14 - Zidderich
- March 17 - Brüel
- March 18 - Zickhusen
- March 19 - Rüting
- March 20 - Hamberge

0 25 50 100 km

Sources: Gross, A., & Geographia Map Company. (1940). Germany and the invasion fronts. New York: Geographia Map Co.
Accessed on 23 Nov 2018 from https://commons.wikimedia.org/wiki/File:Germany_and_its_approaches_(1938-1939).jpg

Map prepared by Martin Chandler
Brock University Map, Data & GIS Library

(Long march to freedom)

FEB. 02

Russians are pretty close to here; explosions from demolitions heard around the town. Rumored that two German divisions positions in woods near the camp. Another party came in today; said all evacuation has been stopped in this province. Sevi came in from Stargard party said Russians issued ultimatum, surrender by noon or else. Noon was supposed to be dead time for this camp. Everyone out looking for the Russians. Rumored that Russians 10 kilos from Stettin. Another American died today. 1:30 heavy explosion. 4:30 lots of explosions; another commando coming in. Russians advancing along Pyritz-Stargard Road and Pyritz-Stettin Road on both sides of lake. All think we are cut off. (8:45 pm) Things have quietened down. Pyritz reported in flames. Russians 80 kilos up the Oder from Frankfurt.

FEB. 03

Heavy barrage heard to the SE at 6 this morning. After the news last night we expected the Russians around here this morning. Heavy air raid on Berlin lasting from 10 am till after 12. Party no. 143 came in this afternoon after traveling two days to come ten miles. They started for Pyritz yesterday morning but were turned back. Americans and French took Kolmar.

FEB. 04

Roll call outside this morning. Cannonading heard this morning around 6. Word of four more Kommandos coming in from the north. I am looking around for Math and Trig books again. Serb kommando in today, left Köslin ½ hour before Russians and an hour after us. Russians forced to plant mines in the fields around here. Obtained a Canadian Legion Trig book from Kitchen. Very heavy cannonading from Pyritz way and Stettin way this evening. Lights went out for 45 minutes tonight. A glow in the sky over Pyritz caused quite a lot of speculation. Still chances that we will move yet; not cut off in west. News is good, Americans almost through the West Wall defences. Pyritz reported as fallen. Russians still advancing on Berlin, which is being heavily bombed by Americans. May move tomorrow.

FEB. 05

Rumors about Pyritz coming in; fighting in the streets; it's fallen; it's still holding out. Also rumors that the Americans and Canadians have broken through on a 150 kilometre front. Miserable weather, foggy and cold. All non-marchers told to report for "Stabartz" inspection right after roll call. Soup and coffee coming up at 7am. Looks like evacuation. Hope not. History repeating itself, kit cutting, shoe greasing, speculation etc., received that we move at 8 in morning. Here we go again. Destination uncertain, some say Danzig (why I don't know). Some say west of Stettin which is more probable. What a commotion. News is good tonight. Americans doing good. Russians forty miles from Berlin. Rumors that they are 24 kilometres from Stettin. Pack is still too heavy; must cut some more.

FEB. 06

Had a big feed of porridge this morning. Called on parade and stood around and waited; a lot of stuff left. Left camp finally at 9:10; went through first town at 10:30. Turned off and followed a swamp road in a large circle finally hitting a small "dorf" (town) where we stopped for lunch. Killed a can of M&Y there. A German woman had all her neighbours boiling water for us. A hard afternoon followed during which walking got harder and harder. Finally reaching a barn on the outskirts of Altdamm 5 kilos from Stettin. A French kommando supplied medical supplies and sanitators. Claude Norman ended with a fever and had to go to bed. Everyone tired and footsore. Sleeping in a big barn full for straw. The road today was strewn with discarded kit. One fellow just dropped his entire kit and walked away from it. Padre still limping along with us. Lord I am stiff. If tomorrow is as hard as today there are a lot of fellows won't make it. Figure about 30 kilos today.

FEB. 07

Up at six, some more kit discarded during night. We were on our way at 7:50. We marched through Altdamm, passed tank traps, and blocks, etc., under construction. Crossed first bridge over the canal at 9:40 and 2nd bridge over Oder at 10:55. After heavy slugging over cobbled stoned side roads we hit Schevenninz, our supposed destination, but as it was only 3:00 the Germans figured on another hour's march. Passed Grabow Station at 4:55;

reached town at 5:15. Not very welcome here. We are sleeping in a light-less barn. Day, Bater and I found a spot on the forbidden side of the barn in some barley. People here don't like Canadians here. The women of the house seemed to be a decent sort. Feet and legs are sore tonight. There was plenty of limping today.

FEB. 8

Up at six and found big blister on my heal. Had salmon and bread for breakfast. Issued with 1/5 of a loaf and a hunk of meat. Started at 9:25 going back by the station. Cobbled stoned roads again. Hard on feet. Passed Bismark at 11:55 on a good road. We got 4 kilos by it when we had to turn back. Before doing so however we had dinner. Back to Bismark then down a side road to a place called Gellin. We are billeted in a barn loft not much light but plenty of hot water. People here pretty accommodating. Last minute warning before going to bed that we may have to evacuate during night as the whole village is on a stand to. Russians are coming fast. This is where we are supposed to stop over for a day's rest.

FEB. 9

We had a couple of air-raids during the night that were pretty good. The whole barn just seemed to move over a couple of feet on two occasions. A shell fragment or shrapnel whined over the barn roof and Kingston yelled "don't get excited, it's only a flare, but put your boots on in case of incendiaries." First raid between 8 and 9 and the second around midnight. Plenty of brews, a hot meal, but hard to prepare on outdoor fires. Kids selling hot water for a couple squares of chocolate or a few cigs. Someone's can of M&D exploded in an outdoor fire, he forgot to puncture the can. Marching order being organized in groups of fifty; 20 kilos a day with a break every hour. Had a good shower and a shave this afternoon. The reflection at Plönzig, target of last night's raid still strong tonight. There is a synthetic oil plant there, or there was.

FEB. 10

We had spuds for breakfast and after a few false starts got under way at 7:30. Passed Bismark at 8:05 on the main highway, icy footing as it rained and froze last night. At 8:40 we passed our old dinner place and were on new ground. We reached Löcknitz at 10 where we met the Serbs coming back; we were ordered off the roads by the military. Turned left, we marched south for about 2 kilos and about 10 we passed a town we didn't get (*Bergholz*) and an hour later Burg Löcknitz. At 12 we stopped for dinner. Finally pulled into a place called Caselow, an evacuated town taken over by evacuees. Billeted in a loft again with no straw, but pinched some from the adjacent barn despite the guards. Received an issue of 1/8 loaf of bread, a block of cheese (4 days) and a little margarine. 3 more guards deserted tonight, totaling five now. Boys are scrounging all over town. People here stopped guards from beating up the Americans. 2 died here. Red and Shorty picked up two women this evening but there regular boyfriends turned up; one carrying a white loaf of bread. Red & Shorty said "bread or the girls"; they got the bread. We stewed up a batch of spuds and a brew of tea on an outdoor fire then later we issued with a brew of hot porridge. We bought choc. bars from Serbs tonight for 50 fags a shot.

FEB. II

Reveille at 5:00, had spuds for breakfast with tea. Lined up in groups of 50 at 7:00 and pulled out at 7:30. Very bad roads, loose sand and mud. Passed Norden, a town at nine finally reaching Zusedom at 9:55. Passed Nieden at 11:45, plenty of evacuees on the roads. On one occasion we had to detour around a dead horse. It's a wonder it wasn't salvaged for meat. Passed Necklin at 12:30. We pulled into Werbelow at 1:00 and were packed into a barn with the Serbs. Scrounging very poor because of the evacuees. No bread ration today and it was cold standing around waiting for hot porridge.

FEB. I2

Reveille at 5:00 with only a cup of tea for breakfast. Formed up into 50 and marched off at 7:23. We were told we had 24 kilos to go. Strasburg is 11. Now that it's not blisters on the heel it's a sore spot on the ball of my foot from cobblestones. Hit paved road at 9:05 where a sign stated 52 kilos to Neubrandenburg, 52 kilos to Stettin. At 10:20 we hit Strasburg and the usual foot race took place. At 1:30 after a hard stretch of road we hit Voigtsdorf, another farming village. Billeted in a draughty barn a short distance from village. Miserable wind blowing. Dave is having a hard time of it with his knee. It's been a long day on a cup of tea and a piece of choc. It didn't take long to locate the vegetable cellar so we had boiled spuds and tea. Bread scarce and difficult to obtain.

FEB. 13

Had a blizzard during the night and snow blew in around eaves, consequently we were covered with fine snow this morning; damp and darn miserable. We managed to whip up a couple of brews and finally received hot porridge from the kitchen. The warmest place is the cow stall, but we were kicked out of there because the Frau said we were disturbing the cows. The other end of the same building is another family and they are just the opposite. The cow stall is crowded, men are in the living rooms serving etc. Eric, Andy, Eddy and Charlie outside brewing up spuds, egg-flakes and porridge. Raining pretty hard. The good Frau donated some peas and spuds so we will have an official pea & spud soup. I figure we are 30-35 kilos from Neubrandenburg, a 3 day march. Had a shave and wash. Issued with 1/7 of a loaf and a bit of cured meat. We've had 4 day bread rations for 8 days. Hear it is 37 kilo march tomorrow. Frau lost her blackouts so found them and after repairs put them up.

FEB. 14

St. Valentines Day. Had a brew, a piece of cheese and a hunk of meat for breakfast. A small meat sandwich for noon. Commenced forming up at 7:00; cold, wet & muddy. We are packing raw spuds, just in case. 26 kilos to go today may hit a Stalag soon, I hope, delousing and a good rest necessary. Pulled out of Voigtsdorf at 7:30. Passed Rattey at 8:00. Heard that an American negro pilot shot down near here, had to dig his own grave then shot. Passed Schönbeck at 9:00 and hit paved roads again. An hour later passed through Heinichwalde. Foot sore as hell and my pack too heavy. Passed some Americans working on the outskirts of Friedland they looked in good shape. Passed through Friedland at 11:24. Another foot race through the town and God help the men behind. Reached Breservitz at 12:45 making darned good time today. Hit Schönbeck, our destination, 26 kilos at 2:20, taking 7 hours big surprise. The village had a piping hot stew waiting for us, so much we couldn't eat it all, altho some men had 7 or 8 helpings, so saved the leftover for evening soup. Also had a brew of German ersatz and a slice of bread. We won't forget Schönbeck in a hurry. Evidently German soldier here repatriated from Canada been home 8 days, he said if he hadn't have been married he would have stayed he was treated so well, consequently the village stew. A full warm stomach on going to bed means a lot. Eric & LaPierre managed to sneak out and buy a loaf of bread for a can of cocoa. It helps a lot.

FEB. 15
Role call 5:00, breakfast consisted of German coffee, bread & jam. We finally got under way at 7:20, with 17 kilos to go. Then we are to wait for further orders. Passed Rehburg at 8:45 having negotiated a swamp road and a field at a very fast pace. Passed Janow at 9:55 then passing through Neuendorf at 10:15, another mad dash over bad roads brought us to Pritzenow, where we went into billets in a big barn apparently for an indefinite period. Scrounging here is pretty bad so far and we are all cold. Dave Cochrane goes to Lazaret (hospital) at Neubrandenburg with acute arthritis of the knee. We stood in line for 1 ½ hours for soup, eating raw carrots & spuds meanwhile. Cassakoff had all his rations box pinched tonight.

FEB. 16
We had German coffee and I shared a can of salmon with Charlie for breakfast. Dave went to Lazaret at Neubrandenburg (II A) this morning. At roll call this AM the German officer said we had reached the end of our journey, at least until further orders were received; and that we would have to pay for all our vegetables while we stayed here. The wagon has gone to Stalag II A to see if some Red Cross can be obtained and other rations. He said he was pleased with the discipline of Canadians and hoped it would continue. He gave us permission to have outdoor fires to boil up spuds we have been packing for 2 days. What an end to a 10 day march. Young Harry, a German kid, has been bringing spuds, carrots and wood for us finally selling us a loaf of bread for a can of cocoa! He spooned the can without even mixing it. We are trying to buy salt, onions and sugar. No dice yet. Bought another loaf from a passing woman for a can of cocoa. Feel a lot better now after 2 lots of spuds. No word

of moving yet. "Harry" says the war will be over in 8 days, because "they" are coming from front and behind. Had 2 helpings of soup tonight. Bates bought some milk; Eric a jacket which we hope to sell for bread.

FEB. 17

This is Charlie's birthday. Wagon came back this morning with 215 American R.C. parcels and 31 bags of flour which will have to be made into bread somehow. The milk bought last night turned out to be flour this morning so we mixed some egg flakes with it and had pancakes, (superb). Much colder today, wind from North. No word of moving as yet. News Russians on 3 sides of Berlin, being bombed and shelled heavily. Big Allied breakthrough in West. Wood is getting scarce. 45 Red Cross just arriving. Received a little less than ½ parcel per man. Trying to make a spud deal at the sheep barn. We managed 1 loaf and a few pieces of bread, also onions, spuds and a little salt today. 2 or 3 brews so far today. Boiling spuds now (3:00) Had the spuds at 4:00 and found them good. Brewing tea now (4:25). Hear that German papers are calling someone the traitor of Europe, possibly another attempt on the little man's life. Everybody out along the stone fence cooking; asking people passing if they will sell bread, stew material etc. Would like to snag a few pigeons but they are too wild.

FEB. 18

Cold and miserable day, peeled spuds for the kitchen this AM. Managed to pick up more spuds and carrots. Bought a chicken for 120 cigs from a Serb. Breakfast; bread, jam & tea. Then a rip snorting stew; followed as soon as possible by a mess of spuds and chicken. Just finished that when soup came up from the kitchen. All this was interspersed with brews apparently we have gone as far as we can for the time being, because at roll call this afternoon arbeiters, NCOs, sanitators etc. were separated and tallied. Sgt. Passmore put Bater and I down as NCOs but I changed back because I didn't like to leave Eric now and Bater did the same because he thought it was too late to change now. It is rumored that there is a group of Canadians a kilo or so behind us. Limey's went through here previous to our arrival hungry and bootless.

FEB. 19

Colder today. Breakfast, bread, jam & tea. Brew biscuits & cheese at 11:00. Soup at 13:00. Now making a stew of peas (hand threshed in next barn) spuds, turnips, carrots, onions, bacon and mustard; it's going to be quite a meal. Müzelburg party asking me to reorganize party just in case. S Company in next village, one kilo back. Fixed my pack today. Had our stew around four and boy what a meal. Fellows from the other farm come down when they like. They left Stargard 2 days after us and could take all the Red Cross they could carry.

FEB. 20

2 weeks on the road. No word of leaving this place yet. Soup from the kitchen will be late today so our midday meal will consist of peas stewed with onions and mashed spuds, bread & tea. Breakfast was bread, sardines & cocoa. The jungle is a busy place these days. Concoctions are varied and of different sizes. We are using the bread faster than it's coming in, must be regulated. Anyone climbing over stone wall will be shot. Have a bad cold. Hear that there will be 30,000 POW in this area soon. Had a big meal this afternoon, too much. Had soup, a brew and a piece of bread this evening. Here there is a break through at Köln, driving NE forward landing at Hamburg.

FEB. 21

Rain during the night. Miserable this AM. Hot water and soup from the kitchen at noon. At roll call more orders: we can only do outside cooking from 1 to 3 in the afternoon. Tony announced at brew time that there is nothing to indicate our future but he is trying to get in touch with Geneva. Bread and other rations are very uncertain. It is very doubtful if we will ever see a Stalag again; apparently we are stuck here. Anthony may be able to talk the farmer into killing a sheep for us but even that is uncertain. Eating in the dark of the barn because it's too cold outside; it's no fun. Apparently we are cut off from everything, Red Cross, mail, German food supplies etc. I hope it doesn't last too long. Sunshine for awhile today. Had a feed of spuds, peas, carrots, onions. Donaldson was down today from the other party. Said boxes and boxes of chocolate left behind, only a few knew it was available. They could have as many R.C. parcels that they were capable of carrying, yet we were only allowed one. Some of last party took parcels, extracted certain articles and left the rest. New order, no smoking in the barnyard.

FEB. 22

I got up for coffee this morning, sandwiches made last night. Fire time changed to 9:30-11:30 to conform with late soup. They are issuing wood now which comes to a small lot per man. Trying to save his property I guess. His threshing machine won't work for some time and fence posts are getting scarce. Rumor that Serbs may move tomorrow and that we will all move. Hear that Stettin officially fell yesterday and that there is fighting in Stargard. Scrounging very poor here now, must move soon. Had spuds & peas for lunch. Told at roll call that we would be moving at 7 in AM to a place 7 kilos away for reorganizing. This was canceled about 9:00, move canceled.

FEB. 23

Managed to buy some onions today. Stomach rolled all night, great relief at latrine this morning. Very good soup from kitchen at noon. News of 19th Canadians & English broke through West wall and close to Münster. We are late cooking our supper. We hear we are going to a camp 2C, pretty close to Isle of Rügen. Supposed to be a clearing camp for Sweden. It's a good rumor, much too good to be true. Can't buy bread today at all; everyone glad we are moving, this place scrounged out. I guess we are off R.C. for some time unless we hit an organized camp. So far we move tomorrow. Spent two hrs in rain trying to buy bread from a Serb for cigarettes, managed to get 1 for cigs and 1 for choc and 10 cigs. Bater got 1 ½ loaves for cigs. No bread issue for two days. At least we will have a breakfast.

FEB. 24

After much standing around finally moved out of barnyard at 7:50; actually left Pritzenow at 8:00. Got on railroad line first thing and followed it the entire way crossing a paved road at 8:30, running at right angles to the track. Good walking. Passed Siedenbüssow at 9:35 and Alt. Tellin station at 9:50. Second toe of left foot giving me hell. After 7 kilos had stretched into 14 had arrived at Schmarsow at 11:20 and more or less billeted by 12:00. There are 2000 here now, 800 or 900 are leaving in the morning. The Russians are still being mistreated unbelievably. One was shot day before yest. another yesterday. The one yesterday was wounded in the chest, so this morning they finished him off and buried him. All Russian guards carry heavy canes and use them freely. Merely spuds seems to be the main food steamed in hog steamers then drawn in a blanket in groups of 30. Apparently we will be here some time 4 to 7 days. An hour after we got here there was 17 chickens and 4 rabbits missing. S.M. Martin and party had to return next village no room here. Germans evidently unable to supply us with bread, marg. etc. All our meals are more or less of our own obtaining, mainly stealing. We are threshing wheat by hand now to make porridge. Turkey reported as entering the war this A.M. (German radio).

FEB. 25
Windy & very cold. Some of the fellows find lice in their clothing. Eric has been boiling wheat for 4 hours this A.M. Spuds hard to get. Scrounging poor. New officer, Hauptmann Hess, seems friendly toward us. Martin & co arrived this afternoon. I have been eating wheat & cold spuds today. Soup coming up later. Pretty sure that we are going to 2C first, 80 kilos from here, then Arbeiters go out on kommandos and attach to other Stalags. Hope war is over by that time. Feet are cold, can't get them warm. Here's the wheat brew. Nearly all II D here now, they have been arriving all afternoon, including Bertrand and Perry. Kline flew the coop 4 days out, not heard of since. Windy, wet & cold, no rations. French cook takes over kitchen tomorrow, whipped out our 4 bags of flour & ½ horse. Soups cooked by Stalag cooks notorious for its unappetizing qualities.

FEB. 26
No brew or water from kitchen this A.M. Made our own brew out in the rain. Received order that Cdns were moving to a place 3 kilos away this afternoon. Brewed up some peas & carrots. NCOs & Privates may be separated soon & we may continue our journey by boxcar. Only Cdn's are supposed to be moving this P.M. Windy & rainy today. Final destination as yet unknown. A man fell off high wheat pile on men below last night but no one hurt. Received horrible soup from kitchen at noon. Latrine quite an ordeal in the rain. Received orders to form up at 1:20, and after standing for an hour in

rain waiting for two axes to turn up we got under way at 2:20. We walked on railway again and finally reached our destination Vanselow. Then issued a mad rush for the barn, it was like a flock of sheep. We didn't get bed space the first rush but by cleaning out the manure from the main aisle got enough room for Eric, Bates & I. Andy & Eddy found holes in the hay. This place is owned & managed by a Baroness & seeing our wet cold conditions gave orders for a stew to be made; but a man then reported some chickens & rabbits were missing so she canceled the stew. We may get something tomorrow, she will think it over. So, we had our piece of bread & bully beef & raw carrots & prepared our bed.

FEB. 27

With plenty of straw over us we slept pretty warm last night. Mint tea (horrible stuff) at 7:30 so we had an onion sandwich for breakfast. Still windy but has stopped raining. Soup may be up at noon. Eating raw carrots when we feel hungry. Rumors are that we go to a place 9 kilos (Demmin) and take 2 boxcars, destination a Baltic sea port. May get R.C. if we go through Demmin. Must get out & do some scrounging. Haven't had an issue of bread for 6 days. Cigs getting scarce. Still have 1 soap & 1 choc, for trading purposes. This A.M. the boys discovered a wagon load of hot boiled spuds intended for pigs. The driver had to move fast to get what was left to the pigs. We got 3 small ones each that Eddy managed to grab. Eddy also managed to get some hot water for some tea. Waiting for Eric & Bates to get back with the soup. There will be another soup this evening. We can't get the flour baked up, so I have heard that they are going to issue it out. Soup finally came up & the quarter of the horse made quite a difference. Eddy tried to boil up carrots, peas & spuds but didn't make it to the fire. Eating raw carrots this P.M. bought a pipe for 50 weed. The wagon went for rations but probably came back empty. Almost bedtime, still waiting for soup. Soup finally came up meager & thin. Resorted to raw carrots again, when they run out, I don't know. No bread for breakfast. Bird announced bread issue in morning. The gang that volunteered for arbeit (work) merely got seconds on soup; mostly NCO apparently 40 men have to work for evening soup.

FEB. 28

Early morning announcement, there is NO BREAD as many times before, they are going to <u>see</u> about getting some. They are having a difficult time raising a gang of 40 arbeiters for the farm this morning. Eating is becoming quite a problem; the line up on the carpenter shop stove was so long by 6 this morning that the last man hasn't a chance of getting on today. A cup of tea & a cigarette not very nourishing. Quite an argument regarding this 40 man arbeit party. There is some pretty ignorant people in this bunch. Volunteered for the party because I like the extra soup at night. Spreading manure not hard. Saw quite a few prisoners on the road this AM. Received a second on the soup at noon. Almost certain we will go by boxcar rest of way. NCO & Privates may separate here. NCO going II B God only knows where we will go. We finally got our stew cooked up reinforced with 2 cans of American M &V. It was good. Also managed a brew of tea. Received 1/5 of a loaf of bread. Also some sugar & barley obtained for the kitchen. Another break issue tomorrow. It's pretty "stimmt" (*correct*) that the NCOs will be leaving day after tomorrow.

MAR. I

Up early for ersatz coffee with the idea of obtaining raw spuds, no luck on the spuds. Had ersatz coffee with chopped ham sandwiches. Last night when everyone was smoking their last cigarette for the night a Feldwebel (*German Sgt.*) walked in. The usual air raid warning went around but few paid any attention to it. He pulled his revolver and fired into the roof, then gave a blast that lasted for some minutes. We got the low down on this move & speculation. 200 or so NCO (Eddy) leave tomorrow to walk to Demmin where they will take boxcars for Stalag II B near Hanover. The privates stay longer but we are destined for II E Schwerin near Lübeck, by train or walking, we don't know. A staff consisting of J.C.M. Anthony & Cordner, Sgt Brown, Dennis & possibly the padre & a few quartermasters. They were unable to have the flour baked up so was issued out this morning. 1 Klim per man. Peeled spuds for soup this morning, managed to pick up a few for the combine. Eddy & Charlie got enough spuds to last for a couple of days. Eddy has been trying to get on the carpenter's stove all morning but Stewart was boiling peas. He got on at 12 but had to leave the spuds on the stove during noon hr while the shop was locked up. Had a very passable soup from the kitchen at noon, combine will be cut to 4 tomorrow; hope we don't stay too long after the NCOs leave. Cold today. Had a mess of plain spuds. Colder this afternoon. Fixed my pack again. Ration wagon came back with NCOs traveling rations & 105 1/5 loaves of ordinary rations. Eric gave the brew pot to the kid for hot water 2 hours ago, she isn't back yet. Soup soon. May get seconds on soup tonight as a spud puller. Wind getting stronger & colder. Had a good second in soup this morning but it was cold waiting for it. Then a piece of bread & the rest of the chopped ham. My tea was practically cold when I got it but it was worth it. Stevie gave his flour & ½ raisins to a woman to cook up, he got a good fair sized cake in return; others are making bannock; we may get ours done tomorrow.

MAR. 1
German coffee for breakfast (burnt barley). We are allowed fires for cooking. Baroness promised enough spuds for soup, steamer, and personal issue. Not issued soon enough so men broke into spud metres. Feldwebel roaring mad, stopped fires and organized restricted area. Issued orders to guards to shoot if restrictions violated. Sgt. Maj. Anthony after a lot of talking, obtained spuds for soup. A little soft soap brought the jungle fires back and a promise that personal spud issue was forthcoming. No fires until 12 noon. Eric and I fried pancakes (flour, raisins, sugar and milk). Heard that our destination was changed to Wismar on the coast. 3 days' marching, 1 day where to take us. Things are a hell of a mess in this country. Crazy refugees traveling in all directions, food shortages, POWs to be housed and fed, which they are not. Had some fair sized spud feeds today and I never cared for boiled spuds. Hear that the sick are going to Wismar in the morning by train.

MAR. 2
Wind stronger & colder. Second on the fire today so we were peeling spuds before breakfast which consisted of ersatz coffee, bread & chopped ham. NCOs probably leaving this afternoon. We had a big mess of potatoes & peas around 15 to 10, the carpenter gave Eric some rock salt, a Godsend. Washed the dishes, God it's cold. Going to try doing a little trig this AM. Bought a 10-carat gold ring with large January birthstone for 70 cig. Because she

couldn't get 40 men to arbeit in the rain yesterday and because she couldn't get 80 today, the 6 (married and 1 kid in Canada) said she needed the big copper for laundry over the weekend. We were told it was known that she only did laundry on Mondays, she said she had to prepare for Monday. Then refused a horse & wagon for rations so the supplies had to be carried by 20 men. Besides she cut the potato ration from 20 to 10 baskets so there's no soup this evening. NCOs didn't go, they are waiting for transportation. Fellows are haying or are cooking their flour up, results are varied. Stevie seems to be the lucky one, a fair sized cake and 31 bannock buns. We got ours cooked by a woman, and flat cakes about 8 or 10 inches across, kind of rubbery but enough to fill a hole. We were last section for coffee this evening so it was 7:30 before we had supper of ersatz & meat sandwiches. Wind still blowing hard. Baroness is persistently awkward. Received 1/5 of a loaf today. News: not much on Russian front but they are on both sides of Köln and within 15 kilos Münster on the west fronts.

MAR. 3

Coffee & the last of our meat for breakfast. More trouble with the Baroness. She gave 8 baskets of spuds some turnips & carrots for evening soup but when it suddenly turned cold & snow thereby stopping the arbiet so she reneged on the vegs. Besides that she deprived us of the use of the large copper pot making it necessary to feed half the men at noon & half in the evening. We were second on fire again this AM so we had a big mess of spuds & wheat. Bates has an upset stomach. No sign of NCOs moving yet and we Privates won't move until after they go. It's about time we moved, things are getting tough again. Alternating snow flurries & sunshine. The first issue of soup served up to No. 3 section, the remaining 3 sections had to wait which included us. Issued with 1/5 of a loaf & a piece of liverwurst & marg. There was hell to pay when a couple of ducks limped home with broken legs. Also a couple of chickens turned up missing and there was something about a 60 lb pig astray. The Baroness was screaming mad, the jungle was stopped. Everyone herded to the vicinity of the 2 barns which put the gong on all buck-shee cooking for a while. Waited for soup until 7:30. Nearly froze! It was only spuds so we reinforced with 2 slices of bread. Wouldn't be surprised if they moved us now.

MAR. 4

German ersatz at 8:00 taken with a meat sandwich. Wind has gone down but snow & rain is the order of the day. No cooking today so stayed in bed until soup time. Horse meat, barley & spuds made a good soup. Unless something happens all remaining eating will be done this evening, a couple pieces of bread. Eddy is going on the bread packing detail for something to do. Jungle *(trading market)* started for a while this AM but change of guards canceled it. Brinkworth (Cpl.) had a sore tooth today but remedied it by the only string method. 6 sick men left at the other place pending transfer to Stalag came in this afternoon. They have been billeted in a sheep barn ever since. There is a rumor that the NCOs will be moving in the next 3 days. Wonder of wonders, soup came up 15 minutes ahead of time at noon and on time tonight. Had a sandwich before going to bed early tonight.

MAR. 5

Bread, German meat & coffee from the kitchen for breakfast. The coffee was barely warm which caused a big beef. The bread had a hard crust which broke another tooth out of my plate; I think I swallowed it this time. Cooked our spuds with Stevie's today thus saved time on the stove and ate about 8:30. Bought some saccharin this morning. Wind has gone down but still cold. Had a wash & a shave around noon. The Baroness discovered the fact that there was a pig missing. Consequently she ordered all families to lay off cooking for us. There was a one-fire jungle just outside of the barn that has gone unnoticed for some time. The soup came up around 2:30, the horse was tough. Eric is down trying to get some brew water & maybe some bread for soup. Anthony has gone down to the next village to see the Hauptmann *(German Capt.)* about Red Cross this morning without much luck, however he had Hess promise to phone various places to try to find some for us. Hess told him to go back in the morning but Anthony went back this afternoon. He came back with the good news, if we can find transport, there is a parcel a man waiting for us at Neubrandenburg. He has to try & bum a team & wagon off the Baroness. He is a good man on this job & will probably reach an agreement with her such as 150 arbeiters tomorrow. The loan fire got by for quite a while so it was very long before the little jungle was growing. The old posten *(watchman)* had to make sure all fires were out before he could go off duty; he did 2 hrs overtime. We had a hot sweet brew with our bread tonight. Word came around that Tony had secured the use of a truck for Red Cross.

MAR. 6

1 month on the road. We had hot coffee & bread for breakfast. Tony put us straight on the Red Cross situation. Apparently he had to see the Hauptmann last night again and found out that a POW relief station had been set up in Neubrandenburg by Red Cross and that the French have a truck which will haul parcels I.R.C. (International Red Cross) supplying the petrol. The Hauptmann said he has phoned the airfield to see if they could spare a plane but the Luftwaffe said they were sorry but they needed all their planes for war service. Then he told Anthony that the Serb, French & Canadian Vertrauensmen would go by train and meet the truck at the Relief Centre. Tony will go early tonight or early tomorrow. Cold at first this morning, cleared up around 11:30. Fires going outside again; the Baroness went past but didn't say anything. When Tony asked her for team & wagon last night, she said she was quite willing to cooperate but it was too far for her horses. Fires going all day. No spuds to boil. Soup is up at noon, had a brew before; coffee up at 4:30 1/5 of a loaf today. Tony gone to Neubrandenburg this morning. Maybe R.C. tomorrow. A late announcement by Tony to the effect that about 200 NCOs would be leaving at 8:00 in the morning. Tony is going to Neubrandenburg at 2 AM. This means that the NCOs won't receive the parcels in time. About 20 Limeys came in late this afternoon. They had been on the road 7 weeks.

MAR. 7

Up at 6:00 getting breakfast ready for Eddy We bought a can of salmon last night which we had on bread for breakfast. Bought another can this AM which we had on spuds. Peeled spuds for the kitchen for a while then went to the kitchen to peel turnips, carrots & parsnips & celery root. Soup at noon, a brew right after. Rumored that we will be moving tomorrow or next day. Bought a can of Bully which we are having this evening. We got spuds from a wagon unloading at the pig feed cooker. A posten raised hell but we got them eventually. When Anthony was talking to the Baroness in regards to the loss of livestock & ducks limping home with broken legs; she said that they were very rare English ducks; Anthony is supposed to have said that the men didn't care what nationality they were when the men were hungry. Anthony is still away. Baroness loaned a horse & wagon for rations today. Went up for soup seconds & a spud peeler but soup ran out 1 man ahead. 3 day's traveling rations in; 1 loaf per man, 1/3 block of marg. per man. We had a big scoff (*meal*) of spuds & Bully; now comes coffee & a piece of bread. May move tomorrow.

MAR. 8
Received orders to pack at 8:45. We received 1 loaf & 75 marg. for 3 days. Then 309 R.C. parcels were dished out haphazardly; 1 fellow getting 6 cans of sardines. Between 4 of us we lost 2 bags of coffee & 1 can of butter, 2 or 3 boxes of prunes, a box of salt. The first section through took a beating. Started at 11:00 hoofing it again; hit paved road at 11:40 walking is okay. At 11:50 passed Eugenienburg & had first break at 12:10. Reached Demmin at 12:50 leaving it behind at 1:20. Passed through Lindenhof at 3:10 & 25 minutes later, Pentz. We reached our billets at 4:25 having walked 23 kilos, feet are sore. Had a really good cup of tea, but spuds & brew from the kitchen pretty late. Had our fill of steamed spuds.

MAR. 9
Had breakfast of tea, bread & jam. Lined up at 8:30. Started off in groups of a hundred at 8:45 mostly on paved roads. Reached a place called Basepohl at 11:25 & passed through Stavenhagen between 11:55 and 12:30. Passed through Jürgenstorf at 1:45 and an hour later were at Rottmannshagen. At 3:10 we got to Zettemin where we went into billets having completed 25 kilos. The steamed spuds which were ready when we got there was nothing but pigswill including rotten spuds, cabbage leaves and spud peelings. Most of the fellows refused to take them so another batch was put on to steam. Hot water was ready however so we had a good cup of tea, bread, biscuits and jam. The farmer put a light in the barn for us but an air raid forced us to turn it out. My feet are very sore tonight! We were told we have 150 kilos to go tomorrow.

MAR. 10

Hot water came up at 6:30 so we had tea, bread and jam for breakfast. Windy with a light rain. Lined up at 8:30 and started at 8:35 over dirt roads. Hit Hungerstorf at 9:45 and Groß Giewitz at 10:55. Passed Rügeband at 1:10. Finally reached the fair city of Waren. It took us until 4:00 to reach our billets outside of this city, having marched 25 kilos again. Here we were told there was a new order out that there was no spuds or transportation for POWs. But the spud meter was handy to the barn so we got spuds for tomorrow. Eric bought a loaf for soap this morning. We had a couple of brews before it got dark. Evidently we stop over tomorrow here. Anthony still away.

MAR. 11

Brew up at 8:00. Pop Mason very sick during the night; so called sanitators; refused to get up and help him. We had a good stew of spuds, carrots, onions and BB. Then a brew at noon. A mess of creamed spuds and a brew, then soup. Washed hands face and feet, had a shave. Fixed the straps on my pack. Cordner asked if we preferred to riding on flat cars and despite probably discomfort decided on riding. Anthony finally re-joined us, apparently after quite an experience. He said there was lots of mail for us at Neubrandenburg which will be sent on to us when and if we ever get permanent billets again. Announced that we are going to II E Schwerin. And we walk no less. Sick go to II A tomorrow while we start on a day march of 20 kilos. The kitchen bought spuds from the pig meister for coffee. Duty section wouldn't peel them. Quite a few of the fellows are lousy. Rations tomorrow at Waren. It's approximately 70 kilos to Schwerin. Orders may be changed before we get there.

MAR. 12

Reveille at 6:00. Hot water at 6:30. Every man is carrying 3 or 4 spuds which he will peel at the end of the day's march just in case spuds are not available at our next stop. We were lined up at 8:20 but 2 missing lanterns had to be found before we could start. Lanterns finally turned up and we got under way at 8:50. Reached Warren again at 9:30 and passed through the town in 20 minutes. Passed Eldenholz at 10:35 and at 11:35 were skirting Binnenmüritz Lake. Passed Klink at 11:45 and stopped for lunch just outside of Sembzin.

621

We had an hour because bread picked up in Waren, was made (350g per day per man for 4 days), one slice than a loaf. At 1:50 passed Sietow and reached Lexow at 3:30 our billets for the night. Steamed spuds and hot water later was issued. Too late for soup tonight so we will have it in the morning.

MAR. 13

We had the soup at 6:00, pretty horrible stuff. Hot water came up soon after. Received the fall in order at 7:30, we were told we had 22 kilos to go. The cover-up men for those who have escaped are having quite a job today. Finally got started at 8:10 and by 8:50 we were passing Kisserow, an hour later we passed through Malchow. At 11:50 Alt. Schwerin was reached where we stopped for lunch. It started to rain while we were eating. At 1:15 we reached a place called Glashütte and at 1:50 Karow, where the wagon passed us carrying the cooks and materials for soups etc. so I guess there is no soup or hot water until late tonight. 3:30 we reached our day's billets called Kleine Wangetin. Raining heavy, blistered heel raising hell, walked 26 to 28 kilos today. Spuds and hot water finally came up. Farm belongs to Director of Police and a Nazi so there's no scrounging here. It's wet and miserable. Porridge came up in 2 or 3 lots and well after dark. Prices here high, 100 cigs for a small loaf of bread. Americans preceding up apparently well-heeled.

MAR. 14

Water came up late but we were lined up ready to go at 8:30, No. 6 section leading. Actually started at 8:45, a heavy mist cleared soon after. We hit paved roads at 9:05. At 10:30 Finkenwelter was reached and 11:25 Goldberg slipped to the rear. We reached Zidderick at 1:30 and went into our usual stable billets. Everything here is forbidden. Another fellow had his Red Cross rations pinched. Things are getting worse as we go along. We might be within 40 kilos of Schwerin our supposed destination.

MAR. 15

It was a long time before the gang settled down to sleep last night. The excitement and satisfaction of receiving the parcels, together with a plain strafing, an ack ack position in full view of our barracks kept everyone awake until the small hours of the morning. Had Eric busy today rigging up a first aid cabinet amply filled with goods filled from the American parcel. Have the highest praise for it. The American drive is getting closer and closer and today we are sure that the rumble that we can hear in the south and south-west must be the front line. Everyone include civvies and guards are sure that it is only a matter of days. Our party disposition took a great change with the coming of the parcels. Everyone is whistling, singing and talking about things other than food. No one really expects to evacuate here simply because there isn't many places to move to. With the Russians at Leipzig and Americans at Magdeburg and Halle, the south is practically cut off. The drive past Hamburg cuts us off from Denmark. The only possible way is by boat to that country and when that becomes necessary the war will be over. We get a wonderful view of the Baltic Sea from our windows nearly every morning. I can see a convoy of 5 or 6 ships passing. The past 2½ year vision of starting for home seems pretty close to a reality now. It seems to be a question whether we be here at the finish or if the advancing Yanks will take us in.

MAR. 16

Reveille at 6:00. Hot water came up soon after, we had tea, cold pancakes and jam for breakfast. Issued with ½ loaf of bread with a promise of more to come. Cloudy and cool today. Lined up at 8:25 and started marching at 8:30. We passed Below at 8:55 and Kläden at 10:00, we hit paved roads at 10:10 which are much better than cobblestones for walking on. Passed Borkow at 12:25 and another large town, Dabel? I missed the name, at 1:24. We arrived at a place called Stietan after struggling through 6 kilometres of sand road. Billeted in a big draughty barn with no straw. No water and no spuds, in fact nothing. We were supposed to come only 17 kilos today but they didn't count 6 kilos through bush this morning and 6 kilos through sand this afternoon. Mighty tired, dirty and hungry. Blistered heel is raising seven varieties of hell. Eric, Day and Bates trying to scrounge hot water for tea. Charlie can't control his bread eating so trying a new system. 1 man rations bread daily for 4.

MAR. 17

Hot water came up at 6:15, issued with 100g of margarine per man. Going to a place called Brüel where there will be another split-up. Raining this morning, lined up at 7:30 started at 8:35, traveled over a bush road passed Hobrow at 9:10, hit Weitendorf and paved roads at 11:00 and arrived Brüel at 11:40. The separation took place right in the street. We are with the 200 Group and are crowded in a very small barn. Soup coming up with hot water later. Bread issued this evening. We are supposed to have 22 kilos to go tomorrow. 3 days' more marching to a place called Scherenburg. Looks like working parties again. Other party of 100 Anthony included, going to a bush working party 10 kilos away. He said he would write to Geneva when he got settled. Crowded in here tonight. May be better when we get out in the country again! French Canadian Q.M.S. (*Quartermaster Sergeant*) in charge of this group. Reorganization in progress. We obtained 2 ½ bags of flour recently so Q.M. traded 1 bag for 63 loaves of bread. Eric managed to buy a loaf off a civvy for cigarettes.

MAR. 18

Hot water came up at 6:15 and lined up at 7:45. Start at 7:50. According to information given by the guards we march 22 kilos today, 18 tomorrow and 8 the next day. We passed through Tempgin at 9:30 and Bibow at 9:40, Neuhof at 10:25 and Dänelow at 10:50 and then Hohen Viecheln at 1:30 and Bad Kleinen at 1:40 are small places. At 2:55 we reached Gallentin and Zickhusen at 3:15. Here we waited for an hour until a barn was found for billets. We received steamed spuds and hot water for supper. There is rumors of another split coming up soon. Came 28 or 30 kilos today instead of 22. Air raid tonight all lanterns and lights doused.

MAR. 19

Lined up at 8:10. Men think there will be a split today so there is plenty of jockeying around for position, friends sticking pretty close together. Actual start at 8:20. Slow pace today, made only 3.5 kilos up to 9:10. Passed Alt-Meteln at 9:30 and arrived Moltenow at 11:28 where were informed of the coming split. Passed Mühlen Eichsen at 11:35. Stopped for lunch at 12:00 where 75 men taken off head of column. At 1:00 the remainder of us started on 6 kilo march to the night's billets. For first time my pack was in the wagon. Arrived at Rüting Kries Schoenberg, Mecklenburg at 1:00 and billeted in the usual barn. Steamed spuds, hot water and porridge coming up soon. Heard of 24 man bush party, some think not enough to eat, some think short hours better than farm. I am not deciding that question. Tomorrow we go 8 kilos to Grevesmühlen for split into working parties. Porridge late and served by lantern.

MAR. 20

Water up early. Going to Grevesmühlen for split. Lined up at 7:30, 2 men missing, we saw them go yesterday afternoon. Guards are mighty riled. We had to clean up barn and yard before leaving. Finally got started at 8:05 and passed Upahl at 8:30. Arrived Grevesmühlen at 9:45. Managed to hit party of 24 for bush party. Registered and inspected for lice. 5 out of the 24 lousy, a good average considering we haven't had our clothes off for nearly 45 days. Trapper White was surprised to find that he had them. Eric and Bates and I escaped the pests. While waiting for inspection a French sanitator heated some water for us. Andy Renny went with NCOs. Marched away Lager. Left town at 1:00 and arrived at village of Hamberge at 1:45. Billets new, no lights, wood, or water. Elected Vertrauensman (Trustee). Rations include 5 lbs of spuds per man per week, 280g per man. Rations less than Stalag rations. Raising hell but getting nowhere. Men must go to work at 7:00 in morning with no rest and clean up. Red Cross may come when our names reach II E Schwerin. Everyone disgusted.

MAR. 21

Merely skimmed milk for breakfast, those who had saved bread and tea lucky. Saved my milk for noon. Made a couple of shelves. Complaining to Germans about lack of lights, wood, water, palaises, blankets, latrine facilities, too little bread, meat, spuds etc. Unteroffizier left for dinner, locking us in and stayed away 3 hours. Complained about that. 5 lousy men are having quite a time boiling their clothes and taking baths. Forester said Feldwebel seeing about Red Cross. Soup was good but not enough. Washing water a problem. The little Posten is a nuisance.

MAR. 22

Tried latrine boxes for night latrine, no good, leaked all over the floor, a hell of a mess. Work in bush seems alright, no set amount yet. Everyone complaining about lack of food. 5 men still trying to boil their clothes. Complained of lack of blankets, was told they had to come from Russian party on other side of bush, guards are all dead-heads. The little squirt is a damned nuisance. ¼ of a pail of cereal mixed with mild comprises breakfast for 24 men. Men refusing to work because they are hungry. Germans threatening but still men won't work as the Hun expects them to. Feldwebel came so complained about everything, principally lack of Red Cross and inadequate rations. No increase in bread but may get more spuds later. May get lights next week. Sick stay in or go to Grevesmühlen. Red Cross may be next week, seeing about more in Neubrandenburg. Had more trouble with the guards, they were butting in when I was speaking to Feldwebel, told guard to keep quiet, that I was speaking to Feldwebel, little guard raised plenty hell. Gary Enouy hit with rifle butt today, Horsborgh hit twice and nearly shot. Complained about it. We had a discussion tonight on rackets and community cooking. By 3 fellows sawing wood Sunday for a neighbor, we can get extra 50 kilos of spuds. By paying 1 cigarette for 1 Red Cross bag of spuds, we can get 2 a night.

MAR. 23

Too much work, especially water carrying to this job. Asked Foresters wife, in charge of our rationing to give us our stuff uncooked, as we need sugar. We are pretty sure she is using our sugar for herself and using saccharin in our stuff. Tried to have 4 men stay in for a good clean up but it was "no soap". New straw comes in today, but no palaises or blankets. Trying to get a pair of hair clippers. Another discussion on rackets tonight. All rackets to be pooled and go to kitchen.

MAR. 24

Lord what a spot. Short rations, 23 men complaining about conditions. German yelling about poor work in the bush, water carrying, ration carrying, cleaning billets, cleaning the yard, complaining to controllers, arguing all day with Germans, getting nowhere. A day's rations for 24 men would leave 6 people hungry, if they ate it at all. Rackets are very poor because of the cigarette shortage. Collected 128 cigs and 1 bar of soap for pool. No lights as yet. A ration cut coming up for all of Germany. 4 men going to neighbours to cut wood for 100 kilos of extra spuds tomorrow. Wood getting scarce, Forester says to carry it from the bush.

MAR. 25

Everyone busy heating water in copper outside for baths, going in groups of 5. Everyone trying to wash and mend clothing. No milk today which means a meager breakfast. Dewulf and I went down to foresters to get something extra. Dewulf lied so well, we got 2½ pails of spuds, ½ pail of carrots and a loaf of bread. Everyone peeled the vegs before lock up. We are complaining all the time about short rations but I think it is useless. Lights coming in next week, will believe it when I see them. We have enough wood for tomorrow.

MAR. 26

Spud and carrot soup for breakfast with no salt, saved some of mine for dinner which consists of roasted mangles, 1 slice of bread (thin) and warmed over German coffee. Trying to get a table for kitchen, no go. Latrine needs fixing, also washroom, billet roof leaks like sieve, plenty of work around here. A Pole is bringing spuds to Larry Emory in the bush, it is a big help. Boys carried quite a bit of wood in tonight. Tempers are short, everyone hungry and beefing is rife. No word of my going to Schwerin for parcels yet. Bates sick with stomach today. Tried to borrow scrub brush from Forester's wife, but she refused.

MAR. 27

Decided to try scrubbing billets, settled for mopping with a piece of sacking tied to a pole. Controller came and said Red Cross isn't at Schwerin yet and saw no reason why I should go. Pointed out that we needed medical supplies, shoe repairs, etc. etc. etc. and he said not many English speaking people there and no supplies. Heard that Sgt. Maj. Martin was Neubrandenburg, is being investigated. Controller admitted rations too low to work on but he couldn't do anything about it. Lights coming this week. One 25 watt in dining room and one 15 watt in bedroom. Received 7 blankets and 12 towels. The men brought enough spuds from bush to equal 2½ days' rations. Pole won't take anything for them, says we haven't anything to give. He is bringing peas tomorrow and eggs Thursday. Skimmed milk again today. Men are beefing about being hungry. Germans beefing about poor work. They lock our shoes up at night now.

MAR. 28

Still no trip to Schwerin. Everyone eating roasted mangles. Everyone hungry all the time and consequently are hungry.

MAR. 29

Unteroffizier is going to try to get some hair cutting tools today. We haven't had haircuts for 2 months. Cleaned latrines today. Rained and roof leaked copiously. Steward stayed in sick today. No sign of Red Cross or mail yet. The grouchy guard said he didn't like it here and the war would be over soon. Mangles are our principle food now.

MAR. 30

Good Friday. Everyone thinking of hot cross buns. Boot inspection at 9:00. Everyone roasting mangles. Grub situation critical. No lights, blankets or Red Cross yet. Nothing to do at night but to sit in dark and talk. Had a lice inspection by German sanitator; Higgins has them.

MAR. 31

One sick and Higgins in with lice. Unteroffizier said I would have to go to the bush and Higgins do my work. Higgins refused and went to work. Had an argument with Unteroffizier about it later, contending that Higgins couldn't possibly boil his clothes and still do work around billets. Fellows came in with bad news, working hours increased on Tuesday. Still no lights.

APR. 1

Sewed a little on my pack today. Conversation centered around food, plenty of speculation on Red Cross supplies, mail and the war. Had boiled mangles syrup and hot milk for dinner. Farmer moved all his mangles but fellows managed to beat him to ¼ of them between loads. Boys seem certain of longer hours on Tuesday. Higgins refusing still, to stay in for delousing and do my work. Another argument with "grouchy" German guard again about it. Pho stayed in sick today.

APR. 2

Had a break today. Lots of fellows around. Higgins deloused himself, a hazardous undertaking. Arrival of Red Cross uncertain. Ernie helped me carry rations today.

APR. 3, MON.

Another holiday and it rained all day. French barbers didn't come so maybe had better buy violins. Forester wanted 4 men to dig potato pits but it rained all day. Have four men for sick parade tomorrow.

APR. 4

Quite a due this morning when Unteroffizier took Bate(r)'s pulse this morning and sent him to work. 2

for dentist and 2 for doctor. Left at 8:00 for Grevesmühlen. Went for rations early this morning and had to dig potato pits. Charlie Stocks, the cook, is plenty mad. Told Charlie I would dig them and for him to return to the kitchen. Received a piece of cake when finished. Just cleaning tables when I had to go and fill pits with spuds, received bacon sandwich this time. Rainy and squally today. Two men got 3 days' excused work. 2 for dentist go back Thursday. We are planning a secret entrance for night scrounging. Another ration cut coming soon. Hear that Hanover has fallen to U.S. so probably on the move again. We can see the Baltic Sea very good from here.

APR. 5

3 men in on excused work period. Heard that the Americans near Hanover and Muenster, big push on. Russians not moving much. Don't think we can move now, except to Denmark. Fellows getting fed up, no food, but they aren't doing much in the bush. Soup is getting almighty thin. Big air raid on factory town near Lübeck. Allied planes strafed air field on edge of bay in sight of billets today. Unteroffizier gone on 3-day leave. Little Grouchy in charge and is a changed man. Lock up at 8:00 tonight.

APR. 6

Jones and Hazeldine went to dentist. Rackets very poor around here. Another cut in rations coming soon, even the German civvies are complaining now. Heard today that Hanover has definitely fallen. Had an egg for breakfast, unusual these days. Roof still leaks. Civvies and guards say war will be over in 3 weeks. Volkssturm getting their uniforms today. Food main topic of conversation these days.

APR. 7

Was told that lights will be in soon. Same old story, stall, stall, stall. Pho and Dewulf in on excused duty. They don't seem to like the way I do things. Forester still yelling about more work in the bush but nothing done about it yet.

APR. 8

Controller here said I could go to Schwerin next week maybe Tuesday or Wednesday. Scrubbed out billets, some job. Lights probably in Monday. Complaining to the Germans about coffee and sugar. Received extra spuds from the Poles.

APR. 9

French men came up and cut our hair, brought some bread and said they would send more. The Big Four, are getting my nerves. May have to go out tomorrow. 2 men on light work. Ran out of cigs today. Cigarette fund useless so returned them to Donors. Poles for power line came today. May have lights tomorrow night. Feel miserable tonight, jumped Pho for no particular reason except that he gets on my nerves. He is one of The Big Four.

APR. 10

Big item of the day. Feldwebel brought the news that 3 car loads of Red Cross bombed at Schwerin on Sat., which means no Red Cross. Will have to try and buy vegetables from farms. Hydro commenced work on light, two poles up, billets almost strung. Heavy Raid to the west about eleven last night. Overheard Pho and Dewulf discussion the way I run things. Decided not to say anything because everyone miserable enough now. Hear that English and

Americans driving fast have taken Bremen, Hanover, Kassel; Russians have taken Vienna. Majority of natives say 2 or 3 weeks will see the end. God are we hoping.

APR. 11

Six men went to Grevesmühlen to see doctor this AM. Went for rations and Forester's wife said she saw 6 Red Cross ships, Red Cross parcels and 18 new Red Cross trucks for distribution being unloaded at Lübeck yesterday. Am right out of smokes now so maybe it is best to quit. Someone pinched 8 fags out of the German electrician's tool bag and is he burnt up. Put up another light pole this afternoon, may have lights tomorrow night. Rumors of another evacuation coming up. If a fellow could smoke, he wouldn't feel the hunger so much.

APR. 12

Informed of the ration cut this AM. From 4½ loaves for 24 men to 4; sugar, syrup, meat, marg. cut proportionately. No milk today, so very slim breakfast tomorrow. Heard that Bremen and Hanover gone. Americans 30 kilos from Hamburg and still moving fast. "Grouchy" left for hospital this AM. No one sorry to see him go. Food crisis is either steal or starve, if caught stealing maybe shot. Can't bank on Red Cross supplies coming.

APR. 13

Great news. I go to Schwerin tomorrow 2 men to pick up Red Cross parcels. Everybody jubilant.

APR. 14

Left early with 2 men for Grevesmühlen and picked up 2 French men and 1 English men to help us carry parcels. Red Cross warehouse in Schwerin packed with parcels, came away with 48. Stored them at Grevesmühlen, phoned for more men to party. We carried enough for an issue 4 kilometers to party. Germans refused to allow issue, must wait for German from Grevesmühlen. Men sore because we have to wait until tomorrow.

APR. 15, SUN.

It was a long time before the gang settled down to sleep last night. The excitement and satisfaction of receiving R.C. parcels together with the excitement of seeing a lone plane and a Ack Ack gun engaged in a dual a short distance from the billets kept everyone awake until the small hours of the morning. Had Eric busy today, rigging up a temporary cabinet for the R.C. medical supply. It's American supply and earns the highest praise. The American drive is coming closer and closer and all day we have been hearing a steady rumble from the south and southwest, which we are sure is the West front. Everyone including civvies and guards are sure that it is only a matter of days before the war is over or the Americans are here. No one expects another evacuation because the Russians being at Leipzig and the Americans at Magdeburg and Halle eliminates the possibility of a southward move while the drive on Hamburg is fast eliminating the possibility of a Denmark move. The only alternative open is by boat to Denmark. It's surprising the change of disposition of the fellows since we received parcels last night and everyone is singing, whistling or acting pleasant.

APR. 16

Dysentery has its grip on me again and Epsom salts is as scarce as hen's teeth. Not feeling so good these days despite the Red Cross food we are eating now. Rackets are starting to come in so we found it advisable to form a price list. Very good news today. It has been my intention since Friday to return to Schwerin as soon as possible to try for some more Red Cross, in case the war ends soon. This morning I was notified by the Unteroffizier that there was four parcels a man for us at Grevesmühlen which we could collect tomorrow. This settles one worry on my mind at least, that of having R.C. to see way through after the fighting stops. Another surprise was the stimmt item that the Americans were only 60 kilos from Berlin, a German report which means that they are only half that distance. The Russians are supposed to be only 50, unconfirmed. Having trouble persuading the Germans that a man doesn't have to have a fever to be sick, no go. Kid bringing spuds to the kitchen. Much speculation regarding the possibility of our evacuating again, if we do, where and how?

APR. 17

Had to go to Grevesmühlen for parcels. Wagon cost 24 Marks. Cy Dervuef says RR yards being strafed plenty there. The little old guard got a shock when he tangled with our new Hauptvertrauensmann, and Frenchie, good man for all that. Ordered to issue second of our 48 parcels this evening which apparently is solely for the purpose of rebuilding us after a long march, then all this new shipment is for April and May, another parcel should be issued tomorrow. Apparently the people this shipment of parcels was for can't be located so it is being issued to anyone in this area; it's kind of tough for the boys caught in the near cut-off of the south. Old guard got another shock when I reported the Unteroffizier taking it upon himself to decide if men should see the Stabarzt *(staff doctor)*. Got back around noon to learn that the U.O. had rousted Pho to work. Pho's fault for not sticking to one complaint. Feldwebel came and said more parcels coming Monday. Wants to racketeer with us for soap. Control came this afternoon and everything I asked for he said to forget it as we wouldn't be needing it. Said he didn't think we would evacuate. Kept talking about after the war and cigarettes received from his good friend Cordner; also said he is coming to Canada immediately after the war period. Said Schwerin would go in 3 days, and said that there was much dead and damaged in Grevesmühlen from strafing. Heavy rain, the place leaks like a sieve. 2 hours sleep in 2 nights.

APR. 18

Am expecting the Hauptvertrauensmann up today. Slit trench must be finished by Friday. Eating good these days and sure notice the difference. The expected visitor arrived and as a result of speaking to the U.O. we got another parcel this evening. That is 3 in 5 days. Frenchie advised against hording as he thinks the stomach is the only safe place for it. He said Hitler is still alive and living in a hunting castle not far from here. Raised a stink over leaky roof and is going to try and get some sacking for palaises. Forester came up wanting four men for unloading wagon, got nobody because 2 men are occupied with business. He went away raving. Neighbours starting to racketeer. Stewie got 1½ loaves for 1 swan soap. Frenchie stayed for supper and until parcels were issued at seven. Eric and I have a large American Red Cross carton over one half full of canned goods in the stores; we don't believe in hording, but we make it last; some believe in eating it as soon as possible. Next issue will be on Sunday.

APR. 19

2 yrs and 8 months today. Forester's wife pretty sore this morning. They cut off all extra vegetables and the milk as retaliation but they even cut off our official ration of vegs. which gives us a legitimate beef. Dug the first corner of the slit trench next door neighbor thought it a great joke. Said she would stay in the house if there was a raid. Hauptvertrauensmann came again bringing a bag of peas, 23 wooden shoes and some shoe repairs. Said Russians were 18 kilos from Berlin, have taken Vienna and surrounded Liepzig; Americans are 15 kilos from Hamburg. Against this is the German news that the Russians have been pushed back to Schneidemühl. Frenchie can't do much about cut of extras but will raise cane if official ration isn't forthcoming. He is going to Schönbeck to see about R.C. and clothing. Decided that Hopkins is about the worst beefer I've met. He beefs about everything. Realized an ambition this evening when we saw 7 Spitfires close enough to see the markings. Spent ½ hour digging steps into the slit trench, came back and found the Dixon had dug them out. No profit planes probably strafing RR at Grevesmühlen; they set fire to something on other side of bush.

APR. 20

U.O. has great ideas about slit trench, he wants to put a roof on it. Wasted a lot of time making a pillow for Charlie. Rations coming in again. Fresh vegetables fine but on a reduced rate. Air raids all day, they don't bother sounding the all-clear anymore. Six or seven Spitfires came in this morning and strafed targets in or near Grevesmühlen; ack ack shrapnel came down; bullets could be heard to ricochet. They came pretty close today. Charlie got quite a scare when he thought shells were hitting the shack; Jimmy Taylor merely walking around in wooden shoes. Bill Rattray dug hole and emptied the latrine in time I thought it would take to dig the hole: five boxes. Am afraid the split graven won't be finished for tonight. Eating pretty good these days. Fixed my bed and started a grub cupboard. I think something is brewing among the gang. Eric planning a big feed for Sunday. Charlie had a run-in with Pho and his gang tonight over potatoes and bannocks. French Vertrauensmann brought nails, studs, heel plates and 24 pr. of wooden shoes. Quite a go-getter, this Lad.

APR. 21

Worked awhile on the Split Graven but not much. Managed to have a fair dinner each day, simply by saving a little of my evening soup, and frying it with the R.C. meats. Raining this morning so the gang didn't go to work until ten o'clock. Milk hasn't come back yet but fresh vegs are increasing to their former quantity. A plane strafed a boat out on the sea this afternoon and the boat had a pretty strong answer. Held a business meeting this evening and ate a lot of dirt, as did Charlie. Many complaints all boiling down to the fellows thinking Charlie and I aren't working hard enough. That coming from those who admit laying around the bush all day. They claimed the billets weren't clean enough, not enough water hauled, etc. despite the fact that Charlie and I work from 5:30 in the morning until nearly 8:00 at night. There were some pretty small dirty remarks passed by certain people which demonstrated the smallness of some minds. Decided on having mashed spuds for tomorrow supper. Boys were very noisy later on, some making shelves etc. The guards yelled for us to quieten down and everyone yelled back. Then Stewie played the mouth organ or sang while I played the drum sticks.

APR. 22

Started the day, not counting arbeit with a porridge, brew, bread, biscuits, cheese for breakfast. The porridge was a week's savings of rations. Men bathing weather turned miserable. Had M & V with a little soup saved from last night, then our old and not recently seen Stalag pudding with a klim and malted milk sauce and a good cup of tea. A very good meal. By a dint of tall maneuvering and pot borrowing from neighbors, we had a good feed of mashed spuds and fried Spam, finished with bread and jam and tea. Actually uncomfortable when we finished. Early this morning I met the Unteroffizier and he gave me hell about the noise last night. Said he was going to lock up at six and everyone must be in bed by 9. On roll call he really raised his voice. Gave Stewie hell, called us all schweinerei and me double schweinerei. He meant what he said. Locked up at 6 and looked in to see if we were in bed at nine. Split graven not finished yet. Recent days marked by plenty of air activity featuring strafing of Grevesmühlen.

APR. 23
Scrubbed the dining room this morning. Very little activity although a rumble heard all day which might have been the fronts. Investigated marg and meat rations; also asked once more for a load of wood which I didn't get and probably won't. Charlie made bannocks today which were a great success but small in quantity. Nothing much else doing. Sanitary Unteroffizier came and left us practically undisturbed. Am expecting the French Vertrauensmann.

APR. 24
Scrubbed bedroom. Very nice day. Air alarm going continually. Village crowded with army who are laying down a communications system. Last night a lone raider dropped 2 bombs on Grevesmühlen which nearly lifted the hut off its foundation, big raid to the northwest. Forester's family more friendly now. Air raids started early again today; climaxing around noon when 6 to 7 Spitfires attacked four ships of various sizes out in the harbor. Saw one shot down and the pilot came down by parachute; don't give him much chance for his life, will probably hung or shot by civvies as soon as he lands. Some of our Red Cross cans have shrapnel holes, Hopkins margarine had the piece of metal still in.

APR. 25
The Spitfire pilot who was shot down yesterday afternoon, turned up here after lock-up. He is a Dutchman in the RAF and he and 3 others attacked an air base a few kilos from here. He was rear guard while 3 other went down to attack. They destroyed a 6-motored bomber. Then he was ordered down. A flack shell struck his motor, he managed to gain enough height to use his parachute. The first thing we asked him was news. Both Russians and Americans in Berlin. Bremen surrounded, Hamburg next, Vienna taken. Then someone got the idea that he was a phoney. Despite divided opinion, we gave him choc, cigs, coffee and lunch and talked until late. He explained lots of things we were wondering about. This morning he seemed worried because he didn't shave before breakfast. The expected orders came around 8:30 and the last I saw of him he was trudging down the road with 2 guards behind him. The next village was strafed today. 6 men and one woman killed. The Aviator left a pr. of leggings behind which I think I will get made into a

purse or a pocket book out of them. This pilot was in Brussels when it was freed. He said there was millions of flags and people were dancing in the streets. People of occupied Germany consider themselves freed people also and that our boys pretty good.

APR. 26

Feeling pretty tough with a cold; very little strafing today. A fast new plane seen in the vicinity is causing a lot of argument. No wood wagon; no kettle; no hot plate, in fact, we get the same answer, "you won't need them!" Issued parcels this evening, the last; trying to get down to Grevesmühlen to see about more, no go yet. Everyone (Ger) thinks it is almost over. The German Leute are in a state of waiting and of expectancy. Couldn't go to Grevesmühlen because Unteroffizier said he wasn't sure if the hauptvertrauensmann was back yet. Would like to know if there are any more parcels coming. German people ordered to stop using motored vehicles. Another ration cut on the 29th; trying to pick up a little German lingo for personal reasons. I'm a bearcat for this chocolate; scoffed nearly two bars this evening. Smokey this morning; visibility very poor.

APR. 27

Smokier today; reminds me of bush fire season back home. Cold is hanging on; sore throat and feeling tough. Length of time for the duration of the war among prisoners and people ranges from Saturday to 2 months. People are asking why the fighting continues as Germany has lost everything now. I have lots to do, but haven't the energy to get at it. Must make start some time. Feldwebel came this afternoon and acted very mysteriously and secretly. On the quiet he told Charlie and I that the war was practically over. The Russians are driving on the north front again, coming this way and Goering and party have flown the coup. Not listening to any requests or complaints. Have a feeling he has told us all he knew. Very quiet around here today; no air activity. Burnt a batch of prunes this PM; practically ruining Higgins' enamel pot. Unteroffizier said Feldwebel was here last night and said that the Hauptvertrauensmann has gone to Schwerin for more Red Cross and we will probably receive word to go to Grevesmühlen and collect same tomorrow or Monday. I wonder how the news will break here; feel like letting things go here now. Started making a drain for the latrine; Forester's kid came up this evening and said there was an armistice between England, America and Germany, but the Russians were still coming. Maybe it is closing at last.

APR. 28

Had four sick; myself, Charlie, Eric and Dixon (cleaning in today). Pithouse went to the dentist. Complete cleaning throughout and it rained. Asked Forester's wife for rackets and got ¾ bread for 1/3 box raisins. Then I bought 5 eggs for 5 cigs from a Pole. Eric went out and brought in over 2 loaves and 2 eggs. A pretty good day. This "Waffenstillstand" is causing a lot of argument. The stories are varied. (1) The Americans and English have stopped coming, but the Russians are coming fast. (2) A 3-day conference in San Francisco, all countries but France, Germany and Japan represented; Russia representing Poland. (If so, it's not an armistice, but only a prelude to an ultimatum to German). (3) German troupes fighting on the West front have about turned and gone to the Russian front. (This sounds extremely unlikely.) All these stories are interspersed with reports that Ribbentrop is in London; that the Nazi party has flown; that the conference broke up because Russia demanded too much. Regardless of that, everyone says that the war is finished. We have been warned by U.O. that it would be wise to keep our kit semi-packed as we may hit the road any time. Troupes are concentrating in this area and getting short of billets; may lose ours. Red Cross is also occupying our minds these days, but the U.O. said that there is another load in Grevesmühlen and we will probably be notified to come and collect any time. Bombing or explosions all day today and the air raid alarm went tonight which means the so-called armistice just isn't. In any event, I must work on my pack tomorrow.

APR. 29

I guess the armistice, if ever in force, is now cancelled. Heavy bombing or cannonading heard all night. About +15 to eight this morning there was a pretty heavy strafing raid in Grevesmühlen direction. Cloudy and overcast early this morning but it seems to be clearing up now (11:40). Young guard watching pretty close here this morning. Went for rations and had a drink of German Schnapps from the Forester's wife. Heard what I think is the straight version of this armistice story. There was only a weapons pause to allow an ultimatum to be issued, to which the Germans said no, as the fighting continues and everything goes. Russians are coming fast. There is no more German radio so most people are getting their news from English or American stations. Could finish any day. Worked all afternoon on my pack; there is more than a hint of more walking coming up. Trying my darnedest to get down to Grevesmühlen to see about more Red Cross, but all I get is the old stall off. Am getting tired of all these dirty hints and cracks some of the fellows are always making. There was a big strafing raid on or near Grevesmühlen in which ten or more planes circled into the attack, time after time. A Frenchman said the war will be finished next Sunday but we have been hearing those kind of predictions for weeks now. Feeling miserable today so am keeping quiet for fear of answering some people out of tone and offending them. God what a set up.

APR. 30

Saw Mosquitoes today, quite a plane. Worked on my pack nearly all day because I had a hunch. Feldwebel came about noon and said we would have to evacuate this place this week or it would be too late as the Russians are this side of Rostock and coming fast. The Americans or English are 40 kilos from here, just west of Lübeck and they were staying there until the Russians joined them. If we move we will walk to Lübeck the area of which is rumored to be proclaimed to be neutral territory. The U.O. says we will probably move in a day or two and we would have to keep off the highways because of the strafing. The Forester's kid came up and said we couldn't get out through Lübeck because the Allies had closed that gap. He said he was going to Lübeck tomorrow and if Russies came here he would stay there; if the Americans got here first, he would come back. 2 loads of evacuees left this village today. Trucks and trailers have been streaming down the highway a little north of here. A little later the U.O. and Feldwebel met in the kitchen and said that the latest news had the Americans were in Schwerin and therefore practically here. Trying my darnedest to get some more Red Cross before we have to move. Activity increasing around here; things are getting hot. When I asked for remainder of R.C. food in stores he said it would be a cinch that we would be here until tomorrow morning at least, therefore wait until then. He said I could go to Grevesmühlen to see about R.C. tomorrow and he went to see if it was a holiday tomorrow. Excitement pretty high here now; opinions variate regarding our moving. Generally, belief is if Russians come first we will move, if Americans come first we won't. Needlessly to say all civvies are hoping the Americans come first. Things are pretty uncertain again and the only solution is to be ready for anything all the time. Have decided that Pho is just an agitator with the main idea of causing trouble. Asked if tomorrow is a holiday, he asked the Forester and the answer was yes.

MAY 1
Guard came at 6 this morning and said "Arbeit Heute," the Forester had changed his mind. 3 men for Stabartz and 2 for Zahnarzt and myself for business went to Grevesmühlen today. Day stayed in my place which means 8 men off. Conditions portrayed in Grevesmühlen indicates complete disorganization of the nation; evacuees from both fronts going in opposite directions; highways and streets congested to a stand still; evacuees sitting on their meager belongings in the middle of the street; soldiers wandering aimlessly around town. Yesterday and today all stores sold goods without ration coupons and the queues were long and waited hours. Enouy went to the dentist and he said "never mind the teeth, where are the Americans?" There is talk of evacuating if the Russians come too close. Found out there will be no more Red Cross. If we don't evacuate we must raise 2 white flags and our own flag, if possible. French wanted us to move down there, with them. Hear that Hitler found dead and Mussy shot by his own men. Everyone hoping Americans come here. Saw typhoon rocket bombers in action from about 3 this afternoon until lock up time; said action getting close and interesting. Some of the fellows hit the split graben today. Prisoners (Russians from Wismar) pulled into the dorf this evening where they are staying the night. Eric made three or four good deals today, for bread, bacon and eggs. Ration woman and son said that, "Mussolini was better than that Hitler," which means something. Unteroffizier asked us if he could lock up tonight. Drew everything out of the stores, pack nearing completion. Russians in Rostock, Americans not yet in Lübeck. If the Americans drive for Wismar, we won't walk; if they drive north for Lübeck it means evacuation. The German intention being to get us beyond reach of the Russians and within the American sphere of operations. I give it until 10:30 Saturday morning.

MAY 2

Great Day. Apparently, we are cut off with either Americans or English at Wismar. We had 5 sick this AM and the U.O. only laughed, but rest had to go to work. U.O. went to Grevesmühlen and returned in a fury around 11:00, packed up; said he had to report to Schönbeck; told us to be ready to move tomorrow morning. Said "Auf Wiedersehen" and took a powder. Russians down in the barn started a jungle. Ober Gefreiter in charge. Worked on my pack nearly all day. At 3 Gefreiter locked three or four of us in and left 3 out; then went to the bush for wood. People of the village are streaming to town buying articles they have been denied for 10 years. At 3:10, a woman coming back from Grevesmühlen told us the Americans were at Wismar and we were surrounded. She was happy because it wasn't Russians; needless to say, we were pleased to hear it. The men came from the bush soon after. Soldiers have been going by all day and they go out of their way to be pleasant. The rumors that Hitler was dead was confirmed this afternoon. He went completely insane, then shot himself. At 5 a woman reported the Yanks at Grevesmühlen. At 6:15 white flags appeared on a windmill a few meters north of here; then another 2 appeared a few minutes later on a house further down the road. We get the news from soldiers on their way home. We had mashed spuds, bacon and eggs, toast, jam and tea for supper. Apparently, we have had it. This village is going to fly a white flag soon. This morning an U.O. took a couple of Russians who were talking to us; the Russian just scratched his head and kept walking. A nurse passing said she had been a prisoner of Hitler for 6 years; a passing U.O. on his way home said the Americans were just taking all decorations of the soldiers, stamping them and sending them home. We are expecting them anytime now. There will be no sleep this night. Getting my pack ready. Women having trouble with toilet papers. Personally, I can't quite believe it. It's a toss-up whether we lock the guards up or they lock us up tonight; kid told us that the white flag was up in Grevesmühlen and the SS shot 5 men who helped raise it. Soon after there was 5 or 6 flags up.

MAY 3

ACTUALLY FREE. Things pretty quiet this morning; young guard went to Grevesmühlen for orders. Then while he was away, the other two guards took

all their arms and equipment down to the Burgomeister, he said "get that
_-_ trash out of here." "Throw it in the pond," so they did. 5 men went to
Grevesmühlen this morning for bread. Went for rations this morning; met
an air force O.G. with a car radio; he said Americans were at Lübeck and
Wismar and a news broadcast would be on in half an hour. A Feldwebel
doffed his hat to us and said, "Bitte Sehr, Amerikans but Russians nicht." He
said he was going to stay in Wismar and be taken by the Yanks, but Russians
came in too, so he is heading well into American-held territory. We are practically free now; men all over town getting eggs and other fresh eatables. Old
Forester said that they will probably feed us well now. Demolition going on
at the airport north of here. Must try to get hold of a small Mauser automatic
pistol. Had rye cereal, toast, eggs and tea for breakfast. Burgomeister has a flag
already here. A woman tried to bum a carrot off of us when we were coming
back with rations. Guards left around noon. (2:00) cutting wood; Charlie
peeling spuds; bus arrived manned by armed Frenchmen and 2 Americans.
Packed in a hurry; went to Grevesmühlen escorted to arms dumping ground
and armed ourselves. Got a 7.65mm automatic pistol and some souvenirs.
Excitement high. Eric Rowat, LaPierre, White and myself obtained upstairs
suite in well to do house, living room, 2 bedrooms, bathroom, kitchen.
All furnishings complete. Had bacon, eggs, coffee, strawberries and cream
for supper. German prisoners streaming in. Yanks going through steadily.
I dreamt of this day for 2 years, 8 months. All Germany taken over, but a
strip 100 miles long by 40 wide in the north. Tomorrow we get identification
papers and may start on our way home. It all seems like a dream. People of
her house heard rumours that Russians were coming in and were scared stiff.
Trapper was trying to pacify them when we came in and he was frantic. They
asked Eric and he said, "No." One of the women threw her arms around Eric's
neck and nearly kissed him. Said they didn't fear the Yanks or English, but
the Russians. This happened 3 or 4 times in half hour. 4 young Hollanders
in bad way. Yanks came 200 miles in 3 days with only 3 wounded. German
people cowtowing horribly to us now. It's like coming back to life again.
Hard to believe.

MAY 4

Up at 20 to 7 after sleeping in a feather bed. Had a good breakfast of eggs, jam and bread, coffee. Owner came home today; she wants to give us everything. Lots of wine. It's a nice day out. Bill and Charlie came up to tell us that they had a truck and were heading for Lübeck as soon as we got the gang together. Cleaned my gun and tidied up my kit. Rowat and Trapper came back and said we would have to wait 2 or 3 days until the main army got over the highway; in the meantime we have to scrounge bread. Louis LaPierre picked up a good car today so we have been endeavoring where, when and how to head out. Received something like definite instructions to go to Wismar, where we would be flown to England. Others want to go to Lübeck. After dallying around all day, Louis and I rode up to Hamburg, saw Limey officer who told us to go to Wismar and report to Military Government. Saw our former neighbours who asked us to bring bread up for the. One woman, wife of an Ober Stabsfeldwebel asked us to locate her husband who had been taken prisoner to Wismar. Got back in time for supper; heard that Yanks will give us good billets, 3 squares a day, clothing, etc. here. Went over to the searching grounds to get some pocket knives and lamps, maybe a camera or compass and when we got back found that Louis and Eric had been driving a Yank Colonel around. He told them that he had received orders that all Canadian, English or Yank ex-POWs were to stay here and he would find us a good billet; gave us good food and every possible comfort and if we wanted to help in some military affairs, all well and good. We could fade out in our own car early tomorrow, but decided to report to the Colonel at nine as requested. Maybe on our way home in a day or two. Thousands of German prisoners coming in for registration and search. It's like good medicine to see them marching from an almost new car. It's a big job gathering, searching and registering our soldiers, airmen, women, cops, evacuees and civvies. If we only had lights here, we would have a fair go. Heard tonight that war over 12 noon today. Early tomorrow last German Army (9th) will give up their arms as will Germans in Denmark and Norway. Once again, Germany has taken a beating and this time she is down properly. Couldn't meet a better bunch of fellow than these in the 7th Armoured.

MAY 5

Heard that the war was officially ended at 8 this AM. Went up to the arms dump for straps, etc. for a shoulder holster harness which I made before 3 this PM. We may move by Yank army transport any time now. Louis LaPierre found a Zeiss camera in the arms dump, the lucky cuss. Had to register with Capt. Bentley this afternoon; sent Rowat up with the names and a request for Yank white bread (cake to us.) Went up for clothing parade this PM, but had to go back at 5 so went down to sand pit to try automatic which works perfectly. Went up for clothing; arrived there just at suppertime. A Yank forced his mess kit at me so got in line to receive hamburg steak with ketchup, pork and beans, sauerkraut, white bread and peaches. Hung around until after six for QM; finally gave up and returned to billets; couldn't eat much supper this evening; called up to give particulars to a Louie and was told to report twice a day. Returned to billets; washed dishes and read Esquire. Lap of luxury. Eric and Louis came in about 10; said Yanks aren't allowed to be on streets unless on duty. Surprising number of Yanks on duty. Yanks say we are lucky because we are allowed cars if we can get them and have free run of the town. Late orders this evening have us reporting at 7:30 for transport to a place 18 kilos back from here, where we will be deloused and sent further back; eventually we might reach England. Feeling miserable with cold, sore throat and a missing heart. Cleaned my gun tonight. May lose it in near future. Cut my kit down some more. 3 aspirins and bed looks good right now; Eric is snoring pretty good.

MAY 6

Loaded onto trucks and taken to Lüneburg; passed temporary prison camps filled with Germans, "Los Immer Weiter" was constantly being yelled to the Yanks. "Take care of those boys, Yank" "Take it easy" etc. Crossed the Elb on a pontoon bridge and by the look of the east side they had quite a scrap to form the bridgehead. A sign on the bridge stated, "dedicated to those who sweated it through and never got a scratch." Arrived camp around five. Registered. QM, delousing, supper. Here for 2 or 3 days; then fly to England.

MAY 7

Nothing much doing this morning except interrogation. This afternoon Jones and I drew 200 Invasion Marks; then went downtown to see a show but was too late so just walked around taking in the sights; got back in time for supper. Heard that "cease fire" goes into effect at midnight and the pact will be signed here in Lüneburg around noon. I saw the building with its guard. May go tomorrow if rumours are true. Took in local show this evening, called "Frenchman's Creek."

MAY 8

Received identification card this morning which means we move today some-time. All packed and on parade square by 8. Lots of standing around. At last Eric and I are split up, LaPierre and I got taken by a newsreel photographer while drinking tea. Very nice day. Waited until 4:00 then returned to billets, drew blankets, salvaged R.C. and went to supper. 15 trucks arrived at 5, but not enough to see us away. Quite a picture, 15 trucks lined up, men swarming around, group numbers being called. Louis took some pictures which I doubt will turn out. Don't expect to go tonight. Heard the King speak tonight. Told that groups from 348 to 375 should have an early breakfast as there is a chance we may leave. Limeys celebrating with big fires, Very flares and a few revolver shots.

MAY 9

Up early, washed, shaved, had breakfast before 7. A dull day which probably means no flying. Navy men getting the runaround and are plenty fed up. Everyone impatient and fed up. Most of us think this part of Germany will be in control of the Germans again in a couple of months. These Limeys are much too soft-hearted. Lined up and waiting for trucks at 10:30. Going straight to England. Left camp 2:30; arrived airport 4:30; enplaned 5:45 "Dakotas" take-off 6:08; crossed Rhine 7:17, bombed area; over coast 8:50; coast of England 9:00; landed RAF Dunsford; good reception 9:30; arrived camp 108 at 10:45. Bacon, egg, potatoes, NAAFI cake, tea.

MAY 10

Up fairly early to wash and clean up before breakfast. Either I can't realize it or there is something wrong with my emotional apparatus but I can't feel any strong enthusiasm at being in England. Glad to be back, "yes," longing for home also yes. Perhaps it's the red tape connected with everything. Pay parade, cable sending, medical and dental inspection, clothing, etc. YMCA gave us 40 weed, 12 bars and a lifesaver, etc. this morning. Leaving at 2:30 for the Canadian camp. Caught a train at Horsham, changed at Guildford, finally arrived Aldershot, Leipzig barracks. Registered, drew pajamas, mess kit, and given a bed. Met Norm Campbell, one of the old originals while waiting for register. Had a good supper of chicken, green salad, boiled spuds. Meeting fellows we left along the road during the great evacuation. It looks as if, where possible, everything is ours for the asking. Can't even volunteer for further service. Langston is a Sgt. Maj. now.

MAY 11

This life is just a series of queues. Getting good meals, however, and am getting fat. Hung around all morning waiting for something to happen. Sent another cable and free airmail letter. Intelligence interrogation this afternoon. Reg Langston came up and we had a great old gab-fest. All old fellows, officers, W.O., Sgt., home or dead. Stood in QM parade from 2 until 6 for clothes. Went looking for Cross, failed to find him.

MAY 12

Decided to do something about these signatures. Got Part II pay book, had a haircut, visited record office, so all that remains is admittance to hospital for the rest of the dope. Nothing doing this evening so Eric and I went down to try to find Geddes. He is on a weekend. Went into Aldershot, met White, had a beer, went to a show, then some fish and chips and back to camp. It's a long walk.

MAY 13

Hung around all morning sewing my service stripes on and reading a little. It is rumored into hospital wards today and after passing our medicals go on leave. About 3:30 we were collected up and moved into wards; chicken and potato salad, stewed raspberries and chocolate cake for supper. Single beds and white sheets competes a realization of a Stalag dream. Louis, Eric, Trapper, Bones and Andy, and myself went to North Camp for a show at the Scala. Got back in time for hot cocoa and biscuits at the hospital. Busy day tomorrow with X-rays, etc.

MAY 14

A few fellows had medicals this morning. It's a slow process. Had X-rays this afternoon, almost missed it by going by the NAAFI for something to eat. Eric and I went down to see Harry Geddes (Cpl.) and we talked for a good many hours, getting back to barracks around 11. Prisoners arriving all the time; faster than they are going out; consequently, we are getting crowded and they are pushing them through the medicals now. I have to get my teeth fixed before I go.

MAY 15

Went through my medical so fast it left me a little dazed, especially when I came out A1. If my heart starts missing again, some MO is going to get a surprise. Eric had to go to hospital for his ear, then his X-ray report showed positive so he moved to Ward 15 as a suspected TB case. Went to dental at 2:00; go back on Thursday. Went downtown for some stuff, didn't get much. Eric and I went down to see Harry Geddes who had contacted Comack. Comack (Lieut.) is quite the lad, not changed a great deal, good conversationalist, good storyteller, good company. Had a good memory rousing.

MAY 16

This morning most of my group left on leave. I was scheduled to go, but I have to return to the dentist tomorrow. Went up to the QM; procured a cap badge and another tie. Visited Eric a while. My name called out again for leave this afternoon; damn it they are persistent. Went up to see Eric again this afternoon. The "Quack" put him to bed pending another X-ray. Went to see W Berg in This Man's Navy at the Ritz. Ate two fruit pies, drank 1 bottle of Pepsi, then had two huge slices of bread, peanut butter and jam with hot cocoa here; then came back and ate a chocolate bar. People say I'm getting fat.

MAY 17

Had to tell him again that I couldn't go on leave, until I had finished with the dentist, which means 2 days gone off my leave. Went to dentist at 9:30; got my repaired plate; returned at 10:05 for grinding. Went down to Aldershot this afternoon and pounded the pavement for 3 ½ hours buying Cameron badges, etc. Got back in time for the fried chicken supper. This evening I sewed new shoulder badges up. There is quite a controversy over whether we can wear the Combined Ops badge. The latest I heard, was we couldn't go home unless we did have them on. The nurses are trying to buy German daggers for souvenirs; no one will sell for offered price. 28 days for calling Zombies, zombies. When going on leave they asked if we wish to volunteer for Japan, or home station or army of occupation. I'll wait until I get home before volunteering. Don't know the score yet.

MAY 18

Now that I am ready for leave, I can't get my papers. This will be 3 days off my leave, unless I can get the date changed. St. Louis taken to another hospital on a stretcher. Maybe it's TB. Went up and exchanged my beret for a Balmoral and drew a pair of braces. Dropped into see Eric; then visited Legion for morning brunch. Met Roy Carlson from Kenora there. He recognized me but I didn't know him. I've got a poor memory for faces. No sign of my pass yet. Got fed up this evening and went to a show at north camp. Met Sid Spite on the way so he came along. He is in 4 CCD, part of this dump. May go on leave tomorrow.

MAY 19

Lord and what a day. Name wasn't called out for leave this morning so decided to chase him. Must (Sgt.) until I got it. Finally located my pass, warrant, etc. in records office. Got everything, including cigarettes pack (no pay) but when it came to pay, no clearance papers so I had to locate them. Found them at the records office. Finally got away at about 4:00. Train from Aldershot 4:14; London at 5:30 or so. Tried to phone Maple Leaf Club but no go. Took tube to Vic.; tram to club. Demeray with me. Jim gone home; club filled; sent to Church Army on Cambridge Square. Ended up at CA on Hyde Park Square. Got a bed. Had sandwich and tea. Went down to Beaver;

too late for supper. Pubs all closed; got lost on tube 2 hours. Came back to bed. Liquor 3 shillings a nip.

MAY 20

Demeray and I got up to go see the Changing of the Guard; disappointed; ate at Beaver Club; still disappointed. Rained, walked around a little. Decided to see Tin Pan Alley but couldn't find the theatre. Ended up at Hyde Park listening to the orator on Speaker's Corner. Quite a show. Found the Ontario Service Club; quite the dump. Dem going north tomorrow.

MAY 21

Up early. Dem taking 10:00 train. Met Pop Miller at Beaver Club with him until 1:00. Put 22 pounds in bank at Beaver Club. Walked around a little; met Harry Pike, Sid Warren, Hodges. Left them at about 7:30; sat in Ontario Club until 9:00. Watched Piccadilly Circus until 10:00. Big crowds on subway. Set out walking from Marble Arch. Town's dead.

MAY 22

Up pretty early and downtown trying to buy a hackle on the way. No soap. Met the Gatton guy on Cockspur Street and surprisingly enough, I recognized him. Went up to Canonbury to Langston's residence, but no one home. Strolled up the Strand; saw all things I had planned on buying, but the prices were two high. It rained hard this afternoon. Went to see "A Medal for Benny"; took the cheapest seat in the house (4/6). Tried to locate Billy this evening with no luck. Walked from Marble Arch in the rain. Met Jack Dale in the Club baggage room and Gendre in the dining room. Swilled everything available; lemonade, Horlicks tea, etc. 2 Canadians left a cafe, two girls and their hats for a minute and then couldn't find their place again. They asked me if I knew where it was, but they couldn't remember the name of the place, the dumb clucks.

MAY 23

Raining this morning, hung around the Club until after ten, then went to Beaver Club hoping to see Eric. Couldn't get anything I wanted down town, saw very few people I knew. Rained heavy around 4:30. Went to see

---

"Sudan" at the Tivoli on the Strand (6) came out and took lunch at Ontario Club. Watched the Circus on Piccadilly. Saw a US Corporal slug a Limey flying officer. Another fight in the Monica required police intervention. With Yanks all around him, a Limey soldier intoxicated, of course, sang the Stars & Stripes will fly over Germany under the Union Jack. A guy picked me out to tell his troubles to; his girl had stood him up. Saw 3 more fights in quick succession. Yanks have town sown up. People getting over their V.E. celebrations and coming out again. Tubes crowded. Showed sailor way to Hyde Park Square.

MAY 24
Fooled around; bought a Balmoral for 1 pound; can't get a hackle. Went window shopping this afternoon; bought nothing except a pair of drum sticks. Met Warren at supper at K of C and spent the night with him and what a night. Finished up with 2 Yanks. Bottled light. One Scotch for 2 pounds; 1 night with 45 years for 3 pounds. Rode home on a Yankee truck.

MAY 25
Saw no one I knew until noon; met Perry at dinner. Decided to draw canned goods from K of C. Carried them in wooden box to club and then packed away and took them up to Aunt Eth's; had to stay the night.

MAY 26
Went to Club; got my bag and took it to Aunt Eth's. Drawing 100 or 110 cigs from Ontario House daily now. Had a breather in Lion & Lamb; met some old friends of mine and Dad's and Jack's. Ernie, Jim Green and Davy, last one is quite a lad.

MAY 27
Slept in; up by 10:30. Had dinner, then went to Petticoat Lane with Jack and Anne. Lion & Lamb this evening.

MAY 28
Tried to locate Jack Fenn, but he isn't at work. Got some more cigs from Ontario House. Met Captain Bell Kent on Cockspur. Kathleen from Luton

came this evening; wants to know why Jack didn't go down and meet also. Told her maybe next 7-day leave. Great do about fatherless babies, etc. Scandal and lots of it. Lion & Lamb with George and Jim.

MAY 29

Drew more cigs; nothing else doing. Met Ernie in Beaver Club; just discharged from the hospital; he is going north tomorrow. Found Reg's wife and her sister, two grand girls and glad I met them. Reg's wife bought lunch, no alternative, date with them and Reg for Saturday at 2. Must go to south end tomorrow. Hear change of address so may be back. Saw Kathy again this AM. Might be good go down there. 70 Berry Park Gardens. Had to run out on her.

MAY 30

Left Aunt Eth's at 8:30; caught 9:05 train to south end; no trouble remembering bus route, except asked for Elm Tree corner instead of Kent Elms. Only Vi at home; recognition was simultaneous and mutual. Met Aunt Pat, Alice, Beat, Jack Mercam and Elsie at Garon's. Went for walk on the Front and pier; very nice. Uncle Jack dead. Rusty came home at 5:30. Opened door for her. Weekend going to be mixed up. Peggy married to a Yankie called Peter. Murph and Jessie apparently that way also.

MAY 31

Sat on lawn all day; did absolutely nil until after tea. Then Vi, Rusty and I sent up to see Harold and Edie. We fell off bike. Grass fight, Vi's glasses broken. Harold showed me many snaps of South African cousins. All cousins want to visit us after the war. Vi and I exchanged antidotes of prisoner life, apparently much the same. People sure took a beating from the V1 and V2.

JUNE 1

Planned on going on a bicycle ride with Rusty this afternoon, but it was very windy and a shower decided us against. However, we did cycle down to Rayleigh for a haircut for me. Barber talkative and very much against marriage. Talked with Vi about Bill for a while. Auntie putting up scrumptious meals. Rusty, Vi and I went to a show at south end at the Ritz, only to find I had seen it at the Scala at North Camp. After tea, Rusty played the piano. At midnight everyone had gone to bed and Rusty was still playing; then we sat in the dark until 2. Psychology and how, great kid, Rusty.

JUNE 2
Rusty, Aunt Pat and I came up to London this morning and we were met at Liverpool by Jack. Had some tea at the Corner house, then Rusty and Auntie went to Jack's while Jack and I went to Aunt Eth's. Then Jack showed me the way to Canonbury where we met Reg. 3 light ales. Received some of my personal stuff from Reg. Mostly books. Jean, Reg and Jack and I travelled to Piccadilly where Jack caught a bus home while we went out to Turnham Green to Jean's stepmother's place. Had a scrumptious supper of roasted rabbit, strawberry and cream, etc. I left off refusing an invite to stay the night, at 9:40. Arrived Aunt Eth's at 11:45. Stayed up and talked until after 2:00. Lily had a scrap with Jim.

JUNE 3
Met Rusty at Liverpool station and we both came to Jack's. Rusty played the piano this evening for a while; then while Jessie, Aunt Pat, Alice and Jack got interested in a game of Brag, Rusty and I went for a walk in the rain. Came back at dusk and had something to eat. Went to bed around midnight.

JUNE 4
Supposed to go back today, but Rusty said, if I stayed, she would, so we stayed. We all went to the Gaumont at Jack's expense and saw "Tonight and Every Night." Came back; had tea. Jack went to bed early; then after the rest had gone, Rusty and I stayed up listening to the radio. Something tells me something is going to happen if I don't get back to camp soon. Rusty told my fortune. Many people all talking at once, a man with a big mustache, a big question to decide, a sum of 52 pounds.

JUNE 7
Long parade this morning. 700 man draft called out. Met Warren; went to see Padre; no leaves until tomorrow. Another parade at 1:15. Tried to see Padre again. Worried about Rusty so started a letter, or rather tried to finish

one started last night. Received letters from home. Tried to write to Rusty again this afternoon, not much good. Did my laundry after supper, wrote a letter to Nelle and one to Mrs. Zanetti. Scared to post the letter to Rusty. Had a shower and washed a pair of shorts.

JUNE 8

Early roll call; name called; interrogated; warned for draft; tried to see Padre for more leave; no go. Tried for fingerprints and photo; too many; can't stand still and wait. Name called for draft at 10:00. Leave in the morning. Got pay book back and exchanged foreign money; fingerprinted and photographed. Saw Padre who after 30 minutes of arguing still said more leave was impossible. Intended to write letters this evening but on an urge caught bus and went to show in Aldershot. Came back in time for lunch in kitchen; finished letters after.

JUNE 9

Up early to wash and shave and mail the 3 letters. On roll call with full pack. Loaded onto trucks and taken to Huron Camp, No 1 Repat Depot, Wing 3. On arrival, informed of the score and that we would get 96 hour pass. This camp well organized. On 1:30 parade; had to listen to what is called intake lectures; then received pass about 3:30. Hassel and I were waiting for bus before 4:00. Caught one to Guildford; straight through to south end; finished journey in taxi. Taxi driver went wrong place. He was plenty embarrassed. Folks very surprised to see me. All home. Rusty and I last to bed. Matters not helped much.

JUNE 10

Didn't do much all day; Rusty and I just lazed around, listening to the radio. Fred, Eileen's husband is home so renewed acquaintance with him. Jessie and Vera came in this afternoon with Harold's youngster; then Harold came in. Promised to call tomorrow night. Jessie and Vera came back again this evening and wouldn't leave until Rusty played the piano for them for ½ hour. Vi is painting dolls at 1 pound for 1 gross. Rusty and I stayed up pretty late, getting things straightened out. Rained all day.

JUNE 11

Rusty and I went down to the front this morning with the idea of getting a hackle, but couldn't find any. We got back in time for the dinner that Vi had cooked; then we took advantage of the sun and patronized the lawn for the rest of the afternoon. Tea was late as it was right before we started for Harold's. We stayed there ten; then caught the last bus half way home and walked the rest. Elsie was washing her hair and Rusty made some tea and sandwiches. We stayed up late again and complications again set in. Poor Rusty. I made a mess of things again.

JUNE 12

We were up pretty early because we had to come up to Jack's. Walked around south end waiting for the train and talking. Everyone seemed to be staring at me. Finally arrived London, got some cigs at the Ontario House; then caught bus for Tooting where we changed for Carshalton. Arrived Jack's just after 3. Rusty lost glove. Sat around and talked after a good dinner. Rusty and I stayed up and talked for quite a while. Quite a girl is Rusty.

JUNE 19

Had quite a time not being picked for fatigues this morning, but I did manage it. Draft 166 is probably going this afternoon. They handed in their blankets and saw the paymaster. He gave them $5 in Canadian money, a Quid or two in English money and a cheque for $100.00 out of their pay so that there will be no delay in going on leave in Canada. Rumors plentiful about 6, 7 and 16 day leaves for personnel struck off draft 167. No foundation for decrease in number or leaves. Interviewed by SPO; told him I wanted radio course. Having medical tomorrow morning. Saw E.G. Robinson in "The Woman in the Window." Theater hot. Finished and mailed letter to Rusty. Put Rosette on ribbon. Did my laundry and had a shower. Service vote beat M. King; can't understand how he can still be in. Missing Rusty these nights.

JUNE 20

First thing this morning we had our last medical. Took my uniform over to be pressed; did some laundry; wrote a letter to Nelle; started another one to Rusty; had a haircut; reclaimed my uniform. Pay parade was started at 2:00

PM and like everything all messed up. Received $5 Canadian money, £1 English, $100 cheque. Turned back the £10 surplus. Had supper; wrote some more to Rusty. Heard Bob Hope on radio. Ate lunch in NAAFI; had a wash, then went for an hour thinking walk. May pull out tomorrow or next day. Rained today.

JUNE 21

Raining hard this morning; continued until noon. No parades. Repacked my kit. 1:30 parade. C-Bed, received train group No 1. 4:00 parade; warned against breaking CB. Told to parade in morning with blankets. 9:45 early lunch; 10:30 move off. Firecrackers on parade. RSM plenty sore. Wrote last letters to Nelle, Rose, Rusty and cousin Jack from this side. Don't know if Rusty will understand the letter. Finished packing. Obtained extra blanket from fellow on parade. He said he didn't want it. Washed out towel and hankies.

JUNE 22

Handed in blankets; had an early lunch; boarded trucks; went to North Farnborough; caught train and pulled out at 1:25. Arrived Southampton; saw our boat, none other than SS "Pasteur", the boat I came over on. Billeted on E deck in hammock. Understand air force came on and walked off again. Supper terrible. Met Ken Peters and Charlie Smalley.

JUNE 23

Troops loading all night; apparently finished loading around 3 this afternoon. Wrote a note to Rusty; caught last mail bag off. Saw Ellison, Tommy Cossin and another fellow, I can't remember name. Met Harold Moreau and talked for long time; he hasn't changed at all. Slipped our mooring while we were eating supper. SS of SS Pasteur means "Starvation Ship." Sat on rail and watched the shore go by. Many people waving good-by. One small craft dipped flag in farewell. Sailed ¾ way around Isle of White, past Portsmouth. Watched England disappear astern until it disappeared.

JUNE 24

Well out to sea, a little rough this morning; a few men sick. Canteen line-up completely around ship. Didn't get anywhere near the Canteen by noon hour, closing time. Loud speaker always blaring. Out of Bounds signs all over the place. Can't go here; can't go there; worse than a prison camp. May get canteen stuff by tables. If not, we'll have to miss a meal and queue up.

JUNE 25

A dull gray day with the sea a little grayer than the sky. Bad news today, we can't land at Halifax until Saturday because of lack of trains and berthing space. Sat outside on A Deck most of the time. Talked a long time with Ellison. Hit the canteen line when it was small and got through in less than an hour. Saw a few ships passing and the odd whale spouting.

JUNE 26

Grey this morning; usual boat drill at 10:15. Loud speaker going continually. Wind rose this afternoon; blew the clouds away, but the sea up. It feels like a storm bearing wind; boat rolling pretty hard tonight. Louis can't stay down in the room and I'll admit the smell is horrible. It takes a strong stomach to stand it. Louis says the stairs are the worse; they're always moving. Someone is putting a concert on in the near future and they were holding a rehearsal in the rec room. It might not be too bad. Rumour tonight says we may land on schedule (Thursday) yet. Writing Rusty an installment letter.

JUNE 27

Did nothing but sit on A Deck with Louis all day. We passed a ship called William Carpenter bound for New York today. Found I can still read lamp pretty fair. Sailing pretty slow this evening. Spent a little time on Fore Deck after dark watching the phosphorous in the water and the stars overhead.

JUNE 28

Very clear and calm this AM. Sea like glass. Speed increased after dinner; passed 4 ships in quick succession, 1 called SS Ilkwas; more lamp reading. At 7:30 this high speed still maintained; rumored we may land tomorrow. Ship's pitching pretty bad on heavy swell. Food still terrible and stuffy down here. Have to rearrange my kit just in case tomorrow is the day. Saw some fish today; had an argument whether they were whales or not. I said no. Anxiously waiting to sight our first seagull.

JUNE 29

Got up to a rough sea, high winds and rain. Few of the fellows not feeling so well. Nothing out of the ordinary took place except the speed of the ship was cut down to a bare 5 knots, which we held throughout the day, much to all aboard's agitation. Decided to go to a concert in the recreation room but someone whistling in my ear drove me out.

JUNE 30, SAT.

All day from Reveille, there has been a feeling of suppressed excitement throughout the ship. Immediately after dinner, men started picking advantage spots all over the ship. We passed through a few dense fogs, the last was the worst. Our whistle was going regularly and we could hear a fog horn on a passing ship. Suddenly the fog began to lift. Our first sight of Canada was the Entrance lighthouse to Halifax (1:20). The mainland appeared soon after. A sight I have dreamed about for years. We got a wonderful reception. A band boat with a goodly compliment of girls, a fire boat with all hoses shooting water high in the air, a flotilla of lighter craft swarmed around. Whistles and horns sounded all the way in. Good natured banter. A great cheer when bowline snubbed; another for the stern line (3:10). Pipe band on the quay. Crowds cheering, etc. No 6 MD unloading now. No. 10 POW tonight at 21:00 and 22:00 hours. We have arrived. Prossit.

S.S. (Louis Pasteur arrives at Halifax, June 30, 1945)

(Posten tower)

(Utensils made by prisoners)

ACKNOWLEDGEMENTS

Many people helped us with research as we transcribed and edited this book. They deserve our deepest thanks. The following organizations provided valuable assistance for which they deserve our thanks and credit.

Brock University, James A. Gibson Library, Geospatial DAT GIS Service

Naval Museum of Halifax for the digital photos of the SS Pasteur.

Library & Archives Canada for the digital photos of Dieppe landing craft.

Edited by James Hyatt and Bonnie (Lodge) Fraser

Wendy Hyatt for the transcription of the diaries.

Printed in Canada